MEDICAL MALPRACTICE EXPERT WITNESSING

INTRODUCTORY GUIDE
FOR
PHYSICIANS
AND
MEDICAL PROFESSIONALS

MEDICAL MALPRACTICE EXPERT WITNESSING

INTRODUCTORY GUIDE
FOR
PHYSICIANS
AND
MEDICAL PROFESSIONALS

PERRY HOOKMAN, MD, MHA
FACP, FACG, FACPE, AGAF, FASGE

Potomac Press
Clinical Research Services

CRS
Potamac Press - Clinical Research Services
9605 Halter Ct.
Potomac, MD 20854

© 2008 by Potomac Press L.L.C.
CRS Press is an imprint of Potomac Press

No claim to original U.S. Government works
Printed in the United States of America on acid-free paper
10 9 8 7 6 5 4 3 2 1

International Standard Book Number-13: 978-1-4200-5895-6 (Hardcover)

This book contains information obtained from authentic and highly regarded sources. Reprinted material is quoted with permission, and sources are indicated. A wide variety of references are listed. Reasonable efforts have been made to publish reliable data and information, but the author and the publisher cannot assume responsibility for the validity of all materials or for the consequences of their use.

Library of Congress Cataloging-in-Publication Data

Hookman, Perry.
    Medical malpractice expert witnessing : introductory guide for physicians and medical
professionals / Perry Hookman.
        p. cm.
    Includes bibliographical references and index.
    ISBN-13: 978-1-4200-5895-6 (alk. paper)
    ISBN-10: 1-4200-5895-9 (alk. paper)
    1. Medical personnel--Malpractice--United States. 2. Physicians--Malpractice--United States. 3.
Evidence, Expert--United States. I. Title.

KF8925.M3H62 2008
344.7304'11--dc22
                                                                              2007036717

Dedication

To Susan—my wife of 40 years—for a marriage made in heaven

Contents

5 Defensive Moves and Strategies to Avoid Medical Malpractice Suits in Primary Medical Care and Specialty Practice   83

18 Medical Malpractice Terms and Tips for the Testifying Physician   301

19 How to Prepare for and Handle Your Deposition: Deposition Preparation for the Physician   311

Preface

Learning successful offense and defensive strategies puts you way ahead in a chess contest.

—Chess Instructor

Who is a potential testifying physician and medical expert witness?

In this malpractice climate, potentially every medical student, house officer, practicing clinician, and full-time as well as part-time academician should be included in this category. A testifying physician is a potential defendant physician, a potential medical expert, or any physician asked by the legal system to help sort out medical facts for an attorney or a jury. I believe this book can serve as a reference to both the physician defendant and the physician medical expert; and that is potentially every practicing physician. It will help you to decide whether or not to accept the case and how to conduct yourself with the attorney prior to taking on the case and after being officially retained. This book is designed to help you know how to conduct yourself at the deposition or in trial testimony in court. It also instructs you on the forms and letters that have taken me several years to develop in communicating with the legal system.

If nothing else, the book will give you a beginner's orientation into the world of medical malpractice—something I sorely needed in my hour of need, but was unable to obtain.

Think of this book as an aid, not as a unique work of originality but simply as a collection—actually several compilations—of my continually updated notes taken during many years of private practice, clinical teaching, medical administration, and managerial training plus current information and inquiry from many sources and Web sites. This is accompanied by my accumulated research of matters relating to what a medical expert does into a CD-ROM to give you an easy way to continually update information you need to survive as a practicing physician and testifying medical expert in today's world of medical malpractice. I present this book and the appendix as a CD-ROM, so that you can not only update current information and the clinical practice guidelines, but delve deeper into the particular subject that interests you.

In this book, I have used an evidence-based medicine (EBM) approach—the same approach I have used for searching out randomized controlled trials (RCTs), clinical practice guidelines (CPGs), and standards of medical care (SOC) published articles for treating patients, as well as for peer-review supported testimony. I have attempted to make the physician comfortable with this book because it is written in the style of the familiar referenced medical journal article.

You should approach this book keeping in mind that this is not a compilation of *ipse dixit** solely personal subjective opinions, theories, speculations, conjectures, and anecdotes. This book attempts to get past the subjective to the objective facts and articles—and to get the best objective information for you as a potential testifying physician or medical expert witness, with an *update just a click away.*

I have added to this EBM technique a filter consisting of my knowledge, experience, training, education, expertise, and note-taking gained from over 30 years of medical and medico-legal experience to get you the information you need not only from my expertise, but also from the broad-ranging peer-reviewed literature. This filter also includes my medical malpractice trial experience, with all the medical malpractice trials in which I have served as a medical expert—both for the defense and plaintiff—along with the constructive opinions and strategic advice given to me by the defendant and plaintiff attorneys who engaged me as a medical expert witness.

I have also used an additional prism for extra analysis. This consists of medical malpractice prevention sessions scheduled by medical malpractice insurance carriers. Looking back, I find that these annual 3-h lecture/seminar sessions given by the malpractice insurance carrier left a lot of free and very useful printed material. Make sure you too attend these sessions, where available, because these meetings continue to give great advice to physicians on how to stay out of medical malpractice difficulties, and once faced with a suit, how to put up the best defense. I not only took good notes from all these sources, but also from my executive master of health administration degree studies. These were good enough for me to give my own risk management seminars to hospital medical house staff and nurses in a former life, when I was director of medical education and then vice president of professional services at a 600-bed community teaching hospital affiliated with a prestigious medical school.

The RCTs and SOC presented here in this book and in the appendix *examples* to instruct you *how* to use these in practice and in court testimony. Please understand that this book is not meant to give any individual medical advice to patients. I must warn you that some published medical care guidelines and RCTs in the appendix will not be up to date more than 1 day after publication. So, use the attached CD-ROM to connect with the changing sources to keep up to date. Remember *an update today is just a click away.*

Having said all this, let me now do the traditional "thank you" that every author gives in the preface. Usually, the author thanks first his spouse, family, then friends, "who have all been so supportive in this endeavor," for their moral support, patience, and understanding during the many months of the author's book writing.

Unfortunately, I cannot do this.

I received no encouragement from my loyal wife of 40 years. Nor have I received the slightest bit of encouragement from any of my friends; certainly none from my attorney friends. Quite the contrary.

My wife's objection was that it would take too much time away from us, and that I would be sitting alone for many hours and days, separated from her, in various law and medical

---

* *Ipse dixit*—"he himself said"—used to characterize a dogmatic statement or dictum totally unsupported except for the speakers' authority. Originally copied to Latin from Greek by Cicero, who quoted from loyal followers of Pythagoras. Currently used also as an expression indicating expert testimony based solely on the "authority" of the expert himself rather than supported by general acceptance of his community or the peer-reviewed literature.

libraries, and also alone at my word processor locked in my study—and that was true. Of my four daughters, daughter #1, the newly minted lawyer and an author in her own right, repeated what all my lawyer friends said, "You are crazy to do this, because everything you say in this book can be used against you on cross-examinations. Every time you testify as a medical expert witness, you are going to have to rememorize this book so as to remember exactly what you said so as to not be in conflict with anything you have written."

My daughter #2, the professional artist, and also an author and illustrator of children's books, sneered at the free clip art that I love so much, rolled her eyes, said "euooo," and explained that this art, though free was "too tacky for any quality book, even for a children's book." But after a few weeks of my selections, she relented and thought it would be a better idea for her to at least edit out some of my more outlandish clip art choices.

Daughter #4, the youngest and the entrepreneur–businesswoman, informed me in no uncertain terms that I would not make one penny of profit on this book, that these books are a dime a dozen, and that "all doctors probably already know what is in the book, and lawyers, judges, and jurors have their own books." I told her that there were no other similar books. Also I did not care to make a profit, and if any profit was made I was thinking of donating all my earnings to charity, specifically our family foundation, which contributes to educational programs in schools and hospitals. She told me she "was proud of her dad."

Only daughter #3, the medical doctor, semiapproved of the idea. She made very constructive suggestions including the addition of the CD-ROM to give the user the chance to update the clinical practice guidelines (CPGs) and RCTs upon which standards of medical care is based. She and one of her esteemed colleagues also contributed a section on psychiatry to the book for which I am grateful. She also suggested beefing up the malpractice prevention chapters with more tips for clinical practitioners. But she also echoed daughter #1 by warning me that the book could and would be used against me by "unscrupulous attorneys" by questioning me on out-of-context book sentences.

So, why did I choose to include humorous snippets and clip art against my artist daughter's advice for this very serious and sober subject? Humor is not something you expect with these somber issues. Medical malpractice is indeed a very tragic event—for the patient and the family; and extremely stressful for the physician and his family. Clip art is free, and can lighten the tone up a bit to make this dark subject less grim. The reader can also take small visual minibreaks while he learns. Visuals are also very good for retention of complex material.

And why the quotations distributed in many sections? To lend a bit of sorely needed wisdom, and to put into a truer context a very sad and stressful event in the life of so many people, especially the plaintiff and defendant.

And if all these months of writing and rewriting does not make me richer, so what? As long as, unlike my traumatic experience, even one physician does not have to face a courtroom without a good and objective orientation as to what to expect, it will be worth it to me. This is not to say that your attorneys may not serve and advise you well, but I believe you need another more independent perspective. So I am giving back to medicine, both patients and physician colleagues, and the community, what it has so generously given to me.

Warning/Disclaimer

This book is sold with the understanding that neither the publisher nor the author are through this book or CD engaged in rendering individual legal services, litigation services, medical services, or any other individual professional service. If expert assistance is required, I emphasize that a competent professional must be sought and retained. It is also not the purpose of this book to reprint all applicable information that is otherwise available to physicians and others professionals.

Readers and users should verify all information and data before treating patients/groups or employing any therapies described in this educational activity. A qualified health care professional should *always* be consulted before using any therapeutic product, treatment, or procedure discussed. In addition, the author and publisher shall have neither liability nor responsibility to any person or entity with respect to any loss or damage caused or alleged to have been caused directly or indirectly by any of the information contained in this book. If you do not wish to be bound by the above, you may return this book to the place where you purchased it for a full refund. This book is designed to provide selected educational information to professionals on preventing, dealing, and testifying in medical malpractice litigation. But I hope this book also entertains you while you learn.

The appendix, on CD-ROM, can be used for further research into the area of medical malpractice and the special needs of medical experts. It is not all inclusive. You will no doubt realize that the information in this book consists of only a fraction of all the information that is available. The appendix is intended, however, to complement, amplify, and supplement at least in a small way, and to give you a jump-start to delve deeper into the various subjects by its updating features, which I hope you regularly use. Remember *an update today is just a click away.*

This book has gone through multiple proof-readings and line editing by myself as well as professional proofreaders and line editors. However, I am sure, with so many hundreds of references, there will probably be at least a few persisting mistakes, both typographical and in content. Also, I cannot guarantee that I have given proper attribution (although I have tried very hard) to each individual source of information in this book.

If I have missed giving appropriate credits, or made any mistake in or missed any quotation, or have missed a coauthor of any of the writings mentioned in this book, I apologize.

If you notice a glaring omission in a name, source, article, lecture, or other; or if I have not given appropriate credit to any of the sources or any of the medical malpractice insurance company lectures I have attended for the past 30 years, I apologize. If you notify me of any of the above, I will make corrections in the next edition, if there is a next edition.

This text contains educational examples that should be used only as a general guide in this field and certainly not as the ultimate source of information on medical malpractice or on any of the medical subjects that appear in this book. As far as the medical guidelines presented in this book go, the same should apply. Remember also that the point frequently made in this book is that the purpose of any clinical guideline is *not to replace, but to support* clinical judgment. Nor are any of the CPGs or RCTs or published standards of care meant for medical self-treatment. All patients must have professionals guiding, supervising, and implementing their individual diagnosis and medical treatment. Nothing in this book is meant for patient or health care provider self-treatment. Your personal physician is the ultimate authority for any medical issue in this book that you think even remotely applies to you or your patients or your family or your friends. Similarly, the ultimate authority for any of the legal or medical issues and information found in this book is, of course, your personal professional—your private attorney and your retaining attorney or your physician.

This book contains sections dealing with my testimony. I know that few people like to admit their own errors, and especially to publish their own mistakes, especially if it is going to be publicly graded as in this book by another expert. However, if these testimony errors serve as an instruction aid to those who will be in my place on the witness stand, so as to not repeat my many mistakes, it will be worth it. My testimony transcripts are presented here in abstracted, digest fashion and are critiqued and graded by an experienced medical malpractice attorney. My past testimony is offered in the sections selected to educate, entertain, stimulate, and provoke your thoughts prior to taking the witness stand. I have destroyed all of the original transcripts in accordance with the Health Insurance Portability and Accountability Act (HIPAA) privacy rules and regulations. However, any attorney in preparation for future malpractice cases in which I will appear as a medical expert witness can obtain all of my prior testimony transcripts from the usual commercial legal transcript services. To avoid any embarrassment to anybody (except myself), I have made every attempt to disguise all the names of all attorneys, courts, locations, and parties to litigation. But if I, or if any of my proofreaders or line editors missed a real name or location somewhere in this text, the buck stops with me. I am responsible. Please accept my full apologies. I assure you I will correct it in the next edition. In fact, if you contact me by e-mail, I will issue a written apology with a copy to anyone you want me to include.

I emphasize again that any similarity in the names or descriptions of places, institutions, organizations, or people living or dead is purely coincidental and completely unintentional.

I will also adapt what I heard Ms. Rosalie Hamilton say, (see Chapter 26) "For simplicity I have used 'he,' 'him,' and 'his' throughout the book. Women readers, please overlook this usage. I, as a father of four wonderful and successful daughters, became an early convert to women's rights and feminism. I look forward to a day when words will be coined in our society that apply equally to either gender."

To those attorneys cross-examining me on my book:

Q: Dr. Hookman, did you not write a book on how to testify in medical malpractice cases? And does not this mean that your main interest is not in medical care but in court testimony as a professional expert witness who derives his major income from litigation-related matters and spinoffs of book profits/royalties/lectures?

A: The short answers to your compound questions are Yes to the first question and to your subsequent compounded questions—No, No, No, and No.

If I may explain, "Yes, I did write this book on advice to the testifying physician."

You will note that I emphasized in this book to "always tell the truth while testifying." And as a matter of fact counselor, I state "Always tell the truth" as the Ten Commandments of medical testimony and I am sure you agree with that advice, don't you?"

Furthermore, as to your subsequent questions, medical expert testimony, as I am sure you know, is now advocated by most medical professional organizations, including the AMA, to be part of the practice of medicine. Indeed the high category of continuing medical education (CME) credits are given to those physicians attending many expert witness lectures and seminars. As a teacher, writer, and researcher in the practice of medicine and postgraduate clinical gastroenterology, the clinical practice of gastroenterology and internal medicine, continues to be my only profession and career, and occupies most of my professional time. I also teach medical students and physicians medical malpractice risk management, to be adequately prepared to testify not only as defendant physicians but also as medical expert witnesses. I believe that my experience as a medical expert makes this instruction part of my responsibility in my medical teaching duties.

As to the latter part of your compound question the majority of my income does not come from "litigation-related matters and spinoffs of book profits/royalties/lectures." In fact I do not personally profit from any book royalties. Any such income is donated directly to an IRS-approved charitable foundation, which gives financial support to programs of interest to the Hookman family such as autism, education, visiting scholars-in-residence, etc.

Q: Dr. Hookman, can you tell the jury what opinions that may directly or indirectly relate to the case at hand, you have expressed in this book?

A: There is not enough time to give you all my opinions in this book but the crux of the book is in agreement with Professor S. Boyarsky of Washington University School of Medicine, who in his article "Practical Measures to Reduce Medical Expert Witness Bias" (*Journal of Forensic Science*, 1989, 34(5), 1259–1265) states that the testifying physician, particularly in professional liability cases, must adhere to the very same measures, I have reiterated throughout the book, i.e., medical expert witnesses should adhere to these seven points:

1. Testify for both the plaintiff and the defense in different cases
2. Assess the merits of the case separately from agreeing to testify
3. Insist on reviewing all the records thoroughly
4. Develop a solid medical posture for each case
5. Review the case in a balanced, critical manner
6. Articulate carefully the standard of care in your own words before expressing it in deposition or at trial
7. Stay within the role and duty as "expert witness" and not as an advocate for either side.

To those attorneys who plan to take any of the sentences in this book either in context or out of context to challenge me during a future cross-examination in a medical malpractice case, I say, as a U.S. president did once to his regret, "Bring 'em on."

My answers about this book will center on the theme of a liberal educational approach by a review of many opinions other than my own. And in particular, my educational techniques in this book center on an evidence based medicine (EBM) approach, that is, collecting published literature on objective studies with a spectrum of other opinions. This offers an array of expert opinions (not necessarily mine), to educate my readers on the spectrum of thought in these matters, for each individual to draw their own conclusions and form their own opinions relying on a background of this spectrum of why I consider a compendium of thought and ideas about medical malpractice and testifying. As stated by the great thinker and essayist Michel de Montaigne, "I quote others only to better express myself;

and although copying from one author is plagiarism, copying from many hundreds of authors is research."

Also, I have designed the book so that one may either read the book in order, or dip into any chapter at random or as the need arises. Each chapter is complete unto itself with its own supporting references (also in the appendix), but cross-references are applied where appropriate. The fact that an occasional sentence or even an occasional paragraph may be repeated in a different chapter is an *intentional duplication* to aid the reader who chooses to dip into only one chapter at a time. The index will also help locate and sort out which subject matter you want to deal with first in this book. Also, the bibliography for the chapter may also be found in the CD-ROM appendix, which can be updated at will in various subjects.

After these explanations, please allow me a sip of water, and a few moments for a rest break, so I can call my daughter #1, the lawyer.

After she tells me "I told you so," I will need some additional time—like maybe the rest of the week—to rememorize the book so I can answer any further questions about it.

Acknowledgments

I thank and offer kudos to the following advisers, content editors, line editors, and contributors of this book.

Jonothan Aronson, Esq., from the law firm of Rodriguez Aronson & Essington PA, Miami, Florida graduated from the Washington University, St. Louis, Missouri (BA, 1980), and the University of Miami School of Law (JD cum laude, 1984). He was admitted to the bar, in 1984, Florida, U.S. District Court, Southern District of Florida, including Trial Bar and U.S. District Court, Middle District of Florida. He is a recipient of the American Jurisprudence Award. He served in the *Florida Bar Journal* editorial board (1997–1998). Mr. Aronson practices primarily in the fields of admiralty and general insurance defense.

Ms. Susan Dufault edited the appendix on the CD-ROM. She is currently the copy editor and proofreader of several peer-reviewed journals, including the *American Journal of Gastroenterology*, official journal of the American College of Gastroenterology, the *Journal of Rapid Methods and Automation in Microbiology*, and *Xenotransplantation*. Ms. Dufault graduated with a BSc (with honors) from Dalhousie University in biology and mathematics. She also obtained an MSc from Dalhousie University in biology. Ms. Dufault is an author herself, having published several peer-reviewed scientific articles based on her ongoing research in marine biology.

Tim Junkin, Esq., is from the Moffet & Junkin law firm, Washington, D.C. Mr. Junkin added many suggestions and did the content editing and proofreading of many of this book's chapters including attorney relations, defendant deposition, trial, and testimony preparation, plus the direct and cross-examination chapters. Mr. Junkin is a graduate of the University of Maryland (with honors) and Georgetown University law school. He has served as defense counsel in criminal and medical malpractice cases. He has taught at Georgetown University, Harvard University, and American University, where he received the adjunct professor of the year award. Tim Junkin is the author of "Bloodsworth" (2004)—the true story of the first death row inmate exonerated by DNA tests.

C. Richard Locke, III, MD, is from the Division of Gastroenterology and Division of Biostatistics, Mayo Clinic College of Medicine, Rochester, Minnesota. Dr. Locke is currently professor of medicine at the Mayo Clinic School of Medicine. He received his MD degree at the Harvard Medical School. Dr. Locke served his internship and residency in internal medicine at the University of Minnesota hospitals where he was also the chief resident. He had a fellowship in gastroenterology at the Mayo Clinic and was a special clinic fellow in epidemiology also at the Mayo Clinic. Dr. Locke's current research at the Mayo Clinic is in the field of applied epidemiologic and outcomes techniques to questions regarding gastrointestinal disorders. He has recently coauthored "Perils and Pitfalls of Small Negative Clinical Trials," which appeared in the *American Journal of Gastroenterology* (2006, 101(10), 2185–2186).

Michael C. Mattson, Esq., has represented dozens of plaintiffs in medical malpractice litigation. He is a partner of the law firm of Cooney, Mattson, Lance, Blackburn, Richards

& O'Connor, P.A. of Ft. Lauderdale, Florida. He graduated (BA) from Dickinson College, Carlisle, Pennsylvania, in 1977 and the University of Miami School of Law, Coral Gables, Florida, in 1980 with a JD (honors: cum laude). He served on the law journal *University of Miami Inter-American Law Journal* from 1979 to 1980. He was admitted to the bar, in 1980, Florida. Mr. Mattson has contributed to this book by his proofreading and modifications of some of the chapters dealing with legal subjects and testimony.

Alan E. Reider, Esq., from the law firm of Arent Fox in Washington, D.C., was named in 2006 as a "leading health care lawyer in Washington, D.C." I thank him for his help and suggestions on the chapter on Qui Tam and HIPPA, as well and advice on other sections of this book. Mr. Reider graduated from the Brown University (AB, 1971), the University of Texas School of Public Health (MPH, 1972), and Boston University School of Law (JD, 1975). He is a partner of the Washington, D.C. law firm of Arent Fox, where he has served as chair of the firm's health care practice section for 20 years. Mr. Reider has been the lead defense counsel in several major government investigation cases, and is currently the defense attorney for several major U.S. hospitals, physicians, and ambulatory surgery centers. He has published other chapters in several health care law books.

Allison Weber Shuren, Esq., graduated from the University of Michigan Law School (JD, 1998), University of Florida (MSN, 1994), and Salem State College (BSN Nursing cum laude, 1987). She is also an Arent Fox law firm member practicing in the health care practice group. Ms. Shuren reviewed the HIPPA chapter in this book and added the generic HIPAA forms recommended for medical offices. She focuses her law practice on a variety of regulatory and legislative health care issues involving Medicare coverage and reimbursement. She is also active in fraud and abuse counseling and investigations including defense of allegations of False Claims Act, Anti-Kickback and Stark Law violations, and review of HIPAA privacy and security standard compliance programs. Ms. Shuren has testified before the U.S. House Energy and Commerce Subcommittee on Health regarding Medicare. She is an active member of the American Health Lawyers Association, and the American Bar Association's health law section.

Carolyn A. Spence is an editor (life sciences) at Taylor & Francis. I thank her for having the faith that this book will be a "big hit."

Special Appreciation

A very special thank you to these individuals for chapter or section contribution.

Elliott A. Alman, Esq., is with the Maryland law firm of Elliott A. Alman, who contributed the section on disciplinary proceedings against physicians. Mr. Allman obtained his JD at the Catholic University Law School in 1979 and MA at State University of New York in 1972 after a BA at the City College of the City University of New York in 1970. Mr. Alman was admitted to the bar, in 1979, District of Columbia, in 1983, Maryland, and also to the U.S. District Court for the District of Columbia, U.S. District Court for the District of Maryland, the U.S. Court of Appeals for the Federal Circuit, and the U.S. Supreme Court. He is active in the American Association for Justice and serves as a section chairman. He is an experienced trial lawyer who represents plaintiffs in medical malpractice cases and physicians at various levels of disciplinary proceedings.

Wendy J. Hookman, MD, coauthor of "Proactive Strategies to Reduce Malpractice Risks in Psychiatry" is currently director of Washington Center for Women's and Children's Wellness in Rockville, MD. Dr. Hookman graduated from the University of Wisconsin with a BA in psychology and received her MD from the Medical College of Virginia in Richmond, VA in 1995. She served her residency in psychiatry at the Beth Israel Medical Center in New York from 1996 to 2000. Dr. Hookman is a former director of the Georgetown University Medical Center's Women's Mood Disorders Clinic. She is also the coauthor of "Maryland Medical History: Was William Osler Responsible for Gertrude Stein's Failure to Graduate From the Johns Hopkins University School of Medicine?" *Maryland Medical Journal* (1999, 48(5), 220–227).

Leigh McMillan, Esq., author of the chapter on maritime malpractice is also of the law firm of Rodriguez Aronson & Essington PA, Miami, Florida. Ms. McMillan graduated from New School University (BA), the City University of New York School of Law (JD, 2001), and the University of Miami School of Law (LLM, International Ocean and Coastal Law Program, 2002). Ms. McMillan was admitted to the bar, in 2003, Florida and New York. Ms. McMillan practices primarily in the fields of admiralty and civil rights law.

Michele T. Pato, MD, coauthor of "Proactive Strategies to Reduce Malpractice Risks in Psychiatry" is currently associate dean for academic scholarship at the Keck School of Medicine of the University of Southern California. She is well known in the field of psychiatry as a teacher of teachers. Dr. Pato received a ScB at the Brown University where she graduated with honors in psychology. She received her MD degree at the University of Cincinnati College of Medicine in 1983 and served her residency in psychiatry at the Harvard-affiliated Massachusetts General Hospital from 1983 to 1986. After completing her postgraduate fellowship in 1990 she became medical director of the Community Mental Health Center in Fall River, Massachusetts, a Brown University affiliate. She then accepted an appointment as residency training director at SUNY, Buffalo from 1996 to 2001, and served as associate chief of staff for research at the Syracuse VA from 2001 to 2002. She later served as director of education for the Department of Psychiatry at Georgetown from

2003 to 2006. Dr. Pato has gained international recognition for her research, lectures, and peer-reviewed published articles in the fields of obsessive compulsive disorder (OCD) and the genetics of mental illness.

The Honorable Judge James M. Vukelic earned his BS, MS, and JD from the University of North Dakota. He served as state's attorney from 1978 to 1986, and then as solicitor general from 1987 to 1994. He was district judge from 1994 to 2000.

Introduction

I wrote this book because this is the kind of book I wish was available to me prior to my first harsh contact with the U.S. medical malpractice tort system. It would have made a world of difference to me to be at least partially immunized against this foreign system. By educating me more, it would have decreased my high stress levels—if only I just knew what to expect in my first and only medical malpractice suit in which I was the defendant physician. Truly, being *forewarned is forearmed. Praemonitus, praemunitus*—the theme of this book is to forewarn you of the opposition's strategies to be used against you as a testifying physician—at least the strategies used against me, and that I have learned about the subject in more than 30 years of experience as a testifying physician on both sides—plaintiff and defendant.

How is this book different from most generic "one size fits all" generic expert witness books? First, this book is written for the medical professional, not for experts in handwriting, lip-reading, accident reconstruction, etc., which may have some common tactical denominators with each other but diverge sharply from medical professionals chiefly because these other books deal with tactics, not strategies. While some of the tactics may bear similar traits, the strategy of a medical professional is and should be very different from the others.

The terms *tactics* and *strategy* are often confused. Tactics are the actual means used to gain a goal, while strategy is the overall plan, which may involve complex patterns of individual tactics. A tactical plan is designed to implement strategic objectives. Tactics can also be isolated actions or events that take advantage of opportunities offered *within a given strategic system* to generate novel and inventive outcomes. Yet the tactician rarely holds onto these advantages in the absence of an overall strategy. This book teaches strategies—knowing at all times who you are, the role you play as the medical expert witness, and yours and the opposition strategies—not just the tactics.

The theme of this book "forewarned is to be forearmed" is to educate you about your opponent and to show you how you can be proactive with your own tactical plan based on an overall strategy in the context of actual medical practice. By knowing in advance yours and your opposition's strategies, you enter with a strategy and not just wait to make non-strategic isolated responses to the opposition's tactical plan designed to achieve his own strategic objectives.

> *"Praemonitus, praemunitus"*—Forewarned is forearmed

In these days of doctors, lawyers and lawsuits, chances of an American physician finishing his or her career without a malpractice claim are growing more remote. Every physician executive overseeing the activities of a group of peers knows this and should be prepared to assist [educate and pre-train] the physician who is sued.[1]

No member of the faculty of my medical school or training institutions ever formally prepared me for the real-world medical malpractice scene or of what I would encounter in medical practice. Nobody ever taught me medical practice risk-reduction strategies. No one ever taught me anything about testifying in court in the U.S. medical malpractice system, as a defendant or medical expert witness. Nor were there any electives I could choose to take in any of my many years of formal study and training.

This lack of preparation by medical education institutions is a significant defect in medical education and needs to be fixed (*see* Addendum: Readings and Quotations).

This book is intended for those physicians who will some day find themselves in a courtroom testifying either as a defendant or as a medical expert. In this era of medical organizational changes and instability that category includes all physicians. Some will be testifying just once or twice in their professional lives; others very skilled in their field of medicine may be asked to continue to testify more frequently. A broader purpose of this book is as a text to serve in a formal medical school and teaching hospital course.

The American Medical Association (AMA) has advocated that medical expert physician testimony should be part of "the practice of medicine." The American College of Physicians in 1990 and the AMA in 1998[2] adopted a policy that medical expert witness testimony by physicians be considered "part of the practice of medicine subject to peer review." But there are no formal courses that I know of either in medical school or in teaching hospitals in this subject. Critics state that this policy is just another attempt by organized medicine to control expert witnesses. Such criticism may be valid if organized medicine does nothing to support this policy through formal mandatory and elective educational programs in medical schools and teaching hospitals.

Nothing of major significance in this regard has yet been accomplished in the past 16 years. The absence of such formal training is a significant defect in medical education and needs to be remedied. As Gorney[1] emphasizes, "In these days of doctors, lawyers and lawsuits, chances of an American physician finishing his or her career without a malpractice claim are growing more remote." It is therefore up to each dean of a medical school, and each medical director or chief administrator of a teaching hospital to implement the appropriate training in preventive and offensive moves in medical malpractice litigation to all students and house staff and the attending physicians who supervise them.

It may also be feasible for physicians good at organizing to establish something similar to an American College of Medical Experts with the high standards of such similar specialty and professional organizations. Such an organization could do much in consolidating the now chaotic and bumbling attempts of many current players—state medical boards, licensing boards, specialty organizations, etc.—at sanctioning "fraudulent testimony." The field of medical expert witness testimony has thus been, for the most part, the tasks falling by default to a minority rather than optimally the majority of physicians.

Physicians have a responsibility to society, their peers, and patients to participate in malpractice litigation in a manner that ensures that medical malpractice cases are properly evaluated. But physicians are reluctant to involve themselves as expert witnesses in medical malpractice litigation because they simply are not educated or trained in "this practice of medicine." In addition, there is a general mistrust of attorneys and misconceptions about expert witnesses and the legal system in general. The authors conclude that if impartial physicians do not evaluate cases for attorneys, other more partisan and less objective physicians will.[2]

Residency programs routinely review cases involving "morbidity and mortality." It would be a "valuable experience to similarly review medical malpractice cases and the associated testimony by medical experts." When available, the cases reviewed in residency programs would be those in which faculty members at the same institution had testified. The faculty member in such cases would be intimately familiar with the case and able to share the knowledge necessary to take part in the legal process. This case review process would expose residents to the legal realities of medical practice, provide a forum for peer review of legal testimony by experts, and show residents how to participate in the legal system should the need arise."[3]

Why should there be special education along these lines? The reasons are that physicians must learn another foreign language—the legal language of the courtroom—as just one example in the education of physicians. Lawyers and physicians—point out that most physicians who are called upon to testify concerning medical issues especially in medical malpractice litigation do not understand the "foreign language of the court and the strange customs of legal proceedings."[4]

For example, judges and attorneys view the word "causation" quite differently than do the members of the medical community. Medical practitioners tend to be concerned with all the possible multiple causes of the patient's current and past medical condition (and differential diagnosis attempt to pinpoint by exclusion the one and only cause of illness). Whereas legal practitioners especially in medical malpractice cases generally focus just on one particular event as a "proximate cause" of an injurious result. This term "proximate cause" is what the legal community defines as "precipitating, hastening, or aggravating a particular aspect of the patient's condition to the injurious event." In fact, courts have interpreted the expression "proximate cause" as a cause, which in natural or probable sequence produced damages. Unlike medical school and postgraduate medical training, courts have ruled that it need not be the only cause. It is sufficient if it is a "substantial factor" concurring with some other cause acting at the same time which in combination causes damages. The proximate cause is considered a "substantial contributing cause" even though the injury, damage, or loss would have occurred anyway without that contributing cause. Thus the courts have ruled that a substantial cause need not be the sole factor, or even the primary factor in causing the plaintiff's injuries, but merely a substantial factor therein—a concept foreign to most well-trained physicians (*Newberry v. Martens*, No. 30967 2005 [Op'n No. 140] [Idaho Sup, Ct. Dec 30, 2005]). To a well-trained physician, this "logic" of "proximate cause" is exactly the opposite of what he learned in medical school and his postgraduate training.

To the physician this sounds like *post hoc ergo propter hoc*, ("after this, therefore because of this") or in other words "The rooster crows; the sun rises; therefore the rooster caused the sun to rise." Physicians have been trained in a scientific discipline that states, "just because events are sequentially related in time, they are not necessarily causally related." The rooster crows in the morning, the sun rises in the morning. This does not mean that the rooster causes the sun to rise.

Similarly, when a physician says, "he admits to..." it simply means to him he says or reveals a fact—not the legal connotation that "having previously denied ... he now admits to ..."

I have demonstrated just two language differences between the legal and medical communities—paradoxically both allegedly speaking English—and in several chapters

I have explained the magic words I have learned that a physician must use in court in order for his testimony not to be stricken by the judge. These are examples of the culture shock faced by the physician in court. With proper orientation, however, the physician can indeed become fluent in legalese.

My reason for writing this book is to help the physician to be more comfortable and more effective in his courtroom role. Whether because of time constraints resulting from being busy practitioners, resentment and distrust toward the legal system, disinterest, or lack of preparation and unfamiliarity with a foreign legal language and culture, many physicians have, up until the mid-1990s, been reluctant to participate in court proceedings and to testify in medical malpractice cases.

The reasons for this reluctance are evaluated by Ashar et al.[5] in the Johns Hopkins study.

The additional factors are the following:

1. Deterioration of the relationship between the medical and legal professions.
2. Conflicting economic interests in legal actions.
3. The reluctance of medical professionals to participate in the legal process was also catalyzed by the perception of increasing (frivolous?) medical malpractice claims ever since the 1970s according to Gibson and Schwartz.[6]
4. This reluctance to participate in testimony (defense or plaintiff) has occurred despite (allegedly encouraging) statements by medical professional associations in favor of such participation.[7]
5. The American College of Physicians[8] and The American College of Surgeons[9] have stated as a matter of policy that physicians "… have a duty to testify in court as expert witnesses."
6. Despite these proclamations there exists no sponsorship of formal training, by either organization to support this policy.
7. On the contrary, despite or because of common law immunity for civil liability for nonfraudulent medical expert witness testimony, *sanctions* for testifying physicians have shifted to forums such as organized medicine and professional medical societies. Medical specialty societies have developed extensive disciplinary proceedings for "violations of expert witness guidelines." Medical licensing boards and state medical societies also have defined medical testimony as the "practice of medicine," thereby also giving themselves jurisdiction to sanction licensees and members for what they in their wisdom decide is "improper testimony." Other professional organizations are starting the process of "monitoring" expert witness testimony as well, including supplying lawyers for legal actions against medical expert witnesses. Private organizations such as Medical Justice Services, Inc., provide specialty assistance to physicians who feel they have been the victims of "false expert witness testimony."
8. Physicians who are members of these organizations may see dissociation from what is proclaimed by their organizations and the many real-life disincentives for practicing physicians to give medical testimony. Unfortunately, this may lead to the opinion held by many physicians that expert testimony is simply not worth it that the cost–benefit ratio is too high to testify.
9. This opinion will bear validity if organized medicine does nothing to augment the policy statement that medical testimony be considered the practice of medicine, with real efforts to support formal educational programs in this subject in all medical

schools and teaching hospitals. And since nothing significant on this matter has been accomplished in the past 16 years, and since the "expert testimony is part of the practice of medicine" policies were proclaimed, perhaps this book will be a call for action. I sincerely hope that this book can serve as one of the textbooks for a formal program to teach young physicians or at least be the catalyst for others to do so.

The purpose of the Johns Hopkins study authored by Ashar et al.[5] was to "qualify and quantify" the current extent of physician participation in legal activities. The good news is that despite these above disincentives to testify, about 25% of the internal medicine physicians in practice or academia are currently actively engaged in legal case review and expert witness testimony. This indicates that there is an interest by physicians for testimony and that involvement in the legal system by physicians may be more widespread, and not dominated by just a few "hired guns" as was previously "alleged by some attorneys."

The Hopkins authors found that the engagement of a doctor to serve as an expert witness was significantly associated with internal medicine specialists. The fact that specialists engaged in these legal activities more frequently than generalists is consistent with a definition of "expert" that includes level of training and education. This study also documented that academic internal medicine physicians were even more likely to take part in expert witness activities than those in practice. Again, the "expert" status attached to academia probably is responsible for this finding, as well as the fact that academics may also have more flexibility in their work schedules to permit more time for medicolegal activities.

In addition, another fact distinguished by this group was that in those more likely to participate in medicolegal activities was

a. self-perception that personal income was higher (not lower as is the myth) than the income of other colleagues; and
b. physicians who have been in practice for more than 5 years were also more likely to participate than younger physicians. This may be due to limited opportunity for younger physicians, since many states require at least 5 years of work in the same specialty of the accused.

The authors concluded that though physician interest in participation in legal review and expert witness activities grows significantly, it appears not to be determined by economic factors, since the study found that economic factors were not associated with physicians engaging in medicolegal activities. This Hopkins study is significant in that it begins to discredit the allegation held by some attorneys, especially defendants' attorneys, that the impetus for an increasing expert witness "industry," is made up of only "a handful of economically motivated physicians."[10,11]

On the contrary, the substantially increasing involvement of physicians in legal review activities demonstrated in this study gives credence to an increased interest and a more widespread demography of medical experts. Previous undocumented allegations about physician experts were also negated by this study, such as physicians take on medicolegal activities because of

A. increasing instability in their historically financially secure profession,
B. limitations on reimbursements,
C. rising educational debt,

    D. escalating malpractice and overhead costs, and

    E. decline in incomes.

All these allegations have been disproven by this statistically valid study. This Hopkins study, on the contrary, found that engagement in legal review activities was not associated with declining or dissatisfaction with income, but suggested that the stimuli for participation in such activities were other than financial with significant noneconomic benefits. The benefits listed by the physicians in the study were

    1. to enhance a physician's reputation,

    2. add variety to routine clinical practice, and

    3. allow for greater understanding of the litigation process.

This study shows a real interest in medical testimony by well-trained physicians and suggests that proper education would increase these numbers for a desirable larger pool of medical experts.

Previous studies, however, have demonstrated marked deficiencies in physicians' knowledge of the legal system. This stems from the limited or no exposure that most medical students and residents have to medicolegal issues while in school and in training.[12]

It is for this reason that I as well as numerous other authors and educators advocate mandatory medical school and postgraduate courses in preventing and dealing with medical malpractice litigation as part of the formal university and teaching hospital curriculum. To my current knowledge, there are, in the main, few 2–3 h courses given annually by medical malpractice insurance carriers on this subject to practicing physicians for their own self-serving purposes of keeping down insurance expenses, but courtroom testimony should be part of the medical school curriculum right next to the medical treatment of the complications of diabetes. Thus, medical organizations, including the AMA, and the professional and specialty societies who advocate that medical testimony "is part of the practice of medicine" ought to add to their credibility by encouraging formal courses in this area. To back up their policy statements, medical school and teaching hospital courses ought to be established and maintained as formal teaching courses, as is with all other practice of medicine subjects. There is no doubt that there needs to be more education and training in this vital area of the "practice of medicine," similar to other courses given to prepare the student for clinical aspects of medical practice and as practicing physicians what they will face in the world outside the ivory tower.

It is not only medical students and physicians that I am addressing in this book; it is especially the thousands of postgraduate physicians working in residency programs throughout the United States—and their training directors—who daily are exposing themselves and their institutions to the risks of medical malpractice litigation, blissfully unaware of the medicolegal dangers surrounding them.

Resident physicians, attending physicians, and graduate medical education (GME) institutions share a collective responsibility. The law does not offer concessions in quality of care to accommodate GME. Resident physicians are generally held to the same standard of care as attending physicians in their respective specialties. Attending physicians face malpractice exposure *not only for the care they provide but also for the care they direct.* In addition, they may be held vicariously liable for the negligence of resident physicians working with them, or directly liable for inadequate supervision. Regardless of the nature of their relationship with the sponsoring institution, attending physicians may also be held liable for improper supervision, as supervising resident physicians is an inherent part of their job. This form of liability is direct. In other words, instead of or in addition to the charge that attending physicians are vicariously liable for the negligent acts of their resident physicians, plaintiffs may allege that the attending physicians are themselves liable for negligent oversight of care provided by resident physicians. GME institutions and programs bear legal responsibility for both the care they deliver and the negligence of their employees. They also face liability for failing to administer safe systems of care. Federal law requires that any payment of a claim against a physician, including resident physicians, be reported to the National Practitioner Data Bank (NPDB). This puts the teaching hospital in the forefront of teaching the preventive moves found in this book.[13]

This book provides the "chess" moves that go into good prevention and treatment strategies for the disorder known as the litigation against medical professionals (LAMP) syndrome. Ask any good chess player and she/he will tell you that most games are won or lost in training preparation or lack of it. This book reviews the beginning, mid-game, and endgame moves and preset maneuvers and strategic plays known to succeed for defense and offense to win or at least to draw, *but not to lose*. In this book, I also attempt to describe the many unique pressures acting on the testifying physician, and how this may be mitigated by adequate preparation.

Often, physicians who are asked to testify either as defendants or medical experts search for printed information to help themselves in this strange world of the courtroom with foreign customs and language. Too often these physicians fall prey to the "one size fits all" generic expert witness books that give generic expert witness advice and that, while perhaps adequate for the handwriting expert or maybe even business, traffic light, and accident reconstruction expert witnesses, are just not appropriate for the medical profession, either in their strategies or recommendations. This book has only the physician and medical professionals in mind. This book may give you, the physician, options you did not know existed, and you will be prepared to make fewer mistakes, or at least fewer than without this book.

Last but not least, the knowledge base and training of a medical expert witness must include a study of those factors that could go wrong in a medical practice, i.e., the factors common to all primary care and specialty practices that may according to Murphy's law*—"if anything can go wrong it will." The corollary with many names attached is "if a slice of bread falls from a table it almost always lands on the buttered side."

The first few chapters in this book are about—"a short history of American medical malpractice" to give the physician a short overview of the U.S. adversarial tort system. I have also included a chapter on "Avoiding Problems with Qui Tam, HIPPA, and Other Disciplinary Actions," which I believe in the coming years will assume a greater share of the LAMP syndrome. Chapters in the spectrum of medical practices risks are also covered. These are titled "Defensive Moves and Strategies to Avoid Medical Malpractice Suits in Primary Medical Care and Specialist Practice"; "Proactive Strategies to Reduce Malpractice Risks in Primary Care and Surgical Practice"; and "Proactive Strategies to Avoid Malpractice in Psychiatry" all dealing with subjects, which will be of interest also to other specialties. Try to remember that history and a review of inevitable medical practice risks are an antidote to delusions of omnipotence and omniscience.

---

* Actually, the original Murphy's law is more relevant. It states "If there are two or more ways to do something, and one of those can result in catastrophe, then someone will do it."—Edward A. Murphy.

These chapters are written to educate the physician within a context of what can and does go wrong in medical practice, because no matter what his specialty, he should not testify as a medical expert in a vacuum.

The medical expert witness must exhibit self-control on the witness stand; thus first and foremost he must know himself and his limitations, and the risks of his profession because self-knowledge is the indispensable prelude to self-control. Next, the medical expert witness must be educated in the strategies of the opposition in the U.S. adversarial tort system. Also, he must know the context of Murphy's law of the common denominators within the whole spectrum of medical practices and most malpractice lawsuits. This knowledge is crucial not only to the medical expert but also to the practicing physician in private or university practice.

These chapters adhere to our theme of preparing the physician not only with a tactical plan but also with the necessary strategies of a risk averse medical practice as well as the strategies leading to effective tactical plans for expert medical testimony.

An ancient Chinese strategist wrote in the sixth century BC:

> If you know your adversaries and know yourself, you will not be imperiled in a hundred battles; if you do not know your adversaries but do know yourself, you will win one and lose one; if you do not know your adversaries nor yourself, you will be imperiled in every single battle. If you know both yourself and your adversaries, you will come out of one hundred battles with one hundred victories.
>
> **—Sun Tzu's**
> *Military Strategy (also known as "The Art of War")*

This book teaches the strategies of knowing at all times who you are, the role you play as the defendant physician, or the medical expert witness, and yours and your *adversarie's* strategies—not just their tactics. We should note that despite the very different and unique specificities in the spectrum of medical practice from surgery to internal medicine and its subspecialties as well as psychiatry; all have common denominators of what can go wrong as well as the preventive and proactive strategies useful in managing these risks. Thus, to be a good medical expert witness you must know the general context of medical practice "on the ground"—before you can understand what medical malpractice is about and make an attempt to testify about it. You must fully understand the "whys, wherefores, limitations, and risks." You must know about medical practice systems that can go wrong—not just mistakes of leaving a sponge in the abdomen, as you will learn by reading these chapters.

The good medical expert witness as well as each practicing physician must be taught effective risk-reduction methods already found to be successful, as per the published literature.

This book starts out then with at least the minimum of what the medical expert witness and all practicing physicians must know about his field and the subject.

The minimum core common denominators to decrease risks in the entire spectrum of medical practice—no matter what the details or specificities of that field of medicine—are these:

- To disclose to the patient any information that a reasonable practitioner in a similar situation would disclose.
- To disclose any information that a reasonable patient would find significant to his or her decision.

- Informed consent should be obtained from all adult patients prior to the initiation of treatment, and from minor patients who are not legally authorized to provide consent. For minors who cannot provide consent, it should be obtained from parents or other legal custodians. Without proper documentation of consent, negligence claims are more likely to be successful.
- To maintain documentation of all communications to and from patients and to and from a third party about a patient with an automatic systematic mechanism for these notes to get into the appropriate patient's chart in a timely manner.
- To carefully choose a colleague to cover your practice when you are unavailable—whom you trust and know to be responsible and whose practice style is similar to your own.
- To be up-to-date in all the published guidelines of your practice, and document the reasons in the medical record of the patient why a treatment has *or has not* been performed according to the appropriate published guidelines for that disorder.
- Finally "a cover-up often has worse consequences than the initial mistake."

Truly, being forewarned is forearmed *"Praemonitus, praemunitus."*

Summary and Conclusions

- More physicians should be expert witnesses.
- The irresponsible expert witness is the product of failure of our current biomedical GME.
- Review and scholarly study of medical negligence cases should be an essential part of medical school and residency programs.
- All physicians must know the minimum core common denominators in decreasing litigation risks in all fields of medicine.
- "In our society it is well for a physician to know something of the workings of court and how to interact with attorneys. One need not go to law school to successfully navigate a legal proceeding as a physician witness. Skillful testifying is simply the transmission of medical information in court in a professional, polite, and compelling manner, an ability within the grasp of any physician who has mastered the art of working with colleagues and patients. Careful, honest assessment of the medical matters in a legal case places a physician in a strong position, which the physician can maintain by remaining polite, even in the face of attempts by an attorney to denigrate the physician's professional abilities. The best witnesses tell the truth in a manner that compels people in the courtroom to listen."[14]

An experienced medical lecturer taught me before I gave my first medical lecture to make sure to quit talking after I had accomplished just three things:

1. Tell them what you are going to tell them
2. Tell them
3. Tell them what you told them

I have just completed first of the three lecture points. Now let us go on to the next two.

Addendum: Readings and Quotations

1. The problems associated with inaccurate, misleading, or biased testimony from expert witnesses are well known. Expert witnesses are actively pursued for their views, their presentation style, and their willingness to tailor their testimony according to the particular needs of the case.[15]

2. The rewards for suits for medical negligence have generated a service industry for plaintiff's lawyers. The provision of "experts" for a contingency fee and the solicitation of plaintiff's attorneys by some physicians to serve as "experts" for large fees may result in highly biased and inaccurate testimony. Ethical expert witness testimony involves knowledge of the commonly accepted principles of treatment at the time of the alleged negligence, recognition of possible multiple accepted avenues of therapy, and testimony that educates the court and jury rather than obfuscates and distorts for personal gain.

3. Physicians have a responsibility to society, their peers, and patients to participate in malpractice litigation in a manner that ensures that medical malpractice cases are properly evaluated. Physicians are reluctant to involve themselves as expert witnesses in medical malpractice litigation because of not wanting to further any malpractice suits, mistrust of attorneys, and misconceptions about expert witnesses and the legal system in general. The expert witness should be an impartial practicing physician who can select those suits that should or should not be filed and identify which parties were negligent in each case. If impartial physicians do not evaluate cases for attorneys, other more partisan and less objective physicians will. The courts are entitled to expect both medical competence and expertise in conveying medical knowledge. Doctors should be familiar with their obligations as competent expert medical witnesses. *There is a pressing need for medical schools to train doctors in the skills required of an expert medical witness.*[2]

4. Many forces have created the epidemic of negligence and malpractice litigation. One of the contributing factors to the rising rate of nonmeritorious litigation is the increasing number of unqualified and irresponsible expert witnesses. The high remuneration has attracted physician-scientists who are unaware of the proper role of an expert witness. They are frequently manipulated by the attorneys and function as partisans rather than scholars. *The role of the expert witness should be taught in medical and graduate school. Testimony should be taught in medical and graduate school. Testimony should be treated as a scholarly endeavor and experts should be encouraged to seek peer review of their opinions and not to testify secretly and in isolation.* It is suggested that greater visibility of experts and their testimony (light of day phenomenon) should raise the quality of expert witness testimony and encourage more qualified experts to participate as expert witnesses, thus removing the stigmata usually associated with unqualified expert witnesses.

5. Residency programs routinely review cases involving "morbidity and mortality." It would be a valuable experience to similarly review medical malpractice cases and the associated testimony by medical experts. *When available, the cases reviewed in residency programs would be those in which faculty members at the same institution had testified.* The faculty member in such cases would be intimately familiar with the case and able to share the knowledge necessary to take part in the legal process. This case review process would expose residents to the *legal realities of medical practice,*

provide a forum for peer review of legal testimony by experts, and show residents how to participate in the legal system should the need arise.[3]

References

1. Gorney M. Coping with bad news: the physician executive's role in a lawsuit. *Physician Exec.* 2002; 28: 26–29.
2. Fish R, Rosen P. Physicians should be expert witnesses. *J. Emerg. Med.* 1990 Sep–Oct; 8: 659–663.
3. Fish R, et al. Review of medical negligence cases: an essential part of residency programs. *J. Emerg. Med.* 1992 Jul–Aug; 10(4): 501–504.
4. Danner D, Sagall EL. Medicolegal causation: a source of professional misunderstanding. *Am. J. Law Med.* 1977 Fall; 3(3): 303–308.
5. Ashar B, et al. Extent and determinants of physician participation in expert witness testimony. *South Med. J.* 2005; 98: 444–449.
6. Gibson JM, Schwartz RL. Physicians and lawyers: science, art, and conflict. *Am. J. Law Med.* 1980; 6: 173–182.
7. Levy DA. Physicians are currently being persuaded to participate as medical witnesses more frequently. *Ann. Intern. Med.* 1996; 125: 140.
8. American College of Physicians. Guidelines for the physician expert witness. *Ann. Intern. Med.* 1990; 113: 789.
9. Professional Liability Committee of the American College of Surgeons' statement on the physician expert witness. *Bull. Am. Coll. Surg.* 2000; 85: 24–25.
10. Weintraub MI. Expert witness testimony. *Neurol. Clin.* 1999; 17: 363–369.
11. McAbee GN. Improper expert witness testimony. *J. Leg. Med.* 1998; 19: 257–272.
12. Darvall L, McMahon M, Piterman L. Medico-legal knowledge of general practitioners: disjunctions, errors and uncertainties. *J. Law Med.* 2001; 9: 167–184.
13. Kachalia G, Studdert DM. Professional liability issues in graduate medical education. *JAMA* 2004; 292: 1051–1056.
14. Davis L. The art of attorney interaction and courtroom testimony. *Arch. Pathol. Lab Med.* 2006; 130: 1305–1308.
15. Spencer FC, Guice KS. The expert medical witness: concerns, limits, and remedies. *Bull. Am. Coll. Surg.* 2000 Jun; 85(6): 22–23.

For Further Reading

American Medical Association. Expert witness testimony (H-265.992). Available at: http://www.amaassn.org/

Asch DA, Jedrziewski MK, Christakis NA. Response rates to mail surveys published in medical journals. *J. Clin. Epidemiol.* 1997; 50: 1129–1136.

Cummings SM, Savitz LA, Konrad TR. Reported response rates to mailed physician questionnaires. *Health Serv. Res.* 2001; 35: 1347–1355.

Goldberg JH. Primary care earning plummet. *Med. Econ.* 2000; 77: 141–157.

Greenberg M. Developing alternative revenue sources. *Med. Group Manage. J.* 2000; 47: 26–29.

May WF. Money and the medical profession. *Kennedy Inst. Ethics J.* 1997; 7: 1–13.

McCrary SV, Swanson JW, Perkins HS et al. Treatment decisions for terminally ill patients: physicians' legal defensiveness and knowledge of medical law. *Law Med. Health Care.* 1992; 20: 364–376.

Moser JW. *Socioeconomic Characteristics of Medical Practice 1997/98*. Chicago, IL: Center for Health Policy Research, American Medical Association, 2000, pp. 5–14.

Pham HH, Devers KJ, May JH et al. Financial pressures spur physician entrepreneurialism. *Health Aff.* 2004; 23: 70–81.

Thompson DF. Understanding financial conflicts of interest. *N. Engl. J. Med.* 1993; 329: 573–576.

Weintraub MI. Expert witness testimony. A time for self-regulation? *Neurology* 1995; 45: 855–858.

Medical Malpractice and Tort Reform in the United States

2

You can't know where you're going if you don't know where you've been.

—Anonymous

That hurts my pride, Watson. It is a petty feeling, no doubt, but it hurts my pride.

—Sherlock Holmes
The Five Orange Pips

The modern concept of professional malpractice started in England following the publication in 1768 of Sir William Blackstone's (1723–1780) *Commentaries on the Laws of England* in which Blackstone linked professional malpractice to physicians. In fact the term malpractice from Blackstone's term originally defined as *mala praxis*, or injuries caused by the neglect or unskillful management by physicians, which breaks the trust between patient and physician. His *Commentaries on the Laws of England* were widely read in the Americas. According to Friedenberg,[1] in the United States prior to 1800, malpractice as we know it today was almost unknown.

But in 1794, 5 years after George Washington was inaugurated as the first president of the United States, the new nation's first medical malpractice lawsuit was adjudicated by a Connecticut court. The husband of a woman who had died as a result of surgery sued the physician for operating in "the most unskillful, ignorant, and cruel manner, contrary to all the well-known rules and principles of practice," and violating "his promise to the plaintiff to perform said operation skillfully and with safety to his wife" (*Gill v. Foster*, 232 3d 768 (Ill App1992)). The lawsuit, the primary allegation of which was breach of contract, was won by the plaintiff. The jury found the physician liable and awarded damages of 40 English pounds.

Benjamin Rush, prominent physician and signer of the Declaration of Independence, called for lectures in medical education that would bring together "those who possess medical knowledge with those who exercise legal authority," and by 1850, such educational programs were instituted in many medical schools in the United States.[2]

However, by the 1890s, cooperation between the two professions degenerated, and acrimony between physicians and attorneys became commonplace. An editorial in the *Journal of the American Medical Association* in 1892 addressed this sad state of affairs and its impact on the quality of expert medical testimony by lashing out at the "disgraceful exhibition of medical experts who are hired . . . [to give] paid theories and opinions": "The lawyers, acting as generals, lead the experts up to conflict, enthused with the idea that the truth is the great object of the struggle. In reality, both sides care nothing for the truth; winning the case is paramount to every other object. The expert physician is seductively drawn up to make statements, then driven to retract or qualify them and pressed to perjury, or so near it that it will be difficult to draw the line. . . . He is made to give a jumbled, confused mass of half-truths and facts open to question. . . . Both sides avoid informing the jury, and are always eager to deceive them." An article published in an 1897 issue of the *Harvard Law Review*[3] also made reference to the low esteem in which expert medical testimony was held by creating a hypothetic opening statement from an attorney to a jury: "Gentlemen of the jury, there are three kinds of liars: the common liar, the damned liar, and the scientific expert."[4]

> The American medical malpractice scene changed in the mid-1800s when aggressive and flamboyant medical advertising became popular, accompanied by a sharp decline in religious fatalism. Concurrently, American courts relaxed the standards for initiating civil tort proceedings for cases such as those of malpractice. The American Medical Association, which was established in 1847, attempted to provide national standards for medical education, licensing, and ethics. This established the first standards of practice for the medical profession, and the standards created an aura of legitimacy for the profession and attempted to enlighten the public about the dangers of nonlicensed healers and quack remedies. An unforeseen complication was that the listing of standards of practice provided an opening for a flood of malpractice cases. It is difficult to prove malpractice without established standards of practice. Licensed physicians now became vulnerable, while alternative healers, who had no established standards, could not really be sued for undesirable results.[1]

Physicians were also making allegations of witch hunts in that era. And some of Blackstone's critics pointed to his oft-mentioned quotation, "Any lawyer who writes so clearly to be intelligible . . . is an enemy to his profession."

However, Blackstone is also reliably quoted as saying, "to deny the actual existence of Witchcraft is to flatly contradict the word of God" (Commentaries IV).

> After the World War II, came the era of specialists. Prior to this time, patients had developed a long-term relationship of trust with their family physician. Now the patient was referred to specialists whom they did not know and with whom there was no particular personal relationship of trust. Patients developed the concept that any medical error was avoidable, and malpractice cases markedly increased in the 1960s and 1970s. As the fear of suits increased, physicians began to practice defensive medicine, which led to marked increases in the cost of health care.[1]

According to University of Oregon history professor J.C. Mohr,[5] medical malpractice litigation appeared in the United States around 1840 for reasons specific to that period.

Medical malpractice litigation, Mohr claims, has since been sustained for a century and a half by an interacting combination of these principal factors:

- The innovative pressures on American medicine
- The spread of uniform standards

- Advent of medical malpractice liability insurance
- Attorney contingent fees
- Citizen juries
- Nature of tort pleading in the United States.

2.1   Evaluation of the Current U.S. Medical Malpractice Tort System

2.1.1   Executive Summary

Health care is too important to be allowed to suffer from misperceptions about the malpractice system. Too much time and energy are wasted on pursuing false devils. Too many people use the problems of patients and providers for their own political ends. We need to bring together providers, lawyers and health policy researchers of good will to find ways to improve the way things work. But their deliberations must be based on reality.[6]

There have been loud shouting matches heard for at least the past 10 years from representatives of medical malpractice trial lawyers, med mal carriers, and physicians about the cost of insurance and who is to blame for it. All have criticized the "system" for terrible state of medical malpractice processes and have advised tort reforms. To clarify the maze of conflicting claims about U.S. medical malpractice issues, several experts (Tom Baker, Connecticut Mutual professor of law, and Director, Insurance Law Center, University of Connecticut School of Law; David Hyman, professor of law and Galowich-Huizenga faculty scholar at the University of Illinois College of Law; and Charles Silver, codirector, Center on Lawyers) reviewed the "crisis." They wrote what I believe is the best review available. This is a summary of their presentation and conclusions.[6]

2.1.2   A Reality Check

2.1.2.1   Background

A 1974 California study by Don Harper Mills and the Harvard Medical Practice Study in 1991 showed, first, that very few patients who had suffered injury from medical malpractice sued, and second, that a considerable amount of medical error took place. A 2000 report by the Institute of Medicine entitled *To Err Is Human* later estimated that malpractice caused approximately 98,000 U.S. deaths per year. The potential solution by the Harvard study authors of no-fault insurance was criticized as impractical and unfair—impractical, because it would be very expensive, and unfair, because the way that the Harvard authors proposed to reduce costs was to cut down dramatically on the amount of compensation for the most seriously injured patients.[7]

2.1.2.2   A Review of Objective Studies

- Virtually all patients who sue (for medical malpractice) suffered adverse outcomes involving serious physical injuries, and most have plausible or valid claims.
- Truly frivolous complaints are rare.
- Far more common are claims that seem strong initially but that turn out to lack merit.

- The U.S. malpractice system weeds out these claims fairly well.
- Patients with meritorious complaints receive payments more often and receive larger amounts.
- The system also appears to be stable in important respects. Claim frequency, payment frequency, payment amount, and jury verdicts have all fallen slightly, held roughly constant, or risen slightly.
- There are no dramatic changes in any of these measures, and the trends that have been noted appear to reflect rising health care costs or the progressive removal of smaller cases from the system.[8]
- "[T]he conclusion that the malpractice system is generally stable and predictable seems surprising only because health care providers and tort reform advocates complain so loudly and so often that it is 'broken' and 'spinning out of control.'"[9]

2.1.2.2.1 The tort system does a good job of sorting medical malpractice claims. After patients file malpractice cases, the system does a reasonably good job of sorting the wheat from the chaff—a much better job than many proponents of tort reform suggest. Many studies report high frequencies of settlement and payment in cases where experts agree that defendants violated the standard of care and low frequencies when experts agree otherwise.[10]

The conclusions in another 2006 analysis was that, "The bottom line is that a strong correlation exists between the likelihood of receiving payment and the merits of malpractice claims. . . . When patients do sue, the malpractice system sorts their claims relatively well,"[11] . . . and that "negligence matters a great deal to the outcome of a medical malpractice claim,"[12] and that "the legal system does a remarkably good job at weeding out weaker claims."[13]

2.1.2.2.2 The U.S. tort system rarely provides compensation to undeserving plaintiffs. Baker points out that the "Harvard data are as likely to support a very different finding, namely that most malpractice claims are reasonably related to medical management injury and provider negligence."[14] What the public heard was that medical malpractice claims are frivolous and that the wrong people get paid. "The investigators found that the (Harvard) and the follow-up study prove no such thing and the rest of the literature suggests exactly the opposite conclusion."[15]

Indeed opine the reviewers, "the malpractice system performs reasonably well in its function of separating claims without merit from those with merit and compensating the latter. In a sense, our findings lend support to this view: three quarters of the litigation outcomes were concordant with the merits of the claim."[16]

2.1.2.2.3 Major points

- ✓ Frivolous lawsuits are not a problem. The profile of nonerror claims observed does not square with the notion of opportunistic trial lawyers pursuing questionable lawsuits in which their chances of winning are reasonable and prospective returns in the event of a win are high.
- ✓ Rather, findings underscore how difficult it may be for plaintiffs and their attorneys to discern what has happened before the initiation of a claim and the acquisition of knowledge that comes from the investigations, consultation with experts, and sharing of information that litigation triggers.[17]

✓ Plaintiffs attorneys do not refuse to settle cases. The refusal to make settlement [named "settlement hardball"], and may explain how it accounts for what may appear to be unmeritorious verdicts.

✓ Some frequency of jury verdicts in favor of plaintiffs with long-shot claims is predictable in a world where providers play "settlement hardball."[18]

✓ There is no good evidence that the tort system is causing problems of defensive medicine or lack of patient access to care. Most defensive-medicine studies have failed to demonstrate any real impacts on medical practice arising from higher malpractice premiums."[19]

✓ Given the uncertainty over what constitutes proper care, the costs of the malpractice system are not excessive: The costs of the malpractice system have little impact on the overall cost of health care.

✓ Even if malpractice insurance premiums decreased nationally by 25–30%, the reduction in overall health care spending would be in the neighborhood of only 0.05%.[20]

✓ Malpractice costs do not make a substantial impact on physician incomes. Surveys by the American Medical Association show that "premiums have consistently been a small percentage of total practice expenses except within anesthesiology, which is a result of its having much lower than average premium expenses. When premium increases occurred between 1970 and 1986, and from 1996 to 2000, they had only a small effect on net income."[21]

✓ The malpractice system does not discourage the disclosure of errors: Reports of near misses and no-harm events are rare even though these errors cannot result in liability. Underreporting and a punitive practice culture were serious problems at VHA hospitals, even though the FTCA protected doctors and nurses who work there from malpractice suits.[22]

✓ Why, then, are providers so reluctant to disclose errors? Northwestern University law professor Steven Lubet explains that doctors, being human are simply reluctant to admit mistakes to their patients, and instead seize upon any available rationalization. "Today, the excuse is malpractice liability. In the old days, it was the patients' own welfare—they would not heal as rapidly, it was said, if they lost confidence in their physicians."[23]

✓ Given the significance of these factors, Hyman and Silver conclude, "it is naive to think that error reporting and health care quality would improve automatically by removing the threat of liability."[24] In short, anesthesiologists worked hard to protect patients because of malpractice exposure, not in spite of it."[25]

✓ The Harvard study found that the experience of being sued "made [doctors] twice as likely to take more time in explaining the risks of treatment to their patients," which is the opposite of the effect that patient safety advocates, who argue that malpractice liability discourages candor, predicted.

✓ Not surprisingly, the Harvard study report recommends that policymakers accept and act on the "indication . . . that malpractice litigation does have an injury prevention effect."[26]

✓ The reason why tort liability promotes patient safety is obvious. "It's the incentives, stupid": Providers are rational . . . when insurance rates go up, they create an incentive for providers to improve the quality of the services they are offering.

2.1.2.2.4   Major points for suggested improvements for the U.S. tort system.   The target should not be the tort system, but the real cause of the crisis: the insurance industry.

- In short, we need to attack the insurance cycle directly.
- Much of the blame for the recent insurance crisis, for example, is attributable to the insurers' practice of reducing premiums in good times to increase market share, only to find themselves without adequate funds when times get bad.
- A solution would be to enable state insurance regulators to control, not only the maximum premium rates, but also the minimum.
- Cushion the blow of sudden changes in the malpractice insurance industry by transferring more of the risk from insurers to reinsurers.
- Subsidize premiums for high-risk specialties, the ones that bear the greatest risk, when premiums rise precipitously.
- Reduce medical uncertainty. The more practitioners know about how to practice good medicine, the lower the rate of error and the more efficient the malpractice system.
- Therefore, we should invest *more in evidence-based medicine* by commissioning more studies on safety and effectiveness.
- Given the degree to which medical mistakes are *drug mistakes*, we also should require drug manufacturers, at a minimum, to conduct safety studies on substantial off-label uses of their products.
- Enhance the effort to create sound medical guidelines, but based on evidence rather than anecdote. For example, only evidence-based guidelines should be given presumptive weight under the law.
- Expand the proper use of apologies and early settlement offers.
- The most obvious way to reduce the costs of the malpractice system is to reduce medical errors and decrease the costs of paying for them.
- Disclosure of error is key to the former. So there must be some incentive to encourage disclosure. This incentive can be positive, such as a financial reward for disclosure, or negative, such as punishing nondisclosure. It can be direct, such as immediate cash payment, or indirect, such as greater profit under a pay-for-performance approach.
- Apologies and settlement offers also can decrease transactions costs, but not the way some apology-and-offer programs work. One model to be avoided is the one used by a physician-owned medical malpractice insurance company in Colorado called COPIC, which coaches the "apologists," offers miniscule settlement amounts, and refuses to deal with patients who involve attorneys.
- Providers should routinely advise patients to consult an attorney before accepting a provider's settlement offer.

2.1.2.2.5   Addendum: signs of the changing times—in the medical-legal environment as of Spring-Summer, 2007

1. Juries are usually able to recognize weak cases, agreeing with legal experts 80–90% of the time.

    In the May 2007 edition of the Michigan Law Review, P.G. Peters, found in a study that when there is any doubt after hearing all the evidence and expert opinions, juries usually return a verdict in favor of the physician. Peters reached this conclusion after conducting an extensive review of studies of malpractice cases from 1989 to 2006, which included cases involving all medical specialties and assessed expert medical opinions as well as the merits of the claims. The data in this study showed that defendants and their medical experts are more successful than plaintiffs and their experts at persuading juries to reach verdicts that are *contrary to the evidence.*"

Key points reached by the Peters review include the following:

- Plaintiffs seldom win weak cases. They are more likely to succeed in toss-up cases and if there is strong evidence of negligence.
- Juries are usually able to recognize weak cases, agreeing with legal experts 80–90% of the time.
- Physicians win 50% of the cases that independent legal experts believed the plaintiff would win.

2. A physician successfully countersued after an insurance company filed a "frivolous" suit for malpractice against physician."

In 1999, Travelers settled a worker's comp claim with a patient. With only a few days to go before the statute of limitations ran out, the patient's insurance carrier in turn sued the physician for medical malpractice, alleging he was responsible for the patient's disability. "The insurance company allegedly was hoping to get back some or all of the $775,000 they had to pay," claimed the physician.

In 2001, a court ruled in favor of the physician who then countersued the insurance carrier for malicious prosecution, alleging that the insurance carrier filed a frivolous lawsuit hoping for a quick settlement to recoup their lost funds from the worker's comp claim. The physician alleged that the suit had cost him personally and professionally as he had to dedicate time and funds to defend. He also alleged that he was passed over for a job at his university because of this malpractice suit.

Though both the trial court and state appeals court initially ruled in favor of the insurance carrier, the Massachusetts Supreme Court ruled otherwise in an April ruling. They decided that the case should go to trial and the physician would have his day in court because there was sufficient evidence to prove malicious intent on the part of the insurance carrier and that a jury should hear the case.

As this case shows, the medico-legal atmosphere in the United States is constantly changing as new laws are passed and new legal precedents are set. Traditionally, doctors targeted by frivolous medical malpractice lawsuits have had little to no recourse, as the legal standard for proving malicious prosecution is often prohibitively high. Though malicious prosecution is difficult to prove, one of the most important components of this court's ruling is updating the standard for "malice" in malicious prosecution.

This Massachusetts court opted to define malice *as a case filed with an "improper purpose,"* an example being a case unfounded on probable cause. This is different from the earlier standard definition of malice, which would allow a plaintiff to prevail in only the rarest of cases.

While this turn of events is certainly encouraging to physicians who feel the need to countersue, physicians should not get the impression that malicious prosecution is easy to prove. Even with this more favorable standard, *of a case filed with an "improper purpose"* and unfounded on probable cause, it is still extremely difficult for "a victimized physician" to prevail in a suit for malicious prosecution.

However, there will be no end of physicians who wish to countersue.

3. A survey conducted by the University of Virginia's Center for Survey Research Center released April 5, 2007 showed that
   - more than 60% of the physician respondents believe lawyers choose their medical expert witnesses based on the physician's willingness to support the lawyer's case,
   - 72% of the physician specialists in the survey personally have seen or heard statements by a medical expert witness in a courtroom they viewed as inaccurate or based on questionable science, and
   - 64% rated the quality of medical expert witness testimony as "poor" or "only fair."
   Other results of this survey include the following:
   - 80% of physicians believe medical expert testimony has a negative impact on the integrity of their profession.
   - 88% of physicians say that physicians who give expert witness testimony should be held to the same standards and sanctioning as they would in their practice or hospital setting.
   - 82% of physicians feel that a medical expert witness found to be giving fraudulent testimony should be sanctioned both in the state where they testified and the state where they practice.
   - 96% of physicians want a code of ethics to govern physician conduct in providing expert witness testimony.
   - 94% of physicians feel it is unethical for an expert witness to receive payment contingent upon the outcome of their testimony.

4. On May 2, 2007 the Maryland Appeals Court upheld the suspension of a physician who misrepresented facts about surgery he performed to investigators and ruled that Maryland's State Board of Physicians (Board) did not err in concluding that the physician engaged in unprofessional conduct in the practice of medicine by misrepresenting to both a hospital peer review investigator and the Board. The Maryland Court of Special Appeals upheld the Board's decision to suspend the physician until he satisfied certain conditions, and to impose a three-year probationary period thereafter. The Board also alleged unprofessional conduct in the practice of medicine in violation of rules, which allow the Board to discipline a licensee who "is guilty of immoral or unprofessional conduct in the practice of medicine," and who "[w]illfully make or files a false report or record in the practice of medicine." In determining that the physician's dishonesty in peer review proceedings qualified as unprofessional conduct in the practice of medicine, the appeals court said that "there can be no debate that a physician's lack of veracity regarding events in an operating room constitutes unprofessional conduct" (*Cornfeld v. State Bd. of Physicians*, No. 0175, Md. Ct. Spec. App. May 2, 2007).

5. On May 3, 2007 the Ohio Appeals Court affirmed sanctions against malpractice attorney for filing a case "With No Merit." The Ohio Court of Appeals noted that *Ohio law provided a mechanism for an award of sanctions for frivolous litigation.* The appeals court held that an attorney "*committed sanctionable conduct by maintaining a matter on the court's active docket long after he knew the medical malpractice case lacked merit.*" In addition, "*the attorney added a punitive damages claim to his re-filed complaint even though it is clear from the record that there was no basis in law for such a claim,*" the appeals court found (*Sigmon v. Southwest Gen. Health Ctr.*, No. 88276, Ohio Ct. App. May 3, 2007).

6. In December 2003, the American College of Physicians (ACP) sponsored a resolution in the American Medical Association's House of Delegates urging the AMA to prohibit the release or sale of doctors' prescribing information. In 2007, the AMA established an opt-out list for physicians who do not want their data shared with pharmaceutical representatives. About 7,000 doctors registered on the opt-out list. New Hampshire was the first state to pass legislation restricting pharmaceutical companies' access to information about individual physicians and their prescriptions in 2006. Shortly after passage of the law, IMS Health and Verispan, two companies which collect, analyze, and sell medical data, sued the state, charging that the law was unconstitutional. *And on May 1, 2007 a year-old law banning prescription data collection was struck down on the basis of restricting free speech and violating the First Amendment.* Thus pharmaceutical companies can continue to collect and use data on physicians' prescribing habits, a federal judge ruled.

References

1. Friedenberg RM. Patient–doctor relationships. *Radiology* 2003; 226: 306–308.
2. Martensen RL, Jones DS. Expert medical testimony. *JAMA* 1997; 272: 1707.
3. Murphy JP. Expert witnesses at trial: where are the ethics? *Georgetown Journal of Legal Ethics* 2000; 14: 217–240.
4. Berlin L. The miasmatic expert witness; *AJR* 2003; 181: 29–35.
5. Mohr JC. American medical malpractice litigation in historical perspective. *JAMA* 2000; 283: 1731–1737.
6. Maxwell J, Mehlman JD. The Truth About Medical Malpractice. Cyberrounds 2006 by (available at data presented in 2006 Cyberounds.com article. (http://www.pewtrusts.org/pdf/vf_medical_malpractice_fairness.pdf).
7. Saying No to No-Fault: What the Harvard Malpractice Study Means For Medical Malpractice Reform (New York State Bar Association, 1991).
8. http://www.cyberounds.com/conf/health_lawbioethics/2006-11-15/reference_51.html
9. http://www.cyberounds.com/conf/health_lawbioethics/2006-11-15/reference_52.html
10. http://www.cyberounds.com/conf/health_lawbioethics/2006-11-15/reference_1.html
11. http://www.cyberounds.com/conf/health_lawbioethics/2006-11-15/reference_2.html
12. http://www.cyberounds.com/conf/health_lawbioethics/2006-11-15/reference_3.html
13. http://www.cyberounds.com/conf/health_lawbioethics/2006-11-15/reference_4.html
14. http://www.cyberounds.com/conf/health_lawbioethics/2006-11-15/reference_8.html
15. http://www.cyberounds.com/conf/health_lawbioethics/2006-11-15/reference_11.html
16. http://www.cyberounds.com/conf/health_lawbioethics/2006-11-15/reference_14.html
17. http://www.cyberounds.com/conf/health_lawbioethics/2006-11-15/reference_17.html
18. http://www.cyberounds.com/conf/health_lawbioethics/2006-11-15/reference_19.html
19. http://www.cyberounds.com/conf/health_lawbioethics/2006-11-15/reference_21.html
20. http://www.cyberounds.com/conf/health_lawbioethics/2006-11-15/reference_28.html
21. http://www.cyberounds.com/conf/health_lawbioethics/2006-11-15/reference_29.html
22. http://www.cyberounds.com/conf/health_lawbioethics/2006-11-15/reference_36.html
23. http://www.cyberounds.com/conf/health_lawbioethics/2006-11-15/reference_39.html
24. http://www.cyberounds.com/conf/health_lawbioethics/2006-11-15/reference_40.html
25. http://www.cyberounds.com/conf/health_lawbioethics/2006-11-15/reference_43.html
26. http://www.cyberounds.com/conf/health_lawbioethics/2006-11-15/reference_46.html

For Further Reading

Abraham KS, Weiler PC. Enterprise medical liability and the evolution of the American health care system. *Harvard Law Rev.* 1994; 108: 381–436.

Baker T. Reconsidering the Harvard medical practice study conclusions about the validity of medical malpractice claims. *J. L. Med. Ethics* 2005; 33: 501–502, 511–512.

Baker T. *The Medical Malpractice Myth*, Vol. 110, Chicago, IL: University of Chicago Press, 2005, 62, 93, 97.

Baldwin L, Hart LG, Lloyd M, Fordyce M, Rosenblatt RA. Defensive medicine and obstetrics. *JAMA* 1995; 274: 1606–1610.

Berwick DM, Leape LL. Reducing errors in medicine. *BMJ* 1999; 319: 136–137.

Blendon RJ, DesRoches CM, Brodie M, et al. Views of practicing physicians and the public on medical errors. *N Engl. J. Med.* 2002; 347: 1933–1940.

Born PH, Viscusi WK. The distribution of the insurance market effects of tort liability reforms. In: *Brookings Papers on Economic Activity: Microeconomics.* Washington, DC: Brookings Institution, 1998, pp. 55–105.

Bovbjerg RR. Legislation on medical malpractice: further developments and a preliminary report card. *Univ. Calif. Davis Law Rev.* 1989; 22: 499–504.

Bovbjerg RR, Berenson RA. Surmounting myths and mindsets in medical malpractice, 5, Urban Institute Health Policy Brief, October 2005.

Bovbjerg RR, Miller RH, Shapiro DW. Paths to reducing medical injury: professional liability and discipline vs. patient safety—and the need for a third way. *J. Law Med. Ethics* 2001; 29: 369–380.

Bovbjerg RR, Sloan FA. No-fault for medical injury: theory and evidence. *Univ. Cincinnati Law Rev.* 1998; 67: 53–123.

Bovbjerg RR, Tancredi LR, Gaylin DS. Obstetrics and malpractice: evidence on the performance of a selective no-fault system. *JAMA* 1991; 265: 2836–2843.

Boyle LV. The truth about medical malpractice. In: *Trial.* April 2002. (Accessed December 23, 2003, at http://www.atla.org/medmal/prez.aspx.)

Brennan TA, Leape LL, Laird NM, et al. Incidence of adverse events and negligence in hospitalized patients: results of the Harvard Medical Practice Study I. *N Engl. J. Med.* 1991; 324: 370–376.

Brennan TA, Soc CM, Burstin HR. Relation between negligent adverse events and the outcomes of medical-malpractice litigation. *N Engl. J. Med.* 1996; 335: 1963–1967.

Brennan TA, Studdert DM, Thomas EJ. Beyond dead reckoning: measures of medical injury burden, malpractice litigation, and alternative compensation models from Utah and Colorado. *Indiana Law Rev.* 2000; 33: 1643–1686.

Calabresi G. The Cost of Accidents: A Legal and Economic Analysis. New Haven, CT: Yale University Press, 1970.

Cheney FW, Posner K, Caplan RA, Ward RJ. Standard of care and anesthesia liability. *JAMA* 1989; 261: 1599–1603.

Corrigan JM, Greiner A, Erickson SM, eds. *Fostering Rapid Advances in Health Care: Learning from System Demonstrations.* Washington, DC: National Academies Press, 2003.

Danzon P. The frequency and severity of medical malpractice claims. *J. Law Econ.* 1984; 27: 115–148.

Danzon P. The frequency and severity of medical malpractice claims: new evidence. *Law Contemp. Probl.* 1986; 49: 57–84.

Danzon PM. Medical Malpractice: Theory, Evidence and Public Policy. Cambridge, MA: Harvard University Press, 1985.

Danzon PM. The Swedish patient compensation system: lessons for the United States. *J. Leg. Med.* 1994; 15: 199–247.

Danzon PM, Pauly MV, Kington RS. The effects of malpractice litigation on physicians' fees and incomes. *Am. Econ. Rev.* 1990; 80: 122–127.

Dauer EA, Marcus LJ. Adapting mediation to link resolution of medical malpractice disputes with health care quality improvement. *Law Contemp. Probl.* 1997; 60: 185–218.

Defensive medicine and medical malpractice. OTA-H-602. Washington, DC: U.S. Congress, Office of Technology Assessment, 1994.

Department of Health, Education, and Welfare. Medical malpractice: report of the Secretary's Commission on Medical Malpractice. Washington, DC: Government Printing Office, January 1973. (DHEW publication no. (OS) 73–88.)

DeVille KA. Medical Malpractice in Nineteenth-Century America: Origins and Legacy. New York: New York University Press, 1990.

Dubay L, Kaestner R, Waidmann T. The impact of malpractice fears on cesarean section rates. *J. Health Econ.* 1999; 18: 491–522.

Entman SS, Glass CA, Hickson GB, Githens PB, Whetten-Goldstein K, Sloan FA. Relationship between malpractice claims history and subsequent obstetric care. *JAMA* 1994; 272: 1588–1591.

Epstein RA. Medical malpractice: the case for contract. *Am. Bar Found. Res. J.* 1976; 1: 87–149.

Gilmour JM. Patient safety, medical error and tort law: an international comparison, 198, Health Canada Project No. 6795-15-203/5760003 2006.

Gostin LO. A public health approach to reducing error: medical malpractice as a barrier. *JAMA* 2000; 283: 1742–1743.

Harvard Medical Practice Study. Patients, doctors, and lawyers: medical injury, malpractice litigation, and patient compensation in New York: report of the Harvard Medical Practice Study to the state of New York. Cambridge, MA: President and Fellows of Harvard College, 1990.

Havighurst CC. Health care choices: private contracts as instruments of health reform. Washington, DC: AEI Press, 1995.

Havighurst CC, Blumstein JF, Brennan TA. Health care law and policy: readings, notes, and questions. 2nd ed. New York: Foundation Press, 1998.

Havighurst CC, Tancredi LR. Medical adversity insurance—a no-fault approach to medical malpractice and quality assurance. *Milbank Mem. Fund Q Health Soc.* 1974; 51: 125–168.

Hellinger FJ, Encinosa WE. *The Impact of State Laws Limiting Malpractice Awards on the Geographic Distribution of Physicians.* Rockville, MD: Agency for Healthcare Research and Quality, Center for Organization and Delivery Studies, July 3, 2003.

Hickson GB, Clayton EW, Githens PB, Sloan FA. Factors that prompted families to file medical malpractice claims following perinatal injuries. *JAMA* 1992; 267: 1359–1363.

Hickson GB, Clayton EW, Entman SS, et al. Obstetricians' prior malpractice experience and patients' satisfaction with care. *JAMA* 1994; 272: 1583–1587.

Hickson GB, Federspiel CF, Pichert JW, Miller CS, Gauld-Jaeger J, Bost P. Patient complaints and malpractice risk. *JAMA* 2002; 287: 2951–2957.

Howard PK. The best course of treatment. *New York Times.* July 21, 2003, p. A15.

Hyams AL, Shapiro DW, Brennan TA. Medical practice guidelines in malpractice litigation: an early retrospective. *J Health Polit. Policy Law* 1996; 21: 289–313.

Hyman DA, Silver C. The poor state of health care quality in the U.S.: is malpractice liability part of the problem or part of the solution? *Cornell L. Rev.* 2005; 90: 897–899, 914, 916–917, 920–921, 925–926, 937, 947–948, 952, 979–980, 991, 1112.

Hyman DA, Silver C. Medical malpractice litigation and tort reform: it's the incentives, stupid. *Vand. L. Rev.* 2006; 59: 1085, 1094, 1098–1099, 1103, 1112, 1129–1131.

Johnson KB, Phillips CG, Orentlicher D, Hatlie MS. A fault-based administrative alternative for resolving medical malpractice claims. *Vanderbilt Law Rev.* 1989; 42: 1365–1406.

Kakalik JS, Pace NM. Costs and compensation paid in tort litigation. R-3391-ICJ. Santa Monica, CA: Institute for Civil Justice, RAND, 1986.

Keeton WP, Dobbs DB, Keeton RE, Owens DG. *Prosser and Keeton on the Law of Torts.* 5th ed. St. Paul, MN: West Publishing, 1984.

Kessler D, McClellan M. Do doctors practice defensive medicine? *Q. J. Econ.* 1996; 111: 353–390.

Kinney ED. Malpractice reform in the 1990s: past disappointments, future success? *J Health Polit. Policy Law* 1995; 20: 99–135.

Kohn LT, Corrigan JM, Donaldson MS, eds. To Err Is Human: Building a Safer Health System. Washington, DC: National Academy Press, 2000.

Kraman SS, Hamm G. Risk management: extreme honesty may be the best policy. *Ann. Intern. Med.* 1999; 131: 963–967.

Kritzer HM. The Justice Broker: Lawyers and Ordinary Litigation. New York: Oxford University Press, 1990.

Lamb RM, Studdert DM, Bohmer RMJ, Berwick DM, Brennan TA. Hospital disclosure practices: results of a national survey. *Health Aff.* (Millwood) 2003; 22: 73–83.

Leape LL. Reporting of adverse events. *N. Eng. J. Med.* 2002; 347: 1633, 1635.

Levinson W, Roter DL, Mullooly JP, Dull VT, Frankel RM. Physician–patient communication: the relationship with malpractice claims among primary care physicians and surgeons. *JAMA* 1997; 277: 553–559.

Liang BA. Risks of reporting sentinel events. *Health Aff.* (Millwood) 2000; 19: 112–120.

Localio AR, Lawthers AG, Bengtson JM, et al. Relationship between malpractice claims and cesarean delivery. *JAMA* 1993; 269: 366–373.

Localio AR, Lawthers AG, Brennan TA, et al. Relation between malpractice claims and adverse events due to negligence: results of the Harvard Medical Practice Study III. *N Engl. J. Med.* 1991; 325: 245–251.

Localio AR, Lawthers AG, Brennan TA, Laird NM, Hebert LE, Peterson LM, Newhouse JP, Weiler PC, Hiatt HH. Relation between malpractice claims and adverse events due to negligence, results of the Harvard Medical Practice Study III. *N. Eng. J. Med.* 1991; 325: 245; Brennan TA, Sox CM, Burstin HR. Relation between negligent adverse events and the outcomes of medical-malpractice litigation. *N. Eng. J. Med.* 1996; 335: 1963.

Mello MM. Of swords and shields: the use of clinical practice guidelines in medical malpractice litigation. *Univ. Penn. Law Rev.* 2000; 149: 645–710.

Mello MM, Brennan TA. Deterrence of medical errors: theory and evidence for malpractice reform. *Tex. Law Rev.* 2002; 80: 1595–1637.

Mello MM, Studdert DM, Brennan TA. The new medical malpractice crisis. *N Engl. J. Med.* 2003; 348: 2281–2284. Erratum, *N Engl. J. Med.* 2003; 349: 1010.

Mills DH, ed. California Medical Association and California Hospital Association report on the Medical Insurance Feasibility Study. San Francisco: Sutter, 1977.

Morlock LL, Lindgren OH, Cassirer C, Mills DH. Medical liability and clinical risk management. In: Goldfield N, Nash D, eds. *Managing Quality of Care in a Cost-Focused Environment.* Tampa, FL: American College of Physician Executives, 1999.

National Conference of State Legislatures. State medical liability laws table. (Accessed December 23, 2003, at http://www.ncsl.org/programs/insur/medliability.pdf.)

Office of the Assistant Secretary for Planning and Evaluation. *Addressing the New Health Care Crisis: Reforming the Medical Litigation System to Improve the Quality of Health Care.* Washington, DC: Department of Health and Human Services, March 3, 2003.

O'Connell J. The Lawsuit Lottery: Only the Lawyers Win. New York: Free Press, 1979.

O'Connell J. Offers that can't be refused: foreclosure of personal injury claims by defendants' prompt tender of claimants' net economic losses. *Northwest Univ. Law Rev.* 1982; 77: 589–632.

O'Connell J. Neo-no-fault remedies for medical injuries: coordinated statutory and contractual alternatives. *Law Contemp. Probl.* 1986; 49: 125–141.

Rabin RL, ed. *Perspectives on Tort Law.* 4th ed. Boston: Little, Brown, 1995.

Reason J. Human error: models and management. *BMJ* 2000; 320: 768–770.

Reed M, Ginsburg PB. Behind the times: physician income, 1995–99. *Data Bull. (Cent. Stud. Health Syst. Change)* 2003; 24: 1–2.

Reliable Medical Justice Act, S. 1518, 108th Congress, 1st session, 2003.

Robinson GO. The medical malpractice crisis of the 1970's: a retrospective. *Law Contemp. Probl.* 1986; 49: 5–35.

Rodwin MA, Chang HJ, Clausen J. Malpractice premiums and physicians' income: perceptions of a crisis conflict with empirical evidence. *Health Aff.* 2006; 25: 750, 757.

Rubin RJ, Mendelson DN. How much does defensive medicine cost? *J. Am. Health Policy* 1994; 4: 7–15.

Rustad ML, Koenig TH. Taming the tort monster: the American civil justice system as a battleground for social theory. *Brooklyn Law Rev.* 2002; 68: 1–105.

Sage WM. Understanding the first malpractice crisis of the 21st century. In: Gosfield AG, ed. *Health Law Handbook.* Eagan, MN: West, 2003, pp. 1–30.

Sage WM. Medical liability and patient safety. *Health Aff. (Millwood)* 2003; 22: 26–36.

Sage WM, Hastings KE, Berenson RA. Enterprise liability for medical malpractice and health care quality improvement. *Am. J. Law Med.* 1994; 20: 1–28.

Schwartz GT. Reality in the economic analysis of tort law: does tort law really deter? *UCLA Law Rev.* 1994; 42: 377–444.

Schwartz GT. Medical malpractice, tort, contract, and managed care. *Univ. Illinois Law Rev.* 1998; 3: 885–907.

Schwartz WB, Mendelson DN. Physicians who have lost their malpractice insurance: their demographic characteristics and the surplus-lines companies that insure them. *JAMA* 1989; 262: 1335–1341.

Shavell S. *Economic Analysis of Accident Law.* Cambridge, MA: Harvard University Press, 1987.

Sloan FA. State responses to the malpractice insurance "crisis" of the 1970s: an empirical assessment. *J. Health Polit. Policy Law* 1985; 9: 629–646.

Sloan FA, Githens PB, Clayton EW, Hickson GB, Gentile DA, Partlett DF. Suing for Medical Malpractice. Chicago: University of Chicago Press, 1993.

Sloan FA, Mergenhagen PM, Bovbjerg RR. Effects of tort reforms on the value of closed medical malpractice claims: a microanalysis. *J. Health Polit. Policy Law* 1989; 14: 663–689.

Sloan FA, Hsieh CR. Variability in medical malpractice payments: is the compensation fair? *Law Soc. Rev.* 1990; 24: 997–1039.

Sloan FA, Whetten-Goldstein K, Githens PB, Entman SS. Effects of the threat of medical malpractice litigation and other factors on birth outcomes. *Med. Care* 1995; 33: 700–714.

Statement by the Physician Insurers Association of America. Rockville, MD: Physician Insurers Association of America, January 29, 2003. (Accessed December 23, 2003, at http://www.thepiaa. org/pdf_files/january_29_piaa_statement.pdf.)

Studdert DM, Brennan TA. No-fault compensation for medical injuries: the prospect for error prevention. *JAMA* 2001; 286: 217–223.

Studdert DM, Mello M, Gawande A, Tejal KG, Kachalia A, Yoon C, Puopolo AL, Brennan TA. Claims, errors, and compensation payments in medical malpractice litigation. *N. Eng. J. Med.* 2006; 354: 1103, 2024, 2030–2031 (emphasis added).

Studdert DM, Thomas EJ, Burstin HR, Zbar BI, Orav EJ, Brennan TA. Negligent care and malpractice claiming behavior in Utah and Colorado. *Med. Care* 2000; 38: 250–260.

Studdert DM, Thomas EJ, Zbar BIW, et al. Can the United States afford a "no-fault" system of compensation for medical injury? *Law Contemp. Probl.* 1997; 60: 1–34.

Taragin MI, Willett LR, Wilczek AP, Trout R, Carson JL. The influence of standard of care and severity of injury on the resolution of medical malpractice claims. *Ann. Intern. Med.* 1992; 117: 780–784.

Thomas EJ, Studdert DM, Burstin HR, et al. Incidence and types of adverse events and negligent care in Utah and Colorado. *Med. Care* 2000; 38: 261–271.

Tussing AD, Wojtowycz MA. The cesarean decision in New York State, 1986: economic and noneconomic aspects. *Med. Care* 1992; 30: 529–540.

Vidmar N. Medical malpractice and the American jury: confronting the myths about jury incompetence, deep pockets, and outrageous damage awards. Ann Arbor: University of Michigan Press, 1995.

Viscusi WK, Zeckhauser RJ, Born P, Blackmon G. The effect of 1980s tort reform legislation on general liability and medical malpractice insurance. *J. Risk Uncertain* 1993; 6: 165–186.

Weiler PC. *Medical Malpractice on Trial.* Cambridge, MA: Harvard University Press, 1991.

Weiler PC. The case for no-fault medical liability. *Maryland Law Rev.* 1993; 52: 908–950.

Weiler PC, Hiatt HH, Newhouse JP, Johnson WG, Brennan T, Leape LL. A Measure of Malpractice: Medical Injury, Malpractice Litigation, and Patient Compensation. Cambridge, MA: Harvard University Press, 1993.

Weiler PC, Newhouse JP, Hiatt HH. *A Measure of Malpractice: Medical Injury, Malpractice Litigation, and Patient Compensation*, Vol. 133. Harvard University Press, 1993.

White MJ. The value of liability in medical malpractice. *Health Aff. (Millwood)* 1994; 13: 75–87.

Zuckerman S, Bovbjerg RR, Sloan F. Effects of tort reforms and other factors on medical malpractice insurance premiums. *Inquiry* 1990; 27: 167–182.

Avoiding Problems with Qui Tam, HIPAA, and Other Disciplinary Actions

3

3.1 Introduction

My mother used to instruct my friends that you should never say on the telephone what you would not want your mother to hear. You should not behave in a way that you would not want your father to know about; and perhaps most important of all, a practicing physician must make absolutely certain that he gives no cause for a whistle-blower in his office to "turn him in."

Whistle-blower claims against physicians can be very time consuming and very expensive. It is predicted that they will increase in frequency as Medicare/Medicaid faxes ever-tighter budget year by year. As the Attorney General and the Office of the Inspector General (OIG) continue to aggressively seek out and prosecute Medicare and Medicaid fraud, it is critical that every physician and health care provider understand what constitutes fraudulent behavior and how to protect your practice from any potential violation.

3.2 Avoiding Whistle-Blower (Qui Tam) Suits

When a doctor does go wrong, he is the first of criminals. He has nerve and he has knowledge.

—**Sherlock Holmes**
The Adventure of The Speckled Band

There are no better instruments than discharged servants with a grievance, and I was lucky enough to find one.

—**Sherlock Holmes**
The Adventure of Wisteria Lodge

Feds Recoup Nearly $1.5 Billion in Fraud Cases
(Reported by J. Young, Capital Hill Executive, 10/6/06)

An interdepartmental program designed to curb waste, fraud and abuse in federal healthcare programs will collect $1.47 billion as a result of criminal or civil cases brought in 2005. With massive and rapidly growing entitlement programs such as Medicare, Medicaid and Social Security, the pressure to control spending is viewed as urgent.

During the year 2005 federal prosecutors secured the convictions of 523 people. The department of Justice began 778 criminal investigations for a total of 1,334 pending cases. Justice also participated in 266 civil cases. The defendants in these the fraud and abuse cases range from individual schemers to some of the largest healthcare companies in the country including several individuals, physicians, small medical groups and small companies which mostly settled charges. Under federal law, private citizens—including whistle-blowers—can file fraud and abuse lawsuits on behalf of federal programs and keep a portion of the financial settlements. In FY 2005, these whistle-blowers collected a total of $136.8 million in these fraud and abuse cases.

The government in just one of these cases agreed to a settlement of $310 million from the defendant medical company over allegedly submitting false claims to Medicare and paying kickbacks to physicians who referred patients to their facilities.

3.2.1   What Is a Whistle-Blower?

What is a whistle-blower? And how can a whistle-blower affect you and your practice? And why are the subjects of Qui Tam and Whistle-blower suits in a medical malpractice book for the testifying physician? Most accusations of health care fraud are currently prosecuted under the False Claims Act (FCA). *The FCA (31 U.S.C. § 3729 et seq.).*

Well you may indeed have to testify in such a suit either as a defendant, but better, as a testifying or medical expert physician. Certainly, if you bill Medicare or Medicaid Insurance for your patients, or own a medical facility, an ambulatory care center (ACS) or other separate medical entity, you should know about these animals and their prey. As a prudent physician you must have some knowledge of this. I thank Alan Reider Esq., Chairman for 20 years of the Health Care division at the top Washington DC law firm of Arent Fox, for the help in contributing and editing this chapter.

3.3   What Is Qui Tam?

3.3.1   The False Claims Act

Congress established the FCA to encourage private citizens to bring action against unscrupulous contractors doing business with the government. It created a special provision to file cases in the name of the United States to recover damages when false and fraudulent claims are submitted to the government.

Sometimes called "whistle-blower" or qui tam lawsuits, these cases under the FCA provide a way for private citizens to share in the recovery of damages recovered. The term "qui tam" is an short for an old Latin phrase, which originally meant "who pursues the action on our Lord the King's behalf as well as his own."

Actually, this is not a new idea. The FCA was enacted in 1863, at President Abraham Lincoln's request. The law's purpose was to "aid in the effort to root out fraud against the government ... [and] to encourage private individuals who are aware of fraud being perpetrated against the Government to bring such information forward."

In 1986, Congress wanted to encourage more whistle-blowing and disclosure of fraud so Congress amended the FCA to increase the damages and penalties that can be recovered, to add protection against retaliation for whistle-blowers, and to make other changes that encouraged greater use of this law to combat fraud against the government. These changes in 1986 to the law created more incentives for private citizens to "blow the whistle" against fraudulent conduct. Congress increased the statutory penalties that may be imposed against those committing fraud against the government to a minimum of $5,000 and a maximum of $10,000 for each violation, plus three times the government's actual damages ("treble damages"). These changes also increased the statute of limitations from 6 years to as much as 10 years under limited circumstances. *See* 31 U.S.C. § 3731(b)(1)-(2). Recent amendments increased the penalty range from a minimum of $5,500 to a maximum of $11,000 for each violation.

Whistle-blower or qui tam lawsuits are an effective tool for recovering damages caused by fraud against the government. Both the government and the private citizen are rewarded if the government gets involved; the private citizen can obtain a recovery of between 15% and 25% of the amount recovered, plus reasonable expenses and attorney's fees. And if the government does not intervene in the case, the private citizen or qui tam plaintiff may recover between 25% and 30% of the damages recovered, plus fees and expenses.

Here are some law-firm advertisements in easy reach of your employees and associates, designed to get a whistle-blower out of the closet and also attract whistle-blower clients—on both sides of the suit—plaintiff and defendant.

3.3.1.1 *Professional Journal Advertisements to Attract Clients*

ADVERTISEMENT 1

Our Firm Has Criminal and Civil Experience in Protecting Whistle-Blowers

Sometimes a "whistle-blower" is afraid to come forward because of fear of what might happen to him or her in any criminal prosecution. Our firm offers unique criminal and civil experience in protecting our clients' interests. Our attorneys have prosecuted and defended civil False Claims Act cases, and thus we can offer our clients both areas of expertise.

Our ability to represent qui tam whistle-blowers is greater because most of our firm's partners are former federal prosecutors. Our attorneys have prosecuted federal criminal cases involving fraud, including high-profile cases. Our attorneys also have represented clients in our white collar criminal defense practice as well. Our qui tam or whistle-blower clients benefit from all of that experience.

Our lawyers use their unique criminal and civil experience in advising and representing "whistle-Blowers." Our goals are to protect our clients from any criminal liability, and also to pursue our clients' claims to recover damages in qui tam or whistle-blower lawsuits. Because of that experience, our clients can help stop dangerous and costly fraud against the government.

These advertisements of whistle-blower "winnings" in the public media whets the appetites of potential winners.

3.4   Qui Tam Adverse Publicity

Even Napoleon had his Watergate.

—**Yogi Berra**

3.4.1   Published Story #1

**Lincare Holdings Pays $526K to Settle Whistle-Blower's Claim
(ASSOCIATED PRESS 1:56 p.m. June 8, 2006)**

SPRINGFIELD, Mass.—Lincare Holdings Inc., a supplier of home oxygen equipment, has agreed to pay $526,000 to end a federal "whistle-blower" lawsuit that claimed three of the company's Massachusetts facilities overbilled Medicare, authorities said Thursday. Authorities had claimed that Clearwater, Fla.-based Lincare's facilities in Marlborough, Dudley and Leicester, Mass., overbilled between January 1999 and March 2004, U.S. Attorney Michael J. Sullivan said. The settlement agreement states that the payment is not an admission of liability by Lincare.

The government's claims were based on allegations by former Lincare sales representative S____ S____ of Holyoke. She worked for Lincare for seven months in 2002.

S ____ will receive $96,680 of Lincare's payment, as part of the federal government's whistle-blower law. Lincare also agreed to pay her attorney $16,890. Lincare, with more than 800 locations nationwide, is one of the nation's largest providers of oxygen and other respiratory therapy services to patients in the home. Last month, Lincare agreed to pay $12 million to resolve federal allegations that it gave kickbacks to providers sometime between January 1993 through December 2000. Under that agreement, Lincare did not admit any wrongdoing.

3.4.2   Published Story #2

The Federal Whistle-Blower Program has brought in $340.3 million in just five years. Since the late 1960s, the program has recovered nearly $3 billion. Typical informants include what one government official calls "the exes" ex-business associates Bookkeepers, accountants and others with access to a business's financial and medical records are often among the most reliable informants. Chief among them are ex-spouses, business partners or ex-employees "seeking revenge." In 2005, the agency handed out 169 rewards totaling $7.6 million to informants. Over the past six years, the average reward has been nearly $24,000. Individuals that represent the "victims" of this program are chiefly especially the self-employed professionals including physicians and/or others who deal in large amounts of cash and where earnings aren't reported to the government and taxes aren't withheld. The chief problems seen with physicians is insurance fraud—typically with Medicare and Medicaid and "upgrading" services and procedures.

3.4.3   Are You in Violation of the FCA?

The above newspaper stories apply to larger medical entities. How about the solo physician's office or the medical group practice?

Are you in violation of the FCA? What constitutes a false claim for the practicing physician?

The FCA prohibits fraudulent activity that goes beyond submitting a claim for payment of a service that was not provided.

It also includes

1. knowingly presenting, or causing to be presented, to the government a false claim for payment;
2. knowingly making, using, or causing to be made or used, a false record or statement to get a false claim paid or approved by the government;
3. conspiring to defraud the government by getting a false claim allowed or paid;
4. falsely certifying the type or amount of property to be used by the government; and
5. fraudulent activity identified and prosecuted under the FCA includes
   - double billing,
   - use of untrained personnel to provide services,

- failure to supervise unlicensed personnel,
- distribution of unapproved devices or drugs,
- forgery of physician's signatures,
- creation of phony insurance companies or employee benefit plans,
- upcoding,
- unbundling,
- kickbacks,
- services provided without medical necessity (Generally considered that which is reasonable, necessary, and appropriate based on evidence-based clinical standards of care. The term "clinical medical necessity" is also used by Medicare as a way to determine if they should pay for goods or services. Under Medicare, medical necessity is defined as that which is reasonable and necessary for the diagnosis or treatment of an illness, injury, or to improve the function of a malformed body member. Medicare has a number of policies, including National Coverage Determinations (NCDs) and Local Medical Review Policy (LMRP) (also known as Local Coverage Determinations [LCDs]), which line out what is and is not covered. Even if a service is accepted as reasonable and necessary, coverage may be limited if the service is *provided more frequently than allowed* under standard policies or standards of care. Also a Letter of Medical Necessity has to be written to justify the need for any medical equipment for a patient.)
- fraudulent cost reports,
- inadequate care, and
- use of substandard equipment.

The following are common examples of medical fraud, which can and often do occur in medical offices:

- Your practice hires a new associate. It takes several months to get all the provider numbers for the plans with which you participate. Until the numbers come in, the new associate is seeing patients and billing for services under the provider number of another physician in the practice.
- The patient's health plan does not cover colon cancer screening. To minimize the patient's out-of-pocket expenses, you include a diagnosis on the claim form that is not supported by the information in the patient's medical record.
- The providers in your practice consistently bill for the same level of service regardless of the documentation in the medical record.
- The level of service billed has no correlation with the seriousness of the problem being addressed.
- You have an arrangement with each of five pharmaceutical representatives to provide lunch for your staff 1 day a week.
- Your physicians bill for consultations provided by the mid-level providers in your practice.
- Your physicians are billing for diagnostic tests performed in your office by the support staff when there is no physician present when the service is provided.
- The date of service on the claim does not match the date of service in the medical record.

- Your practice routinely waives co-pays, coinsurance, and deductibles for physician patients and their families.
- Your practice no longer participates with some managed care plans and bills them as an out-of-network provider. The practice does not bill the patient for the higher co-pay.

3.4.4   Who Usually Initiates the Investigation?

An investigation of fraud can be initiated by the Medicare/Medicaid contractor or other private payer. In fact anyone that has reason to believe that the physician provider is in violation of the FCA, based on the results of a random or targeted audit. A targeted audit can result from aberrant billing patterns or a complaint from a patient to the Medicare carrier. The information captured during the audit is then passed on to the OIG, Attorney General, or Federal Bureau of Investigation (FBI) for further investigation. More often then not, an investigation is triggered by information received by the OIG or Attorney General from a current or former employee of the practice.

3.4.5   What Should the Physician Do When She/He Finds out She/He Is a Target of Investigation?

Physicians and staff should be prepared. Here are some steps that your practice can take:

- Designate a physician or an employee as your compliance officer, to be responsible for managing any request from Medicare, the OIG, Department of Justice, FBI, State Attorney General's office, State Department of Insurance, or any other government entity requesting information from the practice. Ideally, this should be a person who is likely to be in the office at all times during business hours.
- Any inquiries from the above entities, whether in writing, by telephone, facsimile, e-mail, or in person, should be immediately directed to the compliance officer.
- Other than the compliance officer, no one in the practice should respond to any inquiry or provide any information to anyone.
- The practice should identify a backup person to handle any inquiries or requests in the event that the compliance officer is not in the office or immediately available.
- Your practice should take steps now to identify a health care attorney that specializes in fraud and abuse, who can be contacted immediately and who is available to assist the practice, if necessary.
- If the practice receives a written request from Medicare for documentation, try to determine whether the request is a random audit or a targeted audit. Usually, a random audit consists of a request for documentation for 10 services that are pending payment or have been paid within the last year.
- Make copies of everything requested by Medicare or the governmental agency and send the information before the identified deadline. Send only what is requested. If you are having difficulty securing the information, ask for an extension in writing. You might want to get an independent review from a consultant or attorney of those services requested by Medicare or governmental agency to determine whether there are any problems that you need to address proactively.

- If the written request from Medicare is for more than 10 services, or the request comes from any other government agency mentioned above, you should contact your health care attorney immediately.
- If an investigator comes to your practice for an unscheduled visit, refer them to the compliance officer and ask them to wait until you have a chance to contact your health care attorney. You are not required to immediately produce information unless they produce a search warrant; contact your attorney immediately.
- Even with a search warrant, your attorney will probably advise you not to speak to the investigator in the physical absence of your attorney.
- If the agent presents with a subpoena, start collecting the information requested and contact your health care attorney immediately.
- Document all interactions with the investigator as thoroughly as possible.
- Take steps now to prepare a written policy that is distributed to all physicians, nonphysician practitioners, and employees, which include all of the above.

3.4.5.1   *What Should You Do in Case You Are Audited?*

Requests for documentation may come in several forms. If you receive a letter from your Medicare carrier or from a private payer for documentation for a small number of services stating that they are performing a random postpayment audit, it is likely that you have not been targeted but are just among a random sample of audits that is required every year. Take the following actions:

- Make two copies of everything that is requested, one to keep and one to send to the requester.
- Send only what is requested to support the services billed.
- If you cannot get the information together within the required time frame, ask for an extension in writing.
- Review the documentation to see if there are any problems. If there are problems with the documentation, explain the issue in the cover letter and what you are doing to correct the problem.
- Do not expect to receive a response right away. Sometimes it takes months before you get a response.
- If the insurance company asks for a refund because of over-coding, you might want to get an independent audit of the services requested. If the independent audit results in a more favorable review, you might want to challenge the insurance company's results.

If you receive a request for documentation for more than 10 services, or for copies of the complete chart, there is a significant possibility that you have been targeted for an audit.

- Immediately contact a health care attorney that specializes in health care fraud and abuse and follow his advice.
- If someone comes to your office with a subpoena for charts, contact your health care attorney immediately and make copies of everything that is requested.
- Obtain the name of the person with the subpoena and verify their credentials.

- Ask if you can wait to respond until your attorney arrives.
- You might want to cancel appointments and send your staff home.

3.5 Medical Group Harmony: Increase Satisfaction in Your Office and Decreases Qui Tam and Whistle-Blower Activity

There is nothing worse in an office than dissatisfied physicians, associates, partners, and employees. This dissatisfaction often is recognized by the patient and is a fomenter of dangerous complaints and has the potential for the development of whistle-blowers.

Some things to think about in creating harmony and satisfaction: avoid whistle-blowing and which also will reflect on patients' satisfaction.

Since business management is not a topic often discussed in medical training, many physicians are unaware of the problems that can occur in a group practice and how to address them, or better yet, how to prevent them.

The following are some issues that could cause a lot of trouble but which can be prevented with appropriate forethought:

1. *Buyouts.*   Most group practices have a buy-in arrangement specified in their contacts for new associates, but how many have a buy-out clause? The two situations that should be addressed in any contract are: what happens if one partner decides to leave the group for another practice or to go solo, and what happens when a partner approaches retirement. To address these issues, your contracts should include these items to be agreed upon as fair and reasonable by everyone.
2. *A reasonable noncompete clause.*
   a. A section that states that all medical records stay with the practice (copies will be provided at the patient's written request).
   b. A section that states that the physician leaving the practice will pay for letters to be sent to patients informing them of the change.
   c. A description of how on-call will be handled if a physician cuts back on his practice.
   d. A buy-out formula for partners leaving or retiring that identifies how receivables will be handled and who pays for the malpractice trail.

3.5.1 Physician Compensation

Most groups start out small and then grow just like mine did—from a solo gastroenterologist in 1970 to a six physician group practice by the mid-1980s with six satellite offices; a Joint Commission on Accreditation of Health Organizations (JCAHO)-approved ambulatory endoscopy/surgical center with 30 employees; nurses, medical assistants, clerks, and a fully computerized billing system covering all the offices.

I found out very quickly that there were problems in management that no one ever taught me in medical school. So I took a part time "executive" management course leading to a Master of Health Administration (MHA). I come by all this advice I am offering you honestly:

I. The average medical office with two or three physicians who are similar in age and lifestyle and have similar practice styles, so sharing revenue equally seems to make the best sense.

II. However, as the practice grows and the gap in age, lifestyle, and practice style within the group increases, sharing revenue equally may no longer be the best option. And changing the compensation arrangement mid-stream may cause conflict among the partners.

III. So a reasonable compensation agreement that puts the greatest weight on productivity is the most equitable and should be implemented from the onset or at a designated time agreed to by all in the practice.

3.5.2 Strategic Planning

1. Every business (and health care is a business!) should have a written business plan that includes strategic planning.
2. The partners in the practice should meet regularly, at least monthly, to discuss where they want to be in the next 5, 10, 20 years and what needs to happen to get there optimally by consensus of the group.
3. Before making any major decisions, the practice should have someone, whether their own administrator, if they are capable, or an outside consultant, do a cost/benefit analysis to determine whether the change makes sense both in the short and long term.
4. The same would apply to the purchase of expensive equipment. It is a mistake to rely on the equipment salesperson to provide accurate and realistic information on the return on investment as they have a self-interest in having you purchase the equipment. Always perform an independent investigation by speaking with the payers and other practices that have made or considered the purchase.
5. Consensus in decision making is essential to a successful group practice. A group that behaves like multiple solo practices loses all the benefits of a group practice.
6. Successfully integrating the physician extender into your practice.

3.5.3 Reduce Risks in Partnering with a Hospital

Many gastroenterology and other physician group practices are exploring the possibilities of building ambulatory surgical centers (ASCs) or making other large capital investments for additional product lines offered by the practice. In some cases, practices partner with the local hospital in these endeavors, while others go it alone. The following section discusses of the risks associated with each option.

3.5.3.1 Physician/Hospital Partnerships or Joint Ventures

1. Historically, the federal government has looked skeptically at joint ventures between hospitals and physicians. The concern is that a physician or group of physicians that has a financial interest in a hospital or other facility will be motivated to refer more patients to that facility.
2. The Stark and anti-kickback laws are designed to address these issues and restrict financial investments by physicians in other health care entities and by hospitals in physician's practices.
3. However, there are "safe harbors" that have been defined in the law, including physician ownership in ASCs and co-ownership between the physician and the hospital in ASCs and other diagnostic equipment. In addition, hospitals are permitted to pay physicians as medical directors or for other consulting services.

4. However to meet the "safe harbor," for consulting services the following criteria must be met:
   - There must be a written agreement between the hospital and the physician or group that establishes the number of hours expected and the compensation and the proposed services.
   - The financial benefit to both the physician and the hospital cannot be based on the volume of referrals from one to the other.
   - The financial arrangement must be at "fair market value" for services rendered.

One economic advantage of partnering with a hospital, particularly for high-ticket items such as an ASC, is that the hospital shares in the financial investment as well as the risks, relieving some of the burden on the practice. In addition, the hospital may have more clout in negotiating favorable facility fees with private payers. For expensive equipment, the hospital is usually in a better position than the practice to make the financial investment. The main economic disadvantage of partnering with the hospital is that the hospitals are generally less cost efficient than private entities with a higher overhead. In addition, the physicians would have to work within the hospital bureaucracy, which is often frustrating.

The advantages of going solo are that the practice and other physician investors maintain total control of all activities and expenses and are often more cost effective and efficient. The practice would not have to share any revenue with the hospital. The disadvantages of going solo are that the practice has to invest the entire capital required for the venture, hire and manage the staff, and assume any financial risk. The practice also risks alienating the hospital as the practice may be perceived as competing with the hospital for patients.

Before making any decision to partner with the hospital in any endeavor, the practice should consult a health care attorney who specializes in physician/hospital joint ventures; first to educate the physicians about the risks of the "kickback" and Stark laws and then to assure that the arrangement meets all of the requirements as a "safe harbor." Not doing so exposes you, the physician, to the risk of Medicare rules against the Stark and *anti-kickback laws*, which are designed to address these issues and restrict financial investments by physicians in other health care entities and by hospitals in physician's practices.

3.5.4   Would a Physician Extender Be Part of the Problem or Solution?

3.5.4.1   *First the Upside of a Physician Extender*

Given the shortage of physicians in numerous areas of the country and the increased demand for services (e.g., for the gastroenterologist for screening colonoscopy, hepatitis C, and other gastrointestinal disorders, as well as other specialties), many practices are finding it difficult to see all patients in a timely fashion. Many physicians are working long hours, seeing more patients and doing more procedures, but still cannot keep up with the demand. Recruiting another physician is often costly and frustrating. During recruitment of the physician, however, an interview should be performed by someone trained in assessing communication skills. Patient satisfaction has been directly linked to physician communications skills. Communication failures are associated with an increase in medical errors.

Patients who are dissatisfied with their medical care and have filed lawsuits cite communication issues approximately 70% of time. Some physicians are poor communicators and many have never been taught communication skills. Teaching these skills should become a function of risk prevention, as this method of patient interaction does prevent future legal problems. Physicians must be taught proper communication skills and the importance of teamwork. Providers with frequent patient, nursing or medical staff complaints must be critically reviewed. The present system of risk management needs to move from a reactive position to a role of being proactive for both patient and physician. Because of these conditions, many practices are hiring or considering hiring mid-level providers—primarily physician assistants (PAs) and nurse practitioners (NPs)—as a solution to meeting the needs of the patients, staff, and referring physicians.

Mid-level providers have been utilized in primary care practices for a long time, but they are relatively new to the practice of gastroenterology and other specialty practices. Since many physicians have not worked with mid-level providers before, their integration into the practice can be problematic. At times, the mid-level provider can function as little more than a glorified nurse rather than a qualified provider, contributing minimally to relieving the burden on the physicians.

Mid-level providers should be considered providers in the same way that the physicians are providers, and the recruitment and consideration process should be the same as it is when hiring an associate.

Not all mid-level providers are equal. There are subtle differences in the training for NPs and PAs that may affect how they fit into your practice. NPs are registered nurses that go on for a graduate degree and certification. In general, their focus is on managing the needs of the patients and preventive care. PAs usually have a bachelor's degree and 2 years of additional training similar to the training received by medical students. While NPs can work independently of a physician in most states, PAs in most states must work for a physician or hospital. The medical–legal supervision requirements for a PA are usually more stringent than for an NP; both are subject to state regulations associated with scope of practice. Recent mid-level provider graduates with no prior practical experience may take up to 6 months of on-the-job training to get to the point where the physicians are comfortable allowing them to see patients on their own. For others with experience, the learning curve will be shorter. What factors are necessary for a successful PA/MD relationship? What are the characteristics absolutely necessary for a successful MD/PA team? What clinical resources should minimally be provided to a PA?

The traditional pyramid of health care with the physician as the "captain" of the team, responsible for all of the routine care of a patient, is not as solid as it once was. Byington believes that the modern labyrinth of roles and responsibilities can create problems and concerns for both the supervising and supervised caregivers, especially in terms of communication and decision making.

In many settings, PAs now have their own patient panels and more independence about when to seek assistance or consultation. The assumption by some is that this will mean consultations will be fewer because PAs will be capable of handling most patient care problems. Regardless of the validity of this statement, this is an appropriate time to reexamine the essential characteristics of a successful physician/PA team.

Appropriate supervision is the central principle behind successful and competent physician/PA teamwork. Physician supervision means that the PA only performs medical and surgical acts and procedures that have been authorized by state law and the supervising physician. The supervising physician bears both the authority and responsibility for the delegated acts. Obviously, methods of supervision vary with the practice setting, the comfort of the supervising physician, and the experience of the PA. It is common, early in the relationship, for supervision to be more formal and conservative and then to become less rigid as the team works together.

Most physicians and PAs enjoy their professional relationship. The relationship between a PA and the supervising physician should be one of mutual trust and respect. The PA—first and foremost—is a representative of the physician, treating the patient in the style and manner developed and directed by the physician.

3.5.4.2   Now, the Downside to Physician Extenders

There are essentially three legal theories commonly used to ascribe liability to the physician for errors from their nonphysician providers (e.g., medical assistant, PA, NP):

1. Vicarious liability
2. Negligent supervision
3. Negligent hiring

Vicarious liability allows for liability for wrongdoing to be extended beyond the original wrongdoer to persons who have not committed a wrong, but on whose behalf the wrongdoers acted. This provides the plaintiff (patient) with additional financially responsible defendants who may have greater financial resources than the original defendant. The working relationship between physicians and nonphysician providers may determine what liability will be imposed on the physician for the negligence of the nonphysician providers working with them. The employer–employee relationship is the typical relationship between physicians and nonphysician providers. This relationship forms the basis for which the physician will be deemed vicariously liable for the nonphysician provider's negligent acts. When the negligence of a subordinate is imputed to the physician, the physician is said to be vicariously liable.[1-4]

Negligent supervision applies when the nonphysician provider works under a supervising physician. Several states require this direct supervision by statue. State law also determines whether the physician must be in the same physical location as the nonphysician provider. When a physician is designated as a supervisor or has a formal responsibility to oversee and approve the nonphysician provider's work, courts will generally hold the physician responsible for the nonphysician provider's negligent acts. To complicate matters, physicians may also be held directly responsible for their own negligent acts using the theory of negligent supervision. To establish liability, a patient must show a direct connection between the injury and the physician's actions because liability is based on the physician's negligent supervision rather than on the nonphysician provider's actions. It is possible that liability may attach to the physician even when the patient cannot establish negligence by linking the nonphysician provider's acts to the injury.[2,5]

Examples of negligent supervision:

1. Lack of adequate supervision occurs when a nonphysician provider has limited supervision or documentation of supervision by the physician. This often occurs in larger practice settings with multiple physicians which increase the potential for inadequate supervision.
2. Untimely referral occurs when a nonphysician provider attempts to treat complicated conditions beyond his level of training and skill.

3. Failure to properly diagnose occurs when the nonphysician provider misinterprets information provided by the patient or was uncertain about the diagnosis or lack of the skills in managing the case.
4. Inadequate examination usually occurs from the nonphysician provider rushing through the examinations and failing to confirm information with the patient.
5. Negligent misrepresentation occurs when a patient is credibly unaware that the treating physician is not a physician.

These five claims form the basis of the theory of "negligent supervision" used to hold supervisors liable for the wrongful acts of their subordinates. The courts have held time and time again that it is the responsibility of the physician to contact the licensing agency to ensure the existence of the license of those in his employ.[6]

Negligent hiring or negligent selection occurs when an employer hires a nonphysician provider when the physician knows or has reason to know that the nonphysician provider is incompetent or unfit to perform the required duties. Additionally, if employer has failed to use reasonable care to discover the nonphysician provider's incompetence or unfitness before hiring, then they may be found negligent.[2,7]

3.5.4.3 *Preventive Actions*

The physician in hiring any nonphysician provider in his medical practice must focus on the following:

1. Hire only qualified nonphysician providers who meet all education requirements and present the experience and training needed for the physician for which they are hired.
2. Become familiar and knowledgeable with the state rules, regulations, and requirements regarding the type of nonphysician provider that is employed in that state in which the physician practices his profession.
3. Make arrangements to properly train and teach the nonphysician provider in the areas of your practice for which she/he is responsible. Take all the time necessary to also teach the nonphysician provider all systems your practice has in place to ensure high-quality patient care.
4. Do diligence when interviewing and hiring a nonphysician provider. Check all credentials and references to ensure truth and accuracy.
5. Proper supervision of the nonphysician provider is crucial. Limit supervision to the nonphysician providers permitted by statute and more importantly to the number that the physician feels comfortable with even if this number is less than statutorily required.
6. Follow the supervisory requirements as outlined in the state statute governing nonphysician providers.
7. Develop a system to regularly review the work of the nonphysician provider, encourage frequent interaction by the practice's physicians with the nonphysician provider, especially when a question or problem develops involving diagnosis and patient care.
8. Have nonphysician clinicians introduce themselves with appropriate professional titles so patients do not mistake them for physicians and never allow misidentification to remain uncorrected.

9. Set high standards for the nonphysician providers and then make sure goals and procedures are being followed.
10. Act as a positive role model for the nonphysician provider by stressing adequate documentation and patient care at the level you practice.

3.6   What Is Necessary for a Successful Physician/PA Team?

While there are no absolutes, the following are characteristics that I believe are necessary for a successful physician/PA team:

1. Mutual respect. It is important for both the physician and the PA to have professional respect for each other. This means supporting each other with patients, office staff, and colleagues. Disagreements or differences should be ironed out in private.
2. Mutual understanding of state statutes that govern supervision and PA practice. Having a copy of the state statutes and rules that govern the practice of PAs is imperative and should be reviewed on an annual basis, just as we review other standards such as those from the Occupational Safety and Health Administration or standards for advanced life support.
3. Mutual understanding of the PA's scope of practice, including a description of the PA's roles and responsibilities and a list of conditions that require immediate consultation with the supervising physician. Prospective discussion of expectations regarding patient care will assist in later problems or disagreements. The physician should be clear on what conditions, if any, require consultation before discharge. In many emergency centers, for example, there are standing orders that consultation with the supervising physician regarding all chest- or abdominal-pain patients must occur before the patient leaves.
4. Mutual communication such as an "open door" policy or free access to the supervising physician. It is important that the physician and PA avoid obstacles that impede access to discussions of patient care.
5. Mutual recognition of each other's strengths and weaknesses. This is where the physician/PA team can really make a difference. Early on in the relationship the physician and PA should get to know each other's strengths and weaknesses. The practice should cater to the strengths and find ways to address any weaknesses with additional training or continuing medical education.

Minimal clinical resources that should be offered to the PA vary with practice setting and specialty. The physician/PA team should agree upon clinical resources available in the practice setting and, as such, a minimal cookbook list would not be valuable to the reader. At a minimum, however, the PA should have access to, either electronic or hardcopy, reference sources. In addition, appropriate equipment and diagnostic tools should be available depending on the focus of the practice.[8–10]

3.6.1   Hospitalists

Another solution to the problems of short staffing and burnout, which leads to patient dissatisfaction, is the use of hospitalists (suggested by Wachter and Goldman[11]).

In 1996, Wachter and Goldman described a practice model whereby the physician dedicated his professional existence to the care of hospitalized medical patients. They coined the term "hospitalist" and discussed the emerging role of this type of practice. The reasons for development of the hospitalist model included an increase in the serious nature of disease in hospitalized patients, the need for physicians to spend more time in their offices with increasing outpatient volume, the decrease in inpatient admissions, the difficulty for most practitioners to stay at the cutting edge of medical care, and the documented fact that those who do something repetitively do it better and with less expense.

A recent review of this movement demonstrated a remarkable growth in the hospitalist model. Studies have demonstrated that patient satisfaction has been preserved by using a hospitalist and that significant reductions in resource utilization have occurred while good clinical outcomes were maintained. An interesting analysis of hospitalists themselves demonstrated a high level of job satisfaction, low levels of burnout, and a long-term commitment to remain in this field. In their latest study, the authors reviewed data regarding the effect of hospitalists on resource use, quality of care, satisfaction, and teaching, and to analyze the impact of hospitalists on the health care system. The authors found that implementation of hospitalist programs was associated with significant reductions in resource use, usually measured as hospital costs (average decrease, 13.4%) or average length of stay (average decrease, 16.6%).

Several studies found improved outcomes such as inpatient mortality and readmission rates, but these results were inconsistent. Patient satisfaction was generally preserved. Empirical research supports the premise that hospitalists improve inpatient efficiency without harmful effects on quality or patient satisfaction. Education may be improved.

In part, catalyzed by these data, the clinical use of hospitalists is growing rapidly, and hospitalists are also assuming prominent roles as teachers, researchers, and quality leaders. The authors conclude that the hospitalist field has now achieved many of the attributes of traditional medical specialties and seems destined to continue to grow.

3.6.2 The Obstetrics' Laborist

Similar to the hospitalist mentioned in the previous section, Weinstein[12] has proposed a physician extender in the Labor and Delivery area. Weinstein maintains that evidence exists for a marked increase in professional dissatisfaction, substance abuse, poor interpersonal relationships, and burnout. These conditions are now being seen in younger physicians and in Obstetrics–Gynecology training programs. Physicians have stopped practicing obstetrics at a much younger age and are increasingly quitting training programs. These findings, along with the recent professional liability insurance crisis, leave many communities with a shortage of physicians who practice obstetrics.

A potential solution for alleviating some of these conditions is the introduction of a physician whose sole focus of practice is managing the patient in labor.

This physician called the "laborist," may be able to improve patient care and satisfaction because the laborist will have no other distractions during this time. Also, the laborist will remove from the obstetrician the need to be always available to the laboring patient, which potentially may decrease stress, improve physician well being, increase length of professional practice, and decrease burnout.

The most widely quoted legal definition of a profession is that of Justice Louis Brandeis. He listed the following attributes: that it is based on a specialized body of knowledge known only to its practitioners; that it is pursued primarily for the benefit of others rather than for personal gain; and that as a result, its practitioners are granted great autonomy in decision making and self-regulation. The expectation that medicine be pursued for the benefit of others rather than for personal gain may have a hollow ring to it these days. An increasing percentage of health care is now organized for corporate profit, with yields over expenses going to stockholders.

Some practitioners, especially proceduralists in all specialties, make a generous income that considerably exceeds that of most of their patients. Executives of medical companies can be very highly paid, with their compensation packages touted in the newspapers' business pages rather than under medicine or health, and based on patient service cost cutting with denial of benefits that improves the bottom line, but which patients will sign because they are "cheap."

How do we physicians combat this? We begin with a profound regard for the doctor–patient relationship and all that entails: respect for the patient's autonomy, honesty, and integrity in all we do; avoidance of both the fact and the appearance of financial conflict of interest; reasonable standards of what doctors should earn; and an insistence—even when pressed to compromise—that the patient's interests come first. We must continue to maintain high standards of self-regulation; we must also accept shared autonomy of decision making with patients; and we must insist, often against perverse economic incentives, that patients have full information and that we be free to decide with them in their best interests.

To respond to a revolution of shared medical and other information (e.g., the Internet), physicians must continuously pursue new knowledge and apply rigorous standards of evidence, aligned with experienced judgment, to bring the best of medicine to their patients. As compared to Brandeis's day, doctors complain that the most irksome change in medical practice is the loss of autonomy in decision-making and self-regulation. More and more physicians are salaried employees. Physicians are also constrained by the dictates of managed care and malpractice suits are always a risk.

In this regard an Operational Compliance Program is essential.

The Deficit Reduction Act (DRA) of 2005, Pub. L. No. 109–171 also includes a provision requiring all entities that *make* or *receive* at least $5 million in annual Medicaid payments to establish specific written policies and procedures and beginning *Jan 1, 2007*, to inform employees and others about certain federal and state false claims and whistle-blower laws. But even if your practice does not generate the $5 million in Medicaid payments per year, though not mandatory, the OIG of the Department of Health and Human Services has strongly recommended that every health care entity, including physician practices, have a Compliance Program to prevent fraud and abuse.

The DRA includes six new employee training and compliance requirements. The new requirements apply to any entity that *receives* or *makes* annual payments of at least 5 million under a state Medicaid plan. The rule applies to pharmaceutical manufacturers and other entities that pay rebates to state Medicaid programs, as well as providers (hospitals, physicians, nursing homes, etc.) that receive Medicaid payments for services rendered.

The DRA requires *written* policies and procedures. Training is not specifically required, but the provisions contemplate that entities dealing with state Medicaid programs will inform their employees including management, contractors, and agents, of their policies.

The policies and procedures must provide information on the following laws, including the role of such laws in preventing and detecting fraud, waste, and abuse in federal health care programs:

- The Federal FCA
- Federal administrative remedies for false claims and statements
- State laws pertaining to civil or criminal penalties for false claims and statements
- Whistle-blower provisions under the federal and state laws

The policies and procedures must also provide details regarding the entity's policies and procedures for protecting against fraud, waste, and abuse. The entity must include in its employee handbook:

- The specific discussion of applicable fraud and abuse laws
- The rights of employees who are whistle-blowers to be protected from retaliation
- The entity's policies and procedures for detecting and preventing fraud, waste, and abuse

If the entity does not implement appropriate procedures, or if those procedures are not followed, the entity risks the federal or state government contending that the entity is liable under federal and applicable state false claims laws every time it submits claims for Medicaid reimbursement.

Unfortunately, ignorance of the laws is not a defense that will stand up against allegations of violations. Many physicians have found themselves under OIG or Medicare scrutiny for violations that they were totally unaware existed in their practice. An effective compliance program can prevent this situation and goes a long way toward mitigating any penalties.

If you do not have a compliance program documented in a Compliance Plan that meets the requirements for both the Medicaid and Medicare programs, the *AGA Compliance Plan Template for GI Practices* includes all of the elements required under the DRA and the Model Compliance Plan published by the OIG. Other specialties and professional organizations have also implemented templates. Call your organization for information.

The template is designed to allow for customization by your practice and can be used as a training tool for your physicians and staff. It is available for purchase online at www.gastro.org in the Practice Management section under Products and Services.

3.7 Avoiding Problems with HIPAA

This relatively new legislation that came in the 1990s has changed the physician's traditional private office procedures, to say nothing of having to increase his staff and thus overhead. However, the physician must know about these legislative changes and more important he or she must be sure his office staff is properly trained in its implementation.

3.7.1 HIPAA Basics

Other legislation impacting on a private medical practice is the Health Insurance Portability and Accountability Act (HIPAA). The HIPAA of 1996 was signed into law by President Clinton on August 21, 1996.

The act was originally conceived to guarantee that health insurance coverage is available to workers and their families when they change or lose their jobs. The law's original scope has expanded and now requires the Secretary of Health and Human Services to include provisions for standardizing the data content and format for electronic transactions (administrative simplification), privacy of confidential personal health care information, secure physical access to records, and national identifiers for providers, employers, and health plans. HIPAA impacts the physician in at least three ways:

A. *Privacy*—The Privacy Rule for the first time creates national standards to protect individuals' medical records and other personal health information. The rule gives the patients more control over their health information by setting boundaries on the use and release of health records and by establishing appropriate safeguards that health care providers and others must achieve to protect the privacy of health information.

B. *Security*—The purpose of the Security Rule is to adopt national standards for safeguards to protect the confidentiality, integrity, and availability of electronic protected health information and require that measures to be taken to secure this information while in the custody of entities covered by HIPAA (covered entities) as well as in transit between covered entities and from covered entities to others.

C. *HIPAA-mandated transactions*—The law does not require providers to submit transactions electronically. It does require that all transactions submitted electronically comply with the standards. To comply with the transaction standards, health care providers and health plans may exchange the standard transactions directly, or they may contract with a clearinghouse to perform this function.

3.7.2 HIPAA Privacy Rule

3.7.2.1 *What Is the Privacy Rule?*

The rule also holds violators accountable if they violate patients' privacy rights and it strikes a balance when public responsibility requires disclosure of some forms of data, for example, to protect public health. For patients, it means being able to make informed choices when seeking care and reimbursement for care based on how personal health information may be used:

- It enables patients to find out how their information may be used and what disclosures of their information have been made.
- It generally limits release of information to the minimum reasonably needed for the purpose of the disclosure.
- It gives patients the right to examine and obtain a copy of their own health records and request corrections.

The Privacy Rule covers health plans, health care clearinghouses, and those health care providers who conduct electronic financial and administrative transactions covered by HIPAA. Most covered entities must have come into compliance with these standards a few years ago on April 14, 2003.

3.7.2.2   Why Was This Regulation Needed?

When it comes to personal information that moves across hospitals, doctors' offices, insurers or third party payers, and state lines, the United States has relied on a patchwork of federal and state laws. Under the current patchwork of laws, personal health information can be distributed, without either notice or consent, for reasons that have nothing to do with a patient's medical treatment or health care reimbursement. Health care providers have a strong tradition of safeguarding private health information. But in today's world, the old system of paper records in locked filing cabinets is not enough. With information broadly held and transmitted electronically, the rule provides clear standards for all parties regarding protection of personal health information.

3.7.2.3   What Does This Regulation Require an Average Physician Provider or Health Plan to Do?

For an average physician health care provider or health plan, the Privacy Rule requires activities such as

- providing information to patients about their privacy rights and how their information can be used;
- adopting clear privacy procedures for its practice, hospital, or plan;
- training employees so that they understand the privacy procedures;
- designating an individual, a compliance officer, to be responsible for seeing that the privacy procedures are adopted and followed; and
- securing patient records containing individually identifiable health information so that they are not readily available to those who do not need them.

To ease the burden of complying with the new requirements, the Privacy Rule gives needed flexibility for providers and plans to create their own privacy procedures, tailored to fit their size and needs. The scalability of the rules provides a more efficient and appropriate means of safeguarding protected health information than would any single standard. For example

- The privacy official ("compliance officer") at a small physician practice may be the office manager, who will have other nonprivacy-related duties; the privacy official at a large health plan may be a full-time position, and may have the regular support and advice of a privacy staff or board.
- The training requirement may be satisfied by a small physician practice's providing each new member of the workforce with a copy of its privacy policies and documenting that new members have reviewed the policies; whereas a large health plan may provide training through live instruction, video presentations, or interactive software programs.

3.7.3   HIPAA FAQ's

HIPAA Privacy Rules—frequently asked questions (FAQs) and answers about covered entities (the physicians office, ACF, and practice is a "covered entity," i.e., health care providers who conduct certain financial and administrative transactions electronically).

Q: Who must comply with these new HIPAA privacy standards?

A: As required by Congress in HIPAA, the Privacy Rule covers

1. health plans;
2. health care clearinghouses;
3. health care providers who conduct certain financial and administrative transactions electronically; and
4. these electronic transactions are those for which standards have been adopted by the Secretary under HIPAA, such as electronic billing and fund transfers.

These entities (collectively called "covered entities") are bound by the new privacy standards even if they contract with others (called "business associates") to perform some of their essential functions. The law does not give the Department of Health and Human Services (HHS) the authority to regulate other types of private businesses or public agencies through this regulation. For example, HHS does not have the authority to regulate employers, life insurance companies, or public agencies that deliver social security or welfare benefits.

Q: Can covered entities continue to disclose adverse event reports that contain protected health information to the Department of Health and Human Services (HHS) Office for Human Research Protections (OHRP)?

A: Yes. The OHRP is a public health authority under the HIPAA Privacy Rule. Therefore, covered entities can continue to disclose protected health information to report adverse events to the OHRP either with patient authorization as provided at 45 CFR 164.508, or without patient authorization for public health activities as permitted at 45 CFR 164.512(b).

Q: How are covered entities expected to determine what is the minimum necessary information that can be used, disclosed, or requested for a particular purpose?

A: The HIPAA Privacy Rule requires a covered entity to make reasonable efforts to limit use, disclosure of, and requests for protected health information to the minimum necessary to accomplish the intended purpose. To allow covered entities, the flexibility to address their unique circumstances, the Rule requires covered entities to make their own assessment of what protected health information is reasonably necessary for a particular purpose, given the characteristics of their business and workforce, and to implement policies and procedures accordingly. This is not an absolute standard and covered entities need not limit information uses or disclosures to those that are absolutely needed to serve the purpose. Rather, this is a reasonable standard that calls for an approach consistent with the best practices and guidelines already used by many providers and plans today to limit the unnecessary sharing of medical information.

The minimum necessary standard requires covered entities to evaluate their practices and enhance protections as needed to limit unnecessary or inappropriate access to protected health information. It is intended to reflect and be consistent with, not override, professional judgment and standards. Therefore, it is expected that covered entities will utilize the input of prudent professionals involved in health care activities when developing policies and procedures that appropriately limit access to personal health information without sacrificing the quality of health care.

Q: Must the HIPAA Privacy Rule's minimum necessary standard be applied to uses or disclosures that are authorized by an individual?

A: No. Uses and disclosures that are authorized by an individual are exempt from the minimum necessary requirements. For example, if a covered health care provider receives an individual's authorization to disclose medical information to a life insurer for underwriting purposes, the provider is permitted to disclose the information requested on the authorization without making any minimum necessary determination. The authorization must meet the requirements of 45 CFR 164.508.

Q: Does the HIPAA Privacy Rule strictly prohibit the use, disclosure, or request of an entire medical record? If not, are case-by-case justifications required each time an entire medical record is disclosed?

A: No. The Privacy Rule does not prohibit the use, disclosure, or request of an entire medical record; and a covered entity may use, disclose, or request an entire medical record without a case-by-case justification, if the covered entity has documented in its policies and procedures that the entire medical record is the amount reasonably necessary for certain identified purposes. For uses, the policies and procedures would identify those persons or classes of person in the workforce that need to see the entire medical record and the conditions, if any, that are appropriate for such access. Policies and procedures for routine disclosures and requests and the criteria used for nonroutine disclosures and requests would identify the circumstances under which disclosing or requesting the entire medical record is reasonably necessary for particular purposes.

The Privacy Rule does not require that a justification be provided with respect to each distinct medical record. Finally, no justification is needed in those instances where the minimum necessary standard does not apply, such as disclosures to or requests by a health care provider for treatment purposes or disclosures to the individual who is the subject of the protected health information.

Q: Is a covered entity required to apply the HIPAA Privacy Rule's minimum necessary standard to a disclosure of protected health information it makes to another covered entity?

A: Covered entities are required to apply the minimum necessary standard to their own requests for protected health information. One covered entity may reasonably rely on another covered entity's request as the minimum necessary, and then does not need to engage in a separate minimum necessary determination. *See* 45 CFR 164.514(d)(3)(iii). However, if a covered entity does not agree that the amount of information requested by another covered entity is reasonably necessary for the purpose, it is up to both covered entities to negotiate a resolution of the dispute as to the amount of information needed. Nothing in the Privacy Rule prevents a covered entity from discussing its concerns with another covered entity making a request, and negotiating an information exchange that meets the needs of both parties. Such discussions occur today and may continue after the compliance date of the Privacy Rule.

Q: Does the HIPAA Privacy Rule protect genetic information?

A: Yes, genetic information is health information protected by the Privacy Rule. Like other health information to be protected, it must meet the definition of protected health information: it must be individually identifiable and maintained by a covered health care provider, health plan, or health care clearinghouse. *See* 45 C.F.R 160.103 and 164.501.

Q: Can covered entities continue to disclose adverse event reports that contain protected health information to the Department of Health and Human Services (HHS) Office for Human Research Protections (OHRP)?

A: Yes. The OHRP is a public health authority under the HIPAA Privacy Rule. Therefore, covered entities can continue to disclose protected health information to report adverse events to the OHRP either with patient authorization as provided at 45 CFR 164.508, or without patient authorization for public health activities as permitted at 45 CFR 164.512(b).

Q: If a patient or research subject revokes his or her authorization to have protected health information used or disclosed for research, does the HIPAA Privacy Rule permit a researcher/covered health care provider to continue using the protected health information already obtained prior to the time the individual revoked his or her authorization?

A: Covered entities may continue to use and disclose protected health information that was obtained prior to the time the individual revoked his or her authorization, as necessary to maintain the integrity of the research study. An individual may not revoke an authorization to the extent the covered entity has acted in reliance on the authorization. For research uses and disclosures, this reliance exception at 45 CFR 164.508(b)(5)(i) permits the continued use and disclosure of protected health information already obtained pursuant to a valid authorization to the extent necessary to preserve the integrity of the research study. For example, the reliance exception would permit the continued use and disclosure of protected health information to account for a subject's withdrawal from the research study, as necessary to incorporate the information as part of a marketing application submitted to the Food and Drug Administration, to conduct investigations of scientific misconduct, or to report adverse events. However, the reliance exception would not permit a covered entity to continue disclosing additional protected health information to a researcher or to use for its own research purposes information not already gathered at the time an individual withdraws his or her authorization.

Q: Do the HIPAA Privacy Rule's requirements for authorization and the Common Rule's requirements for informed consent differ?

A: Yes. Under the Privacy Rule, a patient's authorization is for the use and disclosure of protected health information for research purposes. In contrast, an individual's informed consent, as required by the Common Rule and the Food and Drug Administration's (FDA) human subjects regulations, is a consent to participate in the research study as a whole, not simply a consent for the research use or disclosure of protected health information. For this reason, there are important differences between the Privacy Rule requirements for individual authorization, and the Common Rule's and FDA's requirements for informed consent. However, the Privacy Rule's authorization elements are compatible with the Common Rule's informed consent elements. Thus, both sets of requirements can be met by use of a single, combined form, which is permitted by the Privacy Rule. For example, the Privacy Rule allows the research authorization to state that the authorization will be valid until the conclusion of the research study, or to state that the authorization will not have an expiration date or event. This is compatible with the Common Rule's requirement for an explanation of the expected duration of the research subject's participation in the study. It should be noted that where the Privacy Rule, the Common Rule, and FDA's human subjects regulations are applicable, each of the applicable regulations will need to be followed.

Q: What Federal agencies are involved in the implementation and enforcement of the HIPAA Privacy Rule?

A: The roles of several Federal agencies regarding the Privacy Rule are described below:

- Office for Civil Rights (OCR)—Oversight and civil enforcement responsibility for the Privacy Rule are under the auspices of OCR, Department of Health and Human Services (HHS).
- Department of Justice (DOJ)—Enforcement of the criminal penalties for violations of the Privacy Rule is under the auspices of DOJ.
- National Institutes of Health (NIH)—Development of educational materials for researchers, in collaboration with other HHS research agencies, is the role of NIH. NIH is not involved in enforcing or monitoring compliance with the Privacy Rule.[13,14]

The final Security Rule, published February 20, 2003, adopts standards for the security of electronic protected health information to be implemented by health plans, health care clearinghouses, and certain health care providers. The compliance date for most covered entities was April 21, 2005 (April 21, 2006 for small health plans). Its purpose is to

- ensure integrity, confidentiality, and availability of electronic-protected health information (EPHI); and
- protect against reasonably anticipated threats or hazards, and improper use or disclosure. This includes all EPHI, protected health information that is transmitted or maintained electronically and applies to all covered entities. All standards should be reviewed with your health attorney.

3.7.4   Helpful HIPAA Hints

1. The answers to the "frequently asked questions" on the HIPAA site are particularly helpful—http://www.hhs.gov/ocr/hipaa/
2. Forms needed in a medical office.

Note: All forms below are presented as examples to smooth the flow of HIPAA matters in the medical office, but all forms seen as in any other book chapter must be reviewed and approved by your attorney before use. These are only examples. Physicians should contact their specialty society for assistance since some specialty societies have developed model forms for their specialty members. If not, then you must consult an attorney who specializes in privacy matters for assistance with respect to these forms. According to our consultants, Attorneys Reider and Shurin, this form "Authorization For Use Or Disclosure Of Information" is required whenever a practice wishes to use or disclose protected health information for any reason not specifically permitted by law. Principal examples for such use are marketing and clinical research. If a patient refuses to sign the form, the practice may not use or disclose the patient's protected health information.

AUTHORIZATION FOR USE OR DISCLOSURE OF INFORMATION

Section A: Must be completed for all authorizations

I hereby authorize the use or disclosure of my individually identifiable health information as described below. I understand that this authorization is voluntary. I understand that if the organization authorized to receive the information is not a health plan or health care provider, the released information may no longer be protected by federal privacy regulations.

Patient Name: _____   DOB: _____

Persons/organizations providing information:

_____

_____

Persons/organizations using or receiving information:

_____

_____

Specific description of information (including date(s), if relevant):

_____

_____

Description of *each* purpose of authorized use or disclosure:

_____

_____

(Note: "At request of [patient's name]" is sufficient when patient initiates authorization and elects not to provide a more detailed statement of purpose.)

Expiration Date

This authorization will expire on _____/_____/_____ (DD/MM/YR) or on the occurrence of the following event:

_____

Revocation

This authorization may be revoked at any time by notifying [Provider Name] in writing at _____ .
If I revoke this authorization, I understand that it will not have any effect on actions [Provider Name] took before it received the revocation.

Section B: Must be completed if health care provider or health plan requested the authorization or authorization is for research

    1. Health care provider or health plan must complete the following:

        a. Will provider or health plan receive financial or in-kind compensation in exchange for using or disclosing the health information described above? Yes ____ No ____

    2. Patient must complete the following:

        a. I understand that I may see and copy the information described on this form if I ask for it, and that I get a copy of this form after I sign it.   Initials _____

        b. I understand that, in most situations, my health care provider will treat me regardless of whether I sign this authorization. If the purpose of the authorization is to allow research-related treatment, I understand I will not be able to get that treatment without signing this form.   Initials _____

        c. I understand that a health plan may condition enrollment or eligibility for benefits on my signing an authorization releasing requested medical records other than psychotherapy notes prior to my enrollment in the plan. However, once I am enrolled, the plan may not refuse to pay for my care, adjust my eligibility for benefits or remove me from the plan if I refuse to sign an authorization.   Initials _____

_____   _____

Signature of patient or patient's representative   **Date**

Printed name of patient's representative _____

Relationship to the patient _____

Witness: _____   **Date** _____

    • *YOU MAY REFUSE TO SIGN THIS AUTHORIZATION* *

The only required form in a physician's office or medical clinic is the above authorization form. The others seen below (e.g., the notice of privacy practices and business associate agreements) are presented for office efficiency. There are many other forms you can have to expedite office practices that are not presented here. These notices/forms must be drafted by individual physicians with their private attorneys so that that they can capture the practices' individualities.The example of the business associate agreement below is a contract. It is strongly recommended that physicians have an attorney familiar with HIPAA draft a model for their own use.

The other documents a physician practice may opt to have is an authorization revocation form, request for an accounting, a request for an amendment, and a request for access in which examples are seen below. All should be individualized by your attorney.

[INSERT PRACTICE NAME]'S

**A. REQUEST FOR HIPAA ACCOUNTING OF DISCLOSURES
OF HEALTH INFORMATION**

[Add Address and Telephone Information for Practice]

Patient Name _____   Date _____

Address _____   Date of Birth _____

_____   SSN_____

INFORMATION REQUESTED

Please provide an accounting of disclosures of health information made by **[insert practice name]** and its business associates from _____ to _____ . I understand that I cannot ask for records going back more than six years. Also, I understand that the practice does not have to list any disclosures made before April 14, 2003.

_____
Signature of Patient or Guardian*

_____
Print Name of Patient or Guardian

* If this request is being signed by an individual's personal representative, please indicate the basis for the representative's authority _____
_____ (e.g., state law, court order, etc.)

[INSERT PRACTICE'S NAME]'S
HIPAA AUTHORIZATION REVOCATION FORM
[Add Address and Telephone Information for Practice]

I wish to revoke an authorization given earlier for certain uses and disclosures of health information.

Patient Name _____   Date _____

Address _____   Date of Birth _____

_____   SSN _____

☐ Check here if you have attached a copy of the authorization being revoked

☐ Check here to identify the authorization you are revoking by describing it below

1. *Description of information authorized for use or disclosure:* _____

_____

_____

2. *Description of each purpose of the requested use or disclosure:* _____

_____

_____

3. *Date the authorization was signed:* _____

_____ **[*Initials of patient or guardian*]** I understand that the uses or disclosures of health information that already have been made based upon the original authorization cannot be taken back.

_____   _____

Signature of Patient or Guardian*   Date

_____

Print Name of Patient or Guardian

* If this revocation is being signed by an individual's personal representative, please indicate the basis for the representative's authority: _____

_____ (e.g., state law, court order, etc.)

AUTHORIZATION FOR USE OR DISCLOSURE OF INFORMATION

Section A: Must be completed for all authorizations

I hereby authorize the use or disclosure of my individually identifiable health information as described below. I understand that this authorization is voluntary. I understand that if the organization authorized to receive the information is not a health plan or health care provider, the released information may no longer be protected by federal privacy regulations.

Patient Name: _____   **DOB:** _____

Persons/organizations providing information:	**Persons/organizations using or receiving information:**
_____	_____
_____	_____

Specific description of information (including date(s), if relevant):

_____

_____

Description of *each* purpose of authorized use or disclosure:

_____

_____

(Note: "At request of [patient's name]" is sufficient when patient initiates authorization and elects not to provide a more detailed statement of purpose.)

Expiration Date

This authorization will expire on _____/_____/_____ (DD/MM/YR) or on the occurrence of the following event:

_____

Revocation

This authorization may be revoked at any time by notifying [Provider Name] in writing at _____ .

If I revoke this authorization, I understand that it will not have any effect on actions [Provider Name] took before it received the revocation.

Section B: Must be completed if health care provider or health plan requested the authorization or authorization is for research

1. Health care provider or health plan must complete the following:
   a. Will provider or health plan receive financial or in-kind compensation in exchange for using or disclosing the health information described above?   Yes ____ No ____
2. Patient must complete the following:
   a. I understand that I may see and copy the information described on this form if I ask for it, and that I get a copy of this form after I sign it.   Initials _____
   b. I understand that, in most situations, my health care provider will treat me regardless of whether I sign this authorization. If the purpose of the authorization is to allow research-related treatment, I understand I will not be able to get that treatment without signing this form.   Initials _____
   c. I understand that a health plan may condition enrollment or eligibility for benefits on my signing an authorization releasing requested medical records other than psychotherapy notes prior to my enrollment in the plan. However, once I am enrolled, the plan may not refuse to pay for my care, adjust my eligibility for benefits or remove me from the plan if I refuse to sign an authorization.   Initials _____

_____   _____
Signature of patient or patient's representative   **Date**

Printed name of patient's representative _____

Relationship to the patient _____

Witness: _____   **Date** _____

- *YOU MAY REFUSE TO SIGN THIS AUTHORIZATION* *

[INSERT PRACTICE NAME]'S

REQUEST FOR ACCESS TO HEALTH INFORMATION

[Add Address and Telephone Information for Practice]

Patient Name _____   Date _____

Date of Birth _____   Telephone _____

Social Security No. _____

Please provide access to health information in the following records:

☐ Medical Records
☐ Billing Records
☐ Other _____

Description of Information: _____

_____

_____ (e.g., type of information, date ranges, etc.).

Please provide the information in the following way:

☐ On-site review of record(s) [*Consider whether practice wants to offer this option*]
☐ Paper copy of record(s)
☐ Electronic copy of record [*Only include this option if practice has the ability
    to provide electronic copies of medical and billing records*]
☐ Check this box to have copies of the records mailed [*if applicable*, or e-mailed] to you

    at: _____

[*If applicable under practice's policies*] I understand that I will be charged a reasonable
copying of [**insert number**] cents per page for hard copies of my records and postage if I
request that my records be mailed.

_____   _____
Signature of Patient or Guardian*   Date

Print Name of Patient or Guardian _____

* If this request is being signed by an individual's personal representative, please state the basis
for the representative's authority:_____ (e.g., state law, court order, etc.).

FOR USE BY PRACTICE

Copy of completed form is to be sent to requester within 30 days *of request for records located on-site and within* 60 days if the relevant records are in storage off-site.

Access granted:

Date records were reviewed or mailed: _____

Access denied:

The following reasons for denial of access are *not* subject to review. Check any that apply:

☐ Requested information is psychotherapy notes.

☐ Requested information was complied in anticipation of litigation.

☐ Requested information is subject to or exempt from the Clinical Laboratory Improvement Amendments of 1988.

☐ Services discussed in the requested records were provided on behalf of a correctional institution.

☐ Requested information involves research that is still ongoing and patient agreed to the denial under such circumstance.

☐ Requested information is subject to the Privacy Act.

☐ Requested information was obtained under a promise of confidentiality and access likely to reveal the source of the information.

The following reasons for denial of access are subject to review upon request. Check any that apply:

☐ Requested information is likely to endanger the life or physical safety of the subject of the information or another person

☐ Requested information references another person and access is likely to cause substantial harm to that person

☐ Access was requested by a personal representative and granting access to the representative is likely to cause substantial harm to the subject of the information or another person

FOR USE BY PATIENT WHEN ACCESS IS DENIED
BASED ON A REVIEWABLE REASON:

I wish to request a review of [insert practice name]'s denial of my request for access to my health information.

_____   _____
Signature of Patient or Guardian*   Date

_____   _____
Print Name of Patient or Guardian   Social Security Number

* If this request is being signed by an individual's personal representative, please state the basis for the authority: _____(e.g., state law, court order, etc.).

FOR USE BY PRACTICE WHEN REVIEW OF ACCESS DENIAL IS REQUESTED

Name and title of the licensed health care provider designated as the reviewing official for

[insert practice name]. _____

[Insert practice name] will abide by the decision of designated reviewing official. That decisions is as follows:

☐ Requested access granted

☐ Requested access denied [circle one] in whole or in part

If access is denied to only part of the requested information, specify the information that

may be provided: _____

_____

_____

As the designated reviewing official for [insert practice name], I certify that I was not involved in the original decision to deny access to the requested health information.

_____   _____
Signature and Title of Reviewer   Date

_____
Print Signature and Title of Reviewer

3.7.5   What the Practicing Physician Should Know about Medical Record Copying Costs and the HIPAA Privacy Rule

Doctors are asked to transfer medical records from one office to another countless times every week. The physician's staff must be alert to the following: the Privacy Rule states that providers "may impose [only] a reasonable, cost-based fee" that includes

1. Only the cost of copying.
2. The cost of supplies.
3. Labor of copying the protected health information requested by the individual.
4. Postage, when the individual has requested the copy, or the summary of explanation, be mailed. As per 45 CFR 164.524(c)(4).

A 12/2000 commentary to the Rule stated served to limit providers to "limit the fee for copying so that it is within reach of all individuals"; "fees for copying and postage provided under state law, but not for other costs excluded under this Rule, are presumed reasonable." (According to Federal Reg, Vol. 65, No. 250, 12/28/00, @ 82557.) But this restriction applied only to copies provided to patients. Therefore, physicians and other health care providers may still charge their State's statutory copying fee (currently, 68 cents per page copied in Maryland) but not the preparation fee (currently $20.52). These fees may still be charged to individuals other than the patient (or the patient's "personal representative" as provided under the Rule).

3.7.5.1   Modification to Medical Records Copying Charges Policies

On October 1, 1994, the law allowing physicians to charge specific sums for preparation and production of medical records went into effect. This law is codified in the Health-General Article § 4-304(c)(3). The law states that these fees may be adjusted annually for inflation using the Consumer Price Index on July 1 of each year. Since the statute does not designate an entity to compute the increases. Maryland and other state medical societies have calculated and published the appropriate adjustment, not in any official capacity, but as a service to its members. The adjusted rates for medical record copying are as follows:

- A preparation fee of no more than $20.52, plus
- A fee of no more than 68 cents per page copied, plus
- The actual cost of shipping and handling

Physicians may demand payment of these fees and charges before turning the records over to a patient or other authorized person (such as the patient's parent, guardian, or lawyer), but probably not before complying with a proper subpoena.

✓ Remember the law says, "Production may not be withheld" in these circumstances:

1. Under an emergency request from a state or local governmental unit concerning child protective services.
2. Or adult protective services case pending payment.
3. Professional Ethics Committee has opined that records should not be withheld from another health practitioner pending payment of the copying fees if to do so would hinder an ill patient from receiving needed medical attention.

4. No fee may be charged to transfer the records of Medicaid recipient to another provider.

5. Finally, the law does not authorize any practitioner to withhold production of the medical records until the fees for medical services themselves have been paid.

3.7.6   A Note of Caution on the Effect of HIPAA on Clinical Research Performed Either in Hospital or in Physicians' Private Office or Clinic

HIPAA was implemented to reduce potential for misuse of personal information and to restrict access to medical records by insurers, employers, and clinical researchers. O'Herrin et al.[15] concluded that HIPAA regulations adversely impact medical records research. Furthermore, HIPAA appears to inhibit medical record and database research. Ethical considerations in health care research are paramount, but current HIPAA implementation strategies increase workload for researchers, and increase the dropout rate for proposed studies when investigators are unable or unwilling to meet the regulatory requirements. It is unclear whether or to what degree the new requirements add to protection of privacy. Studies designed to investigate the costs and effects on quantity and quality of research should be prospectively implemented (prior to implementing and research project).

3.8   Conclusions

To help avoid any problems with Qui Tam or HIPAA, each practicing physician should have a knowledge of the Qui Tam or HIPAA legislation because of the strong impact on his practice. Each physician should have a compliance officer in his office or clinic for managing and coordinating any requests from government, federal or state, Medicare, the OIG, the Department of Justice, FBI, State Attorney General's Office, etc., on either Qui Tam or HIPAA or any other legal matter.

It is important that each physician should have a health care attorney to insure his office is in compliance with this legislation and any subsequent changes. Each physician must have a health care attorney that he and his compliance officer can turn to before any problems turn up and certainly be ready when a potential or actual problem does comes up.

Preventive strategy is described in this chapter on defensive/preventive and proactive moves to avoid these difficulties with implementing these laws and in which experts are predicting will in the future be an increasing problem for practicing physicians. Remember to use the excellent HIPAA web site recommended by Ms. Allison Shuren Esq. —http://www.hhs.gov/ocr/hipaa/—for any other HIPAA questions you may have, but are not addressed in this chapter.

✓ Nothing more than the medical disciplinary procedures in each locality confirms these above summary and conclusions, as does this contribution from Elliott A. Alman Esq.

3.8.1   Physician Ethical Misconduct with Resultant Disciplinary Proceedings

Physicians should be alerted to the potential and numerous situations that may lead to the dire consequences of an expanding area of disciplinary proceedings for ethical misconduct. Most health care professionals believe they can avoid these problems by simply not erring in the provision of medical services. Unfortunately, superior medical and surgical technical skills alone are no guarantee against disciplinary actions. A doctor may in fact be administering the highest level of care to patients, all the while endangering his license to practice medicine. It should be noted that once a state medical board initiates a formal or informal investigation for any reason, every action, inaction, procedure, or patient file of that physician and their office are valid subjects of inquiry. It is therefore extremely important for the practitioner to treat every complaint, regardless of whether it is frivolous, with the utmost seriousness.

3.8.1.1 What Situations Will Most Likely Result in Charges of Misconduct?

Here is a "hypothetical" example based from several law practice cases:

A busy general medical practice office comprised of four internists, a receptionist, an NP, and an assistant/technician got into difficulties when a patient lodged a complaint with the state medical board. The complaint did not allege any specific instance of misconduct on the part of any of the physicians. Instead, the patient complained of "inappropriate" actions by one of the employees of the practice—the assistant/technician. This employee was actually a foreign-trained physician awaiting the results of his licensing examination.

All the physicians immediately conducted their own review. They did not uncover any such conduct from either themselves or the employee. The employee also denied any such conduct, but decided to leave given the environment the complaint produced.

The medical board receiving the complaint referred the complaint to an attorney investigator, hired by the board. The investigator reviewed the allegations, spoke with the complainant, and contacted the practice to schedule an appointment. Upon a visit to the office the investigator conducted a review but did not reach any conclusion regarding the original alleged complaint.

However, the investigator did make other incidental findings not related to the complaint. The investigator took the liberty, permissible in the state code, of reviewing all other aspects of the medical practice. He reviewed files, the office manuals and procedures, and spoke with all the office employees.

The investigator then informed the physicians that he could not reach any conclusion about the complaint that there were other violations of existing regulations. The doctors told the investigator they were ready, willing, and able to implement any of his recommendations. However, rather than offering them their requested suggestions, the investigator reported the "infractions" to the medical board in the form of a formal complaint. Included in the formal complaint were that employees were not adequately identified to the general public by their name, title, and job description.

In this small practice, there had been no formal employee job descriptions. The investigator also determined on the basis of discussions with the employees that the technician was permitted to exceed the scope of his authority in performing certain work in the office.

In addition, while investigating these new allegations, the board demanded copies of complete medical files for other patients of the practice. In effect, the board engaged in a "fishing" expedition designed to locate instances of potential disciplinary breaches. These efforts also included phone calls from individuals identifying themselves as potential patients seeking information and appointments. In actuality the calls were on behalf of the investigator. Appointments were made and selected files were reviewed. In this instance, the board did not find any infractions.

While the doctors were not initially accused or implicated in any action, a formal complaint initiated by the board named them. Under threats to their license they were fined and placed on an extended probation. This eliminated their participation with some medical insurance companies, with a significant financial consequence. In addition, it resulted in a duplication of the charges in all the other states in which the physicians were licensed.

3.8.1.2 Preventive Moves

Contrary to popular belief, a practicing physician must not only "do no harm," but in doing so he must not intentionally, *or unintentionally*, breach any ethical rules while treating patients. To fully understand this, the physician must be acutely aware of the plethora of ethical obligations, some universal and obvious to any practitioner, but others more obscure and unique to their practicing jurisdiction or specialty.

- Each jurisdiction has its own set or sets of rules and regulations governing physician conduct, which may present a dangerous web to the unwary practitioner.
- Each physician must know the importance of understanding the growing maze of rules and regulations impacting each of their actions.
- First and foremost, each practitioner should obtain a set of his local laws and requirements to practice medicine and thoroughly familiarize themselves with the contents. These laws are contained within the respective state legal codes under the sections covering medical licensing, and can be obtained online directly on the website of the respective state as well as the website of the professional board.
- Second, the practitioner should obtain all additional rules and regulations set forth by the respective state regulatory body governing their specialty. Of great importance, the practitioner must also be familiar with the rules and regulations governing any employee of theirs as well (e.g., an x-ray technologist or PA). The physician must not permit the employee to independently perform any work outside of the area specifically defined within their licensure.
- Third, the practitioner should carefully review the publications of the local medical board and local medical society. While patient records are protected by federal and state privacy laws, these do not apply against an offending physician. In fact, it may be a requirement to make public such data. Local medical organizations often provide publications for their membership, which include instances of disciplinary actions taken against the health care professionals in that locality. If your local medical board does not publish disciplinary actions, contact the board directly and inquire regarding obtaining such information. This can be an invaluable resource in determining how certain actions are deemed within each jurisdiction.
- Fourth, review the availability of continuing medical education courses offered by your respective professional organizations and medical schools to seek out courses addressing ethical obligations, rules, and procedures. Such courses are often available locally and an increasing number are available online. Moreover, they may help meet your continuing education requirements.
- Fifth, contact your medical malpractice carrier to make available to you their own publications and informational pamphlets regarding physician discipline.
- Sixth, spend some time online and search for your individual specialty and disciplinary actions. Do not limit yourself to your jurisdiction. The members of state medical boards

interact with other state medical boards. Trends in one jurisdiction are likely to migrate to another. It is therefore important to understand the thinking of all the boards.

- Finally, speak with your colleagues with years of experience in your practice area for a frank discussion about special procedures and requirements in their jurisdiction. This will provide you with a degree of experienced professional peer feedback in your area.

3.8.1.3 Proactive Actions

Have an attorney ready for such an impending disaster.

- It is important to be aware of the severity of the sanctions and the impacts of any disciplinary action.
- Your initial response must be to cooperate fully. Failure to respond or failure to cooperate may often render the practitioner subject to a separate and severe disciplinary violation.
- Medical Boards are organizations staffed by investigators trained to uncover disciplinary infractions. They have a specific mission.
- As soon as you receive notification that a complaint has been filed, obtain counsel skilled in this type of proceeding to help level the playing field.
- As a matter of fact seek out such experienced counsel to have ready for such an event.
- Often, there is a preliminary investigation of virtually all complaints prior to it becoming a formal complaint.
- Meet with your counsel, address the allegations, *and attempt to have the matter dismissed before it is lodged as a formal complaint.*
- Once it becomes a formal complaint, it will be fully investigated with the possibility of discipline rendered against the offending physician.
- The most severe disciplinary actions could result in revocation or suspension of one's license to practice. After the period of suspension, the physician may apply for reinstatement.

Medical boards possess other sanctions that may be levied against the practitioner.

But even the less "onerous" actions may also substantially affect one's ability to practice medicine.

For example, in order to reach a settlement of a pending matter, a physician may agree to be placed on "probation" for a specific period of time. This is often accompanied by the levy of a fine and completion of a course or examination on ethics. On the surface this may appear to be a less severe sanction. But before agreeing to any such probation, the doctor must be aware of the intended, and often unintended, results.

All instances of probation are reported to a national physician database. The database is monitored by each state medical board and by virtually all insurance carriers who provide health insurance coverage to patients. Once a physician's name is included on the database, insurance companies typically revoke that physician's eligibility to be reimbursed for services by that insurance company for treatment rendered to a patient. In short, while a physician may agree to probation for what is perceived to be a minor violation, the ability of that physician to maintain a practice and earn a living will consequently be greatly compromised. Most private practitioners rely on private health insurance or health maintenance organizations (HMOs). If an HMO revokes a physician's right to participate, it could result in a potential loss of a significant portion of that physician's patient base.

3.8.1.4 Good Office Procedures

Note the common denominators in almost all preventive and proactive actions in this chapter:

1. Keep all records intact.
2. Invest in a good computer system, software, and a trained staff who understand the intricacies of a medical practice.
3. All records should be typed and maintained in a computer database. This may appear expensive and duplicative, but it will be of immeasurable assistance.
4. If and when the medical board reviews a file, all information should be available in an easily readable format.
5. The days of scribbling unreadable notes should be long gone.

References

1. Feld AD. Malpractice risks associated with colon cancer and inflammatory bowel disease. *Am. J. Gastroenterol.* 2004; 1999: 1641–1644.
2. Gore CL. A physician's liability for mistakes of a physician assistant. *J. Legal Med.* 2000; 21: 125–142.
3. Cook JH. The legal status of physician extenders in Iowa, reviews, speculations and recommendations. *Iowa Legal Rev.* 1986; 72: 215–239.
4. Feld AD. Vicarious liability, *ASGE Risk Management Manual*, May 2001 (available through the ASGE Office).
5. Saccuzzo DP. Liability for failure to supervise adequately, mental health assistance, unlicensed practitioners and students. *34 Calif. WL Rev.* 1997; 115–151.
6. Khan v Medical Board of California. 16 Cal. Rptr 2d; 385, 392 (Cal. App. 1993).
7. Seariver Maritime v Industrial Medical Services. 983 F. Supp.; 1287, 1297 (N.D. Cal. 1997).
8. Byington M. The changing landscape of supervision. *Forum: Supervision.* Cambridge, MA: Risk Management Foundation of the Harvard Medical Institutions, 1999. Available at http://www.rmf.harvard.edu/ (accessed February 12, 2002).
9. American Academy of Family Physicians. *Non-Physician Providers (NPPs).* Available at: http://www.aafp.org/policy/x1698.xml (accessed March 4, 2002).
10. Danielsen RD, Cassidy BA. Do's and Don'ts for D.O.s who supervise PAs. *Ariz. Osteopath. Med. Assoc. Dig.* 1999; 30: 14–15.
11. Wachter RM, Goldman L. The hospitalist movement 5 years later. *JAMA* 2002; 287: 487–489.
12. Weinstein L. The "laborist": a new focus of practice for the obstetrician. *Am. J. Obstet. Gynecol.* 2003; 188(2): 310–312.
13. U.S. Department of Health and Human Services. Health Insurance Portability and Accountability Act of 1996. http://www.hhs.gov/ocr.hipaa/
14. Standards for Privacy of Individually Identifiable Health Information; Final Rule. Code of Federal Regulations, Title 45, Parts 160 and 164, http://hhs.gov/ocr/combinedregtext.pdf. HIPAA Security Standards.
15. O'Herrin JK, Fost N, Kudsk KA. Health Insurance Portability Accountability Act (HIPAA) regulations: effect on medical record research. *Ann Surg.* 2004; 239: 772–776.

Maritime Medical Malpractice

4.1 Introduction

I spent my 2-week vacation before the completion of my internship at an inner city municipal hospital and the beginning of my residency at the Johns Hopkins Hospital as a ship's doctor cruising the Caribbean. Never had such a very young, very single denizen of the long cold dark nights of the hospital internship, often working round the clock, been so happy even with such little pay. My "girl magnet" rented white uniform with the shiny brass buttons made me look important—especially when sitting for our regular dinner at the captain's table. Maybe it was the Italian captain and all Italian jolly crew that made each day such a happy adventure. It was fortunate that there was nothing more serious that I treated during the 2 clinic hours of each glorious day than a sore throat or occasional sprained ankle. I must admit that during those 2 glorious weeks in the sun, I had second thoughts about returning to a vigorous no sleep medical house-staff training program—no matter how prestigious the hospital.

But I did.

But since then my fantasy has been to return to the sea, as a doctor in another fancy uniform—this time with my wife—to see glorious sunsets from the ship's deck. There are others with the same idea—maybe recent medical school graduates or other house-staff trainees who want to trade their skills as a ship's doctor for a well-earned vacation at no expense except for the uniform.

For this reason, and also because there are so many changes going on in maritime malpractice law, I asked attorneys John Aronson and Leigh McMillan of the law firm Rodriguez Aronson & Essington, P.A., Miami, FL, who in my opinion are the most knowledgeable experts in this subject, to contribute a chapter. To my delight they did—and in the tradition of the cruise lines—for free.

4.2 Alleging, Proving, and Defending Claims of Medical Malpractice under Maritime Law—By Leigh McMillan, J.D., LL.M.

4.2.1 Executive Summary: How Ships' Physicians Are at Medical Malpractice Risk

Cause of action by either seaman or passenger based on failure to treat. The vessel's doctor may be sued personally by a passenger under a cause of action alleging that the doctor

- failed to diagnose,
- failed to properly treat,

- failed to medically advise,
- failed to properly monitor,
- failed in a timely manner to put ashore, and
- resultantly aggravated plaintiff's condition.

4.2.2 What Should a Potential Ship's Physician Look for Prior to Signing on?

Any physician taking a short- or long-term position as a ship's doctor must insist that the ship meets the criteria set by the American College of Emergency Physicians (ACEP), which has drafted a recommended list of medical equipment to be available on board every cruise vessel according to the ACEP's "Health Care Guidelines for Cruise Ship."

4.2.2.1 Physicians Employed by Cruise Ships

Although the laws of the United States do not require cruise vessels calling into ports in the United States to provide physicians aboard the vessel for the passenger's care and convenience,[1] most, if not all, major cruise lines do provide medical staff and equipment to treat passengers during the voyage as a matter of practicality. Federal law does require a physician aboard vessels to care for and treat crew members or at least carry a medicine chest for the care of the crew.[2]

The various cruise and yachting lines, incorporated in the United Kingdom, Norway, the Netherlands, Bermuda, Italy, the Bahamas, Japan, Malaysia, and other countries, sail the seven seas and call into ports worldwide. Cruise lines carry passengers from almost every country and employ crew and personnel from around the world. The operation of each ship entails compliance with the ship's home country and with the laws of each country at which the ship calls into port. In the United States, the Department of Health, the United States Coast Guard, the Department of Homeland Security, the Center for Disease Control, and the state's equivalents all promulgate and enforce rules and laws to which the vessel must adhere. Cruise lines calling into port in United States' ports of call are routinely visited by the Center for Disease Control and rated as to the vessel's cleanliness and adherence to advised standards for safety throughout the entire ship. At all other times, the vessel must comply with international nongovernmental organizations' rules, such as those promulgated by the International Labor Organization, the International Maritime Organization, as well as the numerous international conventions concerning pollution, Safety of Life at Sea (SOLAS), as well as the laws of the vessel's home country.

Cruise ships hire physicians from countries other than the United States because a typical cruise line contract of employment to practice medicine aboard a ship at sea is a short-term (typically 3 months) contract, usually making it impractical for most physicians licensed in the United States. Physicians licensed in a country with a nationalized health care system whose hospitals and clinics are state-owned and operated, such as the United Kingdom, South Africa, Norway, or Italy, allow physicians to go on hiatus or accrue leave time to accept employment with a cruise line for a short-term contract. For cruise lines incorporated in Italy, the Italian Ministry of Health provides that only doctors licensed in Italy and approved of by the ministry may be hired to work aboard Italian-flagged vessels.[3] The Italian Ministry of Health regulations require a ship's doctor to have a degree in medicine from an accredited Italian medical school, 2 years experience as a practicing physician, and successful completion of both the written and oral examinations administered by the Italian Ministry of Health, which also maintains a list of registered ship's physicians.[3]

4.2.2.1.1 Plaintiff passengers who allege a cause of action.

Plaintiff passengers who allege a cause of action for negligence, or "tort," sustained while aboard defendant's vessel in navigable waters state a claim governed by maritime law.[4] All employees and agents of a cruise line, comprising a ship's crew, owe a duty of reasonable care to the passengers.[5] The cruise line's duty of reasonable care under the circumstances includes the duty of the ship's doctor to adhere to the standard of care of a reasonable ship's doctor under the circumstances.[6]

In the event, a passenger suffers an injury and alleges the cruise line and the physician negligent, the cruise line defends and indemnifies the physician under its "protection and indemnity" (P&I) policy, and does not require the physician to carry malpractice insurance for the voyage.

Passengers who do file suit against a cruise vessel for personal injury sustained while aboard the vessel do so under the rights and remedies provided by general maritime law.[7] Passengers may not choose to sue under the statutory law of a state for medical malpractice as to the ship's doctor's alleged misdiagnoses or negligent treatment, so none of the state's statutory laws apply in court, whether the suit is filed in state or federal court.

Historically, the majority of courts, state, and federal, deciding maritime cases in the United States, have followed the same basic rule that if the shipowner decides to employ a ship's doctor to treat passengers who become ill or are injured, then the shipowner has a duty to employ a doctor who is competent and duly qualified. If the carrier negligently hires a doctor who proves to be less than competent, the shipowner is considered to have breached its duty, and will be held liable for its own negligent hiring. If an otherwise competent doctor is negligent in treating a passenger, however, that negligence would not have been imputed to the carrier.[8]

Until recently, the majority rule as set forth by courts sitting in admiralty held that a cruise line could not be held vicariously liable for the negligence of its ship's doctor in the care and treatment of passengers when the cruise line exercised reasonable care in selecting and hiring an otherwise-qualified physician.[9]

The reason for this longstanding rule was the cruise line's lack of control over, and historical noninterference with, the doctor–patient relationship. A cruise line would not be expected to professionally supervise a doctor in the practice of medicine, especially in light of the fact that the physician had usually been employed as an independent contractor.[10] As a result, a plaintiff had little interest in suing a physician when the cruise line could not be held liable and the physician was someone over whom jurisdiction may not likely be had, owing to the fact that a foreign person is not easily haled into court in the United States.

Courts have begun to lean toward allowing plaintiffs to sue cruise lines *in addition to the ship's physician* as cruising has become more popular, more profitable, and the number of Americans who cruise has skyrocketed. Allowing a plaintiff to go forward with a claim of vicarious liability against the cruise line for the physician's alleged negligent failure to render proper treatment makes *claiming against the ship's physician viable economically*. Because the cruise line is the "deep pocket," a plaintiff now has a claim with some likelihood of recovery. The legal concept behind vicarious liability is that an employer may be held responsible for the negligent acts of an employee who, in the course and scope of employment, injures someone.[11]

The modern trend of allowing a plaintiff to plead vicarious liability, on the basis of the physician's status as an employee of the cruise line, has evolved due to the fact that commercial cruise lines do hire their physicians for terms of employment, albeit short, thus giving rise to an employer–employee relationship amenable to a vicarious liability cause of action. The fact that cruise lines now have substantial corporate presences in the United States, evidenced in the passenger ticket "forum and venue clause," mandating that any suit shall be brought in a certain area in the United States, usually California or Florida, makes it easier for a court to entertain a vicarious liability claim against the cruise line itself, *as well as naming the physician personally.*

4.2.2.1.2 Vicarious liability?   A claim of vicarious liability allows the jury to award a plaintiff damages against the cruise line as an employer of the physician, responsible for torts (negligent acts) committed by the cruise line's employee(s). Traditionally, a seaman's negligent acts causing harm to a passenger could be held against the cruise line. The modern trend, therefore, is for a court to not make a distinction between a traditional seaman or a physician who allegedly commits a tort for a plaintiff claiming against a cruise line for the alleged negligence of the ship's physician.[12]

Recent decisions are now citing the once-disfavored 1959 federal court decision from the Northern District of California, *Nietes v. American President Lines, Ltd.*, which allowed the shipowner's liability for a physician's alleged breach of professional standard to be pled. The Southern District of Florida, in *Doonan v. Carnival Corporation*, dismissed plaintiff's causes of action pled under a traditional theory of vicarious liability, but allowed the plaintiff's claim for vicarious liability under "agency-by-estoppel" to survive, because a tort committed by an apparent agent of a corporation is recoverable under Federal Maritime Law.

The court's reasoning in allowing the agency-by-estoppel claim to go forward was that the existence of an agency relationship is a question of fact, and if the ship actually held the doctor out to be its agent, was treating the plaintiff on behalf of the carrier, and the plaintiff relied on the physician to her detriment, then the cruise line could be liable if the ship's doctor was found to have rendered negligent treatment.[13]

The definition for negligence under a claim for failure to treat under the Jones Act is the same as the common law standard articulated in the Restatement (Second) of Torts (1977):

> "Negligence" is the failure to use reasonable care. Reasonable care is that degree of care that a reasonably careful person would use under like circumstances. Negligence may consist either in doing something that a reasonably careful person would not do under like circumstances, or in failing to do something that a reasonably careful person would do under like circumstances.[14]

4.2.2.1.3 The standard of care owed to a passenger.   The standard of care owed to a person who is not a member of the crew was decided by the U.S. Supreme Court in 1959. In *Kermarec v. Compagnie Generale Transatlantique*, a crew member's friend came aboard to visit and was injured while leaving the ship as it prepared to get under way from its berth in a New York city pier. The trial court in New York State had originally decided the case under New York statutory law, using common law land-based premises liability distinctions.

Under land-based law, people are divided into categories classifying the person's status regarding the type of invitation the injured person had to enter the land. If the person entered the land at the owner's request to conduct business, such as a plumber coming to repair pipes, the status was that of an "invitee," and was accorded the highest duty of care; a person entering the land as a social guest, known as a "licensee," was owed a duty of reasonable care, and a person entering the land uninvited, known as a "trespasser," was owed the least duty of care.[4] The duty of care owed is crucial, as the less degree of duty owed to the person injured, the less likely liability might be found by a jury.

After appeals by the parties in Kermarec as to the legally proper standard of care owed by the shipowner and given as a jury instruction to the jury, the United States Supreme Court granted certiorari and ruled on two crucial aspects of maritime torts. One was that the legal rights and liabilities arising from an injury sustained while in navigable waters puts a claim under admiralty jurisdiction and measurable by the standards of maritime law.[4] The second was the ruling that the standard of care owed to passengers by a shipowner is that which is "reasonable under the circumstances." Both of these rulings have remained the applicable legal principles for determining a tort committed upon navigable waters in the United States since that time, whether the case is brought in state or federal court.[15] A passenger's claim against a ship's doctor is therefore, a maritime claim, and governed under maritime law.[16]

Admiralty jurisdiction requires the application of substantive maritime law.[17] Maritime law is historically meant to be uniform throughout the courts of the United States, due to Congress' recognized need for the uniformity of decisions in maritime matters because shipping affects interstate and international commerce. State courts deciding maritime issues must apply maritime substantive law, because substantive state law leads to inconsistencies in court rulings, which are disfavored. General rules of maritime law apply whether a passenger or seaman's causes of action are pled as a maritime claim such as a Jones Act negligence claim or for a cause of action for damages, common law causes of action available to passengers and seamen.[18]

In any suit alleging medical malpractice, then, application of a state medical malpractice statutory law is considered an error by the court.[19] Florida's Third District Court of Appeal in Rand v. Hatch declined to require the plaintiff's compliance with Florida's Medical Malpractice Statute, which requires that the plaintiff notify the alleged tortfeasor of the pending claim before the suit is filed in court and also requires a showing that the claim has merit to go forward in court. The court held that a tort occurring in navigable waters must be determined by maritime law, and that conflicting state law was not permitted. Even though the plaintiff's claim was filed in state court, the malpractice claim did not result in the application of Florida law.[19]

The fact that a shipowner owes a passenger the duty of "reasonable care under the circumstances" does not make the shipowner liable to passengers in the event of an accident, but only for the ship's negligence—the shipowner is not an insurer of the plaintiff's absolute safety.[20] The shipowner also owes its crew members the duty to provide proper medical care under international law and under the Jones Act,[21] and under common law principles embodied in general maritime law. The shipowner's failure to provide proper diagnosis and treatment to a crew member who is injured or becomes ill while employed by the shipowner and is harmed by the lack of proper medical care will give rise to a claim for Jones Act negligence.[22]

A claim for failure to treat may be asserted by either the seaman or a passenger, as "negligent undertaking in a profession or trade" is a traditional cause of action in common law tort.[23] A crew member sues only the shipowner. However, a passenger may sue the ship's doctor personally under a cause of negligence, alleging that the doctor failed to diagnose, properly treat, medically advise, monitor, or put the passenger ashore, and this failure resultantly aggravated the plaintiff's condition.

Conversely, however, a doctor who decides against a passenger's wishes to put that passenger ashore if the passenger is too ill to safely sail with the vessel cannot be successfully sued by the passenger for "negligent decision to medically evacuate." The court in *Metzger v. Italian Line*[24] held that the ship's physician properly decided to refuse to allow a passenger with an ailment requiring surgery to come back aboard the vessel, which was docked in Jamaica. The court held that a medical decision to refuse to allow a seriously ill passenger to come back aboard a ship that did not have adequate medical facilitates for that patient could not legally amount to any actionable kind of negligence.[24] A shipowner is also required, if there is no ship's physician and a passenger requests, to obtain a shoreside doctor for an injured passenger upon reaching port.[25]

4.2.2.2   *The Professional Duty Owed by the Physician*

The duty of a physician in common law tort is to exercise the degree of care, knowledge, and skill ordinarily possessed and exercised by the average member of the profession practicing in the field.[26] There is no "professional" negligence, but simply professional conduct, which is shown to have fallen below the standard of care owed in the relevant circumstance, measured not in the degree of care, but an amount of care measured by the physician's experience, training, and the facilities available.[27] The traditional manner in which a professional, any professional, rendering a service is held to "exercise the skill and knowledge normally possessed by members of that profession or trade in good standing in similar communities."[23]

Under common law, the burden of proof borne by the plaintiff is the showing of (i) facts that give rise to a legal duty on the part of the defendant to conform to the standard of conduct established by law for the protection of the plaintiff; (ii) failure of the defendant to conform to the standard of conduct; (iii) that such failure is a legal cause of the harm suffered by the plaintiff; and (iv) that the plaintiff has in fact suffered harm of a kind legally compensable by damages.[28]

The "burden of proof" that a plaintiff bears upon claiming against a defendant under common law "includes both the burden of introducing sufficient evidence to justify a jury in finding for the party having the burden, and the burden of persuading the jury to find for that party upon the matter in issue. This burden of proof, which concerns the ultimate burden of producing a preponderance of evidence, is to be distinguished from the burden of going forward with evidence, at a particular point in the proceeding, which may shift from one party to the other according to the proof introduced."[29]

The elements that must be proven specifically in a maritime medical malpractice claim are (1) that a physician–patient relationship existed; (2) the standard of care was breached; and (3) that breach of the physician caused harm, provable with a reasonable medical possibility. Maritime law will not hold the physician liable for an adverse result of a reasonable medical diagnoses or treatment, which is generally recognized among a physician's peers, even when the physician could have chosen a different diagnosis or treatment. The U.S. Supreme Court held that "careful and competent men frequently reach different conclusions despite the fullest and most careful examination of all available data."[30]

Physicians are not usually liable for an honest mistake in judgment, only for the departure from the required standard of reasonable care given by a prudent physician in that circumstance.[27] "A physician is not generally liable for errors of judgment if he brings to his treatment that skill and care ordinarily exercised by his professional brethren. If competent medical men can reasonably differ as to the best of several courses, the doctor is not negligent in pursuing one of them though a part of the profession may believe that another course might have produced better results."[31] The applicable standard of care is generally that of a physician who exercises the degree of care and skill of the average doctor licensed to practice medicine. The prevailing professional standard of care for a given health care provider shall be that level of care, skill, and treatment which, in light of all relevant surrounding circumstances, is recognized as acceptable and appropriate by reasonably prudent similar health care providers.[32]

Maritime law bases standards of care on principles as fair as is practicable as to international corporate defendants such as the cruise lines, who are obliged to adhere to the laws of their own countries as to hiring employees. There is no "national maritime standard of care," although two maritime cases reference this theory, both cases involving American seamen treated abroad by physicians licensed in foreign countries. *Fitzgerald v. A.L. Burbank & Co.*,[33] concerned a Jones Act case brought by a seaman injured by negligent medical treatment rendered in Bahrain. In declining to require the seaman to prove that the doctor fell below the accepted standard of care in Bahrain, the court held that the standard should be "free from geographical requirements," as proving the standard of care of the medical profession "in some far distant land" was an unreasonable burden for the seaman, reasoning that some type of general standard of care for all admiralty cases should be implemented, describing the standard as "the degree of care and skill of the average qualified practitioner of the art and science of medicine."[33] In another case, a crew member was rendered substandard medical treatment in India, and the crew member subsequently died.[34] The court cited to a Fitzgerald-type general standard of care such as "the degree of care and skill of the average qualified practitioner of the art and science of medicine," but ultimately applied a "gross negligence" standard because the estate's claim requested punitive damages.[34]

Notwithstanding the presumed application of American federal maritime law, a court of law in the United States may face a choice of law issue when certain circumstances arise. The application of the law of the state of the vessel's flag may sometimes be the correct law to apply in determining the standard of care.[35] When law other than U.S. law is desired by a party, it must be requested and the court must be briefed as to why a conflict of laws would make the application of foreign law appropriate.

The second element that the breach of the applicable standard of care caused harm must be proven "within a reasonable medical possibility" from expert testimony presented by the plaintiff. Case law from either passenger or seaman illustrates this requirement, as expert testimony from the plaintiff passenger or crew member's medical expert witness is necessary to prove a claim for failure to treat.[36] Courts will look to whether the evidence is legally insufficient, and if not, "negligent treatment by the physician will not be found if there is no evidence of it put into the record."[36]

4.2.2.3 A Seaman's Claim for "Failure to Provide Prompt and Adequate Treatment" under the Jones Act

Of the three claims available to a crew member who becomes sick or injured while working, the claim pertaining to a physician's allegedly negligent care is made under a Jones Act negligence basis.[37] The finding of liability for failure to provide prompt and adequate treatment is analyzed under the circumstances of each case, including, the seriousness of the injury or illness, the availability of aid, failure to adequately investigate the cause of the symptoms, obliging the crew member to work in spite of a "no fit for duty" rating, the necessity of the shipowner to turn the ship to the nearest port, arrange for medical evacuation from the ship, or taking other measures, even if the cost incurred is considerable.[38] "The extent of the duty varies with the nature of the injury and the relative availability of medical facilities. In some cases it may be enough to administer first aid without even calling a doctor. There are, however, cases at the other end of the spectrum where the duty is not satisfied by the calling of a competent general practitioner and where the failure to summon a specialist can be negligence."[39]

The cause of action for failure to treat was articulated by the U.S. Supreme Court, in *Cortes v. Baltimore Insular Lines*, and in *DeZon v. American President Lines*, where the Court held that a crew member's aggravation and further harm to the underlying injury caused by negligence was actionable as an additional, separate claim, if a shipowner breaches his/her duty owed to a crew member to provide medical treatment, called "cure," in maritime parlance.[40]

In discussing the nature of this cause of action and remedy in DeZon, the court ruled that recovery must be alleged and proved under the Jones Act for the shipowner's negligence or breach of duty to provide maintenance and cure for a seaman wounded in the service of the ship.[41] The breach of a shipowner's duty to provide "cure" must be shown to have been "medical malpractice," and if the proof was not in the court record, then recovery would be denied.[42] Further, the burden on proof the plaintiff carries is not simply to show that the physician made misdiagnoses based on an array of symptoms, the cause of which differing physicians could have disagreed:

> The doctor apparently made a wrong diagnosis, but that does not provide that it was a negligent one. It seemed to be the obvious diagnosis from the history which the patient gave him, and that appears to have been incomplete and not unlikely to mislead.[42]

Liability for a misdiagnoses will be found when it is shown that the physician failed to test for something that the average physician would have tested for and should have found, but did not, resulting in additional harm to the crew member.[43] Centeno, a Honduran citizen, was hired by Gulf Fleet as a ship's cook for a 1-year contract of employment.[44] During his employment, Centeno became ill and the vessel's agent arranged for Centeno to see Dr. Turner in California, who treated Centeno for the flu.[45]

Centeno's condition deteriorated after his visit to Dr. Turner, and Centeno, still suffering and unable to work, was repatriated to Honduras for other reasons. Centeno saw a local Honduran doctor, who, based upon the same symptoms Centeno described to the Californian doctor, tested Centeno's glucose level, and diagnosed Centeno with diabetes mellitus and diabetic pre-coma.[45] One week later, Centeno developed diarrhea, cramps, and vomiting, apparently ingested from drinking water. Centeno died shortly thereafter from cardiac arrest brought on by the infection and due to "organic exhaustion ... due to diabetic pre-coma" . . ..[46]

At trial, the Honduran doctor testified that Centeno's diabetic pre-coma weakened the body to such a degree that Centeno had no resistance to infection, concluding that Centeno's death was related to the delay in the diagnosis and treatment of his diabetes.[47] Had Centeno stayed in the United States to receive treatment for the diabetes that should have been diagnosed, Centeno would not have gotten so weakened and would have been able to better fight any subsequent infection.[47] The jury found that the ship's officers were liable for Dr. Turner's negligent failure to test for diabetes, and were also liable for failing to seek additional medical treatment for Centeno following his return to the ship from his visit to Dr. Turner, as Centeno continued to physically deteriorate.[47] Liability was affirmed on appeal, as a shipowner is vicariously responsible for the negligence of a physician chosen to treat its seaman.[48]

When a crew member, or seaman, alleges a claim for failure to give proper medical attention, the claim is directed at the shipowner, not the doctor personally. The shipowner is liable for any negligent care or treatment of the shipowner's doctors, either shipboard or shoreside, in the treatment of the crew under the shipowner's maritime duty to provide maintenance and cure under the Jones Act, 46 U.S.C. § 688.[49]

4.2.2.4 Defenses to Claims of Negligent Treatment

There are defenses available to the physician alleged to have given negligent treatment, consisting of "procedural" and "substantive" defenses. Defenses such as the plaintiff's claim being barred by the applicable statute of limitations, or lack of personal jurisdiction, are procedural defenses, arising from laws provided to assure fairness to the defendant in a court of law. The applicable statute of limitations, codified as 46 U.S.C. app. § 763a, provides that "Unless otherwise specified by law, a suit for recovery of damages for personal injury or death, or both, arising out of a maritime tort, shall not be maintained unless commenced within three years from the date the cause of action accrued."[50] The statute of limitations for maritime causes of action occurring aboard a cruise ship may be limited to 1 year under the passenger's ticket/contract under federal law.[51]

Further, once dismissed from a state or federal court based on statute of limitations grounds, the matter is considered adjudicated on the merits for purposes of *res judicata* (settled by judgment). Florida's Third District Court of Appeals held that, given the construction of Federal Rule 41(b) in the federal courts as well as the clear language of Florida Rule of Civil Procedure Rule 1.420(b), neither the state nor the federal court has authority to reinstate plaintiff's cause of action dismissed due to the filing of the claim after the applicable 1 year statute of limitations.[52]

The existence of personal jurisdiction, the ability of a court to command a person to appear before the court on a claim, is also a procedural matter. The difficulties in personally suing the doctor, if the passenger chooses to sue the ship's doctor individually, is the ability to serve the doctor with process and establish that the doctor should be ordered to appear in a court in the United States. Ship's doctors are not usually citizens of the United States and may not be working for the cruise line when the suit is filed. The ability to sue that doctor depends upon whether the doctor can be found, and when found, whether the doctor personally has sufficient contacts with the state for a court to declare personal jurisdiction exists. The plaintiffs in *Carlisle v. Carnival Corporation*[6] were unable to serve process on the ship's doctor, who was a British subject and no longer employed by the cruise line, leaving only the cruise line remaining in the suit. Plaintiffs established personal jurisdiction to sue the doctor personally upon showing that medical treatment occurred while the vessel was in Florida waters and there were multiple contacts with state.[53]

Another court, on similar facts, found differently, ruling that there was no personal jurisdiction over a nonresident ship's doctor who had insufficient Florida contacts;[54] and in another Florida case, the court held that there were sufficient contacts found to support personal jurisdiction, as the cruise line had a corporate presence in Florida and the physician rendered treatment to plaintiff as vessel sailed into Florida waters and docked at Florida port.[55]

Establishing whether the ship was within the state's territorial waters may result in gathering specific ship log information, as well as how the ocean's tide was moving at a particular time and date.[56] The court in *Benson v. Norwegian Cruise Line, Ltd.* ruled that counsel for plaintiff and defendant were most likely obliged to get data from the National Oceanic and Atmospheric Agency (NOAA),[57] holding that Florida's territorial waters, as defined in Florida's 1968 Constitution as waters within the Gulf Stream, move during the year and so must be specifically shown to the court when claiming territorial waters as a basis of jurisdiction.[57]

The procedural defense of lack of personal jurisdiction arises from state law, and both state and federal courts are obliged to apply the state law of the forum state when determining whether personal jurisdiction exists to hale the doctor into court in that state. In *Wurtenberger v. Cunard Line, Ltd.*,[58] the court held that New York's long-arm statute reached to the physician because the vessel docked in New York's pier and the doctor was shown to have been practicing medical care within New York territorial waters. The court in *Corke v. Sameiet M.S. Song of Norway*,[59] ruled that the physician was not subject to personal jurisdiction under the New York long-arm statute because the plaintiff did not show that the physician treated the plaintiff in New York territorial waters and the vessel did not dock in New York. The claim against the physician in *Di Bonaventure v. Home Lines, Inc.*[60] could not go forward when the court found that the vessel was never present in Pennsylvania waters, and so the physician was not subject to personal jurisdiction under Pennsylvania's long-arm statute. The practical effect of a finding that personal jurisdiction does not exist means that the physician is dismissed as a party altogether. If the physician's counsel does not assert this defense, however, the defense may be waived if the physician proceeds to answer the complaint as though the personal jurisdiction did exist.

The substantive defenses to a claim of negligent treatment include the same ones as asserted in land-based suits. If the plaintiff patient did not comply with medical advice or refused to act on the physician's medical advice, or failed to disclose relevant medical history, then the physician may well not likely be found liable for whatever harm the plaintiff alleges occurred as a result of the physician's alleged negligence.

Additionally, the vessel medical center is a limited facility. Standard equipment and staffing, determined proper by the American College of Emergency Physicians' (ACEP) Section of Cruise Ship and Maritime Medicine, and as contained in the "Health Care Guidelines for Cruise Ship Medical Facilities,"[61] was adopted by the International Council of Cruise Lines (ICCL),[62] and is the standard for the cruise lines who are members of the ICCL.

The factors dictating whether a vessel can incorporate the guidelines drafted by the ACEP depends upon the vessel's size; the length of the voyage and how far out to sea and away from shoreside hospital facilities and the ability to evacuate the patient by helicopter, as well as the type of passenger expected to cruise on the vessel; the foreseeable, anticipated number of passenger visits to the sick bay; and the number of medical staff and design and layout of the sick bay will determine how much of the list is feasible.[61]

Ideally, a ship's medical center should be staffed with physicians and registered nurses on call 24 h a day, have examination and treatment areas and an inpatient medical holding unit adequate for the size of the ship, and adequate space for diagnosis and treatment of passengers and crew with 360° patient accessibility around all beds and stretchers. The ship should be accessible by wheelchairs and stretchers; have one examination/stabilization room per ship; one ICU room per ship; a minimum number inpatient beds of 1 bed per 1000 passengers and crew; and an isolation room or the capability to provide isolation of patients. The ship's medical record and communication system should provide well-organized, legible, and consistent documentation of all medical care, in compliance with relevant patient confidentiality requirements.[61]

Every vessel should have a contingency medical plan defining one or more locations on the ship that should be in a different fire zone (from the primary medical center), be easily accessible, and have lighting and power supply on the emergency system, and portable medical equipment and supplies including documentation and planning material; medical waste and personal protective equipment; airway equipment, oxygen, and supplies; IV fluids and supplies; immobilization equipment and supplies; diagnostic and laboratory supplies; dressings; defibrillator and supplies; communication equipment for each member of the medical staff; a clear procedure in case the primary medical space cannot be used, and crew assigned to assist the medical staff.[61]

All ships should employ medical staff who have undergone a credentialing process to verify a current physician or registered nurse licensure; 3 years of postgraduate/post-registration clinical practice in general and emergency medicine; OR Board certification in Emergency Medicine or Family Practice or Internal Medicine; competent skill level in advanced life support and cardiac care; that physicians have minor surgical skills (i.e., for suturing, I&D abscesses, etc.); and that the medical staff is fluent in the official language of the cruise line, the ship, and that of most passengers.[61]

The medical center aboard the ship should have emergency medical equipment including airway equipment (bag valve mask, ET tubes, stylet, lubricant vasoconstrictor, suction equipment), all portable; a cardiac monitor and backup monitor; two portable defibrillators, one of which may be semi-automatic; external cardiac pacing capability; an electrocardiograph; an infusion pump; a pulse oximeter; a nebulizer; automatic or manual respiratory support equipment; oxygen (including portable oxygen); a wheelchair; a stair chair; a stretcher; a refrigerator/freezer; long and short back boards; cervical spine immobilization capabilities; and trauma cart supplies.[61]

Medications on supply should include emergency medications and supplies for management of common medical emergencies, to include thrombolytics and sufficient quantities of advanced life support medications, in accordance with international ALS guidelines, for the management of two complex cardiac arrests; for the gastrointestinal system, cardiovascular system, respiratory system, and central nervous system; infectious diseases, the endocrine system; obstetrics, gynecology, and urinary tract disorders; musculoskeletal and joint diseases; eye, ear, nose, and oropharynx; skin diseases; anesthesia; and immunological products and vaccines.[61]

Procedures for responding to foreseeable medical emergencies, including a medical operations manual as required by international safety management code, a medical staff orientation to the medical center; maintenance for all medical equipment as recommended by manufacturer; code team trained and updated regularly; mock code and contingency medical plan drills on a recurrent basis and as recommended by ships' physician; emergency preparedness plan as required by the international safety management code; and internal and external audits.[61]

The ship should have basic laboratory and x-ray capabilities; hemoglobin/hematocrit estimations, urinalysis, pregnancy tests, blood glucose (all with quality control program as recommended by the manufacturer); x-ray machines; a process whereby passengers, prior to embarkation, are requested to provide information regarding any medical needs that may require medical care on board; and a health, hygiene, and safety program for medical personnel and an annual TB screening program for all medical personnel.

The ability to diagnose and treat a passenger or crew member in an emergency situation is very much affected by the available equipment, supplies, and assistance aboard the vessel. The court takes this into account, as well as the fact that a shipboard physician is an emergency medical worker, not the person's regular doctor with whom a rapport and history is established. Maritime law provides that the analysis must take into account the fact that physicians aboard a cruise ship are working in a facility that, under the best of circumstances, cannot be as fully equipped as a shore side hospital or clinic. "A ship is not a floating hospital."[63] Likewise, a court is likely to conclude that a ship's physician is not negligent in treating an injured passenger where the testimony indicated that the doctor "discharged his duties in a fashion which would be expected of the average doctor under the circumstances, being on board a ship, with somewhat limited facilities."[64]

Passengers who are severely injured or who fall seriously ill onboard a vessel will need to be evacuated, and the ship is obligated to prepare a plan for airlifting the patient to an adequate facility, as was held by the court in *Malin v. Holland Amerca Tours*.[65] A passenger who sustained a severe cranial injury from a fall while shopping on the island of St. Maarten had to be airlifted to Puerto Rico for emergency surgery.[66] She died *en route* to the hospital, and her estate filed suit, alleging that the ship "had not prepared in advance to handle complicated medical emergencies in the event a passenger suffered a serious injury."[66]

In granting summary judgment for the shipowner, the court held that AA carrier has no duty to furnish a doctor or provide medical facilities for its passengers, but it does have an obligation to its sick and injured passengers to use "reasonable care to furnish such aid and assistance as ordinarily prudent persons would render under similar circumstances."[67] The court granted summary judgment in favor of Holland America, ruling:

> There was no question that the ship reasonably prepared for such an emergency, as it was able to procure a flight to the larger island for Mrs. Malin when the ship's doctor determined that Mrs. Malin's injury was far graver than could be accommodated on the island of St. Maarten. "Since a carrier is not charged with guaranteeing its passengers' health or with operating a floating hospital, let alone a hospital with sophisticated neurosurgical facilities and attending specialists, we hold as a matter of law that Holland America acted reasonably under the circumstances by commencing straightaway to arrange for Mrs. Malin's evacuation to San Juan after determining she could not receive adequate treatment in Philipsburg or on the MS Noordam."

The claimant must prove all of the elements under common law negligence, as provided for in the Restatement (Second) of Torts (1977). If the plaintiff cannot prove, via expert testimony, that the physician either caused or aggravated the condition, then the plaintiff will not be able to recover damages. Because the plaintiff's burden of proof is a matter of factual showing and expert witness testimony, a failure to prove a cause of action may be challenged by the physician prior to trial, pursuant to motion for summary judgment, or at trial, as a directed verdict at the close of the parties' evidence, before the question is ever put to the jury.

References

1. *Barbetta v. S/S Bermuda Star* 848 F.2d 1364, 1371 (5th Cir. 1988); *DeRoche v. Commodore Cruise Line, Ltd.*, 31 Cal. App. 4th 802, 808 (Cal. 1st App. Dist. 1994).
2. The Jones Act, 46 U.S.C. § 688 et seq., which provides in relevant part that "Any seaman who shall suffer personal injury in the course of his employment may, at his election, maintain an action for damages at law, with the right of trial by jury, and in such action all statutes of the

United States modifying or extending the common-law right or remedy in cases of personal injury to railway employees shall apply."

3. *Mascolo v. Costa Crociere S.p.A.,* 726 F. Supp. 1285, 1285–86 (S.D. Fla. 1989).
4. *Kermarec,* 358 U.S. at 629.
5. *Carlisle v. Carnival Corp.,* 864 So. 2d 1, 6–8 (Fla. 3rd DCA 2003).
6. 864 So. 2d 1, 6–8 (Fla. 3rd DCA 2003).
7. *Kermarec v. Compagnie Generale Transatlantique,* 358 U.S. 625 (1959) (Torts committed in navigable waters are within maritime jurisdiction and fall within the purview of maritime law).
8. *Barbetta v. S/S Bermuda Star,* 848 F.2d 1364, 1369 (5th Cir. 1988), citing *The Korea Maru,* 254 F. 397, 399 (9th Cir. 1918); *The Great Northern,* 251 F. 826, 830–32 (9th Cir. 1918); *Di Bonaventure v. Home Lines, Inc.,* 536 F. Supp. 100, 103–04 (E.D. Penn. 1982); *Amdur v. Zim Israel Navigation Co.,* 310 F. Supp. 1033, 1042 (S.D.N.Y. 1969); *Churchill v. United Fruit Co.,* 294 F. 400, 402 (D. Mass. 1923); *The Napolitan Prince,* 134 F. 159, 160 (E.D.N.Y. 1904).
9. *Barbetta v. S/S Bermuda Star,* 848 F.2d 1364, 1369 (5th Cir. 1988); *Doonan v. Carnival Corp.,* 404 F. Supp. 2d 1367 (S.D. Fla. 2005) (granting Carnival's motion to dismiss claims for vicarious liability [actual agency], and breach of contract claims), citing *Barbetta,* at 1369; See also, *Warren v. Ajax Navigation Corp.,* 1995 AMC 2609 (S.D. Fla. 1995); *Mascolo v. Costa Crociere, S.p.A.,* 726 F. Supp. 1285, 1286 (S.D. Fla. 1989); *The Korea Maru,* 254 F. 397 (9th Cir. 1918); *The Great Northern,* 251 F. 826 (9th Cir. 1918); *Di Bonaventure v. Home Lines, Inc.,* 536 F. Supp. 100 (E.D. Pa. 1982); *Churchill v. United Fruit Co.,* 294 F. 400 (D. Mass. 1923); *Hilliard v. Kloster Cruise, Ltd.,* 1991 AMC 314 (E.D. Va. 1990) (finding that carriers are not vicariously liable for the negligence of an otherwise qualified doctor, and that plaintiff failed to establish cruise line's negligent hiring of ship's doctor where he failed to produce evidence about cruise line's hiring practices or about cruise line's hiring of physician); *Amdur v. Zim Israel Navigation Co.,* 1969 AMC 2418, 310 F. Supp. 1033 (S.D.N.Y. 1969).
10. *Doonan,* 404 F. Supp. 2d at 1370, *quoting Barbetta,* 848 F.2d at 1369–70.
11. *Nietes v. Am. President Lines, Ltd.,* 188 F. Supp. 219 (N.D. Cal. 1959); See also, *Fairley v. Royal Caribbean Cruises Ltd.,* 1993 AMC 1633, 1640 (S.D. Fla. 1993); *Carlisle v. Carnival Corp.,* 864 So. 2d 1 (Fla. 3d DCA 2003); *Huntley v. Carnival Corp.,* 307 F. Supp. 2d 1372 (S.D. Fla. 2004); *Mack v. Royal Caribbean Cruises Ltd.,* 838 N.E.2d 80 (Ill. App. Ct. 2005).
12. *Nietes v. Am. President Lines, Inc.* 188 F. Supp. 219, 220 (N.D. Cal. 1959) (holding that where a ship's physician is a salaried member of the crew, answerable to the ship's captain and under the direction and supervision of the cruise line, then a shipowner may be liable under the principle of respondeat superior); *Huntley v. Carnival Corp.,* 307 F. Supp. 2d 1372, 1374 (S.D. Fla. 2004) (noting that the issue of respondeat superior has not been directly addressed by the Eleventh Circuit, at 1374 n.5); *Fairley v. Royal Cruise Line, Ltd.,* 1993 AMC 1633, 1635–37 (S.D. Fla. 1993 (criticizing *Barbetta* and discussing with approval the rational of *Nietes*); and *Carlisle v. Carnival Corp.,* 864 So. 2d 1, 7 (Fla. 3d DCA 2003), review granted 904 So. 2d 430 (Fla. 2005).
13. *Doonan,* at 1371–72, citing *Fairley v. Royal Cruise Line Ltd.,* 1993 AMC 1633, 1639–40 (S.D. Fla. 1993).
14. *Gautreaux v. Scurlock Marine, Inc.,* 107 F.3d 331, 338 (5th Cir. 1997).
15. *Rindfleisch v. Carnival Cruise Lines, Inc.,* 498 So. 2d 488, 490 (Fla. 3d DCA 1986), *cert denied,* 508 So. 2d 15 (Fla. 1987).
16. *Carlisle v. Carnival Corp.,* 864 So. 2d 1, 3 (Fla. 3d DCA 2003), *citing Rand v. Hatch,* 762 So. 2d 1001 (Fla. 3d DCA 2000).
17. *East River S.S. Co. v. TransAmerica De Leval, Inc.,* 476 U.S. 85 (1986).
18. *Carlisle Packing Co. v. Sandanger,* 259 U.S. 255 (1922).
19. *Rand v. Hatch,* 762 So. 2d 1001, 1002 (Fla. 3d DCA 2000).
20. *Kermarec v. Compagnie Generale Transatlantique,* 358 U.S. 625, 632 (1959); See also, *Rainey v. Paquet Cruises, Inc.,* 709 F. 2d 169, 171 (2d Cir. 1983); *Monteleone v. Bahamas Cruise Line, Inc.,* 838 F.2d 63, 64–65 (2d Cir. 1988); *Gibboney v. Wright,* 517 F. 2d 1054, 1059 (5th Cir. 1975);

Chan v. Society Expeditions, Inc., 123 F.3d 1287, 1289 (9th Cir. 1997); *Keefe v. Bahama Cruise Line, Inc.*, 867 F.2d 1318, 1320–21 (11th Cir. 1989); *Rindfleisch v. Carnival Cruise Lines, Inc.*, 498 So. 2d 488, 491 (Fla. 3d DCA 1986).

21. Codified as law under United States Code 46 U.S.C. § 688 et seq.
22. *De Zon v. Am, President Lines*, 318 U.S. 660 (1943).
23. Restatement (Second) of Torts, § 299 A (1977).
24. 1976 AMC 453 (S.D.N.Y. 1975).
25. *DeRoche v. Commodore Cruise Line, Ltd.*, 31 Cal. App. 4th 802, 808 (Cal. 1st App. Dist. 1994); *Boston & Yarmouth S. S. Co. v. Francis*, 249 Fed. 450, 452 (1st Cir. 1918).
26. Restatement (Second) of Torts (1977); Modern Tort Law, Medical Malpractice (West Group, 2002), and cases cited therein.
27. Modern Tort Law, Medical Malpractice (West Group, 2002), and cases cited therein.
28. Restatement (Second) of Torts (1977).
29. Restatement (Second) of Torts, Comment a.
30. *DeZon v. Am. President Lines*, 318 U.S. 660, 670 (1943).
31. *Graham v. Alcoa S.S. Co.*, 201 F.2d 423, 426 (3d Cir. 1953).
32. *Zackey v. Am. Exp. Lines, Inc.*, 152 F. Supp. 772, 774 (S.D.N.Y. 1957).
33. 451 F. 2d 670, 680 (2d Cir. 1971).
34. *Osorio v. Waterman S.S. Corp.* 557 So. 2d 999, 1009 (La. Ct. App. 1990).
35. *Amdur v. Zim Israel Navigation Co.*, 310 F. Supp. 1033, 1038 (S.D.N.Y. 1969).
36. *DeZon v. American President Lines*, 318 U.S. at 670.
37. *Joyce v. Atl. Richfield Co.*, 651 F.2d 676, 681 (10th Cir. 1981).
38. *Olsen v. Am. S.S. Co.*, 176 F.3d 891, 894–895 (6th Cir. 1999). The other two claims are for (1) maintenance and cure, which is payment by the ship owner for the seaman's room, board, medicine, treatment, and other expenses relating to his injury while he recuperates; and (2) for the ship's "unseaworthiness," which is a strict liability claim alleging that the defendant ship-owner failed to provide a vessel reasonably fit for its intended use.
39. *Central Gulf S.S. Corp. v. Sambula*, 405 F.2d 291, 300 (5th Cir. OLD 1968).
40. *Cortes v. Baltimore Insular Lines*, 287 U.S. 367 (1932); *DeZon v. Am. President Lines*, 318 U.S. 660, 669 (1943).
41. *DeZon*, 318 U.S. at 665.
42. *DeZon*, 318 U.S. at 671–72.
43. *Centeno v. Gulf Fleet Crews, Inc.*, 798 F.2d 138, 139–40 (5th Cir. 1986).
44. *Centeno*, 798 F.2d at 139.
45. *Centeno*, at 139.
46. *Centeno*, at 139–40.
47. *Centeno*, at 140.
48. *Centeno*, at 140, citing Central Gulf Steamship Corp. v. Sambula, 405 F.2d 291, 302 (5th Cir. 1968); et al., 688 F.2d 256, 262 n.9 (5th Cir. 1982).
49. *De Zon*, 318 U.S. at 664–69.
50. *Wagner v. Apex Ship Management Corp.*, 2000 AMC 2903, 2905 (Cal. 1st App. Dist. 2000).
51. 46 U.S.C. § 183b(a) (making it unlawful for owners of passenger-transport ships to provide a statute of limitations of less than one year for institution of suits for loss of life or bodily injury). See also, *Kientzler v. Sun Line Greece Special Shipping Co.*, 779 F. Supp. 342, 345 (S.D.N.Y. 1991); *Dempsey v. Norwegian Cruise Line*, 972 F.2d 998, 999 (9th Cir. 1992); *Angel v. Royal Caribbean Cruises*, 2002 U.S. Dist. LEXIS 22440, 6–7 (S.D. Fla. 2002).
52. *Carnival Corp. v. Middleton*, 2006 Fla. App. LEXIS 16421 (Fla. 3rd DCA 2006).
53. *Rana v. Flynn*, 823 So. 2d 302 (Fla. 3d DCA 2002).
54. *Elmlund v. Mottershead*, 750 So. 2d 736 (Fla. 3d DCA 2000).
55. *Rossa v. Sills*, 493 So. 2d 1137 (Fla. 4th DCA 1986).
56. *Benson v. Norwegian Cruise Line, Ltd.*, 834 So. 2d 915, 916–17 (Fla. 3d DCA 2003).
57. http://www.noaa.gov/

58. 370 F. Supp. 342, 346–47 (S.D.N.Y. 1974).
59. 435 F. Supp. 308, 310 (S.D.N.Y. 1977).
60. 536 F. Supp. 100 (E.D. Pa. 1982).
61. http://www.acep.org/webportal/membercenter/sections/cruise/default.htm (revised 2000).
62. http://www.iccl.org/policies/medical2.cfm
63. *Barbetta v. S.S. Bermuda Sun*, 848 F.2d 1364, 1369–70 (5th Cir. 1988).
64. *Amdur*, 310 F. Supp. 1033, 1045 (S.D.N.Y. 1969).
65. *Malin v. Holland Am. Tours*, 1990 AMC 1968, 1973 (Cal. 1st App. Dist. 1990).
66. *Malin*, 1990 AMC at 1973.
67. Ibid., quoting *Barbetta v. S/S Bermuda Star*, 1988 AMC 2650, 2661 (5th Cir. 1988), 848 quoting 1 M. Norris, The Law of Maritime Personal Injuries (3d ed. 1975) § 39.

Defensive Moves and Strategies to Avoid Medical Malpractice Suits in Primary Medical Care and Specialty Practice

5

Defensive Strategies Avert the Most Common Causes of Medical Malpractice Lawsuits in Primary Care and Specialty Practice.

5.1 Introduction

In reviewing statistics from various states in the United States on who gets hit the most with medical malpractice suits, the findings are that it is usually the specialists in Obstetrics-Gynecology (Ob-Gyn), orthopedic surgery, and also physicians who specialize in cosmetic procedures.

Ironically, most of these medical malpractice lawsuits can be prevented if only the physician pays particular attention to these known situations, which most often leads to litigation.

This chapter certainly does not list all the different types of lawsuits aimed at physicians, but the chapter lists the more common suits that take place in various hard-hit primary-care and medical/surgical specialties. These include Ob-Gyn, surgery, imaging (x-ray and mammograms), orthopedic surgery, pathology/laboratory, and also the most common suit filed in gastrointestinal endoscopy, based on the ERCP procedure in which a prominent physician has written about his legal experiences with dozens of cases in which he has testified.

Defensive strategies and preventive moves will be presented in these high-risk areas.

I understand, however, from the inquest that there were some objects which you failed to overlook

—Sherlock Holmes
The Adventure of Black Peter

5.2 The Most Common Causes of Medical Malpractice Lawsuits

5.2.1 Preventable Ob-Gyn Errors in Primary-Care Medicine

For the past 15 years, according to national medical malpractice insurance statistics, the most paid claims were those of Ob-Gyn treatment especially performed by the primary-care/general internist/general practitioner/family physician. While malpractice lawsuits against nurse practitioners are rare, nurse practitioners have also been sued for pregnancy-related mishaps. Lawsuits against primary-care clinicians for pregnancy-related mishaps fall into five categories:

1. Failure to diagnose pregnancy before initiating a therapy with potential for fetal damage
2. Failure to get a standard test to diagnose an abnormality in the fetus
3. Failure to inform a pregnant patient of the likelihood of fetal abnormality
4. Failure to treat a maternal illness appropriately
5. Failure to diagnose a maternal illness affecting the fetus

Examples

5.2.1.1 *Insertion of IUD into Pregnant Patient*
Preventive moves:

a. A pregnancy test, careful evaluation of regularity of menses for the past 3 months, and history-taking on the patient's sexual activity and use of contraception is always indicated prior to IUD insertion or any therapy that could cause fetal injury. Some patients have menstruation-like vaginal bleeding in the early stages of pregnancy.
b. A missed period in a patient with a history of irregular menses is almost as likely to be due to pregnancy as a missed period in a patient with regular menses.

5.2.1.2 *Failure to Test for Fetal Abnormality*
A 36-year-old woman claimed that if she had been properly advised by her family doctor she would have had an amniocentesis, it would have revealed that her fetus had Down's syndrome, and she would have chosen an abortion. After a trial and appeal, the patient won the case against the physician.
　　Preventive moves:

a. If a clinician renders care to a patient who is pregnant, the clinician may be held liable for failure to diagnose fetal abnormalities.
b. Any clinician evaluating and managing pregnant patients must remain up to date on the standard of care for screening for fetal abnormalities.
c. If that is not possible, rather than provide primary care, refer pregnant patients to obstetricians, midwives, or Ob-Gyn nurse practitioners.

5.2.1.3 *Failure to Inform Mother of Potential for Birth Defects*
A physician diagnosed a pregnant patient with rubella, but did not inform the woman of the probability that the baby would be born with birth defects. The baby was born with multiple systemic abnormalities and cerebral palsy. The patient sought damages for past and future medical expenses and custodial care, and was successful in getting a judgment against the clinician.
　　Preventive moves:

- The availability of abortion makes it a virtual certainty that a clinician will be sued for wrongful birth and negligence if the clinician knew or should have known that fetal defects were probable, but failed to discuss the patient's options as soon as the probability of defects was known (or should have been known).

5.2.1.4 Failure to Appropriately Treat Maternal Illness

A 27-year-old woman who had had one previous seizure was 24-weeks pregnant when she had a second seizure. The clinician ordered a loading dose of phenytoin and admitted the patient to the hospital, but the patient did not receive the first phenytoin dose until nearly an hour after admission. The patient and fetus were found dead 3 h after the dosage, the result of a seizure that went unnoticed.

The patient's survivors alleged that the phenytoin dosage was too little, too late, and that the hospital had not monitored the patient closely. The defendant clinician argued that a higher dosage would not have prevented the seizure.

Preventive moves:

a. Right medication, right dose, right route, right time, right and timely consultant, and proper monitoring.
b. Damages, as well as emotional trauma, will be extraordinary when the injured patient was pregnant.

5.2.1.5 Using the Wrong Antibiotic in Pregnancy

Because fluoroquinolones have caused arthropathy in young animals, these drugs should be avoided in children and in women who are pregnant or nursing according to Owens and Ambrose.[1]

The fluoroquinolones generally have mild gastrointestinal side effects (nausea, vomiting, or anorexia), central nervous system side effects (light-headedness, dizziness, somnolence, or insomnia), or rash occurring in fewer than 10% of treated patients.[1] But Gemifloxacin used for more than 7 days may be associated with an increased risk of rash, particularly in women younger than 40 years. Sparfloxacin contains a halide at position 8 and is associated with significantly more photosensitivity reactions than the other fluoroquinolones. Sparfloxacin and grepafloxacin were withdrawn from the market because they were shown to prolong the Q-T interval. But this adverse event has also been reported with levofloxacin and moxifloxacin. Risk factors include underlying cardiac disease, advanced age, hypokalemia, hypomagnesemia, and the concomitant use of other agents that may prolong the Q-T interval, such as antiarrhythmics, macrolides, and certain antihistamines. Hyperglycemia or hypoglycemia has also been described in less than 2% of patients treated with fluoroquinolones. Given this finding, dose adjustment should be considered in elderly patients with type 2 diabetes. Tendinitis and tendon rupture may also occur very rarely. Less common side effects include allergic interstitial nephritis, pseudomembranous colitis, and neutropenia.

Preventive moves:

a. Avoid all fluoroquinolones in pregnancy.
b. Also, exposure to selective serotonin reuptake inhibitors (SSRIs) late in pregnancy has been associated with short-term complications in newborns including jitteriness, mild respiratory distress, excessively rapid respiration, and admission to the neonatal intensive care unit (ICU). Use of Paroxetine (Paxil) should be avoided, when possible, by pregnant women or women planning to become pregnant due to the potential risk

of fetal heart defects, newborn persistent pulmonary hypertension, and other negative effects.[2]

5.2.1.6   *Failure to Diagnose Gestational Diabetes*

After a woman gave birth to a baby with macrosomia (a condition related to maternal hyperglycemia/diabetes), the woman filed suit against a nurse practitioner working at a city health clinic, who, she said, had told her she did not have high blood sugar because her urinalysis was normal. An obstetrician was associated with the clinic, but the nurse practitioner did not refer the patient to him. The case settled in favor of the patient.

Preventive moves:

a. Know the standard of care—in this case, a glucose challenge test for all pregnancies at 24–28 weeks' gestation.
b. Refer pregnant patients to Ob/Gyn physicians, midwives, or Ob/Gyn nurse practitioners.
c. Supervising physicians must make regular "records rounds" with nurse practioners and physician assistants because the "buck stops with the supervising physician."

A major problem is the poor quality of vaginal/cervical specimens. In diagnosing cervical cancer, biopsies must be taken from a certain part of the cervix known as the "transformation zone." But physicians and nurses fail to collect cells from the zone often enough to miss lesions 30–40% of the time. Even though it is usually apparent if the proper cells are not present, the lab usually will make a diagnosis on any sample it gets.

Preventive moves:

a. All labs as part of the official report must report the presence or absence of tissue from the "transformation zone."
b. The gynecologist or other referring physician must have an office system in place that will adequately follow up on these reports and redo the test if appropriate. If not redone, the reasons for not repeating the test will be stated in the medical record of the patient.

5.2.2   Preventable Errors in Surgery

Clinical errors are reported almost as frequently and are associated with almost five times as many deaths, as medication errors according to initial data released by DoctorQuality Inc. Adverse clinical events are also nearly three times more likely to require additional treatment than drug-related errors.

According to the *Alert* newsletter from the Joint Commission on Accreditation of Healthcare Organizations (JCAHO), which followed a similar 1998 message reporting on 15 "wrong-site" cases, 136 additional cases were reported in the subsequent 4 years. Most cases involve orthopedic or foot-related surgery—operating on the left knee instead of the right knee, for example. Of 126 cases analyzed by the JCAHO, 76% involved operating on the wrong body part, 13% involved surgery on the wrong patient, and 11% involved the wrong surgical procedure.

Preventive moves:

Since most cases involve a breakdown in communication between the surgical team and the patient and his family, surgical teams should take a "time-out" in the operating room to make sure they have the correct patient, procedure, and surgery site. See hospital procedure protocol.

5.2.2.1 *Errors in Surgery Leading to Liability Payments*

In a major study, all admissions (age >13) of three surgical patient care centers at a single academic medical center between January 1, 1995 and December 6, 1999 were reviewed for significant surgical adverse events. The study group consisted of 130 patients with surgical adverse events resulting in total liabilities of $8.2 million. The incidence of adverse events per 1000 admissions across three patient care centers was similar, but indemnity payments per 1000 admissions varied (cardiothoracic = U.S.$30, women's health = U.S.$90, trauma = U.S.$520). Patient demographics were not predictive of high-risk subgroups for adverse events or litigation.[3]

In terms of medical outcome, 51 patients had permanent disability or death, accounting for 98% of the indemnity payments. In terms of legal outcome, 103 patients received no indemnity payments, 15 patients received indemnity payments, 4 suits remain open, and in 8 cases charges were written off ($0.121 million).

Preventive moves:
Stricter monitoring and "systematizing" of the five categories of major causes which accounted for 75% of the published surgical errors.

1. Patient management, $n = 104$
2. Communication, $n = 89$
3. Administration, $n = 33$
4. Documentation, $n = 32$
5. Behavior, $n = 23$

The current medical review process (in hospital medical review conferences) would have identified only 104 of 390 systems failures (37%).

This study concluded that

a. there were no rational links between the tort system and the reduction of adverse events,
b. sixty-three percent of contributing causes to adverse events were undetected by current medical review processes,
c. adverse events occur at the interface between different systems or disciplines and result from multiple failures, and
d. indemnity costs per hospital day vary dramatically by patient care center (range U.S.$3.60–97.60 a day).

5.2.2.2 *Delayed Surgery is Associated with High Mortality from Acute Abdomen in ICUs*

In medical ICUs, an excess mortality due to acute abdomen is primarily due to delays in surgical evaluation and intervention, according to researchers from the Mayo Clinic in Rochester, MN. Peters et al.[4] retrospectively studied 77 ICU patients who were diagnosed with acute abdomen catastrophe. The most common diagnoses were

i. ischemic bowel,
ii. perforated ulcer,
iii. bowel obstruction, and
iv. cholecystitis.

Mortality rates were higher among these patients than predicted by their APACHE III (acute physiology and chronic health evaluation) scores when they were admitted to the ICU (63% versus 31%), the researchers report. Of the 26 patients who did not have surgery, none survived and of the 51 patients who did undergo surgery, 28 survived.

The factors that were associated with the increased mortality rate among these patients were

   a. delays in surgical evaluation ($p < .01$),
   b. delays in surgery ($p < .03$),
   c. APACHE III scores ($p < .01$),
   d. renal insufficiency ($p < .01$), and
   e. ischemic bowel ($p < .01$).

Preventive moves:
Since delayed surgery, according to this report was more common among patients with altered mental state, few peritoneal signs, previous opioid analgesia, antibiotics, and mechanical ventilation, there should be more focused attention to patients with these characteristics. There should be less of a threshold to do a CT scan and earlier surgical consultation in these patients.

5.2.3   Preventable Anesthesia Morbidity and Mortality

Proper airway management is the worst of the complications—especially if not immediately recognized. It is well known that if a patient is deprived of oxygen for 4–6 min, they will experience brain death. Longer periods will lead to cardiac arrest:

   1. Misplacement of the endotracheal tube. However, if a certain checking device is not present (such as in an office where surgery is performed) or not working, then an error may be made in assessing whether the tube is correctly placed.
   2. Aspiration of gastric contents in a patient with a full stomach is a potential cause of mortality. All pregnant patients, very obese patients, trauma victims, and patients with bowel obstruction have a full stomach. Precautions, through use of drugs to hasten onset of anesthesia and paralysis, along with pressure over the neck to prevent gastric contents from coming up the esophagus, will minimize the risk of aspiration.
   3. Forgetting to reverse certain anesthetics, i.e., their actions must be terminated with the use of antagonists. Patients who are deeply anesthetized or paralyzed will not breathe and may become hypoxic.
   4. Conscious sedation. This sedation should produce only mental relaxation but not loss of consciousness. However, the margin between one effect and the other blurs and the same dose of drug in one patient may produce loss of consciousness in another patient.
   5. Tension pneumothorax from excessive pressure in helping respiration. Unless the pneumothorax is recognized and treated by placing the tube through the chest wall into the area just outside the lung itself, the patient may go on to die.
   6. Allergic reactions:
      a. The drugs that produce allergy with the response of marked drop in blood pressure and wheezing leading to inability to ventilate, are generally drugs that are

used incident to anesthesia, such as muscle relaxants (paralyzing agents), intravenous anesthetic drugs, and antibiotics.

b. Latex may also cause life-threatening allergic reactions. Latex-containing gloves may lead to an allergic response when the surgeon puts his/her hands into the patient's body. These complications must be immediately recognized and dealt with.

7. Dantrolene must be stocked at all times to recognize an infrequent muscle condition called MH, which may flare under anesthesia. However, if the office or facility does not stock dantrolene and is familiar with the signs of the disorder, there could be medical and litigation problems.

8. Not recognizing and quickly treating elevated potassium, which can occur after succinylcholine administration.

9. A liposuction technique has been developed using large amounts of dilute local anesthetics injected under the skin. If the drug is absorbed rapidly or too high a concentration of drug is used, then toxicity may result, which must be immediately recognized and treated.

10. Mechanical problems with anesthetic machines. A check-out list must be followed by every practitioner prior to using the machine. This check-out will detect almost every problem with the machine.

5.2.4 Preventable Imaging Errors

Preventive moves:
In the private sector, the imaging community must take steps to better document the quality of the services it provides. The clinical effectiveness of new forms of imaging technology should be investigated and proved before they are used widely.

It is good policy that General Electric, the largest manufacturer of imaging equipment in the United States, will sponsor clinical trials that will reach beyond earlier industry-sponsored trials. These trials should focus more on the quality of the actual images to test the clinical effectiveness of new forms of technology such as new CT techniques to image the heart and breast.

5.2.4.1 Prevention of Mammography Errors

Recently trained radiologists were more likely to have false positives—or say there were suspicious lesions when none were present—than those with 15 years or more of experience. The radiologist's experience appeared to influence the false-positive rate. Radiologists in their 40s who completed medical school within the last 5–15 years were nearly four times more likely to have a higher false-positive rate than those in their 60s or 70s with more than 20 years since medical school graduation.

Women who were younger, premenopausal, or taking hormone replacement therapy were more likely to get a false-positive result, as were women with a family history of breast cancer or a previous biopsy. Agreement between different radiologists interpreting the same set of mammograms is known to be low. However, few studies have examined just how accurate the readings are for women in the general population who are being screened for breast cancer.

In this new study by Elmore et al.,[5] a comparison was made of the reading accuracy of 24 radiologists who interpreted 8734 screening mammograms from 2169 women.

The researchers' findings were that the interpretation of mammograms varied by radiologist. For example, one radiologist noted no suspicious masses on any of the films read, while another reported that 7.9% of the films contained a mass. Similarly, the proportion of calcifications and fibrocystic changes—other possibly suspicious or benign changes—detected on the films ranged from 0 to 21.3% and 1.6 to 27.8%, respectively. The false-positive rate for the radiologists ranged from 2.6 to 15.9%, the researchers note. However, after adjusting for patient, radiologist, and testing characteristics, this range narrowed to 3.5–7.9%.

Preventive moves:

a. Double reading of mammograms has been shown to cut down on false positives without boosting the rate of missed breast cancer cases. Although double reading has been implemented in 22 countries, but not yet in the United States, Andersen's group points out that the U.S. "public policy needs both a focus on training and an immediate reexamination of double reading as national policy." It would therefore be prudent to implement double reading of all mammograms especially if the radiologist falls into the age group reported above.

b. In addition, Sabel et al. found that a second opinion from a team of specialists after an initial diagnosis of breast cancer resulted in a significant change in the recommended surgical treatment in more than half of cases. Additionally, for 32% of the women, the change in recommendation was based *not on disagreement* about the radiology or pathology findings, but rather on interpretation of the standards for care endorsed by the National Comprehensive Cancer Network. Sabel also emphasizes that these results reinforce the importance of comprehensive breast cancer decision making and care by a multidisciplinary board of specialists in the treatment decisions for breast cancer.

5.2.5 Preventable Errors in Neurology

An in-depth study of neurologic malpractice claims indicate preventable patient harm in 24 of 42 cases. Principal findings included the common occurrence of outpatient events, lapses in communication with patients and other providers, and the need for follow-through by the consultant neurologist.[6]

Preventive moves:

a. Have a system in place to prevent lapses in communication with patients and other providers.

b. Have a system in place for regular follow-through by the consultant neurologist—either through his assistants or by telephone ticklers on his desk.

5.2.6 Orthopedic Medical Malpractice: An Attorney's Perspective

Orthopedic surgeons also have certain procedures and issues related to the physician–patient relationship that could potentially lead to a malpractice lawsuit. In this study, the author performed a randomized nationwide survey of medical malpractice attorneys to evoke their opinion on these issues.[7]

Preventive moves: continuing education and physician awareness in formal courses should be initiated in the lumbar spine, which was the most common anatomic area involved in orthopedic medical malpractice cases.

The author also found that a physician appearing rushed and uninterested is most likely to be the subject of a lawsuit where a poor physician–patient relationship was a contributing factor. Therefore, the preventive move is most evident. Cultivate a good physician–patient relationship even if you must take on few procedures to do this.

5.2.7 Many Errors in Gastroenterology Can Be Prevented by Prudent Patient Selection, Sedation, and Proper Indications for Endoscopic Procedures

In addition, the signed informed consent should include up-to-date information for the patient.

First, with the advent of Medicare approval of screening colonoscopy for colorectal cancer (CRC) and the Katie Couric public colonoscopy seen in millions of homes, the rates of colonoscopic procedures have increased. The usual informed consent process and forms contain much of the warnings common to all such invasive procedures such as perforation, hemorrhage, and even death.

But I have noted in some cases that have come to litigation the absence of some important issues that the patient should also acknowledge by his signature to the informed consent statement.

5.2.7.1 The Missed Cancer Rate with Screening Colonoscopies

One such omission in the informed consent form is the "missed rate" of cancers with colonoscopies—the gold standard of CRC diagnosis from which all other CRC screening and diagnostic procedures are compared. Patients should be informed that there is indeed a "miss rate" of CRC of 1–4% even with this gold standard procedure (somewhat higher with barium enema screening). The reasons for this range from blind areas in the colon, misjudgment that the scope has reached the cecum, poor preparation, and other interpretive errors. It is for that reason that the colonoscopy report should include

- a photographed cecum in each case for adequate documentation,
- appropriate description of preparation,
- examination time (articles have also called attention to higher error rates in colonoscopies of less than 10 min),
- information to the patient that follow-up examination with a repeat colonoscopy or barium enema necessary when the entire colon up to and including the cecum is not well visualized, and
- a complete and detailed discussion in the informed consent statement signed by the patient prior to sedation and prior the procedure.[8-10]

- ask your radiologist who is doing the initial or follow-up Ba enema for a "double reading" to decrease the "missed rate": e.g., 15% of the Ba enema errors were overlooked by the reader and was visible in retrospect.[15]

5.2.7.2 Poor Colonoscopic Technique Is Also Blamed for Colon Cancer Missed Rates in Colonoscopy

As noted, some patients who undergo colonoscopy that appeared to have cleared the colorectum of neoplasia return within a short interval (1–3 years) with CRC. Although several *a priori* mechanisms mentioned could account for this occurrence, wide variation in detection rates of adenomas and cancer at colonoscopy suggests that suboptimal colono-scopic technique is a significant contributor.

Optimal technique with white-light colonoscopy involves these factors, which should be mentioned in the endoscopy report by the endoscopist—especially the time from inser-tion to completion should be carefully noted:

- Taking adequate time for inspection during withdrawal (of at least 6–10 min at a minimum even in normal colons)
- Interrogating the proximal sides of folds, flexures, and valves, clearing fluid and debris
- Distending adequately

Some adjunctive techniques are directed toward exposing more colonic mucosa dur-ing colonoscopy. Wide-angle colonoscopy appears to improve efficiency but does not elim-inate miss rates. Colonoscopy in retroflexion was unsuccessful in reducing miss rates in one study, whereas cap-fitted colonoscopy was successful in reducing miss rates in one small study. Techniques to improve detection of flat lesions include pancolonic chromoen-doscopy (CE). In two randomized controlled trials, CE improved adenoma detection, but CE does not appear to provide substantially greater yields than those obtained by the more sensitive white-light colonoscopists. Adenoma detection rates are an important measure of the quality of colonoscopy and should be reported to endoscopists in quality-improvement programs in colonoscopy.[11]

5.2.7.3 ERCP

Another area of common GI medical malpractice suits are with the ERCP procedure. An important medicolegal study by Peter B. Cotton reports his analysis of his personal series (of his testimony) of 59 cases in which ERCP malpractice was alleged. Half of the cases involved postprocedure pancreatitis, 16 suffered perforation after sphincterotomy (8 of which involved precutting), and 10 had severe biliary infection. In addition, there were two esophageal perforations. Fifteen of the patients died.

The most common allegation (54% of cases) was that the ERCP, or the therapeutic pro-cedure, was not indicated. Disputes about the extent of the education and consent process were common.

Negligent performance was alleged in 19 cases. Inadequate postprocedure care was alleged in 5 cases, including 3 with a delayed diagnosis of perforation.

The final outcome was available in 40 cases. Sixteen were withdrawn and 14 were set-tled. Of the 10 that came to trial, half were defense verdicts.[12–14]

Preventive moves:

1. Make certain that your invasive procedure informed consent statements signed by the patient are up to date, especially those for colonoscopy and ERCP.
2. In addition, ERCP should be done only
   a. For good indications.
   b. By trained endoscopists with standard techniques.
   c. With good documented patient-informed consent and with good communication before and after the procedure.

    d. In major tertiary-care centers.

    e. With the preventive moves that are echoed by Testoni[16] in his article "Preventing post-ERCP pancreatitis: where are we?" in which he points out that post-ERCP pancreatitis can be prevented by proper patient selection.

    f. With each patient having an informed consent form in the chart.

    g. When either diagnostic or therapeutic ERCP is strongly indicated, these high-risk patients should be informed about their own specific risk of postprocedure pancreatitis.

    h. Diagnostic ERCP should be avoided in routine practice.

    i. After magnetic resonance cholangio-pancreatography (MRCP) which should be substituted *as the first diagnostic step.*

5.2.8 Problems with Conscious Sedation Performed by Interventional Specialists—Cardiologists, Radiologists, Gastroenterologists, and Others

Conscious sedation involves intravenous sedative drugs that lower the level of consciousness, but do not put a patient completely under as with general anesthesia; patients can usually breathe on their own and recover more quickly. The most commonly recommended sedation drugs include fentanyl and versed. A newer drug, propofol, is gaining popularity for colonoscopies and other procedures because it works quickly, deeply sedates patients, and lets them recover faster. But while there are drugs that can be given to reverse the effects of versed and fentanyl, there is no antidote to reverse propofol.

- These more powerful sedatives like propofol are more often being administered by medical professionals including gastroenterologists who are not adequately trained in anesthesia and safety practices, increasing the risks of respiratory complications, cardiac arrest, brain damage, and even death.
- The University Health System Consortium, which includes 95 of the nation's largest academic medical centers, reported at a recent meeting that there may be potentially 1690 incidents a year nationwide related to sedation—ranging from an overdose of drugs to a procedure that is started before a patient is adequately sedated.
- In a survey of its members 3 years ago, the consortium found that 42% of hospitals do not require providers to have life-support training, even if a cardiac arrest team may not be available for more than 5 min.
- Only half of the providers allowed to administer moderate sedation were trained in recognizing high-risk airways, or even basic airway management.

Preventive moves:

The nonprofit Joint Commission on Accreditation of Healthcare Organizations has required for the past few years that hospitals have

    a. clear policies for administering moderate and deep sedation;

    b. staffers with appropriate credentials to manage whatever level of sedation occurs. Still, in a survey 2 years ago, JCHAO found that 18% of hospitals were not adhering to those standards. Sedative drugs, however, can be very tricky, even with the care of an anesthesiologist." The journal *Anesthesiology* reported that more than 40% of malpractice claims associated with sedative use (even) monitored by an anesthesiologist

involved death or brain damage. That rate is similar to general anesthesia claims—
and nearly half could have been prevented by better monitoring;

c. medical facilities being inspected by the JCAHO, which must improve its inspection
   systems; and

d. standardized monitoring by physicians, which should be the rule in all endoscopy
   suites.

5.2.9   Preventable Lab Errors

5.2.9.1   Dangerous Lab Errors*

For patients and their physicians, some of the most devastating medical mistakes can start
in the lab, where studies show that 3–5% of the billions of specimens taken each year are
defective, be it a biopsy that does not extract the tumor cells, blood that is not drawn correctly, or a mix-up with another patient's sample.

- The error rate is significantly higher and more dangerous in common tests for many
  cancers, where a false positive may lead to an unnecessary hysterectomy or a false
  negative can miss a deadly skin cancer.
- Malpractice claims for pathology errors are the second-most costly to hospitals after
  neurology payouts.
- In a study of 335 pathology-related published malpractice claims (also see appendix),
  63% of these claims involved the false-negative diagnosis of cancer and 22% involved
  the false-positive diagnosis of cancer.
- Very often the private physician who had nothing to do with these lab errors is also
  named in the malpractice suit.
- For example, clinicians refer to pathologists 300,000 fine needle aspirations annually
  in which a tiny needle is inserted into a growth to extract cells to rule out cancer. But
  25% of the time the tests miss tumor cells.
- In one hospital main lab, blood samples are often unacceptable because phleboto-
  mists (technicians who draw blood), nurses, and other staffers *incorrectly labeled
  blood tubes.*
- At another medical center, out of more than 4.29 million blood specimens taken in
  the 26-month period, there were about 16,000 errors. Most did not cause harm, but
  about 12% were categorized as "critical," such as a requisition form with a specimen
  labeled with another patient's name or an unlabeled specimen.
- More infrequent but more dangerous to patients: "wrong blood in tube" mistakes,
  with one patient's name on another patient's blood. After automating some parts of
  its specimen processing and using an electronic error-reporting system, there was a
  reduction in errors, especially mislabeled specimens.

Preventive moves:

a. Double reading of pathology reports to reduce errors should be mandatory in all pathology labs because a second pathologist usually catches the mistake the first made.

* A link to all the information in Section 5.2.10.1 can be found at www.nap.edu/catalog/11623.html

b. A patient's current medication list should be verified at each medical encounter and each office visit.

c. Also, at times of transition in care setting like hospital admission or transfer to another short- or long-term medical facility (LTMF).*

5.3 Important Points to Remember

- The *severity* of the patient's disability, not the occurrence of an adverse event or an adverse event due to negligence, appears to be predictive of payment to the plaintiff.
- The initiation of malpractice suits correlates poorly with the actual occurrence of adverse events (injuries resulting from medical treatment) and negligence.
- To assess the ability of malpractice litigation to make accurate determinations, 51 malpractice suits were reviewed to identify factors that predict payment to plaintiffs.
- Among these cases, 10 of 24 that they originally identified as involving no adverse event were settled for the plaintiffs (mean payment, $28,760), as were 6 of 13 cases classified as involving adverse events but no negligence (mean payment, $98,192) and 5 of 9 cases in which adverse events due to negligence were found in their assessment (mean payment, $66,944).
- Seven of eight claims involving permanent disability were settled for the plaintiffs (mean payment, $201,250).
- In a multivariate analysis, disability (permanent versus temporary or none) was the only significant predictor of payment ($p = .03$).
- There was no association between the occurrence of an adverse event due to negligence ($p = .32$) or an adverse event of any type ($p = .79$) and payment.
- Thus, the severity of the patient's disability, not the occurrence of an adverse event or an adverse event due to negligence, was predictive of payment to the plaintiff.[17]

Preventive moves:

a. Since the severity of the patient's disability was predictive of payment to the plaintiff, quickly identify and then pay particular attention to and give added supervision and monitoring of medical care to this particular patient group.

b. In addition, in this regard of missing a disease that will markedly increase a patient's disability *screening all adults for HIV is cost effective.* A mathematical decision model study found that screening all adults for HIV with a same-day rapid test was cost effective when the prevalence of HIV in the community was as low as 0.2%.

c. A routine, *voluntary* rapid HIV testing is recommended for all adults, except in settings where evidence shows that the prevalence of undiagnosed HIV infection is below 0.2%. This study entirely supports the shift from targeted screening based on patient risk factors to routine screening based on prevalence and incidence thresholds. The findings support recent CDC guidelines calling for routine HIV screening of

---

* A link to this information can be found at www.nap.edu/catalog/11623.html

all adults and adolescents. Reminiscent of successful screening programs for syphilis and tuberculosis—the cost-effectiveness question will change from whether we should screen for HIV to when we should stop.[18]

For procedures in office, ambulatory care, and also in hospital

- use a routine form similar to this one so that one does not have to reinvent the wheel for each intervention, and
- note that this form has a "time-out" to answer these.

Three questions:

- Is this the correct patient?
- Is this the correct procedure?
- Is this the correct site?

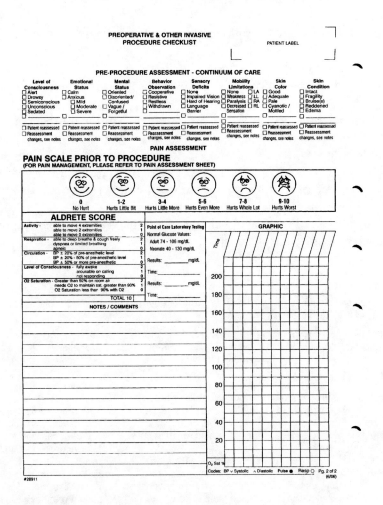

5.4 Summary and Conclusion

- The common denominator of avoiding most preventable causes of medical malpractice suits is good patient selection and good indications for the procedure as well as *double checking the results of the imaging studies.*
- In addition, "wrong-site" surgical cases can be prevented by taking *a routine "time-out" in the or prior to the first cut of the scalpel to double check on answering three questions—whether it is*
  1. the correct patient,
  2. the correct procedure, and
  3. the correct surgical site.

These simple steps performed routinely can avert huge malpractice claims and are certainly not difficult to do. Above all, good physician–patient relationships must be cultivated—not time-rushed—even though "you take on less procedures and see less patients to accomplish this."

Doing so will save you a lot of grief.

5.5   Preventable Hospital Inpatient Errors Applicable to All Specialists

- Studies show that diagnostic errors occur in 10–30% of cases, and generally stem from flaws in doctors' thinking, glitches in the health care system, or some combination of both.
- While many diagnostic errors do not cause serious harm, errors that potentially could have changed a patient's outcome are found in 5–10% of all autopsies according to a 2002 study funded by the Agency for Healthcare Research and Quality.[19]
- Diagnostic errors are among the largest causes of paid malpractice claims at both Kaiser and the veterans administration hospital system (VA), according to the *WSJ*,[20] but studies show an industrywide problem.
- A study of 300 closed malpractice claims found that 59% involved diagnostic errors that harmed patients, and 30% resulted in death.[21]

Dropping the ball

Some examples of diagnostic errors that arose from slip-ups by doctors and hospitals, based on a survey of medical literature:

- **Lack of follow up**–Failure to follow patients after surgery misses recurrent colon cancer

- **Failure to communicate test results**–Biospy report of cancer never communicated to patient who missed appointment

- **Clinician sloppiness**–Doctor known to commonly skip elements of physical misses gangrenous toes

- **Failed oversight of care systems**–Multiple X-rays not read in timely manner; films lost or misplaced

- **Insufficient knowledge or skills**–Missed diagnosis of complete heart block; misread electrocardiogram

- **Faulty data gathering**–Delayed diagnosis of abdominal arotic aneurysm; incomplete history questioning

- **Faulty information processing**–Missed cancer of pancreas in patient with radiating back pain, attributed to reflux

- **Failure to verify diagnosis**–Wrong diagnosis of osteoarthritis in patient found to have drug-induced lupus

- **Failure to gather new data**–Missed colon cancer in patient with declining blood counts, attributed to gastritis

Sources: Department of Veterans Medical Affairs Center, Northport N.Y.; State University of New York, Stoney Brook

---

5.6   Proactive Strategies

Enlist the patient to be part of the solution. This or a similar note should be verbally reviewed, and then given to your patient referred either to another specialist or to the hospital. An initialed copy should be placed in the file.

1. If you are scheduling surgery and can choose where it will be done, select a hospital in your area where the procedure is done frequently. Hopefully, you will have privileges in that hospital. You (as well as your more sophisticated patients) know that patient outcomes are generally better in such hospitals.
2. Ask all health care workers who attend you to *wash their hands*. Hand washing remains a critical way to prevent the spread of infections in hospitals, but studies show it is not done often enough, especially by physicians.
3. Tell your hospitalized patient to *ask questions*. Know what drug and what dose you are being given—and why—before taking it. Never assume it is right just because a

nurse tells you it is what the doctor ordered. Medication errors are the most common mistakes in hospitals.

4. Tell your hospitalized patient to make sure that everyone who gives you medications *checks your hospital ID bracelet* every time. Patient mix-ups are more common than supposed in hospitals.

5. Make sure any *allergies are noted prominently in the chart* and tell your hospitalized patient to mention them to everyone who attends him. Likewise, tell your hospitalized patient to make sure his chart notes every medication you are taking, including over-the-counter medicines and dietary supplements such as vitamins and herbs.

6. Tell your hospitalized patient to *try to have an advocate on hand 24 h a day while you are in the hospital—a trusted friend or family member who can monitor the situation and actively seek help if there is a problem.* Chasing down doctors or care or needed information can be nearly impossible when bed-bound, doped up, or in pain. In some cases, it might be advisable to hire a private-duty nurse overnight when staffing tends to be light and some studies show mistakes are more likely to occur.

7. Tell your hospitalized patient if he is having surgery, to make sure the doctor *marks the proper surgical site clearly*—and initials it, while you are alert. Wrong-site surgery is a highly publicized cause of error.

8. Tell your hospitalized patient to ask the doctor, upon discharge, to *explain the treatment* he or she wants you to follow at home and write it down.

9. Tell your hospitalized patient that if in a teaching hospital and feel that the doctor is not sufficiently knowledgeable or experienced, *ask that a more senior physician be consulted.* Ask that your request be documented in your medical chart. That may be the chief resident or an attending physician. Do not worry about hurting an intern's feelings; your safety is more important.

In solving a problem of this sort, the grand thing is to be able to reason backwards. That is a very useful accomplishment, and a very easy one, but people do not practise it much. In the everyday affairs of life it is more useful to reason forward, and so the other comes to be neglected. There are fifty who can reason synthetically for one who can reason analytically.

—Sherlock Holmes
A Study in Scarlet

References

1. Owens RC, Ambrose PG. Antimicrobial safety: focus on fluoroquinolones. *Clin. Infect. Dis.* 2005; 41: S144.
2. The American College of Obstetricians and Gynecologists' Obstetric Practice Committee, Memo 12/106.
3. Morris JA Jr. et al. Surgical adverse events, risk management, and malpractice outcome: morbidity and mortality review is not enough. Section of Surgical Sciences, Vanderbilt University Medical Center. *Ann. Surg.* 2003; 237(6): 844–851; discussion 851–852.
4. Gajic O, Urrutia LE, Sewani H, Schroeder DR, Cullinane DC, Peters SG. *Crit. Care Med.* 2002; 30(6): 1187–1190.
5. Elmore JG, Fletcher SW. The risk of cancer risk prediction: "what is my risk of getting breast cancer?" *J. Natl. Cancer Inst.* 2006; 98(23): 1673–1675.
6. Glick TH. Neurologic patient safety: an in-depth study of malpractice claims. *Neurology* 2005; 65(8): 1284–1286.

7. Klimo GF. et al. Orthopedic medical malpractice: an attorney's perspective. *Am. J. Orthop.* 2000; 29(2): 93–97.
8. *Am. J. GE* 2002, 97(12): 3183.
9. *Am. J. GE* 2001, 96(12): 3457.
10. *Gastrointest. Endosc.* 1997, 45(6): 451.
11. Rex DK. Maximizing detection of adenomas and cancers during colonoscopy. *Am. J. Gastroenterol.* 2006; 101: 2866–2867.
12. Analysis of 59 ERCP lawsuits; mainly about indications. *Gastrointest. Endosc.* 2006; 63(3): 378–382; quiz 464.
13. *Gastrointest. Endosc.* 2006; 63(3): 383–384.
14. *Gastrointest. Endosc.* 2006; 63(3): 385–388.
15. *Radiology* 1994; 192(2): 373.
16. Testoni PA. Preventing post-ERCP pancreatitis: where are we? *JOP* 2003; 4(1): 22–32.
17. Relation between negligent adverse events and the outcomes of medical-malpractice litigation. *N Engl. J. Med.* 1996; 335(26): 1963–1967.
18. *Ann. Int. Med.* December 5, 2006.
19. Agency for Healthcare Research and Quality, 2002.
20. Wall Street Journal, Health Section, November 29, 2006.
21. *Ann. Int. Med.* October, 2006.

Proactive Strategies to Reduce Malpractice Risks in Primary Medical and Surgical Practices

6

Good advice is always certain to be ignored, but that's no reason not to give it.

—**Agatha Christie**

A man's errors are his portals of discovery.

—**James Joyce**

An ounce of prevention is worth a pound of cure.

—**Anonymous**

6.1 Introduction

No one can promise immunity from lawsuits. However, developing excellent relationships with patients; promoting good communication with patients, colleagues, and other members of the medical care team; maintaining clinical competence; and producing accurate and legible charts can go a long way toward reducing your medical malpractice liability risk.

In this chapter, we will review the chief elements of a good medical malpractice defense, and that is a good offense with proactive strategic moves to reduce risks—both those risks leading to bad medical treatment and those risks leading to patient complaints. These techniques are important as patient complaints have been shown to be the main engine of initiation of medical malpractice suits. The elements of good medical/surgical practice consist of good patient management in the office and avoiding the most preventable in office and post-hospital-discharge errors. We will also discuss low adherence and noncompliance and how this may turn the patient away from being a satisfied patient to being dissatisfied with his treatment regimen and, therefore, more susceptible to complain or sue.

In addition, we will discuss the problem of obtaining a truly informed consent and the most practical ways of getting informed consent from patients. We will also discuss various effective techniques of averting patient complaints, how to deal with them, and how to mitigate patient complaints. Special groups of patients are more susceptible to problems such as the aging and thus special preventive measures are outlined for many of these problems.

Remember, a stitch in time saves nine.

6.2 Patient Complaints Are Linked to Physician Malpractice Risk

1. Unsolicited patient complaints are associated with physicians' risk management experience and lawsuit risk. Data were collected from January 1992 to March 1998. During this period, there were 18,851 patient complaints. Patient complaints and risk management events were higher for surgeons compared with other physicians (i.e., 32% of the nonsurgeons had at least one risk management file compared with 63% of the surgeons). Most physicians get no or very few complaints from their patients over an extended period of time, "A handful of doctors in any area are associated with the majority [of] patient complaints . . . these doctors are also associated with more situations that lead to legal action. These doctors may not know that they are associated with more complaints and may not be aware that they are at higher malpractice risk."

Proactive move:

✓ Someone in the office do "collection, coding, and aggregation of unsolicited complaints in the practice. This offers an excellent tool to help make individual physicians aware of their risk status."

2. Similarly, Beckman et al. (see appendix) looked into the question of why patients sue doctors and hospitals and studied transcripts of discovery depositions of plaintiffs to find out the cause of a patient to file a malpractice claim. Review of a sample of 45 plaintiffs' depositions selected randomly from 67 depositions made available from settled malpractice suits filed between 1985 and 1987 against a large metropolitan medical center was performed.

✓ Four themes emerged from the descriptive review of the 3787 pages of transcript:

1. Deserting the patient (32%)
2. Devaluing patient and family views (29%)
3. Delivering information poorly (26%)
4. Failing to understand the patient and family perspective (13%)

Thirty-one plaintiffs were asked if health professionals suggested maloccurrence. Fifty-four percent ($n = 17$) responded affirmatively.

The postoutcome-consulting specialist was named in 71% ($n = 12$) of the depositions in which maloccurrence was allegedly suggested. The authors concluded that the decision to litigate was often associated with a perceived lack of caring and collaboration in the delivery of health care. The issues identified included

1. perceived unavailability,
2. discounting patient and family concerns,
3. poor delivery of information, and
4. lack of understanding the patient and family perspective.

✓ Proactive moves:

- Particular attention should be paid to the above four common denominators by the practicing physician and his office staff.
- Also, focus on better monitoring of the post-adverse-event and consultant–patient interaction.

3. Sutcliffe et al.[1] (see appendix) described how communication failures contribute to many medical mishaps. In late 1999, a sample of 26 residents stratified by medical specialty, year of residency, and gender was randomly selected from a population of 85 residents at a 600-bed U.S. teaching hospital. The themes reported here emerged from inductive analyses of the data.

4. Residents reported a total of 70 mishap incidents. Aspects of "communication" and "patient management" were the two most commonly cited contributing factors. Recurring patterns of communication appear to be associated with the occurrence of medical mishaps.

- The authors concluded that occurrence of everyday medical mishaps in this study is associated with faulty communication; but, poor communication is not simply the result of poor transmission or exchange of information.
- Communication failures are far more complex and relate to hierarchical differences, concerns with upward influence, conflicting roles and role ambiguity, and interpersonal power and conflict.

✓ Proactive moves:
A clearer understanding of these dynamics highlights possibilities for appropriate interventions in medical education and in health care organizations aimed at improving patient safety. Another study consisted of 160 adults who viewed a videotape of a physician treating a patient while using either positive or negative communication behaviors. Participants were told that the case had a positive result, a bad result through no fault of the physician, a bad result for uncertain reasons, or a bad result that was the physician's fault. Participants then rated their litigious feelings.

- Results showed that the use of negative communication behaviors by the physician increased litigious intentions.
- An increased perception of physician fault for the bad result also increased litigious intentions.
- Uncertainty as to the reason for the bad outcome, however, raised litigious feelings nearly as much as did perceived physician fault.[2]

✓ Proactive moves:
Improving the way physicians communicate with their patients and improving patient education can decrease the risk of malpractice lawsuits.

5. The most common cause of malpractice suits states that the author is failed in communication with the patients and their families.[3]

6. Another study also shows that positive physician communication behaviors increased patients' perceptions of physician competence and decreased malpractice claim intentions toward both the physician and the hospital. This study results also provide empiric evidence for a direct, causal effect of the doctor–patient relationship on medical patients' treatment perceptions and malpractice claim intentions in the event of an adverse medical outcome.[4]

7. The relationship between patients' opinions about their physicians' communication skills and the physicians' history of medical malpractice claims was assessed. The sample

consisted of 107 physicians and 2030 of their patients who had had an operation or a delivery. Although patients tended to give their physicians favorable ratings, they were least satisfied with the amount of explanations they received. Patients gave higher ratings to general surgeons and obstetrician-gynecologists and poorer ratings to orthopedists and anesthesiologists. Women and better-educated patients gave higher ratings on explanations and communication to physicians with fewer claims.[5]

✓ Proactive moves:

- These findings suggest the need for physicians to tailor their communications to a patient's individual needs.
- Improved communication between physicians and patients may result in fewer nonmeritorious malpractice claims while leading to less costly resolution of meritorious claims.

6.3   What Have We Learned about Physician–Patient Relationships and Communication Problems?

Patients don't care how much you know until they know how much you care.

—William Osler

- Nearly every medical malpractice suit addresses some grievance the patient had with the physician, and very often the practice staff.
- They are dissatisfied with their medical care and their treatment in the doctor's office.
- But very few patients who report having a great relationship with the physician will later choose to bring a lawsuit against a well-liked physician.
- The stronger the doctor–patient relationships are, the weaker the legal system becomes an option for patients to resolve the unexpected outcomes that naturally arise in every medical practice.
- Many lawyers report that up to 75% of medical malpractice suits can be attributed to some form of communication problem.
- Many of the attorneys, however, hear from potential plaintiffs who do not want to sue one certain member of their team of doctors involved in a medical mishap leading to damages simply because they like them, they communicate well with each other.
- They like them because *they feel cared for*, which sounds simple but that is the point.
- Although the vast majority of physicians deeply care about their patients, too many do not know how to communicate this effectively to show they care.

Therefore, you should communicate to your patients the *top ten patient satisfaction elements*, which are

- concern,
- friendliness,
- patience,
- sincerity,

- consideration,
- availability,
- technical abilities,
- quality of care outcome,
- cost, and
- practice environment.

Check out your own office and staff.

What is your patient's first experience when they call or arrive in person?
Is the first contact friendly, patient, and attentive?
Or does it feel rushed?
Is the office environment well organized and thoughtful for patients or simply functional?
Is there any plan for addressing problems or complaints?

What attention is given to placing the patient at ease?
Can you identify any individual needs to make the patient more comfortable?
Can you share any personal thoughts, common interests or even humor?
Is there any undelivered communication from the patient? Do you ask?

Is there any effort made to determine whether the patient's needs have been met?
Is there any take-away to instruct, inform, or summarize the office visit?
Is the billing process simple, friendly, and straightforward?
Does the patient feel they are a valued and welcome to call anytime?

6.4 The Dying Patient

Perhaps there is no other single period of heightened medical malpractice risk in the physician–patient relationship than that which occurs with the dying patient. It is in this crucial and high-emotional malpractice risk period that the physician must communicate well with the families of these patients. In recent years, codes of ethics have been developed to provide guidelines for physicians in the application of ethical principles to clinical practice. These organizations include the American Medical Association (AMA), The American College of Emergency Physicians (ACEP), and The Society for Academic Emergency Medicine. Physicians must be at least aware of these codes in general and in particular the codes developed by their individual professional organizations.

Communication with patients and families at the end of life is an essential skill that can improve experiences near the end of life for patients, families, and health care providers and especially mitigate medical malpractice risks.

6.5 Knowing What to Do During the Last Hours

1. Patients in the last hours of life usually need skilled care around the clock. The environment must allow family and friends ready access to their loved one in a setting that is conducive to privacy and intimacy.

2. Advance preparation and education of professional, family, and volunteer caregivers are essential. They should also be knowledgeable about the potential time course, signs, and symptoms of the dying process, and their potential management.

3. The physician or nurse needs to help family members understand that what they see may be very different from what the patient is experiencing.

4. Most patients lose their appetite and reduce food intake long before they reach the last hours of their lives. Anorexia may be protective, and the resulting ketosis can lead to a greater sense of well-being and diminish pain.

5. Most patients also reduce their fluid intake, or stop drinking entirely, long before they die. Dehydration in the last hours of living does not cause distress and may stimulate endorphin release that adds to the patient's sense of well-being.

6. It should be presumed that the unconscious patient hears everything.

7. Planning discussions should cover personal, cultural, and religious traditions; rites; and rituals that may dictate how prayers are to be conducted, how a person's body is to be handled after death, and when/how the body can be moved.

8. Acute grief reactions should be addressed, especially when the body is moved.

In the Room

- You may want to ask the nurse, social worker, or chaplain to accompany you; he/she can give you support and introduce you to the family.
- Introduce yourself (including your relationship to the patient) to the family if they are present. Ask each person their name and relationship to the patient. Shake hands with each.
- Say something empathic: "I'm sorry for your loss ..." or "This must be very difficult for you ..."
- Explain what you are there to do. Tell the family they are welcome to stay, if they wish, while you examine their loved one.
- Ask what questions the family has. If you cannot answer, contact someone who can.
- ✓ Clinical competence, willingness to educate and calm, and empathic reassurance are critical to helping patients and families in the last hours of living.
- Management principles are the same at home or in a health care institution. However, death in an institution requires accommodations that include ensuring privacy, cultural observances, and communication that may not be customary.
- In anticipation of the event, it helps to inform the family and other professionals about what to do and what to expect.
- Care does not end until the clinician has helped the family with their grief reactions and helped those with complicated grief to get care.
- Care at the end of life is an important responsibility for every health professional, and there is a body of knowledge to guide care.

6.6   Terms You Should Know

Despite widespread advocacy and some legal mandates supporting the increased use of advance directives, only a minority of patients have completed these documents. Thus the prudent physician must inquire about this and also make recommendations to the patient and family. To do this the physician must be aware of at least the terms discussed below. The term *advance directive*[6–12] refers to any document stating the patient's wishes regarding medical care, should he be unable to state his or her own wishes in the future. The *living will* is a document used by some terminally ill individuals in which the treating physician accepts the provisions of the living will in advance. Many living wills state that no life-sustaining treatment be used in cases where meaningful recovery is unlikely. The *durable power of attorney* document designates a surrogate decision maker in the event the patient is no longer able to make medical decisions. Most states now have state-approved advance directives, often with specific documents to be completed by patients and physicians, and the Federal Patient Self-Determination Act mandated that all patients who are admitted to hospitals have the opportunity to complete an advance directive.

Since many social and institutional policies still suggest resuscitation attempts for most patients, the development of national and state guidelines to address out-of-hospital care of patients with do-not-attempt-resuscitation (DNR) orders is important in the provision of appropriate medical care for these patients. There have been numerous ethical opinions supportive of the position of providing *only those treatments judged to be of likely medical benefit.*

1. The AMA Council on Ethical and Judicial Affairs states that cardiopulmonary resuscitation (CPR) may be withheld, even if requested by the patient, "when efforts to resuscitate a patient are judged by the treating physician to be futile."
2. Where there is a question the prudent physician should know that the AMA Council on Ethical and Judicial Affairs recommends a *process-based approach to addressing futility, to include such actions as the following*:
   - Deliberation and resolution
   - Joint decision making with physician and patient or proxy
   - Assistance of a consultant, patient representative, or representative from the hospital ethics committee
   - Use of an institutional committee (i.e., ethics committee)

While, in general, it is inappropriate for physicians to suggest specific religious persuasions to dying patients and their families, attention to religious issues that are important to each patient and family can be important in ensuring a meaningful end-of-life experience.

Thus, communication by the physician with the dying patient and family regarding religion, the patient's belief in God, desire to pray or participate in other religious observances, and desire to involve pastoral care services can be vital to meeting spiritual goals at the end of life.

6.7 Death Notification Guidelines

Medical education is deficient in regard to death notification. Inadequate physician education compounds the stress on physicians in these situations. Having a death notification plan and team can lessen physician stress and improve the death notification process for families.

- Informing a family of a patient death begins with the initial contact with the survivors. It is here in the notification process which if deficient may lead to malpractice actions.
- It is therefore crucial for the physician to communicate well. It is the physician's responsibility to inform the family of the death.
- Telephone notification.
- There will be situations in which the people who need to know about the death are not present. In some cases, you may choose to tell someone by telephone that the patient's condition has "changed," and wait for them to come to the bedside in order to tell the news. Factors to consider in weighing whether to break the news over the telephone include whether death was expected, what the anticipated emotional reaction of the person may be, whether the person is alone, whether the person is able to understand, how far away the person is, the availability of transportation for the person, and the time of day (or night). Inevitably, there are times when notification of death by telephone is unavoidable. If this is anticipated, prepare for it. Determine who should be called and in what fashion. It is best to tell the family that the patient is seriously ill and ask them to come to the hospital with a companion who can drive safely.
- Only if the family will not reach the hospital for several hours or are unable to present themselves to the hospital, it may be necessary to inform them of the patient's death over the telephone.
- Extreme care must be taken to accurately identify the deceased person and to notify the correct family.
- If the family is not present, early contact by telephone should occur.
- On arrival, a staff member should be available to greet and escort the family to a private room with a telephone.
- If the patient has not yet died, this allows the family to receive updates on the patient's condition in a secluded setting. The physician should refer to the deceased person by name instead of using terms such as "the patient."
- Families perceive the omission of the patient's name as an indication that the deceased was an object to the physician and not a human life.
- A brief chronology of the events should be given to the family.
- If appropriate, the family should be informed that they acted correctly in the pre- and during the hospital setting, which may decrease their potential guilt.
- They should be informed that all reasonable efforts were made to resuscitate the patient (unless of course the patient was not to be resuscitated (see DNR in Section 6.6).
- A concluding statement that the patient "died" provides the family with a better understanding of the death than does the use of such phrases as "passed on" or "is no longer with us." If appropriate, the family should be reassured that the patient suffered no pain.
- The physician should avoid medical jargon and refrain from providing excessive information, which tends to confuse families.
- The physician should support any decision to view or not view the body.
- The physician or clergy should accompany the family and allow them to touch and speak to the body if they wish.

✓ **Table 6.1   Guidelines for the Approach to Families in Death Notification**

Confirm identity of deceased and family
Private location
Identify oneself
Sit down
Use the patient's name
Brief chronology of events
State that the patient "died"
Reassure that everything possible was done
Avoid medical jargon
Allow for initial grief response
Allow the family to view the body
Ask (if appropriate) about tissue donation/autopsy
Answer family questions
Provide for follow-up with yours, or associates direct telephone number

Source: Olsen, C., et al., *Ann. Emerg. Med.* 31, 6, 1998.

- Several studies have demonstrated that families may later experience regret or anger if they chose not to view or were dissuaded from viewing the deceased. Viewing the body may also help with acceptance of the death.
- The physician and staff should express their sympathy but should not apologize for the death, because survivors may think that more could have been done.
- Staff may find it necessary to tell the family when to leave, because the family may be overwhelmed with the events and not know when it is appropriate to do so.
- The final aspect of death notification is provision of follow-up. Before the physician leaves the department, he should furnish the family with the name and number of a staff person who can answer any further questions. A follow-up telephone call or card may also be helpful.
- Although each physician's approach to families and the circumstances surrounding a death may be somewhat different, the guidelines shown below in Table 6.1 may improve the death notification process.

6.8   Diagnostic Errors as a Source of Dissatisfaction and Malpractice Suits

A total of 181 claims (59%) involved diagnostic errors that harmed patients were reviewed. Fifty-nine percent (106 of 181) of these errors were associated with serious harm, and 30% (55 of 181) resulted in death. For 59% (106 of 181) of the errors, cancer was the diagnosis involved, chiefly breast (44 claims [24%]) and colorectal (13 claims [7%]) cancer. The most common breakdowns in the diagnostic process were

  i. failure to order an appropriate diagnostic test (100 of 181 [55%]),
 ii. failure to create a proper follow-up plan (81 of 181 [45%]),
iii. failure to obtain an adequate history or perform an adequate physical examination (76 of 181 [42%]),
 iv. incorrect interpretation of diagnostic tests (67 of 181 [37%]).

The leading factors that contributed to the errors were

    v. failures in judgment (143 of 181 [79%]), vigilance or memory (106 of 181 [59%]);
   vi. knowledge (86 of 181 [48%]);
  vii. patient-related factors (84 of 181 [46%]); and
 viii. handoffs (36 of 181 [20%]).

Diagnostic errors that harm patients are thus typically the result of multiple breakdowns and individual and system factors.

✓ Proactive moves:
Awareness of the most common types of the above-studied breakdowns should direct the clinician's efforts to identify and prioritize strategies to prevent these common diagnostic errors.

Cancer was the most commonly missed diagnosis.

Most errors occurred at four main "breakdown" points in the diagnostic process, which should be the focus of office systems designed to combat preventive errors causing medical malpractice suits.

- In over half of the cases, a proper diagnostic test was not performed.
- Sometimes test results were not followed up adequately.
- Or the provider did not obtain adequate information from the patient or perform an adequate physical examination.
- Also, providers often incorrectly interpreted results.
- In most cases, more than one breakdown and more than one provider contributed to a missed diagnosis.
- Patients also contributed to the errors in a substantial number of cases by, for example, not providing complete information about their health or not keeping an appointment.
- Errors in diagnosis are not often caused by the failures of a single doctor.
- Instead, they usually have several sources and involve several providers.

6.9   The Key to Good Patient Management

Roberts, calls it the *four winning Cs of risk management*. The key is to develop a risk-management style of practice that involves four Cs: compassion, communication, competence, and charting.

Compassion
When patients do not pay their bills, it may be a signal that they were not happy with their care. It is surprising how often the reason that patients are not paying is because they are angry—angry about the way the nurse acted or something the receptionist said. For these patients, not paying the bill may be their last chance to express their displeasure. Take advantage of these risk-management opportunities. Patients appreciate the chance to have their grievances heard and addressed. Once heard, they are often more willing to work out payment terms. At the least, they are usually happier. Happier patients are less likely to sue.

Also, a low threshold for consultation can be enormously helpful when the patient is not getting better as quickly as expected or wanted; when the patient or the patient's relative expresses dissatisfaction with the care; when the patient's presentation is atypical or the diagnosis obscure; or when the patient is critically ill or dying.

Communication
Physicians practice as part of a team. Communication across teams can be a challenge. Do not write in the chart a disagreement with another physician till you call him to find out why and what he meant.

Competence
Physicians are keenly aware of the need to stay up-to-date on the latest evidence and clinical recommendations. Flow sheets, protocols, and other tools can reduce the chance that important factors are overlooked.

Charting
The greatest charting mistake physicians make is that they fail to note what is important. Often, doctors believe that there is a need to write volumes. Write what is important. We are not expected to be perfect scribes, but we are expected to be honest and thoughtful in how we approach documentation.
Follow these simple proactive moves:

1. Be honest. Never go back and surreptitiously alter a record. Be honest with record keeping. Recording errors, when they occur, are best managed by a single strike through line that is initiated, dated, timed, and identified as an "error." More extensive or significant errors (e.g., "wrong patient") may require more detailed explanation.
2. Be objective. Write the record as though the patient will read it. For example, avoid adjectives such as "drunk and obnoxious" to describe a difficult patient. Instead, use more diplomatic language: "Patient is combative; ethanol-like odor noted." In this case, the patient may be in a state of diabetic ketoacidosis, not alcoholic intoxication, and our description of early impressions will be less likely to haunt us later should our care be challenged as inattentive. The point here is not to sidestep the truth but to choose language that is descriptive, objective and respectful.
3. Be legible. Some physicians actually believe that illegible notes are a good way to prevent lawsuits because they hide any evidence of wrongdoing. In reality, illegible notes provide no protection and are viewed by juries as reflecting sloppy writing and, perhaps, sloppy care. Years later, when the case finally gets to the jury, the medical record can be the doctor's best, and often only, friend as memories fade over time. Legible and logical notes detailing thoughtful care provide the best malpractice defense. Best is to use an electronic medical record system (it brings a wealth of information to the point of care); next best is to have notes dictated and transcribed. If notes must be hand written, make certain they are legible.
4. Key proactive moves:
   To prevent, first and foremost, patient injuries and, secondarily, malpractice claims, physicians should:
   follow their patients' complaints to full diagnosis,
   prepare themselves mentally before procedures,
   know when it is time to consult with a colleague or make a referral,

5. Better care and risk reduction ideas
   - Practice reflective medicine—be mindful of both the harms and inadequacies of care. For example, think of a hospital admission as failed outpatient care. What can we learn about why the patient failed out patient treatment before hospital admission?
   - Think systems—organize care in a way that makes key functions automatic (e.g., "no x-ray or lab report gets into the chart without the doctor's initials").
   - Put people first—when people (patients, family, staff) are unhappy or doing badly, those are the times when we need to be most engaged with them.
   - Make amends—when unexpected and unwanted outcomes occur, we should apologize when we err, go the extra distance to make things right, and always empathize with the patient.

6.9.1   Avoid These Common Denominators of Medical Malpractice Litigation

The decision by the patient to file a malpractice suit frequently is dictated by *insensitive handling by and poor communication from the physician*.

Many patients who file malpractice claims state that their physicians would not listen to them, would not talk openly, attempted to mislead them, and did not warn them about long-term medical problems. The patient then sues because he or she believes that he or she was not informed, was deserted, and was neglected. However, statistics from the IOM show that one-fourth of adults have experienced a medical error within the past 2 years. Like Yogi Berra says, "In theory, there is no difference between theory and practice. In practice there is."

6.10   Avoidable Post-Hospital-Discharge Errors

Adverse events after discharge from the hospital are common. Many of these adverse events were avoidable or ameliorable.

Four hundred consecutive patients discharged home from the general medical service of a tertiary care academic hospital were followed. After discharge, 76 patients (19%) had adverse events, defined as injuries occurring as a result of poor medical management. Of these, 23 patients had preventable adverse events, defined as adverse events judged to have been caused by an error, and 24 patients had ameliorable adverse events, defined as adverse events in which the severity could have been decreased.

Adverse drug events (see Addendum) accounted for 66% of adverse events, and procedure-related injuries for 17%. Of the 25 adverse events that caused a transient or permanent disability, 12 events were preventable and 6 events were ameliorable.

6.10.1   Adverse Drug Events (ADEs) Are Almost as Common Among Outpatients and They Have Important Litigation Consequences

A summary analysis of more than 1500 published case reports of ADEs yielded information on possible risk factors for drug-related deaths, disabilities, and life threats and on which events may have been preventable.

The study showed that the drug categories most commonly involved in ADEs were central nervous system agents, antimicrobials, antineoplastics, and cardiovascular agents.

- Faulty prescribing was the most common reason for medication error, and wrong dosage was the most common type of error.
- Overall, 52% of the cases were judged to have been preventable; of these, 50% could have been prevented by a pharmacist.
- Litigation was reported for 13% of the cases; settlements and judgments averaged $3.1 million.[13]

✓ Proactive moves:

1. Thoroughly evaluate patients at the time of discharge and think ahead as to what the potential problems will be with that particular patient
2. Teach him about his drug side effects, and what to do if specific problems develop
3. Teach him about self-monitoring of his disease(s); and overall medical condition and what to do if certain symptoms develop
4. Make sure there is a companion present who will understand the directions you are giving about the medication regimen the patient is to follow as an outpatient

6.11   Low Adherence and Noncompliance of Patients to Treatment

6.11.1   Impact of Medication Nonadherence

Nonadherence to medications is correlated with a high degree of mortality especially in myocardial infarction and diabetes mellitus patients and is one of the strongest indicators of poor outcomes (*which may ironically lead to medical malpractice suits against the private physician*).[14–17]

One of the reasons of patient complaints may be ironically the patient's perception of lack of success by the physician in the patient's treatment program. Here is where patient noncompliance and lack of adherence to the prescribed treatment regimen plays an important role.

- The adherence rate for medical treatments (or noncompliance rate) averages in some studies about 50%, with a range that extends from 0 to 100%.
- Physicians' estimates of their own patients' adherence have no better than "chance accuracy."
- Thus the problem of low adherence can be almost invisible to the individual practitioner dealing with a specific patient. This is true even for patients whom physicians feel they know well.
- Thus, part of the problem of detecting low adherence is that clinicians often think they know a poor or good complier when they see one, perhaps cueing on such characteristics as age, gender, education, and intelligence—none of which have been shown to have any consistent relationship to adherence.
- Adherence to chronic pharmacological therapies is poor.
- This often leads to worsening disease severity and increased costs associated with higher hospital admission rates.
- Barriers to medication adherence are numerous, and are particularly prevalent among the elderly population, placing them at increased risk for medication nonadherence.

U.S. doctors often fail to discuss costs, prescription drug insurance coverage, and other related issues when they give new prescriptions to patients. A study included 185 patients who had outpatient visits with 15 family doctors, 18 internists, and 11 cardiologists. In total of about 243 new medications were prescribed during these visits.

In only 33% of the cases did the doctors talk with patients about issues related to medication cost, insurance, generic or name-brand, logistics, supply, and refills. All doctors were less likely to do so when prescribing medications to older patients.

Approaches to improve adherence can be complex and labor-intensive. The National Council on Patient Information and Education has termed medication nonadherence "America's other drug problem." The problem of medication nonadherence poses an even greater risk among elderly patients in the United States, among whom poor medication adherence is common, morbid, costly, and difficult to treat. And it is among the elderly, that polypharmacy, which is the use of multiple medications resulting in complicated drug regimens, is an important barrier to medication adherence. Of 4053 patients aged 65 years or older prescribed medications for hypertension and hyperlipidemia, the adherence to both classes of medication decreased rapidly to 40.5% at the 3-month interval, and then to 32.7% at 6 months.[18]

Lee et al.[19] noted that poor medication adherence diminishes the health benefits of pharmacotherapies, especially in elderly patients with coronary risk factors who frequently require treatment with multiple medications, placing them at increased risk for nonadherence. Of a total of 200 elderly patients, a pharmacy care program led to increases in medication adherence, medication persistence, and clinically meaningful reductions in BP, whereas discontinuation of the program was associated with decreased medication adherence and persistence.

Preventive moves to detect and prevent low adherence include the following:

1. Watch for nonresponders (i.e., those whose disorder fails to respond to increments in treatment)
2. Watch for nonattenders (i.e., those who miss appointments), and simply asking patients whether they are taking their medication faithfully.[2]
3. The key question that has been tested in studies is, "Have you ever missed any of your pills (injections, etc.)?"
4. Any affirmative response to this question is associated with taking less than 50% of medications.
5. Unfortunately, only about half of nonadherent patients will acknowledge their nonadherence when questioned, and those who do acknowledge it will overestimate their adherence (by an average of 17%, with a wide variance). However, the combination of monitoring attendance, observing treatment response, and asking patients about adherence will detect most adherence problems.
6. Additional measures include reviewing pharmacy records of prescription refills, if those records are available and, for some medications, measuring levels of drugs or their metabolites in body fluids.
7. Appointment-keeping can be increased by sending reminders, either by mail or by telephone (mailed reminders are less expensive) and by recalling patients who miss appointments.[3]
8. Interventions that are effective for long-term care include
   a. combinations of more convenient care and patient education (about how to take the treatment and for how long),

b. reminders and self-monitoring (e.g., of blood pressure, blood glucose, or International Normalized Ratio),

c. reinforcement, counseling, family therapy, psychological therapy, crisis intervention, individualized telephone follow-up, and supportive care.[4]

Conclusions of all the studies show that there is a deadly combination of medication noncompliance and adverse drug events (ADEs) especially in the elderly. Medication noncompliance contributes significantly to morbidity, mortality, and health care costs, accounting for 33–69% of all medication-related hospital admissions in the United States, at an estimated annual cost of approximately $100 billion. The World Health Organization has responded to the problem of medication noncompliance by publishing an evidence-based guide for clinicians, health managers, and policy makers. Thus,

1. All physicians should realize that ADEs and medication noncompliance are common problems and that their identification and reduction will have a significant impact on the quality of health care. *[Sabate E. Adherence to Long-term Therapies: evidence for action. Geneva, Switzerland; 2003. ISBN: 92 4 154599 2]*.

2. Monitor these patients carefully:
   - Particularly those who miss appointments
   - Those not responding to therapy
   - Those discovered not refilling their medication prescriptions in a timely manner

3. A nonthreatening and nonconfrontational approach when inquiring whether patients are taking their medications has the greatest chance of success in uncovering medication noncompliance.

4. Physicians should ask for the details about patients' medication-taking behavior at all clinic visits and offer practical suggestions that fit within patients' lifestyles on how they can remember to take their medications in the manner prescribed.

5. Identification of medication noncompliance can also help avoid ADEs and optimize treatment of disease.

Patients in the three categories below are likely taking their medications with the degree of compliance necessary for a sufficient therapeutic response for most diseases:

- Near-perfect dosing schedule
- Nearly every dose taken, but with some irregularity in schedule
- Occasional day's doses missed, with some schedule irregularity

In contrast, patients with the following scheduling patterns are not likely to be achieving optimal drug therapy, and in the treatment of certain diseases they may be doing harm:

- Drug holidays taken (missing three or more sequential days of medication) 3–4 times a year with other occasional dosing lapses
- Drug holiday taken at least every month and frequent dosing omissions
- Few or no medications taken while maintaining the outward impression of good medication compliance

Karch and my former mentor at Johns Hopkins Louis Lasagna,[20] almost 30 years ago, proposed a simple, operational algorithm for evaluating possible ADEs. The algorithm consists of three decision tables that identify potential ADEs, assess the certainty of the link between the event and the drug, and evaluate the underlying cause of the ADE (e.g., compliance problem, medication error, drug interaction, etc.). The key questions that are part of all of these algorithms are the following:

- Has the observed reaction been previously documented to be due to the drug taken by the patient?
- Is the time course of the reaction consistent with the time(s) of drug administration?
- Could this reaction be due to another clinical condition in the patient?
- Did the reaction improve when the drug was discontinued?
  - If not discontinued, did the reaction resolve?
  - If the dose was reduced, but not discontinued, did the reaction resolve?
  - If an antidote was given, did the patient improve?
- Did the reaction reoccur when (if) the drug was administered again?
- Was the dose appropriate for the patient in terms of age or organ function?

As part of a national initiative, the Institute for Healthcare Improvement announced in mid-June 2006 that it had successfully achieved a goal of reducing hospital deaths by more than 120,000 in the previous 18 months. The medication reconciliation process for maintaining an accurate and portable record of a patient's medications can be useful in preventing medication errors and potentially reducing ADEs.

Even with maximal efforts, however, the adherence of many patients will not be close to 100%. By learning how to reliably detect low adherence and successfully encourage adherence, clinicians can at least narrow that gap, if not close it.

The new study, referred to above, the Federal Study of Adherence to Medications in the Elderly (FAME), has investigated the effect of a pharmacy care program on medication adherence and persistence at the Walter Reed Army Medical Centers in 200 hundred patients with a mean age of 78 who were taking at least four medications. This program included individualized medication education and drugs which were dispensed in custom package, time-specific blister packs. During the observational study, the mean adherence rose to about 96% and mean blood pressure and LDL cholesterol levels decreased significantly. This study documents not only high rates of adherence, but also the salutary effects on secondary end points including blood pressure and lipid levels.[19,21]

The value of experience is not in seeing much, but in seeing wisely.

—**William Osler**

6.12   Additional Preventive Move to Avert Malpractice Claims

Attempt to follow the rule of three: If you haven't figured out and corrected a patient's problem within three visits, enlist someone to help. Why use only three?

Because it keeps you from temporizing forever while the patient continues to have problems.

✓ *Negligent drug treatment*:   Drug-related iatrogenic injuries cause thousands of hospital admissions each year. Many of these injuries are related to the use of warfarin. Use a written protocol especially in these particular patients to ensure that patients are well educated about using warfarin and are getting their International Normalized Ratios checked regularly.

✓ *Negligent procedures*:   Do not do procedures you for which you were not trained.

✓ *Obtain truly informed consent.*

6.12.1   The Problem of Obtaining Truly Informed Consent

When is a patient truly "informed?"

For patients to be informed, is it sufficient only for doctors to outline the options and share information? The key outcome is not the giving of information, or even information exchange, but the achievement of understanding by the patient.

This understanding should include awareness of particular outcomes of treatment and their characteristics, including benefits, possible harms, the seriousness of the harms and their probabilities (as expressed in absolute and relative terms), the factors that influence susceptibility, and the difficulty of avoiding harmful consequences.

It is more likely that such understanding occurs when decision making is seen as a process and not as an outcome. Proper understanding means that patients can make informed decisions about treatment, based on balancing assessment of information with their own priorities.

✓ **Characteristics of Informed Decisions**

An informed decision about a treatment option is based on

    a. Accurate assessment of information about the relevant alternatives and their consequences

    b. Assessment of the likelihood and desirability of the alternatives in relation to the patients' priorities

    c. A "trade-off" between (a) and (b)

✓ **What to Do**

---

1. Define the problem: clearly specify the problem that requires a decision, taking in your views and the patient's views.
2. Make it clear that professionals may not have a set opinion about which treatment option is the best, even when the patient's priorities are taken into account.
3. Outline the options: describe one or more treatment options and, if relevant, the consequences of no treatment.
4. Provide information in preferred format: also identify the patient's preferences if this will be useful in the decision-making process.
5. Check understanding: ascertain the patient's understanding of the options.
6. Explore ideas: elicit the patient's concerns and expectations about the clinical condition, the possible treatment options, and the outcomes.

7. Ascertain the patient's preferred role: check that the patient accepts the decision sharing process and identify his or her preferred role in the interaction.
8. Involve the patient: involve the patient in the decision-making process to the extent the patient wishes.
9. Defer, if necessary: review the patient's needs and preferences after he or she has had time for further consideration, including with friends or family, if the patient needs it.
10. Review arrangements: review treatment decisions after a specified time period.

According to Elwyn et al.,[22] there are 10 steps to getting truly informed consent.

But in the real world, there are practical problems in this ideal endeavor. According to Physician's First Watch September 7, 2006: Report "Finds Americans Have Middling Medical Literacy," most Americans have an intermediate level of health literacy and may often have difficulty following written health directions, according to a report by the National Center for Educational Statistics. The findings were based on a health literacy test taken by 19,000 adults. On the test, which has a perfect score of 500, men averaged 242, while women averaged 248. An example of intermediate literacy is the ability to determine what time a person can take a medication based on label instructions. An example of proficient literacy is the ability to define a medical term by searching through a complex document. One of the investigators, interviewed by the Associated Press, said insurers, drug makers, and doctors write at a level that is difficult for the general public to understand. For instance, people checking labels for salt content might not understand what "sodium" means. The results showed that adults age 65 and older had lower health literacy than younger people. Whites and Asians had higher literacy than blacks, Hispanics, and American Indians.

6.13 Informed Consent in Intensive Care and Cardiac Care Units

Patients in the intensive care unit who give informed consent to participate in a clinical trial may not truly be capable of making such a decision.

While "80% recalled being in a clinical trial about 10 days later ... only 32% knew the purpose and its risks." These findings call into question current recruitment practices for ICU patients. Informed consent requires complete disclosure of risks and benefits. For that reason the patient's comprehension and voluntary participation should be fully evaluated by a third party. Explain that this study found that ICU patients may have difficulty processing information because the stress, dependence, and anguish inherent to the ICU.[23]

The researchers found that

- complete recall of both risks and purpose of the trial was significantly more common among patients who asked at least one question ($p = .03$);
- ninety-three percent of patients with complete recall, compared with 60% with incomplete recall, had read a one-page informational leaflet about the trial or asked at least one question before signing the consent form (13 of 14 versus 18 of 30, $p = .03$);
- informed consent should be viewed as a process rather than a procedure;
- the informed consent process requires multiple conversations on several occasions while the research is conducted.

The study was performed under the auspices of a larger clinical trial about inflammation. The researchers approached patients admitted to the ICU after a major surgery or trauma with a Glasgow Coma Score of 15, who were not on mechanical ventilation, and were fully oriented. The researchers also found

- 35 of the 44 patients remembered participating in the trial,
- 20 of the 44 patients could recall the purpose of the study,
- 21 of the 44 patients retained a memory of the study risks,
- 14 of the 44 remembered both the purpose and associated risks of the trial.

- Patients with complete recall were similar to those with incomplete recall in demographics, education, admission characteristics, duration of mechanical ventilation, ICU stay, and medications administered during the 24 h before and after giving informed consent.
- These findings were similar to a previous study by the same group in which informed consent was obtained before ICU admission (22% did not recall participation in the trial compared to 20% in the current study). However, only 25% of patients in the pre-ICU informed consent study forgot the trial purpose and related risks compared to 68% of patients approached during ICU stay.
- "It is reasonable to speculate that the rate of recall may be even worse in usual patients in the ICU," the investigators added.

✓ Proactive move:
The researchers suggested that investigators repeat clinical trial information to participants while the research is being conducted and even after discharge from the ICU.

6.13.1 Informed Consent Potential Problems with Attending Physician House Staff

Attending physicians may be sued under a "battery" theory for allowing students, interns, or residents to participate in a surgical procedure after the patient expressly withheld consent to such participation.[24] This Mullins ruling is consistent with other rulings, approving a course of action for battery based on allegations that house staff (the interns and residents) participated in surgical procedures even though the patient allegedly stated prior to the procedure that it was all right for the house staff to observe but not to take part in the procedure. Although other courts have ruled otherwise, you must make absolutely certain that the informed consent statement states that house staff may participate in the surgery and that the patient should be fully aware of that or be given the opportunity to reject that option. The informed consent given by the patient should not be violated.

6.13.2 Potential Solutions to the Problems with Informed Consent, Ades, and Nonadherence

Are all the above practical for a busy physician? Does any practitioner have the time during one office visit that it would take to accomplish the ideal informed consent to medications and procedures? No—for one encounter. Yes—if you take more than one office visit to accomplish this, it can very easily be done as I have done in my own office.

Proactive moves:
All this does not have to be accomplished nor completed in one encounter with the patient. Usually a physician remembers to get informed consent when the procedure or treatment is scheduled and just before the patient leaves the office, he has an assistant get the informed consent signed.

- But it does not have to be that way.
- If during the first visit the patient is given information in a patient brochure that almost all specialty societies print for their memberships' patients; there is plenty of time until the next office visit for the patient to absorb along with the family the entire contents of these very simple brochures written usually at the fifth grade level.
- A copy of such a brochure should be attached to the records simultaneously with the patient and escort(s) receiving it.
- The patient is instructed to have the family read it together and at the next visit(s) all the practitioner has to do is to answer the patient and escort's well thought-out questions.
- After only a short time you will have a lot more informed consent than you had before.
- Avoiding patient noncompliance as a reason for treatment failure with resultant dissatisfaction.
- Finding out whether the patient's wish to take part in the decision-making process is a critical step. Although this may be necessary at various specific decision points (tests or referrals, for example), taking a drug is the ultimate expression of personal decision making as it is something we do to ourselves by ourselves, often every day for many years. Even when patients do not want to take part in decision making their views should be taken into account in the prescribing process—otherwise there is a chance of misunderstanding and of low motivation to use the drug. Interactions in which patients are well informed and satisfied with a decision (whether it is to accept or decline an intervention) is better.

6.14   Summary Points

The way patients take medicines varies widely and is strongly influenced by their beliefs and attitudes.

Concordance describes the process whereby patients and professionals exchange their views on treatment and come to an agreement about the need (or not) for a particular treatment.

Concordance requires that patients are involved in decision-making processes.
Ensuring that patients use drugs effectively sometimes requires additional support, such as involvement of patients' family; support groups and systems for monitoring adherence to treatment.

Published studies have shown that the above methods do indeed decrease the risks of a medical malpractice suit.

These findings highlight the challenge of finding effective ways to reduce diagnostic errors as a component of improving health care quality. The findings that errors are common (59% of all outpatient claims) are sobering, since they do not offer a single target and the promise of a magic bullet. But the study helps point the way to changes in training, practice, and systems that might prevent many of these errors.

In the outpatient setting as compared to the in hospital setting the nature of the patient–provider relationship is different. Because the patient is neither passive nor captive in the office, as he is in the hospital, *patient adherence* is far more important than in the hospital. Gandhi and colleagues found that 46% of errors involved significant patient factors, with nearly half of these reflecting *nonadherence*.

Proactive moves:
In office practice,

- the focus of attention therefore should be involving the patient actively is sure to be a key component of ambulatory safety efforts;
- patient safety initiatives should involve standardizing and simplifying complex care processes;
- also, office practitioners may well see an economic advantage to improved efficiency from thoughtfully applied safety efforts.

Poon et al. surveyed 262 physicians working in 15 internal medicine practices affiliated with two large urban teaching hospitals. Overall, 83% of respondents reported at least one delay in reviewing test results during the previous 2 months. Physicians who actively tracked their test orders to completion were also more likely to be satisfied.[25]

Proactive moves:
Computer tools to help physicians

1. generate result letters to patients,
2. prioritize their workflow,
3. track test orders to completion.

Gurwitz[26] assessed the incidence and preventability of adverse drug events among older persons in the ambulatory clinical setting. There were 1523 identified adverse drug events of which 421 (27.6%) were considered preventable. The overall rate of adverse drug events was 50.1 per 1000 person-years, with a rate of 13.8 preventable adverse drug events per 1000 person-years. Of the adverse drug events, 578 (38.0%) were categorized as serious, life-threatening, or fatal. 244 (42.2%) of these more severe events were deemed preventable compared with 177 (18.7%) of the 945 significant adverse drug events.

✓ Errors associated with preventable adverse drug events occurred most often at the stages of

1. prescribing ($n = 246$, 58.4%),
2. monitoring ($n = 256$, 60.8%),
3. errors involving patient adherence problems ($n = 89$, 21.1%).

The most common medication errors were

1. associated cardiovascular medications (24.5%), followed by
2. diuretics (22.1%),
3. opioid and nonopioid analgesics (15.4%),
4. hypoglycemics (10.9%),
5. anticoagulants (10.2%),
6. preventable adverse drug events associated with problems of electrolyte/renal (26.6%),
7. gastrointestinal tract (21.1%),
8. hemorrhagic (15.9%),
9. metabolic/endocrine (13.8%), and neuropsychiatric (8.6%) (see Addendum).

6.15   Treatment with Strong Analgesics: Points to Remember

Errors often occur:

- When therapeutic conversions use a nonequivalent analgesic dose
- By a calculation mistake (e.g., when converting from Vicodin [hydrocodone and acetaminophen] to MS Contin [controlled-release oral morphine])
- By a misunderstanding regarding the relative potencies of the two products

Other types of errors reported in conjunction with use of opioids include

- name confusion,
- overlapping analgesic regimens.

Thus the dose of the new opioid should first be reduced by 25–50% depending on how well pain is controlled. In addition, rescue medications must be made available for breakthrough pain. To calculate an equianalgesic dose, the following steps should be followed: First, add up the patient's total 24-h analgesic requirement, including all doses for breakthrough pain. Second, convert that total amount to the drug and route desired using a conversion table, such as Table 6.2 below. Third, divide the total 24-h dose of the new drug by the number of daily doses to be administered. The duration of action values in Table 6.2 are helpful in this regard.

Table 6.2   Opioid Equianalgesic Dosage Conversion

Drug	Parenteral (mg)	Oral (mg)	Duration of Action (h)[a]
Codeine phosphate or sulfate	120	200	3–4
Hydromorphone hydrochloride	1.5	7.5	2–4
Meperidine hydrochloride	75	300	2–4
Methadone hydrochloride[b]	5	10	6–8
Morphine sulfate	10	30	2–4
Oxycodone hydrochloride	NA	20	2–4

[a] Values reflect immediate-release products.

[b] Substantial decreases in doses may be needed when converting to methadone (~90%) because of the drug's long elimination half-life and N-methyl-D-aspartate receptor activity.

Respiratory depression is a potentially serious, but uncommon, adverse effect of opioid analgesics. However, fear of respiratory depression should not interfere with provision of appropriate analgesia. Sedation typically precedes respiratory depression; thus, monitoring for sedation should be a routine part of caring for persons who receive opioid analgesics, particularly when starting treatment or changing doses. In general, use of long-acting opioid analgesics should be reserved for persons who are opioid-tolerant, who are expected to require opioid-level analgesia for an extended period, and whose analgesic requirements are relatively stable.

Equianalgesic conversion methods are easily used, but the results are estimates. Reducing the "equipotent" dose of the new analgesic by up to 50% and allowing for liberal rescue doses to treat breakthrough pain may help avoid opioid overdoses. Importantly, patients whose pain is not well controlled at the time of drug conversion may not need to have their dose decreased, or may even require an increased dose.

Nurses and pharmacists should actively evaluate changes in prescribed opioid regimens and question orders that appear to represent a significant increase or decrease in dosage compared with a patient's prior stable analgesic requirement.[27]

✓ Proactive moves:
Since adverse drug events are common and often preventable among older persons in the ambulatory clinical setting, special care must be the focus of the clinician and his office staff in this age group.

Since serious adverse drug events are more likely to be preventable, prevention strategies should target the

    a. prescribing,
    b. monitoring stages of pharmaceutical care,
    c. interventions focused on improving patient adherence with prescribed regimens,
    d. monitoring of prescribed medications—especially of the above most common medications associated with medical errors and medical malpractice suits.

There remains a very disturbing fact in physician communication with patients. This can often lead to nonadherence and poor results leading to marked patient dissatisfaction.

The main problem is improper communication with patients.

Audiotaped office visits from 185 outpatient encounters with 16 family physicians, 18 internists, and 11 cardiologists were transcribed in which 243 new medications were prescribed. The average age of the patients was 55, half of them were men, and most had some college education. Almost all the patients had health insurance. About three-quarters of the doctors were men, and 89% were white. Sixty-six percent of the doctors said nothing about how long to take the medicine, 45% did not say what dosage to take and 42% failed to mention the timing or frequency of doses. Physicians mentioned adverse side effects only 35% of the time.

- When initiating new medications, physicians often fail to communicate critical elements of medication use.
- This might contribute to misunderstandings about medication directions or necessity and, in turn, lead to patient failure to take medications as directed.
- Dr. Neil S. Wenger, a professor of medicine at the University of California, Los Angeles and the senior author on the study, said in an interview that, "The problems

we're seeing are exactly the things we see going wrong in clinical practice. You pre-scribe a cholesterol-lowering medicine, a medicine that has to be taken for a lifetime, and the person never refills the first prescription. And we wonder why. Now it's clear why: we never told them that they were supposed to keep taking it."[28]

6.16　Medical Malpractice Impact of Medication Nonadherence

Nonadherence to medications is correlated with a high degree of mortality especially in myocardial infarction and diabetes mellitus patients and is one of the strongest indicators of poor outcomes (which may ironically lead to medical malpractice suits against the pri-vate physician from the patient's families).

Proactive moves:
It is obvious. Isn't it? You must have a system in place in which patients are not only fully informed about new medications but also are closely monitored for nonadherence to the medications you are prescribing—if not personally by you then at least by someone in your office staff.

6.17　Summary and Conclusion Points

The major theme from the peer-reviewed literature is that increased patient complaints, dissatisfaction, and perceived failures in diagnosis and treatment, are linked to increased physician malpractice risk and, therefore, the prudent physician must devise methods to minimize these issues. They should be handled as soon as they come up without waiting for the next visit or next phone call.

> Complaints about medical care are a warning signal—the canary in the mine.

> Complaints about medical care should be handled by the physician himself.

The keys to good patient management are compassion, communication, competence, and adequate charting. You must be constantly thinking of risk reduction steps both for office patients and especially posthospital-discharged patients in which many preventable errors may occur. The problems of low adherence and patient noncompliance are a major one in ambulatory practice for which the physician should be aware. Finally we have discussed steps to avert adverse drug events especially among the elderly.

6.17.1　Prevention of Adverse Drug Events and Common Medical Errors

> There is a strong family resemblance about misdeeds, and if you have all the details of a thou-sand at your finger ends, it is odd if you can't unravel the thousand and first.
>
> **—Sherlock Holmes**
> *A Study in Scarlet*

As we have seen an important and highly preventable form of medical errors is the adverse drug event (ADES). The objective studies speak for themselves in that these errors are important causes of litigation against all medical providers—the hospital and the physician. Also, the point must be made by objective analysis is that these unfortunate events could have been reversible by early detection and simple system changes. The physician must be acutely aware of the implications of these studies not just for better quality patient care, but also for risk management against medical malpractice litigation. The average physician may assume that if she/he is not directly involved with the medication error (i.e., it occurred beyond her/his control in the hospital setting) then she/he is immune from litigation. But this is not so, as has been documented by many litigation cases in which the physician is also named as a target.

- Adverse drug events represented 6.3% (129/2040) of *medical malpractice claims.*
- Adverse drug events are judged preventable in 73% ($n = 94$) of the cases and are nearly evenly divided between outpatient and inpatient settings.
- The most frequently involved medication classes are antibiotics, antidepressants, or antipsychotics; cardiovascular drugs; and anticoagulants.
- Among these ADEs, 46% were life threatening or fatal.
- System deficiencies and performance errors were the most frequent causes of preventable ADEs.
- The mean costs of defending malpractice claims due to ADEs were comparable for nonpreventable inpatient and outpatient ADEs and preventable outpatient ADEs (mean, $64,700–74,200), but costs were considerably greater for preventable inpatient ADEs (mean, $376,500).

6.17.2 Summary Points

- Adverse drug events associated with malpractice claims were often severe, costly, and preventable and about half occurred in outpatients.
- Many interventions could potentially have prevented ADEs, with error proofing and process standardization covering the greatest proportion of events.[29]

6.18 Be Alert to the Second Epidemic of ADEs in Hospitals and Nursing Homes

The Institute of Medicine (IOM)'s[30] report on the quality of patient care entitled *to err is human* has drawn national attention to the occurrence, clinical consequences, and cost of adverse drug events in hospitals, which is estimated at $2 billion annually in the United States.

Leape et al.[31] (see appendix) found that 44% of ADEs occurred *after* the prescription order was written (i.e., during the medication delivery and administration processes). Drug therapy cannot be successful unless, and until, both the prescribing and medication delivery processes are conducted correctly. Reported errors are a small subset of the totality of errors that signal major system breakdowns with possible grave consequences for patients.[1,32–35] In the early 1980s, the Health Care Financing Administration (HCFA, now the Centers for Medicare & Medicaid Services [CMS])[36] evaluated and adopted a technique involving the observation by HCFA surveyors of selected nurses as they administered medications. The results were considered an outcome indicator of the quality of the drug delivery system. Since then, HCFA has required all 50 states to conduct annual surveys of medication errors in nursing homes and nonaccredited hospitals.

A standard for medication error rates is defined (5%) and must not be exceeded as part of the regulation. (*But 5% of all hospital admissions amount to many thousands of ADEs.*)

6.19 Be Alert to ADEs in Office Patients

The occurrence of ADEs is a significant system problem not only in hospitals, *but also in physician's offices*. In a study of four primary care practices, it was found that one-quarter of outpatients had adverse drug events during a 3-month period. Of these events, 13% were serious, 39% were either ameliorable or preventable, and 6% were serious and preventable or ameliorable.

Ameliorable adverse drug events were attributed to the following:

- Poor communication
- The physician's failure to respond to symptoms reported by the patient
- The patient's failure to report symptoms to the physician
- Preventable adverse drug events are due to prescribing errors, one-third of which could have been prevented by the use of advanced computerized* systems of prescribing medications.
- The characteristics of the patients were not significantly associated with adverse events, except for the number of medications taken.
- Patients reported three times as many events as did trained chart reviewers.
- The longer duration of exposure to medications among outpatients than among inpatients may contribute to the higher rate of events.
- The percentage of outpatients in the study who had serious events was actually higher than the percentage of hospitalized patients who had serious events (3.5% versus 2.6%), because of the higher total rate of outpatient events.
- The frequency of adverse drug events was 5% per year in a population of outpatients who were 65 years of age or older.
- Hernández and Vargas found that 39% of adverse drug events in primary care were either preventable or ameliorable.
- Antidepressant and antihypertensive medications were often implicated in these events, even after accounting for the frequency with which they were prescribed.
- In contrast, analgesics, sedatives, and antibiotics are most commonly implicated in adverse events among inpatients.
- Most of preventable events are due to prescribing errors (an inappropriate choice of drugs, drug interaction, or drug allergy).
- Ameliorable adverse drug events, which were much more common than preventable events, occurred when physicians failed to respond to medication-related symptoms and when patients failed to inform physicians about such symptoms.
- Patients often had symptoms for months without any changes in their medications, and only a small percentage of patients reported that symptoms led to a visit to a physician.
- Patients experience substantial anxiety and discomfort because of drug-related symptoms.

✓ Points to remember:

- More than one-third of such adverse drug events are preventable or ameliorable.
- Improvements in monitoring for and responding to symptoms appear to be especially important for the prevention of adverse drug events in outpatients.
- In addition, improved communication between outpatients and their physicians may reduce the frequency of these events.

✓ Medication errors are common (nearly one of every five doses in the typical hospital and skilled nursing facility). The percentage of errors rated potentially harmful was 7%, or more than 40 per day in a typical 300-patient facility. The problem of defective medication administration systems, although varied, is widespread.[37]

✓ An analysis suggests that medication histories in the hospital medical record are not accurate sources of information in elderly persons. Errors in the history may adversely affect clinical care; researchers and physicians relying on hospital medical records to determine medication use at the time of admission should first validate their data.[38]

✓ Three high-priority preventable ADEs accounted for 50% of all reports:

1. Overdoses of anticoagulants or insufficient monitoring and adjustments (according to laboratory test values) were associated with hemorrhagic events.
2. Overdosing or failure to adjust for drug–drug interactions of opiate agonists was associated with somnolence and respiratory depression.
3. Inappropriate dosing or insufficient monitoring of insulins was associated with hypoglycemia.[39]

✓ In 22 narcotic overdoses that occurred in one study, 14 (64%) were caused by medication prescribing, compounding, or administration errors and were preventable. The causes of overdoses are not limited to prescribing and administration errors. Some patients, despite proper execution of appropriate orders, develop a narcotic overdose. Caregivers must be aware of this problem and monitor patients for a decrease in mental status and respiratory rate.[40]

✓ Of 13,602 emergency department (ED) patients visits, 13,004 records were available. Three hundred twenty-one had suspected and 217 had probable ADEs (1.7% of evaluable encounters); these were compared with visits by 217 age-matched control patients. Insulin and warfarin were the most commonly responsible drugs. Patients with ADEs were older (mean age, 45.1 versus 36.8 years; mean difference, 8.3; 95% confidence interval [CI], 3.7–12.9), were more often women (odds ratio [OR], 1.48; 95% CI, 1.01–2.16), and took more drugs. ADEs encompassed an important segment of ED encounters and annual health care costs.[41]

✓ In a prospective study of 2814 inpatients over 70 years of age who were consecutively admitted to hospital, ADEs were associated with cardiovascular, metabolic, renal, or neuropsychological symptoms. The drugs involved were mainly cardiovascular (43.7%) and psychotropic (31.2%) drugs. One or more risk factors (mainly DDIs and interfering acute diseases) were recorded in 81.2% of ADEs. An interfering acute disorder (usually dehydration) was more frequent in ADEs resulting from drugs or drug combinations administered for 1 month or more ($p < .05$). 41.3% of risk factors were preventable (some DDIs, excess doses, interfering chronic diseases). Therefore

- one risk factor alone or the combination of all risk factors was preventable in 40.2% of ADEs;
- many ADEs in the elderly may be decreased by removing all the preventable risk factors before a drug is prescribed (mainly DDIs and excess doses) and by reinforcing drug monitoring when an interfering acute disease occurs.[42]

6.20   Prescriber's Rule of Thumb: Start Low and Go Slow; Rarely Be the First or the Last to Use a Drug

Findings by Georgetown University researchers Cross et al.[43] support long-standing concerns among some experts that drugs are being studied at excessively high doses to emphasize their effects, and then marketed at the same high doses to maximize profits. Some experts say these patterns may contribute to the high frequency of serious and life-threatening drug side effects. The Georgetown study examined the recommended doses of 354 prescription drugs released from 1980 to 1999. Of those drugs, the instructions on the label were corrected for 73, or 21%, *after the drug came to market.* Eighty percent of the corrections consisted of a reduction in the original dose or a new restriction for certain groups of patients, like those with liver or kidney disease or those taking certain other medications.

- A Georgetown University team found that when its data were adjusted for the length of time a drug was on the market, those released from 1995 to 1999 had a chance of label correction that was roughly *threefold greater* than the rate for those released from 1980 to 1984.
- The corrections occurred after an average of 16 years on the market for the older drugs, but after only 3 years for newer ones.
- Under the FDA's fast-track policy, some watchdog groups have said drugs are being rushed to market without adequate testing.
- But most accelerated drug approvals were in cancer and HIV drugs and that these were no more likely to have labeling corrections than others.
- When a drug is being studied for possible marketing, the recommended dose is set very early in the process, based on small studies, so that manufacturers can efficiently carry out large studies of the drug's safety and efficacy. Because manufacturers have a strong incentive for the drug to show an effect in these studies, they often choose to study a relatively high dose, which may prove to be too high.
- Manufacturers can't test drugs in millions of people, so inevitably things are detected after approval. Indeed, it's "routine" that drug makers and regulatory agencies anticipate learning new details of a drug's effects and interactions after it goes to market. Even the largest clinical trials cannot always identify patterns that emerge when drugs are used by millions of people.
- This is not just an American phenomenon. Data compiled by the World Health Organization show that from 1982 to 2000, 115 drugs used in Europe had their standard doses corrected. Most were reductions, and they became more frequent in the middle to late 1990s.

- Drugs that were first marketed in the United States were no more likely to have dose corrections than were drugs first sold in Europe. Economic factors also come into the equation. Although some drugs have similar prices set for a range of doses, most "are priced on a per-milligram basis." This explains manufacturers' desire to sell as many milligrams as possible, while giving groups that pay for prescription drugs an incentive to finance studies supporting lower doses.For some experts, these results only confirm long-held views that drug-dosing and marketing policies are fundamentally flawed.

- Except in medical emergencies, for many patients a policy of "start low and go slow" is the best way to begin a prescription medicine, with frequent visits to a doctor who is committed to readjusting doses based on the patient's response.

- In the future genetic-based analysis of a patient's metabolic idiosyncrasies may help streamline this process.

- For many people the recommended drug doses especially for the elderly may be too high. Dosage recommendations are based on small studies done on young, healthy people, usually men. But people have such variability in size, shape, age, and patterns of metabolizing drugs, not to mention concurrent illnesses and necessary medicines, that the notion of a single optimal treatment makes no sense. About 75% of serious side effects occur at the recommended doses. If a dose is reduced 7 or 10 years after the drug was first marketed, one wonders how many side effects, what great costs to patients and to the medical system could have been avoided.

When a fact appears to be opposed to a long train of deductions, it invariably proves to be capable of bearing some other interpretation.

—**Sherlock Holmes**
A Study in Scarlet

6.21   Addendum to Patient Compliance and Nonadherence

Lower literacy and multiple medications cause (dangerous) medical misunderstandings. A study, released at the ACP Foundation's National Health Communications Conference, found that patients had difficulty comprehending five common prescription label instructions as to how much and how often medication should be taken. Misunderstanding was particularly high among those with lower literacy (8th grade level or below) and those who took many prescription drugs. In the study, researchers interviewed 395 English-speaking adults in three states. Study findings included the following:

- Although 70.7% of patients with low literacy correctly stated the instructions "Take two tablets by mouth twice daily," only 34.7% could demonstrate the number of pills to be taken daily.

- The rates of understanding individual labels ranged from 67.1% for the instructions for trimethoprim ("Take one tablet by mouth twice daily for seven days") to 91.1% for the instructions on the label for felodipine ("Take one tablet by mouth once each day").

- Most patients did not pay attention to the auxiliary (warning) labels (e.g., "Do not take dairy products within one hour of this medication") and those with low literacy were more likely to ignore them.

The study indicates that currently recommended methods for confirming patient understanding may be inadequate for identifying potential errors in medication administration.[44]
In an accompanying editorial these points were emphasized by Schillinger et al.

- The U.S. health care system largely operates under the assumption that all patients have high English-language literacy skills (1). In fact, many patients do not.
- Davis and coworkers (2) carefully show that a substantial proportion of users of the U.S. health care system do not understand the instructions on prescription bottle labels and are unable to correctly execute these instructions.
- Briefly, in a sample of ethnically diverse primary care patients from community health centers, a high rate of misunderstanding instructions on prescription labels were demonstrated for five common medications.
- Although the highest rates of misunderstanding across each of the five bottle labels (13 to 48%) occurred among patients with the lowest literacy levels.
- Misunderstanding was common even among those with the highest literacy levels (5 to 27%).
- In multivariate analyses, lower literacy and greater number of prescription medications taken were associated with misunderstanding.
- Even worse, among those who seemed to understand a standard prescription label—by correctly reading and restating the instructions.
- More than one-third of patients who take warfarin cannot demonstrate how to follow label instructions on their own medications (5).
- Rates of misunderstanding in a typical internal medicine practice are probably even higher, because greater medication burden, older age, and limited English-language proficiency are all associated with misunderstanding prescription labels (5).
- The practitioner thus must make sure that detailed medication reconciliation takes place—ensuring that the patient knows which medications have been prescribed and can demonstrate how to correctly use all of them.
- This must be part of routine practice.
- Medication reconciliation is important for all patients, but may be especially so for patients taking several medications, those taking medications that require stringent adherence, or those taking medications that cause adverse events if taken incorrectly.
- Providing a visual aid that shows the weekly pill regimen seems to increase comprehension of prescription labels and reduce the risk for medication-related adverse events (9).

You can, for example, never foretell what any one man will do, but you can say with precision what an average number will be up to. Individuals vary, but percentages remain constant. So says the statistician.

—Sherlock Holmes
The Sign of (the) Four

Some of my most interesting cases have come to me in this way.

—Sherlock Holmes
The Greek Interpreter

References

1. Sutcliffe KM, Lewton E, Rosenthal MM. Communication failures: an insidious contributor to medical mishaps. *Acad. Med.* 2004; 79: 186–194.
2. Lester GW, Smith SG. Listening and talking to patients. A similar remedy for managed care malpractice suits? *West J. Med.* 1993; 158(6): 639.
3. Eastaugh SR. Reducing litigation costs through better patient communication. *Phys. Exec.* 2004; 30(3): 36–38.
4. Moore PJ, Adler NE, Robertson PA. Medical malpractice: the effect of doctor-patient relations on medical patient perceptions and malpractice intentions. *West J. Med.* 2000; 173(4): 244–250.
5. Adamson TE, Tschann JM, Gullion DS, Oppenberg AA. Physician communication skills and malpractice claims. A complex relationship. *West J. Med.* 1989; 150(3): 356–360.
6. Johnson SC. Advance directives: from the perspective of the patient and the physician. *J. R Soc. Med.* 1996; 89: 568–570.
7. Ramsey G, Mitty E. Advance directives: protecting patient's rights. In: Mezey M, Fulmer T, Abraham I, Zwicker DA, eds. *Geriatric Nursing Protocols for Best Practice*. 2nd ed. New York: Springer; 2003.
8. Re Quinlan, 355 A.2d. (NJ 1976). *Cruzan v Director*, 110 S.Ct. (1990).
9. Velmans M. *Understanding Consciousness*. London, United Kingdom: Routledge, 2001.
10. Schiff ND, Rodriguez-Moreno D, Kamal A, et al. fMRI reveals large-scale network activation in minimally conscious patients. *Neurology* 2005; 64: 514–523.
11. Bernat JL. Questions remaining about the minimally conscious state. *Neurology* 2002; 58: 337–338.
12. Kelly D. *Critical Care Ethics*. Kansas City, KS: Sheed & Ward, 1991.
13. Bates DW, Cullen DJ, Laird N, et al. Incidence of adverse drug events and potential adverse drug events. Implications for prevention. ADE Prevention Study Group. *Am. J. Health Syst. Pharm.* 2001; 58: 1399–1405.
14. Ho PM, et al. Effect of medication non-adherence on hospitalization and mortality among patients with diabetes mellitus. *Arch. Int. Med.* 2006; 166: 1836–1841.
15. Ho PM, et al. Impact of medication therapy discontinuation. *Arch Int. Med.* 2006; 166: 1842–1847.
16. Tarn DM, et al. Physician communication when prescribing new medications. *Arch Int. Med.* 2006; 166: 1855–1862.
17. O'Conner PJ. Improving medicaltion adherence: challenges for physicians, payers, and policy makers. *Arch Int. Med.* 2006; 166: 1802–1804.
18. Chapman RH, Benner JS, Petrilla AA, et al. Predictors of adherence with antihypertensive and lipid-lowering therapy. *Arch Intern. Med.* 2005; 165: 1147–1152.
19. Lee JK, et al. Effect of a pharmacy care program on medication adherence and persistence, blood pressure, and low-density lipoprotein cholesterol: a randomized control trial. *JAMA* 2006; 296: 2563–2571.
20. Karch FE, Lasagna L. Toward the operational identification of adverse drug reactions. *Clin. Pharmacol. Ther.* 1977; 21: 247–254.
21. Simpson Jr RJ, Challenges for improving medication adherence. *JAMA* 2006; 296: 2614–2616.
22. Elwyn et al. Doing prescribing. *BMJ* 2003; 327: 864–867.
23. Chenaud C, et al. *Crit. Care* December 7, 2006.
24. *Mullins v. Parkview Hospital, Inc.* No. 02A-04-0412-CV-671 Indiana Ct. App., Fourth District, June 30, 2005.
25. Dissatisfaction with test result management systems in primary care. *Arch Intern. Med.* 2004; 164: 2223–2228.
26. Gurwitz JH, et al. Incidence and preventability of adverse drug events among older persons in the ambulatory setting. *JAMA* 2003; 289: 1107–1116.

27. Strassels SN. Miscalculated risk. AHRQ WebM&M [online journal]. August 2006. Available at: http://webmm.ahrq.gov/case.aspx?caseID=132AHRQ WebM&M is produced for the Agency for Healthcare Research and Quality by a team of editors at the University of California, San Francisco. The AHRQ WebM&M site was designed and implemented by Silverchair.

28. Tarn DM, et al. Physician communication when prescribing new medications. *Arch Intern. Med.* 2006; 166: 1855–1862.

29. Rothschild JM, Federico FA, Gandhi TK, et al. Analysis of medication-related malpractice claims: causes, preventability, and costs. *Arch Intern. Med.* 2002; 162: 2414–2420.

30. Institute of Medicine. *To Err Is Human.* Washington, DC: National Academy Press, 1999.

31. Leape LL, Bates DW, Cullen DJ, et al. Systems analysis of adverse drug events. *JAMA* 1995; 274: 35–43.

32. Allan EL, Barker KN. Fundamentals of medication error research. *Am. J. Hosp. Pharm.* 1990; 47: 555–571.

33. Barker KN, Felkey BG, Flynn EA, et al. White paper on automation in pharmacy. *Consult Pharm.* 1998; 13: 256–293.

34. Kubacki RI. Medication pass observation, a new survey technique. *Hosp. Pharm.* 1992; 27: 514–519.

35. Harsanyi CA. Monitoring the medication pass and drug regimen review: a state surveyor's perspective. *Consult Pharm.* 1997; 12: 803–806.

36. Centers for Medicare and Medicaid Services. Surveyor procedures for pharmaceutical service requirements in long term care facilities. Part two: surveyor methodology for detecting medication errors. State operations manual. Available at: http://www.hcfa.gov/pubforms/07_som/somap_n.htm. Accessed December 21, 2001.

37. Barker KN, Flynn EA, Pepper GA, et al. Medication errors observed in 36 health care facilities. *Arch. Intern. Med.* 2002; 9; 162: 1897–1903.

38. Beers MH, Munekata M, Storrie M. The accuracy of medication histories in the hospital medical records of elderly persons. *J. Am. Geriatr. Soc.* 1990; 38: 1183–1187.

39. Winterstein AG, Hatton RC, Gonzalez-Rothi R, et al. Identifying clinically significant preventable adverse drug events through a hospital's database of adverse drug reaction reports. *Am. J. Health Syst. Pharm.* 2002; 15; 59: 1742–1749.

40. Whipple JK, Ausman RK, Quebbeman EJ. Narcotic use in the hospital: reasonably safe? *Ann. Pharmacother.* 1992; 26: 897–901.

41. Hafner Jr JW, Belknap SM, Squillante MD, et al. Adverse drug events in emergency department patients. *Ann. Emerg. Med.* 2002; 39: 258–267.

42. Doucet J, Jego A, Noel D, et al. Preventable and non-preventable risk factors for adverse drug events related to hospital admission in the elderly. A prospective study. *Clin. Drug Invest.* 2002; 22: 385–392.

43. Cross J, Lee H, Westelinck A, et al. Postmarketing drug dosage changes of 499 FDA-approved new molecular entities, 1980–1999. *Pharmacoepidemiol. Drug Saf.* 2002; 11: 439–446.

44. Davis TC, Wolf MS, Bass 3rd PF, Thompson JA, Tilson HH, Neuberger M, et al. Literacy and misunderstanding prescription drug labels. *Ann. Intern. Med.* 2006; 146: 887–894.

For Further Reading

Abughosh SM, Kogut SJ, Andrade SE, Larrat P, Gurwitz JH. Persistence with lipid-lowering therapy: influence of the type of lipid-lowering agent and drug benefit plan option in elderly patients. *J. Manag. Care Pharm.* 2004; 10: 404–411. PUBMED.

Andrade SE, Graham DJ, Staffa JA, et al. Health plan administrative databases can efficiently identify serious myopathy and rhabdomyolysis. *J. Clin. Epidemiol.* 2005; 58: 171–174.

Andrade SE, Walker AM, Gottlieb LK, et al. Discontinuation of antihyperlipidemic drugs–do rates reported in clinical trials reflect rates in primary care settings? *N Engl. J. Med.* 1995; 332: 1125–1131.

Aspden P, Wolcott J, Bootman JL, Cronenwett LR, eds. *Preventing Medication Errors: Quality Chasm Series.* Committee on Identifying and Preventing Medication Errors. Board on Health Care Services. Institute of Medicine of the National Academies. The National Academies Press. Washington, DC, 2006, p. 3. Available at: http://www.iom.edu/CMS/3809/22526/35939. aspx; prepublication copy (uncorrected proofs) available at: http://www.nap.edu/catalog/11623.html#toc. Accessed July 25, 2006; press release (July 20, 2006) available at: http://www8.nationalacademies.org/onpinews/newsitem.aspx?RecordID=11623. Accessed July 26, 2006.

Associated Press. Campaign on hospital errors saves lives. *New York Times.* June 15, 2006. Available at: http://www.nytimes.com/2006/06/15/health/15hospitals.html. Accessed July 25, 2006.

Avorn J, Shrank W. Highlights and a hidden hazard—the FDA's new labeling regulations. *N Engl. J. Med.* 2006; 354: 2409–24011. [PMID: 16760439].

Bates DW, Cullen DJ, Laird N, et al. Incidence of adverse drug events and potential adverse drug events. Implications for prevention. ADE Prevention Study Group. *JAMA* 1995; 274: 29–34.

Bates DW, Spell N, Cullen DJ, et al. The costs of adverse drug events in hospitalized patients. Adverse Drug Events Prevention Study Group. *JAMA* 1997; 277: 307–311. *Abstract.*

Benner JS, Glynn RJ, Mogun H, Neumann PJ, Weinstein MC, Avorn J. Long-term persistence in use of statin therapy in elderly patients. *JAMA* 2002; 288: 455–461.

Berg JS, Dischler J, Wagner DJ, Raia JJ, Palmer-Shevlin N. Medication compliance: a healthcare problem. *Ann. Pharmacother.* 1993; 27(9 suppl): S1–S24.

Blackburn DF, Dobson RT, Blackburn JL, Wilson TW. Cardiovascular morbidity associated with nonadherence to statin therapy. *Pharmacotherapy* 2005; 25: 1035–1043. PUBMED.

Blaschke T. Writing prescriptions. In: Carruthers SG, Hoffman BB, Melmon KL, et al., eds. *Melmon and Morrelli's Clinical Pharmacology: Basic Principles in Therapeutics.* 4th ed. New York: McGraw-Hill, Inc., 2000: 1267–1288.

Buckman R. Breaking bad news: Why is it so difficult? *BMJ* 1984; 288: 159–1599.

Burnier M. Long-term compliance with antihypertensive therapy: another facet of chronotherapeutics in hypertension. *Blood Press. Monit.* 2000; 5(suppl 1): S31–S34.

Chui MA, Deer M, Bennett SJ, et al. Association between adherence to diuretic therapy and health care utilization in patients with heart failure. *Pharmacotherapy* 2003; 23: 326–332.

Classen DC, Pestotnik SL, Evans RS, Lloyd JF, Burke JP. Adverse drug events in hospitalized patients. Excess length of stay, extra costs, and attributable mortality. *JAMA* 1997; 277: 301–306.

Claxton AJ, Cramer J, Pierce C. A systematic review of the associations between dose regimens and medication compliance. *Clin. Ther.* 2001; 23: 1296–1310.

Col N, Fanale JE, Kronholm P. The role of medication noncompliance and adverse drug reactions in hospitalizations of the elderly. *Arch. Intern. Med.* 1990; 150: 841–845.

Cramer JA. Optimizing long-term patient compliance. *Neurology* 1995; 45(2 suppl 1): S25–S28.

Cramer JA, Mattson RH, Prevey ML, Scheyer RD, Ouellette VL. How often is medication taken as prescribed? A novel assessment technique. *JAMA* 1989; 261: 3273–3277.

Cramer JA, Scheyer RD, Mattson RH. Compliance declines between clinic visits. *Arch. Intern. Med.* 1990; 150: 1509–1510.

Crespo-Fierro M. Compliance/adherence and care management in HIV disease. *J. Assoc. Nurses AIDS Care.* 1997; 8: 43–54.

Cullen DJ, Bates DW, Small SD, Cooper JB, Nemeskal AR, Leape LL. The incident reporting system does not detect adverse drug events: a problem for quality improvement. *Jt. Comm. J. Qual. Improv.* 1995; 21: 541–548.

Eisen SA, Miller DK, Woodward RS, Spitznagel E, Przybeck TR. The effect of prescribed daily dose frequency on patient medication compliance. *Arch. Intern. Med.* 1990; 150: 1881–1884.

Esch AF, Inman WH, Westerholm B. WHO Tech Rep Ser, Report No. 498, 1971.

Feinstein AR. On white-coat effects and the electronic monitoring of compliance. *Arch. Intern. Med.* 1990; 150: 1377–1378.

Feldman R, Bacher M, Campbell N, Drover A, Chockalingam A. Adherence to pharmacologic management of hypertension. *Can. J. Public Health* 1998; 89: I16–I18.

Ghose K. The need for a review journal of drug use and the elderly. *Drugs Aging* 1991: 2–5.

Gilbert JR, Evans CE, Haynes RB, et al. Predicting compliance with a regimen of digoxin therapy in family practice. *Can. Med. Assoc. J.* 1980; 123: 119 [PMID 7260749].

Grant RW, O'Leary KM, Weilburg JB, Singer DE, Meigs JB. Impact of concurrent medication use on statin adherence and refill persistence. *Arch. Intern. Med.* 2004; 164: 2343–2348.

Greenberg RN. Overview of patient compliance with medication dosing: a literature review. *Clin. Ther.* 1984; 6: 592–599.

Gurwitz JH, Field TS, Harrold LR, et al. Incidence and preventability of adverse drug events among older persons in the ambulatory setting. *JAMA* 2003; 289: 1107–1116.

Harrold LR, Andrade SE, Eisner M, et al. Identification of patients with Churg-Strauss syndrome (CSS) using automated data. *Pharmacoepidemiol. Drug Saf.* 2004; 13: 661–667.

Haynes RB, McDonald H, Garg AX, Montague P. Interventions for helping patients to follow prescriptions for medications. *Cochrane Database Syst. Rev.* 2002(2): CD000011.

Haynes RB, McDonald HP, Garg AX. Helping patients follow prescribed treatment: clinical applications. *JAMA* 2002; 288: 2880–2883.

Haynes RB, McDonald HP, Garg AX. How can we help patients to follow the treatment we've prescribed? *JAMA* 2002; 288: 2880 [PMID 12472330].

Haynes RB, Yao X, Degani A, et al. Interventions for enhancing medication adherence. *Cochrane Database Syst. Rev.* 2005; 4: CD000011 [PMID 16235271].

Ickovics JR, Meisler AW. Adherence in AIDS clinical trials: a framework for clinical research and clinical care. *J. Clin. Epidemiol.* 1997; 50: 385–391.

Institute for Healthcare Improvement. Preventing Adverse Drug Events through Medication Reconciliation. Saving Lives Web & Action Programs. Begins May 17, 2005. Available at: http://www.ihi.org/IHI/Programs/ConferencesAndTraining/WebandACTIONMedReconciliation.htm. Accessed August 15, 2006.

Institute of Medicine. *Health Literacy: A Prescription to End Confusion.* Washington, DC: National Academy Press, 2004.

Jackevicius CA, Mamdani M, Tu JV. Adherence with statin therapy in elderly patients with and without acute coronary syndromes. *JAMA* 2002; 288: 462–467.

Joint Commission on Accreditation of Healthcare Organizations. Using medication reconciliation to prevent errors. Sentinel Event Alert. Issue 35—January 25, 2006. Available at: http://www.jointcommission.org/SentinelEvents/SentinelEventAlert/sea_35.htm. Accessed August 15, 2006.

Kass MA, Meltzer DW, Gordon M. A miniature compliance monitor for eyedrop medication. *Arch. Ophthalmol.* 1984; 102: 1550–1554.

Kastrissios H, Suarez JR, Hammer S, Katzenstein D, Blaschke TF. The extent of non-adherence in a large AIDS clinical trial using plasma dideoxynucleoside concentrations as a marker. *AIDS* 1998; 12: 2305–2311.

Koh Y, Li SC. A new algorithm to identify the causality of adverse drug reactions. *Drug Saf.* 2005; 28: 1159–1161.

Kohn K, Corrigan JM, Donaldson MS. *To Err Is Human: Building a Safer Health System.* Washington, DC: National Academy of Sciences, National Academy Press, 2000. Available at: http://www.nap.edu/catalog/9728.html. Accessed July 26, 2006.

Kramer MS, Leventhal JM, Hutchinson TA, Feinstein AR. An algorithm for the operational assessment of adverse drug reactions. I. Background, description, and instructions for use. *JAMA* 1979; 242: 623–632.

Kruse W, Rampmaier J, Ullrich G, Weber E. Patterns of drug compliance with medications to be taken once and twice daily assessed by continuous electronic monitoring in primary care. *Int. J. Clin. Pharmacol. Ther.* 1994; 32: 452–457.

Kutner M, Greenberg E, Baer J. *A First Look at the Literacy of America's Adults in the 21st Century.* Washington, DC: National Center for Education Statistics, U.S. Department of Education, 2005.

Leenen FH, Wilson TW, Bolli P, et al. Patterns of compliance with once versus twice daily antihypertensive drug therapy in primary care: a randomized clinical trial using electronic monitoring. *Can. J. Cardiol.* 1997; 13: 914–920.

Lenert LA, Markowitz DR, Blaschke TF. *Primum non nocere?* Valuing of the risk of drug toxicity in therapeutic decision making. *Clin. Pharmacol. Ther.* 1993; 53: 285–291.

Levy G, Zamacona MK, Jusko WJ. Developing compliance instructions for drug labeling. *Clin. Pharmacol. Ther.* 2000; 68: 586–591.

Lisby M, Nielsen LP, Mainz J. Errors in the medication process: frequency, type, and potential clinical consequences. *Int. J. Qual. Health Care* 2005; 17: 15.

Macharia WM, Leon G, Rowe BH, et al. An overview of interventions to improve appointment keeping for medical services. *JAMA* 267: 1813, 1992 [PMID 1532036].

Machtinger E, Wang F, Chen L, Rodríguez M, Wu S, Schillinger D. A visual medication schedule to improve anticoagulant care: a randomized controlled trial [Forthcoming]. *Jt. Comm. J. Qual. Patient Saf.* 2007.

Marcellino K, Kelly WN. Potential risks and prevention, part 3: drug-induced threats to life. *JAMA* 1995; 274: 29–34.

McCannon CJ, Schall MW, Calkins DR, Nazem AG. Saving 100,000 lives in US hospitals. *BMJ* 2006; 332: 1328–1330.

McCarthy D, Blumenthal D. Committed to Safety: Ten Case Studies on Reducing Harm to Patients: The Commonwealth Fund; April 2006. Report No. Publication No. 923.

McDonnell PJ, Jacobs MR. Hospital admissions resulting from preventable adverse drug reactions. *Ann. Pharmacother.* 2002; 36: 1331–1336.

Naranjo CA, Busto U, Sellers EM, et al. A method for estimating the probability of adverse drug reactions. *Clin. Pharmacol. Ther.* 1981; 30: 239–245.

Nebeker JR, Barach P, Samore MH. Clarifying adverse drug events: a clinician's guide to terminology, documentation, and reporting. *Ann. Intern. Med.* 2004; 140: 795–801.

Osterberg L, Blaschke T. Adherence to medication. *N Engl. J. Med.* 2005; 353: 487–497.

Osterberg LG, Rudd P. Medication adherence for antihypertensive therapy. In: Oparil S, Weber MA, eds. *Hypertension: A Companion to Brenner And Rector's The Kidney.* 2nd ed. New York: Elsevier Mosby, 2005, pp. 848.

Paasche-Orlow MK, Riekert KA, Bilderback A, Chanmugam A, Hill P, Rand CS, et al. Tailored education may reduce health literacy disparities in asthma self-management. *Am. J. Respir. Crit. Care Med.* 2005; 172: 980–986. [PMID: 16081544].

Paes AH, Bakker A, Soe-Agnie CJ. Impact of dosage frequency on patient compliance. *Diabetes Care* 1997; 20: 1512–1517.

Pullar T, Kumar S, Tindall H, Feely M. Time to stop counting the tablets? *Clin. Pharmacol. Ther.* 1989; 46: 163–168.

Raebel MA, Carroll NM, Andrade SE, et al. Monitoring of drugs with a narrow therapeutic range in ambulatory care. *Am. J. Manag. Care* 2006; 12: 268–274.

Reducing and Preventing Adverse Drug Events to Decrease Hospital Costs. Rockville, Md: AHRQ; March 2001. Report No. 01-0020.

Rodgers PT, Ruffin DM. Medication nonadherence: Part II—A pilot study in patients with congestive heart failure. *Manag. Care Interface* 1998; 11: 67–69, 75.

Rosen MI, Rigsby MO, Salahi JT, Ryan CE, Cramer JA. Electronic monitoring and counseling to improve medication adherence. *Behav. Res. Ther.* 2004; 42: 409–422.

Rozich JD, Haraden CR, Resar RK. Adverse drug event trigger tool: a practical methodology for measuring medication related harm. *Qual. Saf. Health Care* 2003; 12: 194–200.

Rudd P. Compliance with antihypertensive therapy: raising the bar of expectations. *Am. J. Manag. Care* 1998; 4: 957–966.

Schiff GD, Fung S, Speroff T, McNutt RA. Decompensated heart failure: symptoms, patterns of onset, and contributing factors. *Am. J. Med.* 2003; 114: 625–630.

Schillinger D, Piette J, Grumbach K, Wang F, Wilson C, Daher C, et al. Closing the loop: physician communication with diabetic patients who have low health literacy. *Arch. Intern. Med.* 2003; 163: 83–90. [PMID: 12523921].

Schillinger D, Wang F, Palacios J, et al. Language, literacy, and communication regarding medication in an anticoagulation clinic: a comparison of verbal vs. visual assessment [Forthcoming]. *J. Health Commun.* 2006; 11: 651–654.

Schillinger D, Wang F, Rodriguez M, Bindman A, Machtinger EL. The importance of establishing regimen concordance in preventing medication errors in anticoagulant care. *J. Health Commun.* 2006; 11: 555–567. [PMID: 16950728].

Schmidt TA, Norton RL, Tolle SW: Sudden death in the ED: Educating residents to compassionately inform families. *J. Emerg. Med.* 1992; 10: 643–647.

Schmidt TA, Tolle SW: Emergency physicians' responses to families following patient death. *Ann. Emerg. Med.* 1990; 19: 125–128.

Schroeder K, Fahey T, Ebrahim S. How can we improve adherence to blood pressure-lowering medication in ambulatory care? Systematic review of randomized controlled trials. *Arch. Intern. Med.* 2004; 164: 722–732.

Schumock GT, Thornton JP. Focusing on the preventability of adverse drug reactions. *Hosp. Pharm.* 1992; 27: 538.

Senst BL, Achusim LE, Genest RP, et al. Practical approach to determining costs and frequency of adverse drug events in a health care network. *Am. J. Health Syst. Pharm.* 2001; 58: 1126–1132.

Seravalli EP: The dying patient, the physician, and the fear of death. *N. Engl. J. Med.* 1988; 319: 1728–1730.

Shalansky SJ, Levy AR. Effect of number of medications on cardiovascular therapy adherence. *Ann. Pharmacother.* 2002; 36: 1532–1539.

Sokol MC, McGuigan KA, Verbrugge RR, Epstein RS. Impact of medication adherence on hospitalization risk and healthcare cost. *Med. Care* 2005; 43: 521–530.

Spilker B. Methods of assessing and improving compliance in clinical trials. In: Cramer JA, Spilker B, eds. *Patient Compliance in Medical Practice and Clinical Trials.* New York: Raven. 1991, pp. 37–56.

Stephenson BJ, Rowe BH, Macharia WM, et al. The rational clinical examination: is this patient taking the treatment as prescribed? *JAMA* 1993; 269: 2779 [PMID 8492406].

Stussman BJ. Advance data: National hospital ambulatory medical care survey; 1995 emergency department summary. Advance data from Vital and Health Statistics; no 285. Hyattsville, MD: National Center for Health Statistics, 1997.

Sykes N. Medical students' fears about breaking bad news. *Lancet* 1089; 2: 564.

Tarn DM, Heritage J, Paterniti DA, Hays RD, Kravitz RL, Wenger NS. Physician communication when prescribing new medications. *Arch. Intern. Med.* 2006; 166: 1855–1862. [PMID: 17000942].

Tolle SW. A program to teach residents humanistic skills for notifying survivors of a patient's death. *Acad. Med.* 1989; 64: 505–506.

Tuldra A, Fumaz CR, Ferrer MJ, et al. Prospective randomized two-arm controlled study to determine the efficacy of a specific intervention to improve long-term adherence to highly active antiretroviral therapy. *J. Acquir. Immune Defic. Syndr.* 2000; 25: 221–228.

Urquhart J. The electronic medication event monitor. Lessons for pharmacotherapy. *Clin. Pharmacokinet.* 1997; 32: 345–356.

Urquhart J. The odds of the three nons when an aptly prescribed medicine isn't working: non-compliance, non-absorption, non-response. *Br. J. Clin. Pharmacol.* 2002; 54: 212–220.

US Food and Drug Administration. FDA Clears Genetic Test That Advances Personalized Medicine: Test Helps Determine Safety of Drug Therapy. FDA News. August 22, 2005. Available at: http://www.fda.gov/bbs/topics/NEWS/2005/NEW01220.html (accessed August 15, 2006).

Wheeler AP, Jaquiss RD, Newman JH. Physician practices in the treatment of pulmonary embolism and deep venous thrombosis. *Arch. Intern. Med.* 1988; 148: 1321–1325.

Wilson E, Chen AH, Grumbach K, Wang F, Fernandez A. Effects of limited english proficiency and physician language on health care comprehension. *J. Gen. Intern. Med.* 2005; 20: 800–806. [PMID: 16117746].

Wolf MS, Davis TC, Shrank WH, Neuberger M, Parker RM. A critical review of FDA-approved Medication Guides. *Patient Educ. Couns.* 2006; 62: 316–322. [PMID: 16884888].

Young LR, Wurtzbacher JD, Blankenship CS. Adverse drug reactions: a review for healthcare practitioners. *Am. J. Manag. Care* 1997; 3: 1884–1906; quiz 909–910.

Zygmunt A, Olfson M, Boyer CA, Mechanic D. Interventions to improve medication adherence in schizophrenia. *Am. J. Psychiatry* 2002; 159: 1653–1664.

Proactive Strategies to Reduce Malpractice Risks in Psychiatry

7

WENDY J. HOOKMAN, MD AND MICHELE T. PATO, MD

7.1 Introduction

The most common causes of medical malpractice lawsuits can be averted by simple preventive moves and proactive strategies.

This book teaches strategies—knowing at all times who you are, the role you play as the medical expert witness, and yours and the opposition's strategies—not just the tactics. In that regard, we will now discuss proactive strategies to reduce malpractice risks in psychiatry. We will explore how and why this chapter on *Proactive Strategies to Reduce Malpractice Risks in Psychiatry* is important in forearming the primary care physician, the internist, and also the medical expert witness in this subject.

Common denominators to decrease risks for the spectrum of medical practice including psychiatry are the following:

- Disclose any information that a reasonable practitioner in a similar situation would disclose ("professional standard of disclosure"); or the information that a reasonable patient would find material to his or her decision ("materiality standard").
- Maintain documentation of all communications to and from patients and to and from a third party about a patient with an automatic [system] mechanism for these notes to get into the appropriate patient's chart.
- Carefully choose a colleague to cover your practice whom you trust and know to be responsible and whose practice style is similar to your own.
- Informed consent should be obtained from all adult patients prior to the initiation of treatment, and from minor patients who are not legally authorized to provide consent. For minors who cannot provide consent, it should be obtained from parents or other legal custodians. Without proper documentation, of consent negligence claims are more likely to be successful.
- Know all the published guidelines encompassing the disorders you treat.
- Document the reasons why a treatment has or has not been performed according to the appropriate published guidelines.

7.2   Preventable Psychiatry Errors

Lawsuits against psychiatrists (as well as those physicians using psychotropic medications) fall into five main categories:

1. Failure to comprehensively evaluate and provide a safety plan for suicidal patients
2. Failure to ensure a safe environment for psychotic or suicidal inpatients
3. Failure to warn and protect others from potentially violent patients
4. Failure to inform patients about side-effect risk
5. Failure to follow appropriate procedures when away from your practice

7.2.1   Failure to Provide a Comprehensive Evaluation and Safety Plan for Suicidal Patients

It has been estimated that one in twenty psychiatrists are sued every year.[1] Fifty-one percent of psychiatrists report having had a patient who committed suicide[2] and postsuicide lawsuits account for the largest number of malpractice suits against psychiatrists.[3] Evaluating suicide risk can be difficult even for a well-trained psychiatrist, though, since up to one-third of the general population in the United States have suicidal thoughts at some point[4] and this number increases in a population seeking psychiatric help.

The inability to predict suicide has been demonstrated, so psychiatrists are not negligent for merely failing to predict suicide. To win a psychiatric malpractice suit, the plaintiffs—most often the family of a patient who has committed suicide—must prove that the psychiatrist owed a duty or standard of care to the patient, that the psychiatrist's care fell below that standard, and, as a result, the patient suffered injury or death. The standard of care includes providing a comprehensive evaluation and risk assessment and providing treatment and a safety plan consistent with that risk.[5,6]

7.2.1.1   Proactive Strategies

Conduct and document a comprehensive evaluation of the patient and his or her suicide risk including

1. prior and current suicidal thoughts and whether a plan was/is contemplated,
2. intensity and frequency of suicidal thoughts,
3. previous suicide attempts and gestures, and
4. substance abuse.

Consider hospitalizing high-risk patients. If a patient meets legal commitment criteria, failure to hospitalize the patient would likely violate duty to care. If you decide against hospitalization, you must provide a comprehensive safety plan and document doing so. Safety plans need to be tailored to the individual patient but should include

1. obtaining the patients permission to educate and involve family members or friends;
2. educating patient and family as to symptoms to watch for and what to do if the patient's condition worsens;

3. obtaining and documenting commitment from the patient and family for the safety plan. Make sure the safety plan is accessible to a covering physician in your absence;

4. restricting access to weapons. Make sure any weapons to which the patient has access are locked up by a friend or family member. If possible, it is often best to remove weapons from the house and withhold the knowledge of where they are from the patient; and

5. controlling access to medications that are fatal in overdose.

7.2.2 Failure to Ensure a Safe Environment for Psychotic or Suicidal Inpatients

When a patient is hospitalized with psychosis or suicidality, careful attention to restraint and monitoring systems is mandatory. The law requires us to use the "least-restrictive interventions" to manage patients, but psychiatrists can determine what this term means.[7] It is important to assess patients for dangerousness and to intervene appropriately. For example, a patient who is responding to internal stimuli telling him to hurt himself may need to be restrained, whereas another patient may require only observation.

Decisions about inpatient restraint and monitoring need to be made on a case-by-case basis but the psychiatrists thinking about his or her decision making process should be well documented. A psychiatrist's documentation of a patient's treatment is seen by juries as more factually accurate than subsequent court testimony—"your record was created when your only concern was documenting the facts"—and should include enough information so that someone who looks at the record, would know what services were provided to the patient, and understand why the psychiatrist chose or rejected certain modes of treatment.[8]

7.2.2.1 Proactive Strategies

- Acutely suicidal inpatients should be observed at all times and patient's location, activities, and behavior must be frequently documented.
- Suicidal inpatients' environments must also be evaluated and restricted. Suicidal inpatients may not have access to materials they could use to harm themselves, such as glass objects, shoelaces, plastic bags, and ingestible cleaning supplies.
- Restraints should be used only by trained staff and for only as long as the patient is dangerous to himself or others. The following guidelines must be followed and documented.[9]
  - Ensure the restrained patient's safety and observe him continuously.
  - Check pulse, BP, and range of motion in extremities usually every 15 min or less while patient is in seclusion or restraint.
  - Patient must be able to rotate head freely, and his or her airway must be unobstructed at all times.
  - Keep the patient as comfortable as possible.
  - Provide frequent opportunities for eating, drinking, and elimination, and continually assess physical comfort.
  - Assess the continuing need for restraint, and consider alternatives when possible.

- Alternative restraint systems such as emergency medication, seclusion rooms, or special observation should be considered for patients with the following relative contraindications.[10]
  - breathing problems,
  - head or spinal injuries,
  - history of recent fractures of surgeries,
  - history of sexual or physical abuse,
  - seizure disorder, and
  - pregnancy.

7.2.3   Failure to Warn and Protect Others from Potentially Violent Patients

The precedent for a physician's duty to warn and protect others from potentially violent patients was set by two cases: Tarasoff I and II.[11] The Tarasoff decisions arose when the parents of Tatiana Tarasoff, who had been killed in 1968 by fellow student Prosenjit Poddar, sought to sue Poddar's treating mental health professionals and their employer, the University of California. Before the killing, while Tatiana was visiting Brazil, Poddar had told his psychologist that he was thinking about killing a young woman. The psychologist guessed who the woman was and informed the campus police, who checked on Poddar but did not detain him. Poddar stopped seeing the psychologist, and after Tatiana returned to California, Poddar fatally stabbed her.

In Tarasoff I, the court ruled that a clinician has the duty to warn a potential victim, even if it violates doctor–patient confidentiality, if the clinician has information from a patient that an identified victim is at risk.

Tarasoff II extended the first case and established the clinician's duty to protect, not simply to warn, a potential victim. The ruling states that a clinician must "exercise reasonable care to protect the foreseeable victim." This means that warning the intended victim might not be enough but also may not be necessary, if the clinician takes reasonable care to protect the potential victim by admitting the patient to a secure psychiatric facility, for example.

Not all states have adopted the Tarasoff standard, so clinicians should familiarize themselves with laws in their states (Table 7.1).

7.2.3.1   *Proactive Strategies*

Psychiatrists should exercise their duty to warn and protect when

- a clearly identifiable person or group is at risk;
- risk of harm includes severe injury, death, or severe psychological harm; and
- danger is imminent and creates a sense of urgency.[12]

Risk factors for patient violence[13] should be clearly assessed and documented in making the decision to warn and protect

- personal history of violence is the single most predictive factor for future violence, followed closely by exposure to violence in the immediate family or circle of friends;

Table 7.1 "Warn and Protect" Statutes by State

Require Clinicians to Warn Potential Victims (n = 27 states)

Arizona	Massachusetts	Ohio
California	Mississippi	Oklahoma
Colorado	Minnesota	Pennsylvania
Delaware	Michigan	South Carolina
Idaho	Missouri	Tennessee
Indiana	Montana	Vermont
Kentucky	Nebraska	Washington
Louisiana	New Hampshire	Wisconsin
Maryland	New Jersey	Utah

Allow Clinicians to Warn Potential Victims but Do Not Require It (n = 11 states)

Alaska	Florida	Rhode Island
Connecticut	Illinois	Texas
District of Columbia	New York	West Virginia
Oregon		

No Definitive Law on a Clinician's Duty to Warn and Protect (n = 14 states)

Alabama	Kansas	North Dakota
Arkansas	Maine	South Dakota
Georgia	Nevada	Virginia[a]
Hawaii	New Mexico	Wyoming
Iowa	North Carolina	

Source: Herber, P.B., Young, K.A., *J. Am. Acad. Psychiatr. Law*, 30, 275–281, 2002.
[a] Rejected the "warn and protect" provisions of the Tarasoff rulings.

- gender—Men are 10 times more likely to be violent than women;
- current substance abuse increases the likelihood of violence by reducing inhibitions;
- mental incapacity interferes with judgment; and
- having a detailed plan for violence increases the risk that a threat will be carried out.

When documenting the decision whether or not to warn in a particular case, a psychiatrist should include

- what the patient said;
- the seriousness of the threat;
- the history of the situation; and
- the clinicians actions in response to the threat, such as calling the police or detaining the patient.

A psychiatrist's obligation to take reasonable precautions to prevent harm threatened by a patient may be fulfilled when the clinician has seriously considered the following:

- Communicating the threat to the identified victim or victims.
- Notifying a law enforcement agency where the patient or any potential victim resides.
- Arranging for the patient to be hospitalized voluntarily.
- Taking legally appropriate steps to initiate proceedings for involuntary hospitalization.

- Because laws vary by state, the best course of action is to practice within the proper standard of care and be guided by professional ethics, while maintaining an updated knowledge of the relevant statutory and case law.[14]
- Helping identify any trends in certain states, see Table 7.1.

7.2.4   Failure to Inform Patients about Side-Effect Risk

Failure to inform or adequately inform about side-effect risk is the malpractice area where psychiatrists are often vulnerable, yet these claims can be avoided with careful disclosure and documentation habits.

Informed consent should be obtained from all adult patients prior to the initiation of psychiatric treatment, and from minor patients who are legally authorized to provide consent. For minors who cannot provide consent, it should be obtained from parents or other legal custodians. Without proper documentation, negligence claims are more likely to be successful.

7.2.4.1   Proactive Strategies

Always include the following documentation for each patient in the correct medical record[15]:

- Diagnosis.
- Nature and purpose of the proposed treatment.
- Frequent risks that may pose little danger but might concern the patient or care giver.
- Risks that though infrequent may pose significant harm and thus should be brought to the physicians attention urgently.
- Reasonably expected benefits.
- Alternate treatments, their risks and benefits.
- Risks of no treatment.
- Legal standards may require physicians to disclose the information that a reasonable practitioner in a similar situation would disclose ("professional standard of disclosure"); or the information that a reasonable patient would find material to his or her decision ("materiality standard"); or may specify exactly which information should be disclosed.

7.2.5   Failure to Follow Appropriate Procedures When Away from Your Practice

It is important that patients have access to the same high-quality care from another psychiatrist when you are away or otherwise unavailable. If patients receive substandard care when you are away, both you and the covering psychiatrist may be held liable.

7.2.5.1   Proactive Strategies

If you plan to be away from your practice for an extended period of time, be sure to take the following precautions:

- Inform the covering physician of any cases you are particularly concerned about so they can be better prepared to manage them. If at all possible, prepare a written list of your patients you are concerned about including a brief summary, their medications, and contact information.

- Prepare your patients for scheduled absences. Be specific both verbally and in writing of the time you will be away and instructions to obtain care in your absence. Prepare a written list of contact numbers and instructions, including the instruction to call 911 or proceed to a local emergency room in case of emergency.
- Instruct staff not to release confidential information to anyone without your advance approval.
- Leave written policies for staff on how to handle emergency situations.
- Be aware of potential breaches of confidentiality if you communicate by cellular phone, fax, or voice mail, especially in a hotel or conference center.
- Maintain documentation of all calls to and from patients and to and from a third party about a patient. Be sure to have a mechanism for these notes to get into the appropriate patient's chart upon your return.

References

1. Lowenkopf EL. Memoirs of a malpractice suit. *J. Am. Acad. Psychoanal.* 2003; 23: 731–748.
2. Chemtob CM, Hamada RS, Bauer GB, et al. Patient suicide: frequency and impact on psychiatrists. *Am. J. Psychiatr.* 1988; 125: 224–228.
3. Packman WL, O'Connor PT, Bongar B, Orthwein J. Legal issues of professional negligence in suicide cases. *Behav. Sci. Law* 2004; 22: 697–713.
4. Hirschfeld RM, Russell JM. Assessment and treatment of suicidal patients. *N. Engl. J. Med.* 1997 Sep 25; 337(13): 910–915.
5. Pokoryy AD. Prediction of suicide in psychiatric patient. *Arch. Gen. Psychiatr.* 1983; 40: 249–257.
6. Pokorny AD. Suicide prediction revisited. *Suicide Life Threat Behav.* 1993; 23: 1–10.
7. Grant JE. Restraint and monitoring of psychotic or suicidal patients. *Curr. Psychiatr.* 2005; 11: 144.
8. Bender E. Psychiatrists can minimize malpractice-suit anxiety. Psychiatr. News 2003; 38(16): 11.
9. Joint Commission on Accreditation of Healthcare Organizations. Behavioral healthcare FAQs on special interventions. Available at http://www.jcaho.org/.
10. Sullivan AM, Barron CT, Bezman J, et al. The safe treatment of the suicidal patient in the inpatient setting: a proactive approach. *Psychiatr. Quart.* 2005; 76: 67–83.
11. Tarasoff v. Regents of the University of California, 118 Cal. Rptr. 129 (Cal. 1974) (Tarasoff I), modified by Tarasoff V. Regents of the Univ. Of Cal., 551 P. 2d 334 (Cal. 1976) (Tarasoff II).
12. Chaimowitz G, Glancy G. The duty to protect. *Can. J. Psychiatr.* 2002; 47: 1–4.
13. Buckner F, Firestone M. Where the public peril begins: 25 years after Tarasoff. *J. Legal Med.* 2000; 21: 187–222.
14. Kachigian C, Felthaus ER. Court responses to Tarasoff statutes. *J. Am. Acad. Psychiatr. Law* 2004; 32: 263–273.
15. Principles of Informed Consent in Psychiatry. Resource document available from the APA at http://www.psych.org/edu/other_res/lib_archives/archives/199601.pdf (link checked 4/27/07).

What You Must Know about Managed-Care Snares and Punitive Damages

The future ain't what it used to be.

—**Yogi Berra**

8.1 Managed-Care Liability Suits and Punitive Damages

8.1.1 Introduction

You know the old question about where does an 800-pound gorilla sit? Answer, anywhere he chooses. The Employee Retirement Income Security Act (ERISA) is the big gorilla in the room. This 800-pound gorilla known as managed-care organizations (MCOs) has over the past 25 years dramatically changed the way U.S. medicine has been practiced.

What you should know is that it is difficult to initiate a civil suit like medical malpractice against a medical care organization because of ERISA protections.

This has turned trial lawyers into suing either the physician or the MCO for corporate liability or corporate negligence ranging from such reasons as negligent credentialing of physicians, negligent supervision of physicians, negligence in selecting a health care provider, and negligent decisions to extend or renew the provider's participation status.

In this chapter, we will review how much we really do not know about the future of managed care and where managed care is going with respect to litigation. We will, however, review the physician's risks of liability in MCOs with a summary of points of key articles on this subject. We will especially review the points made about punitive damages, which is a most feared suit by the physician since punitive damages can bankrupt you because these damages are usually not covered by your medical malpractice insurance (for a more detailed reference list of the papers described in this chapter please *see* appendix). In this chapter, we will see how malpractice attorneys are attempting and winning high amounts of punitive damages from physicians by showing that the patient's diagnosis and treatment was "negligent deliberately and intentionally with the conscious disregard for the patient's safety."

The participating physician may justifiably fear that the MCO will not back him since the courts have made it difficult to prove that the MCO is liable for the negligence of the participating physician.

Preventive moves are spelled out on how to avoid managed-care medical malpractice claims.

The authors of the *Legal Answer Book for Managed Care*[1] (Aspen Health Law Center; 1995, ISBN#0-8342-0700) summarize several important points for the physician:

1. Changes in the law concerning liability of MCOs make civil suits still difficult but may allow punitive damages.
2. One of the critical developments in American health care law over the past 25 years has been the expansion of the federal preemption of state insurance law by ERISA of 1974, as amended, 29 U.S.C. §§1001-1461.
3. Congress enacted ERISA in 1974 to safeguard employees' pension and other employment benefit plans and to ease the compliance efforts of national corporations by creating a single federal law. ERISA preempted a broad group of state laws pertaining to employee-benefit plans. *The Employee Retirement Income Security Act of 1974 (ERISA) law preempts any state legislation affecting benefit plans.*
4. Although such a consequence was not envisioned at the time ERISA was passed, the statute has been used to shield organizations that administer employer-sponsored health insurance plans—most notably, managed-care plans—from most types of lawsuits.
5. The Supreme Court has affirmed that the administration of health benefits by self-funded employers is governed by ERISA and, therefore, that claims arising from benefits disputes should be resolved in *federal courts.*
6. But, in a recent decision, *Dukes v. U.S. Health-care Inc.*, the Court of Appeals for the Third Circuit concluded that medical malpractice claims generally do not fall under ERISA preemption. However, it is often unclear states the report whether a particular claim should be considered an ERISA benefits dispute or a traditional medical malpractice claim, based on allegations of poor-quality care.
7. The Dukes decision has identified a number of thorny issues that will likely arise as similar cases are argued in the future: "We recognize," said the court, "that the relevant inquiry is not whether there was an exception of acceptably competent services, but rather whether there was an agreement to displace the quality standard found in the otherwise applicable law with a contract standard."

A summary of conclusions from Horsham and Berlin[2,3] (the median jury award increased by 43% between 1999 and 2000) are as follows:

1. The proportion of awards over $1 million, which was 34% in 1996, increased to 52% in 2000.
2. More than half of all awards are currently over $1 million, with the average award at $3.5 million.
3. Although approximately 70–80% of all medical malpractice actions resulted in no indemnity payments, claims that are dropped have an average cost of $16,745, claims that are settled before trial have an average cost of $39,891, and claims that go to trial average $85,700.
4. These numbers represent only the legal fees.
5. Because of the fear of large jury awards, only 7–13% of cases filed went to trial, and of these only 1–1.5% resulted in a decision for the plaintiff.

6. Overall, 33% of all lawsuits resulted in monetary compensation (32% settled out of court and about 1% settled with jury trial).
7. In 1999, the median time between the negligent incident and the receipt of compensation was 45 months.
8. Only one-third of every dollar awarded to the plaintiff was actually received by the injured party, with the remainder going to pay attorneys and court costs.

8.2   Judicial and Legislative Changes Portend More Frequent Litigation against Managed-Care Organizations

The conclusions of the study on managed care by the Robert Wood Johnson Foundation report are the following:

- The structures of managed-care delivery systems—the internal regulations, relationships, and reimbursement mechanisms—are now being intensively scrutinized by medical malpractice plaintiff attorneys.
- Judicial and legislative changes portend more frequent litigation against MCOs e.g., *the largest malpractice reinsurer of MCOs in the country, Lexington Insurance (Boston), had a 252 percent increase between 1990 and 1997 in claims against such organizations*, whereas the overall number of claims handled by the company was generally flat over that period.
- New types of suits already are emerging, and more surely will follow, as plaintiffs' attorneys and the courts gain a clearer understanding of managed care and the differences among managed-care structures and whether physicians are *employees or independent contractors*.
- Courts have reached a few highly publicized verdicts against MCOs, *but so far these health plans are less likely to be sued than are doctors and hospitals*.
- In the mid-1990s, the Supreme Court began to send signals that the preemption of state laws by ERISA might be less of an open-and-shut matter than was previously thought. The signals have clearly registered with state and lower federal courts, particularly, in the area of claims against MCOs.
- Most legal commentators now see possibilities for the growth of institutional liability in the managed-care arena.
- A number of bills designed to protect patients that are debated in Congress would support suits by plaintiffs, either by bolstering the remedies available under ERISA or by explicitly allowing state jurisdiction over claims based on delay or denial of benefits.

8.3   Liability and Punitive Damages in Managed-Care Medical Malpractice Suits

Physicians fear punitive damages because they are usually not insured for punitive damages in commonly held medical malpractice insurance policies. And when it comes to managed-care suits, the attorneys usually go for the deep pockets. If they cannot get to the deep pockets—they go for the available pockets. Here is how this happens. There are many cases across the country in which patients or their survivors bring medical malpractice actions against physicians and the MCOs:

- Challenging that the patient received substandard care by various defendants.
- Including defendants such as hospitals, nursing facilities, and independent physician associations.
- That the provider defendants, according to the common denominator to these allegations, had
  a. Contracted with the patient's health maintenance organization (HMO) to provide treatment to the HMO's enrollees
  b. Contracted with a treating physician to provide care to HMO enrollees
  c. To contract between the HMO and the physician association, which provided for "capitated fees" based on the (increased) number of patients assumed rather than the (higher quality or) amount of care provided and the contract between the physician association and the treating physician provided for capitated fees.

The plaintiffs not only allege professional negligence, but usually have various other causes of action including

- willful misconduct,
- fraud based on the defendant's alleged conduct,
- withholding essential medical care for the purpose of financial gain, and
- that these financial gains are premised upon the defendant's alleged financial incentives to *withhold care.*

The courts usually hold that where the state law specifically authorizes capitation fee arrangements in the health insurance context, there is *protection (for the patient/plaintiff) against the physician who compromises patient care based on financial incentives or financial considerations.*

The courts usually maintain that "the appropriate remedy is a claim for professional negligence . . . because the physician's professional obligation is to comply with the prevailing professional standard of care in treating his patients."

This is usually when the attorneys go after the physician with grounds that can lead to punitive damages, that is, fraud.

The plaintiffs then

- allege that the defendants breached a fiduciary duty owed to the patient by entering into contracts that create a conflict of interest between the patient's health and their own financial interest;
- allege that the defendants also are committing fraud by failing to disclose this conflict of interest to the patient, thereby, inducing the patient to accept their treatment decisions, which are based on financial and not medical considerations;
- argue that the physician associations commit fraud by falsely assuring the HMO that it would provide enrollees with care that satisfies prevailing professional standards; and
- allege that nursing (LTCF) facilities also commit fraud by making similar false statements in its application for a state license.

And so it goes round and round and where will it stop? At this time nobody really knows.

There are some state laws, which mandate that

a. the right-to-sue provisions in some of these bills exclude punitive damages; others do not preclude them;
b. a wave of proposed state laws would give health care consumers the right to proceed legally against MCOs;
c. HMO contracts with independent medical providers, as held by a California appellate court, to render medical care may be held liable for contracting with provider that the HMO knows or should know is likely to provided substandard care; and
d. entering into a capitation fee arrangement with fees that are so low, it is foreseeable that the provider will deny necessary care.

In this case, *Pagarigan v. Aetna US Healthcare of California* No. NOB167722 (California Court of Appeals 2nd District, Division 7, October 25, 2005), the court while acknowledging that an HMO may indeed enter into capitation fee arrangements that create financial incentives for independent medical providers to minimize care, the court approved the imposition of liability upon an HMO when the fees set by such contracts are unreasonably low. Discussing the standard for liability of the court referred to

a. fees that are so low that the provider will have an undue economic incentive to deny medically necessary services or to deliver below standard care;
b. especially low levels of capitation payments, which foreseeably require or unduly encourage below standard care;
c. fees so low the HMO knows or should know it will require the provider to furnish substandard services or deny any medically necessary care to survive;
d. economic incentives to deny services or furnish low-quality care, which are substantially smaller than those inherent in the capitation system; and
e. HMO acts at its own peril when entering into capitation fee contracts subjecting itself to potential liability for an independent provider's malpractice in the event that a court or jury later determines that the contractual fess were too low to enable the provider to render proper care, under the test and criteria this court rendered.

An MCO will probably defend itself in any malpractice suit caused by a health care provider by attempting to avoid vicarious liability via

- arguing that the provider is not an employee;
- arguing that the provider acted outside the scope of employment (thus shifting the blame and liability on the individual physician);
- arguing that it did not present itself to the public as a direct provider of health care or as a provider of comprehensive health care services;
- joining the provider in arguing that the provider was not negligent;
- arguing that the provider did not cause the subscriber's injury; and
- arguing that a suit based on the malpractice of the healthcare provider is preempted by the ERISA.

8.4   The MCO, However, May Be Liable for Patients Who Reasonably Expect to Look to the MCO Rather Than the Individual Physicians

The data as of this writing is conflicting. According to the summary of opinions submitted in a Robert Wood Johnson (RWJ) report, there will be an increased frequency of future claims against MCOs. The reasons are that the plaintiffs' bar increasingly perceives MCOs to be the deepest pocket. Summary of points in the RWJ report:

1. The report points out the differences between fee for service (FFS) and MCOs.
2. FFS medicine involves a direct buyer–seller relationship: i.e., a physician implicitly agrees to treat a patient competently. The law imposes a duty on physicians who fail to provide their patients with care that meets professional standards and if not can be sued for medical malpractice. But in a managed-care system, patients believing they have suffered an injury may have a grievance not only with physician, but also with the MCO itself.
3. This is done when an MCO is vicariously responsible for the acts of physicians. If they are employees under the organization's control, as in staff model HMOs; or if it creates the appearance that a contract physician is its employee, agent; or under the MCO's control regarding clinical decision making, and the patient relies on this impression to his or her detriment.
4. IPA-model provider contracts sometimes require physicians to hold the MCO harmless for any malpractice-type claim.
5. The courts up to now generally have not found MCOs liable for the actions of independent contractor physicians.
6. The MCO, however, may be liable for patients who reasonably expect to look to the MCO rather than the individual physicians.
7. MCOs also may be found directly liable for their own actions. Liability claims could be made against MCOs by
   - Negligent credentialing of contracted providers
   - Negligent or excessive utilization review
   - Failure to implement specified quality assurance programs or redress identified deficits
   - Use of aggressive cost-control incentives designed to reduce utilization
   - Denial of benefits or "bad faith" by the plan
8. The courts' general reliance on community practice standards for determining professional negligence may put MCOs, particularly HMOs, at a disadvantage.
9. Medical malpractice law has evolved predominantly under FFS medicine and its incentives.
10. FFS practitioners are held to a standard of care that reflects the customary practice of similar practitioners.
11. What drives customary practice in the FFS setting is the expected benefit of a particular procedure to the patient, with little regard for its cost. However, providers in managed-care settings are expected to weigh both costs and benefits in their clinical decisions.
12. Use of a different diagnostic technique or therapy—even if it is cost effective—may be difficult to defend if an untoward outcome occurs, the *RWJ* report said. This is an important point for the physician to remember.

13. In some states, MCOs may find protection by invoking the "reputable minority" defense, which lets them show the acceptable alternatives to customary practice.
14. At least for now, the report said, most medical malpractice cases will be governed by state tort law and remain in state courts.
15. Larger health plans may try to include alternative dispute resolution (ADR) procedures and alternative standards of care in their subscriber contracts (as suggested by the Dukes decision), because in most states
    • the legal environment is uncertain,
    • plaintiff recoveries are more limited under ERISA than under prevailing tort law,
    • federal law is more hospitable to arbitration and other ADR mechanisms.[4-13]

Punitive damages and MCOs. The physician between the devil and the deep blue sea.

Punitive damages have recently occurred in 24% of all verdicts against insurers. This appears to be increasing with the increase in a study of nonmalpractice civil jury verdicts.

As mentioned earlier, there is nothing more threatening to the physician defendant in a medical malpractice suit than a threat of punitive damages, and the managed-care physician may find himself in this difficult position. Why?

• A physician is usually not insured for any actions falling under this category, including fraudulent or criminal acts.
• Punitive damages may mean money directly out of the pocket of a physician, even with excellent medical malpractice insurance.
• The physician feels personally threatened by an attorney on the attack mode for punitive damages.
• That is why it is often the motive for a quick settlement even though the physician's chances of being absolved completely for the alleged medical malpractice are high.
• Punitive damages is a problem that will certainly be growing if some medical malpractice attorneys like David M. Harney have their way.

In an interview, he stated that his "strategy (in medical malpractice suits against physicians) was to help boost the jury award by suing several doctors for punitive as well as compensatory damages" (see Emily Couric[14]). Furthermore he stated, "since Medical Malpractice Insurance Liability does not cover 'punitive damages,' "this promotes early settlement."

How does Harney rationalize punitive damages for the jury? Simple.

Harney believes as do many medical malpractice attorneys that "there is a 'built-in punitive amount for medical malpractices cases' because of the *fiduciary* obligation between the physician and the patient."

Harney's medical expert witnesses will be encouraged to testify that the defendant physician was "guilty of conscious disregard" of the plaintiff's safety. "This is a prerequisite, Harney says, "for awarding punitive damages in addition to compensatory damages."

In addition, Harney's method to attempt to prove that punitive damages should be awarded are by utilizing questions, which force the defendant physician to assume that each and every step of the patient's diagnosis and treatment are "intentionally followed."

So when he puts it all together in the summation, he reasons with the jury that

In order to do all of this "deliberately and intentionally," there had to be a conscious, awake disregard for the plaintiff's safety.

One of his reasons, he says, to attempt to get a punitive damages award from the jury "is because of California's (and other states) Supreme Court's ruling upholding the constitutionality of the state's $250,000 cap on medical malpractice awards."

Since the cap applies only to awards to compensate for noneconomic losses such as pain, suffering, inconvenience, physical impairment, and disfigurement, the malpractice attorneys in those states purposely aim for loss of income or compensation and punitive damages.

As of that 1998 interview with Harney, courts in Idaho, Illinois, Minnesota, Montana, New Hampshire, North Dakota, Ohio, Texas, and Virginia have found the caps unconstitutional. But courts in California, Florida, Indiana, Nebraska, and Wisconsin have upheld the constitutionality of these award limitations.

8.5   The Same Punitive Damages Rationale May Be Followed by Medical Malpractice Attorneys in Claims Against MCOs with the Physician Placed in the Middle of These Dangerous Waters

(Summary of major points from *Legal Answer Book for Managed Care*[1] by the Aspen Health Law Center; 1995, ISBN#0-8342-0700-1 may help to forecast the future of medical malpractice dangers for the managed-care physician.)

1. "As legislative and judicial trends thrust health care insurers into the liability spotlight, they introduce the entity into health care litigation that readily fits the profile of the classic defendant in cases involving *punitive damages*."
2. Consolidation in the insurance market has left a few very large national health insurers. These businesses are so large that juries may believe that punitive damages are necessary to get management to pay attention.
3. Portraying the plaintiff with the theme as David and the managed-care company as Goliath increases the plaintiff's chances of receiving a punitive-damages award, especially against "a corporation perceived as making business decisions, not a human being making simple errors."
4. The MCO can also be sued for corporate negligence—a term that encompasses the legal grounds for MCO liability based on the corporate activities of the MCO itself rather than on the care-related activities of the participating healthcare professionals.
5. What is the interface between corporate negligence and medical malpractice?
   a. Negligent credentialing and negligent supervision are examples of corporate negligence.
   b. An MCO that fails to exercise reasonable care to select a health care provider and who then negligently injures a subscriber can be held liable.
   c. Negligent credentialing can also apply to the decision to extend or renew the provider's participation status.
   d. A plaintiff (patient) must show negligence of the nonemployee provider to recover money from the MCO based on negligence.
   e. The plaintiff will be successful if two things can be accomplished to recover under "apparent agency."

1. The patient *reasonably views* the MCO rather than the individual physician as a source of health care.
2. The MCO engaged in conduct that caused the patient to reasonably believe that the MCO was the source of health care or that the MCO employed the negligent physician.
   i. The courts hold the MCOs liable for the negligence of their participating physicians on the basis of "respondent superior."
   ii. This can be accomplished if there is evidence of an employment contract between the negligent physician and the HMO in which the physician was paid an annual salary, fringe benefits, sick leave, life and health and malpractice insurance, vacation pay, and professional leave, etc.
   iii. To successfully sue an MCO for an injury caused by health care provider based on vicarious liability, the plaintiff must prove these four elements:
   - The negligent actor was the MCO's employee.
   - The employee who committed the negligent act was acting within the scope of employment.
   - The employee was negligent, that is, the employee owed the subscriber duty of care but failed to exercise reasonable care.
   - The employee's negligence caused the subscriber's injury.

Be that as it may, Studdert and Brennan[15] from the Rand Institute in what appears to be a contortionist thought pattern, make the following points:[3]

a. Physicians, insurers, employers, attorneys, and patients may be adversely affected by a rash of verdicts in which punitive damages are awarded.
b. Physicians have expressed increasing concern about the influences of managed care on the medical profession and on the care of patients.
c. Their views are echoed by hospital executives who see declining profit margins, caused in part by reduced payments from managed-care plans.
d. Many physicians would like to regain the control they believe they have lost to managed-care insurers.
e. Opening up managed-care plans to litigation is one way to make this happen. Not only does such litigation comport with many physicians' sense of justice—that health plans should be liable if they are going to be involved in making decisions about health care—but it also disrupts the economics of managed care for the insurer.
f. If the managed-care plans are saddled with the costs of litigation and payment of damages, especially punitive damages, then their management strategies may no longer be economically rational.
g. In this way, a substantial increase in costly litigation could reduce or modify considerably the scope of managed care.
h. The authors truly believe that awards of punitive damages will affect the behavior of insurers. Because of the peculiar interplay of media coverage and the psychological effect of punitive awards, the element of moral judgment appears to weigh heavily in corporate decision making.
i. In particular, the magnitude of punitive damages, the uncertainty surrounding their imposition, and the moral opprobrium attached to them all serve to compound

a special sensitivity that those in the health care field, including insurers and employers, tend to have with regard to litigation.

j. Thus, the authors maintain, "in a way reminiscent of Samuel Johnson's quip that nothing focuses the mind like one's impending execution," there is at least the promise that litigation would lead to a reemphasis on quality and greater attention to responsive care—good outcomes for patients.

k. However, they maintain, "the track record of litigation, at least in the domain of medical malpractice, provides few reasons for optimism." The authors also state that the clearest beneficiaries of an increase in punitive-damages awards in medical malpractice cases will be the attorneys who bring the cases to trial.

l. Arrangements for contingency fees will earn plaintiffs' lawyers a slice of any large award, and the specter of punitive damages will motivate the insurers who are defendants to settle more quickly than they would otherwise and for larger amounts.

m. Either way, the lawyers will win.

Because it has been shown that patient satisfaction varies inversely with frequency of claims.

1. See "Managed care, primary care, and the patient–practitioner relationship."[16] Department of Health Policy and Management, Johns Hopkins Bloomberg School of Public Health patients' ratings of their interpersonal relationships with their PCPs as measured by a scale.

2. This showed that gatekeeping arrangements that require patients to select a primary-care physician or obtain authorization for specialty referrals were associated with lower ratings of the patient–PCP relationship.

3. The authors concluded that managed health plans that loosen restrictions on provider choice, relax gatekeeping arrangements, or promote access to and continuity with PCPs, are likely to experience higher patient satisfaction with their primary-care practitioner relationships. Thus, lack of health insurance impedes the development of patients' relationships with their primary-care practitioners.

4. Grochowski[17] points out that over the past decade, managed care has become the dominant form of health care delivery, because it has reduced the cost of health care; however, it has also created serious conflicts of interest for physicians and has threatened the integrity of the traditional physician–patient relationship. As a preventive move against increasing patient claims

   a. that while rationing of health care is inevitable, physicians must not ration care at the bedside;

   b. that physicians must be advocates for their patients;

   c. that physicians must avoid conflicts of interest whenever possible;

   d. that physicians must put the needs of the patient before their own self-interests;

   e. that physicians must act in ways to promote trust in their relationship with patients.

Managed care uses financial incentives and restrictions on tests and procedures to attempt to influence physician decision making and limit costs. Increasingly, the public is questioning whether physicians are truly making decisions based on the patient's best interest or are unduly influenced by economic incentives. The authors addressed three specific scenarios physicians may encounter

- *Including allocation*: illustrated by a patient who is referred to a different ophthalmologist based on a new arrangement in the physician's group.
- *Access*: illustrated by a patient who wishes to see his own physician for a same-day visit rather than a nurse specialist.
- *Financial incentives*: illustrated by a patient who expects to have a test performed and a physician who does not believe the test is necessary but is afraid the patient will think the physician is not ordering the test because of financial incentives.

Using these scenarios,

- the authors suggest communication strategies that physicians can use to decrease the potential for disagreements; and
- the authors, in addition, propose strategies that health plans or physician groups can use to alleviate or resolve these disagreements.[18]

8.6 Ethics of Medical Practice under Managed Care

The ethics of medical practice under managed care should be examined from a pragmatic perspective that gives physicians more useful guidance in preventing patient claims against them and the MCO.

The following concrete ethical guides can help protect the MCO and the physician from litigation:

i. Financial incentives (by the MCO) should influence physicians to maximize the health of the group of patients under their care.
ii. Physicians should not enter into incentive arrangements that they would be embarrassed to describe accurately to their patients or that are not in common use in the market.
iii. Physicians should treat each patient impartially without regard to source of payment and in a manner consistent with the physician's own treatment style.
iv. If physicians depart from this ideal, they must tell their patients honestly.
v. It is desirable to differentiate medical treatment recommendations from insurance-coverage decisions by clearly assigning authority over these different roles and by having physicians to advocate for recommended treatment that is not covered.[19]

The question as to how far the U.S. Supreme Court would allow punitive damages to increase was answered at least temporarily by its 10/31/06 Philip Morris decision.

- The U.S. Supreme Court has been deeply split on the issue that the Constitution's guarantee of due process places a limit on what states can permit juries to award in punitive damages.
- But the Supreme Court on October 31, 2006, upheld an award of $79.5 million in punitive damages against Philip Morris in a lawsuit brought by the widow of a man

who died 5 months after a diagnosis of inoperable lung cancer in 1996, on the basis of deceptive advertising.

- An Oregon jury had awarded his widow compensatory damages of $821,000, meaning that the ratio of punitive to compensatory damages was 97 to 1. That was far greater than the "single digit" ratio the Supreme Court previously placed at the outer limit of constitutionality in 2003, the last time it decided a punitive damages case.
- The basis for the lawsuit was the claim that Philip Morris's strategy of denying the connection between smoking and cancer deceived the plaintiff. Also "that there was a market-directed fraud driven by their rational and deliberate decisions at the highest levels of the company to deceive customers . . ."

Physicians must be constantly aware of MCO's marketing methods to its subscribers, their patients, because advertising may have dire implications for any MCO with proven market-driven deceptive claims, which is often alleged by patients holding MCO medical insurance policies.

8.7   Physician Temptations of Managed Care: Bonuses and Rewards; Now Emulated by Medicare

The article "Pay for Performance in Commercial HMOs,"[20] points out that as the CMS begins to design a pay-for-performance (P4P) program for Medicare, they may use the models established by the commercial MCOs.

P4P has become an established feature of many payment systems of HMOs in the private sector. Data from a representative national sample document that 52.1% of health plans representing 81.3% of persons enrolled in HMOs used such programs in 2005. Several characteristics of HMOs were associated with the use of P4P, including geographic region, role of PCPs, method of payment for primary care, and whether the plans themselves faced performance incentives. Payment by capitation accounted for the majority of the HMOs' payments to PCPs among 30.6% of the health plans.

When one compares the features of both systems, there are indications that Medicare might have to change other long-standing features in order for this to work and to adapt many of the features of the MCOs.

Why?

1. First, HMOs with a large proportion of enrollees who are not required to select a PCP—a feature not shared by Medicare—were less likely to undertake P4P.
2. This finding may well reflect the challenges of attributing performance to a single doctor or group when many doctors or groups are responsible for a patient's care.
3. The development of appropriate strategies to overcome the current lack of a designated PCP in the Medicare system will be critical to the implementation of a P4P program.
4. As a corollary, private-sector approaches to paying physicians for performance appear to be heavily concentrated in medical groups rather than among individual physicians.
5. This is so perhaps because of the advantages of using groups or systems as the locus for the measurement of quality and improvement.
6. Medicare does not currently recognize groups as contracting entities (with a few notable exceptions).

7. This then may have to change to get closer to the managed-care model.
8. So the CMS may need to consider doing so to take the greatest advantage of P4P.
9. A survey suggests that many private payers use rewards greater than 5% of payments, presumably reflecting their belief that this level of payment to providers is needed to achieve improvement.
10. Given its financial constraints, the CMS may not be able to meet this benchmark without reducing base payments to some physicians, or adding more financial incentives to increasingly reduce Medicare services to its participants.
11. The bonus potential in these plans was typically equivalent to 5% or more of the payments from the plan (according to 41.6% of respondents and 60.0% of those who reported the amount of the bonus).
12. Among the clinical indicators specifically asked about for performance measurements are diabetes care, mammography, and asthma medications, which were most commonly included in measures of clinical care used in physician-oriented P4P programs.
13. Does this mean that those physicians not using long acting beta agonists (LABAs) in those areas where it is in the clinical practice guidelines (CPGs)? Some patients represent a subgroup at risk for life-threatening episodes or death in association with the use of salmeterol.[21] Although uncommon, such reactions provide support for the recent recommendation of Martinez for close medical monitoring of patients with sufficiently severe asthma to justify the addition of a long-acting β_2-agonist to maintenance-inhaled corticosteroids.[22]
14. Will doctors who do not put their asthma patients on LABAs be penalized?
15. Will the temptation and financial incentives in using a drug not indicated for everyone overcome the prudent physician.
16. This is just one of the examples where medical decisions may differ with not yet updated CPGs and reason that the level of medical malpractice risk may rise.

For several years, Medicare officials have advocated a P4P system, noting wide regional variations in the practices of hospitals and medical specialists. It appears that, late in 2006, Medicare had decided to approach P4P with a carrot rather than a stick, this despite the original Medicare law, passed in 1965, said, "Nothing in this title shall be construed to authorize any federal officer or employee to exercise any supervision or control over the practice of medicine."

8.8   July 2007, the Start of Medicare Pay for Performance (P4P)

Commencing July 1, 2007, doctors now qualify for a 1.5% bonus in the second-half of 2007 if they report data on the quality of their care, using measures specified by the government. For example, doctors could be asked to report how often they prescribe a particular drug after a heart attack or how well they control blood pressure in patients with diabetes. Some believe the new initiative is "a backdoor attempt to repeal" the original Medicare 1965 guarantee, "because it's pay for compliance, not pay for performance." Doctors will be financially pressured to comply with government guidelines and standards. Even legislators who support the general idea of P4P express concern with federal agencies setting benchmarks for care. The plan also raises concern among some doctors and lawmakers who specialize in health issues. They said they worried that it could be a step toward cookbook medicine and could erode the professional autonomy of doctors. With these statistics, Medicare officials will, in the near future, be able to reward doctors who follow clinical guidelines and perhaps penalize those who flout such standards without justification. But beyond broader questions about whether the government can accurately measure the quality of care, they are concerned about the feasibility of developing standards for all specialties. They are skeptical that federal officials "do not have the capability, the understanding, the knowledge or the training" to set standards for the quality of care and object to government efforts to define quality. Even the deputy commissioner of the Food and Drug Administration, said he is worried about intrusions into the practice of medicine by federal agencies (2006 speech to the American Medical Association). But be that as it may P4P is here and it should be well understood by the practicing physician.

8.8.1   Pay-for-Performance Financial Terms to Understand

Bonus—A practice would receive a bonus check at the end of the year, based on its ability to meet the performance standards of the particular P4P program.

Quality Grants—These are grants paid to the practice for meeting certain clinical, IT, or efficiency quality measures.

Payment Withholds—A percentage of each regular reimbursement would be kept by the program carrier according to how well the practice met its performance standards.

Increased capitation payment per patient.

8.9   Electronic Medical Record Systems Now Necessary

Although most P4P programs gather performance data from claims, in the future they may begin to rely on practices reporting data separately, which is why P4P programs encourage improvement in health information technology. Most programs build in added incentives for use of advanced health care information technology or electronic medical record (EMR) systems. Many EMR systems can be set up to report data according to the given performance measures, but this capability would have to be programmed into the system, preferably from the beginning. So call your EMR software vendor to ensure your EMR has these capabilities if and when they are needed. If you do not already have EMR, make this one of the requirements when choosing a new system. Even though P4P has not been completely implemented in the market, it would still benefit your practice to know you have the capability to take it on.

Many of the P4P programs are heavily geared toward primary-care physicians, but also include specialists and hospitals. The heart of the P4P is it is focused on clinical performance measurements, although information methodology and efficient measures are now included in many P4P programs. The following is a list of 26 clinical performance measures endorsed by the Ambulatory Quality Alliance. It also includes measures developed by the American Medical Association (AMA) and National Committee for Quality Assurance (NCQA).

✓ I. Preventive measures

1. Breast cancer screening—percentage of women who have had a mammogram during the current year or at least one year prior.

2. Cervical cancer screening—percentage of women who have had at least one Pap test during the current year or the two previous years.
3. Tobacco use—percentage of patients who were questioned about tobacco use one or more times during the current two-year period.
4. Advising smokers to quit—percentage of patients who received advice or counseling to quit smoking.
5. Influenza vaccination—percentage of patients aged 50–64 who have received an influenza vaccination.
6. Pneumonia vaccination—percentage of patients who received an appropriate (i.e., age-specific chronic illness) pneumococcal vaccine.

✓ II. Coronary artery disease

1. Drug therapy for lowering LDL cholesterol—percentage of patients who have coronary artery disease (CAD) who were prescribed lipid-lowering therapy.
2. Beta blocker treatment after heart attack—percentage of patients hospitalized with acute MI who received a prescription for beta blocker therapy within 7 days of discharge.
3. Beta blocker therapy post-MI discharge—percentage of patients hospitalized with acute MI who received persistent beta blocker treatment 6 months after discharge.

✓ III. Heart failure (*see* end note)—Performance measures are intended to be confined to those structural aspects or processes of care for which the evidence is so strong that the failure to perform them reduces the likelihood of optimal patient outcomes. But it may be that the current American College of Cardiology (ACC)/American Hospital Association (AHA) heart failure inpatient performance measures aside from prescription of an angiotensin converting enzyme (inhibitor) (ACE) inhibitor/angiotensin receptor blockers (ARB) at discharge "are not significantly influencing early postdischarge mortality and mortality/rehospitalization." Also, better methods and better performance measures must be identified in heart failure performance (and how many other performance measures?) to more accurately identify practitioners and medical care facilities providing the care that is most closely associated with optimum early postdischarge outcomes.

1. ACE inhibitors/ARB therapy—percentage of patients with heart failure who also have left ventricular septal defect (LVSD) who have been prescribed the ACE inhibitor or ARB therapy.
2. LVT assessment—percentage of patients with heart failure with quantitative or qualitative results of LVT assessment recorded.

✓ IV. Diabetes

1. A1c management—percentage of patients with diabetes with one or more A1c tests conducted during the measurement year.
2. A1c management control—percentage of patients with diabetes with the most recent A1c level greater than 9%.
3. Blood pressure management—percentage of patients with diabetes who had their blood pressure documented in the past year as less than 140/90 mmHg.
4. Lipid measurement—percentage of patients with diabetes with at least one LDL cholesterol test.

5. LDL cholesterol level—percentage of patients with diabetes with the most recent LDL at less than 130 mg/dL.
6. Eye exam—percentage of patients who received a retinal or dilated eye exam by an eye care professional during the current year (or during the prior year if patient is at low risk for retinopathy).

✓ V. Asthma

1. Use of appropriate medications for people with asthma—percentage of individuals who were diagnosed as having chronic asthma during the prior year, and who were appropriately prescribed asthma medications (e.g., inhaled corticosteroids) during the current year.
2. Pharmacologic therapy—percentage of all individuals with mild, moderate, or severe persistent asthma who were prescribed either the preferred long-term control medication (inhaled corticosteroid) or an acceptable alternative treatment.

✓ VI. Depression

1. Antidepressant medication management—percentage of adults who were diagnosed with a new episode of depression and treated with an antidepressant medication during the entire 12-week acute treatment phase.
2. Antidepressant medication management—percentage of adults who were diagnosed with a new episode of depression and treated with an antidepressant drug for at least 180 days (6 months).

✓ VII. Prenatal care

1. Screening for human immunodeficiency virus (HIV)—percentage of patients who were screened for HIV during the first two prenatal visits.
2. Anti-D immunoglobulin—percentage of D (Rh) negative, unsensitized patients who received anti-D immunoglobulin between weeks 26 and 30 of pregnancy.

✓ VIII. Quality measures addressing overuse or misuse. AQA website at http://www.aqaalliance.org/performancewg.htm

1. Appropriate treatment for children with upper respiratory infection (URI)—percentage of patients who were diagnosed with upper respiratory infection and were not dispensed an antibiotic prescription on, or within three days of the date of illness.
2. Appropriate testing for children with pharyngitis—percentage of patients who were diagnosed with pharyngitis who received a group A streptococcus test for the episode, and were prescribed an antibiotic.

8.9.1   Down Sides of P4P

1. If not designed correctly, a P4P plan could place patients from different ethnic, cultural, and socioeconomic groups as well as patients with specific chronic medical conditions (along with the physicians who treat them) at a disadvantage.

2. Also, most of the financial incentives are based on clinical outcomes, which could encourage doctors to drop noncompliant patients or patients with severe chronic illnesses because it will be harder for them to reach performance standards with these types of patients. This may ultimately limit these patients' access to quality care.
3. Another concerning issue is that in most P4P programs, the group, or physician has to meet certain performance standards before they become eligible for bonuses or other types of financial incentives. This places smaller practices at a disadvantage because they may not have the added resources to commit to reaching the standards.
4. It is, however, more important to understand how quickly P4P can adjust to new randomized control trials either proving or disproving some of these performance measures.

As an example, the randomized controlled trial (RCT) "association between performance measures and clinical outcomes for patients hospitalized with heart failure showed that current heart failure performance measures aside from prescription of an ACE inhibitor or ARB at discharge" have little relationship to patient mortality and in combined mortality/rehospitalization in the first 60–90 days after discharge. This study "OPTIMIZE-HF"[23] provided an important opportunity to evaluate whether and to what degree conformity with current performance measures influenced early clinical outcomes in a contemporary cohort of patients hospitalized with heart failure. The authors stressed that better methods are needed for identifying and validating heart failure performance measures to more accurately assess and improve the care of patients with heart failure. Performance measures are intended to be confined to those structural aspects or processes of care for which the evidence is so strong that the failure to perform them reduces the likelihood of optimal patient outcomes.[24]

Of the important criteria, even smoking cessation counseling was one of the performance measures in this OPTIMIZE-HF study that showed no statistical significance either way. The use of anticoagulations in patients with heart failure in this OPTIMIZE-HF study also did not reach statistical significance of this study; therefore, "suggested the authors that the current ACC/AHA heart failure inpatient performance measures aside from prescription of an ACE inhibitor/ARB at discharge are not significantly influencing early postdischarge mortality and mortality/re-hospitalization." The authors conclude that better methods and better performance measures must be identified in heart failure performance to more accurately identify practitioners and medical care facilities providing the care that is most closely associated with optimum early postdischarge outcomes.[25–32]

8.9.2 Summary and Conclusions

Managed care has changed the way the game is played. As part of the new Select Network marketing plan, Regence the BlueShield's insurance program in Washington state had sent letters to members of the Society of Professional Engineering Employees in Aerospace in the Puget Sound area stating that their physicians were lacking in the "quality and efficiency." The move resulted in more than 500 physicians being dropped from the network. Physician groups and the AMA sued because of the "insurer's improper and inaccurate statements' based on the use of unproven efficiency criteria to compare physician performance to patients that certain physicians failed to meet specific quality and efficiency standards." Also alleged was that the insurance carrier' criteria of physician performance was inappropriately driven by economic criteria, and instead raised unfair health insurer restrictions thus jeopardizing patients' access to health care. The physicians' organizations maintained that patients' choice of a physician must not be influenced by a health insurer's mistaken assumption that low cost can be equated with and is the only acceptable measure of high-quality care.

8.10 The MCO Physician Is under Unusual Stresses and Greater Risks

The MCO physician is under unusual stresses and greater risks because of increased conflicts of interest for MCO physicians trapped between corporate MCO decisions and marketing/ advertising and traditional medical ethics which has threatened the integrity of the traditional physician–patient relationship. It also likely that the giant Medicare program might also go the managed-care route starting with its new P4P physician reimbursement.

What can the individual physician do in this unstable medical world do to decrease his malpractice risks?

✓ MCO, managed-care physicians (and also Medicare physicians under new P4P programs) can reduce their medical malpractice risks by the following proactive strategies:

   a. Managed care physicians must not ration care at the bedside.
   b. Managed care physicians must be advocates for their patients.
   c. Managed care physicians must avoid conflicts of interest whenever possible.
   d. Managed care physicians must put the needs of the patient before their own self-interests.
   e. Managed care physicians must act in ways to promote trust in their relationship with patients.
   f. Managed care physicians should strive to maximize the health of the group of patients under their care.
   g. Managed care physicians should not enter into incentive arrangements, which they would be embarrassed to describe accurately to their patients or that are not in common use in the market.
   h. Managed care physicians should treat each patient impartially, without regard to source of payment, and in a manner consistent with the physician's own treatment style.
   i. If managed care physicians depart from this ideal, they must tell their patients honestly.
   j. Managed care physicians must differentiate medical treatment recommendations from insurance-coverage decisions by clearly assigning authority over these different roles.
   k. Managed care physicians should advocate for recommended treatment that is not covered by their patient's MCO insurance if indicated by the disease.
   l. Similarly physicians must keep their patients welfare uppermost in their care by not buying into any of the 5% P4P bonuses given to rigid adherence to CPGs that have been shown not to be ideal for certain patient subgroups or to elderly patients with multiple diseases.
   m. Benefit/risk ratios for any new medication or treatment must always be kept in mind for each individual patient.

8.11   Addendum: Managed-Care Readings

Patients' ratings of their interpersonal relationships with their PCPs as measured by a seven-item scale showed that gatekeeping arrangements that require patients to select a primary-care physician or obtain authorization for specialty referrals were associated with *lower ratings of the patient–PCP relationship*. The authors concluded that managed health plans that loosen restrictions on provider choice, relax gatekeeping arrangements, or promote access to and continuity with PCPs, are likely to experience higher patient satisfaction with their primary-care practitioner relationships. Lack of health insurance impedes the development of patients' relationships with their primary-care practitioners.[16]

Historical views of the patient–physician relationship assumed that the physician's role was to act in the best interests of the patient and to direct care and make decisions about treatment on the patient's behalf. However, under current legal and ethical principles, beneficence is no longer sufficient; respect for autonomy is paramount, necessitating patient participation. Nonetheless, physicians question whether patient participation is realistic in actual clinical situations. The image of a dependent patient who prefers to be sheltered from harsh truths is not supported. It appears that most patients wish to have information, although there is an identifiable proportion who do not. To be understood, health information must be presented in a way that is appropriate to the patient. Format, content, and timing of the material are all important. Mechanisms for incorporating such information into busy clinical practices are crucial.[33]

During the 1990, managed care has become the dominant form of health care delivery, because it has reduced the cost of health care; however, it has also created serious conflicts of interest for physicians and has threatened the integrity of the traditional physician-patient relationship. In this article, Dr. Grochowski argues that the efficiencies created by managed care are one-time savings and will not in the long run reduce the rate of rise of health care expenditures without a concomitant plan to ration health care. He explores the traditional physician–patient relationship and concludes

a. that while rationing of health care is inevitable, physicians must not ration care at the bedside,
b. that physicians must be advocates for their patients,
c. that physicians must avoid conflicts of interest whenever possible,
d. that physicians must put the needs of the patient before their own self-interests, and
e. that physicians must act in ways to promote trust in their relationship with patients.[17]

Patients value the first-contact and coordinating role of primary-care physicians. However, managed-care policies that emphasize primary-care physicians as gatekeepers impeding access to specialists undermine patients' trust and confidence in their primary-care physicians.[34]

In a competitive, monetized medical system, a clash of principles is inevitable; however, amid the tumult in the medical marketplace, the underlying tenets of emergency medical ethics remain inviolate. Although the goals of providing excellent and cost-effective care are not mutually exclusive, the conflicts encountered can only be resolved *by appeal to a higher goal: the good of the patient*. Both MCOs and EPs must function as agents of individual patients first and foremost. The enterprise of health care rests on fidelity, integrity, and trust; therefore, physicians and MCOs must accept and take seriously their important moral, legal, and social obligations to patients and society. *Otherwise, third-party cost considerations and provider greed irreversibly could pervert the practice of medicine and destroy the last vestiges of fidelity in the patient–physician relationship.*[35]

As managed care becomes more prevalent in the United States, concerns have arisen over the business practices of managed-care companies. A particular concern is whether patients should be made aware of the financial incentives and treatment limits of their health care plan. At present, MCOs are not legally required to make such disclosures. However, such disclosures would be advisable for reasons of ethical fidelity, contractual clarity, and practical prudence. Physicians themselves may also have a fiduciary responsibility to discuss incentives and limits with their patients. Once the decision to disclose has been made, the MCO must draft a document that explains, clearly and honestly, limits of care in the plan and physician incentives that might restrict the care a patient receives.[36]

At the heart of ethics in medicine is a solid physician–patient relationship. Managed care has operated to undercut this relationship. Rather than blaming managed care, however, one should identify and modify those social and economic forces that pressure MCOs to (1) undercut the physician–patient relationship and (2) engage in other unjust or unethical practices. Identifying these pressures does not let managed care off the hook for unethical practices. In fact, MCOs have both an ethical and a practical obligation to help define and support national health care legislation—to help reinvent their role in health care.[37]

To explore the nature of managed-care hassles in primary care, 16 internists and 10 family physicians volunteered to collect data about managed-care hassles during or shortly after the office visit for 15 consecutive patients using preprinted data cards. Of 376 total visits for which the physicians completed data cards, 23% of visits generated one or more hassles. On average, a physician who saw 22 patients daily experienced 1 hassle lasting 10 min for every 4–5 patients. More than 40% of hassles were reported as interfering with quality of care, the doctor–patient relationship, or both.[38]

The focus on managed care and the managed-care backlash divert attention from more important national health issues, such as insurance coverage and quality of care. The ongoing public debate often does not accurately convey the key issues or the relevant evidence. Important perceptions of reduced encounter time with physicians, limitations on physicians' ability to communicate options to patients, and blocked access to inpatient care, among others, are either incorrect or exaggerated. The public backlash reflects a lack of trust resulting from cost constraints, explicit rationing, and media coverage. Inevitable errors are now readily attributed to managed-care practices and organizations. Some procedural consumer protections may help restore the eroding trust and refocus public discussion on more central issues.[39]

As managed care proliferates in the United States and other countries, its structure has patterned changes in patient–doctor relationships, including those between older patients and their physicians. The physician as gatekeeper now limits the access of the patient to information and services. Patient's trust in the physician, essential to an effective patient–doctor relationship, will be damaged under this system of care. Additionally, examples from medical encounters demonstrate that many of the problems in the doctor–older patient relationship found under fee for service will remain, including the lack of attention to the contextual issues of health care of older adults.[40]

Many think ethical managed care is an oxymoron. But managed care can be more ethical—and can fulfill it's original pledge of providing broader access and better care by caring prudently—if it is physician-led. Faced with day-to-day ethical decisions that have black and white solutions, physicians are obliged to get more involved in management decisions, create formal ethics programs, report colleagues who are unscrupulous, and learn about new performance tools. Patients angry and suspicious about managed care expect no less from their physician.[41]

Managed care *per se* is a morally neutral concept; however, as practiced today, it raises serious ethical issues at the clinical, managerial, and social levels. This essay focuses on the ethical issues that arise at the bedside, looking first at the ethical conflicts faced by the physician who is charged with responsibility for care of the patient and then turning to the way in which managed care exacts costs that are measured not in dollars but in compromises in the caring dimensions of the patient–physician relationship.[42]

This article examines the ethics of medical practice under managed care from a pragmatic perspective that gives physicians more useful guidance than do existing ethical statements. The article begins with a framework for constructing a realistic set of ethical principles, namely, that medical ethics derives from physicians' role as healers; that ethical statements are primarily aspirational, not regulatory; and that preserving patient trust is the primary objective. The following concrete ethical guidelines are presented: Financial incentives should influence physicians to maximize the health of the group of patients under their care; physicians should not enter into incentive arrangements that they are embarrassed to describe accurately to their patients; physicians should treat each patient impartially without regard to source of payment, consistent with the physician's own treatment style; if physicians depart from this ideal, they should inform their patients honestly; and it is desirable, although not mandatory, to differentiate medical treatment recommendations from insurance-coverage decisions by clearly assigning authority over these different roles and by physicians advocating for recommended treatment that is not covered.[43]

Social trust in health care organizations and interpersonal trust in physicians may be mutually supportive, but they also diverge in important ways. The success of medical care depends most importantly on patients' trust that their physicians are competent, take appropriate responsibility and control, and give their patients' welfare the highest priority. Utilization review and structural arrangements in managed care potentially challenge trust in physicians by restricting choice, contradicting medical decisions and control, and restricting open communication with patients. Gatekeeping and incentives to limit care also raise serious trust issues. We argue that managed-care plans rather than physicians should be required to disclose financial arrangements, that limits be placed on incentives that put physicians at financial risk, and that professional norms and public policies should encourage clear separation between the business aspects and the professional.[44]

Trust, the expectation that institutions and professionals will act in one's interests, contributes to the effectiveness of medical care. With the rapid privatization of medical care and the growth of managed care, trust may be diminished. Five important aspects of trust are examined: technical and interpersonal competence, physician agency, physician control, confidentiality, and open communication and disclosure. In each case, changing health care arrangements increase the risks of trusting and encourage regulatory interventions that substitute for some aspects of trust. With the increased size and centralization of health care plans, inevitable errors are attributed to health plans rather than to failures of individual judgment. Such generalized criticisms exacerbate distrust and encourage micromanagement of medical care processes.[45]

Managed care employs two business tools of managed practice that raise important ethical issues: paying physicians in ways that impose conflicts of interest on them; and regulating physicians' clinical judgment, decision making, and behavior. The literature on the clinical ethics of managed care has begun to develop rapidly in the past several years. Professional organizations of physicians have made important contributions to this literature. The statements on ethical issues in managed care of four such organizations are considered here, the AMA, the American College of Physicians, the American College of Obstetricians and Gynecologists, and the American Academy of Pediatrics. Three themes common to these statements are identified and critically assessed: the primacy of meeting the medical needs of each individual patient; disclosure of conflicts of interest in how physicians are paid; and opposition to gag orders. The paper concludes with an argument for a basic concept in the clinical ethics of managed care: physicians and institutions as economically disciplined moral co-fiduciaries of populations of patients.[46]

References

1. Legal Answer Book for Managed Care. Aspen Health Law Center, 1995, ISBN#0-8342-0700-1.
2. Horsham PA. Medical Malpractice: Verdicts, Settlements and Statistical Analysis. Jury Verdict Research, March 2001.
3. Berlin J. A review of the issues surrounding medical malpractice tort reform. *AJR Am. J. Roentgenol.* 2003; 181(3): A5–A6.
4. Chirba-Martin MA, Brennan TA. The critical role of ERISA in state health reform. *Health Aff. (Millwood)* 1994; 13: 142–156.
5. Mariner WK. State regulation of managed care and the Employee Retirement Income Security Act. *N Engl. J. Med.* 1996; 335: 1986–1990.
6. New York Conference of *Blue Cross and Blue Shield Plans v. Travelers*, 514 U.S. 645 (1995).
7. *DeBuono v. NYSA-ILA and Clinical Service Fund*, 117 S.Ct. 1747 (1997).
8. *California Division of Labor Standards Enforcement v. Dillingham Construction*, 117 S.Ct. 832 (1997).
9. Grosso SM. Rethinking managed care liability and ERISA preemption in the age of managed care. *Stanford Law Policy Rev.* 1998; 9: 433–490.
10. Danzon PM. Tort liability: a minefield for managed care. *J. Legal Stud.* 1997; 6: 491–507.
11. Studdert DM, Sage WM, Gresenz CR, Hensler DR. Expanded managed care liability: what impact on employer coverage? *Health Aff. (Millwood)* 1999; 18: 7–27.
12. Gresenz DR, Pace NM, Dombey-Moore B, Hensler DR, Studdert DM. A flood of litigation? Predicting the consequences of changing legal remedies available to ERISA beneficiaries. Issue Paper IP-184. Santa Monica, CA: RAND, 1999. (See also http://www.rand.org/centers/icj/pubs.html.)
13. Weiler PC. *Medical Malpractice on Trial.* Cambridge, MA: Harvard University Press, 1991.
14. Couric E. *The Trial Lawyers.* St. Martin's Press, New York, 1988, ISBN 0-312-051727.
15. Studdert DM, Brennan TA. The problems with punitive damages and lawsuits against managed-care organizations. *N Engl. J. Med.* 2000; 342: 280–284.
16. Forrest CB, Shi L, von Schrader S, Ng J. *J. Gen. Intern. Med.* 2002; 17(4): 270–277.
17. Grochowski EC. Ethical issues in managed care: can the traditional physician–patient relationship be preserved in the era of managed care or should it be replaced by a group ethic? *Univ. Mich. J. Law Reform.* 1999; 32(4): 619–659.
18. Levinson W. et al. Resolving disagreements in the patient–physician relationship: tools for improving communication in managed care. Section of General Internal Medicine and Program for Physician Patient Communication Research, University of Chicago.
19. Hall MA, Berenson RA. The ethics of managed care: a dose of realism. *Cumberland Law Rev.* 1997–1998; 28(2): 329–332.

20. Rosenthal MB, Landon BE, Normand SL, Frank RG, Epstein AM. Pay for performance in commercial HMOs. *N Engl. J. Med.* 2006; 355(18): 1895–1902.
21. Nelson HS. et al. SMART study group. The salmeterol multicenter asthma research trial: a comparison of usual pharmacotherapy for asthma or usual pharmacotherapy plus salmeterol. *Chest* 2006; 129: 15–26.
22. Martinez FD. Safety of long-acting beta-agonists—an urgent need to clear the air. *N Engl. J. Med.* 2005; 353: 2637–2639.
23. Fonarow GC. et al. Association between performance measures and clinical outcomes for patients hospitalized with heart failure. *JAMA* 2007; 297(1): 61.
24. Bonow RO. et al. ACC/AHA Clinical Performance Measures for Adults with Chronic Heart Failure, A Report of the American College of Cardiology/American Heart Association Task Force on Performance Measures (Writing Committee to Develop Heart Failure Clinical Performance Measures): Endorsed by the Heart Failure Society of America, 2005; 46: 1144–1178, Joint Commission on Accreditation of Healthcare Organizations Specifications Manual for National Hospital Quality Measures, 2006, http://www.jointcommission.org/performancemeasurement/historical+nhqm+manuals.htm)
25. American Medical Association—http://www.ama-assn.org
26. Medical Management Association—http://www.mgma.com
27. The Integrated Healthcare Association—http://www.iha.org
28. Medicare—http://www.cms.hhs.gov
29. National Committee for Quality Assurance—http://www.ncqa.org
30. Bridges to Excellence—http://www.bridgestoexcellence.org
31. The American Medical Association guidelines for Pay for Performance programs.
32. http://www.ama-assn.org/amal/pub/upload/mml-1/finalpfpguidelines.pdf
33. Deber RB. Physicians in health care management: the patient–physician partnership: changing roles and the desire for information. *CMAJ* 1994; 151: 171–176.
34. Grumbach K, Selby JV, Damberg C, Bindman AB, Quesenberry Jr C, Truman A, Uratsu C. Resolving the gatekeeper conundrum: what patients value in primary care and referrals to specialists. *JAMA* 1999; 282: 261–266.
35. Larkin GL. Ethical issues of managed care. *Emerg. Med. Clin. North Am.* 1999; 17: 397–415.
36. Morreim EH. To tell the truth: disclosing the incentives and limits of managed care. *Am. J. Manag. Care* 1997; 3: 35–43.
37. Degnin FD. Between a rock and a hard place: ethics in managed care and the physician–patient relationship. *Manag. Care Q* 1999; 7: 15–22.
38. Sommers LS, Hacker TW, Schneider DM, et al. A descriptive study of managed-care hassles in 26 practices. *West J. Med.* 2001; 174: 175–179.
39. Mechanic D. The managed care backlash: perceptions and rhetoric in health care policy and the potential for health care reform. *Milbank Q* 2001; 79: 35–54, III–IV.
40. Waitzkin H, Cook MA. Managed care and the geriatric patient–physician relationship. *Clin. Geriatr. Med.* 2000; 16: 133–151, x–xi.
41. La Puma J. Integrity in managed care: a short guide. *Med. Group Manage J.* 1998; 45: 53–59.
42. Pellegrino ED. Managed care at the bedside: how do we look in the moral mirror? *Kennedy Inst Ethics J.* 1997; 7: 321–330.
43. Hall MA, Berenson RA. Ethical practice in managed care: a dose of realism. *Ann Intern Med.* 1998; 128: 395–402.
44. Mechanic D, Schlesinger M. The impact of managed care on patients' trust in medical care and their physicians. *JAMA* 1996; 275: 1693–1697.
45. Mechanic D. The functions and limitations of trust in the provision of medical care. *J. Health Polit. Policy Law* 1998; 23: 661–686.
46. McCullough LB. A basic concept in the clinical ethics of managed care: physicians and institutions as economically disciplined moral co-fiduciaries of populations of patients. *J. Med. Philos.* 1999; 24: 77–97.

For Further Reading

Baker G, Carter B. The evolution of pay for performance models for rewarding providers. In: *Case Studies in Health Plan Pay for Performance (Introduction)*. Washington, DC: Atlantic Information Services, 2004.

Berwick DM, DeParle NA, Eddy DM, et al. Paying for performance: Medicare should lead. *Health Aff. (Millwood)* 2003; 22: 8–10.

Census 2000: summary file 1 (SF 1). Washington, DC: U.S. Census Bureau, 2000.

Christianson JB, Knutson DJ, Mazze RS. Physician pay-for-performance: implementation and research issues. *J. Gen. Intern. Med.* 2006; 21(Suppl 2): S9–S13.

Epstein AM, Lee TH, Hamel MB. Paying physicians for high-quality care. *N Engl. J. Med.* 2004; 350: 406–410.

Fisher ES, Wennberg DE, Stukel TA, Gottlieb DJ, Lucas FL, Pinder EL. The implications of regional variations in Medicare spending. Part 1: the content, quality, and accessibility of care. *Ann. Intern. Med.* 2003; 138: 273–287.

Institute of Medicine. *Crossing The Quality Chasm: A New Health System for the 21st Century*. Washington, DC: National Academy Press, 2001.

Landon BE, Epstein AM. For-profit and not-for-profit health plans participating in Medicaid. *Health Aff. (Millwood)* 2001; 20: 162–171.

Landon BE, Normand SL, Blumenthal D, Daley J. Physician clinical performance assessment: prospects and barriers. *JAMA* 2003; 290: 1183–1189.

Leapfrog's incentive and reward compendium guide, 2005. (Accessed October 6, 2006, at http://www.leapfroggroup.org/ircompendium.htm.)

Milgate K, Cheng SB. Pay-for-performance: the MedPAC perspective. *Health Aff. (Millwood)* 2006; 25: 413–419.

Normand SL, Glickman ME, Gatsonis CA. Statistical methods for profiling providers of medical care: issues and applications. *J. Am. Stat. Assoc.* 1997; 92: 803–814.

Rosenthal MB, Fernandopulle R, Song HR, Landon B. Paying for quality: providers' incentives for quality improvement. *Health Aff. (Millwood)* 2004; 23: 127–141.

Schneider EC, Zaslavsky AM, Epstein AM. Quality of care in for-profit and not-for-profit health plans enrolling Medicare beneficiaries. *Am. J. Med.* 2005; 118: 1392–1400.

The competitive edge: HMO database. Bloomington, MN: InterStudy, 2004.

Weber DO. The dark side of P4P. *Physician Exec.* 2005; 31: 20–25.

How to Avert or Deal with a Potential Medical Malpractice Suit

9

Strategies of Averting Medical Malpractice

9.1 Introduction

For a chess match, you need to learn the right defensive and offensive chess moves/strategies. For a medical malpractice contest also, you need to learn the right defensive and offensive moves and strategies.

Successful chess thinking is similar to successful thinking in patient care—differential diagnosis, medical treatment of patients, and medical malpractice. This thinking consists of training yourself to continually run through in your mind the same thoughts or questions in the same order every time. Similar to patient care, in each and every chess position you first of all strive to set targets; and then you must find the ways to achieve those targets. You need to learn the relationship between targets and the means of getting to the targets, which vary according to the phases of the game—opening, middle game, and endgame. This is similar to averting or dealing with medical litigation at different phases of "the game."

Just like in medical practice, every chess move of yours must have a purpose. You must play with a plan. You must seize the initiative, convert weaknesses into strengths, learn from your mistakes, seek small advantages, and above all do not overextend.

This chess match thinking is similar, as we will attempt to show in this book, to dealing with medical malpractice and in learning the successful defensive and offensive moves. As in a chess match, if you know what your trained opponent will try to do in a medical malpractice cross-examination, you are in a much better position to not only react to his actions but to be proactive in your defense.

While a good chess player attempts to learn all the previous successful plays (e.g., English opening, French defense, Kings gambit declined, Nimzo Indian defense, Scandinavian defense, Sicilian defense, Stonewall attack, etc.), a physician must also learn the "plays" that have worked and the "moves" that will successfully prevent or deal with medical malpractice.

While a good chess player knows that the right chess moves are those that take control of the center of the chessboard, the right moves to avoid or deal with medical malpractice is also to take early control of the game—by being proactive and also forewarned as to what your opponent is up to. That is why the motif of this book is "forewarned is forearmed." In chess, for example, the novice player is taught that the contestant whose chess pieces are developed more quickly toward the center will usually control the course of the game. He will be in the best position to avoid an opening trap, because from the center one has the most space to control the rest of the chessboard, greater piece mobility, and better chances for attacking or defending. The loss of the center usually means a cramped and restricted game.

And just like in malpractice defense, losing tempo or not making an effective move could cost you time, space on the board, mobility, or the chess game! Checkmate!

So having learned just one of the basic moves for successful chess, let us now learn some basic practice strategies that a physician should know, and how to avert or deal with medical malpractice.

9.2 Theory and Principles of Medical Malpractice Management

9.2.1 Definition of Medical Risk Management

Risk management is inherently a process in search of balance among competing interests and concerns. Each risk management decision will be a "balancing act" of competing priorities, and trade-offs may sometimes have to be made between seemingly conflicting principles.[1] The following "checklist" helps evaluate that you are making a good risk management decision:

- Make sure you are solving the right problem.
- Consider the problem and the risk within the full context of the situation, using a broad perspective.
- Acknowledge, incorporate, and balance the multiple dimensions of risk.
- Ensure the highest degree of reliability for all components of the risk management process.
- Involve interested and affected parties from the outset of the process.
- Commit to honest and open communication among all parties.
- Employ continuous evaluation throughout the process (formative, process, and outcome evaluation), and be prepared to change the decision if new information becomes available.

9.2.2 Methods of Risk Management

The 10 decision-making principles, with the corresponding ethical principle, are the following:

1. Do more good than harm (beneficence): The ultimate goal of good risk management is to prevent or minimize risk, or to "do good" as much as possible.
2. Fair process of decision making (fairness, natural justice): Risk management must be just, equitable, impartial, unbiased, dispassionate, and objective as far as possible, given the circumstances of each situation.

3. Ensure an equitable distribution of risk (equity): An equitable process of risk management would ensure fair outcomes and equal treatment of all concerned through an equal distribution of benefits and burdens (includes the concept of distributive justice, i.e., equal opportunities for all individuals).

4. Seek optimal use of limited risk management resources (utility): Optimal risk management demands using limited resources where they will achieve the most risk reduction of overall benefit.

5. Promise no more risk management than can be delivered (honesty): Unrealistic expectations of risk management can be avoided with honest and candid public accounting of what we know and do not know, and what we can and cannot do using risk assessment and risk management.

6. Impose no more risk than you would tolerate yourself (the golden rule): This is important in risk management because it forces decision makers to abandon complete detachment from their decisions so they may understand the perspectives of those affected.

7. Be cautious in the face of uncertainty ("better safe than sorry"): Good risk management methods adopt a cautious approach when faced with a potentially serous risk, even if the evidence is uncertain.

8. Foster informed risk decision making for all stakeholders (autonomy): Fostering autonomous decision making involves both providing people with the opportunity to participate, and full and honest disclosure of all the information required for informed decisions.

9. Risk management processes must be flexible and evolutionary to be open to new knowledge and understanding (evolution, evaluation, iterative processes): The incorporation of new evidence requires that risk management be a flexible, evolutionary, and iterative process, and that evaluation is employed at the beginning and throughout the process.

10. The complete elimination of risk is not possible (life is not risk-free): Risk is pervasive in our society and cannot be totally eliminated despite an oft-expressed public desire for "zero risk." However, the level of risk that may be tolerable by any individual is dependent on values or beliefs, as well as scientific information.[1]

Risk management will continue to be a balancing act of competing priorities and needs. Flexibility and good judgment are ultimately the keys to successfully making appropriate risk decisions.

9.2.3   The Physician–Patient Encounter

9.2.3.1   Patient Communication

In May 1999, 21 leaders and representatives from major medical education and professional organizations met. The participants focused on delineating a coherent set of essential elements in physician–patient communication. These broadly supported elements provide a useful framework for communication-oriented curricula and standards. The group identified seven essential sets of communication tasks:

- Build the doctor–patient relationship
- Open the discussion

- Gather information
- Understand the patient's perspective
- Share information
- Reach agreement on problems and plans
- Provide closure[2]

9.2.3.2 Principles of Physician–Patient Communication

Remember this mnemonic. This simple memory aid promotes the key points necessary to optimize a physician–patient encounter.

RADPED, can be used to enhance communication in the radiology or primary care or specialty setting. It reminds us of the salient points and the purpose of enhancing communication.

RADPED reminds the physician to establish rapport with the patient, ask questions as to why the patient and family are presenting for the study, discuss the exam, perform the procedure, use exam distractions in the pediatric age group, and discuss the results with the referring physician and family when appropriate.[3]

9.2.3.3 Closure in the Patient Encounter

Closure is a distinctive phase of the visit. Closure is defined as the final phase of the medical visit in which the doctor and patient shift their perspective to the future, finalize plans, and say good-bye. The frequency of problems in closure suggests that physicians should be concentrating on this phase of the medical encounter. In a study by Goske et al.[3] study, a listening group developed a definition of closure by consensus based on audiotaped data from 22 office visits to physicians. Thirty-six percent of closures were interrupted in some way. Doctors' communication skills for closure are proposed to encompass full attention to the patient without interruptions during this very important phase of the doctor–patient encounter when new medical problems previously unstated may come up.[4]

9.2.3.4 The Companion's Role in the Physician–Patient Encounter

Companions assume important roles in enhancing patient and physician understanding. Patient accompaniment to medical encounters were studied to explore the rationale and influence of the companion on the primary care medical encounter. Academic general internal medicine physicians, patients, and patient companions participated.

The frequency of waiting and examination room companions was measured as were the reasons for accompaniment, their influence on the physician–patient encounter, and the overall helpfulness of the companion as assessed by patients and companions. Companions were in the examination room for 16% of visits, 93% were family members. The rationales for waiting and examination room companions were to help with transportation, provide emotional support, and provide company. Examination room companions helped communicate concerns to the physician, remember the physician's advice, make decisions, and communicate their own concerns to the physician. Patients believed that examination room companions influenced 75% of medical encounters, mainly by improving communication between the physician and the patient. Physicians agreed that examination room companions favorably influenced physician and patient understanding (60% and 46% of encounters, respectively). Patients indicated that waiting and examination room companions were very helpful for 71% and 83% of visits, respectively.[5]

9.2.4   The Practical Aspects of Risk Management

Good advice was given to physicians, especially family practice/primary care general internist physicians, when the Family Practice Management journal published a series of risk management articles from March 2000 to March 2003. This series of articles describe medical risk management "as the style of practice that endeavors first and foremost to prevent patient injuries and, second, to avoid medical malpractice claims." This simple method is performed by developing a routine of reviewing the sequence of care for unexpected or unwanted outcomes.

Others have confirmed the relationship between patient dissatisfaction, complaints, and medical malpractice lawsuits.

1. Medical malpractice lawsuits were significantly related to the total number of patient complaints, even when data were adjusted for clinical activity. The authors concluded that unsolicited patient complaints captured and recorded by a medical group are positively associated with physicians' risk management experiences.[6]
2. Similarly, Beckman et al.[7] looked into the question of why patients sue doctors and hospitals. The authors studied transcripts of discovery depositions of plaintiffs as a source of insight into the issues that prompted individuals to file a malpractice claim. Four themes emerged from the descriptive review of the 3787 pages of transcript: deserting the patient (32%), devaluing patient or family views (29%), delivering information poorly (26%), and failing to understand the patient or family perspective (13%).
3. Sutcliffe et al.[8] also described how communication failures contribute to many medical mishaps. The authors concluded that occurrence of everyday medical mishaps in their study was associated with faulty communication. However, poor communication is not simply the result of poor transmission or exchange of information. Communication failures are complex and relate to hierarchical differences, conflicting roles, role ambiguity, and interpersonal power and conflict.
4. What can hospitalized patients tell us about adverse events? The authors concluded that inpatients can identify adverse events affecting their care. Many patient-identified events are not captured by the hospital incident reporting system or recorded in the medical record. Engaging hospitalized patients as partners in identifying medical errors and injuries is a potentially promising approach for enhancing patient safety.[9]

   As just one example, Shojania et al.[10] describe a patient admitted to a teaching hospital with a mild episode of acute pancreatitis initially improved; but then her condition deteriorated and she subsequently died. The initial deterioration probably reflected bowel obstruction, as shown on an abdominal radiograph that an on-call intern forgot to review. This diagnostic delay was compounded by poor communication that resulted in a medical student inserting a feeding tube—rather than a nasogastric tube—to decompress the bowel, followed by failure to recognize how ill the patient had become. A vicious circle results when the attending physicians fail to provide effective supervision and coaching of housestaff in their charge. Not only is safety compromised but trainees lose the experience of being supervised. Consequently, trainees have no models of effective supervision on which to draw when they become supervisors. They then fall into the same trap as those who taught them, busying themselves with direct patient care and providing supervision only as time allows.

5. Another source of patient complaints is lack of perceived success with the patients' treatment regimen. Ironically it is not the doctor but the patient that bears the responsibility with noncompliance to the treatment prescribed by the physician. The adherence rate for medical treatments (or noncompliance rate) averages about 50%.[11-13]

9.2.4.1 Physicians Must Be Proactive in Detecting Sources of Problems

Some simple ways to detect low adherence (*see* Chapter 10) is by (1) watching for nonresponders (i.e., those whose disorder fails to respond to increments in treatment), (2) watching for nonattenders (i.e., those who miss appointments), and (3) simply asking patients whether they are taking their medication faithfully. The key question is, "Have you ever missed any of your pills (injections, etc.)?" Any affirmative response to this question is associated with taking less than 50% of medications. For some medications, measure the levels of drugs or their metabolites in body fluids (e.g., 5-ASA).

The most common patient dissatisfaction reasons given for medical malpractice suits are as follows:

1. The failure to diagnose or an inordinate delay in making the diagnosis and failure to consult in a timely manner. Risk management methods attempt to avoid medical malpractice claims alleging the failure to consult in a timely manner. Thus the rule of three is strongly recommended "If you haven't figured out and corrected the patient's problem within three visits, enlist help with an appropriate consultation referral."
2. Negligent medication treatment (*see* discussion below).
3. Negligence in invasive procedures (*see* the Mt. Sinai Medical Center preoperative and other invasive procedure checklist, and the discussion in Chapter 10).
4. Failure to obtain and properly document informed consent.
   • Your informed consent discussions with the patient should document expected outcomes, potential risks, and reasonable alternatives, which should be recorded in the medical chart. Now this can be time-consuming. If you allow the medical records to build up, by the end of the day you can have up to 20–30 medical charts on your desk. So a good idea is to extend the duration of the patient encounter by dictating your progress notes on your hand recorder while the patient is listening during each patient encounter and say so in your note.
   • The patient will see how thoroughly you have reviewed his case and findings and also his consent to the new medication or the planned procedure.
   • Since you have recorded that the patient is in the room with you listening and the patient can correct you if you misspeak, you have the necessary documentation of excellent medical treatment.
   • The principle of informed consent is that the physician advises and the patient chooses. This process of patient choice must be documented because if the patient refuses treatment, the documentation must include your discussion of the patient's understanding of the repercussions of the refusal and dictating in his presence reinforces this in the patient, his escort/companion, and in the medical record.
   • The patient's accepted responsibility should be documented in the medical record by the phrase "patient understands and agrees."
   • This is dictated while the patient is present and your dictation will so note the patient's presence.

9.2.4.2 Risk Management Documentation Techniques

- Most doctors use the SOAP outline as a template for their patient encounters (S = subjective complaints, O = objective findings, A = advice, and P = plan).
- The informed consent and discussion about any procedure or new medication used with the patient should include the options discussed with the patient, the opinion you expressed, and the agreed upon plan (add OOA to SOAP).
- Other risk management suggestions is to document "sets of examinations" such as examination of the breasts or genital organs always with a qualified assistant, present and documented in the record by "chaperoned exam of" and "assisted by."
- Every patient should understand that your office policy is a "24-hour, 365-day" policy in which the patient can phone in for any emergency or unexpected change in a medicine's reactions or a procedure's complications. This "24-hour, 365-day" statement should be printed not only on a plaque on the waiting room wall, but also on your prescription blanks and in any printed information given to the patient about a procedure or new medication. Not only it is comforting to the patient to know this, but it is also a risk reduction step when you print this "24-hour, 365-day access" policy to which the office will respond if an emergency arises.
- If you find the rare pharmacist who forgets to give patients automatic handouts with each medication, then at the bottom of your prescription pad you should write, please prescribe "with printed warnings."
- In fact you should proactively enlist the pharmacist into the job he likes to do—that of patient communication of the medications being prescribed—and steer patients to those pharmacists who do so.
- All patients should be given a follow-up appointment, even those with an appointment with another consulting physician.
- The appointment clerk should have a stamp that says, "Patient states will keep appointment."
- If an appointment is missed, there should be a record of at least three calls to make a reappointment.

When asked the question, "How much is enough documentation?" John Davenport, MD, says he usually replies that "When a physician is sued, there was never enough documentation." Obviously, making a full and complete documentation of all patients is ideal but hardly practical. So a special attempt should be made at least on high-risk patients.

This should be especially the case with high-risk clinical conditions that every internist finds in his practice. Davenport,[14] in his article suggests that you remember the acronym Listen to BACH (Lung, breast, appendix/abdominal pain, colon, and heart diseases).

Davenport states that the typical family physician/general internist can expect to be sued about once every 7–10 years and these are the most frequent conditions behind most suits. Therefore, he advises the family practitioner/general internist/primary care physician to make an extra effort and to take a proactive documentation approach—at least in those patients with the greatest malpractice risk such as myocardial infarction, breast cancer, appendicitis, lung cancer, and colon cancer.

- This extra proactive approach should be made with patients with chest pain, heme-occult positive stools, breast lumps, abdominal pain, and smokers (despite recommendations to stop). In these patients especially, you must take special care that every note should be legible.

- Each page should clearly identify the patient, doctor, date of the patient encounter, and date of the note.
- All notes should be dictated, then typed in the case of these high-risk patients.
- You must establish a strong system in your office to follow-up on ANY abnormal result and to order appropriate diagnostic tests in these high-risk patients.
- Chest x-rays should be on the record, according to Davenport, at least once a year on smokers. I would disagree with this and instead recommend in these high-risk patients to obtain an annual chest CT scan report, which should be placed in the medical records of smokers every year. Why? Chest x-rays have been shown to be largely ineffective for early diagnosis of lung cancer.

9.2.4.3 New Studies Perceived by Patients as Standard of Medical Care

Along comes a new study which shows that annual spiral CT screening can detect lung cancer that is curable.[15] Lung cancer ordinarily kills 160,000 people annually, i.e., 95% of its victims, and only 15% live for even 5 years after they receive their diagnosis. However, in this new study, of those who had early stage tumors picked up by CT scan and which were removed within a month of detection, an amazing 92% were calculated by the researchers to survive for 10 years. Since the cost of low-dose CT is below $200 and surgery for stage I lung cancer is less than half the cost of late-stage treatment, the authors conclude CT screening for lung cancer to be highly cost-effective. Other estimates of the cost-effectiveness of CT screening for lung cancer for various risk profiles are similar to that for mammography screening.

The American Cancer Society, the American Society of Clinical Oncology, the International Association for the Study of Lung Cancer, and the U.S. Preventive Services Task Force have not yet, however, recommended chest CT screening as a public policy because of the absence of a control group as a limitation of the above NEJM study. This may be prudent since pitfalls of *uncontrolled screening studies* include *lead-time bias* (i.e., making an earlier diagnosis without necessarily improving outcome) and *over-diagnosis bias* (i.e., detection of lesions that are histologically malignant but clinically indolent and not likely to cause death). Early pickups may also cause problems with needless evaluations using needle biopsy techniques for the lung, which are more dangerous than needle breast lump biopsy. A more definitive answer about the value of CT testing may come in a few years when a National Cancer Institute study is completed. This study will have a control population premised on the fact that because chest x-rays have been shown to be largely ineffective for early diagnosis of lung cancer, the patients chosen for chest x-ray will serve as the controls. So what to do in the meantime?

In my opinion, chest CT screening will soon be the preferred screening procedure in all smokers and others at high risk for lung cancer. And since this CT screening study is readily available, and since CT scanners are so ubiquitous, I believe you will be liable if you do not routinely order it for *your high-risk patients—only with their consent of course.* Other risk reduction strategies are as follows:

- Patients over 50 (even those without heme-occult positive stools) must have screening colonoscopies as should all those with heme-occult positive stools.
- All requests for consults should be fully documented along with your advice and instructions in these high-risk patients.

- All EKGs should not only have a report, but should have a comparison between the most recent and the last EKG.
- Never reassure a patient with a palpated breast lump that it is benign or due to "fibro-cystic disease" without special imaging studies, including mammograms and ultrasounds as well as a referral to a physician who specializes in these matters and in doing cytologies.
- Your office must have a "fail-safe mechanism" to make certain that all scheduled tests are indeed performed and that you initial all the results *before* they are filed in the patient's charts.
- A statement must also be in the medical record documenting that you have informed the patient "to inform you before the next visit whether or not he has competed the tests."

Davenport asserts "Physicians are needlessly frightened by the admonition that if you did not write it down, you did not do it." This is, he says, not true. As a defendant, you are perfectly entitled to testify, "I might not have written it down that I did X, but I certainly remember doing it." You may also testify, "I did not write it down and I do not remember doing it, but I am sure I did it because it is my custom and habit to do X in these situations."

Despite this "Davenport defense," opposing attorneys can demolish your credibility if you have got informed consent recorded in other patients but not in this one. And all things being equal, the jury is much more likely to believe your testimony if it is supported by documentation in the chart.

9.2.5 Handling Stress Is Part of Dealing with a Medical Malpractice Claim

9.2.5.1 The Summons

Sometimes the first clue you have at your being sued is when you receive a summon. At that time, some physicians' initial reaction is shock, disbelief, or denial with intense distress including feelings of depression and anger, which sometimes lasts about 2 weeks and is called the "period of disequilibrium," according to Charles et al.[16] You have got to understand that being sued is truly a traumatic experience, as I felt during my one and only medical malpractice suit about 25 years ago. You have got to understand that medical malpractice suits can occur regardless of whether negligence actually occurred and that your natural reactions may very well be shock, denial, shame, loss of control, anxiety, anger, depression, or physical symptoms.[17]

9.2.5.2 The Stress of an Impending Medical Malpractice Suit

A general understanding of a litigation process can help you decrease the stress of a malpractice suit. Your attorney and malpractice insurance carrier should explain the litigation process to you in detail. You may be feeling extreme self-doubt and guilt even though it is not warranted. Be very careful of excessive self-blame. It can be detrimental to your ability to take corrective action and also to your presentation at the trial. Do not forget that these are natural feelings, which you may also feel even long after your lawsuit is over. Many physicians continue to feel depressed, angry, ashamed, and isolated even after 2 years following a lawsuit.

9.2.5.3 The Discovery Period

During this time interrogatories will be served, which will ask you to respond in writing and under oath the questions from the plaintiff's attorney. Following this is the deposition, again, under oath with questions to respond verbally to the plaintiff attorney's questions. This discovery period could last months or even years after which your case could be dropped or settled or proceed to full trial.

Also, you should know that legal proceedings are commonly subject to postponements and last minute changes. Remember that you may feel that you are on an emotional roller coaster as your feelings intensify every time you are called upon to deal with some aspect of the case. However, know that these feelings are normal.

According to Gabbard,[17] "The trait that serves us well as physicians can also make us susceptible to an exaggerated sense of responsibility and feelings of guilt and self-doubt. Under stress, we are more likely to accept guilt even when it is not warranted. If you are not careful, these traits could make you a poor defendant in your own malpractice case. Instead, answer questions factually and accurately and take care not to assume unwarranted blame. This is important not only during the discovery period, but at all stages of litigation."

If necessary, and even if your attorney has correctly advised you not to discuss the legal or clinical aspects of the medical malpractice suit with anyone else, it is perfectly acceptable, and in fact beneficial, for you to talk with someone about your feelings about being sued. This can either be with your spouse or a trained professional. The professional will help counteract the shame and isolation you may feel. There is also a group that offers workshops and seminars as well as individual assessments and telephone consultations for those needing help in handling the stress of medical malpractice suits. They may also be of help in other physician stresses such as hospital suspension or privilege action, litigation stress management, individual stress burnout, prevention of professional distress, and conflict management training. (The Center for Professional Well-Being, 21, West Colony Place, Suite 150, Durham, North Carolina 27705. Tel: (919) 489-9167, Fax: (919) 419-0011, Website: http://www.cpwb.org.) Sometimes your state's medical association or specialty medical society or your medical malpractice insurance carrier may also know of similar services for support groups with trained professionals in this area.

We must all realize that as physicians, we are human and make mistakes. If you did indeed make a clinical error as a human being you can analyze it and make sure that it is prevented in the future. Christensen et al.[18] writes that "your feelings of frustration, shame, betrayal, and anger should be converted to make something good out of the experience. These feelings if not addressed properly may interfere with your ability to deal with the mistakes constructively."

In addition, you should realize that settling your case out of court is not an embarrassing defeat for you or even necessarily an indication that you are at fault. Remember, however, that any settlement will be listed in the National Practitioner Data Bank and therefore your attorney should be in on this kind of decision.

9.2.5.4 Aftermath of a Medical Malpractice Suit

The aftermath of a medical malpractice suit can continue to leave you with negative memories. Indeed few physicians report symptoms of posttraumatic stress disorder (PTSD) even if they have "won the case."

If at anytime you feel overwhelmed by the stress of your experience and certainly if it lasts longer than 2 years, you may want to seek the help of a mental health professional.

In my own situation, I remember that I had flashbacks about the medical malpractice case for about 2 years after it was successfully defended with the jury finding in my favor.

Martin et al.[19] confirmed that these residual feelings, though less intense than the medical malpractice lawsuit itself, can continue for several years after the end of the suit. The authors suggest that to turn around this terrible experience—both for you and the plaintiff, I will add—and make it constructive, you should "take an active role in medical malpractice prevention or other continuing medical education (CME) activities in the medical malpractice area."

I remember that is what I did. I gave medical malpractice seminars based on my experience. I also noted after "winning" my case the fact that the opposing medical expert was both a medical school and law school graduate who never had a clinical office nor ever saw a private patient nor made a clinical decision. This gave me an incentive to locate medical expert witnesses from academia who actually did practice medicine, clinical practice. I did this gratis for attorneys who needed plaintiff or defendant medical experts.

Many CME courses specifically address courses in improving patient–physician communication as suggested by Levinson et al.[20] Also, professional competency, clear patient communications, and complete documentation of medical records build an additional bulwark against medical malpractice claims.

9.3 The Apology Movement

Recently a movement has arisen toward apology to the patient as integral to risk management. Some of the key papers in this area are as follows:

1. Bismark et al.[21] reports that injured patients who pursue medicolegal action seek various forms of accountability. Compensation is important to some, especially when economic losses are substantial (e.g., with injury during prime working years or severe nonfatal injuries). However, others have purely nonmonetary goals and ensuring alternative options for redress would be an efficient and effective response to their needs.
2. Zimmerman[22] reports in an article that appeared on the front page of the May 18, 2004 edition of the Wall Street Journal. This article supports the proposition that the best tool to minimize the possibility of being sued may be as simple as expressing condolence and empathy when there is a bad outcome. The lawsuit reform bill that recently passed the Oklahoma legislature, H.B. 2661, contains an "I'm Sorry Law" that permits physicians to express condolence without those statements being used against them in court.
3. Finkelstein[23] (who happens to be my ophthalmologist) at the Wilmer Eye Institute, Johns Hopkins Hospital, Baltimore, states that full disclosure of medical errors is in the best interest of patients because it allows them to understand what has occurred, and to gain appropriate compensation for the harm that they have suffered. Physicians have been given little guidance regarding how to conduct a relationship with the patient after such an injury. We argue that the physician must continue to respect the patient and communicate honestly with him or her throughout their relationship, even after the patient has been injured. It is painful to admit our errors, especially to those who have been harmed by them. Nevertheless, offering an apology for harming

a patient should be considered to be one of the ethical responsibilities of those in the profession of medicine. Monetary compensation alone is not to be offered as a charitable gesture; rather, it should be accompanied by an apology to demonstrate the responsibility of the physician to the trusting patient. Full and honest disclosure of errors is most consistent with the mutual respect and trust the patients expect from their physicians. Clearly, physicians' ethical responsibilities sometimes differ from their legal and risk management responsibilities.

4. Virshup et al.[24] of the University of California at Los Angeles, School of Medicine, state that many malpractice suits are brought not because of malpractice nor even because of complaints about the quality of medical care but as an expression of anger about some aspects of patient–doctor relationships and communications. The theory presented is that under the stress of anxiety and physical illness, some patients regress to childhood needs; physicians are not generally trained to fulfill such needs. Thus, these patients, angry because of this, express their anger in malpractice suits. This theory has been taught to physicians and medical students as part of a physician CME seminar on loss prevention/risk management through demonstration of active-listening techniques to seminar participants. Physicians who understand and can respond appropriately to the emotional needs of their patients are less likely to be sued. This may also translate into a more fulfilled practice of medicine by those physicians who are most aware of the importance of a positive relationship.

9.3.1 Thoughts on the Apology Movement

1. Whether or not an apology rendered at the time of medical error—and prior to a medical malpractice attorney entering the case—will ward off a lawsuit is doubtful. It may depend to a large extent on whether the apology occurs upstream (before or early in the suit) or downstream (late in the course of the suit).

2. Whether or not an apology would be successful in warding off a medical malpractice lawsuit once the lawsuit has been launched may be naïve. Therefore, to entertain the idea that after a lawsuit has arisen and accompanied by a plaintiff's attorney ready to earn 30–50% of the (contingency) award that a simple apology will make this all go away also may be naive.

3. So do not take any steps in this direction without consultation with your attorney.

4. You may, however, ask your attorney, if your state has a two-track mediation system (see chapter on ADR).

5. Until an "I'm Sorry Law" that permits physicians to express condolence without those statements being used against them in court is enacted in your state, I doubt that your attorney would advise you to do this and once litigation has started he is the boss.

6. Perhaps an apology will turn out to be the best tool to minimize the possibility of being sued and indeed it may be as simple as expressing contemporaneous condolence and empathy when there is a bad outcome. Certainly the patient deserves nothing less if indeed he has been harmed by your error.

7. However, until one is certain that this is the case, I would suggest letting your attorney call all the shots.

9.3.2   Negligence of Your Physician Replacement

If you leave for the weekend or for vacation, you may be held directly liable for the medical negligence of your physician replacement. If and when you leave at a risky time in the patient's diagnosis or treatment that may be considered negligent or if you failed to select a "competent doctor as a substitute" to cover for you for the weekend or your vacation, you too can be held negligent says the Mississippi Courts *(Partin v. North Mississippi Medical Center, Inc. No. 2003-CA-02206-COA-Mississippi Ct. App., July 19, 2005)*.

9.4   Your Malpractice Insurance Policy

When you take out your malpractice insurance policy, make absolutely certain that your malpractice insurance policy names not only the medical practice as the insured but also the employee's individual malpractice liability. Several state trial courts (specifically Delaware) have ruled that a malpractice insurance policy did not provide coverage for a malpractice claim against an individual physician where only the medical practice that employed the physician was designated by the policy as a named insured *(Delaware Insurance Guarantee Association v. James No. 03C-05-023, Kent Super. Ct. Delaware, July 29, 2005)*.

9.4.1   Computerized Medical Records—Will They Be the Solution or Add to the Problem of Medical Malpractice Risks?

> Don't be hurt, my dear fellow. You know that I am quite impersonal.
>
> **—Sherlock Holmes**
> *The Adventure of the Retired Colourman*

Senator John Ensign (R-Nevada), a member of the Senate health, budget, and science panels, wrote *"The Prescription for Health Information Technology Change"* in the October, 2006 The Hill (a Congressional newspaper) that "Doctors' bad handwriting has been the subject of jokes for years, but sloppy handwriting is no laughing matter." The Institute of Medicine has found that illegible handwriting on prescriptions and the medication errors it causes contribute to as many as 98,000 deaths annually. As my former colleague, ex-House Speaker Newt Gingrich (R-Georgia) said, "It's simple. Paper kills."

In a country that offers the most technological and advanced medical devices to patients, our health care system is dependent on scraps of paper with scribbled medical notes stored in bulky file cabinets. In our outdated paper-based system, a patient's medical history is often scattered across numerous caregivers in different locations. As a result, some, most, or all of the patient's medical information is usually unavailable at the time of care. The fragmentation, disorganization, and inaccessibility of clinical information adversely affect the quality of health care and compromises patient safety. Procedures are unnecessarily duplicated, potential drug interactions are not systematically checked, and preventable medical errors can occur. Patients suffer.

The consequences of this system have proved to be costly, both in terms of lives and dollars. Most health care professionals do not have the information systems necessary to coordinate patient care with multiple providers, monitor compliance with best practices, and measure and improve quality of care. We must focus on making quality health care more streamlined, affordable, and accessible to hardworking Americans. We can do this by encouraging providers to adopt and use health information technology. An interoperable, interconnected health care system will improve quality of care and save patients' and taxpayers' dollars. It can also help us develop a system to reward providers for the quality of outcomes they deliver, as opposed to the volume of services they provide.

If implemented properly, health information technology will reduce medical errors. Interoperable technologies will provide doctors with complete patient histories and allow for *computerized ordering of procedures and prescriptions, so when the doctor types in a prescription there will be little or no question of what is being ordered.

Health care professionals also stand to gain by the improved quality of care through clinical-decision support tools, which can promote best practices. Because of the rapid growth of medical information and new treatment methods, physicians must accumulate a large volume of new knowledge in a short time. It is simply unrealistic to expect doctors to be able to refer to a clinical guideline easily in a busy practice setting. Clinical-decision support tools can provide doctors with evidence-based clinical-practice guidelines at the point of care. If a doctor is examining a patient with diabetes, an electronic reminder can display current, evidence-based protocols and recommendations that also take into account factors unique to the patient. The Department of Health and Human Services estimates that health information technology has the potential to save $140 billion a year. Private-sector entities that have implemented the technology have already realized significant benefits.

Unfortunately, the scoring model at the Congressional Budget Office (CBO) is a significant barrier to meaningful health information technology. The CBO does not recognize that health information technology will reduce medical errors, ultimately keeping people healthy and at home instead of in costly inpatient settings. The CBO also does not recognize that interoperable electronic medical records will improve coordination of care, resulting in less duplication of medical tests and procedures. Current scoring models explain how much a bill would cost the federal government but do not describe the economic benefit. This is unacceptable.

We have an opportunity to modernize our health care system and improve quality of care. It would be neglectful to let this opportunity pass us by. The Senate has taken the first step toward developing a national network for health information technology, and the House of Representatives is making significant progress in this area. However, more needs to be done. It is my hope that the House will pass a health-information-technology bill and a conference committee will be established to address any differences between the House and Senate bills. We must tackle complex issues, including quality measurement, privacy and security, and physician self-referral laws, and we must get the job done soon. We cannot afford to bury our heads in the sand on this important issue. We need a health-information-technology bill that will reduce medical errors, improve quality of care, and cut costs. Ensign ends his essay with "Every patient across the nation deserves this technology."

Comment: Senator Ensign certainly has the information, but does he have the solution?

Koppel et al. state that prescribing errors are the most frequent source of adverse drug events. Computerized physician order entry (CPOE) systems are widely viewed as the answer for reducing prescribing errors and saving hundreds of billions in annual costs. COPE system advocates include not only senators like Senator Ensign but also researchers, clinicians, hospital administrators, pharmacists, business councils, the Institute of Medicine, state legislatures, health care agencies, and the lay public.[25]

In addition to being one of the major applications of technology used in medical care over the past decade, CPOE and the electronic health record (EHR) have been touted to markedly improve medical practice. Desirable components of EHR are secure email with patients and a seamless interface with laboratory and practice management software, in addition to direct order entry. Of extreme importance, at least theoretically, in the prevention of medical malpractice is the ability of easily obtaining practice guidelines with decision support for each patient treatment.

In summary, the touted advantages of CPOE and EHR are as follows:

- E-prescribing: The benefit for writing prescriptions is that you "write it once and you never have to write it again." When refills are needed, a few clicks of the mouse accomplish the task. In theory, fewer mistakes are made because electronic prescriptions are much more legible than handwritten prescriptions.
- Use of reminders for abnormal examinations or when health maintenance examinations are due: This is a function that humans do very poorly and computers do better.
- The ability of finding all patients using a newly recalled medication and alerting them to stop use of this medication.

So what is the evidence that computerization is not as effective as claimed?

In the past few years, a few studies suggested some ways that CPOE might contribute to medication errors (e.g., ignored false alarms, computer crashes, orders in the wrong medical records). Research identified the following:

1. There were 22 situations in which CPOE increased the probability of prescribing errors.
2. Quantitative data revealed that several CPOE-enhanced error risks appear to be common (i.e., observed by 50–90% of house staff) and frequent (i.e., repeatedly observed to occur weekly or more often).
3. Error risks could be grouped as information errors generated by fragmentation of data and failure to integrate the hospital's several computer and information systems (10 error types) and human-machine interface flaws.

CPOE is widely regarded as the crucial technology for reducing hospital medication errors. However, as with any new technology, initial assessments may insufficiently consider risks and organizational accommodations. The literature on CPOE, with few exceptions, is apparently enthusiastic. However, some studies reveal that CPOE systems can facilitate error risks *in addition to* reducing them. Without studies on the advantages and disadvantages of CPOE systems, researchers are looking at only one edge of the sword. This limitation is especially noteworthy because many of the identified problems can be easily corrected. Recommendations to avoid these problems are to concentrate on organizational factors.

9.5   Five Suggestions on New Technology

1. Focus primarily on the organization of work, not on technology; CPOE and EHR must determine clinical actions only if they improve, or at least do not deteriorate, patient care.
2. Aggressively fix technology when it is shown to be counterproductive because failure to do so engenders alienation with dangerous work-arounds in addition to persistent errors. Substitution of technology for people is a misunderstanding of both.
3. Pursue errors' "second stories" and multiple causations to surmount the barriers enhanced by episodic and incomplete error reporting, which is standard, and management belief in these error reports, which may obfuscate and compound the problems.
4. Plan for continuous revisions and quality improvement, recognizing that all changes generate new error risks.
5. It is important to realize that as CPOE and EHR systems are implemented, clinicians and hospitals must attend to the errors they cause in addition to the errors they prevent.[25]

By early 2007, bills to speed the adoption of information technology by hospitals and doctors passed both chambers of Congress. However it is noteworthy that only 1 in 4 doctors used electronic health records the year before in 2005, according to a recent study by researchers at Massachusetts General Hospital and George Washington University, fewer than 1 in 10 doctors used the technology for important tasks like prescribing drugs, ordering tests, and making treatment decisions. Primary-care doctors in the United States were far less likely than doctors in other industrialized countries to use electronic records. In the United Kingdom, however, 89% of doctors use them, according to a recent report in the online edition of the journal Health Affairs, and in the Netherlands, 98% do.

Technology experts have many explanations for the slow adoption of the technology in the United States, including the high initial cost of the equipment, difficulties in communicating among competing systems and fear of lawsuits against hospitals and doctors sharing data.

9.6   Fear of Lawsuits against Hospitals and Doctors' Offices/Practices That Share Data

This is worrisome to American doctors. The Health Insurance Portability and Accountability Act (HIPPA, 1996) made it a federal crime to disclose private medical information improperly (*see* Chapter 8). The Office for Civil Rights in the Department of Health and Human Services had by 2006 received more than 22,000 complaints under the portability law since the federal privacy standards took effect in 2003. Allegations of "impermissible disclosure" have been among the most common complaints. However, the civil rights office has filed only three criminal cases and imposed no civil fines. Instead, it said, it has focused on educating violators about the law and encouraging them to obey it in the future.

Despite this lack of prosecution, critics also say that the law has some worrisome loopholes. The law, for example, allows company representatives review employees' medical records to process health insurance claims. Critics say that it would not be unusual in some companies for the same supervisor to be in charge both of insurance claims and of hiring and firing decisions. (*Personal note: In fact from my personal private medical practice experience with filing insurance claims, this is a very common occurrence—especially in the Washington D.C. area.) This could allow companies to comb their ranks for people with expensive illnesses and find some reason to fire them as a way to keep health costs under control. Easily accessible computerized files would make the job that much easier, the critics say.

Even before the theft in 2006 of a Veterans Affairs official's laptop that contained private medical records of 28 million people, a consumer survey found that repeated security breaches were raising concerns about the safety of personal health records. About 1 in 4 people were aware of those earlier breaches, according to a national telephone survey of 1,000 adults last year for the California Health Care Foundation. The survey also found that 52% were "very concerned" or "somewhat concerned" that insurance claims information might be used by an employer to limit their job opportunities. However, computer technology—the same systems that disseminate data at the click of a mouse—can also enhance security. At NewYork-Presbyterian, when unauthorized people try to gain access to electronic medical records, hospital computers are programmed to ask them to explain why they were seeking information and the computer warns electronic intruders: "Be aware that your user ID and password have been captured."[26]

References

1. Jardine C, Hrudey S, Shortreed J, Craig L, Krewski D, Furgal C, McColl S. Risk management frameworks for human health and environmental risks. *J. Toxicol Environ Health B Crit Rev.* 2003; Nov-Dec 6(6): 569–720.
2. Makoul G. Essential elements of communication in medical encounters: the Kalamazoo consensus statement. *Acad Med.* 2001; Apr 76(4): 390–393.
3. Goske MJ, Reid JR, et al. Epub 2004 Nov 25RADPED: an approach to teaching communication skills to radiology residents. *Pediatr Radiol.* 2005; Apr 35(4): 381–386.
4. White JC, et al. Wrapping things up: a qualitative analysis of the closing moments of the medical visit. *Patient Educ Couns.* 1997; Feb 30(2): 155–165.
5. Schilling LM, et al. The third person in the room: frequency, role, and influence of companions during primary care medical encounters. *J. Fam Pract.* 2002; Aug 51(8): 685–690.
6. Hickson GB, et al. Patient complaints and malpractice risk. *JAMA* 2002; 287(22): 2951–2957.
7. Beckman HB, et al. The doctor-patient relationship and malpractice: Lessons from plaintiff depositions. *Arch Intern Med.* 27 Jun 1994; 154(12): 1365–1370.
8. Sutcliffe KM, Lewton E, Rosenthal MM. Communication failures: an insidious contributor to medical mishaps. *Acad Med.* 2004; 79: 186–194.
9. Weingart SN, et al. Learning from patient-reported incidents. *J Gen Intern Med.* 1 Sep 2005; 20(9): 830–836.
10. Shojania KG, et al. Graduate medical education and patient safety: a busy—and occasionally hazardous—intersection. *Ann. Int. Med.* 2006; 145(8): 592–598.
11. Stephenson BJ, et al. The rational clinical examination: is this patient taking the treatment as prescribed? *JAMA* 1993; 269: 2779.
12. Macharia WM, Leon G, Rowe BH, et al. An overview of interventions to improve appointment keeping for medical services. *JAMA* 1992; 267: 1813.
13. Haynes RB, Yao X, Degani A, et al. Interventions for enhancing medication adherence. *Cochrane Database Syst Rev.* 2005; (4): CD000011.

14. Davenport J. Documenting high risk cases to avoid malpractice liability. *Family Practice Management.* Oct 2000; 7(9): 26–32.

15. The International Early Lung Cancer Action Program Investigators. Survival of Patients with Stage I Lung Cancer Detected on CT Screening. *NEJM* 2006; 355(17): 1763–1771.

16. Charles SC, et al. A sued and nonsued physicians' self-reported reactions to malpractice litigation. *Amer. J. Psychiatry.* 1985; 142: 437–440.

17. Gabbard, GO. The role of compulsiveness in the normal physician. *JAMA.* 1985; 254(20): 2926–2929.

18. Christensen et al. The heart of darkness: the impact of perceived mistakes on physicians. *J. Gen Intern Med.* 1992; 7: 424–431.

19. Martin CA, et al. Physicians' psychologic reactions to malpractice litigation. *Southern Medical J.* 1991; 84: 1300–1304.

20. Levinson et al. Physician–patient communication: the relationship with malpractice claims among primary care physicians and surgeons. *JAMA.* 1997; 277: 553–559.

21. Bismark M, et al. Accountability sought by patients following adverse events from medical care. *CMAJ.* Oct 10, 2006; 175(8): 889–894.

22. Zimmerman R. Doctors' new tool to fight lawsuits: saying "I'm sorry." Malpractice insurers find owning up to errors soothes patient anger. "The risks are extraordinary." *J. Okla State Med Assoc.* Jun 2004; 97(6): 245–247.

23. Finkelstein D. When a physician harms a patient by a medical error: ethical, legal, and risk-management considerations. *J. Clin Ethics.* Winter 1997; 8(4): 330–335.

24. Virshup BB, et al. Strategic risk management: reducing malpractice claims through more effective patient-doctor communication. *Am. J. Med. Qual.* Jul-Aug 1999; 14(4): 153–159.

25. Koppel R, et al. Role of computerized physician order entry systems in facilitating medication errors. *JAMA.* 2005; 293: 1197–1203.

26. Freudenheim M. and Pear R. Health hazard: computers spilling your history. *NYT.* 12 Mar. 2006.

What to Do and Not to Do in a Pending or Ongoing Malpractice Suit

10

I just want to thank everyone who made this day necessary.

—**Yogi Berra**

10.1 What Not to Do If and When You Are Notified about a Malpractice Action

- Do not panic.
- Do not change the records. This may be considered fraudulent and is potential grounds for denial of coverage by the insurance carrier and a risk of punitive damages.
- If you absolutely need to make a change do it only with advice and consent of your attorney.
- Then simply draw a single line through the item and date and initial.
- Remove nothing from the original records.
- Do not accept calls from other attorneys.
- Do not call the plaintiff or his or her lawyer.

10.2 What Should You Do?

1. Be selective in who you talk to about this case.
2. Notify your medical malpractice carrier as early as possible before you receive any official notice of the impending suit.
3. Talk about it only to your medical malpractice attorney and legal representatives.
4. Indeed, notify your private insurance carrier immediately even when you just suspect a medical malpractice case is coming.
5. Review carefully all the medical records on the case.
6. Provide all relevant documents, notes, and diaries to the attorney.
7. Identify pertinent literature dealing with the medical issues of the case.
8. Identify potential expert consultants/witnesses if any.
9. Identify fact witnesses.

10. It may be useful upon approval of your attorney that after performing the steps above to write a letter "for the record" covering the case while the facts are still fresh in your mind. Trying to reconstruct the case, for your attorney, 1 or 2 months or years later, would be much more difficult.

11. This letter for the record would be similar to a complete consultation letter you would write to a referring physician covering the entire history, physical examination, and medical course of the patient—and including in a truthful and brutally frank analysis of any of the factors following.

Make a thorough inspection of the medical records for these possible and potential problems.

Make it a constructive issue and attempt to figure out any possible reasons for the suit from these major reasons physicians are sued and plan for future corrections.

- Failure to communicate or miscommunication
- Wrong procedure
- Wrong, poor indication
- Unwarranted complications
- Failure to document
- Failure to obtain proper consultations
- Inappropriate orders
- Improper delegation of responsibilities
- Failure to follow up
- Loose lips, angry words
- Poor bedside manner
- Premature discharge of patient
- Failure to order indicated tests or studies
- Bad outcome/unreasonable expectations
- Failure to obtain adequate informed consent.

Possible motives of suit

- anger
- guilt
- accountability
- grief
- closure.

10.3   Questions to Answer for Your Attorney

10.3.1   Did You Adhere to Good Charting Criteria?

1. Made sure all documents are in the *correct chart*?
2. Wrote legibly and used approved abbreviations?
3. Used specific and accurate descriptions?
4. Documented all routine office visits?

5. *Documented precautions and preventive measures taken?* Contemporaneous note as to the good reasons why the "standard of care was not followed in this particular patient (i.e., age, multiple medications, multiple diseases).
6. Documented patient refusals of tests, medications and treatment, and patient noncompliance?
7. Documented follow-up instructions, appointments, appointment cancellations, and calls for reappointment reminders, referrals, and telephone communications?

10.3.2   Did You Adhere to Documentation Do's and Don'ts?

- Do not solely rely on boilerplate language in your dictation and medical record charting.
- Personalize each note it to the patient and the case.
- Make sure that there is an accurate time and date, progress note, office notes, and reports.
- Write legibly.
- Dictated notes and reports in a timely manner.

10.4   Warnings

1. *Do not ever alter a record without your initials and date.* This may be interpreted as a criminal act and grounds for denial of insurance coverage.
2. Do not write prejudicial or sarcastic or accusatory statements in the medical records.
3. Do not chart that an incident report was filled out or that risk management was contacted. Those are in separate records.
4. Do not document what someone else said, he or she heard, saw, felt, observed, or smelled unless this information is crucial, in which case quote the statement and give the source.
5. "Harmless terms" can hurt you in a lawsuit. Such terms are
   - by mistake,
   - accidentally,
   - miscalculated,
   - confusing,
   - inadvertently,
   - unintentionally,
   - misinterpreted,
   - erroneously.
6. Remember in the eyes of the law (and Medicare and Medicaid and most medical reimbursement insurance carriers), if you did not document the service and did not charge for it (or indeed in some situations—even if you did charge for the undocumented "service," *you did not do it.*

The usual defense against this (if true) is that it is your routine to do whatever that it is missing from the chart routinely in similar situations—and that you simply do not document what you routinely do. However, the jury believes more in what you have recorded than what you say "you do routinely but did not document."

10.5   Preventive Moves

1. Each doctor needs to establish standard operating procedures for consultation letter, lab, and x-ray report processing to reduce opportunity for separation of reports and patient ID information.
2. Implement consistent staffing for specific high-risk tasks and ensure consistency in procedures.
3. Process analysis to build in red flags, steps in accessing, testing, and review protocols to eliminate deviations from standard protocol.
4. When pathology or x-ray reports are inconsistent with the clinical history, *pause before filing.* Consider repeat or additional testing.
5. Personal communication should be made as soon as possible with referring and consulting physicians when results are unexpected or inconsistent.
6. Document all communications with colleagues and patients.

10.6   Deviations from Clinical Practice Guidelines and the Standard of Medical Care

Inform your attorney of any potential problems with possible patient. Also tell him of known deviations from medical guidelines and standards of are in this patient—note why you did not think it was beneficial for the patient for you to adhere to that particular clinical practice guideline (CPG).

Although deviations from the clinical guidelines occur frequently and are not unique (only) to those who are being sued for medical malpractice, a suit may follow if the specific deviation(s) results in damages.

Most medical malpractice lawsuits are brought to trial when a physician's deviations from the standard of care and medical guidelines are documented to cause damages.

10.6.1   Examples of Published Nonadherence to Medical Guidelines by Physicians*

10.6.1.1   Example 1

Patients at highest mortality risk after non-ST-segment elevation (NSTE) Acute Coronary Syndrome (ACS) receive less aggressive care reports the *American Heart Journal.*[1]

Evidence-based practice guidelines have been developed for managing patients with NSTE ACS.

Yet patients with NSTE ACS who are at the highest risk of mortality are actually less likely to receive guideline-recommended treatment, according to the American Heart Journal. Lead author Dr. Matthew T. Roe and colleagues examined in-hospital treatments and outcomes for 77,760 patients with NSTE ACS participating in the CRUSADE (Can Rapid Risk Stratification of Unstable Angina Patients Suppress Adverse Outcomes

---

* *See* attached CD-ROM appendix for other guidelines and standard of care.

With Early Implementation of the ACC/AHA Guidelines) Quality Improvement Initiative. Compliance with American College of Cardiology/American Heart Association Class guidelines for the management of NSTE ACS was examined according to risk categories for in-hospital mortality; the latter were based on an adaptation of the PURSUIT risk model.

In-hospital mortality rates were significantly higher in patients ≥75 years old (8.6% versus 2.7%) and in those with diabetes mellitus (5.8% versus 4.3%), renal insufficiency (10.0% versus 3.9%), or signs of congestive heart failure at presentation (10.6% versus 3.1%) than in patients who did not have that feature. Yet guideline-recommended acute medications, invasive cardiac procedures, and discharge medications and interventions were used significantly *less often in these high-risk patients.*

For example, patients ≥75 years old were significantly less likely to receive aspirin (89.8% versus 93.0%), glycoprotein IIb/IIIa inhibitors (45.2% versus 57.3%), and catheterization (29.8% versus 53.8%) within 48 h of enrollment than were patients <75 years old.

10.6.1.2   Example 2

At discharge, the above patients with renal insufficiency were significantly less likely to receive counseling about smoking cessation (51.1% versus 66.7%), dietary counseling (68.7% versus 72.1%), or cardiac rehabilitation (31.8% versus 42.8%) than were patients without renal insufficiency.

10.6.1.3   Example 3

Similarly, these patients categorized as high risk for in-hospital mortality were significantly less likely to receive guideline-recommended therapies than were patients with low or moderate risk. The authors called for a new quality-improvement approach to target these undertreated, high-risk subgroups of patients.

10.6.2   Reasons Why Physicians Do Not Adhere to CPGs and the Standards of Care?

This question was addressed by Mottur-Pilson et al.[2] They found that noncompliance "with best practices in diabetes is *common.*"

Physician volunteers reported about their diabetic patients that they were not complying with the annual foot examination in 13% of encounters.

A similar level of noncompliance was reported for the annual lipid profile (15%) and retinal examination (17%). Among the five measures examined, noncompliance was most common for screening urinalysis (26%) and screening microalbuminuria (46%). The physicians' open-ended comments suggested that lack of physician oversight, patient nonadherence, and systems issues were common reasons for noncompliance with guidelines.

Noncompliance with nephropathy screening, established renal disease; and angiotensin-converting enzyme inhibitors guidelines also resulted from a conscious decision by the physician, because of patient's age and comorbid illness. Although physician forgetfulness and external factors are frequently offered as reasons for noncompliance, it may also result from a conscious decision, as physicians may disagree about what constitutes "best practices."

So it was concluded by the Mottur-Pilson et al. that even among a self-selected group of physicians, that noncompliance "with best practices in diabetes is *common*."

The reasons for physician noncompliance with guidelines were also published,[3] which points out that adherence to good clinical guidelines is critical to improved patient outcomes.

However, a variety of barriers undermine this process. Lack of clinician awareness and familiarity affect physician's knowledge of a guideline. In terms of physician's attitudes, lack of agreement with the guidelines, or differences with outcome expectancy, as well as the inertia of previous practice are barriers. Despite adequate knowledge and attitudes, external barriers can affect a physician's ability to execute guideline recommendations.

Mottur-Pilson et al. describe these "barriers to physician adherence" to guidelines:

1. *Lack of awareness*: Although many guidelines have achieved wide awareness (i.e., immunization guidelines, recommendations for infant sleeping position). More than 10% of physicians are not aware of the existence for 78% of the guidelines.
2. *Lack of familiarity*: In all cases, lack of familiarity was more common than lack of awareness.
3. *Lack of agreement*: Physicians may not agree with a specific guideline or the concept of guidelines in general. In that case a contemporaneous note is often placed into the medical records.
4. *Lack of self-efficacy*: For example, higher self-efficacy in prescribing cholesterol-lowering medications was associated with physicians initiating therapy consistent with national guidelines. Low self-efficacy (due to a lack of confidence in ability or a lack of preparation) may lead to poor adherence. Sixty-eight percent of the surveys reported that this barrier involved preventive health education and counseling, which suggest that poor self-efficacy may be a common barrier to adherence for such guidelines.
5. *Lack of outcome expectancy*: If a physician believes that a recommendation in the guidelines will not lead to an improved outcome, the physician will be less likely to adhere. For example, the United States preventive services task force (USPSTF) recommends that physicians provide smoking cessation counseling. Although most physicians are aware of and agree with the recommendation, many smokers are not counseled to quit during a physician's visit.
6. An important reason for physician nonadherence is a belief that the physician will not succeed. Seventy-five percent of surveys report lack of good outcome expectancy.
7. *Inertia of previous practice*: Physicians may not be able to overcome the inertia of previous practice, or they may not have the motivation to change. More than 20% of respondents indicated that it was a barrier to adherence. The results suggest that close to half of physicians surveyed were not ready to change behavior (i.e., adopt guideline recommendations for a variety of reasons).

8. *External barriers*: A physician may still encounter barriers that limit his/her ability to perform the recommended behavior due to other (patient, guideline, or environmental) factors.
9. Even well-trained physicians confident about their counseling skills can be affected by external barriers (such as time limitations, lack of a reminder system) that prevent them from adhering to a counseling guideline.
10. *Guideline-related barriers*: Physicians were more likely to describe guidelines as not easy to use or not convenient when asked about guidelines in theory. When physicians were asked about barriers for specific guidelines, a significant percentage (more than 10% of respondents) described them as inconvenient or difficult to use.
11. Guidelines recommending elimination of an established behavior may be more difficult to follow than guidelines that recommend adding a new behavior.
12. Trialability of a guideline and its complexity are also described as significant predictors of adoption. Trialability is "the degree to which an innovation may be experimented with on a limited basis."
13. *Patient-related barriers*: The inability to reconcile patient preferences with guideline recommendations is a marked barrier to adherence. Patients may be resistant or perceive no need for guideline recommendations.
14. In addition, a patient may perceive the recommendation as offensive or embarrassing. In all the surveys that included patient-related factors, more than 10% of physicians indicated them as a barrier to adherence.
15. *Environmental-related barriers*: Adherence to practice guidelines may require changes not under physician control, such as acquisition of new resources or facilities. For example, unavailability of an anesthesiologist 24 h a day may interfere with physician's ability to adhere to guidelines aimed at decreasing the rate of elective cesarean deliveries.
16. Many factors described as barriers by more than 10% of respondents, such as lack of a reminder system, lack of counseling materials, insufficient staff or consultant support, poor reimbursement, increased practice costs, and increased liability, may also be factors beyond physician's control.
17. *Lack of time*: Although, it is commonly described as a barrier to adherence by more than 10% of respondents (11/17 cases), time limitations were not a barrier for mammography referral or breast examination guidelines, management of fever, and hyperbilirubinemia.

If indeed there was a deviation from the guidelines and you did not explain why in a contemporaneous progress note in the medical record, use the above 17 items as a learning experience.

10.6.3 Ten Preventive Moves

1. Since you now know that there are a variety of barriers to guideline adherence, summarized by a lack of awareness, lack of familiarity, lack of agreement, lack of self-efficacy, lack of outcome expectancy, the inertia of previous practice, and external barriers your continuing medical education (CME) selections must deal with these barriers.

2. You must ask yourself which of these categories fit you and take constructive action to modify them.

3. By focusing on these specific barriers to adherence, you may also be more direct in improving your behavior to avert medical malpractice suit.

4. You should be attending all the CME courses designed to keep you abreast of changes in your field particularly as applies to CPGs.

5. You should be reading at least your own specialty journal to keep up with these changes, now that CPGs are so much a part of the standard of medical care.

6. An important record-keeping point is this: you must document for each patient a contemporaneous note as to why you chose not to adhere to a CPG, since there are many good reasons for doing so (e.g., elderly patient taking multiple medications).

7. You must inform your attorney of the potentially important CPG, which will probably be pointed out by the opposing medical expert in this particular medical malpractice case.

8. Your attorney may ask you to add your written summary of the case and its issues that explain your actions or inactions relating to a particular CPG that you did not follow. Remember there are many published reasons for not following certain CPGs.

9. Your attorney will also need to know all the pertinent medical issues to select from among medical experts in that area the best one to testify for you.

10. Your medical expert would certainly also want to read your rationale of the patient's (now the plaintiff) medical treatment, and all your reasons for not adhering to the CPG recommendations, preferably with a contemporaneous note in the medical records—but in its absence the summary letter will do.

10.7 Miscellaneous Preventive Protection Methods Used by Physicians against Medical Malpractice Litigation Threats[*]

10.7.1 Going Bare[†]

Many physicians are advised on going bare, i.e., saving money by not purchasing medical malpractice insurance and also providing less of an incentive for anybody to sue them.

This is true especially in those states with the highest insurance premiums. Many of the "going bare doctors" are advised to make themselves malpractice suit proof. This is not my advice.

I have never been and never will be without medical malpractice protection from a good company. However, those readers who choose the "going bare approach" should do a "due diligence" and may be interested in reading Silverman's article.[4]

10.7.2 Asset Protection

Asset protection, or placing your money where it is safe from lawsuits or creditors, appears to be moving into the mainstream. People who are vulnerable to a lawsuit, bankruptcy

---

[*] From my notes on options offered to physicians by various medical society speakers—written here to give you the whole picture.

[†] I definitely do not recommend this ill advised move!

or divorce—including doctors, corporate executives, business owners, real-estate investors, and even families with teenage drivers—have grown increasingly concerned about protecting their property. Fanning the flames, financial-services companies and lawyers have been aggressively marketing complex trusts, partnerships, insurance products, limited-liability companies, and other vehicles to move those assets out of the reach of others.

Insurance companies are also boosting their excess-liability, or "umbrella," products, which protect policyholders from personal-injury claims above the limits in standard home or auto policies.

It is not necessary to shell out tens of thousands of dollars to set up a complex offshore trust or partnership. Some effective asset-protection strategies can be both simple and cheap, such as putting more money into a *401(k) plan, which is off-limits from most creditors* under federal law. A person at risk of liability could also transfer money to his or her spouse's name, but beware: if your marriage breaks up, so will this strategy.

Another emerging technique, called "accounts-receivable financing"—in which you take out bank loans against your business's receivables, in order to make the debt-laden assets less attractive to creditors—is being considered. In recent years, states such as Alaska and Delaware have started permitting asset-protection trusts.

The federal bankruptcy law enacted last year also changed the asset-protection landscape—making it tougher, in some instances, to protect your home from creditors. The goal of any plan like this is simple: to create as many hurdles as possible for potential creditors to jump through. Most plans are also designed to encourage your creditors to make a favorable settlement with you, rather than face long and perhaps expensive litigation.

One big caveat: If you know you have a potential legal action looming, do not transfer a big chunk of assets out of your hands. It is too late, because courts are likely to rule it a "fraudulent transfer." There are scores of questionable asset-protection "experts" who are hawking their tactics in seminars online and in cookie-cutter kits. It can be tough to detect them, but there are a couple of warning signs: Be careful if you are required to sign a nondisclosure form, since if something is done in accordance with applicable laws, you should be able to show it to your adviser. Be wary if the plan seems too complicated. And make sure to work with a lawyer who is well versed in your own state's laws.

Keep in mind that asset-protection techniques cannot be used to evade taxes—although some strategies such as family limited partnerships, insurance, and trusts can have attractive tax benefits. The most effective plans layer multiple tactics, to create as many steps as possible.

Here are some of the other asset-protection strategies that some advisers are now recommending:

1. Segregate business and personal risks.
2. Place businesses including family businesses inside a corporate shell such as a limited-liability company or a family-limited partnership. If creditors go after your company because of a business problem, they will have a hard time taking any personal assets.
3. Buy "umbrella insurance." One of the first lines of defense is to shift your risks to another entity such as an insurance company. Umbrella insurance protects assets from personal-injury claims above the liability limits set by standard-issue home or auto policies.
4. *Maximize state exemptions.* The laws governing protection of assets such as homes and insurance policies vary by state. In Florida and Texas, you can transfer your wealth into your home (building an addition, say, or paying off a mortgage), life insurance policy, annuity, or retirement plan, all of which are generally exempt from creditors.

5. In some states, married couples can title their property in a special way called "tenancy by the entirety," which can make it tough to reach for a creditor of one spouse. (More details about your state's laws are available online.)[5]
6. *Use trusts.* Doctors, executives, and other professionals are increasingly turning to asset-protection trusts, in which you transfer a portion of your own money into a trust run by an independent trustee, who can give you occasional distributions.
7. If set up properly, these trusts are supposed to be out of reach of creditors. The trusts have long been created in offshore jurisdictions such as the Cook Islands and Nevis. The idea is to put money in a foreign place that does not recognize a U.S. court order. But with new pending legislation I would not count on this for long.
8. In recent years, a growing number of people are setting up *asset-protection trusts* in the United States, as several states including Alaska, Delaware, Rhode Island, Nevada, and South Dakota have started permitting them over the past decade. You do not have to be a resident of one of these states to set up a trust there. Offshore trusts generally cost at least $25,000 to set up; domestic asset-protection trusts generally can cost less than half of that. But domestic trusts have not been adequately tested in court, and it is not clear whether they will be upheld.
9. Another well-established tactic is to set up a trust to benefit your children and generations beyond. Because the trust, rather than your heirs, legally holds the money, trust assets should be safeguarded from creditors.
10. *"Equity-strip" your assets.* That is a fancy term for loading your property with debt, so it is less attractive to creditors. Let us say you have a vacation home you want to safeguard. Take out a bank loan against the value of the property and place the loan proceeds into an asset, such as an insurance policy or annuity, if such assets are exempt from creditors in your state.

The theory: If the house is loaded with debt, it isn't going to be attractive to another creditor. *The downside*: You'll have to come up with a way to pay back the loan.[4,5]

10.7.3   Medical Malpractice Insurance

If I were to give any advice based on my 40 years of practice purchasing a medical malpractice policy is one of the best "peace of mind" steps a practitioner can take and expensive as it is it is worth every penny. Caveats are as follows:

1. Do your due diligence on the malpractice carrier in your locality.
2. Do not be the first nor the last to use a medical malpractice carrier.
3. Physician sponsored plans are on the whole (with some few exceptions) the way to go.

If you are truly worried about litigation—"an ounce of prevention is worth more than a pound of cure."

10.8   Why Be Ethical?

As Michael P. McQuillen MD, of the University of Rochester, reflected upon the "business of being human," he wondered whether all the effort, all the pain, all the frustration, and all the embarrassment of being human (and also a pending malpractice case) is worth it.

To paraphrase Sesame Street, he thought, "it isn't easy!" But then, it never has been. William Osler[6] the great nineteenth century physician who introduced modern medicine to America in his essay "Aequanimitas" advised maintaining a "gravidas" a stoicism through trouble. He never implied isolation, distancing, a lack of feeling or concern; only levelheadedness, self-control, and perspective through the stress of a medical practice.

Osler said

"To do that and to remain human is first and foremost to respect the humanity of those for whom you are privileged to care; to do your best for each and every one of them; being ever vigilant not to cause harm in the process; to do so in fairness and with respect and concern for the rest of humanity."

Osler added that

"The physician must bring the particular skills and insights of [Medicine] to bear upon the problems at hand. Furthermore, you must avoid mistakes as much as you can but then have the courage and humility to admit them when you make them. Whatever you do, you must do with the knowledge and consent of those for whom you do it. In the most dreadful of circumstances, whatever you do—even if it is only to stand there—you must do so with respect, even for the humanity you cannot see."

To which Michael P. McQuillen adds

"When in situations theat causes more pain and more frustration, you must bear the pain and frustration in the cause of those for whom you care. You not only must, but you can do all of this with guidance from the business of being human—the discipline and reasoning of whatever bioethical framework you choose. If so, then the effort, pain, frustration—even the embarrassment—become fun, as the profession was when first we were drawn to it. That is reason enough to be ethical!"

The observer who has thoroughly understood one link in a series of incidents, should be able accurately to state all the other ones, both before and after.

—Sherlock Holmes
The Five Orange Pips

References

1. *Am. Heart J.* 2006; 151: 1205–1213.
2. Mottur-Pilson C, Snow V, Bartlett K. Physician explanations for failing to comply with "best practices." *Eff. Clin. Pract.* September/October 2001; 4(5): 207–213.
3. Cabana M, et al. Why don't physicians follow clinical practice guidelines? A framework for improvement" *JAMA*; 282: 1458–1465.
4. Silverman RE. A fortress for your money how to guard against lawsuits and other claims on assets; the 'equity strip' maneuver. *Wall Street J.* 2006; B1.
5. http://www.assetprotectionbook.com/state_resources.html.
6. Osler W. *Aequanimitas with Other Addresses.* Philadelphia: Blakiston, 1952.

Alternate Dispute Resolution as an Alternative to Medical Malpractice Litigation

11

Alternate Dispute Resolution, Mediation, and Other Options for the Defendant Physician

A clever counsel would tear it all to rags.

—**Sherlock Holmes**
Silver Blaze

11.1 Your Options as a Physician Defendant

You should know at least something about alternate dispute resolution (ADR) rather than to go the full length of medical malpractice litigation without knowing this possible option. If you feel not up to the rigors, stress, and strain of litigation you might suggest another option to your attorney—whether he can look into ADR and mediation, and whether it is feasible in your state or locality. Sometimes, when the patient really wants an apology or wants to find out what really happened to him or his relative, this may work.

There are states that run a very successful program with ADR as an alternative to medical malpractice litigation. One such state is Wisconsin. Also, Colorado and other states are trying to get into this position to decrease the load on the courts.

In this chapter, we will discuss various options and substitutes for medical malpractice litigation as well as ADR terms and definitions you need to know. You should be aware of this process, especially the two-track system in which two tracks, i.e., mediation and litigation start off at the same time with one ultimately taking preference over the other. It is not as difficult or expensive as it sounds; in fact costs are lower when you take into consideration that upto 50% of the money paid on a liability claim goes to attorney fees alone.[1]

Prior to making any decision as to whether you should opt for ADR, you must know yourself first. Are you selecting ADR out of your anxiety and fear of the stress of litigation? If that is so you do not need another reason. Your peace of mind is worth a lot. However, this is not a decision to be made unilaterally. It may be preferable to review with your private attorney—not the insurance attorney—the pros and cons. Perhaps to calm your anxiety, you might ask for further study of your case with a focus group and check out other options you may not know about till now.

11.2   Litigation Focus Groups

Litigation focus groups use paid "jurors" to sit in for the real ones in a "mock" rehearsal of the medical malpractice trial. This method may allow a testing of your attorney's potential theory and themes of your defense and how it would go over with the jury.

11.2.1   Mock Trials

Mock trials include both adversarial, in which "opposing" lawyers are present and non-adversarial without opposing attorneys. In the former, lawyers for both sides of the issues render only their concise summaries of their positions; sometimes with additional real witnesses to rehearse their testimony. An advantage of mock trials is it prepares you and your witnesses to testify in court along the basic theme of your trial strategy with a reduction of anxiety. The "focus group-jury" can give some information as to the effectiveness of you and your expert's exhibits and perhaps ideas on how to modify them.

11.2.2   The Mock Jury: The Mock Jury Graduates from Law School

Mock trials are no longer classroom-only exercises. They are increasingly being used, sometimes well in advance of an actual trial, to help parties assess strategy, determine the manner of presentation of the cases, and evaluate settlement as an alternative to litigation. Real attorneys watch the mock jury deliberations through one-way mirrors or on live-feed monitors or videotape. The mock jury's members often are asked to complete questionnaires about each witness so that the lawyers can gain insight as to how real jurors at an actual trial may react.

How can a mock jury help lawyers and experts? By answering questions such as

- does the jury comprehend what the expert witness is saying?
- how does the jury perceive the expert witness—knowledgeable? believable? fair? pompous? candid? nice? biased? defensive?
- does the expert's testimony help the jury come to the right conclusion?
- should the expert also use some demonstrative evidence? Or would it distract from the expert's explanation?
- what else would be helpful to better convey an understanding of the case to the jury?

A mock jury carries more weight with you, the medical expert witness than all the words and warnings that the attorney can give. For example, if the jurors do not understand the "big words" the expert is using, the expert can try to "dumb it down" at trial. If the mock jury reads the expert's ongoing referring to her notes as "reading from a script," the lawyer sometimes can blow the notes up as an exhibit, so the jury sees there is nothing to hide. If the expert takes undue pains to carefully qualify his answers, yet the jurors see that as "evasive," the expert can adjust his trial presentation.

If you are to be an expert, you should welcome the opportunity to participate in a mock trial. The experience provides guidance and suggestions for improving and clarifying your testimony and delivery to become a more effective expert witness. Watching your own testimony on videotape, and hearing and seeing how jurors react to your testimony, and how they reach their decisions, can be invaluable to you as a witness. It often helps you to present a clearer, more focused picture during the actual trial and in the future.

11.3 Tort Reforms

Various solutions have been proposed to reform the tort system and thereby reduce the rippling effects of the malpractice crises on the cost and delivery of health care. The impetus for tort reforms come from the heavy costs of litigation to the U.S. health care system. According to *2006 AHA Hospital Statistics, 2004 Aon Hospital Professional Liability and Physician Benchmark Analysis, 2004 Best's Aggregates & Averages*, and *Price Waterhouse-Coopers 2006*, the numbers are staggering.

- Ten percent of all U.S. annual expenditures for health care goes to medical liability and defensive medicine.
- Annually, $32.6 billion is spent for professional liability claims and expenses for hospitals, long-term care facilities (LTCF), and physicians' malpractice awards.
- Total annual allocation to the legal industry is $246 billion/year.
- Medical malpractice litigation costs are growing 7.5% annually.
- Fifty to eighty percent of payouts by self-insured hospitals, LTCFs, and medical malpractice insurance companies go directly to attorney' fees, both defense and plaintiff, and their "administrative costs."
- Twenty-five percent goes to adjusted loss allocation expenses.
- Of the amount awarded to the injured patient (the plaintiff), 35–50% goes to the plaintiff's attorney as a contingency fee award.
- While tort reform in several states may keep some cases from entering the pipeline, for any case that does enter the pipeline more than 50% goes to the plaintiff's and defendants' attorney fees.

Least intrusive	Voluntary	Nonbinding

Negotiation

    Mediation

       Moderated settlement conference

           Mini-trial

             Summary jury trial

               Arbitration ◆

Most intrusive	Involuntary	Binding

These tort reform strategies are best understood when these reforms are considered as first- and second-generations.

Early interventions, first-generation tort reforms, attempted to reduce the frequency and severity of malpractice claims. Later efforts, second-generation tort reforms, were aimed at streamlining adjudication and compensation systems.

It is important to note that 50% of the award payout still goes to attorney fees even if mediation/arbitration is chosen. That is because plaintiffs and defendants are still represented by trial attorneys whose revenues go up with either the contingency fee in the former or billable hours of preparation by the latter, especially if ADR occurs downstream, i.e., late in the process, after the lions' share of the money has already been spent on adversarial discovery, depositions, medical experts, and other trial preparations.

11.4 Alternative Dispute Resolution

ADR refers to a group of processes through which a dispute can be resolved short of litigation and procedures for settling disputes by means other than litigation. ADR is increasingly used in commercial and labor disputes, divorce actions, motor vehicle claims, and more recently, medical malpractice tort claims. Various ADR methods are available to resolve medical malpractice claims.

11.4.1 Terms in Use in ADR

Arbitration: A form of ADR, in which the parties agree to have one or more trained arbitrators hear the evidence of the case and make a determination on liability or damages. The disputing parties may specify the rules of evidence and other procedural matters. Arbitration can be binding (i.e., subject to limited judicial review) or nonbinding (i.e., the parties may proceed to trials if not satisfied with the outcome of the arbitration).

In arbitration, the parties agree to submit their dispute to a neutral third party, usually an arbitrator or an arbitration panel. The arbitrator conducts a hearing in which each side presents evidence. The arbitrator then makes a determination on liability and renders a decision of award. Often, the parties agree in advance whether the arbitrator's decision will be binding. However, the decision of the arbitrator is subject to limited appellate review for procedural error, arbitrator bias, or fraud. Arbitration can be private, arising from the terms of a contract between the parties, or judicially mandated (court-annexed) by statute or rule.

Potential advantages of arbitration over judicial trials for resolving malpractice claims are speed (arbitration can be initiated as soon as the dispute arises), simpler and less-expensive proceedings (in arbitration, the rules of evidence are less stringent and the processes are often more streamlined than court proceedings), and privacy (arbitration hearings are more private than judicial trials, which can become media events).

An advantage not to be overlooked is the opportunity to use a uniquely skilled arbitrator. Unlike a judge, the arbitrator may possess technical skills or scientific knowledge directly related to the subject of the dispute; this could be a distinct advantage when the dispute is enmeshed in an extremely complex or esoteric content area such as medicine. However, by choosing an arbitration panel over a court trial, the defendant physician sets aside certain rights. For example, in arbitration there is no right to a trial by jury and no judicial instruction on the law. Similarly, documents from arbitration proceedings are not as complete as court proceedings. This can become problematic, as arbitration panels need not explain the basis of their decisions.

11.5   Alternate Dispute Resolution Definitions

Arbitration has been applied in medical malpractice for more than 20 years. In the state of Michigan, it is required by statute and in California by contract between managed-care organizations and enrollees. Challenges to medical malpractice arbitration awards in both states have been upheld by their highest courts. Despite this, arbitration remains an underutilized ADR method in medical malpractice cases across the country.

Caps on damages: Legislative limitations on the amount of money that can be awarded to the plaintiff for economic or noneconomic damages in personal injury claims, such as medical malpractice. The limit is imposed regardless of the actual amount of economic and noneconomic damages.

Damages: The sum of money a court or jury awards as compensation for a tort or breach of contract. The law recognizes several categories of damages. General damages: typically intangible damages, such as pain and suffering, disfigurement, interference with ordinary enjoyment of life, or loss of consortium. Special damages: out-of-pocket damages that can be quantified, such as medical expenses, lost wages, or rehabilitation costs.

Punitive/exemplary damages: Damages awarded to the plaintiff in cases of intentional tort or gross negligence to punish the defendant or act as a deterrent to others.

Defensive medicine: Physician behavior intended to prevent patients from filing medical malpractice claims. Attempts to make more accurate diagnosis by ordering extra laboratory tests, medical procedures, and visits. The term can also be used to describe physician avoidance of high-risk patients or procedures primarily to reduce the risk of malpractice claims being filed against the physician. The performance of extra procedures for defensive purposes is sometimes called positive defensive medicine. The avoidance of high-risk patients or procedures can be referred to as negative defensive medicine.

Early neutral evaluation: A panel of one to three neutral advisors hears a presentation of the disputants' positions. The panel reports its evaluation of the merits of each side's case, then facilitates further settlement discussions. This term is synonymous with the term *moderated settlement conference* when lawyers are the neutrals.

Example of how it works in one state (Wisconsin): Medical mediation panels in Wisconsin provide an objective assessment of the strengths and weaknesses of a medical malpractice claim. By law, all medical malpractice claims must go through this process before they can proceed to court. Each panel consists of a lawyer, a health care provider, and a layperson. The early neutral evaluation they provide can reduce litigation costs by identifying claims without merit as early as possible and by expediting the resolution of those claims that do have merit. The medical mediation panels were created by the legislature in 1986 in an effort to provide "an informal, inexpensive and expedient means for resolving medical malpractice disputes without litigation," Wis. Stat. § 655.42(1). Although referred to in the legislation as "mediation," the work of the panels is more accurately described as "early neutral evaluation."

Enterprise liability: A system under which a health care institution or health insurance plan assumes full legal liability for the actions of physicians acting as their agents and individual physicians cannot be named as defendants.

Malpractice: Professional negligence resulting from improper discharge of professional duties or failure to meet the standard of care of a professional, resulting in harm to another. The legal standard for malpractice requires (a) a physician–patient relationship that establishes the duty of care, (b) an adverse outcome with actual injury or harm, (c) negligence by the provider (often interpreted as failure to provide the standard of care), and (d) direct causality between negligence and outcome.

Mediation: It is really an extension of direct negotiation between the parties, using a neutral third party to facilitate the negotiation process. As a facilitator, the mediator has neither the authority to impose a solution on the parties nor the results of the process binding on the disputing parties. The mediator acts by identifying issues, proposing solutions, and encouraging accommodation on both sides. Mediation can be effective in medical malpractice cases in which the patient and physician want to preserve their relationship or in which poor communications has led to the dispute.

The advantages of mediation over litigation are its decreased costs, more confidential proceedings, and the degree of control enjoyed by the disputing parties over the process and outcome. In resolving allegations of medical negligence, patients tend to favor mediation because it provides a forum in which they can express their concerns and may lead to an acknowledgment of the problem sometimes in the form of an apology.

Mediation, however, has its limitations. In many jurisdictions, mediation is voluntary and can only be pursued if both parties agree to it. Mediators do not have the same authority as judges and therefore cannot compel the release of information nor can their decisions be imposed. The mediator has only as much power as the disputing parties permit and as such can go no further than the disputants themselves are willing to go.

The Two-Track System—upstream, i.e., in the early phases of the impending malpractice suit may save you a lot of time and stress and is not so expensive if done early.

Track 1 = Negotiation or mediation by separate attorneys paid on an hourly basis.

Track 2 = The traditional method of litigation with contingency fees for the plaintiff's attorney and the same hourly reimbursement for the defendant's attorney only if track 1 fails.

11.6   How Mediation/ADR Works and Saves Time and Money

A discussion from Slaikeu is presented.[2–4]

Of the many models of mediation, some emphasize shuttle diplomacy, others joint talk, and yet others an integration of the two. Any mediation, however, stands to save money by helping in the following ways:

1. Overall, the mediator serves as a buffer and helps control adversarial posturing. In litigation, mediation can control discovery costs (depositions of key witnesses, exchange of records, assessments of damages, etc.) by providing a forum for collaborative resolution of issues along the way to court.
2. After an opening meeting, the mediator might meet with the parties privately to hear interests and "matters of the heart" that they and their attorneys may be unwilling to

disclose to the other side. To the extent that the mediator uses private caucuses, the mediator will have a greater data set (private information from each party) than the parties themselves had when the mediation began. The mediator uses this information very carefully and does not disclose what the parties do not want to be disclosed to the other side.

3. In joint meetings, the mediator can assist the parties as they discuss problems and underlying interests and as they create solutions. Both parties are assisted by having a monitoring process that allows them to get back to the table should there be any difficulty in implementing the agreement.

4. The mediator can float options for resolution that the parties are unwilling to declare or even discuss with the other side for fear of sending the wrong signal. The private caucus gives both the mediator and the party more freedom to explore options than arbitration or litigation ever does.

5. Mediation takes fewer person hours than a hearing, as the primary players are the conflicting parties.

6. They might consult with attorneys in the early stages; attorneys might even be present in mediation in certain cases. Still, two parties, two attorneys, and one mediator are considerably fewer people than a full-scale hearing. The savings in attorney time (a key indication of expense) using this approach are significant. The reduction in legal expenses usually falls in the range of 50–80%.

11.7   Who Decides on ADR?

Attorneys on both sides can argue forever with one another—"a game without end" as someone once put it—about whether a case is "right for ADR." Can you imagine that attorneys who do not agree over the facts of the case, liability, and damages will somehow reach agreement on whether or not to take a case to mediation or ADR? Especially when, by going to mediation or arbitration, they fear showing "weakness," and their fees as litigation counsel may be one-fifth or less of what they would be if the case went to trial or settled on the courthouse steps? The decision should be up to you, the physician defendant, who must make the decision to undergo a very rigorous courtroom litigation battle versus a quieter medication session with the patient along with the mediation attorneys.

In *litigation*, the idea is to convince a judge or jury of the rightness of one's argument according to a point of law. There is no interest in getting cooperation from the other side. Litigation is a battle. Litigation takes more money.

Mediation, in contrast, is just the opposite. Instead of using the adversary model to try to convince somebody else that one is right or wrong, the mediation model helps the parties and their advocates to understand and appreciate one another's points of view and key interests, acknowledge any mistakes or wrongdoing, and then fashion solutions that can be accepted by both sides. How the parties will relate (or not) to each other at the end is very important.

When *mediation* is done well, the parties may settle their dispute with appropriate restitution, and, in some cases, even reconcile with one another through acknowledgments, apologies, and by making mutually agreeable changes in a possible doctor–patient working relationship in the future.

11.8   Why Litigate the Case in Court?

There are really only two reasons to be in court these days:

1. To establish a legal precedent (case law).
2. To send a message to the world (very public dispute resolution). If you win the case there is no settlement or transfer of money to the plaintiff. This saves your insurance carrier the award to the plaintiff (minus of course the legal fees of discovery, expert witnesses, attorney billable hours, legal research, etc.). But more important to you it saves you from being reported to the National Practitioner Data Bank (NPDB), which will be kept in your record during your entire professional life. This has to be weighed very carefully by you in this decision. But remember this that over 90% of malpractice cases get settled before trial and literally on the courthouse steps. Even that settlement after all your stress and preparation for the trial still means a report to the Data Bank. You should know and at least ask whether you have the right to block any settlement decided by the malpractice insurance company without your permission. Otherwise, all that time in discovery and stress all the way up to the trial date will be for naught and out of your control.

But there is an advantage, where insurance carriers allow mediation of maximizing the benefits of mediation by adopting the "two-track" model for attorney representation in dispute resolution.

11.9   Should Your Malpractice Attorney Suggest or Decide on ADR?

Litigation and mediation are very different processes, and the attorney role in each is very different. If you send in the litigation attorney whose main talent is the adversary model, and who will make more in legal fees if the case goes to court rather than if it is resolved earlier in mediation, you shoot yourself in the foot in at least two ways. First, with few exceptions, this type of advocate would not be as good in the "work together to work it out" part as would an advocate who is trained and paid only to "work it out." Second, if you follow the money, the old model effectively allows a financial conflict of interest to run freely in the mediation, since the financial compensation for the attorney advocate is always greater in litigation (or settling on the courthouse steps) than in mediation, which typically entails fewer billable hours per case for attorneys.

This is not lawyer bashing. What is being bashed is the use of the litigation model when you may not need it. Here is another way to put it. In our culture, the lawyer jokes are actually grounded in disgust at the litigation/adversary model wreaking havoc to relationships—the divorce, the partnership split, the personal injury case, and even the medical malpractice case—after which the two "adversaries" go out for a drink and a talk about their golf scores.

The traditional view of lawyers, are as spoilers who say no because of legal liability issues, or who inflame a case by escalating it with their adversarial/litigation tools, which are used in relating to the other side as an "opponent."

A far better approach perhaps in your case is to appropriately use one set of attorneys (to maximize the counselor at law role) for the "work it out," mediation, or settlement phase, and then hand it to true litigators for going to court, if necessary.

Indeed, there will be many lawyers who will be equipped to do both services, *although not both services for the same client.* As a bonus, you can tell your malpractice insurance carrier that if their litigation expenses go down with ADR, then so will your insurance costs and malpractice premiums, since the insurance rates are influenced heavily by the litigation expenses.

11.10   The Two-Track Model

As a solution to this problem, the "two-track" model uses separate attorneys for the two tracks.

If you get into mediation, you or your insurance carrier will hire one attorney to represent you in the mediation, and use an attorney from another law firm to pick up the case for litigation, if necessary. "This is not as inefficient as it may at first sound, i.e., two attorneys instead of one," claims Slaikeu. "You can build in an appropriate transfer of the case if you need it. And, even more important, you can actually have the litigation counsel give a private opinion to you and the insurance carrier, and your mediation counsel, regarding your chances in court, so a comparison can be made of a potential mediation settlement with your chances of success in court. The difference is that the one predicting the success of the court path will not be allowed to represent you in the bridge-building, talk it out for resolution phase of mediation. As a client, you will then have the best of both worlds: a highly skilled collaborative type to reach a win/win agreement if at all possible (sometimes called "the last nice person you will talk to on this matter") versus the aggressive litigator."

11.11   Attorney Fees in the Two-Track System

How about the plaintiff's side? The plaintiff's side takes a percentage of whatever the settlement is, however they get it, whether through direct negotiations or mediation, or failing that, a court award. It is actually to their advantage to get many of these cases resolved earlier to reduce their upfront expenses on contingency fee cases. Some plaintiffs' attorneys may also see the value in representing clients in negotiations and mediations on an hourly fee basis.

In summary, claims Slaikeu, "Instead of continuing the tort reform battle why not move upstream and implement solutions that will reduce to a trickle the number of [medical malpractice] cases that will end up in litigation. Thinking of the interests of patients, physician, and [medical] provider institutions for solutions that allow them to continue as partners even in the face of unanticipated outcomes. Why not invest in systems that address human needs and professional interests while also reducing the inordinately high litigation expense component of medical malpractice insurance?"

Medical arbitration: This is a hybrid form of dispute resolution. It starts with mediation, which if unsuccessful, is followed by arbitration.

Mini-trial: Senior officials of corporate entities in the dispute meet with a neutral advisor and after hearing each party's presentation, proceed to develop a voluntary settlement.

Moderated settlement conference: Sometimes referred to as "early neutral evaluation" or "advisory opinions," this procedure is similar to nonbinding arbitration with certain exceptions: no rules of evidence, no cross-examination, and no formality in how the neutral entity communicates the outcome. This venue is often used in cases with heavy application-of-law content.

Negotiation: The most frequently used method of ADR is defined as the process whereby two or more disputing parties confer together in good faith so as to settle a matter of mutual concern. The approach to negotiation may be positional or principled. In positional negotiation, divergent parties incrementally concede their position until a compromise is reached. In principled negotiation, the parties generate options focused on their interests to arrive at an agreement based on objective criteria. Negotiation serves as the basis for mediation, an important ADR method used in medical malpractice cases.

Negotiation has its advantages. The disputants remain in control of the process. Negotiated resolutions tend to have greater durability than agreements reached by other methods. The process of negotiation can be educational for both parties and therefore may prevent subsequent discord in the relationship. However, sometimes negotiation alone is not enough to resolve medical malpractice actions.

Neutral fact finder: A neutral entity with expertise in the disputed subject matter examines critical facts in the dispute and renders an advisory opinion on the matter.

No-fault compensation: A method for compensating persons injured during the course of medical treatment, regardless of whether the injury was caused by the negligence or fault of a health care provider.

11.12 National Practitioner Data Bank

A major impediment to physician use of ADR in medical malpractice is the mandatory reporting of all malpractice payments to the NPDB. It is important that physicians understand that any malpractice payment (e.g., settlement or award) made on their behalf, even those derived from an ADR process, must be reported to the NPDB. Entries in the NPDB are specific to the physician on whose behalf the payment was made and are permanent. Every time a physician seeks or renews clinical privileges at a hospital or new employment, his or her NPDB may be queried by authorized entities. Although physicians can furnish a note of explanation in their NPDB files, many prefer to take the odds of litigation, which tend to favor the physician's defendant. Repeated efforts to open the NPDB to the public have not succeeded thus far. This could change as patient rights initiatives continue to gain momentum and other databanks of disciplinary actions taken against health care practitioners that are already open to the public (e.g., Medicare/Medicaid programs exclusions, Occupational Safety and Health Act/Clinical Laboratories Improvement Act sanctions, adverse actions taken by state medical licensing boards) continue to proliferate.

Ombudsman: A neutral third party investigates facts involved in a complaint or grievance within an institution and makes a nonbinding advisory recommendation to senior managers regarding resolution of the problem.

Practice guidelines: Generally refers to clinical practice guidelines (CPGs), which is defined by the Institute of Medicine as systematically developed statements to assist practitioner and patient decisions about appropriate health care for specific clinical circumstances.

Pretrial screening panel: An ADR procedure in which a screening panel hears the evidence of a malpractice claim including expert testimony, and determines liability before the plaintiff files a malpractice suit. In some instances, the pretrial screening panel also determines damages in the claim. The pretrial screening panel may be composed of health care professionals, legal experts, and health care consumers. The use of the screening panel and its method of operation are determined legislatively, thus it may be mandatory or voluntary depending on the law. However, the decision of the pretrial screening panels is not binding. Therefore, the parties may subsequently pursue the claim through the legal system.

The pretrial screening panel is an ADR method that was uniquely developed for medical malpractice cases. About half of the states have statutes establishing pretrial screening panels, which review malpractice claims and render a nonbinding advisory opinion on the merits of the claim before a suit being filed. Panel composition varies considerably from state to state. In some states, only physicians sit on pretrial screening panels. Other states restrict panels to attorneys. And some others require that the members of a pretrial screening panel include physicians, attorneys, judges, and laypersons. The panel reviews the merits of the malpractice case and offers an opinion on the physician's liability. In some states, the panel reviews the claim before legal action is taken. In other states, the suit must be filed in court before it is sent to the panel. States also vary on whether the panel renders an opinion on damages. Furthermore, state law determines whether the findings of the pretrial screening panel can be admitted as evidence should the claim go to trial, and if so, how much weight the panel's findings should be given.

The purpose of the pretrial screening process is twofold:

1. To eliminate nonmeritorious claims
2. To encourage settlement of meritorious claims before litigation

The earliest malpractice pretrial screening panels date back to the 1960s. In New Mexico, a 1962 statute introduced a voluntary pretrial review panel; in the mid-1970s, during the malpractice litigation crisis, the statute was revised to make pretrial screening mandatory. Consequently, from 1976 to 1996, New Mexico panels have heard more than 2,100 medical malpractice cases; nearly three-quarters of those cases were resolved without trial.

A major disadvantage of pretrial screening panels is the nonbinding nature of most ADR methods. In many states, the plaintiff can still litigate after the pretrial screening panel decision is made. Thus, the pretrial screening panel may, in effect, further delay final resolution of the claim. Although there is some evidence that screening panels are effective in eliminating low-merit cases, others contend that panels are victims of their own existence, as they can become clogged with frivolous claims that otherwise would not be pursued.

Private judging: Also known as "rent-a-judge," parties hire a retired judge to hear the case, following court-like procedures. The judge's decision is as enforceable as a regular court decision would be.

Statute of limitations: The time period established by law during which a plaintiff may file a lawsuit; the period for reporting malpractice is longer for minor patients than adults. Once this period expires, the plaintiff's lawsuit can be barred. In some states, the time period does not begin until the injury is discovered. The discovery rule states that the date of the injury, from which the time period is measured, is the date that it was reasonable for the plaintiff to have discovered the injury rather than the actual date of injury. Injuries may be discovered years after the treatment was provided. Therefore, the time period for filing actions may be extensive and difficult to verify. The long tail associated with pediatric care is an important consideration in resolving malpractice allegations. The more time that has passed, the more difficult it is to obtain pertinent evidence and available witnesses.

Summary jury trial: The parties' lawyers present summaries of evidence and arguments to a jury in a 1-day hearing. After a nonbinding jury verdict is rendered, the parties may interview jurors about how they perceived the merits of each side's position. A regular trial may follow if the parties do not subsequently settle based on the information received.

Tort: A civil wrong for which an action can be filed in court to recover damages for personal injury or property damage resulting from negligent acts of intentional misconduct.

Tort law: A body of law that provides citizens a private, judicially enforced remedy for injuries caused by another person. Legal actions based in tort have three elements: (1) existence of a legal duty from the defendant to the plaintiff; (2) breach of that duty; and (3) injury to the plaintiff as a result of that breach.

Tort reform: A term used to describe collectively a number of legislative and judicial modifications to traditional tort law.

11.13   Summary of Points Made in the Peer-Reviewed Literature*

1. ADR techniques are often described as bilateral tort reforms because they can make it cheaper for physicians to defend unfounded claims and easier for plaintiffs to prevail on meritorious claims. Given the persistent problems in medical malpractice litigation for both sides, it is surprising that ADR methods remain underutilized, especially when reforms based on ADR potentially make the tort system more equitable and affordable to both plaintiffs and defendants.[5]

2. The use of arbitration in the commercial arena has increased tremendously in recent years, yet there has been a reluctance to adopt arbitration of medical malpractice claims in place of litigation. After discussing the benefits of arbitration in medical malpractice cases, Professor Metzloff[6] examines why the use of arbitration has not become predominant, discussing factors such as judicial hostility, failure of state statutes designed to encourage arbitration, and lack of hard evidence that arbitration works. Professor Metzloff then explores the future of arbitration in medical malpractice cases, citing examples from his own work experience with Duke Law School's Private Adjudication Center, and discusses attributes, which would make malpractice arbitration successful in the future.

3. Dr. J.J. Fraser[7] from the Department of Emergency Medicine, University of Texas (Houston) Medical School compares the different ADR systems in this summary article. The medical malpractice crises and ensuing tort reform efforts, including methods of alternative dispute resolution (ADR), are generally reviewed. Arbitration in the context of medical malpractice is examined from the perspective of other states' experiences.

---

* *See* Appendix attached CD for other references and readings.

Fraser reports that Michigan has one of the nation's oldest medical malpractice arbitration programs, but it suffers from underutilization. California's experience derives from the use of arbitration in the managed-care setting. While Texas has statutory provisions for medical malpractice arbitration, in light of public policy favoring ADR, the statute could be perceived as antipublic policy, resulting in underuse. Fraser also believes that the NPDB also serves to discourage physician participation.

4. In the 1970s, Michigan and other states were confronted with a medical malpractice crisis. The escalating number of medical malpractice lawsuits and concomitant increase in malpractice premiums for health care providers fostered a divisive climate among doctors, lawyers, and patients. In response to this crisis, the Michigan legislature enacted the Medical Malpractice Arbitration Act. The Act establishes a process whereby patients may agree to arbitrate any claims rather than pursue them through the courts. Bedekian[8] believes that as the law-respecting arbitration becomes less vulnerable to judicial perforation, other jurisdictions will treat the Michigan Medical Arbitration Program as an archetype, susceptible to replication.

5. Lehrman proposes a two-pronged legislative response to the current debate over medical malpractice insurance. The author does not advocate mandatory caps on malpractice damages, nor the imposition of a uniform regime on the field of medicine. Rather, he articulates some of the important legal, medical, and societal benefits that would come from embracing arbitration in the nonemergent medical malpractice context. The author also calls for the reformulation of the NPDB.

6. The wide variety of economic cooperative arrangements in which hospitals and physicians engage can lead to disputes. As methods of dispute resolution, litigation, and arbitration are costly and time-consuming and can have long-lasting adverse effects on relationships between the disputing parties, an alternative method of dispute resolution is mediation, the process of voluntarily negotiating a settlement with the help of a mediator. Mediation generally is quicker, less costly, and less likely to be adversarial than litigation or arbitration. In addition, mediation offers privacy regarding the nature of the dispute, thus preserving valuable reputations.[9]

7. An increasingly complex health care system undergoing rapid changes is an ideal set up for frequent conflicts among the numerous participants. While conflict is inevitable, the manner in which it is handled can markedly affect the outcome of the dispute and the future relationship of the parties, as well as the emotional and financial cost of the dispute. This article presents an overview of the principles and processes of ADR, and describes how these processes are currently used to resolve health care disputes.[10]

8. Provider–patient disputes are inevitable in the health care sector. Health care providers and regulators should recognize this and plan opportunities to enforce ADR as early as possible in the care delivery process. Negotiation is often the main dispute resolution method used by local health care providers, failing which litigation would usually follow. The role of mediation in resolving malpractice disputes has been minimal. Health care providers, administrators, and regulators should therefore look toward a postevent communication-cum-mediation framework as the key national strategy to resolving malpractice disputes.[11]

9. The wide variety of economic cooperative arrangements in which hospitals and physicians engage can lead to disputes. As methods of dispute resolution, litigation, and arbitration are costly and time-consuming and can have long-lasting adverse effects on relationships between the disputing parties. An alternative method of dispute resolution is mediation, the process of voluntarily negotiating a settlement with the help of a mediator.

Mediation generally is quicker, less costly, and less likely to be adversarial than litigation or arbitration. In addition, mediation offers privacy regarding the nature of the dispute, thus preserving valuable reputations.[12]

10. Malpractice litigation is felt to provide a standard for practice. It can be costly both in terms of settlement awards and detrimental impact on the physician. Mediation offers opportunities to bypass that stringent legal process, yet allows a resolution of disputes and allows proper redress of grievances.

11. Conflict thrives and grows in the increasingly competitive and uncertain health care environment. Conflict impacts health care organizations' performance in several areas: (1) patient grievances and health plan member disputes; (2) internal employee and management disputes; and (3) payer, provider, and vendor disputes. "Grief budgets," the hard and soft costs due to disputes that are poorly handled and conflicts that are ignored, detract from an organization's health mission and erode its bottom line. This article offers a strategy to solve conflict at an early stage in all three areas, with measurable results that strengthen profits and improve customer service by instilling a mediation-based conflict resolution culture throughout the organization. Mediation is nonadversarial, neutral, proactive, and collaborative. It is also confidential and always protects the future relationship between the parties. The challenge, therefore, is to strategically implant mediation into the health care organization's structure, to intercept and solve conflict early on. The article provides an overview of the steps needed to install a dispute resolution program.[13]

References

1. Slaikeu KA. *ADR in Health Care*. Austin: Chorda Conflict Mgmt., 1988.
2. Slaikeu KA. *When Push Comes to Shove*. San Francisco: Jossey-Bass Pub., 1996.
3. Slaikeu KA. *Controlling the Costs of Conflict*. San Francisco: Jossey-Bass Pub., 1998.
4. Slaikeu KA. *Two Track Model for Attorney Representation in Dispute Resolution*. Austin, TX: Chorda Conflict Management, 2004.
5. Fraser JJ. Technical Report: Alternative Dispute Resolution in Medical Malpractice pediatrics. Committee on Medical Liability, 1999–2000. Vol. 107, No. 3 March 2001, pp. 602–607.
6. Metzloff TB. The Unrealized Potential of Malpractice Arbitration. *Spec. Law Dig. Health Care Law* 1997(215): 9–36. USA: Duke University School of Law.
7. Fraser Jr JJ. Medical malpractice arbitration: a primer for Texas physicians. *Tex. Med.* 1997; 93(1): 76–80.
8. Bedikian M. Medical Malpractice Arbitration Act: Michigan's experience with arbitration. *Am. J. Law Med.* 1984; 10(3): 287–306.
9. Duncheon MA. Using mediation to resolve disputes among hospitals and physicians. *Healthc. Financ. Manage.* 1999; 53(6): 78–79.
10. Joseph DM. The role of health care ADR (alternative dispute resolution) in reducing legal fees. *Physician Exec.* 1995; 21(11): 26–30.
11. Harold TK. Minimizing medical litigation. *J. Med. Pract. Manage.* 2006; 21(5): 257–261.
12. Gorton C. Using mediation to resolve disputes in health care. *Physician Exec.* 2005; 31(4): 34–37.
13. Brown H et al. Alternative dispute resolution and mediation. *Qual. Health Care* 1995; 4(2): 151–158.

Caveats on Testifying Physicians–Attorney Relationships

12

A physician's reputation takes many years to develop and only seconds to destroy.

—**Anon**

If you accept the responsibility of serving as an expert witness, it should be one of the best consultations you have ever given.

—**Kunin, CM**
Annals of Internal Medicine, January 1984, 100(1): 139–43

12.1   Introduction

The first thing you should know as the defendant or testifying physician is not only is the opposing attorney no friend of yours, but neither is your retaining attorney. And you are no friend of his. Your relationship is and must be purely professional. Therefore you must adhere to certain guidelines outlined in this chapter:

- All contacts with the attorney should preferably be verbal, unless you are documenting your relationship terms in writing.
- Your financial relationship should always be documented in a letter or signed agreement.
- When you are first contacted by the attorney to be a testifying medical expert, it is often advisable to spell out your role in a very short one-page summary outlined below in this chapter.
- When both of you agree that you should act as a testifying physician, I strongly advise a mutually signed medical expert witness engagement agreement, also included below in this chapter. Your individual written agreement may differ as per your needs and as your own private attorney suggests. However, at least show your private attorney the example demonstrated below in this chapter and build from it.
- You must also document your invoices and billable hours on permanent time sheets.

Several key phrases should be used in the note accompanying the invoice. I also include advice on avoiding other key phrases. Suggestions are made on the statements you should make during the deposition to spell out your role and your needs. This chapter also includes a sample report so that you can see how to dovetail the peer-reviewed literature citations to support your medical opinions so as to surmount a Daubert attack. I have also included suggestions as to potential advertising and promotion.

Also included in this chapter is an example of a medical expert's letter/report to the defendant physician's attorney on preparation for the deposition. This includes certain key elements, which must be present in each report. In addition, there is a discussion of the unethical DWP syndrome or "designation without permission" methods used by some unethical attorneys you may encounter. Also be on the lookout for opinion shopping attorneys. They can easily be identified and this chapter shows how.

What does the attorney need from you, the defendant physician or the medical expert consultant?

1. Help in developing a (medical) theme for the case (see chapter on themes and analogies) and to help him understand the relevant medical issues in the case—assemble, review, and analyze the medical data.
2. Think through the analysis of each of his complaints and each individual aspect of his claim.
3. List the strengths and weaknesses of his and his opponent's case.
4. Your assistance during deposition on questioning the opposing parties, defendant physician, or medical experts.
5. As a skilled physician you can expose weaknesses of the opposing parties and support your own fact-gathering process.
6. He needs information on
   - what you know about the opposing expert physicians?
   - how they are perceived by their peers?
   - whether they have been involved in any medical controversies?
7. To help organize his questions to you on direct testimony.
8. List all your weaknesses and that of the case so it can be handled on direct testimony.

First, as to the above questions that the retaining attorney will ask you, my advice to you is never report gossip about any opposing medical witnesses. As gossip goes it is usually wrong. It is my policy to analyze for the retaining attorney only what is published about the opposing expert—his articles, lectures, etc. Anything more is contrary to the code of ethics, or should be.

Now let us discuss some simple advices that I have learned the very hard way.

12.2   Attorney's Initial Relationship with the Potential Medical Expert

A good attorney will want to know all you have testified relating to the subject at hand. You should review any available articles, deposition, or trial testimony given by you on this subject.

If your opinion is unfavorable to the interviewing attorney's case or your past publications or testimony are contrary, then termination of the interview may be appropriate. He will want to know if you appear to be a "hip shooter" who quickly takes firm positions based only on the minimal materials sent to you about the candidate. If so, he may then decide that you are simply attempting to obtain the engagement at all costs rather than to provide honest opinions. The potential retaining attorney will also provide you with the opportunity for brainstorming many issues in the case. The results of that brainstorming could serve as a basis for providing ideas or guidance as a consultant-expert.

✓ In accepting retention, you must not assume that all materials were provided to you. You should ask (preferably in writing to keep for your records) for every document generated and all materials circulated among the parties; every item in the medical file, as well as the content of every conversation among the other experts, counsel, and the client, or anyone else concerning your work in the case. Also take precautions from the very inception of the relationship between counsel and you, to minimize the generation of written material that could be used to impeach you.

12.2.1 What Background and Characteristics Is the Potential Retaining Attorney Looking for in You?

- Court system knowledge and awareness of the legal intricacies of the case for that geographic area.
- Understanding the issues, including the subtle differences that the opposition counsel may be probing.
- The ability to quickly go to the heart of the case—find the medical strengths and weaknesses of a case, and to advise in that regard. This sometimes involves further research in the area, but this extra attention, you should point out, can pay enormous dividends for the retaining attorney—whether for the defense or the plaintiff.
- He wants his expert needs to be incisive enough to pick up the limitations and strengths of the case in the context of his or her specialty.
- These limitations commonly may not be realized by the retaining team initially, because they are not expert physicians.
- The medical expert's skills often translate into expertise in court, coherent expressions to a judge, and persuasiveness for a jury.
- The expert has to be able to communicate information clearly and appropriately.
- This witness needs to be able to interact with juries effectively when applicable.
- Interaction skills can sometimes be reflected by expertise in public speaking—this is seldom asked about.
- Testimony involves situations that frequently require the expert to quickly and appropriately think on his feet.
- Positive pointers may be the ability to communicate in conversation with the attorney and experience in public speaking—e.g., lecturing reputation.
- *Balance*: An expert who earns his or her principal income as an "expert witness," particularly one who always testifies for the plaintiffs or always for the defense, will be regarded as somewhat suspect by the judge and jurors. Thus he will find that an expert who "works both sides of the street" is trusted by both sides.

A good summary of what a retaining attorney looks for in a medical expert is a medical expert witness who currently is in active patient care and doing the same procedures in the issues in the case as well as holding a medical school faculty appointment, an author of peer-reviewed medical articles, and who is able to teach and present well before a jury.

12.3   Rules of Thumb on Accepting Cases

1. As part of the process of deciding on whether to accept a new case as a medical expert, you should find out how much is at stake in the litigation and if the attorney has a reasonable budget for your expert work. One symptom of an underfunded or overly cost-sensitive lawyer is the retaining attorney's refusal to provide you with an advance retainer fee. Do not be persuaded by the attorney's blandishments "to help out with this one case" because I will give you a lot more work later or "Don't worry. The case will settle and never go to court."

2. You should also find out about the case's probable time lines—e.g., when you are likely to be deposed, the deadlines for written reports, and when the case is likely to go to trial to determine whether you may have scheduling conflicts.

3. *Written agreements*: Insist upon a written agreement written by *your personal attorney* that clearly defines the scope of the engagement, including fees and when the fees are to be paid. (See my written agreement in the forms and communications chapter.) This should include a compensation agreement.

In either capacity, consulting or testifying, the expert should obtain a written agreement spelling out his compensation and a clear understanding as to who is responsible for payment. Such a written agreement should be reviewed by your own private attorney so as to eliminate any potential misunderstandings as to your compensation or to whom you should look to for payment. The terms of your consultant's fees should be based on (1) rate per hour, (2) experience and expertise, (3) out-of-pocket expenses (such as travel, etc.), and (4) the nature of the task assigned (e.g., if it requires time-consuming efforts on the part of the expert).

Your expert activity should never-ever be compensated on a contingency basis. Contingent compensation, which you must always avoid, may take several forms:

1. It is not always an overt percentage of the recovery.
2. It may consist of "abnormally" higher hourly rate payments, or "bonuses," or "premiums," or "fringe benefits," or any other direct or indirect form of contingent financial incentive or reward if the case is won.
3. Any agreement to pay witness fees, which in any way is contingent upon the outcome of the case, is unethical and void as against public policy (and also may be unenforceable).
4. Instead, your fee for testifying in a trial or a deposition should be based *only* on (1) the rate per hour, including waiting time in court; (2) your experience and expertise; and (3) out-of-pocket expenses (such as travel, etc.).

Therefore I strongly advise that your mutually signed written agreement with the retaining attorney or, at minimum, a written letter from you acknowledged by the attorney should stipulate the following:

- You have the right to abide by the "Code of Ethics" of your profession or professional society.
- You have the right also to receive adequate and fair compensation for your services; to assist the fact finder (jury) in reaching a just and fair determination of the matters

in dispute (Rule 702, Federal Rules of Evidence); and render your opinions based on your knowledge, granting, and experience (Rule 702).

- You have the right to be able to rely on other professionals to support your conclusions (radiologists, pathologists) if it is usual for physicians such as you to regularly rely on such information (Rule 703).
- You have the right to be given all relevant data by your retaining attorney.
- You have the right to be kept informed as to a new development and new evidence in the case, which could alter your expert opinion.
- You have the right to have adequate time to prepare and complete all assignments free from undue influence by any attorney.
- You have the right to have a deposition conducted in a comfortable and physically agreeable setting with reasonable time to prepare and to schedule.
- You have the right to adequate notice of your endorsement as an expert witness in any proceeding in which you are selected.

My own written agreement with the retaining attorney covers the above points and more, with my accompanying letter #2 insisting on a 10-h advance for billable hours as a medical expert witness. Note that this is subsequent to the already expended 3-h advance for a preliminary review of the medical records, which was accompanied by letter #1.

Warning: Do not adapt this or any of my letters and communications without your attorney's input!

Letter #1 to the attorney with whom I have agreed on the phone after a preliminary telephone discussion to hear about the major points in the case so as to know whether it fits my specialty, my interests, and whether there appears the potential of some merit in the case so as to review the medical records. This is a request for an advance to review those medical records.

Thank you for your inquiry.

I will be glad to review the medical records. I have attached my CV.

I charge a minimum fee of $1500 per case. This represents my hourly fee of $475/h for expert consultant medical record review.

The check should be sent with the medical records to the address seen on the CV. My tax Federal tax id # is _____.

This amount usually covers a complete and confidential review of all the initial documents as a consultant medical expert, with my analysis of this case, and the rendering of a preliminary verbal medical opinion on the merits of the case.

To summarize my CV, I am Board Certified in both Internal Medicine and Gastroenterology.

The decision of whether I will also act as an expert testifying witness will depend on whether I believe the case has merit and if you and I wish to extend the scope of the engagement to include expert witness testimony in connection with the matter to which the preliminary opinion relates.

Until such time that I have agreed to the merits of the case and to testify as an Expert Witness in this case, I cannot be named as an Expert Witness. Nor can my name appear on any documents outside of confidential attorney work products.

And if the initial inquiry came from a paralegal of RN or other staff member in the attorney's office, I add the following:

I would like to talk to the attorney supervising the case before I receive any records. Please let me know which weekday and telephone number, between 10:30 a.m. and 12:00 p.m., that I can call him.

Letter #2 accompanying my agreement to testify after I have decided, post-medical-record review and conference call with attorney, that the case has merit. This agreement is to be reviewed and signed by the retaining attorney.

Re: _____ CASE

It was a pleasure talking to you today.

As I informed you, I have completed the initial review of this case as a consultant medical expert and expended the minimum $1500 advance @ my fee of $475/h.

At your request I have attached my Expert Witness agreement for your review. If you approve please fax back your signed agreement to the above fax number. Please call me for any questions.

Please refer to Section IIIA, which requires a minimum 10 h advance payment of $4,750 with the signing of this agreement. Please send the check to me by overnight mail to the Potomac Maryland address above. When I receive the check I will fax the agreement back to you with both our signatures.

Until an agreement is mutually accepted and signed by both of us, my name cannot be used as an Expert Witness.

Please note our above addresses, phone and fax numbers. You should always phone for the proper address for overnight and/or mail delivery *each* time *prior* to sending me any other additional documents/materials. And please indicate on all overnight mail/deliveries that no accepting signature is required.

Also please continue to make sure your office staff send me ONLY COPIES of medical records or other documents and no original or "must return" document/records (including x-rays or any other original imaging films).

Given below is my expert witness agreement developed by a lot of trial and error +30 years of experience with attorneys.

Warning: Do not adopt this agreement without your attorney's input.

✓   **Health Care Consultant, Medical Expert Engagement Agreement**

THIS HEALTH CARE CONSULTANT, MEDICAL EXPERT WITNESS ENGAGE-MENT AGREEMENT ("Agreement") is made and entered into as of this ____ day of ____, 2007 by and between: PERRY HOOKMAN, MD, PA ("Physician") and ____, Esquire and the law firm of ____ (collectively, "Attorney" or "Firm"), for purposes of engaging Physician to consult with Attorney in the matter of ____ v. ____ (the "Case") in which Attorney represents ____ ("Client" or "Clients").

Recitals

R-1   Physician is knowledgeable in medical and health care subject areas and disciplines, that Attorney acknowledges are germane fields to Attorney's representation of Client.

R-2   Attorney wishes to engage Physician to consult with Attorney respecting Attorney's representation of Client and/or to serve as an expert witness or health care consultant.

NOW, THEREFORE, Physician and Attorney, intending to be legally bound, hereby agree, as follows:

Section (Phase) I—Initial Consultation

During this time Physician acts in the capacity of a consultant to review the merits of a case for Attorney and render an oral report as an Attorney Work product. During this consultation Attorney provides to Physician case files and other documents pertinent to the medical issues entailed in Attorney's representation of Client. After receipt of the aforesaid materials, Physician reviews same, and consults with Attorney respecting same, and helps analyze the health care and other issues entailed thereby. A $1500 advance fee @ $475/h for the initial consultation as a consultant medical expert has been paid.

Section (Phase/Option) II—Engagement of Physician as Expert Witness, Federal Health Insurance Portability and Accountability Act (HIPAA) Regulations, Independence, and Code of Conduct of Expert Witness

If Attorney determines that Physician should serve as an Expert Witness and, if based on the merits of the case, Physician agrees to serve as an Expert Witness, Attorney acknowledges and agrees that at all times Physician retains full autonomy and independence in the formulation and rendering of Physician's professional opinions.

To better facilitate Physician's total independence from any direct or indirect financial considerations, Attorney and Firm shall, prior to Physician's giving of deposition or trial testimony in the Case, pay to Physician all amounts owed to Physician hereunder.

At no time during Physician's engagement hereunder will Attorney or Firm take or permit any action that has the purpose or effect of causing or seeking to cause Physician to deviate from the Code of Conduct for Expert Witnesses for either plaintiff or defense as promulgated by the American College of Gastroenterology and formulated, with the recognition of the American College of Gastroenterology and the American Medical Association, such that the professional responsibility of Physicians is to serve the needs of the public in settings and legal proceedings where a Physician's expertise is required.

It is acknowledged that Physician is not an advocate for any party in the proceedings involving Attorney's Client to which Physician's services herein relate. Physician shall at all times have the right to exercise his own independent judgment free from control or influence by Attorney or any other person. This includes but is not limited to the type of independent research performed by Physician, and the amount of preparation for any written opinions, testimony, or reports. Physician may, in Physician's sole and unreviewable discretion and for any reason whatsoever, terminate this Agreement and resign his appointment hereunder without penalty or further obligations or liabilities to Attorney, Attorney's Firm, or their Clients.

Physician acknowledges that, in circumstances where Attorney's Client is a "covered entity" as defined in federal regulations published at 45 C.F.R. Parts 160 and 164 ("the Privacy Standards"), promulgated pursuant to the Health Insurance Portability and Accountability Act of 1996, certain medical records provided to Physician by Attorney or Attorney's Client may constitute protected health information (PHI) within the meaning of these Privacy Standards. In each such instance, prior to the time of disclosure of PHI to Physician, Attorney shall so certify to Physician in writing, designate as "protected and confidential" all such PHI and describe in detail for Physician all of the use and disclosure restrictions applicable to same under the Privacy Standards, in which event Physician will use reasonable efforts to manage the PHI consistent with the applicable Privacy Standards so described. Physician will use reasonable efforts in attempting to avoid divulging such designated PHI to persons other than those whom Physician determines in Physician's sole opinion have a need to know or have access to same, including without limitation, clerical, administrative, professional, or other staff employed or engaged by Physician, Attorney, or Attorney's Client. At the conclusion of Physician's work under this Agreement it is agreed that Physician will destroy such designated PHI in Physician's possession. It is mutually acknowledged and agreed that Physician will then be deemed to have fully discharged all obligations under the Privacy Standards respecting such designated PHI.

Section III—Fees

The following fee schedule is mutually agreed to.

A. **Medical written reports, affidavits, conferences, transcripts review, and research**: Personal or telephone interview with Attorney, Client, or others related to case plus Research by Physician @ $475/h. The first 10 h of $4750 shall be prepaid to Physician as an advance to cover partial future or past unpaid billable hours with the signing of this agreement. Any unused hours will be credited but not refunded. Physician's services hereunder beyond an additional 50 billable hours for each of the services below must first be approved by Attorney:
   - Medical records/transcripts review/study
   - Medical literature research
   - Preparation for deposition
   - Preparation for trial testimony

B. **Testimony**:
   - For the benefit of the parties hereto, Attorney and Firm shall, to the maximum extent permissible under applicable court rules, orders, and other regulations and laws, schedule Physician's testimony and use best efforts to whenever possible arrange for either deposition or trial testimony either preferably as phone conference, or by live-videoconference, or videotaped testimony so that Physician minimizes travel away from the metropolitan area of Expert's in-town residence or office and also thereby decreases this case's expenditures, including travel plus other overall expenses disbursed to or for the Physician expert.

- Notwithstanding the efforts of Attorney and Firm as aforesaid regarding the place for Physician's giving of testimony, if out-of-town travel by Physician cannot be avoided, Attorney and Firm will use best efforts to give Physician at least 12 weeks advance notice to schedule in-town (e.g., deposition) testimony so that Physician can prudently schedule time away from his normal agenda of activities. For like reasons, Attorney and Firm will use best efforts to give Physician not less than 16 weeks advance notice to schedule out-of-town trial testimony.
- Advances for out-of-town testimony will be based on the anticipated length of estimated time away from Physician's normal activities—up to 4 days minimum depending on distance for out-of-town testimony @ $600/h (8 h = $4800 flat rate per day). This includes waiting time; time spent in office, video center, or courtroom locations, or elsewhere.
- Advance payments for Physician time relating to the giving of testimony shall be paid by Attorney and Firm not later than the date when Physician consents to give testimony (deposition or trial) and shall be received by Physician by overnight delivery not later than three (3) days after such date. Physician is released from any duty or obligation to appear for deposition or trial if this advance payment is not received by Physician within three (3) days after such date. Any unexpended advance fees for rescheduled court or deposition dates will be credited to future dates as per *section V* below.
- Attorney acknowledges and agrees that whenever Physician is engaged to give testimony at deposition, hearings, trial, or otherwise at any location outside the County where he then resides, Physician shall not be called on to travel to or from the site of testimony on the same day when the testimony is scheduled, but is authorized to travel to and from same on the day before and the day after same.

C. **Deposition testimony**:
- Fee for phone deposition to Physician's home or office without the necessity of Physician's physical proximity to attorneys and court stenographer, $475/h with minimum flat 4 h fee of $1900 paid as an advance.
- For personal appearance at in-town deposition, $600/h with the minimum 4 h flat fee of $2400 paid as an advance.
- For in-town videotape deposition or in-town live videoconference deposition $600/h with the minimum 8 h flat fee of $4800 paid as an advance.

D. **Trial testimony**: Fees for attendance at court or video center for trial testimony, including waiting time and time spent at video center, courthouse, or elsewhere $600/h (minimum 8 h flat fee of $4800/day) shall be paid by Attorney and Firm in advance not later than the date when Physician consents to appear for trial testimony. Advance(s) for testimony shall be received by Physician not later than three (3) days after agreement by Physician to testimony date. All instances involving the giving of out-of-town testimony by Physician are subject to additional out-of-town advances which shall be paid by Attorney and Firm to Physician based on Physician's estimate of the anticipated number of days away from Physician's normal activities up to 4 days minimum depending on distance for out-of-town testimony @ $600/h (8 h = $4800 flat rate per day).

E. Prior to the commencement of Physician's preparation for the giving of testimony, and promptly after the materials become available to Attorney and Firm, Attorney and Firm shall provide to Physician, at no cost, copies of any and all as yet unreviewed medical records, relevant pleadings, or other relevant documents, interrogatories, responses, depositions, trial transcripts, and exhibits as they become available to Attorney. All such records shall remain the property of the Physician. Physician may later dispose of all such records and other materials at a time solely of his own discretion according to applicable HIPAA requirements.

Section IV—Travel and Reimbursement of Out-of-Pocket Expenses of Physician

A. Advances to Physician for testimony time are exclusively for time spent at his hourly rate in a "testimony room" (e.g., courtroom, video center, office, meeting room, or elsewhere) away from the Physician's normal scheduled activities. Advances for testimony do not include billable hours for Physician's pretestimony preparation. Under no circumstances are advances directly or indirectly contingent on the content or context of expert opinions expressed by the Physician.

B. In addition to the fees set forth above, Attorney will on demand reimburse Physician for all reasonable out-of-pocket expenses associated with furnishing Attorney the services covered by this Agreement, including without limitation, postage, long-distance telephone, telecopy, photocopying, printing, exhibit preparation, fee and expense collection, and the like. Air travel of more than 2 h in duration, including connecting flight, airport waiting, and traveling time, will be in first class unless business class is available. All estimated travel expenses, including hotel expenses, transit expenses, and ground transportation, will be paid by Attorney in advance.

Section V—Invoicing, Payment, and Liability

A. It is acknowledged that all fees detailed in this Agreement are within the guidelines from the 2004 National Guide to Expert Witness Fees and Billing Procedures [ISBN 1-892904-25-X].

B. No downward adjustment of fees or other change in terms will be effective without the parties' advance mutual written agreement. Physician's invoices for time and expenses and Physician's statements of billable hours and expenses incurred shall be deemed conclusively and irrevocably accepted and approved by Attorney and Firm unless, not more than five (5) days of Physician's rendering of such invoices or statements Attorney and Firm deliver written notice to Physician objecting to same and stating in detail the factual and legal basis for such objection. Failure by Attorney or Firm to make such objection timely in strict compliance with this Section (V-B) shall absolutely bar Attorney and Firm from thereafter objecting to or otherwise contesting Physician's invoices, statements, and charges for billable hours and expenses.

C. All fees specified in this Agreement will be billed by fax or e-mail to Attorney. Attorney shall pay the same by overnight mail within two (2) days after the date of Physician's invoices. Payments delivered to Physician after three (3) days are considered delayed. If at any time any payments become delayed for any reason, then all future projected payments shall be made in advance. Payment(s) late by more than seven (7) days are delinquent. Unexpended advance fees for scheduled meetings, depositions, trials, or other proceedings will be credited if Attorney gives written notification of the cancellation and the same is received by Physician at least twenty one (21) working days in advance of the scheduled date of the event, and Physician can restore his professional schedule of activities and appointments for that cancelled time. There will be no credit for any unused hours of testimony after the deposition or trial. All invoiced amounts shall be paid to Physician on a timely basis and without reduction, setoff, or delay for any reason.

D. Attorney acknowledges that payment(s) are for the quantity of billable hours only and are in no way contingent on the content of the Physician's opinion or outcome of Attorney's case to which Physician's services relate.

E. Physician provides no guarantee or assurances on any trial outcome, nor on the outcome of any case or settlement, nor on any qualification to serve as an expert witness in any local, state, or federal court or in any arbitration, mediation, administrative, legislative or other nonjudicial proceeding. Notwithstanding anything to the contrary contained in this agreement, under no circumstances and in no event shall Physician, under or in connection with this agreement or the performance of any service hereunder, incur or have any monetary, financial, or other liability to Attorney, Firm, or Attorney's or Firm's Clients, whether based on contract, tort, or otherwise, other than for the return of any unused portion of any advanced fees paid to Physician hereunder. Attorney and Firm hereby unconditionally waive, and covenant never to assert, any claims for same and agree to indemnify and on demand reimburse Physician for and hold Physician harmless from and against damage, injury, or expense arising from claims, actions, or proceedings asserted against Physician by any Client of Attorney or Firm, or by any opposing party in the Case, or by any other person, firm, or entity, including counsel fees and the costs of investigating and defending against same arising from or in any way relating to any opinion rendered, or testimony given by Physician, or any other conduct by Physician in connection with this Agreement or the Case.

F. The payment of all fees and expenses is the responsibility of Attorney and Firm, jointly and severally, notwithstanding Attorney's relationship with Clients and third parties, contingency arrangements, etc. As a convenience, Physician may agree to prepare separate billing for anyone taking Physician's deposition, or for other charges, so that the Attorney may be more easily reimbursed. However the responsibility for making all payments to Physician, in full and on time remains that of the Attorney. Original time records will be maintained by Physician who will make them available for inspection at Physician's office during regular business hours. Copies of these original time records will be sent to Attorney upon request.

Section VI—Material Change or Payment Delinquency

In the event of any "Material Change" (as that term is defined below in relation to events or occurrences affecting or relating to Attorney, Firm, or the Case or matter to which this Agreement relates), Attorney and/or Firm shall, not later then three (3) days after the occurrence of same, give Physician telephonic and written facsimile notice of same setting forth the full particulars.

This Agreement shall automatically terminate as of the date of Physician's receipt of such written notice unless, within ten (10) days after Physician's receipt of such telephonic and written facsimile notice, Physician advises Attorney and Firm in writing that notwithstanding the occurrence of the Material Change Physician has elected, at Physician's option, to continue under this Agreement (or an updated form of agreement proposed by Physician) and upon the execution of same by the persons and entities who have assumed responsibility in connection with the Case or representation of Client as a result of the Material Change.

Whether or not the Physician elects to continue this Agreement in effect upon the occurrence of a Material Change, upon Physician's receipt of Attorney and Firm's written notice of same, Physician will ascertain and fax to Attorney the amount of any remaining balance of Physician's billable hours in the Case, which balance shall be then due and paid to Physician within two (2) days and received no later than three (3) days after Physician's sending of such fax, or e-mail, together with all remaining and yet unpaid fees and/or other amounts due for services rendered hereunder up to and including the day of documented receipt by Physician.

For purposes of this Agreement, the term "Material Change" refers to each of the following events and occurrences: the death, retirement, or disability of the Attorney signatory to this agreement; the termination of Attorney signatory's employment or association with Firm; the substitution or addition of other Firms or counsel in the Case on behalf of Attorney's or Firm's Clients; the withdrawal or the removal of signatory Attorney and/or Firm from the Case and/or as counsel for Attorney's or Firm's Clients in the Case; the entry of appearance in the Case on behalf of Attorney's or Firm's Clients of other counsel not currently employed by or associated with Attorney or Firm as of the date of this Agreement and/or who are not signatories to this Agreement; the insolvency or dissolution of Firm or Firm's merger with another law firm or group of Attorneys not signatories to this Agreement; and any other material change in the composition of Firm in the legal representation of Firm's Clients in the Case; or in the status of the Case whether by way of full or partial settlement or dismissal of the Case to which Physician's work under this Agreement relates.

Attorney acknowledges and agrees that failure by Attorney or Firm to give such notice and make such payment(s) in a timely and full fashion or any other payment delinquency by Attorney or Firm shall constitute a material breach of this Agreement, and shall conclusively be deemed an admission by Attorney and Firm that same constitutes a material breach of this Agreement, whereupon Physician may, in his sole discretion, thereafter elect to withdraw from the engagement provided for hereunder without penalty or other liability on the part of Physician to Attorney, Firm, or Client. In the event of a termination of this Agreement on account of the occurrence of a Material Change or in the event of Physician's resignation for any other reason or other termination of this Agreement, Attorney and Firm shall give notice of same and Physician is authorized to give notice of same to all parties and counsel in the case to which Plaintiff's services relate. Physician is authorized to notify all parties of Physician's resignation or the termination of this Agreement for any reason.

Section VII—Alternative Dispute Resolution

All disputes arising from or relating to this Agreement and any and all other disputes of whatever nature between Physician and Attorney or Firm, or Attorney's or Firm's Clients (whether in tort or in contract or otherwise, and whether relating to or arising from conduct, events, or occurrences occurring before, during, or after the term of this Agreement) shall, at the request of either party, be referred to and adjudicated through binding arbitration before the American Arbitration Association, sitting in the American Arbitration Association offices closest to the Physician's residence.

Physician and Attorney agree that any arbitration award issued shall be final and binding. Judgment upon any arbitration award may be entered in any court having jurisdiction over the parties. In any arbitration proceeding initiated by Physician or seeking to enforce Physician's rights or Attorney's Firm's responsibilities, the Attorney and Firm shall pay to the Physician all of Physician's legal fees and costs incurred in connection with the arbitration and post-arbitration judicial enforcement proceedings. Attorney and Firm unconditionally and irrevocably covenant never to file or make any complaint or file or institute any judicial, administrative, governmental, or nongovernmental proceeding against Physician, other than arbitration proceedings instituted in strict accordance with the alternative dispute resolution procedures set forth in this Section VII or in any forum other than the American Arbitration Association offices referred to above.

In the event of any breach of any of the foregoing covenants by Attorney or Firm, Attorney and Firm shall, in addition to all other legal remedies available to Physician, hold Physician harmless from and against, indemnify Physician for and on demand reimburse Physician for all damage, injury, and expense incurred by Physician—including without limitation Physician's counsel fees, court costs, travel and lodging expenses—in connection with investigating, defending against, and otherwise opposing any such lawsuit, complaint, or other proceeding.

This Agreement is fully integrated and supersedes all prior and contemporaneous written or oral agreements and understandings and all other negotiations, promises, representations, assurances, discussions, or other commitments or communications of whatever kind, and cannot be modified except in writing and mutually signed and dated by Physician and all other parties who are signatories to this and/or any future agreement.

This Agreement shall be construed and enforced in accordance with the laws of the State of Maryland.

IN WITNESS WHEREOF, Physician and Attorney have entered into this 8 page Agreement as of the date first written above.

PERRY HOOKMAN, MD, P.A.

By:_____

Date: _____

Perry Hookman, MD.
Information for W-9;
Perry Hookman, MD. PA
5607 NW 24th Terrace
Boca Raton Fl 33496
IRS [W-9] TAX ID # _____

Attorney/Firm

Date: _____   _____

_____

Firm Name

Updtd. 3.26.0

Examples of further correspondence to attorneys are those prior to making an expenditure of many billable hours. The attorney should never be surprised by your bill.

So this is an example of my note to the attorney asking for permission prior to doing the Rule 26 report.

Dear Mr. _____

You have requested the Rule 26 report from me. I also understood that under Fed. R. Civ. P. 37(c)(1) the sanctions for nondisclosure include prohibition against use of the undisclosed testimony at trial, unless the nondisclosure was "harmless."
   As I understand it, the report must include six things:

- A "complete statement of all opinions to be expressed and the basis and reasons therefor."
- All "data or other information" that the expert has "considered" in forming his or her opinions.
- Any exhibits to be used as a summary or support for the opinions.
- The qualifications of the witness, including a list of all publications authored in the last 10 years.
- The compensation to be paid for "the study and the testimony."
- A "listing" of any other "cases" in which the witness has testified as an expert "at trial or by deposition" within the previous four years. Because of Daubert, Rule 26(a)(2)(B) demands, as I understand it, even closer attention, because the rule requires a "complete" statement not only of the expert's opinions, but also of the "basis and reasons" for them. The methods employed by the expert (me) are naturally regarded as part of the expert's "basis and reasons" and of course those methods are the touchstone of reliability analysis under Daubert.

I project an expenditure of _____ billable hours to accomplish this. Do I have your permission to do this?

   Respectfully yours,

Example of Rule 26 report: Every sentence has significance. For any questions I'll be glad to communicate by e-mail only (hookman@hookman.com).

Your stationary heading

Date:_____

Name and address of retaining attorney.

Dear Mr. Retaining Attorney

Re: Mr.[Dr.] Your Client

I. *Establishing your qualifications to render your expert medical opinion*

I am a physician, Board certified in Internal Medicine and also in Gastroenterology.
   I am licensed to practice medicine in the states of Maryland, Florida, and the District of Columbia. I practice medicine in Florida.

As a teacher of Physicians on the teaching staff and faculty of a major teaching Hospital and Medical School, I am familiar with the standards of medical care for internists, nurses, E.R. Physicians, surgeons and gastroenterologists from all sections in the U.S., on the standard of care for the diagnosis and treatment of _____ and the complications from these diseases. I also train and teach in seminars in this subject of _____ for health care providers in a major teaching hospital.

These include nurses, physicians of most specialties including radiologists interested in the gastrointestinal tract, Physicians' assistants, nurse practitioners, & gastroenterologists in post graduate training as well as certified gastroenterologists and nurses from different parts of the US.

At the time the patient was under the care of the defendant physician[s], the national standard of care was consistent with the standard of care for internists, surgeons, nurses, gastroenterologists and other physicians as well as nurse practitioners and physician assistants in the state of Florida for the treatment of the medical problems of _____.

These medical standards in Florida [or your state] for the diagnosis and treatment of _____ and its complications and other associated gastrointestinal disorders were also the same as the national standards.

These national medical standards of care were and are applicable to and consistent with standards in the diagnosis and treatment of _____ in the year of the occurrence of _____.

These teaching rounds and seminars I supervise include patients with _____ gastrointestinal disorders and medical and gastrointestinal complications including post-operative problems. I do this at an accredited health care institution, currently; and also at the same time this patient was treated.

Furthermore I see and help treat such problems on a regular basis.

A copy of my up-dated curriculum vitae is attached.

II. A review of the medical expert-retaining attorney engagement to show all the documents you considered in your opinion and to preempt questions on whether or not you formed your expert medical opinion with less than a full set of documents. Note the difference made between when you found that there was merit in the case; and when you finalized your expert medical opinion

On _____ you contacted me regarding a review of the records (listed below) with a request for my opinion on whether this case met the standard of medical care.

The list of documents you sent to me included:

1. _____
2. _____ etc.

I previously informed you that this engagement was for a preliminary review of the records as a Consultant medical expert [not as a testifying medical expert witness] and the rendering to you of a preliminary verbal medical opinion about the merits of the case [not written] based on the records you had sent me.

On _____ we had a conference call. I informed you, I had completed the initial review of this case as a consultant medical expert. I told you that my initial review concluded that case had merit. You asked for and I subsequently agreed to be a testifying medical expert in this case.

I also requested any and all additional documents that I had not yet thoroughly reviewed including all depositions in this case transcribed up to the conference call date to aid in the further formulation of my expert medical opinion[s].

On _____, I received the following requested additional documents from you: These included:

1. _____
2. _____ etc.

After my review of all these records, we had a telephone conversation on _____ in which I reviewed with you my medical expert opinions about this case based on a reasonable degree of medical probability.

You subsequently asked me to write a report to you about this case on _____.

I agreed based on your assurance that I was sent all the documents in this case taken so far to this date

III. *Medical summary of case*

Who, what, when, why, where, & how.

IV. *Using the magic words*

All the opinions expressed herein are the product of reliable principles and methods developed as a result of my professional knowledge, experience, education and training in the fields of internal medicine and gastroenterology. Furthermore, I applied said principles and methods reliably to the facts of this case in reaching the opinions expressed herein based on a reasonable degree of medical probability and supported by the peer reviewed literature.

V. *Summary and conclusions*

From my review of the records, it is in my opinion based upon a reasonable degree of medical probability that, _____ did [not] receive appropriate and timely management for _____ from these doctors _____.

These physicians deviated [did not deviate] from the medical standards of care.

For delayed or missed diagnosis:

Had _____ been treated at this earlier stage and according to the standard of care, it is my opinion held to a reasonable degree of medical probability that s/he would not have had _____, followed by complications of stormy septic problems secondary to perforation of the _____.

The unnecessarily delayed surgery was proximate cause of complications which included multiple organ failure and death.

VI. For preemption of a Daubert challenge

Review of the peer reviewed literature supporting my medical expert opinion

A. Survival & mortality rates of CRC

According to the J NAT CANCER INST. 2004; 96:1420—Five-year survival rates in a contemporary series of over 119,000 patients treated between 1991 and 2000 stratified according to the most recent modification of the TNM staging system were as follows:

- Stage I (T1-2N0)—93 percent
- Stage IIA (T3N0)—85 percent
- Stage IIB (T4N0)—72 percent
- Stage IIIA (Tl-2 Nl)—83 percent
- Stage IIIB (T3-4N1)—64 percent
- Stage IIIC (N2)—44 percent
- Stage IV—8 percent

B.

Sources: CANCER 1998; 78: 918; CANCER 1998 83: 2408

At initial presentation, the distribution of disease extent for colon cancer is as follows:

- Localized to the mucosa and submucosa (Dukes' A or TNM stage I)—23 percent
- Extending into or through the muscle layer without lymph node involvement (Dukes' B or TNM stage II)—31 percent
- Lymph node involvement (Dukes' C or TNM stage III)—26 percent
- Distant metastases (Dukes' D or TNM stage IV)—20 percent

The distribution of disease extent for rectal cancers in the United States is as follows:

- Localized to the mucosa and submucosa (Dukes' A or TNM stage I)—34 percent
- Extending into or through the muscle layer without lymph node involvement (Dukes' B or TNM stage II)—25 percent
- Lymph node involvement (Dukes' C or TNM stage III)—26 percent
- Distant metastases (Dukes' D or TNM stage IV)—15 percent

The major screening tests then and now available to detect polyps or CRC are the regularly performed fecal occult blood test (FOBT), flexible sigmoidoscopy, double-contrast enema, and/or colonoscopy.

The pathogenesis of CRC allows two opportunities to prevent cancer:

1. Finding and removing polyps to prevent the onset of cancer
2. Finding and removing early cancers to improve prognosis.

C. Scientific rationale for early diagnosis of CRC

Sources: SMJ 1991; 84: 575; CANCER 1986: 57: 1866; DIS.COLON AND RECTUM 2000; 43: 303

The majority of patients with CRC have hematochezia or melena, abdominal pain, and/or a change in bowel habits. Some patients have more than one abnormality:

- Abdominal pain—44 percent
- Change in bowel habit—43 percent
- Hematochezia or melena—40 percent
- Weakness—20 percent
- Anemia without other gastrointestinal symptoms—11 percent
- Weight loss—6 percent

Colonoscopy—The majority of colon and rectal cancers are endoluminal adenocarcinomas that arise from the mucosa. Colonoscopy is the single best diagnostic test in symptomatic individuals, since it can localize lesions throughout the large bowel, biopsy mass lesions, detect synchronous neoplasms, and remove polyps. The air contrast enema, supplemented with flexible sigmoidoscopy, is also used, but the diagnostic yield of this combination is less than that of colonoscopy for the evaluation of lower tract. From AJR 1999; 173: 561

Colorectal cancer (CRC) is a common and lethal disease. Approximately 145,290 new cases of large bowel cancer are diagnosed each year in the United States, of which 104,950 are colon and the remainder rectal cancers.

Colorectal cancer (CRC) is a common, lethal, and preventable disease. It is infrequent before age 40; the incidence rises progressively thereafter to 3.7/1000 per year by age 80. The lifetime incidence for patients at average risk is 5 percent, with 90 percent of cases occurring after age 50.

CRC is the third most common cancer and the third leading cause of cancer death in both sexes, accounting for approximately 10 percent of cancer deaths overall. Approximately one in three people who develop CRC die of this disease [because of delay in dx]. From CANCER J CLIN 2005;55: 10; MMR 2003; 52: 193

VII. Preemption of attempts to "freeze" you opinion before testimony

In the event that other information is brought to my attention, I reserve the right to supplement and modify my opinion if necessary.

And in the future, if I am asked to discuss auxiliary or supplementary issue[s], I will do so at the time, with of course, any additional information made available to me.

Respectfully yours,

Perry Hookman, MD

---

1. Sign in different color ink to document this as your original report.
2. Do not ever significantly vary your testimony from the details or opinions within this report despite opposing attorney subtle or strenuous attempts.
3. There should not be any other significant additional information for your review to change your testimony from this report other than additional future depositions or other documents sent to you after you have submitted this report.

4. Do not forget your above documentation (a & b) that you asked your retaining attorney for everything to neutralize any question about this:
   a. "I also requested any and all additional documents including all depositions in this case transcribed up to this conference date to aid in the further formulation of my expert medical opinion[s]."
   b. "I agreed based on your assurance that I reviewed all the documents in this case taken so far to this date."

12.4 My Advice to You on Advertising

Don't. Not that there is anything wrong with advertising. Lawyers do it all the time—on TV and even as part of the prevues in the movie theatres. However, it is not appropriate for physicians. So my advice to you the beginner is that you should limit all "advertising" *to listings in expert directories*. Listing your name in Expert witness directories is an ethical and legitimate way to document that you are available to review medical cases. Having your own web site is also a legitimate and ethical way to have a source of present and future patients to obtain information about you.

Thousands of doctors now have their own web sites.

However "paying a search engine to list you as the number 1 expert in your field could be an issue in your cross examination. Even a beginner is capable of handling questions posed by the cross-examiners.

12.5 My Advice to You on Unsolicited Letters to Attorneys for Referrals

Don't. You will find suggestions in many books, written not by physicians or lawyers, to "enhance your expert Witness business" by using "tried and true good marketing rules."

One such recommended marketing suggestion is an unsolicited "Introductory Mailings to Attorneys" or an *introductory/solicitation* letter of a brief cover letter, a business card, and or an abbreviated curriculum vitae tailored to the potential retaining attorney's "needs."

I do not believe this is not suitable for physicians.

Some other advice given for by *other* marketing consultants is to offer a trial of free or reduced rates for the first case.

That is the main problem with generic expert witness and Expert marketing books that do not recognize the special nature and unique and vital role of the *physician in and out of court*. While the jurors may be familiar with the commercial aspects of other trades and semiprofessionals, this taint of commercialism in a physician will not go down well in court.

A physician testifying in a medical malpractice case and translating for the jury the nuances of the medical aspects of the case should be extremely professional and without any appearance of bias or commercialism.

What do you think the effect would be of an answer to the usual first question of the cross-examiner as to how you came into this case, which reveals an unsolicited letter to the attorney? What would the average juror think of you? Could you be biased? Could you want the attorney's continued business and therefore give him any opinion he needs?

Imagine the follow-up questions, and these are mild compared to a really tough cross-examiner intent on demolishing you (*see* chapters on cross examination):

- Why did you select this attorney and not the hundreds of others?
- Have you changed the usual way you bill for your testimony?
- Why is this retaining attorney being charged less than your usual rate?
- Really? How many attorneys received you soliciting letter?
- Are you favoring a defendant's rather than a plaintiff's attorney?
- Doctor, you did know who the attorney was representing when you sent the letter didn't you, etc. all designed to show you as a biased expert hungry for cases and willing to testify in such a manner as to satisfy the case issues for the attorney and his client so you can get more "business."

Now this may be OK for a business consultant/expert because these business methods are discounted by the jury as the norm for business—but not for medicine!

Medical experts must avoid even the appearance of a relationship between parties, even though no relationship exists.

The opposing counsel's job is to discredit your testimony and thus attempt to impeach an expert because of relationships with counsel or the client, the amount of fees charged, or contingent fee arrangements. These impeachment attempts are common in the malpractice adversarial legal environment.

Potential conflicts of interest which will lead to impeachment attempts (to discredit you) by the opposing attorney include any relationships direct or indirect with either the retaining attorney, or any of his law firm partners and associates.

These relationships can include financial relationships, family relationships, either directly or in-law; or any other close personal relationships or commercial links with anyone in the firm.

✓ You must also avoid billing relationships that are not your standard practice and at your standard rates. Implications of other conflicts of interest can also arise if, as the medical expert, you are seen to represent only one side—either plaintiff or defendant. I found to my surprise that some attorneys believe that a medical expert who always previously represented a defendant physician probably will not ever take a case to represent a plaintiff for the reason that to always see fault one way or always can raise the issue of bias.

To summarize, the steps you should take to minimize impeachment attempts include

- not sending "commercial type letters asking for business,"
- not altering your billing rate and practices for different client–attorneys,
- keeping a balance of plaintiff and defendant work,
- discuss any potential "gray areas" about possible impeachable relationships upfront with your retaining attorney at the very beginning.

12.6   Summary of My Advice to You on Expert Directories

- Listing your name with a directory is a perfectly professional thing to do as long as you list your name with "Expert Witness directories"—*no TV or radio or bill-post commercials* like the personal injury attorneys do, no newspaper ads or other similar commercial advertising.

- List your name with an expert witness directory (and there are at least 100 at last count) but do not show listing favoritism to only one side (plaintiff or defendant).
- Find out which directories in your area are focused to which side and try to balance between the two—plaintiff and defendant.
- Do list your name on both sides of the legal divide between defendant and plaintiff attorneys to show you are also available to review medical records from *both*—plaintiff and defendant Attorneys. They really are specialized into those two camps, a fact I learned years ago to my surprise. Some good defendant professional directories are sponsored by the American Association of Health Attorneys based in Washington D.C. and also DHI based in Chicago. Both of these defendant directories (as most of them) have an Internet presence. American Trial Lawyers Association (ATLA) is the plaintiff's organization which has recently changed its name to the American Association for Justice (AAJ), which may also sponsor its directories. So it is OK to list your name to show your availability to review medical records, but to both sides.

✓ Another way that attorneys seek you out for your expert opinion is the way I have discovered that most now find me. I do not know if you realize this but most, if not all, peer-reviewed medical journals have an Internet presence and **almost** all articles written on any medical subject is available on the easily researched Web by name of study, journal, and *author's name and e-mail address*. Most of the time when I get a call or e-mail from an attorney or someone on his staff they ask whether I am the author of the so and so medical article about _____ (e.g., Crohn's disease; or hiatal hernia), etc. So publish or perish should not apply just to academia.

Most attorneys—both plaintiff and defendant—are now sophisticated enough that they direct a search for a medical expert by matching the client's illness or medical problem/issues that led to the alleged negligence with the author of a recent medical article dealing with that issue in the peer-reviewed medical literature. In fact attorneys on both sides look to medical articles written by the potential medical expert as a key selection tool in requesting and retaining a medical expert.

12.7 *Verbum sat sapienti*—A Word to the Wise

One caveat. Read what you have published on that issue before testifying on the matter to refresh your memory of what you wrote. Your opposing cross-examining attorney will have already reviewed your publications prior to you testimony, as well as any transcripts of previous testimony you have given relating to the issues at hand. Some additional caveats are given below.

12.7.1 The DWP Syndrome

The DWP syndrome is a <u>d</u>esignation of an expert by an (unethical) attorney <u>w</u>ithout the expert's <u>p</u>ermission and many times even without the expert's knowledge. The unethical attorney does this in the hopes that his case can be settled on favorable terms before the expert even becomes aware of the use of his name and therefore does not have to pay a retainer to the expert.

There have been numerous blogs in the "expert witness blogosphere," yes there is such a thing, about this unethical syndrome. The issue seems to be coming up more and more frequently in that the attorney will name you as an expert without your permission, many times without your knowledge and frequently without ever having communicated with you to begin with. There are hundreds of e-mails on just this subject more recently compiled by Expert Communications (www.expertcommunications.com). Meredith Hamilton deserves a lot of credit in publicizing this unethical practice on her blog.

If you read these blogs, you will see how frequently this happens. And if you check with one of the Internet services which names expert witnesses in medical malpractice cases, such as IDEX, you may also find your name associated with cases you were never consulted on or even imagined or that you knew about.

According the blog writers, most of the time you will not know about it. The DWP syndrome, which happens unknowingly to most experts, can be difficult to discover since the majority of cases successfully settle prior to any depositions or trial testimony or a subpoena to the expert to alert him to the problem. These unethical attorneys are thereby using the expert's name for an advantage without compensation to the expert.

The attorney somehow gets a copy of your CV, either from some previous case or from the Web or even after requesting your CV in the guise of choosing an expert for his case. He then goes ahead with his case by naming you as his expert without your knowledge, thus advancing his case to a later stage where settlement can take place. Unless you find out about this by a surprise subpoena to testify, you will never know it ever happened.

The lawyer finds that it is a great (and cheap) way to settle early. They get the expert's credentials, name him and he is none the wiser. This happens to me frequently, says one blogger. If I become aware of it, I immediately contact the attorney. When I notice that an attorney I am working for has listed more than one expert in my field, I always ask how he intends the work to be divided up, so that I do not duplicate the work of the other expert. If the attorney tells me he just listed a bunch of experts so they are not available to work for the opposition, I ask if he has actually retained the experts. If the answer is no, I call the experts and tell them about it.

One blogger writes, "I have had experiences in which I was listed on the IDEX.com database as having been involved with cases in which I was never retained." I only discovered this, he says, because an attorney assisting another client in preparing for possible litigation contacted me and asked if I could review some medical records and possibly serve as an expert. Then he called back and said that his client had some concerns after reviewing the IDEX database, which show that I have been involved in multiple cases not having anything to do with my specialty. I asked for specifics and to my surprise, the IDEX entries were all erroneous.

The same thing happened to me, says another. I wrote a letter to IDEX, but I have heard nothing since. After calling them, I was informed that IDEX simply adds the consultant's name to any case in which the attorney is calling to ask about the expert. Even if the expert is not involved any further, the name is permanently associated with that attorney and the case.

Questions come up as to what you should do about it, if you do find out you are such a victim. Suggestions in the blogs range from reporting the attorney to his bar association's discipline and grievance committee or even originating a lawsuit using section

"652C Appropriation of Name or Likeness—one who appropriates to his own use or benefit the name or likeness of another is subject to liability to the other for invasion of privacy."

Gutheil et al. described this problem as the "phantom expert" in his article in the American Psychiatric Association Press, 2002. The authors suggest that the ethical complaints filed with the local bar association "are worthless." Their suggestion is for you to instead threaten to contact the attorney on the other side of the case against whom your phantom testimony is intended or a civil suit, "which may prevent the unethical attorney from ever doing it again." You may point out to the attorney the bar association's model Rules of Professional Conduct.

Rule 4.1—Truthfulness in statements to others

In the course of representing a client, a lawyer shall not knowingly

- make a false statement of material fact or law to a third person; or
- fail to disclose a material fact to a third person when disclosure is necessary to avoid assisting a criminal or fraudulent act by a client, unless disclosure is prohibited by Rule 1.6.

Rule 7.1—Communications concerning a lawyer's services

A lawyer shall not make a false or misleading communication about the lawyer or the lawyer's services. A communication is false or misleading if it contains a material misrepresentation of fact or law, or omits a fact necessary to make the statement considered as a whole not materially misleading.

Rule 8.4—Misconduct

It is professional misconduct for a lawyer to

- violate or attempt to violate the Rules of Professional Conduct, knowingly assist or induce another to do so, or do so through the acts of another;
- commit a criminal act that reflects adversely on the lawyer's honesty, trust, worthiness, or fitness as a lawyer in other respects;
- engage in conduct involving dishonesty, fraud, deceit, or misrepresentation;
- engage in conduct that is prejudicial to the administration of justice;
- state or imply an ability to influence improperly a government agency or official or to achieve results by means that violate the Rules of Professional Conduct or other law;
- knowingly assist a judge or judicial officer in conduct that is a violation of applicable rules of judicial conduct or other law.

Most of the bloggers state that despite these rules this unethical practice is widespread. Very few believe that the effort to contact the court or disciplinary committees "is worth it." "Notifying the bar of this lapse in ethics is not necessarily effective either since this association tends to lean backwards to protect their own," say most of the bloggers. Therefore, the consensus is, "Sometimes, we just have to suck it up." We cannot control what the bottom of the barrel in the legal profession will do or say. Eventually the word gets around in the marketplace."

However, comment others, was this falsehood put into court documents? If so, is that not a misrepresentation to the judge, grounds for a grievance or ethical complaint?

Is it not a clear example of "conduct prejudicial to the administration of justice?" Ethical complaints are significant pain for everyone involved regardless of the outcome, but sometimes, say the minority of writers on this problem, that investment is warranted to confront and abuse what seems to have become a new low as a community standard.

In general, it is very time-consuming and expensive to take legal action in the form of a lawsuit against that attorney even in small claims court. The odds of winning are not with you because the attorney will often not show up at court by faxing the court and asking for an adjournment without telling you. It will take multiple appearances before the case is heard. Bringing your own attorney is helpful, but certainly not cost justified. For me, says another, it is a matter of right and wrong and not just a matter of a loss in earnings allegedly stolen by the offending attorney. You must consider if the personal loss of time involved in pursuing the matter outweighs the less than 50-50 chance for you being reimbursed through legal actions. If the loss income is your only concern, you probably would be better served to avoid spending time to pursue the matter legally.

With physicians listing their CVs on their website for their patients and other referring physicians, it is very easy now for an attorney to "steal" a CV and pretend he has an expert witness in an effort to settle very quickly. Finally, it may be appropriate to have one of the expert organizations review how DWP can be monitored and penalized, and whether stronger regulations or an attorney awareness campaign is needed to make this possible.

I have experienced the DWP syndrome several times in my career spanning 30+ years. However there was one horror story in which I found it difficult to extricate myself from the attorney's clutches.

✓ This was an attorney who insisted that I be his expert witness despite the fact that I told him I would not testify. He then went ahead and designated me without my permission. When I found out, I continually wrote to him, telling him that I would not testify. I finally went to my private attorney who helped me write this letter, for the surreal situation.

CERTIFIED MAIL RETURN RECEIPT REQUESTED TO

XXXXXXXXXX.Esq.

XXXXXXXXC

XXXXXXXXXX

Dear Mr. XXXXX

Frankly I am perplexed that you believe we have a continuing "professional collaboration." In fact, we do not.

Please let me remind you again of what we discussed at the very beginning when you first phoned me. I told you last May when you first asked me to review the M_____ medical records that I would do so only with the understanding that my long-standing policy in these matters was that this was a consultation only, and that my reviewing the case did not mean that I would accept being a testifying expert witness. And I further informed you that during this consultation, I would act only in the capacity of a consultant to review the merits of the case for you.

Then, as I told you, after this Consultation period ended and if you requested my testimony and my service as an Expert Witness, and *if I were to agree to serve as an Expert Witness* it would be under a mutually signed written agreement which would spell out in writing our responsibilities and obligations towards each other.

In addition, my standard agreement provides that you as the Attorney would acknowledge and agree that at all times I as the Physician would retain full autonomy and independence in the formulation and rendering of my professional opinions. Consistent with this unvarying approach to my consulting work, I told you several times that you would have to recognize that I as the Physician would not be your or your Client's advocate; and that I was not an advocate for any party in the proceedings in which I was engaged. Also I would at all times have the right to exercise my own independent judgment free from the control or influence by you the Attorney or any other person.

It seems that you have feigned a lack of recollection of our above discussion as, but also now, you state that you "cannot imagine . . . negotiations *de novo* at the completion of every phase." Other than the case-specific elements of my standard written agreement (which was never entered into in this instance) there never was anything to negotiate and that remains the case now.

In the context of our past communications, your 10/11/02 blatant claim that I was engaged "for the M _____ case in all of its phases" and in that same letter your denial of my completed services with your statement that you "will not burden your client with such distractions" is, with all respect, nothing short of outrageous.

At no time between May, the first time we talked, up to the present day did I ever agree to continue on beyond the consultation phase. You should remember that I resigned my nontestifying consultancy on 8/1/02 because of nonpayment of my bill; and on 8/15/02 I told you I would have to attempt collection in small claims court.

However, on 8/21/02 after you paid my bill and apologized for your "mistakes" while at the same time you threatened action against me if I did not continue until late August when you belatedly informed me of a court-imposed deadline never previously disclosed, the opinion-letter deadline of 8/30/02.

I did tell you after your apology on 8/21/02 that I would continue with the matter on a limited nontestifying basis until 8/30/02, and we both acknowledged at that time that my engagement would end at the end of August after my opinion letter was completed.

However, there is now a continuing darker side to what appears to becoming a looming litigious conflict between us. Your latest 10/11/02 letter again hints of your threat of litigation against me if I do not do what you want me to do and by continuing past my engagement as a Consultant Expert and on through the next phase of being a testifying expert witness for you, without any written agreement.

You are using methods of intimidation towards me with your statement of my "exposure to the risk of causing your client pain and suffering," if I did not do as you say.

Your 10/11/02 letter is now yet another instance when you have informed me in no uncertain terms that unless I cave in to your demands and on your terms that I will be sued by you. The first time on 8/21/02 is detailed above. The second time was 8/23/02 when I refused your demands that I sign on to all your suggested modifications to my opinion letter on the medical aspects of the case that you were to take to your state's tribunal.

You do remember that you left out of my initial review the most vital information. You said it was "an oversight" that you did not send those key records to me with all the rest of the M _____ medical records sent in May. Instead it was sent to me (perhaps accidentally) by your clerk just a few days before the 8/30/02 letter deadline. These most important of the M _____ medical records—her stay at the B _____ Hospital—changed my expert opinion and necessitated a drastic revision of the preliminary draft I sent you, away from what was your theory and complaint in this case. Your strident demands that I should not change my original opinion or anything else but "simply send the original draft containing the opinion you wanted as "provisional" and pretend that I did not yet receive or review the vital B _____ Hospital medical records" was unethical as I told you and wrote to you on 8/23/02.

You again apologized profusely for your statements, demands, and threats. You said it was because of the medications you were taking for Parkinson's disease. I actually felt sorry for you, but more so for your Client. However, now your latest 10/11/02 letter of intimidation is the last straw. I tell you now I cannot ethically and in good conscience continue any association with you in this case. Indeed I really do not understand why at this point you insist that I should continue in this case.

I have informed you several times that my engagement as a consultant is over, and I am no longer involved in this case on any basis. You must understand this and not continue to harass and threaten me. I have advised you several times to obtain a different testifying expert during these next available months prior to settlement or potential litigation—from the many dozens potentially available for this case.

However you continue to ignore all this and mistakenly claim we are still somehow in "this professional collaboration . . . [up] . . . through to a successful conclusion." I simply can not imagine rationally why you are doing this and thereby also increasing your Client's risk, *unless you have, without my consent and contrary to our relationship, designated me without my permission as your testifying medical expert and filed with the Court or served on defendant's counsel some statement indicating that I am your designated testifying expert in the case.*

Please confirm for me that you have not done so. Or if you have done so, kindly provide me with identifying information (name, address, telephone, fax, and e-mail numbers and addresses) of the judge and opposing counsel involved so that the record can be set straight.

Perhaps it is irrational but I have exhausted all the rational reasons here in this "twilight zone" of a situation. I am quite afraid now that what you may also be planning is to string this out and not even bother to obtain another testifying medical expert in this lengthy period before trial several months from now. Perhaps you are planning to not even bother to do any work in this case but then exact retribution from me claiming you did not do as well without me as your testifying witness.

Not only that, I fear that even if I was to be your testifying expert witness and if the case is not as "successful" as you want you will somehow try to regain it from me.

However, one thing is certain.

Your threats and intimidations and your harassment of me must come to an end. Because of your threats and my fears about your motives, I have consulted my attorney

S___ S___ Esq.

Work: (xxx) xxx-xxxx

Fax: (xxx) xxx-xxxx

Mobile: (xxx) xxx-xxxx

E-mail: s___@aol.com

Address: xxxT___ St., N.W.
            Suite 425 West
            Wash, D.C. 20007-5201

I insist that you do not send me any further communications. Indeed any further communications from you to me—if there should be any—should go through my attorney.

Respectfully yours,

Perry Hookman, MD

12.7.2 E-mail Scams

I am certain that you would have received this or a similar e-mail and have immediately recognized it for what it is.

BARRISTER ABDULAHI DIENG & ASSOCIATE
(Ivory Right Chambers)

SOLICITORS & ADVOCATES, NOTARY PUBLIC
Head Office: No. 45 Clegg St.,
Dakar, Senegal

Our Ref: JUSTICE/FG2006

Dear Good Friend,

I am Abdulahi Dieng (Esq.) a solicitor at law. I am the personal Attorney to Mr. David Moussa, who lived in Dakar, Senegal, hereinafter shall be referred to as my Client. On the 20th of December 2000, my client was involved in a car accident along Place Independence Road, Rue Lamine Guaye, Dakar, Senegal. All occupants of the vehicle unfortunately lost their lives. I have contacted you to assist in repatriating the money and property left behind by my client before they get confiscated by the Security Company where this huge deposit was lodged.

Particularly, the financial insist where the deceased had an account valued at about $19.5 million has issued me a notice to provide the next of kin or have the account confiscated within the next twenty official working days. Since I have been unsuccessful in locating relatives, I now seek your consent to present you as the next of kin of the deceased so that the proceeds of this account valued at $19.5 million can be paid to you. If you agree, we can share the fund in a ratio of 50% to you and 50% to me. I have all necessary legal documents that can be used to back up any claim we may make.

All I require is your honest cooperation to enable us see this deal through. I guarantee that this will be executed under a legitimate arrangement that will protect you from any breach of the law. I will like you to send me your full name and address, private telephone and fax number for easy communication.

Please copy your reply to: dieng_abdul2006@yahoo.fr

Best regards,

Abdulahi Dieng (Esq.)

No virus found in this incoming message.
Checked by AVG Free Edition.
Version: 7.1.409 / Virus Database: 268.15.15/580 – Release Date: 12/8/2006

Now you would not respond to this e-mail would you? It is so obvious. Yet many Americans do respond and lose a lot of money. You should also be aware of other tricks used in the e-mail world so you can also recognize them.

You must guard against the attorney shopper syndrome (ASS) attorneys who shop for opinions.

With the advent of e-mail, this becomes very simple. You do not know whether the attorney has written only to you or to several other experts, shopping for an opinion favorable to him. Here is a recent example of one such attorney who may have read my article on *C. Difficile* and other GI infections, and my response to him.

12.7.2.1 *Example of Attorneys Fishing for Favorable Opinions*

----- Original Message -----
From: L. C. B.
Sent: Monday, October 09, 2006 5:01 PM
Subject: Expert Consulting Inquiry

Dear Dr. Hookman,

My client Mrs. H _____ first complained to Dr. B_____, the family physician, about her problems in October of 2000. On August 13, 2001, Dr. B_____, noted that "[Mrs. H _____was] complaining of significant stomach upset to the point that she has post prandial [after eating] nausea and vomiting." She was seen again by Dr. B_____ in June of 2003 and complained of "loose stools" and "crampy, lower segment abdominal pain."

Mrs. H _____ continued to complain of nausea, chronic diarrhea—including night symptoms, upset stomach, and vomiting through October of 2003. On October 24, 2003, she underwent a colonoscopy, but this procedure discovered nothing that would identify the root cause of her symptoms. However, Mrs. H _____ was diagnosed with "collagenous colitis" which, according to my research, can be caused by exposure to *E. coli* bacteria as was detected in the H _____ s' tainted water supply. Fairly early on, a consulting gastroenterologist, Dr. Q_____, noted, unknowingly but inaccurately, in a medical record dated September 29, 2003, that Mrs. H _____ "had no obvious history of contaminated water, etc."

Subsequent medical records note, such as that dated February 24, 2004 from Dr. Q_____, that biopsies "did show microscopic colitis." In July of 2004, Mrs. H_____ was admitted to the emergency room at G- H.C. Hospital because her abdomen felt like it was "on fire."

Subsequent surgeries included splenectomy, hernia repair, and hemicolectomy—removal of the right half of her colon. The diarrhea continued, however, leading to a diagnosis of anemia in early 2005. Another gastroenterologist, Dr. T_____ at the University Hospital of _____, was consulted in August of 2005. On August 23, 2005, just days before the problem with the water supply was discovered, Dr. T_____ noted that the "cause of her chronic diarrhea is unclear" and that "I would recommend a repeat colonoscopy to try and document whether the patient still has ongoing evidence of microscopic colitis on biopsies." Thereafter, having been unable to properly ingest food or maintain weight, Mrs. H _____ suffered a stroke on September 8, 2005. This stroke has rendered Mrs. H _____ partially paralyzed and unable to care for herself. She is currently confined to a group living facility in A _____ where she receives nursing care. Please let me know if you would like to offer an opinion in relation to causation.

Thank you, L. C. B Esq.

My Standard Response to Such an Inquiry was Sent.
From: Perry Hookman [mailto:hookman@hookman.com]
Sent: Mon 10/9/2006 2:44 PM
To: L. C. B
Subject: Re: Expert Consulting Inquiry

Thank you for your inquiry. I will be glad to review the medical records. I have attached my C.V.

I charge a minimum fee of $1500 per case. This represents my hourly fee of $475/h for expert consultant medical record review. This check should be sent with the medical records to my address seen on the C.V. My tax Federal tax id # is _____ . This amount usually covers a complete and confidential review of all the initial documents as a consultant medical expert, with my analysis of this case and the rendering of a preliminary verbal medical opinion on the merits of the case. The decision of whether I will also act as an expert testifying witness will depend on whether I believe the case has merit and if you and I wish to extend the scope of the engagement to include expert witness testimony in connection with the matter to which the preliminary opinion relates.

Until such time that I have agreed to the merits of the case and to testify as an Expert Witness in this case, I cannot be named as an Expert Witness. Nor can my name appear on any documents outside of confidential attorney work products.

His Response to My E-mail
----- Original Message -----
From: L. C. B
To: "Perry Hookman" <hookman@hookman.com>
Sent: Monday, October 09, 2006 5:47 PM
Subject: RE: Expert Consulting Inquiry

Thanks. You seem to have a very impressive background. I would send the materials if you gave me some sort of first impression on the case beforehand.

L.C. B

My Response to the above E-mail
From: Perry Hookman [mailto:hookman@hookman.com]
Sent: Mon 10/9/2006 3:12 PM
To: L. C. B
Subject: Re: Expert Consulting Inquiry

With this question you have eliminated me from this case. Good luck on finding an expert but don't hire one who gives you his opinion before reviewing all the facts because that's the first question asked during testimony.

L. C. B.

Another One

This time it's given away by the address listing four doctors. The chances of one of the four fishing lines are greater for success. Needless to say, I never heard further from this attorney.

---- Original Message -----
From: M. D. P
To: A. Z. ; L. R.; C.P; G.C; Perry Hookman
Sent: Saturday, November 11, 2006 8:32 PM
Subject: W_____ v. M _____ Pending in State Court of _____

Dear Internal Medicine Doctors,

I represent the interest of a deceased patient of MCCG hospital. The patient was 63 years of age at the time of his death. He died from a massive subdural hematoma he received at M _____ hospital. He entered the hospital on 9/12/99 due to bilateral leg swelling, was oriented x3, but had a low platelet count.

I looked up your names in SEAK national directory of experts. I need an internal medicine doctor who has at least five years experience as an internal medicine doctor or has five years of experience teaching internal medicine in a school or institution from at least September 17, 1994 to September 1999.

Georgia has a national standard for physicians, basically what physicians are required to provide the care that physicians would generally provide to a patient in the same or similar situation. If you have the experience or the education expertise that I described above, you may be able to testify in a Georgia Court. If you do have the expertise, please consider the following facts.

Summary of facts.

Client was on various medicines and was admitted to the hospital on the 6th floor. On the morning of September 15, 1999, the intern performs a lumbar puncture on my client. On the afternoon and evening of the 16th he had two Paracentesis performed, one at 1600 and another at 2130. My client was given ativan at about 21:00.

He fell out of bed before 0100 am September 17, 1999, it is unknown how long he was on the floor, but it could have been up to four hours.

Nurse tells intern doctor that my client fell out of bed at 0120 am; Doctor does not come to bedside but accepts the assessment of the nurse that cranial nerves II through XII are intact. The assessment the nurse gave to the intern is not written in the medical records. The intern doctor does not tell the resident and does not tell the attending that my client fell out of bed. Two hours later, 03:00 am my client's tongue is hanging out of his mouth and he is unresponsive to painful stimuli.

Nurse Calls intern doctor again at 0315, intern doctor tells resident. Both the intern and the resident doctors arrive at bedside at 03:30. They assess my client and order a stat CAT scan. My client undergoes the CAT scan, and neurology states that my client does not have any brain activity.

Operative intervention was not offered to my client due to neurology's recommendation. Client was placed on Category IV, care and comfort only. He was not fed, and no medical interventions were used, and he died on September 20, 1999.

The attending physician has testified in his deposition that the internist doctor violated the standard of care for physicians generally under the same or similar circumstances in relying on the Cranial Nerve II-XII assessment of the nurse. He states that the standard of care required the internist to perform the Cranial Nerve assessment herself, or notify the resident or himself as the attending about the fall.

What I need now is to get an opinion as to whether or not, to a reasonable degree of medical certainty if the internist had came to the bedside, or told the resident or the attending about the fall at 01:00 am, would my client's injuries and death been avoided, by giving him closer observation, an earlier CAT Scan, or by giving him earlier surgical intervention.

Please send me back an email if you are interested in the case, along with your compensation requirements for reviewing the case.

Thank you for your time in reviewing the brief facts above.

M. D. P., Esq.
The C _____ Firm, XXXX
Xxx xxxxStreet, NE, Suite xxx
Xxx xxx
xxx-xxx-xxxx

No virus found in this incoming message.

My Response:

Thank you for your inquiry.

I will be glad to review the medical records. I have attached my C.V.

I charge a minimum fee of $1500 per case. This represents my hourly fee of $475/h for expert consultant medical record review.

This check should be sent with the medical records to the Potomac Maryland address seen on the C.V.

My tax Federal tax id # is 52-0915376

This amount usually covers a complete and confidential review of all the initial documents as a consultant medical expert, with my analysis of this case, and the rendering of a preliminary verbal medical opinion on the merits of the case. I do this before I can render any opinion one way or the other. Asking me to give you an opinion now on the basis of your outline of the case no matter how indirect my answer or even my accepting the case for review under your guidelines for taking the case is not useful for either of us, and not fair to your client.

To summarize my C.V., I am Board Certified in both Internal Medicine and Gastro-enterology.

The decision of whether I'll also act as an expert testifying witness will depend on whether I believe the case has merit and if you and I wish to extend the scope of the engagement to include expert witness testimony in connection with the matter to which the preliminary opinion relates.

Until such time that I have agreed to the merits of the case and to testify as an Expert Witness in this case, I cannot be named as an Expert Witness.

Nor can my name appear on any documents outside of confidential attorney work products.

How Physicians Can Be Investigated Prior to Trial

13

Investigating the Medical Expert Witness

Half the lies they tell about me aren't true.

—**Yogi Berra**

Observe, record, tabulate, communicate. Use your five senses. … Learn to see, learn to hear, learn to feel, learn to smell, and know that by practice alone you can become expert.

—**William Osler**

13.1   Investigating the Testifying Physician: *Forewarned Is Forearmed*

13.1.1   Introduction

This is the electronic age. Most of you know that your entire life and lives are out on the Web, constantly stealing identities so that they can make money from using your credit card, your social security number, etc. While this is not in the same league, the opposing attorneys in the medical malpractice case want to know about you, whether you are the defendant physician or whether you are the opposing plaintiff's medical expert scheduled to be an expert witness. There are many ways to investigate you. The cheapest and most efficient is through the Internet and Web searches where an amazing amount of information about you can be found. The important point to remember is if there are any "skeletons" about you, it has probably already been revealed and you should not try to cover it up. You should, in all cases, report this to your attorney and let him figure out a way of how to handle it during your testimony. This chapter includes sources of information that can be obtained by attorneys or people they hire such as hackers investigating your past, any gaps in your curriculum vitae (CV), checking into your past testimonies with all the modern techniques of investigating you as a physician and an opposing expert.

13.2   First a Warning

You should be aware of a common scam.

Phishing: Obtaining someone's personal information under false pretenses, i.e., sending an e-mail to a user falsely claiming to be an established legitimate enterprise in an attempt to scam the user into divulging private information that will be used for identity theft and other information gathering. Invariably these e-mails contain a link, or a Web address to copy, paste, and go to. Never use them.

Also, in Adobe versions prior to version 8 Adobe Acrobat, plug-in fails to properly validate user-supplied content, which may allow for cross-site scripting. An attacker may be able to obtain sensitive data from a user who visits a Web site hosting a PDF document. Depending on the nature of the Web site, this data may include passwords, credit card numbers, and any arbitrary information provided by the user. Likewise, information stored in cookies could be stolen or corrupted. This issue has been addressed in Adobe Reader 8. Adobe has issued updates for Adobe Reader versions prior to 8. See Adobe security bulletin APSB07-01 for more details.[1-7]

And, as to the question, how safe is your e-mail? Or how safe is secure mail? In December 2006, Google fixed a bug that caused the disappearance of "some or all" of the stored mail of around 60 users. A week later, it acknowledged a security hole that could have exposed its users' address books to Internet attackers. So if those contained private and confidential hospital records—those records would have been at risk.

E-mail accounts use servers or Internet Service Providers [ISPs]. Those servers have backup schedules and your e-mail may be getting saved there—whether or not you delete it from your personal computer! Google, you may not know, reserves "the right to access, read, preserve, and disclose any information as it reasonably believes is necessary." Hotmail and Yahoo may do the same. Using an e-mail program (such as Outlook) located on your personal computer does not change the situation much. There are some actions you should consider to reduce your exposure to e-mail problems:

- First, do not write crazy things into e-mails and then hit that Send button!
- We all know that people will write into e-mails words they would never say in person, let alone want saved forever. This phenomenon is called "flaming."
- Even a sophisticated e-mail encryption scheme does not relieve you from thinking carefully about what you write in e-mails.
- The very nature of e-mail is that you send it to someone else. Once you send it, that e-mail is out of your control.
- Who knows what that person might do with it? They might save it, they might forward it to the *New York Times* or they might print it and post it on the bulletin board at the county courthouse.
- Next you must develop your own e-mail retention policy. Depending on how you read the Federal Rules of Civil Procedure, you may be required to have an e-mail retention policy if you are doing any consulting in the USA. An e-mail retention policy specifies how long you will save e-mails. Some suggest seven years if taxes are involved. If you are using e-mail during your litigation support work, you should ask one of the attorneys how long they suggest you save the e-mails.

Hospital records are also at risk even from the most surprising sources. B Stone wrote in the *New York Times*, January 10, that when DeKalb Medical Center in Atlanta started monitoring its staff use of Web-based e-mail, it found that doctors and nurses routinely forwarded confidential medical records to their personal Web mail accounts—not for nefarious purposes, but so they could continue to work from home. How dangerous is this? The flimsier security defenses of home Web mail systems could allow viruses or spyware to get through, and employees could unwittingly download them at the office and infect the corporate network. Also, because messages sent from Web-based accounts do not pass through the hospital mail system, hospitals could run afoul of federal laws that require them to archive all mail and turn it over during litigation. Lawyers in particular wring their hands over employees using outside e-mail services. In the months after the hospital began monitoring traffic to Web e-mail services, it identified "a couple hundred incidents," according to DeKalb's information security administrator. DeKalb now forbids the practice, and uses several software systems that monitor the hospital's outbound e-mail and Web traffic, but still catches four to five perpetrators a month trying to forward hospital e-mail. Even the security experts most knowledgeable about the risks of e-mail forwarding to personal accounts acknowledge doing so themselves. In addition to other things going wrong—the Web mail services may also be prone to glitches.

13.3 Sources of Information on Testifying Physicians That Can Be Obtained by Attorneys

Once a physician defendant or potential medical expert has been identified, that physician's past can be researched to check for "skeletons in the closet." (*See also* attached appendix-CD for further references on opposing medical experts and conflicts of interest.)

Do not forget that any investigation about you also means research of the opposing medical experts. How do attorneys and others investigate you and check out opposing experts? Section 13.3 focuses on the preliminary investigation of the testifying physician, which can be done by any para legal, or for that matter anyone with access to the Internet, and especially a computer hacker who can sell his services to an attorney or intermediary. Modern technology has so far advanced that even a teenage computer hacker can get tons of information about you.

Information about you is not limited to all the homes you have lived in; the mortgages you have paid; your divorces, separations, child support, your income/salary; any civil or criminal actions against you; how many traffic violations you or your family have, the cost of the clothes you bought; your credit card expenses in Las Vegas (it is not true that "anything you do in Las Vegas stays there"); your credit card balances; and much more!

13.3.1 Investigating Your Past; Any Gaps in Your CV?

13.3.1.1 Checking into Your Past Testimony

1. What will their research on your background and writings provide in response to these questions?
2. Google yourself periodically. Bring up any potential problems to your retaining attorney.

3. You can be sure of this. Any bad stuff they find will probably not come up in your deposition—unless they are aiming for a quick surrender or settlement. It will be saved to discredit you in front of the jury during your cross-exam.

4. Even judges now insist that it is the attorney's job to verify the expert's CV. According to Hassmyer[8] in preparing a case for trial, a Judge stated, "It is the attorney's job to learn as much as possible about an adverse party's expert witness including verifying his qualifications as an expert."

Indeed, the failure of an attorney to adequately research the qualifications of his expert could subject that attorney to claim of professional negligence according to "The Lawyers Weekly on 8/17/01."

13.3.1.2 Checking into Your Disciplinary Record; Checking Your Past Hospital Medical Staff Health Maintenance Organization (HMO) Affiliations and Terminations

Public records are also easy targets for ID thieves. And where do investigators look? Well you would be surprised.

Government Web sites contain millions of searchable records brimming with social security numbers, dates of birth, etc. As an example, a quick search of the Miami-Dade County Clerk's Web site, by an investigative reporter at the Miami Herald yielded the social security numbers of several prominent Florida citizens.

Also in Austin, Texas, an index of personal documents remains online. Indeed, some county clerks have questioned whether taking down the images at this point, or even redacting them, would make any difference, since it is already in the public domain.

You may also be surprised that government jurisdictions regularly sell the information to data brokers, direct marketing, title-search, and mortgage companies. Millions of older documents containing sensitive information were recorded before the public's sensibilities were heightened to the growing danger of identity fraud. Other government Web sites, such as the Florida Department of State's Secured Transaction Registry, contain hundreds of thousands of additional social security numbers. Anyone can go to the Web site, type in a name and rummage through scanned images of deeds, mortgages, liens, judgments, and other records containing signatures, social security numbers, credit card, charge card and bank account numbers, and notary stamps, among other choice information.

So, never make the obvious attempt to hide anything, because they may already have the information and evidence of what you may try to hide. Often the cover-up is worse than the problem uncovered by a computer search of your private life. That is another reason why the first rule you must adhere to as a physician testifying under oath is to "tell the truth." Cover-ups are far more damaging than the truth-as bad as you think the truth could be.

The easiest and quickest way in this computer age is in deep pockets of Internet information. (See attached appendix-CD to learn how conflicts of interest of testifying physicians can be revealed.)

Not many physicians know that medical insurance carriers such as Blue Cross/Blue Shield can track health records. For example, "Independence Blue Cross," Philadelphia's largest health insurer, with 19 other Blue plans across the nation forms a massive database of health care records to provide more detailed performance data on their doctors and hospitals based on bills submitted to these insurers.

Even curious consumers could learn, for example, which primary-care doctors are most consistent at ordering mammograms or which surgeons have the fewest (or most) postoperative complications. The Blue Health Intelligence database is composed of all medical procedures and other care—allegedly stripped of information identifying individual subscribers—from Blue Cross Blue Shield members in 34 states. The insurers use the data to give doctors and hospitals reports on their own quality of care, using widely accepted measurements, such as whether they have given heart attack patients beta blockers or ensured that diabetic patients received recommended blood tests on time.

In addition, we now also know a lot about AOL's misstep in August 2006, which revealed 19 million Internet search queries made by more than 600,000 of its unwitting customers. This has reminded many Americans that their private Internet searches are often monitored.

Most of the major search engines such as Google, Yahoo, and MSN collect and store information on what terms are searched, when they were queried, and what computer and browser was used. Information can be used to match historic search behavior emanating from a specific computer by a good computer specialist. As of this writing, little with regard to search queries are private.

No laws clearly place search requests off-limits to advertisers, law enforcement agencies, or academic researchers, beyond the terms that companies set themselves. But the detailed records of searches conducted by 657,000 Americans, copies of which continue to circulate online, underscore how many people unintentionally reveal about themselves when they use search engines. Bloggers claim they can identify AOL users by examining data, while others hunt for particularly entertaining or shocking search histories. Some programmers made this easier by setting up Web sites that let people search the database of searches. The fact is, travelers also take certain risks with the things they do on most trips and if followed, a lot of private and confidential information could be detected. Wireless networks at airports—or for that matter, hotels, or cafes—are not as secure as most people think. Someone may have some software on their computer that allows them to look at all the wireless transactions going on around them and capture packets that are floating between the laptop and the wireless access point. These software programs are called packet sniffers and many can be downloaded free online. They are typically set up to capture passwords, credit card numbers, and bank account information.

Info-World magazine wrote about a security researcher who managed to collect more than 100 passwords, per stay, at hotels with lax security (about half the hotels she tested). The most recent computer crime and security survey, conducted annually by the Computer Security Institute with the Federal Bureau of Investigation, found that the average loss from computer security incidents in 2005 was $167,713. Using a public computer can also mean your life is an open book, because data viewed while surfing the Web, printing a document or opening an e-mail attachment is generally stored on the computer. This means it could be accessible to the next person who sits down unless you delete any documents you have viewed, clear the browser cache and the history file, and empty the trash before you walk away.

At several Kinko's locations, you also run the risk that somebody has loaded a program on there that can capture your log-ins and passwords. But the most common snoop that business travelers encounter is someone nearby "shoulder surfing" to see what is on a laptop.

There are also many Web sites, which can elicit not only personal but professional information about a physician so as to discover any skeletons. In addition, many search engines can be used to research any physician. A physician's personal Web page, articles, research projects, presentations, speaking engagements, and even postings on discussion boards can be found by simply conducting a search for the physician's name on a search engine such as Google.[9]

13.3.2   Yes, Your Life Is Really an Open Book

Yahoo has a computer system that uses complex models to analyze records of what each of its 500 million users do on its site: what they search for, what pages they read, and what ads they click on. It then tries to show them advertisements that speak directly to their interests and the events in their lives, reports Hansell S. in the August 15, 2006 *New York Times*.

Collectively, a person's Web searches can create an intimate portrait. Web companies continue refining their techniques. Yahoo's system is meant to use search queries and other actions to select ads people see while checking their e-mail and reading other pages. AOL and MSN from Microsoft have similar systems to display ads for products related to a person's Web search history. Other companies use systems that bring together information about users from across many sites. Internet companies call this "behavioral targeting," and it is based on the insight that knowing what people do online can be more valuable to a marketer than knowing how old they are or what they do for a living. "Search behavior is the closest thing we have to a window onto people's intent," they say.

Many Internet users have no idea that records of their actions are being collected and used. They might find out about these practices only if they read the fine print of Web site privacy policies.

Not all of the behavioral marketing involves search engines. Technology from companies like Double-Click and AOL's Advertising.com unit allows marketing messages to follow people around the Web. Starwood Hotels, for example, alerts members of its frequent-guest program to new promotions by placing ads that will be shown only to people who have previously visited its Web site. These ads can find customers in unlikely places, like the vast social networking site MySpace.

Cingular Wireless uses a similar approach to advertise to people who have started shopping for a phone. How do they do this? Most of these marketing systems use cookies, unique numbers that a Web site can place on a computer to spot return visitors. Cookies are also used by companies such as Advertising.com[10] that place ads and track visitors across many sites. Shopping sites like Amazon.com[11] use cookies to greet returning customers by name. Yahoo and most of the major Internet companies do not sell profile information to others, but magazine publishers and credit card companies often do. They want to profit directly from the information they gather. Web publishers do sometimes trade information among themselves—often simply what sites a particular computer has visited. For example, Seevast, an Internet advertising company, pays Web sites to place its cookies on the computers of users that visit them. That way, Seevast will know more about those users when it chooses which advertisements to display on sites in its network. Yahoo's new system is based on monitoring for 300 types of behavior—some as detailed as having shopped for flowers in the last two days—but allegedly does not keep records on more sensitive topics, such as specific medical conditions. Yahoo and many other sites see this sort of targeting as a way to increase advertising rates for material that otherwise would have little appeal to advertisers. Even the *Los Angeles Times* targets car buyers when they are surfing the local news on its Web site.

Tacoda runs a network across 3500 sites, so Weather.com,[12] for example, can show lucrative auto ads to its users who recently visited Car.com.[13]

Google, which runs both the largest search engine and largest advertising network, sells advertisements that appear on other Web sites. It selects the ad by analyzing the subject matter of the page the ads appear on. Those sites can send Google additional hints for use in ad targeting, such as ZIP codes. Although Google claims it has not used information about the past behavior of searchers to target advertisements, the company keeps logs of all searches and its privacy policy allows it to use these for advertising. Although Google claimed it did not collect the names of most searchers, it has lately been doing so increasingly as it offers more personal services like e-mail. Panasonic uses technology to show ads to people who had once visited those sites while they surfed elsewhere. Even LendingTree, an online loan broker, has experimented with aiming ads at some of the 300 categories of users in Yahoo's new system, such as newlyweds and people who have just moved. It had by far the best results advertising to people who had searched for and read information about borrowing money.

What one man can invent, another can discover.

—Sherlock Holmes
The Adventure of The Dancing Men

I think, Watson, that you are now standing in the presence of one of the absolute fools in Europe.

—Sherlock Holmes
The Man with the Twisted Lip

13.4 Other Techniques to Investigate the Physician

13.4.1 Investigation of the Testifying Physician

USA Today on October 12, 2006 described the "Wal-Mart of the underground," in which hackers can get almost anything to commit identity theft and investigation of your life routing through an Iranian server so that law enforcement is difficult.

Hackers have cost U.S. business $67.2 billion according to the FBI; $93.8 million in stolen personal records since 2005. For $500 a hacker can buy a credit card number with a PIN and expiration date, social security number, and a birthdate. A driver's license or birth certificate cost $150; a pay pal account with log-in cost $7.00.

Also, according to the October 17, 2006 *New York Times* commercial databases are fast undoing the process of expungement, which means that with a judge's consent, the records are supposed to be destroyed or sealed. But records once held only in paper form of people convicted of minor crimes like possessing marijuana, shoplifting, or disorderly conduct by law enforcement agencies, courts, and corrections departments are now routinely digitized and sold in bulk to the private sector. Some commercial databases now contain more than 100 million criminal records, which often turn up in criminal background checks ordered by employers and landlords. Although some ethical private database companies update their records to reflect expungement of criminal records, critics claim that even the biggest vendors do not always update their records promptly and thoroughly. They also assert that in this electronic age, people should understand that once they have been convicted or arrested that information will never go away.

"Drug companies have been buying prescription records [on your prescription habits] since the 1990s, yet the practice is still not widely known. Even many doctors don't know it occurs," writes Jake Whitney in the *SF Chronicle* August 6, 2006. This data is given to drug reps calling on physician offices to gauge the extent of the incentive process.

Data mining companies such as IMS Health play the role of middleman in tracking prescription records. These firms buy records from pharmacy chains and other sources before repackaging them and selling them to drug companies. When pharmacy chains sell the records, however, they allegedly do not include patient names and, in some cases, the doctors who wrote the prescriptions. So drug companies turn to a surprising source to complete the prescription profiles: the AMA.

The AMA leases its "physicians' masterfile" to data mining companies and, through them, subleases it to pharmaceutical companies. This masterfile contains personal and professional information, including the Drug Enforcement Agency number on all doctors practicing in the United States. And since every prescription written in the United States must include the prescribing physician's DEA number, drug companies use these physician-unique numbers on the masterfile to match prescription records to doctors. The AMA justifies its role because these data can be analyzed by researchers to identify poor prescribing habits. Analyzing prescribing data is another way the AMA wants to make sure patients all over the country receive the best possible care.

The AMA generates millions of dollars per year with the lease of its masterfile. The AMA has absolutely no incentive to stop the practice. Drug companies lay out hefty sums for the profiles. IMS Health, just one of a handful of data mining companies, generated $1.7 billion in revenues last year, $847 million from its "sales force effectiveness offerings."

13.5   What Other Investigation Tools Does the Opposition Have to Uncover Facts about You?

a. The individual physician's own Web site: A physician's personal Web site is carefully reviewed. Many physicians post their full "CV," prior litigation experience, speaking engagements, references, memberships and professional organization affiliations, articles, and newsletters on their Web sites.

b. When reviewing a physician's Web site, keep in mind that opposing counsel can do so as well.

c. Is there anything embarrassing or contradictory on the site?

d. Does the physician advertise that he or she is "the leader in the medical field" or put forth similar bravado that could affect how the jury perceives the physician?

e. Imagine how the jury would react if the pages of the physician's Web site were displayed as exhibits at trial, because they very well might be.

f. A researcher cannot depend on the physician to have posted all of his or her published works on the Web site, and should search himself.

g. Full text articles from over 300 periodicals dating back to 1998 can be found at findarticles.com.[14]

h. Some legal portals, such as Heros Gamos,[15] post articles written by physicians.

i. Although not a free search, Idex[16] has created an internal database of physicians who have been reviewed and disciplined by jurisdictional licensing boards. To access this database, one must be an Idex member and a defense attorney (or work on behalf of a defense attorney). According to its Web site, 6,000 records are added each month to Idex's database of over 800,000 records of physician involvement.

j. From queries in news sources, researchers can often find quotes made by the physician and learn a physician's opinions. A list of newspapers and magazines and their links can be found at Newslink.[17] It is worthwhile to run a search for a physician's name on these news Web sites, especially in the newspapers in the physician's locality.

k. Google can find Usenet Discussion postings by physician or medical experts. By clicking on the "Groups" tab on the Google home page, one can access more than 700 million messages dating back to 1981.

l. Information about physician defendants or physician experts can often be found in litigation briefs. *The Brief Reporter*[18] publishes legal briefs from previously litigated cases in all state and federal jurisdictions.

m. Juritas[19] provides a fee-based, searchable database to the complete text of briefs, pleadings, motions, affidavits, orders, verdicts, judgments, jury instructions, and physician or medical expert testimony. According to its Web site, these papers come directly from state and federal trial courts across the United States. The documents also cover the most litigated practice areas, including medical malpractice, and white-collar crime.

n. Jury verdicts and settlements are unofficially reported in a variety of locations on the Internet, and often provide information about the physicians used in the case. Morelaw[20] is one of the only free, searchable nationwide jury verdicts Web sites. This site has verdicts and settlements dating back to December 1996.

o. Some free information for physician defendants or physician/medical experts is available on the National Association of State Jury Verdict Publishers (NASJV),[21] a portal site for many jury verdict publications. According to its Web site, their "physician witness directory" contains the names of nearly 40,000 physicians who have testified in civil trials across the United States.

p. Physician's names often appear in reported decisions. Searchable, free case law can be accessed at Findlaw[22] or LexisOne.[23]

q. To date, there is no free, centralized database for physician witness transcripts. For defense attorneys, full text copies of the physician's testimony are available for a fee from Idex. Physician defendants and physician or medical expert transcripts are also available for a fee to defense attorneys who are members of the Defense Research Institute.[24]

r. On the plaintiff's side, the ATLA Exchange[25] makes available to its members a database of over 10,000 physician witnesses and over 15,000 transcripts.

s. The commercial site TrialSmith[26] states that it hosts the nation's largest online deposition bank, with more than 147,000 depositions.

Now that you know what the other side really knows, you must make certain that all your CV and other data you hand over is accurate and that there are no skeletons you think you can hide.

If there are skeletons tell your retaining attorney about it—do not try a cover-up. The attorney will probably handle it—to put the best face on it—during your direct or redirect testimony. Remember again the cover-up is often worse than the crime.

13.6 Summary and Conclusions

The important point to remember in this chapter is the major point made in the beginning and that is, do not try to cover up any "skeletons" or other perceived deficiencies in your background. The other side knows it probably and you can get into a lot more trouble by covering it up than by telling your attorney frankly what the problem is or problems are and having your attorney handle it.

> In seeking absolute truth we aim at the unattainable and must be content with broken portions.
>
> **—William Osler**

References

1. http://www.cert.org/advisories/CA-2000-02.html.
2. http://www.adobe.com/support/security/advisories/apsa07-01.html.
3. http://events.ccc.de/congress/2006/Fahrplan/attachments/1158-Subverting_Ajax.pdf.
4. http://www.wisec.it/vulns.php?page=9.
5. http://secunia.com/advisories/23483/.
6. http://www.adobe.com/devnet/acrobat/pdfs/PDFOpenParameters.pdf.
7. http://en.wikipedia.org/wiki/Reverse_proxy.
8. Hassmyer D. Surgeons credentials scrutinized. *San Diego Union Tribune* 2005; December.
9. www.google.com.
10. www.Advertising.com.
11. www.Amazon.com.
12. www.Weather.com.
13. www.Car.com.
14. www.findarticles.com.
15. www.hg.org.
16. www.Idex.com.
17. http://newslink.org.
18. www.briefreporter.com.
19. www.juritas.com.
20. www.morelaw.com.
21. www.juryverdicts.com.
22. www.findlaw.com.
23. www.lexisone.com.
24. www.dri.org.
25. www.atla.org.
26. www.trialsmith.com.

Overview of a Medical Malpractice Trial

14

You wouldn't have won if we'd beaten you.

—**Yogi Berra**

14.1   Introduction

A testifying physician must know what is coming. He must know the strategy of the contest and the questions that he is going to be asked. He must know the trick questions, the trap questions, and the questions designed to discredit him (impeachment). This is the theme of this book. *Forewarned is forearmed.*

In this chapter including its six sections, you will get a reasonably good description as to what strategies against you to expect as a testifying physician, and how to handle it.

14.2   A Trial Has a Definite Format and Order

Think of it as a Shakespearean play in several acts with the attorneys as the leading men and women, the judge as the director, the producers—the framers of the U.S. constitution, and the jury as the voting audience and critics. As far as your ego is concerned you have to realize that you—the medical expert—are not even a bit player.

Your sole role in this production is to act in perhaps only one scene as a part-time interpreter for the audience so as to help translate some difficult parts of Shakespearean language into modern day English. Most of the play's actions, drama, and decisive moments take place completely in your absence from the stage.

So do not inflate your own importance. And do not try to be more than you are—you are definitely not even close to the star or even the understudy of this production.

Thus keep your distance "and speak the speech, I pray you, . . . trippingly on the tongue," "sincerely, humbly and without dramatic gestures or false emotions . . .," but if you mouth it as many players do, "I had as lief the town crier speak the lines."

And if I have to tell you who spoke these lines, you have been too narrowly trained in only your own specialty and should never accept the task to be an expert witness.

The trial starts with

Act 1—*The opening statements.*

The attorney for each party makes an opening statement. First the plaintiff who tells his story first and last (in the summation). Usually, each attorney tells the jury what she/he intends to prove—perhaps saving a few surprises for the trial.

Act 2—*The Plaintiff's case* in which she/he presents the evidence and witnesses favoring their side of the story.

Scene 1:   Direct testimony (with a friendly witness).
Scene 2:   Cross-examination.
Scene 4:   Opposing attorney cross-examines the friendly witness.
Scene 5:   Redirect examination.
Scene 6:   Re-cross-examination.
Scene 7:   Motion for dismissal at the end of the Plaintiff's case. This *pro forma* motion is always made by the defendant on the grounds that the plaintiff failed to fulfill the burden of proof. If the motion has merit and is accepted by the judge the case is over. This is rare because most judges fear an appellate reversal due to reversible error (an error that substantially prejudiced the appealing party). In such instances, the appellate court will overrule the trial judge and order a new trial. So the trial judge usually denies the motion or "reserves" his decision, thereby forcing the case to proceed with the defense putting on its case.

Act 3—*The defendant's case.*

Scene 1:   *Possible rebuttal* by the plaintiff on evidence not previously introduced.
Scene 2:   *Possible surrebuttal* by the defendant when the defendant can challenge the new evidence to refute the above new evidence.
Scene 3:   Both side have rested their case and now the court can hear *end of case motions.*
   A.   The plaintiff for a redirected verdict—that the defendant did not controvert the plaintiff's evidence establishing malpractice and the damages it caused.
   B.   The defendant can move for
      1.   dismissal of the plaintiff's case because the plaintiff's proof is insufficient as a matter of law;
      2.   a directed verdict in behalf of the defendant on the grounds that the judge set aside any verdict for the plaintiff as against the weight of evidence; therefore there is no point in sending the case to the jury (which is the opposite of the plaintiff's motion for a directed verdict).

Act 4—*Summations* now take place once the judge has denied or reserved the above motions.

14.3   The Closing Argument

The party with the burden of proof is given the opportunity to open and close in both the opening statement and closing argument. During the closing argument, both attorneys again tell their story or their theme. Both attorneys should have broadly developed their themes even before discovery begins and should have honed down as the trial day approach to a concise cogent explanation of how and why these events occurred. In addition, Waites[1] states that the attorney as a part of the theme must include a suggestion to the jury that it will be doing "the right thing" in adopting their respective positions. The "right thing" guides the jury to that attorney position; thus, the closing argument concludes with a theme that consists of one side of the facts and one view as to how the facts should resolve in the jury during the "right thing" a favorable verdict for your client.

Actually, the theme is used by a smart attorney once a jury is selected as a major role in his opening statement and in examining nearly every one of his witnesses including you—the medical expert. Each attorney knows that "the key" is to convince each juror that by adopting his position, it is the "right thing" to do.

That is another reason why you, the medical expert, should understand that if the jury senses any effort in you or your retaining attorney to be insincere, artificial, or deceitful, that credibility is immediately lost, and possibly the trial because the jury wants to make the "right decision." The "right decision" does not include aligning themselves with a team who appears to be "dishonest and disingenuous."

Scene 1: First the defendant's then the plaintiff's attorney makes the last summation or final arguments to the jury. Each attorney must confine their arguments only to the evidence introduced in the case and cannot discuss anything new. They are not supposed to incorrectly paraphrase or summarize testimony.

It is here that any mistakes by the retaining attorney or you or unnecessary concessions you made in either deposition or trial testimony will be fully taken advantage of by the opposing attorney.

She/he has been knitting like Mme. DeFarge a string of yarn to clothe the arguments with (partial?) "truths," because "nothing hath an uglier look to us that facts, when it is not on our side."

Remember, also I have heard from losing attorneys that "there was never a cause yet, right or wrong, that ever wanted an advocate to defend it." It is in the summation or closing argument that a web of partial truths to which you had agreed during your testimony, has been spun to convince the jury that you have actually agreed with the opposing expert or "authoritative" text.

It is here that any successful impeachment tactics from the deposition or the trial will be announced as from the public square of the guillotine while the jurors are knitting.

If and when objections are raised by either attorney to "indiscretions" by the other attorney, the judge usually just reminds the jury not to pay heed to the attorney's last statement and that it is their recollection of the testimony that controls. Only if the summation is extreme in its inaccuracies or prejudice will the judge sustain an objection.

But most attorneys know that once a "mis"-statement is made to the jury they really do not forget it, as shown in study by Lee.[2]

There appear to be no significant restrictions on a medical expert witness in many states on his opinions, i.e., whether or not hearsay evidence is allowed.

As an aside stay tuned to the chapter on the Daubert challenge for a discussion of whether an expert witness in a malpractice action can testify that his opinion was formed or documented by the medical and surgical literature, and not violate his state's rule on *hearsay evidence*. You must check with your retaining attorney about the law in your state.

Ohio and Florida are some of the states that do not recognize an exception to the hear-say rule for learned treatises even in medical malpractice cases. Also stay tuned for the discussion on whether you can be asked by a cross examiner as to whether you have nightly sex with a parrot(sic).

But as for this discussion a study by Lee is presented here to demonstrate that despite attempted neutralization by the judge, the jury still remembers statements or "mis-statements."

Using a simulated civil case, Lee's experiment investigated whether mock jurors

a. are able to disregard hearsay evidence when admonished to do so?
b. experience psychological reactance and "backfire effects" in proportion to the strength of judicial admonition instructing them to disregard hearsay evidence?
c. are able to recognize and disregard hearsay evidence without judicial instructions?

Results indicate that jurors were *unable to disregard inadmissible hearsay testimony* in some legal decisions regardless of whether there were judicial instructions to do so. Jurors exhibited backfire effects *paying more attention* to inadmissible hearsay evidence when they were strongly instructed to disregard it. These juror backfire effects were evident in both their confidence in their liability verdicts and in their punitive damage awards.

So you must inform your attorney when such partial truths will hurt the case that you have sworn to tell the truth (no lies) the whole truth (not the partial truth) and nothing but the truth (no guessing or speculating). And you must have your retaining attorney prepared to take on "the parrot question" aimed to undermine you as well as the "hearsay" in your medical opinion.

You must let him know that when you signal by your answer to the cross examiner "Yes, but" and you are cut off in the questioning that he has to return to that subject in the Redirect so you can explain the full truth as you know it, but more about this in the following chapters.

Scene 2:   The charge of the court

Scene 3:   The judge instructs the jury

Scene 4:   Exceptions and requests to the charge

Scene 5:   The verdict

Scene 6:   Postverdict motions

14.4   Subpoena

If the expert is subpoenaed—without any agreement for professional compensation—and is later qualified by the presiding judge as an expert witness, he may not be required to perform any special service without an agreement for payment for the expert's professional fees. In the event that the expert is subpoenaed and is given only the statutory fee, he will probably not be as cooperative a witness as one who voluntarily agreed to testify as an expert witness. However, often times an attorney will serve a subpoena to his own expert to indicate that the witness has appeared under court order.

14.5   The Oath

> No human being is constituted to know the truth, the whole truth and nothing but the truth; and even the best of men must be content with fragments, with partial glimpses, never the full fruition.
>
> **—William Osler**

An expert who gives testimony in deposition or trial is administered an oath requiring that he vouch for the truthfulness of his testimony. For example, Federal Rule of Evidence 603 requires that:

> Before testifying, every witness shall be required to declare that the witness will testify truthfully, by oath or affirmation administered in a form calculated to waken the witness' conscience and impress the witness' mind with the duty to do so.

Similarly, experts are occasionally required to sign declarations in support of summary judgment motions "declaring under penalty of perjury that their statements are true and correct" (28 U.S.C. § 1746).

All oaths or declarations inherently represent a witness's commitment to the system that he or she will tell the truth. Sounds simple, but what is the truth?

Experts give "opinions." The "truth" of an opinion is open to debate. Philosophers and theologians have written tomes on this subject, all disagreeing on what is true. Accordingly, oaths and Declarations Under Penalty of Perjury, may not effectively guarantee an expert will tell the truth. Moreover, all experts do not have the same commitment to our system of justice to guarantee unadulterated truth. Perhaps the most significant consequence of an expert's failure to testify truthfully, is that the trier of fact (the jury) may disregard the expert's opinion.

Thus, it is the layperson's perception of truthfulness that is critical. The real effectiveness of the oath is the expert's implied promise of truthfulness and the penalty, which will result if the expert is not perceived as truthful.

14.5.1   Maxims

A. In deposition testimony—be accurate, brief, and responsive.
B. In trial testimony—be accurate, clear, persuasive, and memorable.
C. In cross-examination—listen, concentrate, and be extremely careful with your answers. Take George Washington's advice—Think before you speak! Also take my advice—Think before you think.

14.6   Trial Testimony

> There is nothing more stimulating than a case where everything goes against you.
>
> **—Sherlock Holmes**
> *The Hound of the Baskervilles*

14.6.1 Your Direct Examination

14.6.1.1 *Puff and Stuff*

Puff is the puffing out of your excellent credentials experience, training, expertise, and everything short of the Nobel Prize—that too if you won it—by your retaining attorney. Stuff is the facts elicited from you on direct examination, which leads to your opinion.

14.6.1.2 *Helpful Hints*

1. Check into analogies for the jury.
   Agency: Walmart truck passes a red light. Kills someone. Walmart says only the driver is at fault.
   Early action: Train coming down the track will smash a person on the tracks. Get the person off the tracks or stop the train. Do not wait.
   Time bomb waiting to go off. Do something about it quickly.
2. Rehearse the story with the attorney and condense into a 10-word theme. Tell a story—the three things you want the jury to remember. Know the timeline. I read that you should buy a train ticket to home for the weekend. Not your current house, but home–home, to your parents or your sister and brother-in-law. Now sit with them down at the kitchen table and, in 50 words or less, tell them what this case is about, what your opinion is, why and how you came to your opinion, and what is good about it. Do not use medical words or any words with lots of syllables. Do not quit till they understand your opinion.
3. The main reason physician testimony is presented to the jury is to offer a medical opinion. Accordingly, physicians can anticipate being closely cross-examined on their opinions. They should also expect to be closely questioned on the bases of these opinions because a medical physician opinion is only as strong as the facts and reasoning upon which it is based.

Specter[3] states that the important points on direct examination by your retaining attorney are as follows:

1. Convey the fact that you are a professional dedicated to accurate and detailed work.
2. You must avoid any impression at all that you are a hired gun by not being drawn into any biased or exaggerated statements.
3. Emphasize the peer-reviewed medical literature that you reviewed in this case.
4. Your testimony represents your professional opinion done by careful analysis of the medical records and supported by the peer-reviewed medical literature.
5. Remember that the courtroom is a serious place. Your appearance occupies only a relatively small amount of time, but it is significant.

14.6.1.3 *Trial Tips*

1. Say what you mean and mean what you say after a thorough preparation.
2. Do not be intimidated, boring, or making your jury wish they were somewhere else.
3. Show them that you are relaxed and not tense.
4. Do not frown, make exaggerated gesticulations, sound like you memorized words from a page, preach or orate, and do not present a wordy recitation.

5. If you use visuals, which I advise to do all the time, keep the visuals simple.
6. Make the diagrams large, clear, and very visible.
7. Make sure they are prepared professionally.
8. Do not try to do it yourself.

It is true that though in your mission you have missed everything of importance, yet even those things which have obtruded themselves upon your notice give rise to serious thought.

—Sherlock Holmes
The Adventure of The Retired Colourman

References

1. Waites RC. *Courtroom Psychology and Trial Advocacy*, 2003, pp. 535–537.
2. Lee D., et al. The effects of judicial admonitions on hearsay evidence. *Int. J. Law Psychiatr.* Nov–Dec 2005; 28(6): 589–603 (Epub 2005 Aug 25).
3. Specter A. What does it take to be a good expert witness? *ASTM Stand. News* February 1988; 38.

Introducing the Physician to Legal Testimony
Preparing the Defendant Physician for Testimony

15

15.1 Introduction

In our next and more advanced text for advanced medical expert witness testimony including advanced strategies in responding to very aggressive cross-examination from hyper-combative opposing attorneys, we will cover the applications of medical expert testimony in more detail and from the point of view of more assertive defensive and offensive strategies in your medical expert testimony. However, now for introductory purposes, we will explore how and why this chapter on "Preparing the Defendant Physician for Testimony" is important in forearming the physician and medical expert witness in the subject of court testimony.

It is important for the defendant physician to understand what may be coming at him in the courtroom. This introduction to physician testimony cannot contain everything you need to know. So it is important to sit down with the attorney selected by your medical malpractice insurer or your own personal attorney to find out all the upcoming events and what the scenario will be. Always ask for the best-case and the worst-case scenario so that you can be *forearmed by being forewarned* and be able to make decisions. Sometimes the insurance carrier insists on not settling the case because they do not want to set an example as an easy mark for settlement. Other times they will try to settle a case quickly even though you do not want the settlement because most settlements are reported to the National Data Bank. In this chapter, we first introduce you to how you, as a physician, should be prepared for a deposition. Also included is a section on how to prepare the defendant physician for trial testimony and an article "Advice to the Testifying Physician on Enhancing Credibility in Court" contributed by The Honorable James M. Vukelic, JD, who has presided as the Judge over many medical malpractice trials.

15.2 Gold Nuggets Executive Summary

1. For the cross-examination, good advice for the defendant physician is to answer directly and simply with a "yes" or "no" if appropriate and not to volunteer information or attempt to explain an answer.

2. If your attorney wants you to explain something, he will ask it on redirect examination if he thinks it is appropriate.
3. If your answer is compete and truthful, simply remain quiet.
4. Do not say more even if the cross-examiner looks at you expecting you to say more.
5. If the examiner asks you if that is all you recall, say yes (if that is the truth).
6. Testify to only what you have personally seen, done, said, or heard from the patient–plaintiff.
7. Do not speculate, guess, or assume anything.
8. If you do not know something because you have not seen it, done it, said it, or heard it, your answer should be, "I don't know."
9. Testify only to your best recollection.
10. If you do not recall something, do not hesitate to say so even if you fear this may make you appear to look foolish.
11. Do not exaggerate.
12. Take your time if you need in answering the question.
13. If the information is contained in a document that you are uncertain of, ask to see the document or state you do not recall the answer.
14. If you are asked a question, which was asked during the deposition or a prior statement, answer the question if you recall the answer; otherwise, say you do not recall.
15. Do not allow the cross-examiner to put words in your mouth.
16. Do not accept the cross-examiner's characterization of time or events.
17. If a question is inaccurate, state "I cannot answer that question" even if the cross-examiner tries to force you into agreeing or disagreeing with the question or saying "yes" or "no."
18. If you say something that is inconsistent with your prior testimony, do not be panic—mistakes will happen. Remember Tiger Woods' rule " just don't think about the last bad hole."
19. If you make a misstatement, correct it as soon as you can. If you make a mistake, admit it.
20. Expect the cross-examiner to obtain some information that may weaken your story. Do not worry about it.
21. If the cross-examiner apparently seems (appears) confused, do not ever attempt to help him.
22. Answer all questions properly.
23. **Q. "Have you talked to anybody about this case?"**
    A. You may identify whom you have talked to about the case, including your attorney or other witnesses or anyone else. It is normal and expected to talk with these individuals.
24. The defendant physician should be reminded that she/he will be constantly watched by the jury and should always be calmly conscious of being observed.
25. Do not fidget or make any body language that appears to the jury as being nonconfident in your testimony—or worse yet, evasive or dissembling. (See Judge Vukelic, next chapter: rubbing or wringing of hands, shifting leg posture or alignment coinciding with pertinent questions, wiping sweat, locking feet together under chair, turning the body away from the questioner, rhythmic drumming of fingers, and closed body position with arms and elbows particularly close to the body.)

26. Periodically maintain eye contact with the jury. This helps to personalize you.
27. The defendant physician should not interrupt the attorney unless necessary or when the attorney seeks advice.
28. It may be preferable to write a note with a question or idea.
29. The defendant physician must pay attention and concentrate on the evidence and arguments.
30. The defendant physician should never eat in the hearing room.
31. When you are addressing and answering questions, in addition to telling the truth you must speak clearly and loudly. And do not cover your mouth with your hand.
32. If you will be testifying regarding an event, attempt to recreate in your mind the details of that event, picture the scene, the persons present, what happened, and what was said.
33. Listen very carefully to the questions and make sure you understand them before answering.
34. If you do not understand, ask to repeat the question.
35. If you still do not understand the question, say so.
36. Never answer a question you do not fully understand or before you have thought your answer through.
37. Answer with positive, definite answers.
38. Avoid saying, "I think, I believe, I am not really sure, or In my opinion" when you actually know the facts.
39. If you are uncertain or do not know the answer, say so.
40. If your answer was incorrect or unclear, correct it.
41. It is appropriate to say, "I want to clarify something."
42. Use your own words and language, not anybody else's language or somebody else's words.
43. When testifying, imagine you are having a conversation with the jury.
44. Look at the jury when testifying, answer the questions asked and do not second-guess why the attorney asked the question.
45. Be aware of your body posture at all times. Do not make gestures or facial expressions that are distracting (see Vukelic body postures above).
46. Dress neatly and appropriately as if this trial was a serious and an important business meeting.
47. Do not bring any written notes or material to the witness stand.
48. Immediately stop when there is an objection. Do not try to sneak in an answer.
49. If there is an objection to the question, listen to the objection and what was said. You may learn something about the questions and how it should be answered from these statements.
50. Be serious and avoid disagreeing with the attorney.
51. Do not make jokes.
52. Do not ask the judge for advice.
53. Anticipate being nervous, it is normal and expected.
54. If you feel ill, nervous, or fatigued, ask for a break or for a glass of water.
55. Try to *always* avoid absolutes, adjectives, and superlatives such as never or always, every time, anytime, etc.[1]

15.3   Strategies for First Time Medical Expert Witnesses

If this is the first time you have been called as a medical expert witness, you must at least have some idea of what can happen. Expert witnesses are persons whose special knowledge, skill, experience, training, or education permits them to testify to an opinion that will aid a judge or jury in resolving a question that is beyond the understanding or competence of laypersons. In the realm of medical malpractice litigation, the expert witness is asked to define the applicable standard of medical care in a given case and then to offer his or her opinion as to whether the defendant physician deviated from that standard.

Notwithstanding that expert witnesses are expected to be sufficiently knowledgeable to proffer realistic assessments of the appropriate standard of medical care and whether a defendant physician complied with or breached it, many in the legal and medical communities have often expressed doubts that physicians inexperienced in the language and culture of our legal system are competent to do so.

A perusal of the excerpts shown here may prove the point (Gill *v.* Foster, 232 3d 768 [Ill App1992]). Here is an example of terrible testimony.[2]

Defense attorney (A): Doctor, what is the standard of care for a radiologist?

Plaintiff's expert witness (W): To make the correct diagnosis on an x-ray.

This is the ideal and not the standard of care. This response is not correct. The standard of care is what a prudent physician of similar training would do or read an x-ray under similar circumstances. It is what a similar trained physician would do in a similar circumstance. In this case the opposing attorney smells blood.

A: Are you saying, Doctor, that *every* time a radiologist misses a diagnosis on an x-ray, he or she is guilty of malpractice?

W: Yes.

By answering yes to the absolute word "every" the expert has entered the trap; all the opposing attorney has to do now is spring the trap.

A: Have you ever missed an abnormality on an x-ray?

W: Not that I'm aware of.

A: Doctor, you have told us you are an examiner for the American Board of Radiology. If you were testing a resident for board certification and there was this abnormality on the chest radiograph, and that resident didn't describe that abnormality on the report, are you saying that the resident would fail the examination?

W: Absolutely.

Again he uses an absolute word. This expert will soon be taught a lesson he will not forget.

A: Doctor, tell us again what position you hold in the American College of Radiology and how that helps you to form an opinion in this case.

W: I have been elected to the Board of the American College of Radiology and my assignment is to be in charge of quality assurance for all the United States. As such, I will tell you that this radiologist's report is inadequate. Furthermore, it would not suffice if this man were in my radiology group.

A: Doctor, please tell us why you feel that the missing of this radiographic abnormality amounts to *negligence*.

Did he say anything about negligence? He is not listening carefully to the question.

W: I looked at this film as a neutral and with complete disinterest, and saw the lesion immediately—cold—without a history or clinical information.

A: Doctor, do you think the missed lesion is *subtle?*

W: No, *even* a student could see a lesion on these films.

A: Doctor, would you call this lesion *obvious?*

W: Yes, *the abnormality was so obvious, my secretary saw it from across the room.*

He should have left everything out after "yes." Don't try to gild the lily.

A: So, Doctor, *unless* a radiologist is certified by the American Board of Radiology, that
radiologist would not be qualified to interpret x-rays?

W: Correct.

A: And if a radiologist who *is not board-certified* was to review x-rays, in your opinion that
physician is not qualified to do so?

W: Correct.

A: Doctor, in your experience, do you know if you have ever had occasion to miss a nodule
on a chest x-ray?

W: Yes.

A: On how many occasions?

W: I don't know. Unfortunately, I see the ones other people miss and they see the ones that
I miss.

A: Do you have any estimate?

W: Very rarely.

A: What does that mean?

W: Maybe once or twice in my life.

A: So, Doctor, *any time,* even retrospectively, an abnormality is missed then, in your opinion, that is a deviation from the standard of care?

W: Yes, a miss is not the standard of care. It's a mistake and you can't say a mistake is the
standard of care.

A: Doctor, isn't it true in the field of radiology oftentimes radiologists make a diagnosis of
cancer and they look back at prior mammograms and they may see signs of that
cancer earlier that they did not note initially?

W: Yes, that is true.

A: Okay. In your opinion, if that happens with microcalcifications that were not reported
on an earlier mammogram, do you believe that in 100% of the cases the radiologist who did not call the calcifications deviated from the standard of care?

W: Yes, they have deviated from the standard of care.

A: And so that I understand then, at least in your opinion, you think *it is reasonable* to
expect *every radiologist* to recall any grouping of microcalcifications that later
turns out to have been malignant?

W: The answer is yes.

A: So in your opinion that is a *reasonable standard* to hold all radiologists to, and you would
expect other radiologists who specialize in mammography to agree with you?

W: I would expect that.

A: Doctor, does the failure to observe any calcifications on any mammogram constitute
malpractice?

W: Yes.

A: Have you ever missed calcifications on a mammogram?

W: I wouldn't say I missed them. We're talking about sensitivity levels. There is a difference between a sensitivity and a miss. *A miss is a mistake. A miss is malpractice, if it has some detrimental effect.* You look back to all the previous films when you are dealing with a newly diagnosed cancer to see if it may have been discoverable earlier or whether your sensitivity level was at a higher or lower bar . . .

A: Okay.

W: . . . and if you see something looking back and say to yourself, it was a cancer then and I diagnosed it now, then you've got a miss.

A: That's never happened to you?

W: No.

A: Okay.

W: If you look back at the earlier films, and you say, well, this is the area, could I have called it, do I see something in retrospect, might there be something in retrospect, then that is not a miss. That is a sensitivity.

A: All right. That latter description has occurred to you?

W: That has occurred to everybody.

A: Okay. And that latter description can occur and that is not malpractice?

W: No, that is not.

A: Okay. Very good.

Let us see what went wrong.

1. The question, the medical expert must address *is not whether a physician has made a mistake; rather the question is whether he was negligent.* In simple terms, the baseline for establishing a standard of care is the standard of a "reasonably prudent person."

   In other words, if the defendant physician fails to exercise the degree of care and prudence that a reasonable physician in similar circumstances would exercise and the patient is injured, then the defendant physician is negligent.[3]

2. One concept remains absolute, however, a concept with which no court has ever taken issue: "Perfection is the social aspiration, but not a legal requirement; an honest effort in conformity with customary standards is all that can be demanded of physicians."[4]

3. (Some) physicians serving as medical expert witnesses who, either deliberately because of "opportunism and greed" or inadvertently, exploit the judicial system—in other words, physicians become "miasmatic experts." The ideal expert witness is knowledgeable about the standard of care in a given case; the miasmatic expert is not. The ideal expert witness is objective and nonpartisan; the miasmatic expert is not. The ideal medical expert witness presents the community at large with the best of what his specialty has to offer; the miasmatic expert does not. In the final analysis, the medical profession must look to itself.[5]

References

1. Haydock RS and Sonsteng JO. *Advocacy, Examining Witnesses: "Direct, Cross and Expert Examination."* Professional Education Edition. West Publishing Company. New York, 1994.
2. Berlin L. On being an expert witness. *AJR* 1997; 168: 607–610.
3. Finder JM. The future of practice guidelines: should they constitute conclusive evidence of the standard of care? *Health Matrix: J. Law—Medicine* 2000; 10: 67.
4. Mello MM. Of swords and shields: the role of clinical practice guidelines in medical malpractice litigation. *Univ. Penn. Law Rev.* 2001; 149: 645.
5. Berlin L. The miasmatic expert witness. *AJR* 2003; 181: 29–35.

A Trial Judge's Advice to the Testifying Physician on Enhancing Credibility in Court

16

HON. JAMES M. VUKELIC, J.D.

A modern court trial is a civilized form of battle. Instead of using sticks or swords, lawyers fight in court with witnesses and exhibits. In every battle, civilized or not, there are two opponents. The premise underlying our judicial system is that two evenly matched adversaries will bring out the strengths of their own cause and the weaknesses of the other. It is hoped this adversarial system will illuminate the truth for the finder-of-fact, whether that be a judge or jury.

A witness will always be seen by one party as a friend; the opposing party will take a contrary view. Regardless of how professional you appear, how unbiased and impartial your view of the case, you will be treated by one side as a comrade and as an adversary by the other.

The simple truth is that your testimony helps one side and hurts the other. If this were not so, you would not be called to testify in the first place. If you do not fully appreciate the battleground for what it is, you may be surprised, affronted, or both when you take the witness stand. To be forewarned is to be forearmed.

When you testify, your credibility is at stake. Indeed, it is one of the useful targets for the opposing counsel. Common forms of attack are based on your perception, knowledge of the facts, any bias or prejudice you may have, or your recollection of the events about which you are called upon to testify. These modes of attack, or impeachment as it is called in court, make the courtroom a stressful arena.

Psychologists have long identified the reaction to stressful situations as the "flight-or-fight response." When faced with acute stress, the heart beats faster, the digestive system shuts down so more blood can flow to the arms and legs, and adrenalin level increases. We gear up to fight or skedaddle just as our ancestors did when faced with saber-toothed tigers and other menaces.

On the witness stand, even those who have testified many times will admit that they experience anxiety. Part of that is created by the atmosphere: a room devoid of personality

Some of the material in this chapter is updated from J.M. Vukelic "Testifying Under Oath: How to be an Effective Witness," Volcano Press ©2005.

and warmth, a stern-looking judge in a black robe peering down at you from on high, and an opposing attorney poised to attack every word you utter in pursuit of a client's cause.

Unfortunately, there is no opportunity for "flight." Witnesses usually come to court under subpoena, failure to attend will result in contempt of court charges. The alternative is to "fight." Although no physical altercation is anticipated, a battle of wits may ensue between the witness and opposing counsel. Many witnesses are partially "disarmed" in this battle because the stress induced by testifying hampers the ability to recall events clearly.

Humans manifest what has been labeled "state-dependant memory."[1] We can access memories easily when we are in a relaxed state, say, at home talking with our spouse or friends. But when we are "under the gun" aimed at us by a bright, sharp-tongued attorney as we occupy the witness stand, our recall may be diminished.

There are several ways to reduce the stress associated with testifying in court. One is to reduce the fear of the unknown. Another is to control the environment to the greatest extent possible. Third is to anticipate the tactics used by attorneys to impeach, or discredit witnesses.

16.1   Reducing the Fear of the Unknown

16.1.1   Visit the Courtroom

To reduce stress, you can become familiar with the courtroom setting, the "battleground." You need to know where this search for the truth, this civilized warfare will take place. Fortunately, our courthouses and courtrooms are generally accessible to the public.

There is no reason why you cannot or should not visit a courtroom before trial, preferably the one where you will later testify. Go to the courthouse and ask to speak to the court administrator. Explain your purpose and ask for permission to visit the courtroom. Unless it is in use, most court administrators will accommodate you. When you get there, look around. Take a seat on the witness stand.

In the best of all worlds, your attorney will make the arrangements for your courtroom visit and accompany you. Ask your attorney how the oath is administered to witnesses in this judge's court. Is it done by the bailiff? A clerk? The judge? It can be unnerving to walk into a room full of strangers and not know where to stand, whom to address, or what to do.

On the witness stand, try out the sound system (almost all courtrooms use microphones and amplification so witnesses, attorneys, and the judge can be easily heard). If the system is turned off, do not be afraid to walk up to the judge's chair where the sound system controls typically are found. Turn it on and try it out.

16.1.2   Go through a Dry Run

The best preparation you can make for testifying is to have your attorney take you through a dry run. The attorney should put you on the witness stand and ask you the very questions that will be asked at trial, offering a critique as you answer. When done with direct examination, the attorney should assume the role of the cross-examining attorney and ask you questions a defense counsel is likely to ask.

This will give you a good idea of how the interrogation will proceed during the actual trial. Some witnesses have asked if it is proper to go over your testimony in advance of trial. The short answer is an unequivocal "Yes." It is not only ethical, it is encouraged.

Attorneys who are well prepared for trial will have conducted dry runs, or at a minimum, given witnesses a list of questions they intend to ask on direct examination. Some attorneys, after interviewing the witnesses and reviewing pertinent reports, will send each witness a list of questions and anticipated responses to those questions. The list is typically accompanied by a caveat to the effect that the enclosed responses are based on information received from the witness previously and that if any of the anticipated responses are incomplete or inaccurate, the witness should contact the attorney to discuss them.

Every attorney has an ethical obligation to refrain from presenting perjured testimony. But attorneys are also required to represent their clients "zealously." This means so long as the answers are truthful, attorneys and witnesses are free to rehearse them before trial.

16.1.3 Use Imagery

Imagery is the process of imagining through any sense: hearing, sight, smell, taste, or touch. Imagery has been used since ancient times as a technique to encourage changes in attitudes, behavior, or physiological reactions. Today it is used in a wide variety of therapies and as a form of meditation. Health care professionals have demonstrated through scientific studies that imagery can affect a number of physiological functions including brain-wave activity, blood glucose levels, cardiovascular function, gastrointestinal activity, and oxygen supply in tissues.

Coaches have long recognized the importance of imagery, also called visualization, in preparing athletes for competition. One swimming coach wrote

> To perform well in a big meet, you have to "experience" the whole thing in advance! This means you must "feel" the atmosphere of the big occasion, "see" your competitors, the coaches, the pool, and your friends, "smell" the water, "hear" the crowd—I could go on and on, you have to immerse yourself into the entire meet if you want to be truly prepared for it. If you do not do this, you can find yourself becoming overwhelmed on the day by the big occasion. This is exactly what so many swimmers do—they train brilliantly all week and then get stressed out at the meets and do not perform at their best.

A martial arts expert advises his students to

- visualize yourself executing a technique with perfect balance, accuracy, and coordination;
- imagine how to react to a specific self-defense situation. Visualize your opponent or attacker delivering a front kick or right cross. Think about how you should react. See yourself reacting confidently with strong counters and strikes;
- create a strong visualization for greater impact. Use all of your senses to observe the detail of sensations, such as the feel and movement of a kick, the texture of your uniform, and the sounds of your feet moving;
- imagine yourself within your body rather than looking at yourself from a distance. It creates a more realistic visualization;
- anticipate the anxiety and stress that comes with competition and promotion testing. Visualize yourself using deep-breathing techniques and performing confidently to reduce your stress level.

All proponents of imagery advise that you begin the process by finding a quiet place to sit or lie down. Relax muscle groups of your body by tensing them for 5 s and then letting them go. Start with your feet and work your way up the body. By the time you have flexed and released your facial muscles, your body and mind should be more receptive to the imagery exercise.

As with athletic contests, imagine the setting. Yours will not be a swimming pool or gymnasium, but a courtroom. After you have visited the courtroom, you will find it much easier to prepare for trial by using imagery. Go through the relaxation sequence, then visualize the courtroom. "See" the attorneys, jurors, clerk of court, judge, and perhaps some people in the audience watching the whole thing. Remember the ambiance of the place, the color of the carpet and woodwork. "Hear" the official administers the oath. "Feel" what it is like to sit in the chair on the witness stand, adjusting the microphone, and listening to how your first answer comes across the public address system.

Then imagine yourself being cool, calm, and collected. In your mind, see yourself as an unflappable witness speaking to the jurors as if they were interested neighbors and friends leaning on every word you utter. Visualize a confident, smooth delivery with just the right amount of inflection and a serious tone to your voice. Picture yourself handling cross-examination with measured, matter-of-fact responses. Then see yourself thanking the judge, stepping down from the witness stand and walking confidently out of the courtroom.

There, you have done it! Your body will associate the calm you are experiencing in your resting, imaging setting with the mental environment of the courtroom you have created. Believe it or not, your brain cannot distinguish this "dry run" from the real thing. If you repeat the imaging exercise, when it comes time to actually testify, you will enter the courtroom with the confidence that you have "been there, done that."

16.2   Control the Environment

Many aspects of testifying are beyond the control of a witness. But one can control the communication in a courtroom using verbal and nonverbal methods that enhance the witness's credibility.

16.2.1   Dress Professionally to Persuade

At one time, I would have urged witnesses to dress as if they were going to church. But with today's relaxed standard, this is no longer safe advice. I have seen folks in church wearing jeans and tank tops, definitely inappropriate attire for the witness stand.

You must project the image of a professional. Dr. James Rasicot,[2] a psychologist, studied the impact of dress on the credibility of witnesses. He had actors recite the same testimony in a mock trial setting while wearing different sets of clothes. He then asked several groups of mock jurors to rate the actors on credibility. The results were illuminating, though not surprising. They could best be summarized this way: the more conservative the attire, the more powerful, authoritative, and credible the witness was perceived as being.

For men, the most credible witness was one who wore a dark suit with a white shirt and red or burgundy tie. The least credible witness was one who wore jeans and a T-shirt. Persons wearing a sport coat, colored shirt, and tie were viewed as more credible than someone wearing slacks and a sport shirt, but less credible than one wearing a suit. Solid colors or pinstripes are fine; plaids are not. John T. Molloy, in his book, *Dress For Success*, says, "There are only three appropriate colors for men in a business setting—'dull, dark, and drab.'" Navy and gray-colored suits are recommended by Susan Bixler in her book, *The New Professional Image*.

For women, wearing a matched-skirt suit with a white blouse proved to be the most credibly enhancing attire. Low-cut necklines seem more common today than 20 years ago but still connote someone out to impress with her body, not her mind. A tailored, as opposed to loose fitting, look is more authoritative. Solid colors are preferred to mixed. Red and black are generally preferable colors for professional women. Wearing shoes with heels, not spikes, gives an air of sophistication while wearing flats does not. Women who put their hair up and pull it away from the face look more powerful than those who do not.

For both men and women, wearing glasses connotes you read more and are more intelligent than those who do not wear them. So if you have contact lenses, leave them at home and wear your glasses to court. Shoes should be polished, clothes cleaned and pressed.

Any hairstyle, makeup, jewelry or clothing that calls attention away from the substance of your testimony should be avoided. You want to make it easy for the jury and judge to concentrate on what you say.

16.2.2 Maintain a "Powerful" Posture on the Witness Stand

Dr. Rasicot[2] also studied the effects of posture on witness credibility. His research supported mom's advice: "Sit up, don't slouch." In general, Dr. Rasicot concluded, the more space you take up when standing or sitting, the more powerful you are perceived as being. Power, he noted, enhances credibility. So, within reason, assume a posture that uses more space rather than less. For example, if you sit sloop-shouldered or hunched forward, you will be perceived as being less credible than if you sit erectly.

Both feet should be on the floor. Arms should be at your side, not draped over the back of the chair or resting with your hands more than a few inches apart. You do not want to give the impression that these proceedings are informal or unimportant. A sprawling appearance tells the jury you lack self-discipline or are insensitive to social norms.

Do not cross your legs or arms. Crossing your legs indicates an informality generally foreign to the courtroom. Crossed arms send the signal that you are smug or unwilling to speak openly. Good attorneys will take note of the psychological discomfort, which led to the crossed-arms response. It is like waving a red flag at them. As soon as the attorney notes the arms crossing or the body shifting away from the attorney, a question comes immediately to mind: "Why is this person so anxious about this particular subject?" The attorney then silently concludes, "I think this area deserves further attention." Your objective is to keep the questioning by opposing counsel as short and painless as possible. If, through your body language, you prod opposing counsel to keep you on the stand to question you about a subject that evidently causes your anxiety, you may regret it.

16.2.3 Make Eye Contact

Generally speaking, maintaining eye contact with your listeners is a good method of increasing credibility. It helps establish rapport and assures your audience of your sincerity. Lawyers know this and, if the judge allows it, often stand at the corner of the jury box while questioning an important witness. This requires the witness to look at or in the general direction of the jurors while testifying.

I once prosecuted a divorced father for molesting his 5- and 6-year-old daughters during a weekend visitation. There was scant physical evidence. The father adamantly denied fondling the girls. Worse, a judge allowed the visitations to continue even after the charges were filed and, sure enough, the girls recanted.

This kind of case is a prosecutor's nightmare but I was fortunate to have as one of my witnesses Joan Senzek Solheim. Joan had impeccable credentials as a child psychologist, having been trained at the world-renowned Kemp Institute in Denver. She had studied child sexual abuse extensively and had worked with hundreds of abused children. I wanted Joan to explain to the jury the phenomenon of "recanting" and what it meant, or rather, what it did not mean.

Joan took the witness stand and looked at me directly as she answered preliminary questions about her education and experience. But when I got to the crucial question, the one that asked her to explain recantation in children, her body shifted. She turned 30° or so in the witness chair so that she was facing the jury directly. Then, with confidence and skill, she leaned forward and looked at each juror in turn as she summarized the professional literature on the topic and explained that children often recant their previous statements when faced with unpleasant repercussions from their disclosure. It did not mean the sexual abuse did not happen.

Her explanation took 3 or 4 min. I watched in awe as she nonverbally communicated her sincerity to each juror. She meant every word she said and she wanted them to know it. They did. I could see that Joan had them eating out of the palm of her hand. When she was done, I wanted to stand up and applaud her, she was so effective. The jury convicted.

There is no rule that says you must look at opposing counsel while being cross-examined. If the question allows you to give anything but a "yes" or "no" answer, you are free to turn to the jury and tell them forthrightly whatever you can honestly say in answer to the query. Pick your moment, though it looks a bit awkward if you turn to the jury after being asked questions that require only a brief answer like: "How long have you worked in the health field?" (turn, face jury) "7 years" (turn back, face attorney).

It is always wise to take your cues from your listener. If you notice a juror avert your eye contact, do not linger and make him or her uncomfortable. Let common sense be your guide.

16.2.4   Avoid Indicators of Deception

Many of us have had the experience of questioning a child about a broken object or some missing cookies. When the youngster's face flushes and the eyes dart, we suspect the child's response may be something less than truthful.

Ken Lanning is a retired FBI agent who was a specialist in interrogating criminals. At one of his training sessions, Lanning taught attendees to look for the "indicators of deception" when interviewing suspects. The following list of indicators is representative, though not all-inclusive:

Rubbing or wringing of hands
Scratching oneself
Pulling on earlobes or nose

Stroking or grooming hair
Inspecting or picking fingernails
Adjusting clothing
Taking eyeglasses off or cleaning them
Picking lint or pulling threads from clothing
Putting hand to back of head or neck
Wiping lips or eyes
Shuffling, tapping, or swinging feet
Probing ears or nose
Shifting leg posture or alignment coinciding with pertinent questions
Wiping sweat
Locking feet together under chair
Turning the body away from the questioner
Removing or adjusting watches or jewelry
Rhythmic drumming of fingers
Closed body position with arms and elbows particularly close to the body
Hiding of mouth or eyes with hands

Lanning hypothesized that these deception indicators arise from the unconscious need to relieve anxiety and reduce stress through some motor activity. When a suspect engages in deceptive conduct, interrogators make a note to explore that area in greater detail.

Can jurors really tell when you are not telling the truth? In some research studies, law enforcement officers were accurate only half of the time when guessing which statements were truthful and which were fabricated.[3] Other studies support the hypothesis that all of us have a built-in lie detector.[4,5] Deception detection studies indicate that many subjects can do better than chance in detecting falsehood. One researcher[6] found that aphasics—people who do not understand the meaning of words but can still communicate because they gather meaning from nonverbal cues—were particularly adept at recognizing lies from the speaker's tone, emphasis, facial expression, and gestures. If aphasics have this ability, the rest of us most probably possess it too, though we may not recognize it. In short, jurors probably have a subconscious feel for whether or not a witness is lying, based on body language and speech inflection.

The trouble is, your body language, while indicative of lying, may simply be the result of nervousness. Appearance is reality. If jurors do not believe you, it makes no difference whether their perception about your body language is correct or not.

You need to be comfortable on the witness stand. That comfort level will rise with experience and with the knowledge of how jurors perceive you. Going through a "dry run" and using imagery as discussed earlier will reduce anxiety and lessen the chance that you will unwittingly exhibit indicators of deception.

16.2.5 Speak Clearly and Confidently

Obviously, any witness who is not easily heard and understood by the jury will have minimal positive impact. A moderately loud voice indicates confidence. Jurors favor confident witnesses and tend to believe them. Research has shown that people who speak in a lower register are perceived as more credible than those who do not; listeners equated high-pitched voices with nervousness and less truthfulness than lower-pitched voices.[7]

Participants in another study rated witnesses using the powerful style of speech as more convincing, more competent, more intelligent, and more trustworthy than witnesses using the powerless style.[7] Powerless language is typified by comments such as, "I guess," "sort of," "kind of," "in my opinion," "it seems like," and "I believe." Hesitations, hemming or hawing, the use of intensifiers,* and a slow cadence or speech delivery are also associated with powerless language.

16.3   Anticipating the Trips and Traps Used to Discredit Witnesses

16.3.1   Nonverbal Techniques to Unnerve a Witness

One respected legal scholar[8] wrote that witnesses can be categorized into three ways. In one group are witnesses who testify calmly and confidently on both direct and cross-examination. They are unflappable and the cross-examining attorney is wise to get them off the witness stand as quickly as possible.

In the second group are those witnesses who always display marked negative mannerisms while testifying. Attorneys will try to keep these witnesses on the stand longer than usual in order to allow them to discredit themselves through their behavior.

The last group is comprised of witnesses who normally testify convincingly but who display negative mannerisms when pressured. Attorneys may use tactics intended to frustrate and unnerve these witnesses.

One such technique is to simply exclude the witness from the courtroom until he or she testifies. This is accomplished through a request for sequestration which, in most jurisdictions, must be granted by the judge. The theory is that if the witness is allowed to remain in the courtroom to observe other witnesses testify, the witness may become more familiar with trial procedure and relax.[8] When the witness is kept out of the courtroom, or sequestered, the witness is more likely to remain anxious because of the fear of the unknown. Anxious witnesses have a greater tendency to display unfavorable demeanor.

Another technique is to stare at the witness while the witness is answering questions from the other attorney. This aggressive, intrusive act can make an already uncomfortable witness more nervous.

The attorney may take notes with great flourish, often drawing the jurors' attention to the attorney in the process. The intended nonverbal message is that the lawyer has "discovered" some great flaw in the witness's last statement and will be exposing that flaw shortly. This may be pure fiction; the lawyer has no means of discrediting the statement but the dramatic note-taking may distract and unnerve the witness, producing the desired effect.

In jurisdictions where attorneys are allowed to question witnesses from anywhere in the courtroom, an attorney may use physical proximity to intimidate a witness. We all have our personal zone of privacy that space around us, which is violated when strangers come too close. Even in jurisdictions where attorneys are supposed to do all of their questioning while seated at counsel table, there are exceptions where, for example, the attorney wants the witness to examine an exhibit.

---

* Intensifiers are words which are intended to persuade but which have the opposite effect. They include: really, extremely, absolutely, entirely, certainly, obviously, highly, greatly, and totally.

As the attorney closes in on the witness, the effect is exacerbated by the fact that the attorney is standing while the witness is seated below. Sometimes, the attorney will stand slightly behind the witness while the exhibit is being examined, again with the intent of causing discomfort.

Recognizing these activities for what they are lessens their impact. One witness, a seasoned veteran, related how he was being badgered by an attorney who "got in his face" during cross-examination in a bench trial. When the attorney got very close to the witness and was almost shouting his questions, the witness calmly used his foot to affectionately rub it up and down the lawyer's leg! The lawyer jumped back and never tried to intimidate that witness again.

16.3.2 Why Can't You Just Answer "Yes" or "No"?

In a typical cross-examination, questions are designed to confirm the information contained in the query. "Isn't it true that you worked two shifts in a row on September 20th?" Not only does the leading question put into the record information phrased exactly as desired, the technique has the additional benefit of allowing the questioner to control the witness. In most cases, questions are framed so that the only appropriate answer is "yes" or "no." While a witness is never bound to answer in this fashion, it is usually appropriate to do so.

Questions about observable activities almost always must be answered "yes" or "no." But often the focal issue in the case revolves around intent or some other state of mind. The attorney may try to hem in the witness with questions about conduct, gaining concession after concession. Then the attorney moves to seek an admission of what was in the witness's mind at the time. A vigilant witness can, and often should, refuse to answer "yes" or "no" if that would not be a truthful answer.

If a witness cannot honestly answer the question "Yes" or "No," the best response is to say something to the effect that "I cannot truthfully answer your question 'yes' or 'no.'" If the lawyer persists, you may turn to the judge and say, "Your Honor, I take very seriously the oath I swore and I cannot truthfully answer that question 'yes' or 'no.' What should I do?"

The judge may ask the cross-examiner to rephrase the question. But if the judge orders you to answer the question "yes" or "no," follow the judge's instruction. In these circumstances, rest assured that your attorney will have an opportunity to explore the matter later on redirect examination.

16.3.3 Jargon

Some medical experts are surprised to find that the attorney knows a great deal about a particular aspect of medicine. This becomes obvious from the phrasing of the lawyer's questions to the witness. Assuming that the lawyer is no more knowledgeable than the average layperson about some scientific or medical matter is unwise.

Nevertheless, the witness must bear in mind the intended audience for all of this sometimes esoteric dialogue between counsel and the medical expert. That audience is the jury, which typically is comprised of people with a high school education. To be sure, some on the jury may have advance college degrees but it is the rare jury that does not have a few jurors who are not well educated.

This is important because a frequent criticism of medical experts is that they are arrogant or condescending. To prevent a juror from drawing this conclusion, the witness does not have to "dumb down" testimony but rather explain medical terms immediately after using them and in ways that common people can understand. Analogies and examples are the best way to do this. Using a visual aid can work wonders as well.

Jurors enjoy entering the world of the medical expert, even if it is only briefly, but they do not like being "talked down to" by anyone. Albert Einstein said, "You never truly understand a thing until you can explain it to your grandmother." The best witness is one who knows the subject matter well enough to teach jurors without coming across as patronizing.

16.3.4   "Always," "Never," and "Isn't It Possible . . ." Questions

It has often been said that medicine is as much an art as it is a science. There are some absolutes, but more often there are exceptions to every rule. Attorneys often use a funnel technique when cross-examining witnesses. Initial questioning involves asking the expert to agree with some broad principle. Later, the questions are designed to force the expert to agree that the broad principle applies to the specific facts of the case at hand.

Witnesses should make note during those initial questions when an attorney uses words like "always" or "never" in a query. It is best to give yourself some leeway by answering, "That is usually true" rather than "yes" if there is any possible exception to the fact assumed by the question.

Another ploy is to ask the witness, "Isn't it possible that ..." It does no good to get sarcastic and say, "I suppose it's possible that the moon is made of green cheese so anything is possible, counselor." The cross-examiner salivates when a witness becomes sarcastic. A better response might be, "I really don't know the answer to that question and I would simply have to guess." This should prompt your attorney to object that the question calls for speculation. Such questions are typically disallowed by the judge. The point is not to answer the question affirmatively unless you absolutely know it to be true.

16.3.5   Implying the Witness Is Biased

Here is an example of how opposing counsel may attempt to show the bias of a medical expert witness in court:

Attorney: Is this the first time you've ever testified in court?
Witness: No, it's not.
Attorney: Would it be fair to say you testified numerous times before?
Witness: Yes, that would be fair.
Attorney: Of those times you've testified before, would it also be fair to say that you have typically testified in support of a plaintiff?
Witness: Yes, I'd say that's true.
Attorney: Are you aware that attorneys who represent plaintiffs keep a list of witnesses like you who can be called to testify in a particular case?
Witness: I wasn't aware of that, no.
Attorney: But you do get paid for your testimony, don't you?
Witness: I charge a fee for my services, yes.

Attorney: You get paid quite handsomely?

Witness: I don't know what you mean by handsomely, but I do get paid for my time and expertise.

Attorney: Well, come now. If the average citizen makes $9.50 an hour in this country, you'll admit you are paid considerably better than that?

Witness: Yes, I guess so.

Attorney: You guess so. How much do you charge for an hour of your services?

Witness: Four hundred dollars an hour.

Attorney: Whew! More than forty times the amount an average citizen makes. And I don't suppose the plaintiffs' lawyers would keep hiring you if you didn't get results for them, would they?

Witness: I wouldn't know about that.

Attorney: No further questions. *Checkmate!*

This style of examination will almost always be permitted. A witness may respond, "I resent the implication" in answer to the questions about witness fees but should expect little sympathy from jurors whose income is comparatively small.

An expert is better advised to simply answer these questions unemotionally and without apparent resentment. Knowing they are coming will help a witness keep calm on the witness stand.

16.4 Conclusion

When witnesses are secure in their facts and have a better understanding of how court works, their comfort level goes up. When the unknown court processes become known and witnesses take a measure of control over the court environment, they testify more effectively. Armed with cogent testimony, judges and jurors are better able to make good decisions and our judicial system operates as it was designed to do. Then, we all win.

References

1. Perry BD, Welch L. Testifying in juvenile and family court: preparing for depositions, hearings and trials. *Interdisciplinary Education Series.* Vol. 4, Number 7. Child Trauma Academy, December 1999.
2. Rasicot J. *New Techniques for Winning Jury Trials.* Minneapolis: AP Publications, 1990.
3. Ekman P, et al. A few can catch a liar. *Psychol. Sci.* 1999; 10: 263–265.
4. Jeremy A, Blumenthal A. Wipe of the hands, a lick of the lips: the validity of demeanor evidence in assessing witness credibility. *Neb. Law Rev.* 1993; 72: 1157, 1189.
5. Wellborn III OG. Demeanor. *Cornell Law. Rev.* 1991; 76: 1075, 1088.
6. Sacks OW. *The Man Who Mistook His Wife for a Hat: And Other Clinical Tales.* New York: Harper Perennial, 1990.
7. Smith JD. The advocates use of social science research into nonverbal and verbal communication: zealous advocacy or unethical conduct? *Mil. Law. Rev.* 1991; 134: 175–176, 180.
8. Imwinkelried EJ. Demeanor impeachment: law and tactics. *Am. J. Trial Advoc.* 1985; 9: 183, 211.

Medical Malpractice Terms and Definitions for the Testifying Physician

17

17.1 Medical Malpractice

Medical malpractice law is based on concepts drawn from tort and contract law. It is commonly understood as liabilities arising from the delivery of medical care.

Causes of action are typically based on

1. negligence,
2. intentional misconduct,
3. breach of a contract (i.e., guaranteeing a specific therapeutic result),
4. defamation,
5. divulgence of confidential information,
6. insufficient informed consent,
7. failure to prevent foreseeable injuries to third parties.

Negligence according to *Black's Law Dictionary*, requires that the plaintiff establish the following elements:

1. The existence of the physician's duty to the plaintiff, usually based on the existence of the physician–patient relationship
2. The applicable standard of care and its violation
3. Damages (a compensable injury)
4. A causal connection between the violation of the standard of care and the harm complained of

Negligence: Failure to use "ordinary care," or failing to do what a professional of ordinary prudence would have done in similar circumstances.

Proximate cause: The cause (or sequence of causes) that produces the undesirable or catastrophic event/consequence.

We all understand that no cure is guaranteed in medicine. A medical complication is not synonymous with medical negligence. So for a claim of medical negligence to be proven, the plaintiff's attorney must be able to demonstrate one of several possibilities:

1. The physician departed from commonly accepted standards of medical practice. Although the medical defendant may not follow the majority standards, the physician must at least follow the standard of what is called the respected minority.
2. The physician failed to keep abreast with changes in medical practice.
3. The physician employed a new but unproved and unaccepted method of treatment.
4. The physician did not take proper precautions against risks.
5. The physician did not perform to the standards expected of a reasonably competent (and prudent physician) specialist.

In summary, medical malpractice suits must prove

1. the physician had a duty to care for the plaintiff;
2. the physician failed in the duty to care;
3. the failure to care resulted in damage to the plaintiff;
4. the damage can be measured for monetary compensation;
5. medical negligence occurs when the acceptable standards of medical practice is not adhered to, and, when the physician's failure in the duty to care led to significant damages to the plaintiff;
6. however, the plaintiff must at first establish the appropriate medical standard of care (by the use of a medical expert) so that the fact finder (jury) can determine whether the defendant's conduct was a deviation constituting negligence.

17.2   Burden of Proof

The plaintiff bears the burden of proof and must convince a jury by a preponderance of the evidence that his case is more plausible. A preponderance of the evidence is at least 51%. The plaintiff and defense attorneys will present their respective experts, each side hoping their witnesses will appear more knowledgeable, objective, and credible than their counterparts. Unlike criminal cases, in which the fact at issue must be proven beyond a reasonable doubt, the jurors or triers of a medical negligence case must base their decision on the preponderance of the evidence. That means that jurors in a medical negligence case must be persuaded that the evidence presented by the plaintiff is more plausible as the proximate cause of the injury than any counterargument offered by the defendant.

17.3   How Are Standards of Medical Care Determined?

In the law of negligence, the standard of care is generally thought of as "that degree of care, which a reasonably prudent person should exercise in same or similar circumstances." If the defendant's conduct falls outside the standards, then he or she may be found liable for any damages that resulted from his or her conduct. In medical negligence disputes, the defendant's behavior is compared with the applicable standard of care.

Generally, this is understood to be "that reasonable and ordinary care, skill, and diligence as physicians and surgeons in good standing in the same locality, in the same general line of practice, exercise the same prudent care in similar cases." Many courts have held that the increased specialization of medicine and establishment of national boards is more significant than geographic differences in establishing the standard of care. These courts contend that board-certified medical or surgical specialists should adhere to standards of their respective specialty boards.

17.4 Was the Standard of Care Breached?

In medical liability cases, the roles of the expert witness are the following:

1. To establish standards of care applicable for the case at hand.
2. The expert may also be asked to evaluate whether the factual testimony provided by other witnesses indicates any deviation from acceptable standards.
3. When care has been deemed "substandard," the expert witness may be asked to opine whether that deviation from the standard of care could have been the proximate cause of the patient's alleged injury.
4. Because courts and juries depend on medical experts to make medical standards understandable, the testimony should be clear, coherent, and consistent with the standards applicable at the time of the incident.
5. Although experts may testify as to what they think the most appropriate standard of care was at the time of occurrence, they should know and *consider alternative acceptable standards*. These alternatives may be raised during direct testimony or under cross-examination.
6. Expert witnesses should not define the standard so narrowly that it only encompasses their opinion on the standard of care to the exclusion of other acceptable treatment options.

Whenever a medical intervention is undertaken, several outcomes can occur—the patient's condition can improve, stay the same, or deteriorate.

A negative outcome alone is not sufficient to indicate professional negligence. Even when the appropriate treatment is performed properly, sometimes the patient will get better, sometimes the patient will stay the same, and sometimes the patient will get worse.

These same outcomes are possible when the medical treatment is performed improperly. This is the reason for the prudent physician rule, i.e., which treatment would a prudent physician pursue?

17.5 What Is the Standard of Medical Care for the Prudent Physician?

Medicine is learned by the bedside and not in the classroom. Let not your conceptions of disease come from words heard in the lecture room or read from the book. See, and then reason and compare and control. But see first.

—William Osler

The standard of medical care is usually defined as what a prudent physician with similar training would do in similar circumstances. In simple terms, the baseline for establishing a standard of care is the standard of a "reasonably prudent person." In other words, if the defendant physician fails to exercise the degree of care and prudence that a reasonable physician in similar circumstances would exercise and the patient is injured, then the defendant physician is negligent.[1] That is how most state and federal statutes interpret the standard of care.

A deviation from the standard of care that leads to damages to a patient is defined as medical malpractice or medical negligence. In our litigation system, the burden of proof falls on the plaintiff (injured patient) to document how the standard of care was breached. So how does the plaintiff bring on a medical malpractice case before a jury? The plaintiff must have a physician of the same specialty to testify under oath that the standard of care was breached; and it was specifically that breach that led to the damages.

How does one defend against the medical malpractice lawsuit? Another physician of the same specialty must testify that the standard of care was adhered to in all respects, also based on a reasonable degree of medical probability (more likely than not) and supported these days under the Daubert rules by the proper methodology and PEAT—i.e., guidelines were peer reviewed; the error rate is known; the guidelines or medical standard of care is accepted by the medical community, and the guideline has been tested.

This leads us to the important question of what elements do the standards of medical care consist? How can a standard of medical care become a generally accepted guideline by the medical community?

How is it developed and published as guidelines?

This section discusses these issues from the point of view not of the academic professor medical researcher, but of the prudent practicing physician trying to take care of his patients according to the standard of care in his community and the physician who has to testify about this in court.

First, the (published) standard of care is established by random controlled studies (RCT'S) and meta-analysis of multiple studies, which establish medical guidelines. We read about them every week in peer-reviewed journals in our profession and specialty.

For example, here are just a small sample published guidelines you would receive in the mail or on the Web with a subscription to *Journal Watch*—which I would recommend to every practicing and testifying physician. For a more complete update of many more guidelines/standard of medical care please refer to Book II's chapter on guideline modification publications.

17.6   Changing Standards of Medical Care Examples

You must keep up with them. But remember that the standard of care is what it was during the year of the alleged medical malpractice. But to know the difference, you must find a way during your busy day and keep up with the constantly changing clinical practice guideline literature.

Four examples of rapidly changing guidelines: (for others *see* appendix).

17.6.1 Treatment of Sexually Transmitted Diseases*

An update of the CDC's 2002 guidelines; target population: infectious disease, emergency medicine, obstetrics/gynecology, internal medicine, and family medicine physicians, as well as public health workers sponsoring organization: The centers for disease control and prevention type: consensus statements are based on a systematic evidence-based review of the medical literature on each of the major sexually transmitted diseases (STDs). Reviews are conducted by CDC personnel, with input from outside consultants. Recommendations on management of hepatitis A and B from the Advisory Committee on Immunization Practices are also incorporated.

Key points: This revision of the CDC recommendations for STD management contains an expanded discussion on the management of cervicitis/urethritis, including new information on the roles of *Mycoplasma genitalium* and *Trichomonas vaginalis* in such infections; new recommendations for antimicrobial therapy for trichomoniasis; and updated information on lymphogranuloma venereum in men who have sex with men (MSM).

1. One- and two-day courses of antiviral medications are now among the recommended regimens for managing recurrent genital herpes.
2. Additionally, it is noted that the risk for transmitting herpes simplex virus 2 to sexual partners can be reduced with daily valacyclovir therapy.
3. Updated information is provided on azithromycin resistance in *Treponema pallidum* and quinolone resistance in *Neisseria gonorrhoeae*.
4. Fluoroquinolones are no longer recommended for treating gonorrhea in MSM or in anyone who acquired the infection in an area with known high rates of resistance. Although the recommended regimens for bacterial vaginosis are unchanged, single-dose metronidazole treatment is no longer considered a potential alternative due its low cure rate.
5. Lindane is no longer recommended as a first-line therapy for pediculosis pubis due to potential toxicity.
6. Updated information is provided on sexual transmission of hepatitis C, on postexposure prophylaxis for HIV following sexual assault, and on general measures for preventing STDs.
7. Comment: These guidelines† were not compiled using strict evidence-based medicine-grading criteria. Nonetheless, for more than two decades, CDC guidelines have been the standard of care in the United States for managing STDs, and they should be reviewed carefully by all clinicians working in this field.[2]

17.6.2 New AHA Diet and Lifestyle Recommendations

The new advice includes specific maximums for daily saturated and trans fat intake. Sponsoring Organizations: American Heart Association Nutrition Committee Background and Purpose: when the AHA last revised these recommendations in 2000, diet was

---

* *See* appendix.
† Available at http://www.cdc.gov/mmwr/pdf/wk/mm5614.pdf

the near-exclusive emphasis. In the 2006 statement, the authors attempt to be more comprehensive by emphasizing diet and including broader lifestyle recommendations.

Key points:

1. The committee recommends a diet high in "deeply colored" fruits and vegetables (e.g., berries and spinach), whole grains, oily fish (eaten at least twice weekly), low-fat dairy products, and lean meats. Low-carbohydrate diets are not specifically discussed.
2. The committee now advises that <7% of daily energy intake come from saturated fat and <1% from trans fat. (In 2000, saturated and trans fats combined were recommended to be <10% of daily energy intake.)
3. The committee now suggests limiting consumption of drinks with added sugars and still recommends reducing salt intake and achieving previously defined optimal blood pressure and lipid goals, although a normal fasting glucose level is now specified as ≤100 mg/dL.
4. Unlike in 2000, the committee does not recommend antioxidant supplements and questions the value of soy products, folate, and other B vitamin supplements, and phytochemicals for reducing cardiovascular risk.
5. Specific lifestyle recommendations include
   • Avoidance of tobacco products (both use and exposure)
   • Physical activity >30 min/day to maintain a healthy weight and >60 min/day to achieve or maintain weight loss
6. The new statement acknowledges that lifestyle recommendations might need to be tailored to other individual circumstances—socioeconomic, cultural, and environmental (e.g., lack of sidewalks). Comment: These updated recommendations cast diet and lifestyle as components of overall health, although reducing fat intake (especially saturated and trans fats) remains a central feature. We still do not have clear evidence that limiting saturated and trans fats improves cardiovascular outcomes. However, epidemiologic research suggests that this approach is reasonable until we have more robust clinical trial data on the subject.[3]

17.6.3   New Guidelines for Evaluating and Managing Diverticulitis

The latest guidelines from the American Society of Colon and Rectal Surgeons are consistent with the approach taken by most gastroenterologists.

The American Society of Colon and Rectal Surgeons recently released new guidelines on the evaluation and management of diverticulitis. The following recommendations are of interest to gastroenterologists:

   • After resolution of an initial episode of acute diverticulitis, the colon should be imaged by colonoscopy or contrast enema x-ray to confirm the diagnosis.
   • The decision to recommend elective sigmoid colectomy after recovery from acute diverticulitis should be made on a case-by-case basis. The decision should be influenced by the patient's age and medical condition, the frequency and severity of attacks, and the persistence of symptoms after the acute episode. After one attack, about a third of patients will have a second one, and then a third of those patients will

have yet another attack. Most patients who present with complicated diverticulitis do so at the time of their first attack.

- Elective colon resection should usually be advised when an episode of complicated diverticulitis is treated nonoperatively, including by radiographic drainage.
- A laparoscopic approach to surgical treatment of diverticular disease is appropriate in select patients. Comment: Diverticulitis can often be managed more conservatively than is recommended in surgical guidelines. However, these new guidelines are very sensible and are consistent with the approach taken by most gastroenterologists. In particular, the decision to perform elective surgery in a patient with repeat episodes is not based on the number of episodes but on the frequency and severity of attacks.[4]

17.6.4   Metronidazole Plus Rifampin for *Clostridium difficile—Primum Non Nocere*

- Adding rifampin to metronidazole does not improve outcomes in *C. difficile*-associated diarrhea (CDAD) and may increase patients' risk for death.
- The incidence of CDAD is increasing in both hospital and outpatient settings. This development, coupled with the emergence of a hypervirulent *C. difficile* strain that produces high levels of toxins A and B, has spurred the quest for more effective CDAD treatments. In a recent multicenter, randomized, single-blind study involving 39 CDAD patients, researchers in Canada studied the effects of adding oral rifampin (300 mg twice daily) to the commonly used 10-day course of oral metronidazole (500 mg three times daily). Rifampin is highly effective against *C. difficile in vitro*, and has excellent penetration into intestinal tissue. Time to symptom improvement, time to first relapse, relapse rate at 40 days, and proportion of patients with nonfatal adverse events were similar between regimens.
- However, the proportion of patients who died was significantly greater in the metronidazole/rifampin group than in the metronidazole-alone group (32% versus 5%). Only 32 patients could be fully evaluated, but cure rates (63% in the rifampin/metronidazole group, 65% in the metronidazole-alone group) were considerably lower than the ~95% previously reported for metronidazole.
- Comment: *Adding rifampin to metronidazole yielded no benefit in the treatment of CDAD.* However, the authors and an editorialist note that the study was inadequately powered because of its small sample size. In addition, the factors leading to suboptimal cure rates in both study arms are unclear.
- Routine addition of rifampin to metronidazole treatment for CDAD is unwarranted at this time. Other agents under study, especially those that inactivate the toxins, may be more effective.[2]

Hippocrates' first law *primum non nocere* (your first duty is to do no harm). So what should a prudent physician do to make certain he adheres to Hippocrates' first law *primum non nocere*?

1. A prudent physician would first know the published RCT'S, meta-analysis, and changing guidelines that make up the standards of medical care.

2. She/he should also know the defects and weaknesses of these RCT'S and meta-analysis upon which the standards of care are based.
3. She/he should be an avid reader of the peer-reviewed literature in her field.
4. She/he would be able to spot defective studies and biased journals.
5. She/he would record in the patient's medical records the reasons why she/he was deviating from the "guideline" or the "standard of care."
6. But above all she/he would do what is best for the patient with a risk benefit analysis (recorded in the medicial records) of the individual combination of diseases that make up the individual patient.
7. For the most part, his patients "will be not the first for whom the new are tried—nor yet the last to lay the old aside" (Alexander Pope).

17.7   Definitions

Answer: A paper (or pleading), which recites a civil defendant's response to claims of plaintiff and which may include defenses and claims on behalf of defendant against the plaintiff.

Assumption: Factor or information not actually known, but believed to be so. Assumption should almost never be used by the expert.

Attorney work product: The thought processes of an attorney preparing a case for trial including trial strategy, books, papers, writings, notes, and other tangible things that evidence the attorney's effort. These items are generally privileged and cannot be obtained during discovery.

Case decision: Determinations by courts, which provide guidance to attorneys and experts on the legal requirements of evidence, testimony, and substance of law.

Comparative faults: A legal doctrine, which waives the fault or liability of various parties to an extent. A method by which the responsibility of a party to an event is proportion based upon their respective conduct.

Complaint: A paper (pleading), which sets forth the civil plaintiff's claims.

Contributory negligence: A doctrine or law providing that a party who participates in conduct, which causes the injury, loss or damage, can make no recovery whatsoever in a court proceeding.

Cross examination: That phase of the trial in which opposing counsel ask questions of the witness to test the truth, accuracy, or thoroughness of direct testimony.

Defendant: A person or entity against whom a civil action or criminal action has been brought.

Deposition: Testimony given outside the presence of the jury in the presence of a court reporter, the attorney, and the parties for the purpose of finding out what you know, to determine what sort of witness you will be, and to lock you into a position prior to the trial.

Direct examination: That procedure during a trial or hearing, which first presents the witnesses' testimony to the jury.

Discovery: Those processes used before a trial to uncover the facts of the case.

Engagement letter: A contract of employment used by the expert witness when engaged by a retaining attorney for consultation or testimony purposes.

"Is this really necessary, Your Honor? I'm an expert."

(From *The New Yorker* Collection, 1979, Arnie Levin, www.cartoonbank.com.)

Expert witness: An expert witness is someone who has been qualified as an authority to assist others (e.g., attorneys, judges, and juries) in understanding complicated and technical subjects beyond the understanding of the average layperson. In medical malpractice, expert witness testimony may be used (and is required in some jurisdictions) to evaluate the merits of a malpractice claim before filing legal action. The expert responds to questions posed by an attorney during the course of a legal proceeding. Some states have enacted laws requiring that a competent medical professional in the same area of expertise as the defendant review the claim and be willing to testify that the standard of care was breached. Thus in summary, an expert witness is a person who by reason of education, training, or experience has special knowledge not held by the general public.

The image of the medical expert witness has suffered because of a few bad apples. One of the purposes of this book is to increase the number of good apples in huge numbers.[5]

17.8 Concern by the Public about the Credibility of Medical Expert Testimony in Malpractice Litigation[5]

17.8.1 First, the Bad News

Concern about the credibility of medical expert testimony in malpractice litigation is nothing new. Nearly two centuries ago, Benjamin Rush, prominent physician and signer of the Declaration of Independence, called for lectures in medical education that would bring together 'those who possess medical knowledge with "those who exercise legal authority,"' and by 1850, such educational programs were instituted in many medical schools in the United States.[6,7]

However, by the 1890s, cooperation between the two professions degenerated, and acrimony between physicians and attorneys became commonplace. An editorial in the *Journal of the American Medical Association* in 1892 addressed this sad state of affairs and its impact on the quality of expert medical testimony by lashing out at the "disgraceful exhibition of medical experts who are hired ... [to give] paid theories and opinions"[8]: "The lawyers, acting as generals, lead the experts up to conflict, enthused with the idea that the truth is the great object of the struggle. In reality, both sides care nothing for the truth; winning the case is paramount to every other object. The expert physician is seductively drawn up to make statements, then driven to retract or qualify them and pressed to perjury, or so near it that it will be difficult to draw the line.... He is made to give a jumbled, confused mass of half truths and facts open to question...."

"Both sides avoid informing the jury, and are always eager to deceive them." An article published in an 1897 issue of the *Harvard Law Review*[8] also made reference to the low esteem in which expert medical testimony was held by creating a hypothetic opening statement from an attorney to a jury: "Gentlemen of the jury, there are three kinds of liars: the common liar, the damned liar, and the scientific expert." Many things in our society have changed in the past 100-plus years, but concerns surrounding the quality of medical expert testimony, and the low esteem in which many expert witnesses are held, remain as strong as ever.

Expert witnesses are still referred to by certain legal scholars as "jukebox experts . . . who sing the tunes they are paid for."[8]

A penetrating but insightful perspective of the role played by expert witnesses in the current medical malpractice quagmire has been rendered by an Ohio court (*Kirby v. Ahmad*, 635 NE2d 98 (Ohio Misc1994)):

> In the context of the frequent polemics that occur between the legal and medical professions with reference to medical malpractice, the common perception exists that the recent proliferation of medical malpractice cases somehow is due to the onerous efforts of lawyers. Without being drawn into that argument, it has been the experience and observation of this Court that in all the medical malpractice trials over which it has presided, the ultimate beneficiaries in an economic sense are truly the physicians who demand and usually obtain exorbitant compensation for their testimony as expert witnesses. Ordinary checks and balances, state the above authors, are non-existent in medical malpractice cases and the standard appears to be to get whatever the traffic will bear. In too many medical malpractice cases, unfortunately, the Hippocratic Oath has been supplanted by opportunism and greed by those who participate as medical expert witnesses.

17.8.2 The Facts: Expert Witness Testimony

The expert witness plays an essential role in determining medical negligence under the U.S. system of jurisprudence. By and large, courts rely on expert witness testimony to establish the standards of care germane to a malpractice suit. Generally, the purpose of expert witness testimony in medical malpractice is to describe standards of care relevant to a given case, identify any breaches in those standards, and if so noted, render an opinion as to whether those breaches are the most likely cause of injury. In addition, an expert may be needed to testify about the current clinical state of a patient to assist the process of determining damages.

In civil litigation, expert witness testimony is much different from that of other witnesses. In legal proceedings involving allegations of medical negligence, "witnesses of fact" (those testifying because they have personal knowledge of the incident or people involved in the lawsuit) must restrict their testimony to the facts of the case at issue.

The expert witness is given more latitude. The expert witness is allowed to compare the applicable standards of care with the facts of the case and interpret whether the evidence indicates a deviation from the standards of care. The medical expert also provides an opinion (within a reasonable degree of medical probability/certainty) as to whether that breach in care is the most likely cause of the patient's injury.

17.8.3   The Better News

Without the medical expert's explanation of the range of acceptable treatment modalities within the standard of medical care and interpretation of medical facts and issues in the case, juries would not have the technical expertise needed to distinguish malpractice (an adverse event caused by negligent care or "bad care") from maloccurrence (an adverse event or "bad outcome"). Most medical experts perform this job well, and despite the allegation of no checks and balances in medical expert witness testimony this book documents many such mechanisms currently in place to do this (*see* chapter on sanctions).

Expertise: Special skill or knowledge in a particular field.

17.8.4   Expert's Liability for Negligence

Case law has imposed legal liability on expert witnesses for negligence if the expert deviates from accepted standards of professional competence. In one case, *Levine v. Wiss*, 478A.2d397 (NJ, 1984), the plaintiff sued that the experts did not "exercise that degree of skill and knowledge normally possessed by members of their profession in similar communities." The appellate decision remanded the matter for another trial (against the experts).

Fact witness: A person who testifies in a dispute resolution trial about information gained from the senses: touch, sight, smell, and sound and whose task it is to adherently report those observations.

17.8.5   Federal and State Rules

Standards of admissibility of expert witness testimony vary with state and federal rules of procedures and evidence. Although most state laws conform with the federal rules of procedure and evidence, some do not. The same testimony from a given expert witness, therefore, might be admissible in some state courts but not in federal court and *vice versa*.

Federal rules of civil procedure: Those organized processes that govern trials and preliminary matters in United States Courts.

Federal rules of evidence: A body of evidentiary rules used in Federal Court adopted in many state courts and generally constituting a summary of the law of evidence in many jurisdictions.

Final status conference: A process by which expert witnesses can fine tune preparation for trial or hearing testimony.

Forensic witness: A person who testifies at a dispute resolution trial or hearing based upon scientific professional, technical or specialized knowledge, and training or experience. A person who is allowed by law to give opinions of law-related settings rather than merely recite facts gained from the senses. Forensic opinions are sought to explain past, present, and future events.

Frye rule: A rule of the court which provides that for an expert witness to testify concerning scientific, medical, professional, or specialized matters, the opinion testimony must be based upon a reasonable degree of acceptance within the scientific, technical, professional, or specialized field of the processes utilized by the witness to which the conclusion is tendered. To a great extent even with the Daubert requirements, this rule still applies for medical experts.

In fact the phrase "must be based upon a reasonable degree of acceptance within the scientific, technical, professional, or specialized field of the processes utilized by the witness to which the conclusion is tendered" is satisfied to a great extent if your professional expert medical opinion is supported by the peer-reviewed literature—which it can be argued by definition satisfies the Daubert requirements of PEAT—peer reviewed, error rate known (p-value and standard deviations), acceptability by the medical community, testability (RCT's).

But stay tuned for the next chapters for a discussion of questions regarding biased guidelines, clinical studies, and evidence-based medicine, the terms of which you must be familiar in a Daubert challenge.

Hearing: An organized process by which the contesting parties present their evidence and testimony.

Hearsay: A statement of conduct made by a witness outside the presence of the trier of fact (jury) with no opportunity for cross-examination by the opposition. There are certain exceptions to the hearsay exclusion, which are based on indicators of reliability, attending such declarations or conduct, which makes them admissible.

Hypothesis: A rational configuration of assumed facts subject to establishment by specific proof.

Hypothetical question: Question posed to an expert based on assumed theories of factual events. For example, if A, B, and C exist, what is your opinion as to D?

Impeachment: An attack on a witness that questions his credibility, believability.

In Camara: An "in chambers" hearing which is conducted in the judge's chambers without the presence of the jury.

Interrogatories: Written questions proposed to a part and which specific written responses under oath are required.

Judgment: The decision by trial or appellate court.

Learned Treatise: A book, publication, journal, or any other professional, scientific, technical, or specialized writing, which is considered authoritative in a particular field.

17.8.6   Medical Review Panels

State laws governing the timing and process for review panels also vary. Depending on the state, the review can take place before or after the claim has been filed; it can be conducted by a review panel or by some other method. States also differ in their use of such reviews.

Review panel findings can be binding or nonbinding. The opinion of the review panel may or may not be admissible should the matter proceed to litigation. Those seeking regulation of expert witness testimony note that the expert opinions provided during the review panel process are subject to even less scrutiny and accountability than testimony provided later. Critics believe that the lack of oversight of experts during the pretrial reviews allows too many nonmeritorious cases to proceed, thereby defeating the purpose of having pretrial reviews.

Motion in limine: A motion to limit testimony or evidence in a contested proceeding.

Negligence: Failure to exercise that degree of care, which a reasonably prudent person would have exercised under the usual circumstances and conditions and conduct marked by carelessness or neglect.

Plaintiff: A person or entity that brings a civil action.

Pleading: A paper prepared by an attorney which is filed with the court which contains a factual or legal position for a litigant usually with copies provided to all other parties to a case.

Preliminary opinion: The first stage of an expert witness' opinion forming process. Early judgments are made by the case subject to later verification based upon additional investigation.

Presumption: A rule of law which states that if certain facts exist, that another conclusion as a matter law are deemed to exist. For example, if A and B are true, then C as a matter of law must also be true.

The prevailing professional standard of care for a health provider is that level of ordinary care, skill, and treatment which in light of all relevant surrounding circumstances are recognized as acceptable and appropriate by a reasonably prudent, similar health care provider.

"Ordinary care" means that degree of care that a person of ordinary prudence would use under the same or similar circumstance.

"Negligence" means failure to use ordinary care, that is, failing to do that which a person of ordinary prudence would have done under the same or similar circumstances or doing that which a person of ordinary prudence would not have done under the same circumstances. The legal definition of *negligence*—is a tort that is defined as a civil wrong for which a remedy may be obtained usually in the form of damages. The most common form of medical malpractice action against the health care provider is the tort of "negligence." The plaintiff (patient) negligence attorney must prove for elements to be successful in a medical malpractice lawsuit, (1) that the provider has an obligation or duty of care for the individual, (2) that the duty was violated or breached by the practice below the accepted standard of medical care, (3) that the substandard practice caused the alleged harm (this approximate cause), and (4) that the plaintiff suffered compensable harm or damages. To establish the standard of medical care, medical expert testimony is used. Usually, a medical malpractice lawsuit occurs when a patient experiences a negative outcome as a result of negligent medical care provided by a physician. However, the physician may also have liability from a nonphysician provider used in the physician's practice either for vicarious liability, negligent supervision, or negligent hiring. These claims against physicians are for mistakes of their employees (e.g., nonphysician providers) that usually take the form of (1) lack of adequate supervision by a physician, (2) untimely referral to a consultant, (3) failure to diagnose properly, (4) inadequate examination, and (5) negligent misrepresentation.[9]

"Proximate cause" means that cause which, in a natural and continuous sequence, produces an event, and without which cause such event would not have occurred. To be a proximate cause, the act or omission (or commission) complained of must be such that a person using ordinary care would have foreseen that the event, or some similar event, might reasonably result therefrom.

Privilege: Those communications written or verbal between certain (unintelligible) persons, which cannot be reached by the opposition in the dispute resolution process.

Professional negligence: Failure of a professional person to perform or conduct themselves in accordance with the standards of care and attention usually displayed by persons in that field in the same (unintelligible) circumstances.

Reasonable probability: That degree of "certainty" necessary to support expert opinion, which suggests that an event is *more likely than not* to occur.

Request for admission: A discovery process by which one party requests the other party to admit that particular facts or circumstances are true or certain events actually occurred.

Request for production: A written request to a party to produce documents and other tangible things for copying or inspection.

Rules of evidence: Rules that determine what is and what is not admissible in various dispute resolution processes. They may be enacted by the legislative body determined by appellate decision or controlled by court order.

Rules of practice: Guidelines for conduct of parties who appear before courts and tribunals. These rules direct how certain steps are to be accomplished.

Sanction: The process by which a court punishes parties, witnesses, or attorneys for failure to comply with the rules of the forum.

Statute: An enactment by a legislative body, which constitutes the law of a particular state or country.

Testimony: The process of conveying information from a witness to a judge, jury, arbitration, or other hearing panel.

Testing: A means of analysis, examination, or diagnosis.

Fere libenter homines id quod volunt credunt—people are generally glad to believe that what they want true is so.

Tort: A wrongful act involving injury or damage to persons or property for which a civil action may exist.

Transcript: A written version of verbal statements.

Trial: The method by which disputes are resolved in the court system with either a judge or jury as the trier of fact.

Trier of fact: The judge, jury, administrative body, board, or arbitration panel, which determines the fact issues of the controversy in the dispute resolution process.

Vicarious liability: Is the absolute liability of one party—generally the legal "principal"—for misconduct of another party—her "agent"—the actor, whose activities she directs. In the common law, the legal doctrine of respondent superior is the principal vehicle for *holding principals liable for the torts and other delicts of their agents*. Under this doctrine, principals are jointly and severally liable for the wrongs committed within the "scope of employment" by agents whose behavior they have the legal right to control. Vicarious liability is a form of strict liability: the principal is absolutely liable for the delicts of the agent as if the principal actually were the agent. Moreover, the agent and the principal share exactly the same liability: *the principal simply steps into the shoes of the agent*.

It is based on "apparent or ostensible agency" principles, which holds, the hospital represents that the physician is its agent and that the patient being treated reasonably believes that he was being treated by a hospital employee, then the hospital is the one liable for damages. This usually comes up in the hospitals' emergency rooms where the physicians may all be independent contractors, i.e., not the hospital's employees.

Although there have been few exceptions (Virginia is one of them), most states hold that a hospital has vicarious liability for the malpractice of an independent physician in its emergency room even though that independent physician is working under an independent contractor arrangement. This is based on "apparent or ostensible agency" principles, which holds, if the hospital represents that the physician is its agent and that the patient being treated in the emergency room reasonably believed that he was being treated by a hospital employee.

In addition, the same argument holds for nonphysician employees of physicians.

There are essentially three legal theories commonly used to ascribe liability to the physician for errors from their nonphysician providers (e.g., medical assistant, physician's assistant, and nurse practitioner):

1. Vicarious liability
2. Negligent supervision
3. Negligent hiring

Vicarious liability, which allows for liability for wrongdoing to be extended beyond the original wrongdoer to persons who have not committed a wrong, but on whose behalf the wrongdoers acted. This provides the plaintiff (patient) with additional financially responsible defendants who may have greater financial resources than the original defendant. The working relationship between physicians and nonphysician providers may determine what liability will be imposed on the physician for the negligence of the nonphysician providers working with them. The employer–employee relationship is the typical relationship between physicians and nonphysician providers. This relationship forms the basis for which the physician will be deemed vicariously liable for the nonphysician provider's negligent acts. When the negligence of a subordinate is imputed to the physician, the physician is said to be vicariously liable.[10–13]

Negligent supervision applies when the nonphysician provider works under a supervising physician. Several states require this direct supervision by statute. State law also determines whether the physician must be in the same physical location as the nonphysician provider. When a physician is designated as a supervisor or has a formal responsibility to oversee and approve the nonphysician provider's work, courts will generally hold the physician responsible for the nonphysician provider's negligent acts. To complicate matters, physicians may also be held directly responsible for their own negligent acts using the theory of negligent supervision. To establish liability, a patient must show a direct connection between the injury and the physician's actions because liability is based on the physician's negligent supervision rather than on the nonphysician provider's actions. It is possible that liability may attach to the physician even when the patient cannot establish negligence by linking the nonphysician provider's acts to the injury.[11,14]

Negligent hiring or negligent selection occurs when an employer hires a nonphysician provider when the physician knows or has reason to know that the nonphysician provider is incompetent or unfit to perform the required duties. Additionally, if an employer has failed to use reasonable care to discover the nonphysician provider's incompetence or unfitness before hiring, then they may be found negligent[11] (*Seariver Maritime v. Industrial Medical Services*, 983 F.Supp. 1287, 1297 (N.D. Cal. 1997)).

17.8.7   Sources on Vicarious Liability for Further Reading

Jackson v. Power, 743 P.2d 1376 (Alaska 1987); *Mejia v. Community Hospital of San Bernardino*, 122 Cal.Rptr.2d 233 (App. 2002); *Tadlock v. Mercy Healthcare Sacramento* No. C0447777 (Cal. Ct. App., 3d Dist. June 2, 2004), 26 MLR 126 (June 2004); *Schagrin v. Wilmington Medical Center, Inc.*, 304 A.2d 61 (Del. Super. 1973); *Vannaman v. Milford Memorial Hospital, Inc.*, 272 A.2d 718 (Del. Super. 1970); *Orlando Regional Medical Center v. Chmeilewski*, 573 So.2d 876 (Fla. App. 1990); *Irving v. Doctors hospital of Lake Worth, Inc.*, 415 So.2d 55 (Fla. App. 1982), rev. denied, 422 So.2d 842 (Fla. 1982); *Webb v. Priest*, 413 So.2d 23 (Fla. App. 1982); *Richmond County Hospital Authority v. Brown*, 361 S.E.2d 164 (Ga. 1987); *Cooper v. Binion*, 598 S.E.2d 6 (Ga. App. 2004); *Stewart v. Midoni*, 525 F. Supp. 843 (N.D. Ga. 1981); *Gilbert v. Sycamore Municipal Hospital*, 622 N.E.2d 788 (III. 1993); *Tierney v. Community Memorial General Hospital*, 645 N.E.2d 284 (III. App. 1994); *Monti v. Silvet Cross Hospital*, 673 N.E.2d 427 (III. App. 1994); *Chicago Title & Trust Company v. Sisters of St. Mary*, 637 N.E.2d 543 (III. App. 1994); *Paintsville Hospital Community v. Rose*, 683 S.W.2d 255 (Ky. 1985); *Arrington v. Galen-Med, Inc.*, 838 So.2d 895 (La. App. 2003); *Mehlman v. Powell*, 378 A.2d 1121 (Md. 20050); *Hardy v. Brantley*, 471 So.2d 358 (Miss. 1985); *Arthur v. St. Peters Hospital*, 405 A.2d 443 (N.J. Super. 1979); *Houghland v. Grant*, 891 P.2d 563 (N.M. App. 1995); *Casucci v. Kenmore Mercy Hospital*, 534 N.Y.S.2d 606 (App. Div. 1988); *Mduba v. Benedictine Hospital*, 384 N.Y.S.2d 527 (App. Div. 1976); *Heinsohn v. Putnam Community Hospital*, 409 N.Y.S.2d 785 (App. Div. 1987); *Clark v. Southview Hospital & Family health Center*, 628 N.E.2d 46 (Ohio 1994); *Smith v. St. Francis Hospital*, 676 P.2d 279 (Okla. App. 1973); *Creech v. Roberts*, 908 F.2d 75 (6th Cir. 1990) (applying Oklahoma law); *Coleman v. McCurtain Memorial Medical Management, Inc.*, 771 F.Supp. 343 (E.D. Okla. 1991); *Themins v. Emanuel Lutheran Charity Board*, 637 P.2d 155 (Or. App. 1981), *rev. denied*, 644 P.2d 1129 (Or. 1982); *Capan v. Divine Providence hospital*, 430 A.2d 647 (Pa. Super. 1980); *Calderone v. Kent County Memorial hospital*, 360 F.Supp.2d 397 (D. R.I. 2005); *Edmonds v. Chamberlain Memorial Hospital*, 692 S.W.2d 28 (Tenn. App. 1981); *Baptist Memorial Hospital System v. Sampson*, 969 S.W.2d 945 (Tex. 1998); *Adamski v. Tacoma General Hospital*, 579 P.2d 970 (Wash. App. 1978); and *Torrence v. Kusminsky*, 408 S.E.2d 684 (W.Va. 1991).[15] Also see "Further Reading."

Verdict: A trial decision by a jury in a criminal or a civil case.

Voir dire: The examination by which attorneys or the court are allowed to question jurors as to their fitness to serve as impartial triers of fact. Also, the examination conducted by an attorney or the court in a trial or hearing by which a witness or a document is tested for reliability. Expert witnesses are sometimes subjected to voir dire examination before allowing to render opinions.

> I have three personal ideals. One, to do the day's work well and not to bother about tomorrow.... The second ideal has been to act the Golden Rule, as far as in me lay, toward my professional brethren and toward the patients committed to my care. And the third has been to cultivate such a measure of equanimity as would enable me to bear success with humility,

the affection of my friends without pride, and to be ready when the day of sorrow and grief came to meet it with the courage befitting a man.

—William Osler
Farewell Dinner (from Johns Hopkins; May 2, 1905)

References

1. Finder JM. The future of practice guidelines: should they constitute conclusive evidence of the standard of care? *Health Matrix: J. Law–Med.* 2000; 10: 67.
2. *J. Watch Infect. Dis.* September 6, 2006
3. *J. Watch Cardiol.* July 12, 2006.
4. *J. Watch Gastroenterol.* August 18, 2006
5. Berlin L. The Miasmatic expert witness. *AJR* 2003; 181: 29–35.
6. Martensen RL, Jones DS. Expert medical testimony. *JAMA* 1997; 272: 1707.
7. Martensen RL, Jones DS. Expert medical testimony in jury trials. *JAMA* 1992; 18: 304.
8. Murphy JP. Expert witnesses at trial: where are the ethics? *Georgetown J. Legal Ethics* 2000; 14: 217–240.
9. Delman JL. The use and misuse of physician extenders. *J. Legal Med.* 2003; 24: 249–280.
10. Feld AD. Malpractice risks associated with colon cancer and inflammatory bowel disease. *Am. J. Gastroenterol.* 2004; 1999: 1641–1644.
11. Gore CL. A physician's liability for mistakes of a physician assistant. *J. Legal Med.* 2000; 21: 125–142.
12. Cook JH. The legal status of physician extenders in Iowa, reviews, speculations and recommendations. *Iowa Legal Rev.* 1986; 72: 215–239.
13. Feld AD. Vicarious Liability, ASGE Risk Management Manual, May 2001 (available through the ASGE Office).
14. Saccuzzo DP. Liability for failure to supervise adequately, mental health assistance, unlicensed practitioners and students. *Calif. WL Rev.* 1997; 34: 115–151.
15. *Medical Liability Reporter*, September 10, 2005, pp. 193–194.

For Further Reading

Arlen JH, Carney WJ. *Vicarious Liability for Fraud on the Market: Theory*, 1992.
Arlen, JH. Commentary on Rewarding Whistleblowers: The costs and benefits of an incentive-based compliance strategy. In Daniels R, Morck R, eds. *Corporate Decision-Making in Canada.* 1995, pp. 635–647.
Croley SP. Vicarious liability in tort: On the sources and limits of employee reasonableness. *South. Calif. Law Rev.* 1996; 69: 1705–1738.
Shavell S. *Economic Analysis of Accident Law.* Cambridge, MA: Harvard University Press. Restatement (Second) of Agency (1958), American Law Institute, 1987.
Sykes AO An efficiency analysis of vicarious liability under the law of agency. *Yale Law J.* 1981; 91: 168–206.
Sykes AO. The economics of vicarious liability *Yale Law J.* 1984; 93: 1231–1280.
Sykes AO. The boundaries of vicarious liability: an economic analysis of the scope of employment rule and related legal doctrines. *Harvard Law Rev.* 1988; 101: 563–609.

Medical Malpractice Terms and Tips for the Testifying Physician

18

18.1   The Judge: *Paucis verbis*—in Few Words

The judge decides on the questions of the law, rules, regulation, statutes, courtroom procedure, etiquette, etc. He is not always, as Edmund Burke said, "a man of cold neutrality." She/he decides which questions are proper, rules on objections by the opposing attorneys, etc. The judge also instructs the jury on the applicable law in the case; she/he gives the jury rules and guidelines to reach a verdict. The judge explains to the jury that the plaintiff has the burden of proof and explains various other legal principles to guide the jury to its verdict.

*"We all make mistakes, as Your Honor knows,
having been twice reprimanded by the New York
State Commission on Judicial Conduct."*

(From *The New Yorker* Collection, 1981, James Stevenson, www.cartoonbank.com.)

So "integrity, above all things," said Francis Bacon "is their proper virtue." A judge will not permit a medical expert to testify unless satisfied that she/he not only has sufficient and valid credentials as an expert in the field (generally board certified in the same field as the defendant), but also that the expert's methodology is valid. Guthrie et al.[1] showed that the quality of the judicial system depends upon the quality of decisions that judges make. Even the most talented and dedicated judges surely commit occasional mistakes, say the authors, but the public understandably expects judges to avoid systematic errors. This expectation however, might be unrealistic.

Psychologists who study human judgment and choice have learned that people frequently fall prey to cognitive illusions that produce systematic errors in judgment. Even though judges are experienced, well-trained, and highly motivated decision makers, they too might be vulnerable to cognitive illusions.

The authors report the results of an empirical study designed to determine whether five common cognitive illusions (anchoring, framing, hindsight bids, the representativeness heuristic, and egocentric biases) would influence the decision-making processes of a sample of 167 federal magistrate judges. Although the judges in the study appeared somewhat less susceptible to two of these illusions (framing effects and the representativeness heuristic) than lay decision makers, the authors found that each of the five illusions tested had a significant impact on judicial decision making. "Judges, it seems," say the authors "are human." "Like the rest of us, a judge's judgment is affected by cognitive illusions that can produce systematic errors in judgment," concluded the authors.

Judges really are human. And thus any human judge can be biased. A biased judge can "marshall the evidence" and review the case to the jury his way. A biased judge can sway the jury by the manner of his explanations and body language, which does not get into the record. The judge may protect himself by ending his remarks to the jury with the statement that their "recollections and opinions take *precedence* over his."

Judges, it is said, are more likely to follow precedent while juries are more likely to follow group decision-making patterns.

What is the relevance of this observation?

An individual judge may be especially susceptible to the "anchoring and adjustment" patterns described by Garb.[2] This decision making comes to a provisional judgment on the basis of first heard testimony. His opinion is readjusted on the basis of later testimony. However, the earlier testimony remains dominant; or his decision making can be "conservative," which is influenced by earlier examples such that he will be continually influenced by "an opinion he held earlier" even though that may not be accurate according to Perlin.[3]

For "common sense" we depend on the jury—*ab honesto virum bonum nihil deterret*: *nothing deters good people from acting honorably.*

So be verr-y very careful on how you present yourself and what and how you say anything to the jury!

> "There, Watson, this infernal case had haunted me for ten days. I hereby banish it completely from my presence."

> **—Sherlock Holmes**
> *The Adventure of Black Peter*

> "No lesson seems so deeply inculcated by the experience of life that you should never trust experts. If you believe the doctors, nothing is wholesome: if you believe the theologians, nothing is innocent: if you believe the soldiers, nothing is safe. They all require to have their strong wine diluted by a very large admixture of insipid common sense."

> *Letter to Lord Lytton 15 June 1877 in Life of Robert,*
> *Marquis of Salisbury (1921–32), vol. 2, chapter 4.*

That is why our American framers of the constitution gave us the jury. Remember that the jury is the trier, judges the facts, and the sole judge of the facts and credibility of all witnesses, including experts. The jury decides whether the defendant physician is guilty of malpractice (liability) and how much the injuries are worth in dollars (damages).

The attorneys select the jurors by a selection process known as *voir dire* in which they excluded from a pool of potential jurors anyone each intuitively feels would not vote for them. This is why the great American poet Robert Frost who was picked to deliver his poem at President Kennedy's 1960 inauguration said *"A jury is 12 persons chosen to decide who has the better lawyer"—to which I will add also the better medical expert.*

Be that as it may, most jurors are honest and diligent and work hard to ascertain what they feel is the truth. Verdicts are reached after honest deliberation according to the judge's guidelines. The strength of the American process is the jury. You and I know that no human is completely without bias. However, the American jury—by its multiethnic, multicultural multi-experienced experience—seem to cancel out the individual biases. The jury can really see through dishonesty and insincerity. That is why the physician who testifies must do so with complete honesty and candor. Jurors can recognize a phony. Just like you, they ask themselves about anyone they meet—what do I like or dislike about this person emotionally, physically?

18.2 Tips for the Medical Expert Witness

One of the main duties you have in a medical malpractice case is to get the jury (and the judge) to understand that negligence cannot be inferred *solely* from an unexpected result, a bad result, failure to cure, failure to recover, or any other circumstance showing merely a lack of success. Negligence, if found, must be based on a reasonable degree of medical probability and a deviation in the standard of medical care must be supported by unbiased guidelines and the published standard of care. The judge will also explain to the jury the elements of true medical negligence.

Another word of advice is—do not ever get the judge mad at you. Keep admonitions from the judge to a minimum *as I did not do in two cases.*

I try to remember these acronyms before testifying before a judge and jury, and so should you:

1. PSCHH (Positive Statements Carry High Honors): Be Professional, Sincere, Courteous, Honest and Human.
2. *Also, try to avoid being* Combative, Impolite, Pompous, Arrogant, Sarcastic, Cynical, Overconfident, Verbose, Evasive or the Acronym "C i pas cove," imagined by seeing a boat passing a cove.

Never talk down to a jury. Learn to communicate with nonphysicians better, as if you are speaking to your patients—be yourself. Be sincere especially if you are giving testimony at a videoconference. In that case a few helpful tips to help you with the jury is as follows:

1. Dress well, top to bottom, for the video-testimony, deposition, or trial.
2. Refrain from wearing busy patterns during any video meeting.
3. Remember to speak in crisp, conversational tones and pay close attention.

4. It helps to lean a bit toward the camera.
5. Maintain eye contact with remote viewers. You appear stiff if you stare at the screen constantly.
6. Be careful not to frown, slouch, put your chin in your hands, or bob in the conference chair.
7. Calm your video interview jitters by practicing. You might rehearse at a Kinko's. Enlist a distant friend to play the role of attorney at his local Kinkos; critique your body language and sharpen your delivery.
8. *Remember this*—the single most important thing a jury can recognize quickly is insincerity.

And also remember, while you are an expert in medicine, each person on the jury is an expert on people and combined they can act as a human lie detector. Do not ever forget that your demeanor should be that of a calm teacher. Take every opportunity you can to get out of the witness stand to educate from a clear simple diagram or exhibit so that your students can understand the medical issues and why you hold your expert opinion. A jury of 12 people at an average age of 40 has already had a combined experience of 480 years in dealing with

1. authority (of parents, teachers, and ministers),
2. false claims (of advertising from the reams of media hours spent with newspapers, radio, TV, etc.),
3. empty promises (of politicians and other authority figures),
4. false guarantees (of used car and other salesmen), and
5. a host of other people acting "sincerely, in their interest."

You can also be sure, as Mark Twain said, "that they have previously dealt with hucksters, hookers, and hackers trying to separate them from their money." *Believe this and believe this well*—if any group can differentiate a phony huckster, then that group certainly can do it. And, for however long the trial may last, as a matter of law they are also the experts on the facts of the case being tried and especially on the credibility of each witness, including you.

Currently, juries can generally award three types of damages: (a) compensatory damages, which represent an injured plaintiff's economic losses, including the cost of health care and lost wages; (b) compensatory damages for noneconomic losses, including pain, suffering, and other emotional losses associated with injury; and (c) punitive damages in cases in which the defendant has acted in a willful fashion or has demonstrated wanton disregard for the plaintiff's well-being. Punitive damages have been historically relatively rare in medical malpractice litigation, having been awarded in fewer than 1.5% of individual physician verdicts in malpractice cases. Juries appear hesitant about awarding punitive damages in medical practice, perceiving that physicians are human beings who commit regrettable but not repeated errors of oversight.[4] However, you can see in Chapter 8 "Managed Care Snares and Punitive Damages" that some attorneys are now attempting to get verdicts of punitive damages from juries under the theory that malpractice is not just a mistake, but a deliberate disregard of clinical guidelines. *Punitive damages can be a great burden to physicians because the usual medical malpractice policy does not cover this.*

18.3 The Medical Expert and Consultant Expert

Experto credite—believe an expert who speaks from experience. Often times, a "lucky" expert consultant will mature into an expert witness after first employed by attorneys as a consultant.

An expert witness must be objective. Does that mean impartial? Yes.

Make sure you fit the definition of impartial defined in "The Devil's Dictionary" by the American author Ambrose Pierce (1842—1914). "Impartial means unable to perceive any promise of personal advantage from espousing either side of a controversy."

Do not qualify for Oscar Wilde's 1891 definition in "The Critic as an Artist" that "the man who sees both sides of an issue is a man who sees absolutely nothing at all."

The role of the medical expert is to provide the jurors his opinions of the medical treatment rendered to the plaintiff, the effect of that treatment, and the injuries to the plaintiff; whether the treating physician acted as a prudent physician would under similar circumstances in the best interests of the patient. Except in cases where the negligence speaks for itself (*res ipsa loquitur*) expert testimony is vital because of the jury's lack of medical knowledge.

The jury will quickly detect any specialized agenda the expert may have, and the expert's credibility is directly proportional to the extent of the jury's belief, i.e., its perception, in his or her objectivity. An objective expert views all facts and underlying data unemotionally and without regard to how the client or attorney wants them viewed.

An expert witness is someone who has been qualified as an authority to assist others (e.g., attorneys, judges, juries) in understanding complicated and technical subjects beyond the understanding of the average layperson. In medical malpractice, expert witness testimony may be used (and is required in some jurisdictions) to evaluate the merits of a malpractice claim before filing legal action. The expert responds to questions posed by an attorney during the course of a legal proceeding. Some states have enacted laws requiring that a competent medical professional in the same area of expertise as the defendant review the claim and be willing to testify that the standard of care was breached.

18.4 More Tips for the Medical Expert Witness

18.4.1 Question: How Much Are You Being Paid?

If, on cross-examination, you are asked—"Are you being paid for your testimony?"—A suggested answer might be "I am being paid for my time, experience, expertise, and out-of-pocket expenses."

18.4.2 Your Written Communications

Do not put your questions, assertions, comments, and opinions in writing too casually. *Why?*

It is because "discovery" is the process of forcing the other side (including experts) to divulge every fact and thought about a lawsuit long before the dispute ever sees the inside of a courtroom. *In discovery, there is one fundamental rule: If it is in writing, it can be obtained by the opposing attorneys.* That includes any written communication between the expert and the attorney in which the expert expresses his or her opinions, even in preliminary form. So instead of writing every message to the attorney, use the telephone and call to discuss a point or make a statement or reveal a doubt or weakness about a position. And things written—like love letters—have the potential to embarrass you.

Only the court, by direct order or a federal rule requirement (e.g., FRCP-Rule 26) or scheduling order, can make you—the medical expert—prepare a written report.

Since you do not use anyone else to write your medical consultations, you should research/ prepare/write all reports bearing your name by yourself.

1. You may not have to prepare a report, but if you do you should prepare it yourself!
2. Do not let an attorney write "your" report for you nor should you permit him to revise your report.
3. If you need advice on the structure of the report conforming to local statutes or rules of a particular state, discuss a verbal report as you think it will read and then discuss it with the attorney.
4. If anything needs to be clearer or maybe placed elsewhere for greater emphasis or persuasiveness, then talk about it; do not write about it.
5. And never stamp the word "draft" on any of your reports, unless you do not mind explaining who, what, when, where, and why for each draft and to prove that there was no contribution by the retaining attorney.

18.4.2.1 Reports

According to Federal Rules of Civil Procedures 26 (b)(2), A, B, and C, the expert witness' report must be prepared by the witness, signed by the witness, and contain a complete statement of all opinions to be expressed plus the basis and the reasoning included. The data or other significant information as needed by the expert in forming the opinion must be included as well as any exhibits to be used or as a summary or as support. All publications authored by the witness within the last 10 years, regardless of relevance, must be listed plus the compensation to be paid for the expert's time and study, and a list of all cases where the expert gave deposition or trial testimony within the last 4 years, which is a report without regard to relevance or relationship to the subject matter and issue. See Federal Rules of Civil Procedure 26(b)(3).

FRCP rule 26, General Provisions Governing Discovery; Duty of Disclosure:

(a) Required Disclosures
(2) Disclosure of Expert Testimony
(B) Except as otherwise stipulated or directed by the court, the disclosure with respect to a witness who is retained or specially employed to provide expert testimony in the case or his duties as an employee of the party regularly involve giving expert testimony, be accompanied by a written report prepared and signed by the witness.

A sample of my way of introducing a medical report is as follows:

Name of retaining attorney Esq.
Address

Dear Mr. Retaining Attorney

I am a practicing Board Certified Internist who also serves as a consultant and teacher to physicians that provide direct patient care—currently—as well as during the time period of this case. I am also involved in teaching and academic activities including training medical and surgical resident physicians and medical students at an accredited U.S. medical school outlined by my enclosed curriculum vitae.

I have a knowledge of the accepted national and local standards of care for the diagnosis and treatment of conditions associated with _____ which is the condition(s) at issue. I am qualified on the basis of training and experience to discuss the pertinent medical issues involved in this case.

I have reviewed the medical records you sent me on _____ (the patient) medically treated by _____ (the physician) and others. The opinions I render in this case are to the best of my ability, objective, and strictly impartial. My opinions are expressed to a reasonable degree of medical certainty.

Then go on to the body, substance, opinions, and conclusions of the report.

Signed

Respectfully yours,

Make certain you have full knowledge of all the underlying facts in every case.

Do not rely only upon information provided by the attorney. The expert witness should never blindly accept the lawyer's word that she/he has sent you *all of the documents* critical to the medical records and depositions. Merely accepting the word of the attorney, without verification, can have a devastating effect upon your credibility if proved wrong (see my Southern prisoner case).

It is the physician's first responsibility, therefore, to ensure that she/he has a full knowledge of all the underlying facts (at the very least those that impact the area of the opinion solicited) and full access to all relevant records. The attorney may have a tendency (overtly or possibly even subconsciously) to mold or restrict the retained medical expert's work to ensure a favorable opinion. Never put total faith and reliance in what you are told or shown as to the relevant medical records and other significant documents by the retaining attorney.

I usually make it my policy to document in writing an independent request for *all* the documents to prove that at least I made the attempt to independently evaluate all the underlying facts and assumptions I was given (see chapter on my forms, letters, and agreements).

Furthermore, the dismal potential is out there that if your credibility is successfully impeached on any point in the minds of the jury, it may impeach on every point in their eyes and not only those jurors but even those who ask to read the transcripts of that trial, as is routinely done by future attorneys in future cases.

Always remember that the plaintiff's or defendant's attorney is not your friend; and is certainly not your attorney. All she/he cares about is winning the case. She/he does not give a hoot about you after the case is over.

The attorney is an advocate *only* for his client—*not you*. It is his job to take a side and argue it with passion and conviction or with "perilous mouths," as Shakespeare described lawyers' arguments.

Remember always you are the medical expert. You are not the client's or the attorney's *advocate*. It is not the expert's job to be an advocate for the client; the medical expert advocates only for the objective truth. Trying to fit an opinion into a preconceived objective or goal will be dangerous to the expert's credibility and, therefore, the case. While your retaining attorney is his client's advocate for legal rights, you the medical expert are not the client's or the attorney's advocate. You are an advocate only for your own opinions, but not for the case itself. Expert witnesses should tell the truth, simply, directly, and with sincerity and I am not talking about the famous George Burns quote that "acting is not difficult once you learn how to act really sincere."

You must know about the significance of Daubert rules even if (believe it or not) your attorney does not—as per *Daubert v. Merrill Dow Pharmaceuticals, Inc.*, 509 U.S. 579, 113 S. Ct. 2786 (1993) and *E. I. duPont De Nemours and Company, Inc. v. Robinson*, 923 S.W.2d 549 Tex. (1995), respectively. These cases changed the standard of proof for admitting expert testimony and caused the legal world to focus more and more upon the expert witness' methodology. With this Daubert case the judge became the "gatekeeper" of expert testimony (*peat-peer* reviewed material, with knowledge of the *error rate*, generally *accepted* by the medical community and *tested*) rather than merely upon his or her credentials as an "expert."

As I describe in the chapter on Daubert, show your sophistication by the correct pronunciation of Daubert. The way the family pronounced the name was Duh-bert, not the fancy French pronunciation of Dow-berrr.

18.5 Summary of Recommendations

Remember that all of your writing and speaking is discoverable and can be discussed with you in deposition and in court. So

- Be careful
- Be consistent
- Investigate
- Verify and cross-examine your writings and lectures
- Proofread, and proofread again, any and every paper you wrote and your cases:
  - How many times have you been hired by attorney for the plaintiff and defense?
  - Did any of the previous cases involve the same issues? How many and which ones?
  - Have you ever worked for this particular law firm before?
  - Have you performed/consulted for this client before?
  - Have you ever worked for the client in any other (regular) capacity?
  - What percentage of the physician's time is spent in clinical practice/teaching and what percentage as a litigation consultant?
  - A copy of the physician's curriculum vitae will be requested as an exhibit. Remember that litigators are looking for mistakes or chronology lapses in credentials. If found they will be revealed with devastating results on cross-examination.
  - About what you published?
  - And whether you have any experience particularly relevant to the subject?

Arrogant Experts

There are some people who, if they don't already know, you can't tell 'em.

—*Yogi Berra*

Remember: Medical experts should not advocate.

"I consider that a man's brain originally is like a little empty attic, and you have to stock it with such furniture as you choose. A fool takes in all the lumber of every sort that he comes across, so that the knowledge which might be useful to him gets crowded out, or at best is jumbled up with a lot of other things, so that he has a difficulty in laying his hands upon it. Now the skilful workman is very careful indeed as to what he takes into his brain-attic. He will have nothing but the tools which may help him in doing his work, but of these he has a large assortment, and all in the most perfect order. It is a mistake to think that that little room has elastic walls and can distend to any extent. Depend upon it—there comes a time when for every addition of knowledge you forget something that you knew before. It is of the highest importance, therefore, not to have useless facts elbowing out the useful ones."

—**Sherlock Holmes**
A Study in Scarlet

"I assure you, Watson, without affectation, that the status of my client is a matter of less moment to me than the interest of his case."

—**Sherlock Holmes**
The Adventure of The Noble Bachelor

"Although he may be absolutely devoid of reason, he is as tenacious as a bulldog when he once understands what he has to do."

—**Sherlock Holmes**
The Adventure of The Cardboard Box

References

1. Guthrie C, Rachlinski JJ, Wistrich AJ, Cornell L. Inside the Judicial Mind. *Law Rev.* May 2001; 86(4): 777–830.
2. Garb H. Clinical Decision Making 1. *Ann Rev Clin Psych.* April 2005; 67: 30–40.
3. Perlin ML. Pretexts and Mental Disability Law. *Univ. of Miami L. Rev.* 2003; 47: 625, 659.
4. Moller E, Pace NM, Carroll SJ. Punitive damages in financial injury jury verdicts: document no MR-888-ICJ. Santa Monica, Calif Rand, 1997.

For Further Reading

Herman R. Going by the Book—Directing Cross Examination of Medical Experts. Trial Magazine, *ATLA*, August 1991.
Mark AD. *Expert Witnesses in Civil Trials.* Bancroft-Whitney Co., 1989.
Nancy H. and Lauren B. Winning with Experts. Trial Magazine, *ATLA*, March 1993; 16.
William GM. *Expert Witnesses: Directing Cross Examination.* Wiley Law Publications, 1987.

How to Prepare for and Handle Your Deposition
Deposition Preparation for the Physician

19

19.1 Part I: General Orientation

It gets late early out there.

—**Yogi Berra**

Observe, record, tabulate, communicate. Use your five senses. . . . Learn to see, learn to hear, learn to feel, learn to smell, and know that by practice alone you can become expert.

—**Sir William Osler**

This introductory section will include general orientation, questions you can expect, suggested answers to possible trick questions including a core outline of basic deposition questions. The next section will be on answering questions designed to trap you and the third section on how to handle abuse.

In our next and more advanced text for advanced medical expert witness testimony including advanced strategies in responding to very aggressive cross-examination from hyper combative opposing attorneys, we will cover the applications of depositions in more detail and from the point of view of more assertive defensive and offensive strategies in your medical expert testimony. But now for introductory purposes, we will explore how and why this chapter on how to prepare for your deposition is important in forearming the physician and medical expert witness in the subject of discovery and depositions.

19.2 Discovery

The purpose of discovery is to identify all the facts related to the case. Both sides of the dispute retain experts to provide opinions on the merits of the claim at issue.

19.2.1 Be Prepared for Your Deposition

A deposition is a discovery proceeding in the form of oral testimony taken by the opposing attorney in advance of the trial. Although interrogatories are used to acquire initial information, depositions are used to develop and expand on this information.

The opposition has a right to depose you and you cannot be properly deposed unless you are prepared. Insist on a conference with your client-attorney in advance of the deposition. Discuss the questions either of you expect the opposing attorney to ask. Too many busy attorneys meet with their experts for only half an hour or so, prior to the deposition. This is not enough time.

Prepare to be asked about your qualifications. The opposing attorney hopes to expose potential bias or lack of qualifications or experience. Tell your client-attorney if you have ever expressed a contrary opinion in a previous case, a magazine article or book. How long ago was it? Has thinking, teaching, or equipment changed? Is there new information? New technology? Can you justify a change of thought now? Be prepared and read everything again. Remember, the majority of cases never go to trial—the plaintiff gives up or the defendant makes a settlement. Therefore, you must be prepared for the deposition. Be ready to list all the things you did and read before forming an opinion. Do not try to "wing it." If you are sure of your material, you will not feel threatened.

19.3 Depositions: Preparation of the Defendant Physician for Deposition

19.3.1 Defending Your Patient Care

Being forewarned is forearmed.

You should look at the deposition as an opportunity because the deposition offers the defendant physician a chance to rebut erroneous claims while demonstrating the merits of his care.

The deposition, which occurs during the discovery phase of litigations follows a question and answer format. It is given under oath and recorded by a stenographer. Seeing every word of yours recorded is somewhat unnerving and adds to what will probably be the most stressful event other than a jury trial.

The patient's attorney also called the plaintiff's attorney is the interrogator. Attorneys for co-defendants may also have the right to ask you questions, which they may do if attempting to distance their clients from the care provided by you. The patient's attorney (plaintiff's attorney) holds two essential purposes in mind when taking your deposition:

One, to commit you to a set of facts.
Two, assess your strengths and weaknesses of your capabilities of being a witness.

Consistent testimony is good. Inconsistent testimony or unexplained changes in testimony is bad because it permits the opponent attorney to discredit you (impeach you in the legal parlance).

Your strategy should be the following:

1. Prepare and practice with your defense attorney to maximize your presentation of the facts of your case in the most beneficial manner.

2. To also promote the impression that you are a competent and confident witness.
- The deposition should ideally be in a neutral location and I would advise never in your office where the opposing attorney can make additional notations for anything that might serve his client (patient handouts displayed in the reception area, medical texts you have on your bookshelves, etc., which can be later used against you). Also, not having the deposition in your office hinders the opposing attorney from requesting additional records or documents from you during the deposition.
- If this is your first case hold a mock deposition with your attorney. Face his tough questions before your answers really count, and have a full critique afterwards to guide you toward effective and persuasive communication with the jury, and to accurately answer questions. Remember that this type of dress rehearsal is protected by client-attorney privilege.
- Review again and again all the medical records, in the malpractice case. You must be fully familiar with every aspect of your documented treatment even though the events may have occurred years earlier. You must thoroughly review the records, which augment your ability to explain what you said and what you did and the rationale behind the treatment you provided. You do not want to look unfamiliar with your own care because this can damage your case.
- Your role, though limited, must be factual and provide a solid foundation for your supporting medical expert witness to defend the care that you provided.
- Do not argue in your own defense that is left for your attorney.
- Do not be an advocate.
- Think about *all* your answers. Your responses should be clear, concise, and directed only to the specific question asked.
- If the question is unclear, vague, or couched in language that lacks a sound medical basis, do not even try to answer it.
- Do not think out loud.
- Admit you do not know or that you do not recall.
- Do not speculate or guess.
- Explain the circumstances. You must explain the (poor) medical outcome. Prepare to offer an explanation as to why the patient did not fare well with sincerity and reasonableness of your explanation as the key to what the jury will be looking to. The outcome may have been affected by patient noncompliance, which should have been documented in the chart or an unavoidable risk associated with a new medication or surgery, which the patient had previously been warned about.
- Keep cool.
- Remain calm under the stress of cross-examination.
- Do not become defensive, combative, argumentative, or evasive.
- Indeed, if the attorney during the deposition senses that you can easily be provoked and therefore, convey an adverse impression on the jury, the patient's attorney will more likely proceed to trial rather than settling before trial.

19.3.2 Present Yourself as Confident and Competent

In preparing for the deposition, work with our attorney to identify any areas of vulnerability and be prepared to explain any of those areas.

In summary, be forearmed by being forewarned:

1. Be prepared: Know the patient, the chart, and the medicines given. This requires advance preparation that is well worth the time and effort.
2. Be confident: If your care was appropriate, you should be able to withstand the challenges of cross-examination.
3. Be patient: Let the fight come to you. There is no need to be aggressive. In a medical claim, you are the "home team."
4. Be alert: Do not allow a faulty premise in the questions, medical or factual, to lay a foundation for an equally faulty response.
5. Be considerate: Convey empathy and sympathy for the patient's poor outcome while maintaining your belief in the quality of the care provided.
6. Be professional: From your appearance, demeanor, and verbal responses. Let it be clear you are a true professional. You can disagree without being argumentative or disrespectful. If the patient's attorney respects you, he will realize that the jury will respect you too according to Teichman.[1]

19.4 Deposition Testimony

The deposition is arguably the most important facet of the discovery process in malpractice cases. A deposition is a witness's recorded testimony, given under oath, on being questioned by attorneys for the parties in the case. Throughout the deposition process, attorneys gather information on what factual and expert witnesses will say and assess the relative effectiveness of their testimony. Crucial decisions in determining the next phase of the case (e.g., seeking a settlement, going to trial, moving for summary judgment) are often based on the strength of the expert witness testimony.

I find that all depositions no matter how many I have been to and attended that there is much agitation and anxiety that you live through and in my opinion you are not being paid enough for that kind of stress and strain.

Make sure you take regular breaks. And if anybody tells you, you do not deserve to be paid well for this stress ought to try it just once.

No matter what anybody says about getting used to depositions; and no matter how experienced you are in talking in front of audience, this intense and focused questioning by an examiner is extremely stressful. It is especially draining because you must focus on every single question and think about thinking before you even answer any question. Like making moves on a chess board—you must ask yourself where is he going and what will be my countermoves. Keep your eyes at the examining attorney at all times and maintain eye contact with him whenever possible.

If you have reviewed all the facts and all the medical files and you are comfortable with the issues at hand, do not forget that you know more about this case than anyone else in that room.

a. So display the air of confidence and composure no matter how you feel internally.
b. Your demeanor should be that of a person who is familiar with all the material and sufficiently at ease with himself and to be very comfortable.
c. Avoid fraternizing with anyone in the room or out of the room.

d. I like to sit at the head of the table with the window or light at my back, so that I see very clearly any of the notes that I have and that the "enemy" is facing the sun (according to the strategy of Hannibal).

This document contains the magic words to use at most depositions. Of course, I do not hand them this paper; but I know all of the points and try to make them during the deposition. Notice in item 6, it is important to emphasize that you are familiar with the national standards of care of the diagnosis and that this standard is the same in the locality of the alleged medical negligence.

You should make these points verbally for the record (if applicable):

1. Though I would not repeat the same terminology each time I offer my expert medical opinion today—I state now that any medical opinion I set forth in this deposition today were finalized after my review of all the medical records I have here today, and together with the reasons for those opinions are based on a reasonable degree of medical probability. These opinions relied on my education, training, experience, expertise, and analysis, and rooted in the science of medicine as supported by the Peer-Reviewed Medical Literature that I have researched and summarized for today's testimony.

2. As of today, I do not recall any other information related to this case other than the materials I brought with me today, but if other information about this case is brought to my attention, I reserve the right to supplement and modify my opinion if necessary.

3. And in the future, if I am asked to discuss auxiliary or supplementary issue(s), I will do so at the time, with of course, any additional information made available to me.

4. I am a licensed physician, board-certified in both internal medicine and gastroenterology. I am licensed to practice medicine in the states of Maryland, Florida, Virginia, and also in the District of Columbia. I currently see patients in Florida.

5. I train health care providers at an accredited health care institution in similar (Internal Medicine) and also allied fields (gastrointestinal dx, follow-up, and complications) with medical conditions similar to this patient. I have past experience in seeing consultations in the diagnosis of _____. I do so currently and also at the same time the patient was treated.

6. As a teacher of physicians, medical students and nurses on a teaching staff and faculty of a teaching hospital, I am familiar with the national standards of care of the diagnosis, screening and treatment of _____ in the years prior to and concurrent with the treatment of this patient.

7. These national standards were and are applicable to and consistent with local _____ standards in the diagnosis and treatment of _____. At the time the patient was under the care of the defendant(s), the national standard of care was consistent with the standard of care for internists, surgeons, gastroenterologists and other physicians, and nurses in the state of _____ for the treatment of the medical problems of the patient _____ and the diagnosis and treatment of the patient's clinical problems and other associated medical disorders.

8. A copy of my updated curriculum vitae (CV) is attached.

9. All titles of my publications are listed in my CV under "Publications." I currently have no copies of any of the articles. You have my permission to obtain any of them from a medical library.

10. Also attached is a copy of my testimony chronology. I have been qualified as an expert by a court of law in all cases. I have never been disqualified from rendering any expert opinion in any court of law.

11. None of my medical licenses or hospital privileges have ever been withdrawn or challenged. Nor have I have ever had any disciplinary actions against me.

You may find that at the beginning, the questions are extremely easy. The lawyer is not so bad. He could be extremely polite. He is friendly. He also seems to want to help you get through all of this so he can catch his plane in time. He will tell you so several times. You find you are becoming relaxed—perhaps too relaxed.

The initial questions are relatively simple and you are beginning to think this is a snap, but this is the point where you should be most alert.

No matter how many times I warn myself, there is always a time during the deposition where the attorney, if she/he is good makes me feel so relaxed that I volunteer more information than is necessary.

For example, in one of my depositions, the opposing attorney got me to feel that he was a southern good old boy. During the breaks cracked jokes so funny and raunchy that people in the other conference room looked in to see what all the laughter was about. He was extremely amiable and the kind of guy you would like to have a beer in a bar.

He got me so loose that I began discussing and volunteering information that had really nothing to do with the case and fortunately did not hurt.

But in reading the case you will see where I start go off on a tangent about a movie with an actor who has irritable bowel syndrome (IBS) and so on.

After realizing what I was doing, I stopped myself and got right back into the case at hand. Remember:

- These attorneys are professionals.
- They are actors.
- They are excellent psychologists.
- They can read you.
- They know how to relax you to the point where you will volunteer information that they have not even asked for.
- Any unnecessary information you volunteer can and most likely will be used against you.

19.5 Your Report

Federal Rules of Civil Procedures—Rule 26 (FRCP) General Provisions Governing Discovery; Duty of Disclosure

(a) Required Disclosures (2) Disclosure of Expert Testimony (B) Except as otherwise stipulated or directed by the court, the disclosure with respect to a witness who is retained or specially employed to provide expert testimony in the case, or his duties as an employee of the party regularly involve giving expert testimony, be accompanied by a written report prepared and signed by the witness.

This report shall contain

1. a complete statement of all opinions to be expressed,
2. the basis and reasons,
3. the data or other information considered by the witness in forming the opinions,
4. any exhibits to be used as a summary of or support for the opinions,
5. the qualification of the witness, including a list of all publications authored by the witness within the preceding 10 years,
6. the compensation to be paid for the study and testimony,
7. a listing of any other cases in which the witness has testified as an expert at trial or by deposition within the preceding 4 years.

This requires an expert witness to provide a written report that includes all opinions, the basis for the opinions, and the information that was considered in coming to the opinions. The report must include exhibits such as photographs or diagrams, which will be used. Along with the basic qualifications of the witness, education, training, and experience, a listing of all publications authored by the witness for the preceding 10 years must be provided.

The rule does not differentiate between material that may or may not be germane to the case at hand; all published material for the preceding 10 years must be listed. Copies of the publications or articles do not need to be attached, just a list which includes the title, publisher, and date of publication. This is usually on every physician's CV.

If you have been retained as a medical expert by the defendant's attorney, it would be helpful that all your opinions should be written down and bring it with you to the deposition in order to ensure that all opinions that have been formed are actually given during the course of the deposition with your retaining attorney.

If you have an opinion that you do not establish during the course of the deposition, you run the risk of not being able to raise this opinion at the trial. Having all your opinions written down serves another function. Because you may sometimes have more opinions that maybe outside the scope for which you were retained and extraneous opinions can create more harm than good for the defendant physician. So you should limit your opinions to those that have been set out in writing during the course of the deposition.

The written report usually should include the following features:

1. Identify each doctor or health care provider named in the report.
2. For each one named, individually, state the standard of care. Thus, the perfect sentence would be one that says, "The standard of care for a radiologist/physician/dentist such as Dr. X requires Dr. X to do X, Y, and Z."
3. For each one named, individually, state the specific conduct that shows that they breached the standard of care. Thus, the perfect sentence would be one that says, "Since Dr. X failed to do X, Y, and Z, he breached the standard of care."
4. For each one named, individually, link the conduct that was a breach of the standard of care directly to the injuries suffered by the plaintiff. Thus, the perfect sentence would be one that says, "Dr. X's failure to do X, Y, and Z, proximately caused, within reasonable medical probability, the A, B, and C suffered by Plaintiff."

5. Lastly, it is necessary to explain *how* the conduct caused the injuries. Thus, the perfect sentence would be one that says, "The use of X, Y, and Z ensures that Plaintiff is protected from Q during surgery/treatment, and since X, Y, and Z were not used in this case, the lack of X, Y, and Z caused Plaintiff to suffer Q."

19.6   Example of Rule 26 Reports

19.6.1   Introduction: Example

I am a practicing Board Certified Internist who also serves as a consultant and teacher to physicians that provide direct patient care currently as well as during the time period of this case. I am also involved in teaching and academic activities including training medical and surgical resident physicians and medical students at an accredited U.S. medical school outlined by my enclosed CV.

I have a knowledge of the accepted national and local standards of care for the diagnosis and treatment of conditions associated with _____ which is the condition(s) at issue. I am qualified on the basis of training and experience to discuss the pertinent medical issues involved in this case.

I have reviewed the medical records you sent me on _____ (the patient) medically treated by _____ (the physician) and others. The opinions I render in this case are to the best of my ability, objective, and strictly impartial. My opinions are expressed to a reasonable degree of medical probability.

19.6.2   Example of a Medical Report for the Retaining Attorney Representing the Plaintiff

Medical expert reports take a certain form:

1. The first paragraph summarizes pertinent credentials and qualifications for being an expert witness in this particular issue.
2. The next paragraph summarizes the medical history of the plaintiff and the consequence of the alleged negligence.
3. The next paragraphs are reasons for the opinion.
4. The paragraph of conclusions gives all five conclusions starting with number one, the valid indication, going to number five, "based on a reasonable degree of medical probability" (remember those magic words) that the alleged act of negligence proximate cause (look up proximate in the definitions) of the medical complications.
5. The very last paragraph is I always put in the report and that is in the event other information is brought to my attention, I reserve the right to supplement and modify my opinion if necessary.

Now, that is there to give you plenty of wiggle room, so that if other records come into your review, you are not frozen into this opinion.

It is important to throw away your stamps containing the word draft. In fact do not print out separately dated drafts. Why? Here is the reason:

Q: Your draft report is dated 01/01/05, correct?
A: Yes.

Q: You faxed it to your retaining attorney on that date?

A: Yes.

Q: It says "draft" on the top of the report?

A: Yes.

Q: Do you have any subsequent reports?

A: Yes.

Q: What dates?

A: Well, I have another draft on 01/07/05 and a third draft on 02/01/05.

Q: Did your retaining attorney talk to you in the interim between these drafts?

A: Yes, but we did not discuss the substantive parts of the reports.

Q: Come now, Dr. Hookman, you are telling me that he never asked you to change or modify any parts of the report?

A: Yes, well there was one change, one small, insignificant modification that I changed having to do with the correct date of his last hospitalization.

Q: Come now, Dr. Hookman, that is not all the suggested changes and tell me why you made 15 different changes that appear on your final draft and did not appear on all your other three preliminary drafts?

A: Du-uh-

19.6.3 Examples of a Medical Report for the Plaintiff's Retaining Attorney (All Names Disguised)

I am a physician, Board certified in Internal Medicine and also in Gastroenterology and licensed to practice medicine in the states of Maryland, Florida, and the District of Columbia. As a teacher of physicians on the teaching staff and faculty of a major Hospital, I am familiar with the standards of care for physicians from all sections in the U.S., for ERCP and Sphincterotomy, and including the standard of care for the diagnosis and treatment of abdominal pain.

I reviewed the records that you sent me on August 19, 2003 on Lynda Jo Watkins. In summary, Lynda Jo Watkins was a 58-year-old diabetic female, who on February 21, 2003, developed a post-ERCP sphincterotomy perforation while having the procedure performed by Dr. I. Randolph (gastroenterologist) and Drs. K. Sanders and B. Rogers (radiologists).

The iatrogenic perforation of the Duodenum, which developed at the Digestive Disease Center of Biloxie, Memorial Harrison Hospital, necessitated an ER admission to Mid J_____ Hospital, as well as as an admission to C_____ Hospital, for a surgical exploratory laparatomy, deuodenal exclusion, gastrojejunostomy, a feeding jejunostomy with drainage of a duodenal perforation on February 23, 2003. Sepsis, which subsequently developed, was treated with antibiotics. The patient was discharged on March 24, 2003, after duodenostomy and jejunostomy tubes were removed by Dr. S_____ K_____.

This procedure was done for the diagnosis of "abdominal pain." This patient had been very well worked up several times in the past and in fact went through a previous January 14, 1994, ERCP which was negative for very similar clinical and laboratory findings.

A likely diagnosis of nonalcoholic steatohepatitis [NASH] was made on October 8, 1999 to explain all the patients' findings.

She had a previous cholecystectomy for a positive HIDA scan even though the patient had a negative sonogram.

Despite December 23, 2002 laboratory data similar to the January 18, 1994 laboratories, an ERCP/sphincterotomy was performed on this very well worked up diabetic female for no apparent real indication that I can determine. The standard of care for a gastroenterologist such as Dr. Randolph requires him to avoid performing unnecessary medical procedures. Dr. Randolph instead performed the above described unnecessary medical procedure on Mrs. Watkins, which is a breach in the standard of care. It is my expert opinion, held to a reasonable degree of medical probability, that had Dr. Randolph not conducted the unnecessary sphincterotomy on Mrs. Watkins, she would not have developed the perforation. The perforation, and resulting complications described above, were the proximate cause of Mrs. Watkins's subsequent injuries.

The standard of care for radiologists such as Drs. Sanders and Rogers calls for prompt and thorough review of x-rays, recognition of medical complications, and notification to the physician of obvious medical complications, before and instead of discharge of the patient. In this case, the perforation should have been picked up by the extravasation which was plainly visible and apparent on the x-rays taken coincident with the ERCP and sphincterotomy.

However, this abnormal finding was apparently missed or ignored by Dr. Randolph and by Drs. Sanders and Rogers, who reviewed the films, thus causing Mrs. Watkins to be prematurely discharged.

This failure to thoroughly review this x-ray, the failure to recognize the extravasation and perforation, and the failure to notify the physician and act on the extravasation and perforation were all separate breaches of the standard of care. Mrs. Watkins should have been hospitalized and observed, rather than discharged. It is in my opinion, based on a reasonable degree of medical probability that these failures caused Mrs. Watkins to be denied necessary medical attention, and thus were a proximate cause of her injuries.

19.6.3.1 Conclusions

In my opinion:

1. There was no valid indication for performing this endoscopic retrograde cannulation of pancreas (ERCP) and especially the sphincterotomy.
2. There was no clinical evidence to suggest that the patient had any common bile duct obstruction.
3. There was no evidence of sphincter of Oddi (SOD) dysfunction based on any objective studies.
4. These very same symptoms were diagnosed almost 10 years previously as being secondary to NASH, and therefore, a sphincterotomy should not have been performed on this diabetic female with probably hyperalgesia and NASH.

5. Based on a reasonable degree of medical probability that there was no proper indication for the sphincterotomy. The sphincterotomy was proximate cause of the duodenal perforation with all the resultant complications that ensued.

   In the event other information is brought to my attention, I reserve the right to supplement and modify my opinion, if necessary.

   Respectfully yours,

   Perry Hookman, MD, FACP, FACG

6. It is important to include all of your credentials (CV), which show that you are qualified to make all of the opinions made in your report.

7. In addition, the report should include the amount paid for the expert's efforts for the matter.

8. Listing of all other cases in which you have testified, in trial and deposition as an expert, for the preceding 4 years. This does not include cases where you acted as a consultant and did not provide expert testimony; *it is only those cases where you have testified as an expert.*

   In this regard, I personally keep records only of cases in which I have given testimony. I keep no previous medical records—medical or attorney calls, or letters, or affidavits.

9. Survey results show that reports of physicians resolve many medical malpractice cases. 20% of cases require deposition testimony and about 12% require actual trial testimony.

10. Do not be fooled by a retaining attorney who wants to keep your preparation fees low and who will tell you the deposition will probably be short and all he needs is your opinion. In my experience this is rarely true.

19.7   Deposition "Routine" Questions

In a deposition, the physician has the responsibility to provide all the documents and treatises that he relied on, all case materials supplied to the physician, and all of the physician's notes and written reports and opinions. So when retained by an attorney, as a consultant, the best policy for the physician is to begin to act immediately as if she/he will become a disclosed expert. This means to keep records as if they will be disclosed during the deposition.

The purpose of the discovery deposition is for the opposition to learn as much as you know. I usually prefer to present the entire case as I would a consultation report to the referring physician—with citations of all medical articles that support my opinion. This is desirable when the retaining attorney really does not want to go to trial and looks for a speedier settlement. But other retaining attorneys do not like giving up all information prior to trial on the basis of their experience with certain attorneys and insurance carriers that preclude any settlement whatsoever before trial. Thus in a deposition in these situations you are advised to tell as little as you must.

You can expect that the opposing attorney during the deposition will start with very broad questions in a "funnel" fashion and then narrow the areas covered only as you give your opinions. Typical open-ended questions are as follows:

Tell us how you saw this assignment at the beginning of your engagement.
What medical records did you check?
Issues of the standard of care were involved as you saw it?
How did you arrive at your opinion?

The opposing attorney might appear friendly, courteous, extremely curious, and act like a very naïve and eager student.

This demeanor is dangerous to a medical schoolteacher because the goal of the deposition for the expert is not to display how much he knows about his field.

The goal of the opposing attorney is to find out what the physician knows and what he reviewed with respect to the matters important in the case.

The opposing attorney will not worry about appearing ignorant at the deposition by asking very basic questions and explanations and for definitions of even very simple terms—even those he already knows.

The opposing attorney will appear very interested in every word you say to help lower your defenses and so that you would be stimulated as a teacher would with a student to fully educate him. Therefore, the opposing attorney will put the medical expert into a teaching mode especially if the opposing expert is a member of a medical school faculty.

You will also be asked to use whatever materials you need to show your opinions on paper, to draw you are saying, to specify the anatomic area that you are discussing. You can be sure, however, that during the cross-examination at trial, you as the medical expert will not be invited to leave the witness chair to teach and impress the jury with your knowledge. The opposing attorney during his cross-examination of you will use everything he has learned during the deposition. He will press to keep you in your chair. You will have to remain in the witness chair and answer his questions-based on the knowledge he has gained from and about you in the preceding deposition.

19.8   Preparation for These Deposition Questions

You should always be prepared to accurately answer these routine deposition questions:

1. The length of time you have worked as a physician or medical expert.
2. The number and identity of cases in which you were involved.

Always have an updated summary of those cases in which you have testified during at least the past 4 years.

19.8.1   Questions on Your Expert Report

Remember that the inclusion of material in your expert report does not preclude questioning on that and related material at the deposition, but as Nordberg[2] points out on his web site:

> Inexplicably, experts who have devoted Herculean Labors to perfecting the placement of every comma in his expert's report, during the deposition the expert may change his report by testifying differently. . . . This will in effect alter or even negate some parts of his report during the deposition because every reformulation of the expert's language posses some risk of inconsistency or misunderstanding and as the reformulations mount, so do the risks.

Attorneys, therefore, may act very ignorant and eager to lap up any information you give. If you are a professor, they will begin to act like students swallowing every one of your words and interested more in asking questions that continue to reformulate your written report.

"You as the expert though should understand that depositions are really not seminars teaching sessions for any of the attorneys. There is no requirement for you, the expert, to rephrase any of the required reading of your report to the satisfaction of opposing counsel." There is in fact, says Nordberg, "no requirement that the opposing counsel even admit to understanding the report by the time the deposition concludes." This does not mean that you as the expert should be evasive, but you should stick to your report in your deposition and in your trial testimony without making any errors in reformulating the text of your report so that any individuals will understand it better.

So, the opposing attorneys can feign total ignorance to lead the expert on to explaining ad absurdum to the point where at some points the expert actually changes his report by repeated reformulations.

This is not a good idea and you should avoid it.

19.8.2 Suggested Response Preparation to Deposing Attorney's Predeposition Requests

---

A requested chronology of my testimony is attached. I have no copies of any previous medical records or transcripts of prior depositions or trial testimony on any patient given by me as a medical expert witness.

In accordance with the medical privacy provisions of Federal Health Insurance Portability and Accountability Act (HIPAA) regulations, all records of previous medical malpractice cases for which I was retained have been discarded via HIPPA standards.

I will do the same with the records here after completion of this case.

   i. I am not affiliated with any expert witness recruiting organizations.
  ii. I brought with me the complete file(s) I have in this matter including copies of medical records provided to me, including all the written materials and correspondence that I have in my possession and a copy of written materials prepared by me for this deposition. I have no other documents here. What I have brought here with me today are copies of all documents in my possession relating to this case. I recall receiving no other records or documents.
 iii. All the documents which I have brought with me today are everything pertaining to this case in my possession. I currently have no copies of medical texts, articles, exhibits, diagrams, photos, x-rays, and literature. I have reviewed except for the references listed in my Notes included into what I have brought with me today.
  iv. All reports, notes, etc. are here with me today.
   v. My CV is attached.
  vi. All titles of my publications are listed in my CV under "Publications." Please note publications that may directly or indirectly relate to this case. #s _____

I currently have no copies of any of the articles. You have my permission to obtain any of them from a medical library.

This is faxed when I send with my total billable hours spent in preparation for deposition. Note the five important points:

1. I explain why I needed the preparation time.
2. I ask for the attorney to reacquaint himself with all the facts and reiterate that the advance for the deposition time does not include preparation time.
3. "These notes are not and should not be construed as a medical expert report," i.e., this is not disclosed till the deposition.
4. A memory aid during the oral examination as to the facts, and chronology, plus references of the peer-reviewed medical literature on the standard of care—"this the reason I need the notes . . ."
5. "No changes in these notes are requested. Nor can any changes be suggested or made except by me." To show, this is entirely my own product without any input by retaining attorney.

RE: _____CASE

I have attached my Notes for and my total of all billable hours I have expended in this case so far in review, research, and preparation for the _____ deposition in the E _____ offices in Boca Raton.

I understand that one of the goals of a deposition is to "freeze my testimony." That is why I have put a lot of work and research into my Notes on this case so as to make certain my opinions, which are based on my training, experience, and expertise are also "Daubert proof" and supported by the peer-reviewed medical literature. These notes are not and should not be construed as a medical expert report.

These notes are a cumulative summary and analysis of my opinions based on review of the medical records, and work, study, and research in this case, and a memory aid during the oral examination as to the facts, and chronology, plus references of the peer-reviewed medical literature on the standard of care.

No changes in these notes are requested. Nor can any changes be suggested or made except by me.

I have also attached my updated CV.

19.9   Deposition Goals of the Opposing Attorney

When taking an adversary expert's deposition, the opposing attorney's goals are to establish everything prior to the trial that the jury is going to consider to force you, the opponent's expert, to divulge absolutely all information that you have reviewed and all opinions that you intend to present at the trial so that there is no surprise at the trial.

In summary, the purposes of deposition testimony are

1. to gather new information or confirm existing facts,
2. to lock you into a position for trial or hearing,
3. to size you up as a witness,
4. to develop what appears to be a lie or an inconsistency and then use that point for purposes of impeachment (to discredit you).

Your response as a testifying physician is to simplify his expert testimony by doing the following:

1. Tell the truth.
2. Prepare, prepare, prepare by reviewing of all the facts and the peer-reviewed literature on the issues involved in the case.
3. Remember that most questions on deposition can be answered yes, I do not know, I do not remember, I do not understand, or by stating a single fact.
4. If yes or no will do, that should be your answer.
5. Limit your answer to the narrow question asked and then stop talking.
6. Never volunteer information or answers on depositions.
7. Do not assume you must have an answer for every question.
8. Be cautious of repeated questions about the same point.
9. Do not ever lose your temper or show your tense emotions, speak slowly, clearly, naturally, and coolly.
10. Your posture should be positive, forward, upright, and alert.
11. Do not nod or gesture in lieu of an answer.
12. Do not be afraid to ask for clarification of unclear questions.
13. Do not be intimidated by any of the examining attorneys.
14. Be accurate about all facts, conditions, and damages.
15. Restrict your answers only to the medical records that you actually have reviewed. Admit it when you are shown records that you have not reviewed.
16. State the basic facts on those records, not your opinions, until they are asked for.
17. Be extremely careful of any questions that include the word absolutely or positively.
18. Remember absolute means forever and without exception.
19. Do not make any guesses. If you do not know the answer, do not second-guess the examining counsel.
20. Admit that you discussed your testimony previously, if you did even if the question is asked in a sarcastic way to intimate some irregularity on your part.
21. Do not memorize a story.
22. Avoid the wussy phrases such as I think, I guess, I believe, or I assume.
23. Maintain a relaxed, but alert attitude at all times.
24. Do not answer too quickly. Take a breath before answering each question.
25. Do not look to the retaining counsel for any assistance.
26. Make sure you understand the question before answering.
27. Do not answer if you were told not to do so.
28. Never joke during a deposition or testimony and never try to pull any tricks that you have read about in "how to be a dangerous expert" books or courses.
29. Do not exaggerate, underestimate, or minimize.
30. Dress neatly in clean clothes.
31. Be serious before, after, and during the testimony.
32. If you make a mistake, correct it as soon as possible.
33. Remain silent if the attorneys object during the examination.
34. Listen carefully to dialogue between the attorneys.
35. Avoid mannerism by signaled nervousness. Do not use "evasive" body language discussed by Judge Vucelic in his chapter.

36. Do not use medicalese without translating it for the lay jury.
37. Speak simply and clearly.
38. Do not discuss the case in the hallways or restrooms.
39. Do not even converse with any opposing parties, attorneys, or jurors.
40. Tell the truth.

You should always learn as much as possible about the opposing expert and where the opposing expert disagrees with you and why.

Your preparation, therefore, should be focussed on any points of disagreement so as to adequately answer any questions on those issues.

As an example of focussing your work on the differing issues of the opposing medical experts, let us take a look at one of my cases (the McCoy case).

In this case, the opposing expert, a prominent professor of medicine specializing in liver diseases at a very prestigious university hospital differed with my opinion. His opinion was that the intestinal malabsorbtion suffered by the patient with the obvious sequelae of malnutrition was secondary to a mucosal defect in the intestine because of celiac sprue.

The opposing expert acknowledged the malabsorbing effects of the numerous gastric surgical operations of this patient and how this could contribute to malnutrition and malabsorption. But his major point was based on the fact that this patient had a positive lab test (positive endomysial antibody); therefore this proved that the patient, had to have celiac sprue as the predominant feature of her disease, which caused her malnutrition.

However, the "gold standard" test of celiac sprue is not one positive blood test (see themes "one swallow does not make it summer") but a positive small bowel biopsy, which shows villous atrophy of the mucosa.

In this case, the patient had several biopsies, none of which showed villous atrophy. She also had an additional biopsy of the small intestine taken 4 weeks after being placed on a gluten-free diet, which also showed normal villous architecture—opposite to that of celiac sprue.

The opposing expert explained away this normal small bowel biopsy with normal villous architecture by stating that the gluten-free diet that she had been started on 4 weeks earlier was responsible for the complete restoration to normality of the small bowel intestinal villi. He offered no peer-reviewed literature to support for his opinion. This then became my focus in the preparation leading up to the deposition.

My review of the medical literature was the question as to the length of time for a small bowel biopsy to become normal after a gluten-free diet is started in the gluten-sensitive celiac sprue patients. I urge you to review the testimony to see how this issue developed.

19.10   Deposing the Opposing Expert

You may be asked as a defendant physician to assist the attorney in gaining a better understanding of the medical issues in the case. This way the deposition of the opposing expert is likely to yield better results. The defendant physician can suggest lines of questioning that might further expose weaknesses in the opposing expert's training and/or review of the literature.

19.10.1 What Are You Going to Be Asked to Bring Along with You to the Deposition?

1. All your reports in writing reflecting your assessments and conclusions (if not previously produced by rule or other discovery requests).
2. All your communications relating to the expert's involvement in the case including those with any witnesses.
3. All your documents relating to any preliminary opinions or conclusions even if those opinions or conclusions were ultimately rejected.
4. All your documents consulted or relied upon by the expert.
5. All your documents reflecting the expert's educational employment (CV) and professional history and other qualifications.
6. All your copies of all publications written in whole or in part by the expert.
7. All your documents relating to other cases in which he has testified as an expert including transcripts of his testimony, engagement terms, etc.
8. All your documents relating to the engagement including the terms of the current engagement.

19.10.2 At the Deposition

In summary, the opposing attorney's goals at the deposition are (1) to obtain full disclosure of your qualifications to testify, (2) to get complete and full disclosure of your work on the case, (3) to fully capture and exhaust all your opinions and the assumptions and facts supporting them, and (4) to freeze your testimony before trial. Another goal is to explore your possible biases, prejudices, and admissions that might lead to impeachment. Therefore make sure your CV is accurate and up-to-date. You can be certain your CV will be targeted in its entirety, detail by detail, and differences will be looked for between your experience and how they apply to this case.

You will be asked questions in a meticulous fashion going step by step through everything that you did to prepare to render your opinion. You then may be asked specific questions about what was not done, why it was not done, and whether the result might have been different had you done so.

It is important to proofread again and again your CV and anything else you bring into the deposition by someone else. Otherwise the questioning could go something like this.

Q: Dr. Hookman, are you a careful expert?
A: Yes.

Q: Were you careful when you drafted your CV?
A: Yes.

Q: I have one question on your CV, if you could help me.
A: Okay.

Q: On page one it says you received your MD degree in 19588?
A: I'm sorry, that's a typo.

Q: Are you saying, Dr. Hookman, that's a mistake?
A: Yes.

Q: Like everyone else, Dr. Hookman, you make mistakes?
A: Yes.

Q: But you do not know what year it is now?
A: Yes.

Q: And do you know the actual year you received your MD?
A: Yes.

Q: Do you know how many other mistakes you had made on your CV?
A: No, I hope there were none.

Q: Dr. Hookman, you have at the head of your CV the statement that this your Curriculum Vitae?
A: Yes.

Q: Do you know what the term Curriculum Vitae means?
A: Well, you know, I'm not really sure. I'm not a Latin student.

Q: It means, "academic life." Did you know that?
A: No, I just learned that today.

Q: Dr. Hookman, do you ordinarily title papers with expressions you do not understand?
A: Well, this is an exception.

Q: Doctor, you're saying this is an exception? How do we know that?
A: I can't answer that question.

Q: Did you carefully check your CV for accuracy before you sent it to me?
A: Yes.

Q: Are you aware the court, the jury, and everyone depend upon accuracy of your CV?
A: Yes.

Q: Dr. Hookman, you state that your article on "Crohn's Disease in Adolescents" appeared in the Journal of Gastrointestinal Endoscopy, do you not?
A: Yes.

Q: Is it not true, Dr. Hookman, that the journal was not the Journal of Gastrointestinal Endoscopy, but instead it was the Journal of Digestive Diseases?
A: Well, yes. That must be a typographical error.

Q: That article shows that your CV is not complete and accurate, does it, Dr. Hookman?
A: I'm sorry for the typographical error.

Q: Do you know if there's anything else you forgot to add or omit or change or modify on your CV?
A: I don't know.

Q: Why not, Dr. Hookman? You seemed to be very verbal in all the other answers you have given.

Next, the goal of the opposing attorney is to get the corresponding basis and factual support and assumptions for each opinion to prevent you from developing "new" opinions following the deposition, or opinions you will recast or reframe assumptions.

Also, the deposing attorney must find out whether there are particular facts, which have changed (or can potentially change) that would change your opinion—hypothetical questions.

At the end of each series of questions, he will attempt to lock in your testimony with this question. The opposing attorney wants to lock you into a position or story, which will be difficult for you to either change or maintain at trial, with these questions—"Do you have any other opinions regarding this incident that we have discussed?" and "Is there any other training, experience, education, or knowledge that you believe qualifies you to render an opinion in this matter that we have *not* discussed?"

Obviously, you should not accept the burden of knowing what was *not* discussed to lock you in.

Your answer could be "I do not know."

For that reason, you should also get into the record before the end of every deposition a statement so to maintain flexibility and a lot of wiggle room.

You can say your opinion is *up to date as of the date of the deposition*, but if you learn of other facts and data, then you will be flexible enough to modify your opinion and discuss all auxiliary issues raised by the new information.

19.10.3 Do Not Forget the Other Objectives of the Opposing Attorney in Taking Your Deposition

Try to figure out a way during the deposition to attempt to impeach (discredit your testimony or yourself) either during the deposition or most probably at the trial. So, it is crucial for you to go to the deposition with *substantial preparation*. It is a good idea to

1. again, review your entire file;
2. carefully keep the accuracy of all of your reports, preliminary or final, if present;
3. "sanitize" your file for work product memos or correspondence, which can legally and properly be removed;
4. confer with your attorney prior to the deposition for any last minute information;
5. get a good night's sleep before the deposition, the most important of all.

Also, I usually prepare a list of items asked for by the opposing attorney. This answers most, if not all, of the questions usually asked of you when you appear for the deposition. You do not have to write any of this. I have written it out so that you can see what you are generally asked for and your potential answers at the deposition to these requests.

Routine questions during the deposition are as follows:

1. Who retained you, when?
2. What are you being paid?
3. How many hours have you spent in reviewing the records?
4. What records have you reviewed?
5. Who have you spoken to about the issues?
6. What did they tell you?
7. What did your attorney tell you about this case?
8. Show me every communication you have had with the retaining attorney.
9. Have you consulted any other medical experts or physicians about these issues?

10. What did they say?
11. What text or periodicals did you review or rely on (this is a code word for authoritative in which they can ask you anything about that text once you admit that you either relied on it or was authoritative)?

19.10.4 Prepare for This Core Outline of Basic Deposition Questions

1. What is your area of expertise that describes your current practice?
2. What hospital do you practice in?
3. Do you have an administrative job in that hospital?
4. Is most of your time spent in patient care?
5. How much of your time is spent in research?
6. Has your hospital privileges ever been suspended or revoked?
7. What number of beds in the hospital?
8. What kind or level of facility is it?
9. Have you ever taken a course in CPR (or extra courses in any of the issues in the case)? When? Where? Why?
10. Are you as a practicing physician qualified to be able to take part in a cardiac arrest with defibrillator procedure?
11. When did you begin to review litigation matters?
12. How did you get started—defense or plaintiff—and why?
13. How many cases have you reviewed?
14. How many cases have you given depositions in?
15. Of those time that you have actually been given deposition testimony, what percentage were you testifying on behalf of defendant?
16. How many times have you testified in trial?
17. All those times that you have testified in trial, what percentage was on behalf of the defendant?
18. Have you been retained by the defendant's counsel or his firm before?
19. How many times?
20. What are the names of those cases?
21. What were the issues in those cases?
22. Have you testified in a trial or deposition for them?
23. How did your retaining attorney learned of your availability for litigation matters?
24. What records are you relying upon in support of your opinion?
25. Were you provided with any documentation, records, e-mails, films that you have not brought with you today?
26. Did you generate any documentation, e-mails that you have not brought with you today?
27. If so, why do you not have them?
28. Has anything been deliberately removed from your file on this matter?
29. Do you have any notes that you made while reviewing this case and the materials that you have identified today?
30. Are you prepared to render a full and complete opinion?
31. Is there anything that you feel you have not been provided or have not reviewed that would prevent you from rendering a full and final opinion on this matter?
32. If so, why is that important?

33. Have you been retained as an expert on behalf of the defendant for cases filed in states other than your home state?
34. If yes, list them.
35. Has your percentage regarding your retention as an expert for defendant changed in the last 10 years?
36. What percentage of your income is derived from being retained as an expert in litigation matters?
37. Has your percentage of income derived from being retained as an expert in litigation matters changed in the last 10 years?
38. What percentage of your time is spent reviewing cases in litigation matters where you have been retained as an expert?
39. Have you ever produced a report in any federal case that listed a listing of cases in which you have testified as an expert at a trial or by deposition (Federal Rule of Civil Procedures Rule 26)?
40. How do you keep information regarding who has retained you so you can check for conflicts?
41. Do you personally know of any of the parties to the case?
42. Do you personally know of any of the potential witnesses in this case?
43. Do you have a personal as opposed to a professional relationship with anyone connected to this case?
44. Do you know any of the other retained experts in this case?
45. Have you communicated in any way with any of the other retained experts in this case?
46. Have you communicated with any potential witnesses in this case?
47. Have you prepared a written report?
48. If not, why not?
49. Has *your* attorney told you not to prepare a written report?
50. Have you discussed this case with anyone other than the retaining attorney or his representatives?
51. How many hours have you spent on this case?
52. Have you billed for your time?
53. What are your billing charges?
54. Will you bring your updated charges when you come to trial?
55. Have you written any papers or given any lectures that dealt with the medical issues in this case?
56. The standard of care in this case.
57. Did you review any articles or textbooks or other written materials regarding the issues in this case in preparation for rendering your opinions?
58. Do you consider any person an authority on the issues in this case?
59. Do you consider any document authoritative on any of the issues in this case?
60. Are there any positions, statements, or guidelines published by any of the organizations that you belong to that relate to the issues in this case?
61. Do you advertise your services?
62. Have you ever rendered any opinions and depositions or a trial on the issues in this case?
63. If the answer is yes, give me the information.

64. Have you ever been sued for professional negligence?
65. Have you ever been disqualified as an expert witness?
66. If yes, what are the details?
67. Have you ever had your license to practice medicine suspended or revoked?
68. Have you ever been censured, expelled, or fined from a medical society, medical organization, or a hospital?
69. Have you ever been warned to receive any other adverse ruling from any of the professional societies or medical organizations or hospitals that you belong to or of any jurisdiction?

19.11   Spot Quiz

Your demeanor

(a)    (b)    (c)

(d) None of the above   (e) All of the above

Answer: If you have chosen (a), (b), or (c) please go back to Chapter 1 and reread the entire book. Then take this test again and repeat the process and take this test again.

     If you have chosen (e):

Stop reading now!
Do not ever accept a case from any attorney whatsoever.
Never admit you bought this book.
In fact, return the book for full amount paid.

During the deposition:

1. Keep your eyes focused on the examining attorney, and not your retaining attorney. If you do, will make the opposing attorney believe that you need the retaining attorney for some help or aid and that perhaps at the time of the trial you will not be able to stand up alone to the rigors of the cross-examination.
2. The opposing attorney's questions sometimes may border on the harassing or irrelevant and many questions will look like a fishing expedition.
3. But remain cool under fire.
4. Do not become ruffled even by seemingly needless questions.
5. If at any time you feel nervous or feel that the deposition is not going the way you want, you can do several things.
   a. One, you can ask for a recess or constant break.
   b. Use the time to relax.
   c. Also, use a slow, relaxing abdominal breathing and slow nasal exhalation to calm you down.

d. Do not get perplexed by attempting to search your files and answer questions at the same time.

e. Try to go back by giving only short, curt answers.

f. If you have made any mistakes, try to correct any previous misstatements.

g. Know that you will also have a chance, if you do not waive the rights to the deposition by signing an erratum sheet in which you can make corrections.

h. But it is far better to make the corrections at the deposition.

i. Once you have done that, block any of those mistakes from your mind.

j. If you play golf, you know what Tiger Woods says about golf mistakes that "every next hole is a new hole. Don't even think about your terrible shot from the last hole."

19.12   Additional Questions

You can also be certain if you are being deposed by the opposing attorney that you will be asked the following questions:

1. Your background and qualifications, everything on your CV.

2. Your education and training; your schools and postgraduate education; all your degrees; the licensing, especially certification; professional accreditation received and when.

3. Have your physician accreditations or hospital privileges ever been questioned, investigated, suspended, or removed?

4. Have you ever been sued for medical malpractice?

5. Have you ever testified in a lawsuit before, where, when, and how often?

6. Do you have a deposition or any written transcripts? If you do, please let me see them.

7. How much of your income is derived from testifying and preparing to do so?

8. Do you advertise your services and if so, where and when?

9. How did you get into this case?

10. Have you ever served for this particular attorney before or his or her firm before and how often?

11. Have you published any original work on the issues in this medical malpractice case? Let us go through your medical writings and tell me whether any of these and how directly or indirectly they bear on the issues?

12. Have you ever done research relevant to the subject at issue? If so, let me have the details as to when, where, under what circumstances, and for whom.

13. Where were your articles published and if so, can we have a copy?

14. What hospital staffs do you belong to?

15. Which organizations do you belong to and what positions have you held?

16. Have you had any privileges or memberships, questioned, investigated, suspended, or removed? Let me have the details.

17. Of all the materials that you have seen, let me have a complete list. Where did you get them? Are they copies or originals?

18. If you are expecting to examine more records, which records, when and from where? Were there any records you wanted, but could not get?

19. Of the peer-reviewed literature that you have reviewed for this case, what articles were they? Where were they obtained? Who obtained them? Were any obtained by the lawyer's office or did you obtain all of them? Were any copies retained by you and if so, let me have them? Is any of this material authoritative, useful, persuasive, or generally relied on by the medical profession?

20. Are you aware of any medical literature that is relevant, but still in preparation for the process of being published? Let me have those details.

21. Have you obtained any verbal information? From whom was the information obtained and when? What information was obtained? What part of the information plays in your opinion? What notes or records were made of any oral information, which you have received about this case?

22. What other materials or information did you gather and used? When, where, and from whom were they obtained? Where are these materials now and if anything else is expected and if so, what, when, and from whom?

23. What was the task that the retaining attorney has told you to perform? Have you ever done this before? What are the details of when you did this and where? Did you do what you were asked to do in this case? Did you do anything beyond what you were asked to do?

24. What are the defects in this case, if you know of any, and what are the defects in your opinion?

25. What is your definition of a standard of care? How do you know what the standard of care is in this case? Describe any patients that you have in your practice that you have performed these standards in and in any of them did you deviate from any of these standards. If the standards are derived from publications, which one specifically? Have you ever helped to prepare such standards? Was there any help in preparing these standards from industry, corporations, drug companies, or drug representative? Were they financed by any of the drug representatives? Did any drug representatives or statisticians from the drug company play a role in performing any of the tasks in correlating the statistics, if it was a meta-analysis or in correlating the numbers if this was a random-controlled trial?

26. Do you get any income from drug companies? Do you lecture for drug companies? What is the total amount of lectures you do? What is the year, for which companies, and for which drugs have you ever prepared standard of care statements involving any of these drugs from any of the companies that you have received any income and if you have not received income from any of these drug companies, have any of these drug companies contributed to any charitable agencies that you asked them to or did any of the drug companies contribute to any medical education activities by you or your office?

27. Who gathered all your information? Did you personally do all the work and researched that led to your opinions? Did the lawyer's firm do any of the work at all in writing up any chronology sheets or any other work products? Let me have the full names, address, titles, and qualifications of anybody else involved in gathering and evaluating this data. Describe what every one of these persons did. Were you actually involved in all the work or did you supervise? Was any of your work done in a medical library and where and when? Were you present at all times when all the others performed their work? Were full names, addresses, titles, and qualifications of any independent consultants' input received? What did they produce? How was it used?

28. Describe all the records you reviewed, the times spent on their review, and what part did the records play in the formation of your opinions? Did you obtain any manuals or peer-reviewed medical articles from the library, which library, which librarian? Do you have copies and if you do, may we see them? What part did any of these publications play in the formation of your opinions? Did you actually yourself view any of the original x-rays, pathology slides, videotapes, or any of the lab findings?

29. Did you use computers in gathering all your information? Describe the computer used. Who used the computer? What special software did you use? Describe how you got the information from the computer. Do you have any copies of any printouts or results and how are those results significant to your opinion?

30. Was anything else other than what we just talked about done to reach your opinion? What was done? When was it done? Who did it? What were the results and what are these results' significance to your opinions?

31. Please lay out every single one of your professional opinions. Let me read you the list of your opinions so we have it right. Do you agree that you have given me all your opinions and that your list is accurate?

32. With respect to each opinion, please discuss what operative facts upon which it was based in the medical records. If you have used any of the medical literature, please let me have the citation and source of each fact. Do you have a list of any assumptions that you have made about any of the facts? What is the basis of the assumptions? Do you agree that these are all the relevant facts for each of the opinions on this list that I will read to you?

33. With respect to each of your opinions, please explain whether it is causal or what other relationship it is to the case. Give me an explanation of the interrelation of these multiple factors. Are all of your opinions based on reasonable medical probability? Are all your opinions based and supported by your professional standards? Would the majority of your peers agree with these opinions? Are there any respected minority opinions in your profession based on these issues? Do you as a medical expert concede the legitimacy of minority or different views on this issue?

34. What additional responsibilities or participation do you expect to undertake in this case? When is it to be done? Do you feel that everything has been done and do you now have a total sufficient basis for all opinions that you have rendered? Have all your professional opinions and conclusions reached in this case been explored in this deposition? If not, what else is there? Do you feel that you have had a fair chance to state these and other opinions or conclusions and is there anything you would like to add so as not to be misunderstood.[3]

References

1. Teichman PG. Defending your care. *Family Practice Manage.* July/August 2001; 8(7): 34–36.
2. http://www.daubertontheweb.com/
3. For the defense. *Defense Research Institute.* July 1989; 31(7): 24.

How to Manage Attorney Abuse

It ain't the heat, it's the humility.

—**Yogi Berra**

20.1 Abuse of Experts

20.1.1 What Constitutes Abuse and How Will You Recognize It?

Abuse can consist of:

1. repetitive, invasive questioning;
2. disregard for personal comfort; and
3. unreasonable time constraints.

Fortunately, physician abuse is rare. But have this ready for your retaining attorney to use if she/he is asleep at the wheel; "pursuant to Fed R Civ Proc 30(d)(4) I will suspend[terminate] the deposition to file a motion for a protective order from the court."

If and when abuse of expert witnesses occurs, it does so most of the time in depositions; however, it can also happen to you during your trial testimony.

You should know that you never have to be subject to any coercion from either your retaining attorney or the opposing attorney at least on the following issues:

1. You should not be encouraged to corrupt a scientific fact; i.e., to reach a predetermined result determined by the attorney.
2. You should not be forced to use particular text; e.g., that you do not want to use or researched material by someone else and that are outside of your control.
3. You should not be pressurized to be an advocate.
4. You should never be asked to use questionable scientific or professional methods to support your opinion.
5. You should never ever be denied written documentation of the results of other experts.

337

6. You should never be subjected to any kind of pressure, which would alter your judgment.
7. You should never be subjected to any withholding of key documents or facts by your retaining attorney.
8. You should never be subjected to having your private life inquired into with improper ways during any questioning by any opposing attorney.
9. You should never be subjected to frivolous discovery request (Disciplinary Rule 304).
10. You should never be tricked or misled by your retaining attorney or the opposing attorney.
11. You should never be subjected to being "blindsided" by inadequate presentation of facts or false presentation of facts.
12. You should not be a subject of inquiry into your personal finances (unless that inquiry directly relates to a strong suggestion of your bias, prejudice, or partiality in this case).
13. You should not be subjected to repetitive, argumentative, redundant, or insignificant questioning.
14. You should not be subjected to badgering.
15. You should never ever be physically threatened in any way.
16. Your payment for your services should *never be made contingent* on a specific answer or opinion favorable to the retaining attorney.
17. You should not be forced to reveal the names or other identification concerning other retaining attorneys when such information is protected by Rules of Confidentiality.
18. You should not be forced to give out any medical information about any named plaintiffs (HIPAA).
19. You should never ever be contacted by the opposing counsel without notice to your retaining attorney.
20. You should never be subjected into inquiry into any aspect of your personal and private life or habits, which would embarrass, humiliate, intimidate, or harass you where such questions do not relate to your competency as an expert witness.
21. This includes the following:
    a. You should not be inquired about religion, political beliefs, sexual preference, health, and finances.
    b. You should not be forced to make disclosure or confidential business, commercial, industrial, or others of secret financial information.
    c. You should never be subjected to an examination protocol, which is designed to wear you down and not really to discover relevant information.
    d. You should never ever be subjected to any examination or treatment, which is beyond the bounds of professional common sense and courtesy.[1-3]

Genius may have its limitations, but stupidity is not thus handicapped.

—Elbert Hubbard
American writer and publisher

20.2   How to Recognize the Beginning of Subtle Attorney Abuse Either at Deposition or Trial

Medical witness abuse by attorneys, like domestic verbal abuse, often starts in a subtle manner with a slow "turning of the screw" before becoming overt abuse. Medical expert witness abuse may start with these or similar opposing attorney's techniques and demeaning questions.

Repeating a question twice or three times after your answers to show that you are not answering the question completely, plus these 10 or similar questions with a sarcastic tone develops the opposing attorney's progressively demeaning questions.

If the opposing attorney is not checked by either your retaining attorney, or you, it gets even worse.

1. Are you really saying Dr. Hookman that . . .?
2. So, Dr. Hookman why can't you be reasonable and agree that . . .?
3. Thank you, Dr. Hookman [before you have completed your answer] you have answered my question.
4. Do you not understand Dr. Hookman what I am asking you? I am asking you a very simple question whether or not . . .?
5. Why do you not understand the difference between a question which asks X and not Y, Dr. Hookman?
6. Doctor, the question I asked you which you have not yet answered is did you perform a blood test? This can certainly be answered with a yes or no, can't it, Dr. Hookman?
7. Dr. Hookman you have been so responsive to your retaining attorney, Mr. Retaining Attorney. May I ask you to be just as responsive to me as you have been to him?
8. Dr. Hookman, can't you reasonably concede that . . .?
9. Dr. Hookman, did you come in to this courtroom favoring only one side or did you come in to honestly answer whatever questions were asked by whatever lawyer asked them?
10. Dr. Hookman, I did not ask you to give me any other details. The question I simply asked you was did you actually read the EKG, the answer to which is either yes I did or no. Why in the world can't you cooperate on just this simple question. Do you not understand it?

In the absence of any successful objections or other moves from your retaining attorney, you may have to continue to respond to sarcastic, even facetious questioning. You may choose to use these answers to show some resistance, but not disrespect, while always maintaining your cool.

Q: Dr. Hookman haven't you ever been wrong?
A: Of course, but not today.

Q: Dr. Hookman, wouldn't it be fair to say . . .
A: What does the word fair mean in your question?

Q: Dr. Hookman isn't it a fact that . . .?
A: Under all circumstances?

Q: Dr. Hookman Wouldn't you reasonably agree that . . .?

A: How much agreement on a scale of 0–100?

Q: Dr. Hookman do you really want us to believe that position?

A: Yes, I'm glad you asked me that question, permit me to explain this additional point . . .

Q: Dr. Hookman you have been hired to be your client's advocate haven't you? In other words doctor you are a "hired gun"?

A: I don't advocate for patients in court.

I'm here to testify as to the standard of medical care in this case.

I am not being paid for my testimony.

I'm being paid for my expertise based on the time I spend in court.

I am not an advocate for anyone's side, as an attorney must be.

If I am an advocate, I'm an advocate for the truth as I know it.

Q: In the past, Dr. Hookman, haven't you also differed in your opinions with many other doctors?

A: Doctors do not always agree in their diagnoses and opinions. I don't know about the other two doctors in this case, who are your medical experts, but I am certain that my diagnosis and evaluation are based on objective findings and a thorough evaluation of the medical records and research of the peer-reviewed literature.

Q: Be reasonable Dr. Hookman; isn't it just barely possible that . . .?

A: No, sir, it is not possible, not under the facts of this case, not from what I know.

Q: Isn't this book used as an authoritative source, a recognized source of professional knowledge by most doctors?

A: If you mean by authoritative in this book with a lot of good information? Yes. But if you mean have I read the entire book recently and do I agree with everything in it? No.

Q: Why are you not familiar Dr. Hookman with this very well-known article?

A: With over 600 journals and 30,000 articles each year, no one can read them all, but I will read it now and give you my opinion.

Q: Isn't my expert Dr. Nobel Prize with whom you do not agree, not the universally recognized authority on this subject?

A: I am familiar with Dr. Prize's writings, but not everyone agrees with every statement he has ever made.

Q: Doctor, isn't your profession simply an art and not a science?

A: Medicine is not nuclear physics, but medicine is based on scientific theory and my research and the opinions I offered today are rooted in medical science.

Q: Dr. Hookman, who is better qualified to render an opinion—my client who is the patient's long-standing treating physician or you the "Johnny come lately" medical expert who just recently came in to this case and hired to give an opinion even before you completely reviewed the records?

A: The treating doctor has more experience with the patient. Nevertheless, because of the many hours of research I've done on this case including the review of all the patient's past medical records, I am in the position to offer my expert opinion regarding the medical issues in this trial along with all the research, which supports my opinions from the peer-reviewed medical literature after this complete review.

You may ask how much worse can his questions get if he does not get the message; or if your resistance has no effect.

How about this question?

Is it not a fact doctor, that you commit sodomy every night with a parrot? (*see* chapter discussing attorney Irving Younger's advice to cross-examiners).

At this point, you will no doubt think of very improper and individual ways of handling abuse. My method is to repeat in my mind at least one of my feisty grandmother's old world curses to many of the scammers, cheaters, and abusers she encountered in the new world.

One of these days I may shout one of these out!

When your mother called you a bastard she was telling the truth for the first and last time.

May characters like you be sown thickly and germinate thinly.

May all your teeth fall out, except one to give you a toothache.

May your guts freeze so hard that only hellfire will be able to thaw them.

May you own 10 ships full of gold and may you spend it all on your illnesses.

May you have a hundred houses, in every house a hundred rooms, and in every room 20 beds, and a delirious fever should drive you from bed to bed.

May you have a brain, but remain a simpleton, the juiciest goose, but only one tooth; the best wine, but no sense of taste; the most beautiful wife, but be impotent and cuckolded.

May you be consumed by leprosy and your nose drop off.

May worms hold a wedding in your stomach and invite their relatives from all over.

May you be a lamp; hang by day, burn by night, and be snuffed out in the morning.

You should be transformed into a chandelier, to hang by day and burn by night.

May you be buried like an onion, with your head in the ground, and your feet in the air.

20.3   Fight Your Impulses and Do Not Yield to Temptation

Although you are thinking of your grandmother's Yiddish curses, you have got to act out British verses of self-discipline and self-control plus a stiff upper lip to act completely calm and cool and collected.

Ask for a break. Or if not, while you are sitting in the witness chair you can fill your lungs slowly with air. Let your lower abdomen relax and inflate as you continue breathing in slowly through your nose. Slowly breath out through your mouth and, as your abdomen contracts visualize your diaphragm collapsing. Repeat again once or twice more.

Do not stop abruptly; you can train yourself to do this even while you are responding to questions. Practice with a friend.

20.4   So How Should You Properly Handle Abuse?

Using the mentioned guidelines in Section 20.1.1, plus additional rules seen in Federal Rules of Evidence (Rules 104, 403, 702, 703), plus Federal Rules of Civil Procedure Rule 26, you are entitled under certain conditions of abuse to do the following:

1. Develop a prearranged signal between you and your retaining attorney to alert him in the event you think a particular line of questioning is outside the scope of propriety

by simply adding to the answer "Is that a proper question?" to clue your counsel to either object or take other action.

2. Your retaining attorney has a considerable obligation to maintain your examination either in deposition or trial on a proper course.

3. You may also ask the court reporter in a deposition to mark a particular question and answer for future reference in the event you believe a question is calculated either to be improper, or for some other reason.

4. In a polite and professional way, you could also refuse to answer an objection or question or be examined in any objectional way.

5. You should "be cool" about this.

6. Never become emotional or angry or otherwise upset.

7. Repeat the breathing exercise as described in Section 20.3.

8. If things go very far, you may ask during your testimony to ask for a recess for purpose of consulting with your own private attorney who you may call long distance about your question.

9. Do not forget that your personal *attorney is not your retaining attorney who has engaged you to be his expert witness.*

10. Since you have the right to your own attorney in and out of deposition, you should follow the telephone advice of your private attorney.

11. During this entire abuse process, you must, and I emphasize, *you must maintain professional politeness, calmness and a very cool demeanor,* especially when you tell the examining attorney on the record that you believe the questioning or the question is abusive, uncalled for, improper, badgering, harassing, or otherwise outside the scope of propriety.

12. Repeat the breathing exercise.

13. You may respectfully request the line of questioning be stopped and new matters be inquired into by the examining counsel.

   If things go even further and nothing works as discussed above and improper questioning continues or gets worse,

   a. You should ask for the opportunity to contact the trial judge before whom the case is pending, so the matter may be resolved by the judge literally from the deposition room by telephone.

   b. It would be important for your own private attorney to be conferenced in during this communication.

   c. All of the proceedings should be conducted on the record during this deposition.

   d. The judge will need to hear which questions you think are objectionable to determine whether they are indeed abusive.

   e. If the above cannot be accomplished, then you can ask for a recess.

   f. Repeat the breathing exercise.

   g. The offending question transcribed by the court reporter is literally carried to the court for ruling on a "forthwith" basis.

   h. In the most extreme circumstances, it is even possible for you, if abusive and improper questioning does not cease, to make a *quiet, calm, clear, polite, and professional record with the court reporter to this effect.* You believe "the questioning is abusive, harassing, improper, intimidating, threatening, or otherwise beyond the scope of propriety."

i. If worse comes to worse, you can then *respectfully, quietly, calmly, and politely terminate the deposition and leave the deposition room.* Repeat the breathing exercise.

j. *A caveat:* If the event you erroneously evaluate the deposition should be terminated and do so in such a way that the judge finds you responsible for additional expenses by reconvening the deposition, such expenses could be placed on your shoulders. *So, if you must terminate do so at your own risk with great care and caution and only as a last resort, while acting in a very cool calm way.*

14. Above all, as a medical expert, you should treat even a very abusive opposing counsel courteously no matter how abusive or aggressive the attorney might become.

15. *Never, never, never* should you, as the expert, engaged in a one-upmanship discourse with the opposing attorney as advised in some instruction/guidebooks for generic expert witnesses which define the "dangerous expert witness" as an expert witness "who puts fear into opposing counsel." "Dangerous experts in the opinion of these authors understand how to defeat opposing counsel's tactics and are capable of turning the tables on the opposing attorney."

16. With over 30 years experience as a medical expert witness, I can say with great assurance that such a demeanor from a physician will antagonize the judge who may read the transcript of the deposition testimony or see those nonprofessional activities in the courtroom, with very negative results for you, especially from the jury.

17. Jurors do not expect respected physicians to act in this undignified manner no matter what the provocation.

18. Perhaps jurors would accept this behavior from other trades and experts, i.e., business, political, bankruptcy lip reading, handwriting expert witnesses because they enjoy seeing these courtroom antics on TV.

19. However, this action from a physician dealing with the life and death decisions of patients and relatives of jurors may often not be found acceptable by the jury.

References

1. Horowitz EB. The use and abuse of expert witnesses. *Practicing Law Institute Corporate Law and Practice Course Handbook*, Series PLI, Order No. B4-7072, July–October 1994.

2. Malone DM. *The Use, Misuse, and Abuse of Expert Witnesses, Dealing with Experts from Discovery Through Summation.* NITA, 4858, Monograph, p. 34, 1991.

3. Pierce S. et al. Expert testimony in technically complex litigation. *Cooley L. Rev. 7;* 1990: 429.

Ten Examples on the Daubert Impact on Physician Testimony 21

There is no doubt that the Daubert (actually Daubert, Joiner, and Kumho cases) directly impact physician medical expert testimony as well as all expert testimonies.

As just an example, doctors have a long-held maxim that "the earlier the better" when it comes to diagnosis and treatment. Before Daubert, one could simply state this dictum during medical testimony, which would be accepted in your medical opinion. But let us look at this dictum post-Daubert, in which three medical expert witnesses testified that "the earlier the better" as part of their expert medical opinion, but could not document "the earlier the better" opinion in the peer-reviewed medical literature.

In a Daubert challenge in the *McDowell v. Brown Case*, 392 F3d 1283, 6, 1294 n.9 (11th Cir. 2004), each of three plaintiff's medical experts expressed confidence in his "the earlier the better" opinion, but none could offer any empirical data, survey, study, or literature to support the rendered opinion for the particular case at hand.

The testimony established that the standard of care for treatment that the case required was surgical decompression of the abscess as soon as possible. The expert testimony established, however, that many factors such as, the duration and severity of the abscess at the time of examination, greatly impacted the prognosis. Indeed the literature and testimony established that prognosis is negatively affected by the presence of symptoms for greater than 24 h before examination.

The defense theory was that it was essentially too late to reverse the damage by the injury at the time the plaintiff presented for medical care. The plaintiff's case relied on the testimony of three plaintiff's experts—a neurologist, a neurosurgeon, and an infectious disease specialist. All three experts testified that the alleged delay in diagnosis and treatment of the plaintiff's spinal epidural abscess injury caused or worsened his condition.

Common sense; according to the old and established dictum, right?

This, "the earlier the better," theme of the plaintiff's medical experts was based largely on the experts' observation of their own patients' recoveries. Each of these experts expressed confidence in his opinion, *but none could offer any empirical data, survey, study, or literature to support the theory.* Indeed, the plaintiff's experts testified that the "earlier, the better" theory was a "universal axiom" based on "common sense," "understanding," and "medical logic" and that it did not "rise to the level where someone would bother reporting (the results of this theme as a randomized controlled trial [RCT] test)".

Ultimately, the experts when pressed conceded that the theory was based primarily on their personal or anecdotal experience, which lacked any supportive testing, peer-reviewed and published studies.

At the close of discovery, the defendants filed a (Daubert challenge) motion to exclude the testimony of the plaintiff's three experts as being neither relevant nor reliable under Federal Rules of Evidence 702, 703, and 403.

The district court granted the motion, finding that the expert's testimony failed to pass Daubert scrutiny, and thus excluded the causation testimony of the plaintiff's experts.

In affirming the exclusion, the Eleventh Circuit held that the experts had made an "inappropriate and unreliable leap from the 'presumably accepted scientific principle' earlier surgical intervention would be preferable to the 'unsupported scientific principle' that a delay of more than four hours caused plaintiffs problems." The Eleventh Circuit emphasized that "'this leap of faith' was supported by little more than the fact that early treatment begets improved recovery." The Circuit found that the "earlier the better" theory added nothing absent some testimony connecting the delay to the causation or aggravation of the medical problem.

However, even though this Daubert challenge went for the plaintiff, the plaintiff attorneys are frustrated by Daubert. Groups like the American Tort Reform Association and the Defense Research Institute are urging defense lawyers to file Daubert motions whenever possible. These groups advise that the motions provide a relatively low-cost way to exhaust the finances and patience of all but the most well-funded and persistent plaintiff lawyers. It is thus not surprising that the great majority of Daubert motions are filed by civil *defendants*, and they have been winning nearly 70% of the time.

Most plaintiff attorneys are frustrated with the gatekeeper role of the trial judge. Take for example this diatribe from an Association of Trial Lawyers of America (ATLA) spokesman Ned Mittenberg Esq. Miltenberg, writing in *TRIAL* (March 2001), a journal of ATLA, makes the following points. This will give the medical expert witness some idea of how threatening Daubert is to the plaintiff's attorneys—at least as opined by a spokesman for ATLA—a group that represents the views of most plaintiff attorneys (recent change of name to American Attorneys for Freedom).

1. Plaintiffs should sidestep the ever-growing dangers posed by Daubert, Joiner, and Kumho by taking a page from the successful strategy developed by ATLA's Legal Affairs Department for challenging tort "reform" statutes, which has been successful in striking down statutes in Illinois, Indiana, Ohio, and Oregon.
2. Plaintiffs should consider filing suit in state courts, particularly in jurisdictions that follow the traditional "general acceptance" test established by *Frye v. United States* [293 F. 1013, 1014 (D.C. Cir. 1923)].
3. Because as many states have adopted their own versions of Federal Rules of Evidence, not all of these states have adopted Daubert, Joiner, and Kumho, or all aspects of these cases.
4. The Supreme Court will not reverse or even revisit the Daubert–Joiner–Kumho trilogy anytime soon, particularly in light of the newly effective amendments to Federal Rule of Evidence 702, in which Congress codified Daubert.
5. Daubert has made trying cases in federal court a *riskier* and more expensive enterprise than at any time in the last 50 years.

6. The strategy simply involves taking pains to file suit in (and avoid removal from) state court, where the constitutions, rules of evidence, and judicial precedents tend to be much more hospitable.

7. These options are available because Daubert involved an interpretation of a federal rule—Federal Rule of Evidence 702—"not the U.S. Constitution," and thus *is not binding on the states.*

✓ It is important to medical expert witnesses to see how Daubert disadvantages are perceived by plaintiff's attorneys. Perhaps no better way to understand this is to review Miltenberg's following points as to why he favors non-Daubert courts:

- There are two crucial differences between jurisdictions that apply Frye and those (both federal and state) that apply Daubert.
- The first difference concerns the types of evidence to which Frye and Daubert apply.
- And the second lies in who ultimately determines admissibility.
- Whereas, Kumho extended Daubert's reach to all types of expert testimony, many Frye jurisdictions limit "validity/reliability" challenges to the 10% of experts who offer purely scientific testimony.
- And in those cases, Daubert identified five factors that could be used to evaluate whether a particular testimony was "scientifically valid" and therefore reliable as evidence, that is whether the method or technique
  1. was falsifiable or testable,
  2. had been peer reviewed,
  3. had a known (or potentially knowable) rate of error,
  4. was accompanied by established standards controlling the technique's operation and accuracy,
  5. was generally accepted.
- What Miltenberg finds objectionable is that "a technique that would have passed muster under Frye as 'generally accepted' might fail under Daubert if a court concluded that an entire discipline was somehow lacking in scientific rigor."
- He also believes that Daubert makes judges into "executioners" rather than "gatekeepers," and that conservative judges are less concerned with gatekeeping than with "industry safekeeping."

Why? Because

- These courts *do not allow these challenges against the 40% who furnish medical expertise*, let alone the remaining 50%, who supply all other kinds of expert testimony.
- Moreover, many of the state courts that apply Frye typically allow the "general acceptance" *test to be used solely to challenge the admissibility of scientific testimony.*
- The advantages of this approach (Frye) are obvious. Plaintiffs enjoy a greater chance of having a jury hear their experts testify, and they are spared the considerable expense of conducting endless admissibility hearings.
- The second crucial difference between Daubert and Frye lies in who ultimately makes the call on admissibility. Daubert entrusts federal judges with responsibility for "gatekeeping." That term may have been intended to describe a relatively benign

presence—as noted earlier, Daubert was ostensibly designed to liberal(ize) admissibility standards—and it conjured up images of friendly functionaries checking tickets at a county fair.

- But the reality is that the gatekeepers tend to view themselves as the Spartans at Thermopylae or, to use a modern analogy, as Cold War GIs at Checkpoint Charlie (this was written before the Berlin Wall came down).
- Frye certainly is not a panacea, and it may be inherently, unavoidable amorphous—no theory can be admitted into evidence unless it has been approved by some vaguely defined consensus among a vaguely defined "relevant community" of scientists. But at least Frye courts tend not to *play amateur scientist* and tend not to devise ever more numerous hurdles to be placed in front of expert witnesses.
- It may be difficult to win the "general acceptance" of the scientific community, as Frye requires, but it is even more difficult to win general acceptance (which is still a Daubert factor) and meet the dozens of other tests thrown up by inventive and hostile judges.
- Thus, under Frye, trial judges do not evaluate the reliability of all preferred testimony. They merely assess whether a restricted class of testimony is based on generally accepted principles and is therefore admissible.

✓ Medical experts can learn from Miltenberg's conclusions and recommendations to plaintiff attorneys:

- Unless a plaintiff happens to be in a state that follows the Daubert trilogy "hook, line, and sinker," or in a state whose application of Frye offers more malevolent treatment of expert witnesses than they might receive in federal court, the plaintiff should file in state court if at all possible, and avoid removal to federal court at all costs.
- The easiest way to avoid removal is to sue at least in an in-state defendant (to defeat complete diversity and thus to deprive a federal court of jurisdiction).
- And to make sure that you serve that defendant first.
- And if you cannot avoid federal court, you should take pains to try to anticipate—and satisfy—all the myriad tests that might be used to challenge the admissibility of your expert's testimony.
- In addition, you might argue that if your expert's testimony satisfies what the Daubert Court regards as Frye's more restrictive "general acceptance" test, that fact alone should guarantee the validity and reliability of the testimony.

21.1 Summary of the Daubert Trilogy

Viewed together, the *Daubert–Joiner–Kumho trilogy* stands for the following criteria:

- Federal trial judges must act as vigilant "gatekeepers" regarding the admissibility of expert testimony (*Daubert*).
- They must do so regarding expert testimony of all types, both scientific and nonscientific (*Kumho*).
- They must ensure, at minimum, that testifying experts honor the same theories, employ the same methodologies, use the same tools, and follow the same standards as they do in the course of their ordinary, nonlitigation work (*Kumho*).

- And trial court decisions to exclude expert witness testimony will be reversed only for abuse of discretion (*Joiner*).
- Federal judges are not only hearing many more motions to exclude experts, but they are becoming ever more willing to grant them.

PEAT for peer reviewed; error rate known; accepted by the medical community; testability.

Let us see examples of the application of Daubert by the Courts and why a plaintiff's lawyer in a medical malpractice case may want to avoid a Daubert Court or why a medical expert must be careful to have his/her opinions supported by PEAT and the peer-reviewed medical literature.

Again memorize—PEAT for peer reviewed; error rate known; accepted by the medical community; testability.

Let us review 10 examples of the application of Daubert in medical cases by the Courts and why a medical expert must be careful to have his/her opinions supported by PEAT and the peer-reviewed medical literature.[1]

21.1.1 Example 1

In *Cooper v. Smith & Nephew, Inc.*, 259 F.3d 194 (4th Cir. 2001), plaintiff was allegedly injured by the use of defective pedicle screw in spinal fusion surgery, and sued the manufacturer. Plaintiff offered causation testimony from physician expert who performed differential diagnosis. District court excludes testimony and awarded summary judgment to defendant.

Exclusion was affirmed on the basis that reliable differential diagnoses satisfy Daubert, but this expert's differential diagnosis was unreliable.

Expert's opinion was conclusory and *not supported by any scientific method*. Expert appears to have concluded that the defect in pedicle screw caused disunion on the sole basis that disunion occurred after pedicle screw was used, but the expert himself acknowledged that disunion is a well-known risk of spinal fusion whether instruments are used or not.

Indeed, he estimated plaintiff's chances of completely successful fusion at only 25%. Moreover, expert did not satisfactorily address plaintiff's smoking as possible cause of disunion. Ordinarily, differential diagnosis is not rendered inadmissible merely because physician cannot rule out every alternative cause. However, differential diagnoses that fail to take serious account of alternative causes can be so lacking that they cannot afford reliable basis for causal attribution. Here, plaintiff's treating physician thought smoking significant, with substantial support from medical literature, and expert refused to read more than two articles on causal relation between smoking and disunion because, he said, no number of articles would change his mind. Finally, expert did not perform physical examination of plaintiff, and admitted that this was inconsistent with his own clinical practice.

21.1.2 Example 2

Pipitone v. Biomatrix, Inc., 288 F.3d 239 (5th Cir. 2002). Patient with osteoarthritic pain develops salmonella after his knee is injected with Synvisc (replacement synovial fluid made from rendered rooster combs). In suit against Synvisc's manufacturer, plaintiff offers causation testimony from Dr. Chad Millet (patient's orthopedist) and Dr. Jeffrey Coco (infectious disease specialist). District court strikes both physicians' testimony and grants summary judgment to defendant. Exclusion affirmed; exclusion reversed. Dr. Millet testified it was "as likely as not" that Synvisc injection was source of salmonella, but conceded he had no "scientific evidence" to support conclusion that it was more likely than not. Thus, even if Dr. Millet's testimony were assumed to be reliable, it would fail Daubert's "relevancy" criteria.

As for Dr. Coco, district court excluded his testimony because Dr. Coco conducted no epidemiological study and discovered no reports of injectable knee products causing salmonella infections in his literature review. But Dr. Coco explained why epidemiological studies would be inappropriate for rare or unique events such as this, and his failure to find other reports of infection after knee injections actually tends to negate defendant's theory that salmonella resulted from medical personnel's unsterile injection procedures (because if those procedures were plausible source of salmonella infection, other reports of such infections would be expected). Dr. Coco properly relied on his considerable expertise in infectious diseases in ruling out other potential causes of infection. His testimony should have been admitted, and summary judgment therefore should have been denied.

21.1.3   Example 3

Stahl v. Novartis Pharmaceuticals Corp., 283 F.3d 254 (5th Cir. 2002). Patient develops cholestatic hepatitis after his dermatologist prescribes Lamisil. In products liability claim against manufacturer, district court awards summary judgment for defendant in partial reliance on affidavit from patient's treating physician stating that manufacturer's warning was clear and reasonably apprised him of risks. Affirmed. *Plaintiff argues that treating physician is not expert in liver disease or adequacy of pharmaceutical warnings, and that district court should not have considered physician's affidavit without first conducting Daubert hearing.* But in testifying that warnings reasonably notified him of risks, physician was testifying to personal knowledge, not as an expert documenting with peer-reviewed material.

21.1.4   Example 4

Nelson v. Tennessee Gas Pipeline Co., 243 F.3d 244 (6th Cir.), cert. denied, 122 S. Ct. 56 (2001). In putative class action arising from exposure to polychlorinated biphenyls (PCBs), seven bellwether plaintiffs agree to trial of their personal-injury claims before magistrate judge. Plaintiffs offer two physician experts on medical causation: Dr. Kilburn, whose study analyzes sample of 98 persons from allegedly contaminated area (including bellwether plaintiffs) versus control group of 58 persons from elsewhere in Tennessee; and Dr. Hirsch, who has examined plaintiffs and testifies that their conditions were more likely than not caused by PCBs. Magistrate excludes testimony from both physicians and awards summary judgment to defendants. Exclusion affirmed. *Magistrate did not abuse discretion by failing to hold Daubert hearing, where matter was fully briefed and plaintiffs requested no hearing (citing Kumho Tire).* Nor did magistrate err by refusing to permit plaintiffs to cure deficiencies in their proofs (citing Weisgram). Plaintiffs were on notice that their experts' testimony was challenged and had adequate opportunity to develop expert testimony and respond to challenges, yet never attempted to offer additional or substitute testimony.

Dr. Kilburn's testimony was properly found unreliable, because he failed to account for confounding factors, did not establish temporal relationship between exposure and illnesses, failed to show sufficient dose to make plaintiffs ill, and did not demonstrate general acceptance of his theories. Magistrate properly gave weight to lack of peer review or publication of Dr. Kilburn's litigation study, even though Dr. Kilburn had authored and published other peer-reviewed studies. Dr. Hirsch may have used valid diagnostic procedures to ascertain neurological impairment, but failed to offer reliable scientific support for his conclusion that PCB exposure caused those impairments. In particular, Dr. Hirsch had no knowledge concerning plaintiffs' PCB exposures or their temporal relationship to onset of symptoms. He also failed to account for confounding factors or identify specific scientific literature supporting his opinion on causation. Magistrate properly rejected Dr. Hirsch's "circular reasoning" that because plaintiffs exhibited symptomatology and PCBs had been in plaintiffs' environment, PCBs must have caused plaintiffs' conditions.

21.1.5   Example 5

Austin v. American Ass'n of Neurological Surgeons, 253 F.3d 967 (7th Cir. 2001), cert. denied, 122 S. Ct. 807 (2002). In this chilling case for medical experts, neurosurgeon is suspended by his professional association after it is complained by the defendant and others allied with the physician defendant that this medical expert's testimony in this medical malpractice suit was "irresponsible."

Neurosurgeon sues professional association, arguing that trial judge in underlying malpractice suit held that neurosurgeon's testimony satisfied Daubert. Dismissal affirmed. Federal courts are bound by Daubert, but professional associations are not. Judges rely on professional associations to screen experts. Just as testimony held inadmissible under Daubert does not automatically result in discipline by professional association, so too admissibility of physician's testimony under Daubert does not preclude professional discipline therefore.

21.1.6   Example 6

Turner v. Iowa Fire Equipment Co., 229 F.3d 1202 (8th Cir. 2000). Fire extinguishing system at delicatessen accidentally activates during inspection, releasing large quantities of sodium bicarbonate (baking soda). Exposed employee develops respiratory symptoms later diagnosed as hyperreactive airway disorder. District court excludes causation testimony from treating physician and awards summary judgment to defendant. Exclusion affirmed. Proper differential diagnoses satisfy Daubert, but plaintiff's physician admitted he was more interested in identifying her condition than in ascertaining its cause, and he did nothing to rule out alternative causes.

21.1.7   Example 7

Domingo v. T.K., 276 F.3d 1083 (9th Cir. 2002). After hip replacement surgery, patient suffers from fat embolism syndrome, FES, goes into coma, and suffers severe brain damage. Did unusual length of time required to mallet prosthesis during surgery cause patient's injury? Plaintiff's expert physician so testifies in medical malpractice action, based on expert's experience, observation, and review of pertinent studies. Defendants move to exclude expert's testimony and for appointment of special master. District court appoints board-certified orthopedic surgeon as technical advisor, and advisor issues report concluding that plaintiff's expert's testimony is neither scientifically derived nor based on objectively verifiable scientific principles. After parties have opportunity to respond to advisor's report, district court excludes plaintiff's expert testimony. Plaintiff then argues that causation is supported by portions of defense experts' testimony, but district court concludes otherwise, and further holds that relevant testimony from defense experts is subject to exclusion under Daubert in any event. There being no expert evidence from any quarter to support causation, district court awards summary judgment to defendants. Exclusion affirmed. Plaintiff's expert reasoned that unusual malleting time was only unusual aspect of plaintiff's surgery, but FES is risk associated with all hip replacement surgery, and nothing in literature cited suggests that risk increases when some aspect of surgery proceeds atypically. Expert's malleting theory was not published, peer reviewed, or clinically tested, does not enjoy general acceptance, and is not otherwise supported by objective and verifiable scientific principles. District court acted within sound discretion in excluding plaintiff's expert's testimony. As for defense experts, district court correctly ruled that their testimony would not support permissible jury inference of causation, and so summary judgment was properly awarded. Accordingly, Ninth Circuit need not reach question whether district court's exclusion of defense experts' testimony under Daubert was appropriate.

21.1.8   Example 8

Sallahdin v. Gibson, 275 F.3d 1211 (10th Cir. 2002). Man convicted of murder in state court petitions for *habeas corpus*, alleging that state trial court erred in barring testimony from petitioner's physician re "steroid rage syndrome" (SRS), and that counsel rendered ineffective assistance by not presenting expert's more general testimony reeffects of steroids on petitioner's state of mind. District court denies petition. Reversed. District court determined that state trial court did not err in barring testimony re-SRS, because defense counsel: (a) failed to establish reliability of SRS theory under either Daubert or Frye; (b) expressly disclaimed any intent to use SRS evidence in guilt phase; (c) did not seek to offer steroid evidence in sentencing phase. Tenth Circuit agrees with district court's conclusions, but dispositive fact is that state trial court barred only testimony relating specifically to SRS, leaving admissibility of other steroid evidence open, and never barring the latter. Remaining question is whether trial counsel rendered ineffective assistance in failing to offer any steroid evidence. As to guilt phase, petitioner has failed to show that counsel's performance fell sufficiently far below par to constitute ineffective assistance; steroid evidence would not have lessened defendant's culpability. As for penalty phase, however, physician's testimony reeffects of steroid usage was relevant and reflected emerging scientific consensus (although physician conceded that SRS was not specifically recognized). Testimony was therefore admissible under Daubert. District court should determine on remand whether counsel's failure to offer that testimony during sentencing phase amounted to ineffective assistance.

21.1.9   Example 9

Ralston v. Smith & Nephew Richards, Inc., 275 F.3d 965 (10th Cir. 2001). After surgery for cancer of femur, patient trips and fractures femur. Device is surgically implanted to hold bones together so they can heal. Patient subsequently twists leg at work, and physical examination reveals that implanted device has broken. Original surgeon replaces original device with intramedullary nail. Plaintiff subsequently complains of pain. Specialist in oncologic orthopedics examines patient and concludes that original fractures have failed to heal, though not by reason of any failure of original device. New orthopedic surgeon removes intramedullary nail and performs total knee replacement. Patient brings failure to warn claim against manufacturer of original device and offers second surgeon as expert. District court excludes testimony from second surgeon because she is unqualified and also for want of reliability under Daubert. Summary judgment is then awarded to defendant. Exclusion affirmed. Court of appeals need not reach reliability issues, because district court properly excluded witness as unqualified. Expert's sole qualification was that she was orthopedic surgeon. Expert admitted she was not expert in intramedullary nailing, had done no research on subject, was not retained as expert on warnings, and had never drafted any warnings for this or any other medical product.

21.1.10 Example 10

Meister v. Medical Engineering Corp., 267 F.3d 1123 (D.C. Cir. 2001). Silicone breast-implant plaintiff with scleroderma offers treating physician and pathologist as causation experts. Trial court initially denies defendants' Daubert motions but later grants defendants' motion for judgment as matter of law or new trial after jury returns verdict for plaintiff. Exclusion affirmed. Treating physician performed differential diagnosis, but case study reports were not sufficient to "rule in" silicone as potential cause of scleroderma in face of strong body of epidemiological research showing no causal nexus, and pathologist's causation opinion was tentative and insufficient; "chemical, *in vitro*, and *in vivo* . . . studies . . . singly or in combination, are not capable of proving causation in human beings in the face of the overwhelming body of contradictory epidemiological evidence." Courts elsewhere are unanimous in rejecting similar causation evidence in silicone breast-implant cases.

21.2 How to Help Prevent an Effective Daubert Challenge to Your Testimony

Questions on the Standard of medical care:

- Opinions regarding standard of care, as well as all other opinions, should be backed up by research and facts to be persuasive.
- In medical malpractice cases, the medical standard of care the physician can expect to be asked is how he defines "standard of care" and how he arrived at his opinion as to what the standard of care was.
- In terms of defining the standard of care, the physician needs to be aware that this opinion may not be admissible and will certainly be challenged on cross-examination if it is based *only* on the physician's personal opinion, anecdotal experience, speculation, or conjecture.
- Once on the stand, physicians need to be prepared to justify the reasons for their opinions on the standard of care in a cool, calm teaching manner.
- If the expert witness testifies in a partisan manner, he ceases to be an independent witness and has become an advocate, which challenges his credibility. (See my

routine statement prepared to be given each time I testify in the chapter of forms and communications with the legal system.)

- The physician's testimony on the standard of care may not be based on his or her personal opinion, nor on mere speculation or conjecture; and the physician's opinion must reflect some evidence of a national standard, such as attendance at national seminars or meetings or conventions, or reference to published materials, when assessing a medical course of action or treatment.

- Be sure to add that the national standard of care in this issue "is compatible with the local standard of care in Podunk Nebraska."

- It would be desirable if you had in the past either lectured at Podunk hospital or conventioned in that town or had communication or contact in your teaching CME activities with at least some Podunk physicians at national conventions.

- During the deposition preparation with retaining counsel, a physician should carefully review his opinion on the applicable standard of care. A physician's opinion should be based on reliable methodology (according to the Daubert–Joiner–Kumho rulings and criteria), and physicians should be prepared to precisely and articulately recite the methodology used (e.g., review of the peer-reviewed medical literature).

- You must also be extremely careful when expressing your medical opinion about causation. In one case (*Clerc v. Chippewa County War Memorial Hospital* No. 254940, Michigan Ct. App., August 4, 2005), the defendants moved to strike a medical expert's causation testimony on the grounds that it lacked a scientifically reliable basis because the expert opined on a proposed "backward staging" hypothesis in which 7 months after a chest x-ray was mistakenly interpreted as normal by a radiologist, the patient died with lung cancer. The medical expert "reasoning backwards" opined that a patient's cancer would have been either stage I or stage II at the time of the x-ray with a higher survival rate. The medical expert's opinion, therefore, that the patient would have had a better chance of survival had the cancer been definitively diagnosed at the time of the x-ray 7 months earlier based on backward staging of stages I, II, and III invited a Daubert challenge.

- Remember in Daubert, the acronym PEAT, P for peer review, E for error rate, A for acceptance by the medical community, and T for testability of the data. If a hypothesis of "backward staging" is to be opined by medical expert, then he must definitely have scientific data to satisfy PEAT in the Daubert challenge.

- As to the Daubert challenging questions from the opposing side at deposition, you must prepare for the following questions:

Q: Is your opinion supported by the peer-reviewed medical publications?

Q: What is the error rate attributable to these articles?

Fortunately, most peer-reviewed articles to be published in peer-reviewed journals will reveal the confidence level and the probability (*p*-value) factor and all the other important accompanied statistics (*see* chapter on Evidence-Based Medicine and attached appendix CD).

Q: The additional question is, have all the Daubert criteria been met (PEAT)?

Q: As to general acceptance in the relevant medical field, if RCTs and meta-analysis support your opinion, it is indeed accepted as a relevant Daubert criteria.

Q: How are the results applicable is a question, which you should be able to answer by your opinion on the standard of care.

If you remember the acronym PEAT (see discussion) in the Daubert questions (peer review, error rate, acceptance by the medical community, and testability of data), you will be safely ahead of the game. Your retaining attorney should establish the relevance and reliability to summarize the legal foundation needed for the admission of your testimony.

You must, therefore, make sure that each of your opinions is supported by the above Daubert (PEAT) criteria especially if your scientific testimony comes under attack by the opposing medical expert witness.

Reference

1. http://www.Daubertontheweb.com.

The Use of Evidence-Based Medicine to Fend Off a Daubert and Cross-Examination Challenge of Your Medical Opinion(s)

22

22.1 Introduction

In our next and more advanced text for advanced medical expert witness testimony, including advanced strategies in responding to very aggressive cross-examination from hypercombative opposing attorneys, we will cover the applications of answers to cross-examination challenges in greater detail and from the point of view of more assertive defensive and offensive strategies in your medical expert testimony. But now, for introductory purposes, we will explore how and why this chapter on evidence-based medicine (EBM) use in Daubert is important in forearming the physician and medical expert witness in the subject of the Daubert Challenge. Remember, when Daubert is discussed *vis-á-vis* medical expert testimony, we are really referring to the Daubert trilogy of Daubert–Joiner–Kumho decisions by the U.S. Supreme Court.

Any physician who testifies in court must be adept at knowing the appropriate peer-reviewed articles and other sources to support his opinions on the standard of care.

The way to do this is explained in this chapter with the description of the terms of EBM-randomized controlled trials (RCTs), and clinical practice guidelines (CPGs) and how they relate to PEAT (peer reviewed, error rate, acceptability to the profession, testability).

PEAT must be documented in a Daubert or other cross-examination challenge to your scientific or testimony quoting the peer-reviewed medical literature.

A testifying physician in a Daubert or cross-examination challenge to your testimony must know the ins and outs of EBM, and be able to explain its use in the establishment of published standards of care. Since the published standard of care is almost wholly based on published randomized controlled studies one must know how to obtain and process that information. The medical expert of the twenty-first century must know the language of EBM, RCTs (randomized controlled studies), and CPGs.

22.2   You Must Understand Evidence-Based Medicine (EBM), Randomized Controlled Trial (RCT), and Clinical Practice Guideline (CPG) Terms

At the risk of repeating what all of us have learned as medical students, here is a very short summary as a reminder. This necessary information for all medical expert witnesses has been very much abbreviated and it is strongly recommended that you go to the sources for a more detailed understanding of these concepts.[1-5]

In our next and more advanced text for advanced medical expert witness testimony, including advanced strategies in responding to very aggressive cross-examination from combative opposing attorneys, we will cover the subjects of EBM, RCTs, and CPGs in more detail and from the point of view of more assertive defensive and offensive strategies in medical expert testimony.

But for now and for introductory purposes, the basic understanding of EBM necessitates an understanding of terms *sensitivity* and *specificity*.

Sensitivity: The proportion of patients with the target disorder who have a positive test result.

Specificity: The proportion of patients without the target disorder who have a negative test result.

Test sensitivity is the likelihood that a diseased patient has a positive test. If all patients with a given disease have a positive test (i.e., no disease patients have negative test), the test sensitivity is 100%.

A test with a high sensitivity is useful to exclude the diagnosis because the highly sensitive test will render few results that are falsely negative.

To exclude infection with the AIDS virus, for example, a clinician might choose a highly sensitive test such as the HIV antibody test. Test specificity is the likelihood that a healthy patient has a negative test. If all patients who do not have a given disease have negative tests (i.e., no healthy patients have positive tests), the test specificity is 100%. A test with high specificity is useful to confirm a diagnosis because a highly specific test will have few results that are falsely positive.

To determine test sensitivity and specificity for a particular disease, the test must be compared against a "gold standard," *a procedure or test that defines the true disease state of the patient at a particular time and circumstance*.

Sensitivity and specificity, however, can be affected by the population from which these values are derived. Many diagnostic tests are evaluated by first using patients who have severe disease and control groups who are young and well. Compared with the general population, the study group will have more results that are truly positive (because patients have more advanced disease) and the control group will have more results that are truly negative (because the controlled group is healthy). Thus, test sensitivity and specificity will be higher than would be expected in the general population when more of the spectrum of health and disease are found.

Clinicians and testifying physicians must be aware of the spectrum bias when generalizing published test results to their own clinical practice treating their own patients.

There is additional information that must be understood about the use of test sensitivity and specificity in a particular clinical situation. The value of a test in a particular clinical situation depends *not only on the test sensitivity and specificity,* but also *on the probability that the patient has the disease before the test result is known (pretest probability).* The results of a valuable test will substantially change the probability that the patient has the disease (posttest probability). For example, the pretest probability of a disease has a profound effect on the posttest probability of disease. When a test with 90% sensitivity and specificity is used, the posttest probability can vary from 1% to 99% depending on the pretest probability of the disease. Furthermore, as the pretest probability of disease decreases, it becomes less likely that someone with a positive test actually has the disease and more likely that the results represent a false positive.

22.3   Additional EBM Terms to Understand

Odds ratio (OR):   How many times more frequently a factor is associated with one group, as opposed to another (used in case control studies, cross-sectional studies, and meta-analyses).

Positive likelihood ratio: How many times more frequently a positive test is seen in the diseased population, as compared to those who are disease-free.

Positive predictive value (PPV):   Quantifies how frequently patients with abnormal test values have a certain disease.

Relative risk (RR):   Proportional risk for a dichotomous outcome when one group is compared to another.

Relative risk reduction (RRR):   The decrease in the proportion of adverse events when the experimental group is compared to the control group or alternative treatment arm.

22.4   EBM Grades

EBM or practice is usually interpreted by assigning grades to the recommendation, which are primarily based on the level of the evaluated study(ies). Generally, grades range from A (best) to D (worst).

A hierarchy exists starting from the bottom (grade D) with expert opinion statements, followed, in successive order, by case series, case control comparisons, and cohort studies. At the other side of the spectrum are single high-quality RCTs, surpassed by heterogeneous (in terms of variations in the directions and degrees of results between individual studies) systematic reviews, to the ultimate—grade A recommendations—that are based on consistent results from large number of high-quality RCTs (e.g., double-blind, intention-to-treat, or complete follow-up).

EBM has four main steps:

1. Defining a structured question about the target population, outcomes, and (usually) intervention or exposure.
2. Searching (by a Medline survey or other similar method) the published (and occasionally unpublished) literature for sources of data that might answer the question.
3. Appraising or evaluating the data for methodologic rigor and relevance to the question (typically, *this process weeds out about 90–99% of studies*).
4. Describing and analyzing the resulting data *to answer the question posed.*

22.5 How Do We Get to EBM the Long Way?

Let us take as an example that we want to answer the question as to which proton pump inhibitor (PPI) medication is best for erosive esophagitis (EE). Because all PPIs are effective, head-to-head clinical trials must be extremely large to demonstrate statistically significant and clinically relevant differences between competing agents.

Also, it has been shown that it is not efficacious to rely on small studies. Why? Because small studies can exaggerate bias even in nonindustry-sponsored studies. Egger[6] believes that funnel plots, which are plots of effect estimates against sample size, are useful to detect bias in meta-analyses that were later contradicted by large trials. The authors examined whether a simple test of asymmetry of funnel plots predicts discordance of results when meta-analyses are compared to large trials. How is this done? Medline is searched to identify pairs consisting of a meta-analysis and a single large trial. Concordance of results is assumed if effects were in the same direction and the meta-analytic estimate was within 30% of the trial. Analysis of funnel plots from 37 meta-analyses identified from a hand search of four leading general medicine journals, 1993–1996, and 38 meta-analyses from the second 1996 issue of the Cochrane Database of Systematic Reviews showed that funnel plot asymmetry was present in three out of four discordant pairs but in none of concordant pairs. In 14 (38%) journal meta-analyses and 5 (13%) Cochrane reviews, funnel plot asymmetry indicated that there was bias. A simple analysis of funnel plots provides a useful test for the likely presence of bias in meta-analyses, but as the capacity to detect bias will be limited when meta-analyses are based on a limited number of small trials, the results from such analyses should be treated with considerable caution.

Therefore, relying on underpowered comparative studies might lead to a type II error, in which a true difference between agents exists but cannot be detected because of inadequate sample size. The risk of committing a type II error might be overcome by performing a meta-analysis of pooled data, an accepted methodology that increases the ability to detect small yet statistically significant and perhaps clinically relevant differences. So Ian M. Gralnek et al.[7] performed a meta-analysis to calculate the pooled effect of esomeprazole on healing rates, symptom relief, and adverse events versus competing PPIs in EE the long manual way. The authors performed a time-consuming but structured electronic search of medline and embase and reviewed published abstracts to identify English language, randomized clinical trials from 1995–2005, comparing rates of endoscopic healing, symptom relief, and adverse events with esomeprazole versus alternative PPIs in the treatment of gastroesophageal reflux disease (GERD)/EE. This structured electronic search of medline and embase yielded a review of published abstracts from three major subspecialty journals to identify English language, randomized clinical trials from 1995–2005, comparing rates of endoscopic healing, symptom relief, and adverse events with esomeprazole versus alternative PPIs in the treatment of GERD/EE. In addition, the authors manually searched the bibliographies of key review articles for references not captured by this search strategy and even reviewed the Web sites of the manufacturers of the PPIs to search for other unpublished clinical trial data that might have existed.

They then performed meta-analysis to compare the RR of EE healing, symptom relief, and adverse events between study arms and calculated the absolute risk reduction and number needed to treat (NNT) for each outcome. Their results showed that with the meta-analysis performed on 10 studies ($n = 15,316$), at 8 weeks, there was a 5% (RR, 1.05; 95% confidence interval, 1.02–1.08) relative increase in the probability of healing of EE with esomeprazole, yielding an absolute risk reduction of 4% and NNT of 25. The calculated NNTs by Los Angeles grade of EE (grades A–D) were 50, 33, 14, and 8, respectively. Last, esomeprazole conferred an 8% (RR, 1.08; 95% confidence interval, 1.05–1.11) relative increase in the probability of GERD symptom relief at 4 weeks. Thus, the authors could conclude that, "As compared with other PPIs, esomeprazole confers a statistically significant improvement, yet, clinically, only a modest overall benefit in 8-week healing and symptom relief in all-comers with EE."

In addition, the abstractors assigned a score for methodologic quality by applying the Jadad scale. This is a standardized instrument focusing on features related to internal validity. Disagreements were settled by discussion and consensus between the two primary reviewers and a third arbiter. These data indicate that although esomeprazole is a more effective agent in healing and symptom relief in patients with EE, any advantage is largely found in those with more severe disease.

22.6 How Do We Get to EBM the Easier Way?

Today, the most useful Web-based resources make EBM techniques quicker and easier.

1. Clinical Evidence
2. DynaMed
3. InfoRetriever
4. PDxMD
5. UpToDate
6. NICE—(U.K.) the National Institute for Health and Clinical Excellence
7. Journal Watch On Line from the Massachusetts Medical Society

✓ 1. Clinical Evidence

Clinical Evidence[8] identifies important clinical questions and answers them by systematically searching for randomized controlled trials and then summarizing the best evidence. The initial literature search includes the Cochrane Library, medline, and Embase.

A word about Cochrane: Findings suggest that compared with industry-sponsored reviews, Cochrane reviews are more transparent; more often consider the potential for bias; and more often include reservations in recommending drugs, despite similar estimated treatment effects. The conclusions of industry-sponsored reviews and meta-analyses should be read with caution. Why? As an example cited in a thorough review compared with industry-supported and undeclared support reviews, Cochrane reviews more often considered the potential for bias in the review by describing the method of concealment of allocation and describing excluded patients or studies. The seven industry-supported reviews with conclusion sections recommended the drug without reservations. Whereas none of the Cochrane review recommendations lacked reservations, despite similar estimated treatment effects in the two types of reviews with undeclared or nonprofit support in the Cochrane reviews.[9]

✓ 2. DynaMed

DynaMed[10] systematically surveys original research reports, journal review services, systematic review sources (such as Clinical Evidence and the Cochrane Library), drug information sources, and guideline collections as well as accompanying letters, editorials, or review articles that may also be clinically useful, selecting information based on relevance and validity. A key advantage of DynaMed is that it is updated daily, typically within days of publication of the original research. A key disadvantage is that although DynaMed's editors write article summaries from peer-reviewed information, not all resultant summaries have been peer reviewed. The annual subscription to DynaMed is $200 for a practicing health care professional, and access is also provided for health care professionals who assist with peer review. DynaMed is primarily used via the Internet, but a desktop version is available. A free 30-day trial is also offered.

✓ 3. InfoRetriever

InfoRetriever[11] is a search engine that allows you to search multiple databases, including InfoPOEMs (concise evidence-based summaries selected for clinical relevance and validity from more than 100 journals), Cochrane Database abstracts, selected guidelines, clinical decision rules, diagnostic test calculators, and the complete "Griffith's 5-Minute Clinical Consult." Information from these resources is cataloged according to clinical topic. A keyadvantage to InfoRetriever is that it includes clinical calculators, allowing interactive lookups with numerically dependent data, such as calculating risks for specific diseases. A key disadvantage is the need to read multiple hits from different sources to synthesize the available evidence. A 1-year subscription costs $249 and includes online access as well as InfoRetriever versions for the desktop computer and either Palm or Pocket PC PDAs. A free 30-day trial is also available.

✓ 4. PDxMD

PDxMD[12] is designed for intuitive browsing. Topics are created using information from Cochrane Reviews, Clinical Evidence, and the National Guideline Clearinghouse. References are hyperlinked to the home pages of these sites, making it easier to search for the relevant report or article. PDxMD also searches for information in reference books, journals, guidelines, and position papers. Content is assessed and updated on a rolling basis, and certain updates (e.g., drug approvals or withdrawals) are posted immediately, if necessary. A key advantage to PDxMD is its differential diagnosis section, which organizes potential conditions by age and prevalence within a signs-and-symptoms matrix. A key disadvantage is that it does not provide direct references for many assertions, except in the treatment section.

✓ 5. UpToDate

UpToDate[13] is a collection of well-referenced reviews. Beginning as a specialty resource, it has grown considerably by identifying "the most eminent physicians" in multiple specialties. UpToDate is more valid than most textbooks because authors are asked to include up-to-date evidence where there is any process. Although UpToDate presents reviews in a dense text format, a key advantage to UpToDate is that it contains specialty-focused information and includes multiple specialties. A key disadvantage is the lack of an explicit, systematic method for identifying and analyzing the relevant literature.

An individual subscription to UpToDate costs $495 for the first year (plus shipping and handling) and includes three CD releases per year as well as online access. Renewal rate is $395/year. A PDA version (for Pocket PCs only) and a free online demo are also available.

✓ 6. Another good standard-of-care Web site (from England) is NICE—the National Institute for Health and Clinical Excellence.

✓ 7. Last but not least—"the lazy man's method" of reviewing up-to-date and rapidly changing guidelines. A subscription to *Journal Watch On Line* from the Massachusetts Medical Society. I find this no effort Web site the easiest and quickest (if not the most completely thorough) way to keep up with rapidly changing guidelines based on newer RCTs. It is well worth the annual subscription to its many resources and journals. See Appendix i for Journal Watch 2006 guidelines in various specialties. You must remember, however, to follow up these published changes with the references literature listed at the end of the article. Still, I must admit this is my favorite way to keep updated.

22.7 EBM Conclusions

Evidence-based clinical resources make searching for medical information on the Web much faster and easier.

Caveats:

The term "evidence-based" is used loosely by many Web sites. It can describe anything from information based on rigorous evaluation of scientific research to "We cite articles."

22.8 The Use of Clinical Practice Guidelines in Testimony

CPGs are systematically developed statements intended to assist practitioners and patients in making decisions about health care.

Clinical algorithms and CPGs are now ubiquitous in medicine; however, the utility and validity depend on

1. the quality of the evidence that shaped the recommendations,
2. their being kept current, and on their acceptance,
3. appropriate application by clinicians.

22.9 What Is Your Minimum Task in a Daubert and Cross-Examination Challenge to Your Testimony

First remember, PEAT = peer reviewed, error rate, acceptability to the profession, testability. You must be able to interpret the "evidence-based" results. Interpretation usually involves understanding common measures of risk (such as RR, OR, and absolute risk) and measures of uncertainty in the study's results (such as confidence interval and probability [p] value).

For example, if you know that the RR of an outcome is 1.5 with, say, a psychological treatment versus a medicine, then, in plain English, this means that the outcome is 50% more likely.

If the published confidence interval around this RR is 1.5–2.5, this means that the psychological treatment's effect is most likely to be between 1.5 and 2.5 times greater than the medicine's effect. Because this confidence interval does not include one (which would mean that the two treatments have equal effect on the outcome), the result is statistically significant (and you do not need a *p*-value in this instance).

22.10 Documenting the Scientific Studies Supporting Your Testimony on the Standard of Care in a Daubert and Cross-Examination Challenge

First, it is important to know from the point of view of a medical expert that the standard of care is not the word-for-word published guidelines even from a highly regarded and respected specialty or cross-specialty professional organization(s).

Indeed almost every published CPG states in the preamble, or extreme end of the publication that the CPG does not replace, but is a supplement to support the *clinical judgment* of the treating physician. CPGs usually state they are intended to be advisory in nature and are rarely phrased in mandatory language.

If you testify that a published CPG is indeed the recognized standard of care in your field then this scientific substitution of your expert opinion can be challenged by Daubert. This is a double-edged sword if you forget to use the magic words necessary in your particular state.

It is best that your opinion is supported by the peer-reviewed literature. The danger of not having such scientific support arises when an opposing expert testifies that you are wrong on the standard of care and does indeed back up his opinion with the scientific literature. You must admit these published CPGs into evidence when you state that it is accepted as reliable by the medical profession. You cannot just proclaim that the applicable standard of medical care lies in those guidelines and is the standard of care for that particular case. You must present evidence in your testimony that the CPGs at issue are indeed generally accepted by the medical community and represent the standard of care at the time of the alleged malpractice.

If not, the court will usually hold that the CPGs are advisory in nature, even if you assert its reliability by the fact that it was published by an appropriate group of experts in the peer-reviewed literature to establish appropriate guidelines for the standard of care (*Missan v. Dillon*, No. 121379/02. New York County Sup. Ct.N.Y.3/23/06).

You can be certain that your testimony will be challenged by the opposing medical expert via the opposing attorney if you do not have such scientific support. It is when you testify on the presence (or absence of a) CPG or RCT or any other scientific piece of information that your testimony also can be Daubert-challenged. If the other side suspects that you have no, insufficient, or more important biased RCT scientific support, they will make a motion that you be ordered by the court to submit Daubert-type evidence to support your opinion.

Daubert reliability standards apply only to scientific facts or "factoids" upon which the medical expert witness bases his opinion on the standard of medical care. And it is when medical expert testimony sets forth a standard of care that incorporates scientific fact(s) it is the scientific fact(s) itself, not the expert's opinion, that is subject to a Daubert challenge (see discussion of PEAT).

As an example, you will see in the chapter on the Daubert impact on medical expert testimony (Chapter 21) that if you state that the "earlier the better" (to diagnose and treat a medical condition) as a dictum of medicine without citing any scientific support you can be challenged by the Daubert court via the opposing medical expert witness (*McDowell v. Brown Case*, 392 F3d 1283, 6, 1294 n.9 [11th Cir. 2004]).

If, however, you state that the peer-reviewed medical literature supports your opinion that the "earlier the better" in the diagnosis and treatment of disease (e.g., cancer and infections), you can also be ordered to cite the specific literature which documents your scientific support. You must then present the Daubert evidence for any such deviation from the standard of care, which ignores or supports this dictum.

Some courts are very vigorous in Daubert challenging any medical expert who incorporates a scientific fact into a statement regarding the standard of care, especially if the expert attempts to introduce an unsupported "scientific fact" or "factoid" in his opinion on the standard of care (*Palandjian v. Foster*, No. 09562 [Mass. Sup. Jud. Ct. 2/21/06]).

The Importance of Legal Language and Legally "Magic" or Secret Words

Can a medical expert witness in a malpractice action testify that his opinion *was formed* or *documented* by the medical and surgical literature, and not violate his state's rule on hearsay evidence?

You must check with your retaining attorney about the law in your state.

Ohio and Florida are some of the states that do not recognize an exception to the hearsay rule for learned treatises even in medical malpractice cases.

Case 1

A surgeon in Ohio testified that he met the standard of care in operating on this particular patient and that his "opinion *was documented* in the medical and surgical literature."

The plaintiff objected, arguing that a reference to the medical literature by the defendant's medical expert violated the hearsay rule (*in establishing the expert's opinion*). The trial court overruled the objection and the jury later returned a verdict in favor of the defendant surgeon.

However, the Ohio State Intermediate Court reversed the trial court's ruling, holding that the trial court had erred in allowing the surgeon *to refer to medical literature (outside his opinion) during his expert testimony.*

Subsequently, the Ohio State Supreme Court reinstated the jury's verdict ruling that an expert in a medical malpractice action may make a generalized statement that his opinion *is supported* by the medical literature without violating the hearsay rule.

So, even though Ohio does not recognize exceptions to the hearsay rule, the Ohio Supreme Court determined that the statement made in this case did not constitute hearsay.

Their reasoning was that it was a reference to the general body of medical literature that *informed* the expert's opinion rather than a *specific article* that was being indirectly presented *as substantive evidence* through the expert as *a conduit* (*Beard v. Meridia Huron Hospital* No. 2004-0048, Ohio Supreme Court, September 28, 2005).

Case 2

In Florida, physicians who testify as medical experts (as in all states) will need to carefully watch their words during their medical expert testimony. The Florida Supreme Court ruled that medical experts cannot base their expert opinions on *consultations with colleagues or other experts when they testify about the standard of care in medical liability cases.* "Such second hand testimony would amount to hearsay," the high court said in an 11/02/06 ruling . . . "[This hearsay] could mislead a jury into believing that the witness' opinion has the approval of others in the field who themselves may not be qualified experts. . . ."

"Referring to consultations with other experts creates the danger of bolstering the credibility of the testifying expert's opinion without providing the opposing party the ability to effectively cross-examine the expert as to the basis for the opinion," wrote Justice Barbara J. Pariente for the majority, "because 'Florida laws require medical experts to base *their testimony on their own education, training and experience.*'" In either event, the magic or secret words may be different in your state so you must check with your retaining attorney about your state's peculiarities.

Make certain you may say "My opinion is based on my education, training, expertise and experience and is within a reasonable medical degree of probability. My opinion [thus formed], is also *supported* by the peer reviewed medical literature."

So in response to this question you should always rehearse your response with the retaining attorney who will advise you of the magic words of that particular state and will give you his preference of the verbs, adverbs, and nouns below based on that state's law.

If this reminds you of Groucho Marx's secret woids [sic] on the old 1950's show now in cable TV re-runs "You Bet Your Life" I don't blame you.

My take on what's correct in most states is—

Q: Dr. Hookman, did you rely on [hearsay-i.e.] *the opinions expressed by any another doctor, treatise, publication or experts in forming your expert opinion expressed here today?*

A: I did not rely on *the opinions expressed by any another doctor, treatise, publication or experts in forming my expert opinion expressed here today.* My medical expert opinion is based on my education, training, expertise and experience and is within a reasonable medical degree of probability. My opinion is *supported* by the peer reviewed medical literature [optional in whole or part-as per your retaining attorney who may choose one of these italic words appropriate to the individual state] At no time was my opinion *formed, originated, commenced, derived, emanated, emerged, conceived, formulated initiated or spawned* by the peer reviewed medical literature *nor* has my expert medical opinion been *formed, originated, commenced, derived, emanated, emerged, conceived, formulated, initiated or spawned* any other expert, treatise, publication or from anybody else's opinions.

22.11   What Is the Standard of Medical Care?

You should remember that in most American jurisdictions the standard of care, according to the definition of many states, is "what a *prudent* physician in the same specialty with similar training would do under similar circumstances." The traditional synonyms for "prudent" according to "Sissons" synonyms are alert, careful, cautious, heedful, judicious, reliable, sagacious, sensible, shrewd, solid, wary, well-advised, and wise.[14]

With these definitions of the term "prudent physician," one should assume that the prudent physician keeps up with the literature in his field at least on published guidelines. And it should also be assumed that the prudent physician keeps up with the literature in his field which contains randomized controlled trials (RCTs) on the diseases of the patient he medically treats. These RCTs give direction and are actually the building blocks of CPGs for the appropriate diagnosis and treatment of his patients.

22.12   Biased RCTs and Guidelines

The testifying physician must also understand the impact of how different guidelines, some of which are constructed by biased RCTs, can impact his testimony.

In our next and more advanced text for advanced medical expert witness testimony including advanced strategies in responding to very aggressive cross-examination from combative opposing attorneys, we will cover the subjects of biased RCTs and guidelines in more detail and from the point of view of more assertive defensive and offensive strategies in medical expert testimony. But for now and for introductory purposes, the basic understanding of EBM necessitates an understanding of elements of biased RCTs and guidelines.

1. The proportion of research funded by industry has more than doubled during the past decade and comprises almost half the funding for clinical research. An "extremely high" percentage of these published studies reported positive results favorable to the industry supporting the project.[15]
2. Sixty five percent of the experts used in clinical guideline panel members have conflicts of interest.
3. Also, 75% of all experts eligible to sit on those panels have links to the industry (drugs, med appliances, etc.).[16]
4. Unlike relationships that individual authors or physicians have with the pharmaceutical industry, financial conflicts of interest for authors of CPGs are of particular importance since they may not only influence the specific practice of these authors but also those of the physicians following the recommendations contained within the guidelines.
5. Based on these results and the considerable debate that has taken place about the relationships between clinical researchers and the pharmaceutical industry, the medical expert in his opinion of the standard of medical care must have these bottom line questions answered.
6. What potential financial conflicts of interest acted on the authors of CPGs?

Experts and guideline authors should be sensitive to the possibility that the influence of these relationships may subconsciously affect their judgments. The following *North England Journal of Medicine* articles in November, 2006 say it all when it comes to the "duplicity of drug companies and the physicians who allow themselves to be used by them in an adverse manner, contrary to the ethics of the medical profession."

"Many of the Drug companies have contracts not only with researchers, but also clinical physicians and even Medical schools and hospitals who many times think twice before offending their patrons."

This has ominous connotations for these physicians who also act as medical expert witnesses, either for the plaintiff, the defendant, or even if court appointed from the faculty of a medical school or hospital with such drug company contracts, especially if the issues in the case revolve around the treatment medications and if any medical expert quotes from these studies.

Carefully performed observational studies may provide the best information available about side effects, but propensity scores and other multivariable techniques applied to good epidemiologic research still cannot always control for all the inevitable selection bias, making the transparency of methods and raw data even more important than in randomized trials.

Rather than yielding "virtual randomized trials," the methods available for controlling confounding in observational research can sometimes look better than they work.

Thus, these studies can inform our understanding only after their methods have been scrutinized closely, fairly, and objectively—*but only if the data are available.*[17]

22.13 Potential Daubert and Cross-Examination Challenges to Your Testimony Especially for Academics, RCT, and CPG Authors

- Was there complete disclosure to the readers of CPGs of individual authors' financial relationships with the pharmaceutical industry?
- Questions will also be asked of medical experts testifying on the standard of care and randomized controlled trials (RCTs) whether conflicts of interest were present from financial ties with industry or to outside companies or self-owned businesses such as honorariums for speaking or writing about a company's product.
- Payment for participating in clinic-based research.
- Referrals to medical resources.
- Were any of the CPGs and relied-upon articles authored or coauthored by ghost-writers who worked for pharmaceutical companies or medical education companies hired by pharmaceutical companies?

22.14 You Must Also Know the Implications and Challenges to Multiple, Biased, and Even Small Nonbiased CPGs and RCTs

1. We discussed the exaggerated statistical bias found in small and underpowered studies in our discussion of EBM.
2. But we must also understand that the results of a randomized clinical trial (RCT) cannot always be extrapolated to the individual patient. As an example of such RCT's, physicians, who according to CPGs stopped using steroids in sepsis and ARDS for years until they realized the RCTs were partially wrong, and began using it again.
3. The potential for undetected adverse long-term consequences is a particular concern for patients with multiple conditions, who are exposed to ever-increasing numbers of medications and whose response to medications may be altered by the presence of coexisting conditions.
4. Drug recommendations for patients with multiple conditions are presented usually in the RCT report, but rarely rated in terms of priority. With notable exceptions such as end-of-life care for patients with congestive heart failure, the health preferences of patients and the outcomes related to their quality of life are seldom mentioned.

5. Comorbid conditions (i.e., those present that are in addition to the condition of interest) in RCTs fall into three categories[18]:
   a. Those clusters of comorbidities that are pathophysiologically related to the condition of interest and require congruent treatment plans. (These conditions might be called positive-effect modifiers of the disease-specific outcome of interest.)
   b. Comorbid conditions that have discordant (and potentially competing) treatment recommendations (negative-effect modifiers of the outcome of interest).
   c. And comorbid conditions that do not modify the outcome of interest at all.

Ultimately, the problem that multiple maladies in the same patient raises for clinicians is a problem of illness management. This is a problem of how to make decisions in the context of ill-defined problems and fragmentary evidence; a problem of how to design adaptive responses to unpredictable aspects of the illnesses; and a problem of how to organize multiple resources to achieve specific health goals. Information in this context, belong to the realms of experience, practice, intuition, and creativity. At the end of the line, the ultimate test is relevance (of specific treatment) to the patient's specific needs, goals, and wants. Clinicians must realize that textbooks and published RCT articles do not contain all the information they need. *What is needed most is good clinical judgement.*[19]

1. Also, there is much redundancy and significant variation in recommendations across multiple CPGs for single conditions, such as the 386 diabetes-related CPGs now listed as active at the National Guideline Clearinghouse. The Agency for Healthcare Research and Quality listed about 650 CPGs in 1999 and more than 1650 active CPGs in July 2005. Evidence-based recommendations from CPGs have often been proposed as measures of quality of care. Federal law will soon mandate use of such quality measures to assess clinical performance for accountability purposes and for pay-for-performance initiatives.
2. The most "onerous problems that physicians who use CPGs now face include too many evidence-based recommendations that are sometimes inappropriate in particular clinical situations, and recommendations not ranked in terms of their clinical value."[20]
3. Physicians must understand when applying results of clinical trials in practice, that all evidence-based recommendations are not of equal clinical benefit to a patient but that benefits documented in clinical trials are "average" benefits.
4. Even within the trials the degree of benefit received from an intervention depends on many patient-specific factors.
5. Practicing physicians care for patients with even greater patient-specific variation (because of restrictive eligibility criteria in most clinical trials), so it is not surprising to find wide variation in the benefits obtained from even nonbiased RCTs.
6. When treating elderly patients with multiple comorbid conditions, the complexity of care is compounded by the need to simultaneously address multiple clinical domains.[20]
7. In addition, Locke and Zinsmeister of the Mayo Clinic document in their succinct article that small negative clinical trials have several important "perils and pitfalls," since small trials "do not show that two treatments are different *but they do not prove that they are the same either.*" They prove little, *and therefore these studies cannot be relied upon by the treating or testifying physician.*[21]

22.15   Summary and Conclusions

In a Daubert and cross-examination challenge to your testimony, RCTs are the best methods. We have to determine what medical guidelines should be in certain groups of patients with certain diseases. RCTs, however, have not only advantages, but many disadvantages, some of which being learned by potential jurors from the newspapers and, therefore, will be the subject of the intensive questioning of opposing medical experts who are quoting RCTs to support their opinions in the standard of care. All medical expert witnesses should by alert to cross-examiner's questions regarding the above details of the RCTs or CPGs being quoted as supporting their version of the standard of medical care. In our next and more advanced text for advanced medical expert witness testimony including advanced strategies in responding to very aggressive cross-examination from combative opposing attorneys, we will cover the applications of themes in more detail and from the point of view of more assertive defensive and offensive strategies in medical expert testimony.

But for now and for introductory purposes, we will explore how and why themes are important to the medical expert witness.

Weaknesses of RCTs and CPGs that are outlined in this chapter are as follows:

- Bias.
- Other factors such as subgroup analyses.
- Meta-analyses, which may not cover specific subgroups of patients can also be a major problem.
- Whereas RCTs deal with clearly and narrowly defined alternatives, real world clinicians treating real world patients have to deal with a complex real world numerous, often ill-defined rival alternatives.
- Real world patients have comorbid conditions and may be in subgroups that either are not covered by the RCT or covered incorrectly by the RCT in terms of statistical significance.
- With the logarithmic growth of many medical guidelines listed in the National Guideline Clearinghouse, the treating and testifying physician must be certain that he is dealing with the appropriate guideline for the appropriate patient.
- Above all, as in treatment situations as well as a Daubert and cross-examination challenge to your testimony-risk/benefit analyses should be explained by the testifying physician, to ascertain the appropriateness of any medical guidelines applicable or not applicable to the particular patient with a particular disease = +/– comorbidities and other issues in the case.

References

1. DeKay ML, et al. Is the defensive use of diagnostic tests good for patients, or bad? *Medical Decision Making* 1998; 18: 19.
2. Jadad AR, et al. Cochrane collaboration: advances and challenges in improving evidence-based decision making. In: *Medical Decision Making* 1998; 18: 2.
3. Panzer RJ, et al. *Diagnostic Strategies for Common Medical Problems,* Second Edition. American College of Physicians. 1999.
4. Sackett DL, et al. *Clinical Epidemiology: A Basic Science for Clinical Medicine,* Second Edition. Ed. Little, Brown 1991.

5. Sox HC. The evaluation of diagnostic test: principles, problems, and new developments. *Annu. Rev. Med.* 1996; 47: 463.

6. Egger M, et al. Bias in meta-analysis detected by a simple, graphical test. *BMJ* 1997; 315: 629–634.

7. Ian MG, et al. Esomeprazole versus other proton pump inhibitors in erosive esophagitis: a meta-analysis of randomized clinical trials. *Clin. Gastroenterol. Hepatol.* 2006; 4(12): 1452–1458 (http://journals.elsevierhealth.com/periodicals/yjcgh/issues/contents?issue_key=TOC@@ JOURNALS@YJCGH@0004@0012) http://journals.elsevierhealth.com/periodicals/yjcgh/article/PIIS1542356506009414/fulltext#.

8. http://www.clinicalevidence.com/.

9. Jorgensen AW, et al. Cochrane reviews compared with industry supported meta-analyses and other meta-analyses of the same drugs: systematic review. *BMJ* 2006; 333: 782–785.

10. http://www.dynamicmedical.com/.

11. http://www.infopoems.com/.

12. http://www.pdxmd.com/.

13. http://www.uptodate.com/.

14. Sisson AF. *Sissons Synonyms*, Parker Publishing, New York, 1969.

15. Brown, et al. Association of Industry Sponsorship to Published Outcomes in Gastrointestinal Research. *Clin. Gastroenterol. Hepatol.* 2006; 4: 1445.

16. Taylor G, Giles A. *Nature*. 2005; 437: 1070–1071.

17. Avorn J. Dangerous deception—hiding the evidence of adverse drug effects. *N Engl. J. Med.* 2006; 355: (21): 2169–2171.

18. Boyd CM, Darer J, Boult C, Fried LP, Boult L, Wu AW. Clinical practice guidelines and quality of care for older patients with multiple comorbid diseases: implications for pay for performance. *JAMA* 2005; 294(6): 716–724.

19. Fortin M, Hudon C, Dubois MF, Almirall J, Lapointe L, Soubhi H. Comparative assessment of three different indices of multimorbidity for studies on health-related quality of life. *Health Qual Life Outcome* 2005; 3: 74.

20. O'Conner PJ. Adding value to evidence-based clinical guidelines. *JAMA* 2005; 294: 741–743.

21. Locke GR, Zinsmeister AR. *Am. J. Gastroenterol.* 2006; 101: 2185–2186.

For Further Reading

Berenson A. Trial lawyers are now focusing on lawsuits against drug makers. *New York Times* May 18, 2003.

Burton TM. Merck takes author's name off Vioxx study. *Wall Street J.* May 18, 2004.

Mangano DT, Tudor IC, Dietzel C. The risk associated with aprotinin in cardiac surgery. *N Engl. J. Med.* 2006; 354: 353–365.

Statement on Aprotinin. Rockville, MD: Food and Drug Administration, December 30, 1993.

Sturmer T, Schneeweiss S, Brookhart MA, Rothman KJ, Avorn J, Glynn RJ. Analytic strategies to adjust confounding using exposure propensity scores and disease risk scores. *Am. J. Epidemiol.* 2005; 161: 891–898.

Resource of Legal Theories, Themes, and Analogies for the Medical Expert Witness

23

"Take it away. This pudding has no theme" said Winston Churchill to the cook.

23.1 Introduction

In our next and more advanced text for advanced medical expert witness testimony including advanced strategies in responding to very aggressive cross-examination from hyper combative opposing attorneys, we will cover the applications of themes in more detail and from the point of view of more assertive, defensive, and offensive strategies in your medical expert testimony.

But for now and for introductory purposes, we will explore how and why themes are important to the medical expert witness. Can anybody forget the theme of the late Johnnie Cochran, in that notorious murder trial?

If the glove doesn't fit, you've got to acquit.

That, my dear reader, is a powerful and effective theme. That is what each lawyer strives to accomplish.

Those of us who were raised in the television age of 15–30-second commercials know that the most effective commercials are those with a theme you can remember and that will relate to the product being sold.

No one can forget the theme of Hebrew National, a picture of Uncle Sam with a somber voice—over declaiming, "We have to answer to a higher authority." In just that one theme, of eight words, the message came through about higher-quality frankfurters than the competitors who must satisfy the minimum criteria.

What this has got to do with medical malpractice litigation?

A lot!

As we know, Johnnie Cochran used this theme effectively.

Why?

It was the theory of Cochran's that the jurors would easily remember. Cochran's theme was that his client was being framed by the L.A. police by slipshod "evidence." The analogy he used to get the theme into the jurors' memory was "if the glove doesn't fit, you've got to acquit."

The analogy/theme very strikingly showed the limitations of that piece of the prosecution's evidence. And most important, it raised an element of doubt in the minds of the jurors—that element of doubt, which decreased the certainty of a guilty verdict—even if a juror was just looking for an excuse to vote not guilty—because if the prosecution was wrong on that one, what about everything else? We will learn later in the chapter how to formulate an effective theme and analogy.

Effective medical malpractice lawyers also try to achieve an effective theme.

And it is your job as the testifying physician to help construct a theme.

Why?

You have the medical knowledge of the standard of medical care. And you will hear that theme throughout the case. As a matter of fact, as a medical expert, it is your job to help the retaining attorney construct a theme but also to implement the theme in your testimony, because you will touch on this theme during your direct testimony and you will try to maintain this theme during your cross-examination. Let us see what this is all about.

A theme in a trial as in a story is the essence of the story. Concentrating on the theme is focusing on the story for the jury, because a story format is remembered more clearly and has a more vivid impact than list of facts, dates, and events.

The story can provide a framework with which jurors can hang all the facts. The juror as does anyone else needs a method by which he can organize myriads of information and to remember the relationships among all the facts.

The trial theme in our adversary litigation system is one side of the story.

Examples:

"Don't look a gift horse in the mouth": do not be critical of what you get for free
"That's water under the bridge": whatever happened is over now
"Behind the 8-ball": being in a bad position
"The apple doesn't fall far from the apple tree": like father like son
"A stitch in time saves nine": it is better to fix a problem now than later

("A stitch in time saves nine" is using sewing as an example. If there was a small hole in your jacket and you did not repair it, then it would gradually get bigger. If you had not left it, and repaired it straight away, then the hole would only take one stitch. If you leave it for a week, it would take nine stitches.)

Also a little preventive maintenance can eliminate the need for major repairs later. "An ounce of prevention is worth a pound of cure."

A theme encapsulates the theory of the case and should at its essence be a concise sentence—approximately 10 words or less—which can hang a "moral" or point to the story. This "moral" or "point" of the story preferably should be founded on a well-known maxim or proverb—the more widely known the better because it is easier to remember.

And as a testifying physician you should be able to encapsulate the medical story in a theme, by explaining it to your grandmother so she completely understands it. In fact you should be able to make her understand your expert opinion in a 30-second story/theme—and do not testify if you cannot.

It is this trial story of the medical facts—the merits of the case you found on reviewing all the records, the reason you took this case—that must be communicated by you, the physician, to the jury. This story line should be established in the jury's mind by the conclusion of your direct examination and ideally reconfirmed at the conclusion of your cross-examination.

What sources can you draw on for a theme? It is basically so simple many educated and sophisticated minds find it difficult to believe and to implement.

The chief sources are stories everyone knows simple stories from childhood, proverbs and maxims—or even a rhyme that is easy to remember (*see* Section 23.3).

Themes can be found in your favorite story plots.

It is said that there are only 13 basic plots in the history of the entire world's literature. This includes all the novels, stories, etc., and myths which have multiple permutations, combinations and variations of the same 13 plots—even seen in the Bible. Similarly, with themes, one can refer to the Bible (e.g., *David v. Goliath*) Aesop's fables, or proverbs, or maxims that we learned in school.

These short stories are part of our universal common culture and are present in almost every ethnic group and simply by looking at each cartoon you can supply the entire story.

Now just in case you think that relating complex facts to a simple story/theme or even a fairy tale is a simplistic mechanism designed for simple unsophisticated jurors, think again about how our Washington D.C. lawmakers organize multiple and complex facts.

The Wall Street Journal reported on 9/29/06 that the corporate spying scandal at Hewlett-Packard (H-P) was so "shocking and complicated, that Congressmen had trouble even describing it as they grilled the company executives on their spying on leakers of confidential information." Congressional grilling of the deposed H-P Chairman, H-P CEO, and the company's outside lawyer, were so complex that congressmen had to explain it to themselves in terms of a story upon which to hang all the facts together. Rep. Diana DeGette said, "It seemed like 'a made-for-TV movie.'"

All these members of Congress have attained a high level of education; college graduates as well as postgraduate degrees. Yet when it came to their thinking about the testimony they heard these were the themes they relied upon commonly held prototypes and examples. To Rep. Tammy Baldwin the story was "more of a third-rate detective novel," to Rep. Edward Markey he thought "H-P might be suffering from *Sergeant Schultz syndrome*," in reference to the "Hogans Heroes" character who frequently intones "I know noth-ing!" In addition, he said, "The evidence we've seen shows that this investigation is part 'Keystone Kops.'" And Rep. Cliff Stearns refused to restrict himself to just one comparison story or theme. "It's part 'Mission: Impossible,' and part 'All the President's Men' all tied together." Rep. John Dingell (D-Mich.) said "Calling the folks who did or allowed or participated in this Keystone Kops is an insult of the grossest sort to the original Keystone Kops."

Congressmen are not the only ones who think in prototypes. So do physicians. According to research in medical education, knowledge of a given category is structured in memory around *key cases or clear examples, referred to as the prototypes, which capture the core meaning of the category*. It is argued that the prototype view may help facilitate the understanding of the learning and problem-solving process in medicine. It is likely that experienced physicians use a hypothetico-deductive strategy only with difficult cases and that *clinical reasoning is more a matter of pattern recognition or direct automatic retrieval*. Clinicians approach problems flexibly; the method they select depends upon the perceived characteristics of the problem. "Easy cases" can be solved by *pattern recognition*: difficult cases need systematic generation and testing of hypotheses. Whether a diagnostic problem is easy or difficult is a function of the knowledge and experience of the clinician.[1]

Now you have got to remember that this story telling is the job of the attorney. It does not have you as its star actor of chief storyteller. That role belongs to the lawyers who advocate for their clients. Do not get taken in by the fantasy that all depends on you—and without you the show cannot go on. Although yours is a vital role it is one of a translator of the story or theme from Medicalese to the English language.

This show has several acts as in a Shakespeare play where you, the expert, come on for a bit role—important as it may be in the translating role. You as the medical expert should take Shakespeare's advice to the bit players—"do not saw the air too much with your hand, thus, but use all gently; for in the very torrent, tempest, and, as I may say, the whirlwind of passion, you must acquire and beget a temperance that may give it smoothness."

> Suit the action to the word, the word to the action; with this special observance, that you o'erstep not the modesty of nature.
>
> **—Shakespeare**
> *Hamlet III.ii*

The play's director makes sure that even the bit players are an integral part of the theme of the story.

Every trial story has a beginning with sequencing of the underlying issues. Every story has appropriate analogies/maxims/proverbs, which comport with the education and life experiences of the average person—especially a juror.

It is the attorney who is the main actor that determines the theme of the story; and as the testifying physician you should help him develop this theme to fit the medical facts.

One of the major attributes of a good medical expert is to be able to abstract the medical issues and his opinion into such a trial theme. It should match that of the retaining attorney's theme because it is a theme that is returned to by the attorney and yourself in the beginning and end of summations to the jury and also, it is a theme that recurs in your testimony.

Present your theme to the retaining attorney, and if he agrees, that is great. But if he does not agree, I would want to hear what his theme is. If it was not compatible with the facts or your ethics, I would not agree to continue. It is as simple as that. Only if there is mutual agreement, then I would continue in that case as a testifying expert. It is crucially important to be in mutual agreement because of the relevance and importance of the theme to all your testimony. If you cannot agree with a common theme and get him to understand a different theme to fit the medical facts in the case, then it is best not to continue. The reason is that the theme of the trial story is returned to, time and time again, during the course of the trial. It should recur with your direct testimony and also your cross-examination. It is augmented by exhibits and visuals with the use of simple diagrams, preferably in color.

As the bit actor testifying on this theme—and actually the translator from Shakespearean English to modern English—you should not come on as a know-it-all, either in your verbal or body language. You should never appear to be the slightest bit arrogant. You should act as a teacher that you are to your patients, as a trustworthy, reliable family doctor. You should be a humble actor and as Hamlet advised his players do not wave your hands or employ too many body movements to tell your story, which should be told in an appropriate manner.

The opposing attorney as well as your own will have a major theme of attack that will recur again and again and finally in both summations.

The trial theme is a powerful instrument of delivery. Do not ever sell it short. As an example of the power of a good theme ask yourself how many of the hundreds if not thousands of advertising themes pushed at you from all media do you really remember? Probably you forget 99.9% of it—even if you do not turn your mind off to screen out all the advertising directed at you.

23.2   What Is an Analogy?

Examples:

Agency—who is ultimately responsible?
   Walmart truck passes a red light
   Kills someone
   Walmart says only the driver is at fault—not the company.
For respondent superior themes
   The surgeon says the nurse made the operation mistake; therefore he is not at fault for
      leaving the clamp in the abdomen.
   Who is the *captain of the ship*?

Early action examples:

1. Train coming down the track will smash a person on the tracks; get the person off the tracks; or stop the train. Do not wait.
2. That hoped for light in the tunnel is a freight train speeding at us. Get off the tracks now.
3. Time bomb waiting to go off; do something about it.

These analogies can easily be adapted to medical issues in obvious ways.

23.3   What Is a Jingle?

A jingle is a memorable *slogan* or theme that contains the essence of the message in a very easy to remember tune.

While a jingle is set to a catchy tune, the tune and the words are constructed to stay in one's *memory* (colloquially, "ringing a bell"). Good jingles or themes stay in memory even without the melody. Advertisers know that it is the nature of people to remember jingles *decades* later, even after the advertised *brand* has ceased to exist.

23.4   What Is a Theme?—Examples

Here are the ones I remember well. Note that the best themes are ones that revolve around some type of action you want the listener to take. Who, as mentioned in the Introduction, does not remember the late Johnnie Cochran's trial theme—"if the glove doesn't fit you've got to acquit." This pointed out the feckless gathering and presentation of evidence in the trial by the prosecution.

Other memorable themes/slogans I am sure you remember depending on your age. Many themes will lose impact and gradually disappear according to the age of the target audience. But as time goes by they will be replaced by other themes. So the age of the jurors is an important consideration in the selection of a theme based on TV programs and movies. I will bet you remember these jingles/slogans/themes:

- Burger King—"Have it your way."
- Campbell's Soup—"M'm! M'm! Good!"
- Folgers—"The best part of waking up is Folgers in your cup!"
- Rice Krispies—"Snap! Crackle! Pop!"
- The Pepsi generation.
- "Got milk?"
- This Bud's for you.
- Double your pleasure; double your fun with Doublemint gum.
- Nobody doesn't like Sara Lee.
- I can't believe I ate the whole thing. Plop plop, fizz fizz: Alka Seltzer.
- Mama mia, thatsa spicy meatball! Alka Seltzer.
- So you should never ever put ban-anas in the refrig-er-ator. NO, NO, NO, NO!
- Chiquita Banana.
- Pardon me; do you have any Grey Poupon?
- When it rains, it pours. Morton's salt.
- Rice-a-Roni, the San Francisco treat.
- See the USA in your Chevrolet.
- A little dab'll do ya. Bryll Creme.
- Winston tastes good like a cigarette should.

As examples of trial themes let us take just a few of my cases in which you can review my testimony transcripts (*see* chapter on my testimony—along with my comments on what I did wrong and sometimes did correctly).

The themes of these cases can be better transmitted to a jury than a mass of disconnected facts. The jury as well as everyone else needs a theme upon which to hang all the assorted facts and to better understand them. The themes I used were classic themes and can be seen in italic.

1. *Quis custodiet ipsos custodes* (who will guard the guardians themselves?).
   This was the theme for a Southern jailhouse guard who permitted the prisoner to die before getting him hospital help for his rapid UGI bleeding while in Diabetic keto-acidosis.
2. *Venienti occurrite morbo* (run to meet disease as it comes, i.e., do not wait for the sickness to develop, nip it in the bud).

And especially

3. *Nulla umquam de morte hominis cunctatio longa est* (when a human life is at stake, no delay is ever excessive).

And certainly

4. *A decision delayed until it is too late is not a decision, it is an evasion.* Also appropriate to that kind of situation.
5. *Wherever a doctor cannot do good, he must be kept from doing harm* (*Primum Non Nocerum—Hippocrates*).

    This latter theme can be used in many instances of overt medical negligence or an iatrogenic event in which a doctor's action or inaction cause a catastrophy.
6. Caveat emptor—let the buyer beware is also a recurring theme especially in elective cosmetic surgery cases.

Now let us evaluate another theme for another of my cases—one of the very few more than 10 words.

> For the want of a nail, the shoe was lost. For the want of a shoe, the horse was lost. For the want of a horse, the rider was lost. For the want of a rider, the battle was lost. For the want of a battle, the kingdom was lost, and all for the want of a horse, the horseshoe, nail.
>
> **—Benjamin Franklin**

Ben Franklin's homily has also been engrained into our culture. It is a simple story to understand. Yet it makes its important point in the case involving the doctor whose clerk forgot to mail a prepared reminder letter and thus failed to follow through on his colonoscopy for a patient who ultimately died of metastatic colon cancer.

> He who will not be ruled by the rudder, must be ruled by the rock.

This can be used in cases of outright deviations of the published guidelines and standards of care.

> "The horror of that moment," the King went on, "I shall never, never forget!" "You will though," the Queen if you don't make a memoranda.
>
> **—Lewis Carrol**

In situations where medical note does not conform to the actual event and has not been recorded in the doctor's operative (op) report, or its corollary:

> It's no use trying to hide what can't be hidden.

These following themes can be universally understood by juries everywhere when it fits into the case:

> Wherever the art of medicine is loved, there is also love of humanity (Hippocrates).
> An ounce of prevention is worth a pound of cure.
> A stitch in time saves nine.

Prior to writing this chapter, I discussed this chapter with my content editor attorney Tim Junkin. I told him my doubts about this chapter because it would be seen as so elementary that an attorney would develop the trial's theme even before he sent the case to a potential testifying physician. And certainly I thought, we need go no further in this chapter as that would be gilding the lily.

But he emphasized the necessity of this chapter to educate all testifying physicians. He even encouraged me to expand it into a resource and repository for trial themes so that in his opinion a potential testifying physician for him or any other attorney would add extra value to the case by checking into a "menu of potential themes" without having to reinvent the wheel.

So here is my continued research into the sources of potential themes to be used a resource for you as you would do with ethnic restaurant menus to take from columns A, B, etc.

23.5 Ethnic Restaurant Menus of a Variety of Potential Themes; Pick from Columns A–H

23.5.1 Column A: Aesop's Fables: The Goose That Laid the Golden Egg

The classic themes in Aesop's fables occur in the myths and stories of all of the world's cultures. For example, these are the following stories:

The Tortoise and the Hare
The Fox and the Grapes
The Boy Who Cried Wolf
The Two Pots, the Wolf, and the Lamb (the innocent are always the injured ones)
The Cat and the Birds (the villain in disguise will not deceive the wise)
The Spendthrift and the Swallow (one swallow does not make a whole summer)
The Moon and Her Mother (changeable people are not easily satisfied)
The Lion and the Mouse (no good deed goes unrewarded and the corollary, no bad deed goes unpunished)
The Flies and the Honey Pot (the greedy never know when they have had enough)
The North Wind and the Sun (persuasion is better than force)
The Hares and the Frogs (there are always others worse off than you are)
The Fox and the Goat (look before you leap)
The Fisherman and the Little Fish (a bird in the hand is worth two in the bush)
The Boasting Traveler (deeds not words count)
The Crab and His Mother (example is better than precept)
The Monkey as King (there is more than one way to set a trap)
The Old Lion (your own eyes may be your best witness)
The Boy Bathing (give assistance not advice in a crisis)
The Quack Frog (physician, heal thyself)
The Swallow and Fox (do not get too big for your breeches)
The Mouse, the Frog, and the Hawk (start wrong, end wrong)
The Boy and the Nettles (hold strongly to what you want)
The Jackdaw and the Pigeons (to thine own self be true)
The Oxen and the Axle (they who complain most, suffer least)
The Boy and the Filberts (do not attempt too much all at once)

The Fox without a Tail (beware of those who wish to bring you down, not up)
The Traveler and His Dog (sometimes the slow ones blame the active for the delay)
The Shipwrecked Man and the Sea (the blame does not always lie with the obvious)
The Wild Boar and the Fox (prepare your defenses before the enemy appears)
Mercury and the Sculptor (nobody can judge his own worth)
The Fawn and His Mother (a coward cannot be taught courage)
The Stag at the Pool (what is worth most is often valued least)
The Dog and the Shadow (if you grasp the shadow, you may lose the substance)

23.5.2 Column B: Mottos/Morals from Aesop's Fables[2]

The farthest you go is with using your own gifts
Misfortunes we bring on ourselves are doubly bitter
Kindness is thrown away upon the evil
There can be great danger in falling in a rut
One man's pat is another man's swat
Don't play both sides against the middle
He who gives in to others' wants will have no principle of his own
Even a brute may sometimes listen to reason
Gratitude sometimes brings its own punishment
Advice from the greedy is best ignored
Give a wide berth to those who can do damage at a distance
Thoughtless friends can be as bad as enemies
Goodness is the greatest strength of all
A willful beast must go his own way
Be content with what you are sure of
Traitors richly deserve their fate
Repeat the wisdom of those who came before you
When the rich surrender the rights of the poor, they endanger their own privileges
You can look at the stars, but watch where you are going
Advantages that are dearly bought are double blessings
You may punish a thief, but his habits remain
Think twice before you act
Be happy with what you have
Flattery should get you nowhere
To each his own
It's no use trying to hide what can't be hidden
The other fellow's plate always looks fuller than your own
It's easy to cry coward when it's not you in danger
Some people find fault even with things that benefit them
Misfortune awaits those who love unwisely
When you hit back, make sure you have the right man
There is no virtue in giving to others what is useless to oneself
The whole world doesn't dance to your own tune
The good you do should always outweigh the bad
Live and let live
Better a certain enemy than a doubtful friend

Of what use is it to pretend there is choice when there is none
Clothes do not make the man
Appearances are often very deceiving
It's easy to fight someone who can't fight back
The flower in the vase smiles, but it can no longer laugh
Those who pretend to be something they are not only make themselves ridiculous
Unused riches create no good
Vengeance may be worse than the deed that provoked it
One good turn deserves another
It's better by far to bend than to break
Evil tendencies are early shown
We may often be more important in our own eyes than in the eyes of others
Better poverty without a care than wealth with its many obligations
Nature never disobeys her own laws
Necessity is the mother of invention
One man's meat is another's poison
Looks aren't everything
The enemy you know is better than the enemy you don't
Those who live by thievery can't complain of robbers
Position is everything in life
Be most kind to those who are most giving
There are two sides to every question
Friendship is a hedge against adversity
For everything, there is a season and a purpose
That governs best which governs least
In union there is strength
Our own vanity is the worst flatterers
People who fight give opportunities to their enemies
It's easier to make a suggestion than carry it out
There are two sides to every truth
See how the wind blows before making a commitment
Kindness is better given to the living than to the dead
The advice of an enemy is not to be trusted
Once bitten, twice shy
Fine feathers do not make fine birds
Much wants more and loses all

23.5.3   Column C: Maxims/Proverbs

A proverb is the wit of one and the wisdom of many

—Anon

1. One mother can take care of 10 children, but 10 children cannot take care of one mother.
2. You can believe some people even when they swear they are lying. Or no one can lie like a man with a secondhand car to sell.

3. Lots of folks confuse bad management with bad luck.
4. It is easier to know mankind in general than to understand one man in particular.
5. Man is the only animal that blushes. Or needs to (Mark Twain).
6. He that marries for wealth sells his liberty.
7. When you hear hoof beats, think of horses before zebras. (Medical Maxim quoted by Harley S. Smyth, Rhodes Scholar at Oxford; University, Professor in the Department of Surgery, University of Toronto, originally from William Dock MD.)
8. He who tastes every man's broth sometimes burns his mouth.
9. Most things get better by themselves. Most things, in fact, are better by morning (Lewis Thomas).
10. Wherever the art of medicine is loved, there is also love of humanity (Hippocrates).
11. An ounce of prevention is worth a pound of cure.
12. It is part of the cure to wish to be cured.
13. Writing things down is the best secret of a good memory.
14. The right honorable gentleman is indebted to his memory for his jests and to his imagination for his facts (R.B. Sheridan).
15. It is not so astonishing, the number of things that I can remember, as the number of things I can remember that are not so (Mark Twain).
16. "The horror of that moment," the King went on, "I shall never, never forget!" "You will though," the Queen said, "if you don't make a memorandum of it" (Lewis Carroll).
17. That which is bitter to endure may be sweet to remember.
18. The true art of memory is the art of attention.
19. The mind is like the stomach. It is not how much you put into it that counts, but how much it digests.
20. Another's misfortune does not cure my pain (Portuguese proverb).
21. Any man may make a mistake; none better fool will persist in it.
22. To err is human, but when the eraser wears out ahead of the pencil, you are over-doing it.
23. Great services are not canceled out by one act or by one single error.
24. Things could be worse. Suppose your errors were counted and published everyday like those of a baseball player.
25. Even brute beasts and wandering birds do not fall into the same traps or net twice (Saint Ambrose).
26. Money talks, but it does not always talk sense.
27. When money speaks, the truth is silent (Russian proverb).
28. Money is a good servant, but a bad master.
29. The love of money and the love of learning seldom meet.
30. The price we pay for money is paid in liberty.
31. God could not be everywhere and, therefore, he made mothers (Hebrew proverb).
32. If you do not scale the mountain, you cannot view the plain.
33. He who is in the mud likes to pull another into it.
34. A good name is rather to be chosen than great riches (Proverbs 22:1).
35. He who has a bad name is half hanged (Italian proverb).
36. The beginning of wisdom is to call things by their right names (Chinese proverb).
37. When elephants fight, it is the grass that suffers.

38. When I am getting ready to reason with a man, I spend one-third of my time thinking about myself and what I am going to say and two-thirds thinking about him and what he is going to say (Abraham Lincoln).
39. It is difference of opinion that makes horse races (Mark Twain).
40. He thinks by infection, catching an opinion like a cold (John Ruskin).
41. He that never changes his opinions, never corrects his mistakes, and will never be wiser on the morrow than he is today (Tryon Edwards).
42. Do not be afraid of opposition. Remember, a kite rises against and not with the wind.
43. He is a good orator who convinces himself.
44. If you give me six lines written by the hand of the most honest of men, I will find something in them, which will hang him (A. Richelieu).
45. People are better persuaded by the reasons, which they have themselves discovered than by those which have come into the mind of others (Blaise Pascal).

23.5.4   Column D: Proverbs/Famous Quotations

1. There is only one thing that a philosopher can be relied on to do and that is to contradict other philosophers (William James).
2. He is like a blind man in a dark room looking for a black hat, which is not there.
3. You can fool too many of the people too much of the time (James Thurber).
4. MacDonald's Law: Never write a letter if you can help it, and never destroy one (John A. MacDonald).
5. A proverb is the wit of one and the wisdom of many.
6. A proverb is short sentence based on long experience.
7. Few sinners are saved after the first 20 minutes of a sermon (Mark Twain).
8. Forewarned, forearmed; to be prepared is half the victory (Spanish proverb).
9. An ounce of prevention is worth a pound of cure.
10. As proud as a pig with two tails.
11. The difficulty is to know conscience from self-interest (W.D. Howells).
12. In the final analysis, your worth to your company comes not only in solving problems, but in anticipating them (H.H. Ross).
13. Comrades, you have lost a good captain to make him an ill general (Michel de Montaigne) (*see also* Peter's principle).
14. The most dangerous of all falsehoods is a slightly distorted truth.
15. The longer I live, the more convincing proofs I see of this truth, that God governs in the affairs of men; and if a sparrow cannot fall to the ground without his notice, is it probable that an empire can rise without His aid? (Benjamin Franklin).
16. He that goes barefoot must not plant thorns.
17. Conceal a flaw and the world will imagine the worst.
18. A fool may ask more questions in an hour than a wise man can answer in seven years.
19. It is not every question that deserves an answer.
20. Never answer a question until it is asked.
21. The uncreative mind can spot long answers, but it takes a creative mind to spot wrong questions.
22. I quote others only the better to express myself; copying from just one or two authors is plagiarism, however, copying from a hundred authors is research (Michel de Montaigne).

23. Employ your time in improving yourself by other men's writings so that you shall come easily by what others have labored hard for (Socrates).
24. There is only one step from the sublime to the ridiculous (Napoleon Bonaparte).
25. Enough research will tend to support your theory.
26. Scratch where it itches.
27. To keep your secret is wisdom, but to expect others to keep it is a folly (Samuel Johnson).
28. He who will not be ruled by the rudder, must be ruled by the rock.
29. One may smile, and smile, and be a villain (William Shakespeare).
30. A soft answer turneth away wrath (Proverbs 15:1).
31. Beware of still water, a still dog, and a still enemy.
32. You cannot make a satin purse of a sow's ear.
33. Feed a pig and you will have hog.
34. A teacher affects eternity. He can never tell where his influence stops (Henry Adams).
35. True teaching is not that which gives knowledge, but that which stimulates students to gain it.
36. Keep thy tongue from evil and thy lips from speaking guile (Psalm 34:13).
37. A slip of the foot may soon be recovered, but that of the tongue, perhaps never.
38. For the want of a nail, the shoe was lost. For the want of a shoe, the horse was lost. For the want of a horse, the rider was lost. For the want of a rider, the battle was lost. For the want of a battle, the kingdom was lost, and all for the want of a horse, the shoe, nail (Benjamin Franklin).
39. A striking expression with the aid of a small amount of truth can surprise us into accepting falsehood (Marquis de Vauvenargues).
40. Half a truth is often a great lie.
41. Truth is the anvil, which has worn out many a hammer.
42. Truth needs no memory.
43. When in doubt, tell the truth (Mark Twain).
44. The truth is always the strongest argument.
45. Men occasionally stumble over the truth, but most of them pick themselves up and hurry off as if nothing happened (Winston Churchill).
46. The better part of valor is discretion.
47. The farther back which you can look, the farther forward you are likely to see (Winston Churchill).
48. Words, once spoken, can be never be recalled (Wentworth Dillon).
49. Let thy words be few (Ecclesiastes 5:2).
50. Sharp words make more wounds than surgeons can heal.
51. Always keep your words soft and sweet—one day you may have to eat them.
52. It is a sobering thought that each of us gives his hearers and his readers a chance to look into the inner working of his mind when he speaks or writes (J.M. Barker).
53. A fault confessed is half redressed.
54. A fault once denied is twice committed.
55. The first faults are theirs that commit them; the second theirs that permit them.
56. Those who live in glass houses should not throw stones.
57. Make three correct guesses consecutively and you will establish your reputation as an expert (Laurence Peter) (also see Peter's principle above).

58. The fox should not be on the jury at a goose's trial.
59. The best executive is the one who has sense enough to pick good men to do what he wants done and self-restraint enough to keep from meddling with them while they do it (Theodore Roosevelt).
60. You can discover what your enemy fears most by observing the means he uses to frighten you (Eric Hoffer).
61. We never forgive those who make us blush.
62. The purpose of education is to teach one's self how to study on their own.
63. One doctor makes work for another.
64. Wherever a doctor cannot do good, he must be kept from doing harm (Hippocrates).
65. A man who is his own doctor has a fool for his patient.
66. Dilemma is being between the devil and the deep blue sea, or between the hammer and the anvil.
67. A decision delayed until it is too late is not a decision, it is an evasion.
68. Some disguised untruths counterfeit truths so perfectly that not to be taken in by them would be an error of judgment (La Rochefoucauld).
69. It is always darkest just before the dawn.
70. Boast not thyself of tomorrow; for thou knowest not what a day may bring forth (Proverbs 27:1).
71. A critic [expert?] is a legless man who teaches running.
72. Let us believe neither half of the good people tell us of ourselves nor half of the evil they say of others.
73. Birds of a feather flock together.
74. He is known by his companions.
75. When a dove begins to associate with crows, its feathers remain white, but its heart grows black.
76. Tell me thy company and I will tell thee what thou art (Miguel de Cervantes).
77. He that walketh with wise men shall be wise (Proverbs 13:20).
78. He that lies down with dogs will rise up with fleas.
79. Everyone is a moon and has a dark side, which he never shows to anybody (Mark Twain).
80. Learn to say no. It will be of more use to you than to be able to read Latin.
81. Life is like riding a bicycle, either you keep moving or you fall down.
82. People are strange. They want the front of the bus, the back of the church and the center of attention.
83. Honesty stands at the gate and knocks and bribery enters in.
84. Every horse thinks his own pack heaviest.
85. None knows the weight of another's burden.
86. Draw not your bow until your arrow is fixed.
87. The borrower is server to the lender (Proverbs 22:7).
88. I read part of it all the way through (Sam Goldwyn).
89. Some books are to be tasted, others to be swallowed, and some few to be chewed and digested.
90. A good title is the title of a successful book.
91. Judge not a book by its cover.
92. A room without books is a body without a soul.
93. None so blind as those who will not see.

94. When the blind man carries the banner, woe to those who follow.
95. In the country of the blind, the one-eyed man is king.
96. He that blows on the fire will get sparks in his eyes.
97. Empty barrels make the most noise.
98. The pot called the kettle black.
99. He must be pure who would blame another.
100. The early bird catches the worm.
101. A bird in the hand is worth two in the bush.
102. A bird is known by its feathers.
103. Better to wear out than to rest out.
104. Beware of no man more than of thyself.
105. What a man desires, he easily believes.
106. Seeing is believing.
107. To accept the benefit is to sell one's freedom.
108. Good to begin well, better to end well.
109. He who begins many things, finishes but few.
110. The beginning is half of a whole.
111. Before beginning, prepare carefully.
112. I start where the last man left off.
113. Begin it and the work will be completed.
114. Once began, the task is easy.
115. Great is the art of beginning, but greater is the art of ending.
116. The beginning is the most important part of the work (Plato).
117. Bad luck is bending over to pick up a four-leaf clover and being infected by poison ivy.
118. If you wish to know what a man is, place him in authority.
119. He who covets is always poor.
120. I do not mind being average because it means I am as close to the top as I am to the bottom.
121. As long as a man imagines that he cannot do a certain thing, it is impossible for him to do it (Spinoza).
122. Every ass loves to hear himself bray.
123. Do not ask a blind man which is the right way.
124. A long dispute means both parties are wrong (Voltaire).
125. I learned long ago never to wrestle with a pig, you get dirty and besides, the pig likes it (for those medical experts who engage in a battle of wits with the cross-examiner).
126. We never know the worth of water until the well is dry.
127. I now perceive one immense omission in my psychology—the deepest principle of human nature is the craving to be appreciated.
128. When arguing with a stupid person, be sure he is not doing the same thing.
129. Appearances can be very deceitful.
130. Things are not always what they seem.
131. All that glitters is not gold.
132. The proof of the pudding is in the eating, not in its looks.
133. Appeasers believe that if you keep on throwing steaks to a tiger, the tiger will turn vegetarian.
134. Solomon made the book of Proverbs, but the book of Proverbs never made a Solomon.

135. Neurotic means he is not as sensible as I am and psychotic means he is even worse than my brother-in-law.
136. Anger punishes itself.
137. Never answer a letter when you are angry.
138. He that is slow to anger is better than the mighty and he that ruleth his spirit than he that taketh a city (Proverbs 16:32).
139. An angry man stirreth up strife (Proverbs 29:2).
140. Show me an amateur and I will show a person who is always willing to give you the benefit of his inexperience.
141. Most people would succeed in small things if they were not troubled with great ambitions.
142. I have never, in my life, learned anything from any man who agreed with me.
143. Some men have alarm clocks, I have my wife's elbow.
144. Not only strike while the iron is hot, but make it hot by striking (Oliver Cromwell).
145. Nobody loves life like him who is growing old (Sophocles).
146. Few people know how to be old (La Rouchefoucauld).
147. He who builds to every man's advice will have a crooked house.
148. Advice when most needed is least heeded.
149. Advice is like snow, the softer it falls, the longer it dwells upon and the deeper it sinks into the mind (Coleridge).
150. The harder you work, the luckier you get (Gary Player).
151. Behold the turtle. He makes progress only when he sticks his neck out (James Conant).
152. The absent are always wrong.
153. Everyone excels in something in which another fails.
154. Out of sight, out of mind (Homer).

23.5.5 Column E: Latin Quotations Found in Operas and Classic Literature

23.5.5.1 Roman Menu

Caveat emptor—let the buyer beware
Ante tubam trepidat (before the trumpet for battle sounds, he trembles with fear).[3]
Argumentum ad hominem. (This is an argument directed towards the man addressed, i.e., an argument founded on the principles, practices or character of an opponent.)
Cavendo tutus (safe by being on one's guard).
Diem perdidi (I have lost a day).
Ex cathedra (with authority).
Fere libenter homines id quod volunt credunt (people are generally glad to believe what they want to be true is so).
Fidem qui perdit, nihil pote ultra perdere (the man who loses his honor can lose nothing further).
Impari marte (with Mars, the god of war, unequal, i.e., with unequal military strength).
In actu (in practice as opposed to theory or potentiality).
In cauda venenum (the poison is in the tail, i.e., one should look beyond first impressions and guard against the lurking peril which could await us or bland smiles may be followed by vicious onslaught).
Ipsa quidem virtus pretium (literally means virtue itself pays the price to itself, i.e., virtue is its own reward).

Locus desperatus (means a hopeless passage, i.e., a passage in a text transmitted via manuscript whose meaning is so corrupt as to be almost beyond conjecture).

Magna est veritas et praevalet (literally means truth is great and it prevails).

Memoriter (i.e., memorized by heart).

Mundus vult decipi, ergo decipiatur (the world wants to be deceived, so let it be deceived).

Nescit vox missa reverti (a word once published cannot be recalled).

Ne sutor ultra crepidam (let not the shoemaker go beyond his last; a wooden or metal model which a shoemaker fashions shoes or boots) (from Pliny's Natural History xxxv.85. The elder Pliny tells how a cobbler criticized the painting of a sandal and the work of Apelles, the most famous of Greek painters. When he went on to criticize the subject's legs, Apelles burst out with this response which is the basis of the English proverb, "Let the cobbler stick to his last.")

Nihil ad rem (nothing to do with the point in hand).

Non sequitur (does not follow, i.e., an inference or a conclusion which does not follow from the premises).

Nosce te ipsum (know thyself).

Nulla umquam de morte hominis cunctatio longa est (when a human life is at stake, no delay is ever excessive).

Nunquam non paratus (never unprepared).

Obiter dictum (literally, a thing said by the way an incidental statement or remark).

Obscurum per obscurius (explaining the unclear by means of the more unclear; an unclear argument or proposition expressed in terms of one that is even less clear).

Omnia mutantur nos et nutanur in illis (all things are in the process of change, we also are in the process of change among them).

Onus probandi (the burden of proof, the obligation under which one who makes an assertion, allegation or charge is of proving the same).

Quae nocent, docent (things that injure, teach).

Quaere verum (seek the truth).

Quantum meruit (as much as he has deserved, i.e., a reasonable amount of money to be paid for services rendered or work done when the amount is due is not determined by any provision of a legally enforceable contract).

Qui docet discit (he who teaches, learns).

Quis custodiet ipsos custodes (who will guard the guardians themselves?).

Quot hominess, tot sententiae (there are as many opinions as men).

Reductio ad absurdum (reduction of a debate, discussion, argument to the absurd).

Res ipsa loquitur (the thing itself speaks, i.e., the matter speaks for itself).

Salva veritate (saving the truth, i.e., without infringement of truth).

Satis eloquentiae, sapientiae parum (plenty of eloquence, but too little wisdom).

Sed haec hactentenus (but enough of this—now we can move on to something else).

Suggestio falsi (suggestion of what is false, i.e., a misrepresentation of the truth whereby something incorrect is implied to be true, an indirect lie).

Sutor ne supra crepidam iudicaret (let not the cobbler criticize a work of art about the sandal).

Ubi mel ibi apes (where there is honey, there are bees).

Venienti occurrite morbo (run to meet disease as it comes, i.e., do not wait for the sickness to develop, nip it in the bud).

Verbum sat sapienti (a word is sufficient to a wise person, i.e., an expression used in place of making a full statement or explanation implying that an intelligent person may easily understand what is left unsaid or understand the reasons for reticence).

Veritas nunquam perit (the truth never dies).

Post hoc ergo propter hoc is a Latin expression, which when literally translated means "after this, therefore because of this."

Because events are *sequentially* related in time, they are not necessarily *causally* related. The rooster crows in the morning, the sun rises in the morning. It does not necessarily mean that the rooster causes the sun to rise. Physicians have a hard time with this when they are asked to give an expert opinion on "causation, or proximate cause."

23.5.6 Column E: Proverbs/Maxims from Ancient Rome and Greece

23.5.6.1 *Greek Menu*

Better late than never.
A bird in the hand is worth two in the bush.
Between the devil and the deep blue sea.
Birds of a feather flock together.
Blood from a stone.
To carry coals to [the ancient equivalent of Newcastle].
Every man to his taste.
Example is better than precept.
Familiarity breeds contempt.
Forewarned is forearmed.
The game is not worth the candle.
I'll scratch your back if you scratch mine.
Kill two birds with one stone.
The leopard does not change its spots.
Let sleeping dogs lie.
Moderation in all things [Aristotle].
Necessity is the mother of invention.
Out of sight, out of mind.
Out of the frying pan, into the fire.
Pearls before swine.
Still waters run deep.
Strike while the iron is hot.
Talk of the devil.
Many a slip betwixed a cup and a lip.
No accounting for taste.
No smoke without a fire.
Virtue is its own reward.
You have hit the nail on the head.
Strike while the iron is hot (occasionem cognosce).
Where there's life, there's hope (Dum spiro, spero).
One more such victory and we are lost (Plutarch on defeating the Romans at Asculum, 279 BC).

23.5.7 Column F: More Modern Quotations That Can Be Used as Themes

My definition of an expert in any field is a person who knows enough about what really is going on to be scared.

—**PJ Plauger**
Computer Language, March 1983

As Samuel Goldwyn once said,

A verbal contract isn't worth the paper it's written on. [for verbal agreement or " informed consent"].

An expert can be found to testify to the truth of almost any factual theory, no matter how frivolous . . . At the trial itself, an expert's testimony can be used to obfuscate what would otherwise be a simple case . . . Juries and judges can be and sometimes are misled by such experts for hire.[4]

An expert is someone who knows some of the worst mistakes that can be made in his subject and who manages to avoid them.

—**Werner Heisenberg**
Physics and Beyond, 1901–1976

Swimming for his life, a man does not see much of the country through which the river winds.

—**WE Gladstone**
British Prime Minister, 1809–1898

The first thing we do, let us kill all the lawyers.

In defense of lawyers, let me explain that famous quotation of Shakespeare in Henry VI Part 2 written in 1592, Act IV Scene 2, which so often is mistakenly used in a negative instead of the positive Shakespeare meant. The previous actors' dialogue is usually ignored to make it appear that the last sentence of the conversation "first thing we do is let us kill all the lawyers" stands alone. But the actual dialogue goes like this:

And when I am king, as king I will be [says the character Gade] . . . There shall be no money; all shall eat and drink on my score; and I will apparel them all in one livery that they may agree like brothers and worship me, their lord.

It was the character Dick's response to that statement that in order to fulfill Gade's anarchic fantasy to become enriched and powerful is that the "first thing we do is let us kill all the lawyers," meaning those who are the obstacles standing in the way of anarchy which would enable Gade to be worshipped as a lord by everyone else.

However, how does an attorney-phile explain away?

Woe unto you lawyers! For ye have taken away the key of knowledge.

St. Luke 11:52

In general, the great can protect themselves but the poor and humble require the arm and shield of the law.

—**Andrew Jackson**
Letters of John Quincy Adams August 26, 1821

I don't want to know what the law is. I want to know who the judge is.

> —**Roy Cohn**
> *Quoted by Tom Wolfe in the*
> *New York Times Book Review, April 3, 1988*

Next to the confrontation between two highly honed batteries of lawyers, jungle warfare is a stately minuet.

> —**Bill Veeck**
> *The Hunter's Handbook, 1965*

23.5.8　Column G: The Classics

Speak the speech, I pray you, as I pronounced it to you, trippingly on the tongue, but if you mouth it, as many of your players do, I had as lief the town-crier spoke my lines. Nor do not saw the air too much with your hand, thus, but use all gently; for in the very torrent, tempest, and, as I may say, the whirlwind of passion, you must acquire and beget a temperance that may give it smoothness.

> —**Shakespeare**
> *Hamlet III.ii*

Suit the action to the word, the word to the action; with this special observance, that you o'erstep not the modesty of nature.

> —**Shakespeare**
> *Hamlet III.ii*

To hold, as'twere, the mirror up to nature; to show virtue her own feature, scorn her own image, and the very age and body of the time his form and pressure.

> —**Shakespeare**
> *Hamlet III.ii*

23.5.9　Column H: Litigation Combat

To fight the enemy bravely with the prospect of victory is nothing, but to fight with intrepidity (resolute courage) under the constant impression of defeat and to inspire irregular troops to do it is a talent peculiar to yourself.

> —**Nathaniel Greene**
> *American revolutionary war General*
> *To Brigadier Francis Marion (the Swamp Fox)*

As the proposition advanced . . . That hereafter war will be made altogether with artillery, I consider that this observation is wholly erroneous . . . For whoever wishes to train a good army must . . . Train his troops to attack the enemy sword in hand and seize hold of him boldly.

> —**Niccolo Machiavelli**
> *(in advising his prince)*

Everything which the enemy least expects will succeed the best.

> —**Frederick the Great**

Ruses are of the greatest usefulness; they are detours which often lead more surely to the object than the wide road which goes straight ahead.

—Frederick the Great

It is always more difficult to defend a coast than to invade it.

—Sir Walter Raleigh

"You know you never defeated us on the battlefield," said the American colonel. The North Vietnamese colonel pondered this remark a moment, "That may be so," he replied, "but it is also irrelevant."

As per conversation between Colonel Harry G. Summers Jr.
and Colonel Tu, North Vietnamese Army

Happiness often sneaks in through a door you didn't know you left open.

—John Barrymore
Actor

23.5.10 Yiddish Menu of Proverbs and Common Sayings

A friend you have to buy, an enemy you can get for nothing
A wise man knows what he says, a fool says what he knows
As you make your bed so shall you sleep in it
Better a crooked foot than a crooked mind
Better to do nothing than to make something into nothing
From fortune to misfortune is a short step; from misfortune to fortune is a long way
From litigation you can never recover your loss
God helps the poor man; he protects him from expensive sins
He who always keeps quiet is half a fool; he who talks much is a complete fool
He who throws stones on another gets them back on his own bones
If you don't save the penny, you'll not have the dollar
If you have the money, you have the say
If you keep talking you will end up saying what you didn't intend to say
If you lie down with dogs, you'll get up with fleas
If you repeat often enough that you are right you eventually will discover you are wrong
If you wait to please everybody; you'll die before your time
If you're a child at 20 you're an ass at 21
If you're at odds with your rabbi, make peace with your bartender
Lost years are worse than lost dollars
Money buys everything except brains
Money lost; nothing lost; reputation lost, everything lost
Poverty is no disgrace; but also no great honor
Rich men are often lean; poor men are fat
The first time it's smart, the second time it's cute, the third time you get a sock in the teeth
The heaviest burden is an empty pocket
The poor man's enemies are few, the rich man's friends are fewer
Those who can't bite should not show their teeth
When does a wealthy man go hungry? When the doctor orders him
When the stomach is empty so is the brain
When you sow money you reap fools
You cannot pay a debt with a noble pedigree

23.6   Let All Who Testify Remember These Words of Caution

Cavendo tutus (be safe by being on one's guard) and *Caveat emptor* (let the buyer beware).

There is a danger in oversimplification of the truth. There are great risks in *Salva veritate* (saving the truth, i.e., without infringement of truth), in which a theme, jingle, motto, analogy can be so striking and memorable as to enable falsity to submerge the truth.

The Romans had a phrase for it—*Suggestio falsi* (suggestion of what is false, i.e., a misrepresentation of the truth whereby something incorrect is implied to be true, an indirect lie). The medical expert witness must balance the need to communicate well to the jury while at the same time maintain his validity as a scientist upholding the truth of the issues. It is essential that medical experts insulate themselves from what Perlin[5] calls the "pernicious" use of heuristic* devices in their testimony.

So what should the ethical medical expert do to guard against false simplification? The medical expert must realize that many people operate according to *Mundus vult decipi, ergo decipiatur* (which means the world wants to be deceived, so let it be deceived), and *Fere libenter homines id quod volunt credunt* (people are generally glad to believe what they want to be true is so).

Therefore, the ethical expert must have integrity, i.e., testifying physicians must be independent, and objective in this very adversarial legal process. The medical expert must avoid conflicts of interest and even the perception of a conflict of interest in providing reliable testimony. That is the major reason for my policy of referencing my professional organizations guidelines in my written agreement with retaining attorneys and also my policy to never to accept another case from the same attorney or firm.

The medical expert must have and show competence by documenting credible expertise and experience in the practice of his medical field. He must show an in-depth understanding of all the relevant facts in the case along with *transparent analyses*, methods and research of the peer-reviewed literature, so that his opinions have a strong scientific foundation.

The medical expert witness must also understand his role as a teacher and educator. He must be able to communicate to many different audiences while maintaining his objectivity. He must be able to articulate clear concise coherent and compelling narrative with respect, and sincerity to the jury using analogies and themes but always aware that "In cauda venenum" (the poison is in the tail, i.e., one should look beyond the apparently simple explanation and guard against the lurking peril of oversimplification). The medical expert importantly also has an ethical responsibility to his retaining attorney.

The testifying physician must also teach the attorney to ensure that upon direct questioning the attorney asks the correct questions that permit simplification of complex medical issues yet not absent the analyses that must go with the analogies.

Furthermore, the medical expert must also provide his retaining attorney insights on how his simplifications on direct testimony may be distorted on cross-examination so that

---

* Heuristics refers to implicit "rule of thumb" reasoning that people use to oversimplify complex information-processing tasks. The good news: these devices enable decision making in real time. The bad news: used out of context, decision makers can ignore or misuse useful rational information leading to erroneous decisions.[6] As an example over-reliance even on just one vivid memorable clause or case can swamp subsequent mountains of relevant data. (e.g., "If the glove doesn't fit you've got to acquit?")

the attorney can go back to those potential distortions on redirect to clarify for the jury again.

Finally, the ethical medical expert does not allow the cross-examiner to undermine his opinions to the nonbelievable to the benefit of the opposition's themes and analogy to a "Reductio ad absurdum" simplification (reduction of a debate, discussion, testimony, argument to an absurd) conclusion and thereby noncredible.

And in his explanations to the jury the medical expert should not allow for any false heuristic devices to creep in, e.g., "Post hoc ergo propter hoc," which means "after this, therefore because of this," or just because events are sequentially related in time, they are not necessarily causally related. The rooster crows in the morning, the sun rises in the morning. It does not mean that the rooster causes the sun to rise, yet at the same time balance this with a consideration of the legal definitions of causation. The medical expert must also remember always that it is his job to teach by documenting the truth in a transparent fashion and not to succumb to the adversarial process so as to persuade or to advocate for either side, i.e., "Truth persuades by teaching, but lawyers teach by persuading" (from Quintus Septimius Tertuillianu).

References

1. Bordage G, Zacks R. The structure of medical knowledge in the memories of medical students and general practitioners: categories and prototypes. *Med. Educ.* November 1984; 18(6): 406–416.
2. Larkin R (Ed.). *Great Illuminated Classics.* New York: Playmore, Inc., Publishers and Waldman Publishing Company, Baronet Books, ISBN: 0-86611-678-8.
3. Virgil's Aeneid xi, 424.
4. Weinstein JV. *9th Symposium on Statistics and the Environment.* National Academy of Sciences, October 27, 1986.
5. Perlin ML. There's no success like failure. Exposing the pretexuality of *Kansas v. Hendricks. Northwest. Univ. L. Rev.* 1998; 92: 1247.
6. Garb H. Clinical judgement and decision making. *Ann. Rev. Clin. Psych.* April 2005; 1: 67.

Example of Translating for the Jury; Medicalese into Understandable English

24

We made too many wrong mistakes.

—**Yogi Berra**

24.1   Jury Translations into English

Mintz[1] believes that medical language frequently contains linguistic forms that serve to create a social distance between physicians and patients. This distance develops not only out of poor communication with the patient, but also, and more importantly, arises as the language that a physician uses comes to modulate his or her experience of the patient. It is suggested that some of the problem lies in the very nature of language itself, and that further fault can be found in the particular structures of Western language. Unfortunately, however, medical language has adopted special forms and metaphors, which further serve to create distance.

The same applies to the legal culture.

If a doctor says that a patient "admits" to something, he does not mean that the person previously tried to deny it as it means in the legal culture. Used in that way, "admit" just means "said." Similarly, when an attorney talks about causation or proximate cause he does not mean medical cause defined that condition or pathophysiology stimulating an abnormal physiological function. The medical culture as does the legal culture has "jargon" or a language that a physician uses to describe or to modulate his or her medical experiences in the shortcut terms used by the medical culture. Just watch a couple of TV episodes of emergency room (E.R.) and you will be amused as I am of the mangling of medical terms and jargon by tongues unfamiliar with the language despite language coaches on the set.

Remember you have a role as the translator from Shakespearean English to plain modern English to the audience?

The medical expert's role is to translate medicalese into plain English for the jury.

How the testifying physician should translate from medicalese to English for the jury. The best way is to present an example.

24.2   First a Case Discussion in Medicalese

24.2.1   CC and HPI

A father brought his 15-year-old son to the emergency department because of a large hematoma over the left upper quadrant (LUQ) from being struck by a lacrosse ball.

In addition to complaining of pain in the LUQ, the patient also has pain in his left shoulder, aggravated by movement. He is ambulatory and in no acute distress. The triage nurse orders a chest radiograph, which is normal.

The patient is triaged to fast-track care.

Physical examination (P.E.) showed a blood pressure (BP) = 125/78; heart rate (HR) = 106; and a RR@ 12. Temperature and O_2 are normal. He had no trouble walking, but he seemed to have a lot of pain while positioning him on the bed. Findings from cardiorespiratory examination were unremarkable.

Diffuse abdominal tenderness was most pronounced in the LUQ. There was no rebound or guarding. The patient had no tenderness to palpation over the left shoulder or clavicle, with full ROM in that joint.

24.2.2   Medical Course

When an intravenous (I.V.) line was started in the E.R., the patient's systolic temporarily decreased to about 90, thought to be due to a vasovagal episode.

However, suspicion of splenic trauma prompted bedside ultrasonography (US), which showed free fluid in the splenorenal space.

The patient was immediately transferred from the fast-track area to the trauma section of the ED, where CT scan confirmed a splenic grade 2–3 laceration. Intraperitoneal blood was indicated by a vascular contrast blush medial to the spleen consistent with active intraperitoneal bleeding.

Angiographic embolization, instead of open laparotomy, was chosen as the modality to control the bleeding, and coils were placed in the mid portion of the splenic artery beyond the origin of the dorsal pancreatic artery with repeat angiography showing reperfusion of the spleen via collateral vessels.

The patient's condition was stabilized without the use of blood products.

24.2.3   Standard of Medical Care Discussion

24.2.3.1   Introduction

In blunt trauma, the most commonly injured abdominal organ is the spleen, closely followed by the liver. Mechanisms of injury include motor vehicle crashes, assault, sports injuries, and bicycle injuries. Even minor trauma can cause splenic rupture in patients with previous splenomegaly due to mononucleosis, malaria, leukemia, or other conditions. The spleen is a highly vascular organ with the potential to contribute to severe blood loss in the setting of trauma. Patients with splenic injuries may present with isolated LUQ pain or diffuse abdominal tenderness. Referred pain (the "Kehr sign") was positive to the left shoulder.

Severe hemorrhage may cause abdominal distension and frank shock. A presentation delayed by more than 48 h after trauma may cause additional findings, such as jaundice or left pleural effusion.

Traumatic splenic injuries are graded I–V according to their severity, as evaluated on CT imaging. A grade I injury is a subcapsular hematoma of less than 10% of the surface area or a laceration that is less than 1 cm deep. If both of these findings are present, the injury is grade II. A grade II injury is also a subcapsular hematoma of 10–50% of the surface area, an intraparenchymal hematoma of 5 cm diameter, or a laceration 1–3 cm deep. If two grade II injuries are present, the severity is grade III. A grade III injury is also defined as a subcapsular hematoma of greater than 50% of the surface area, a parenchymal hematoma that is larger than 5 cm in diameter, or a laceration that is deeper than 3 cm or that involves the trabecular vessels. A grade IV injury is a laceration that involves segmental or hilar vessels that produces >25% organ devascularization. A grade V injury is a completely shattered or completely devascularized spleen.

24.2.3.2 Standard of Medical Care

Details:

1. Patients in hemodynamically unstable condition with signs of intraperitoneal bleeding should receive aggressive fluid resuscitation and/or blood products.
2. These patients should be sent directly to the operating room, a technique known as focused abdominal sonography in trauma (FAST).
3. Bedside US may be useful to determine the presence of intraabdominal blood. Most patients with splenic injuries have stable vital signs and may undergo an imaging study for diagnosing and defining the injury.
4. CT of the abdomen is the modality of choice.
5. For patients in stable condition, serial hematocrit determinations and serial bedside US studies may be performed as part of expectant management.
6. As part of stabilization after potential intraabdominal injuries, two I.V. lines should be placed in all patients.
7. Blood should be sent to the blood bank for typing and screening if the patient is stable.
8. Or for typing and cross matching for 4–6 units if the patient has any signs of hemodynamic instability or evidence of a decreasing hematocrit.
9. Surgical management by means of laparotomy is indicated if hemodynamic instability is observed or if the patient requires massive transfusion (transfusion of packed red blood cells of >40 ml/kg in a child or of >2 units in an adult). Overall, less than 10% of children with splenic injuries ultimately require surgery.
10. In the hemodynamically stable patient, the higher the grade of injury, the more likely the need for surgery. Most grade IV or V injuries require surgical care, as do some low-grade injuries depending on a variety of circumstances, including comorbidity, concomitant injury, hospital resources (e.g., angiographic and surgical capabilities), and acceptability of blood transfusion to the patient.
11. Nonsurgical observation is a safe practice that improves outcomes in for hemodynamically stable patients with blunt solid-organ injuries. In addition, preservation of the spleen avoids the subsequent risk of infections with encapsulated organisms, such as *Streptococcus*, *Neisseria*, and *Haemophilus* species.
12. Some grade III injuries and all grade IV or V injuries should be initially managed in an ICU setting because sudden decompensation is an ever-present possibility.

13. Most grade I or II injuries can be observed in a step-down unit or a regular surgical unit.
14. Splenic injuries in stable patients that used to be treated surgically are increasingly being managed nonoperatively in trauma centers with 24-h surgical capabilities.
15. Angiographic embolization may increase the likelihood for success with nonoperative treatment, especially when a vascular blush is seen on CT scans, as this procedure may help to stop bleeding and avoid surgery.

Resources must be available to take the patient to the operating room if unexpected or sudden decompensation occurs.[2]

24.3   Translating the Same Case to a Jury from Medicalese to Understandable English

First obtain; explain exhibit with pointer to left upper quadrant of the abdomen and the location of the spleen

> It is much more important to know what sort of a patient has a disease than what sort of a disease a patient has.
>
> **—William Osler**

Winston Churchill said that "short words are the best, and the old words best of all." Mark Twain knew it is best to use short sentences when he declared that "I didn't have time to write a short speech, so I wrote a long one instead." You must also sincerely believe what you are saying because credibility is in your voice. Consistency of theme and repetition of language hones the message. Above all you must visualize by painting a vivid picture with words. It would not hurt to have a simple exhibit that does not further complicate your story.

Explain the relevance of your story in such a way that it is remembered. Dr. Frank Lutz[3] summarizes his points of good communication with lay people as "rules for effective communication":

- Simplicity.
- Brevity.
- Credibility.
- Good sound.
- Visualization.
- Appropriate context.
- Relevance.
- Consistency.
- Visual imagery—symbols and exhibits.
- Never use a long word where a short word will do.
- If it is possible to cut a word out—cut it out.
- Never use a foreign phrase, a scientific word or word of jargon if you can possibly think of an everyday equivalent.

According to Lutz, there are differences in outlook and perspective between the genders. "Women respond better to stories anecdotes, and metaphors. Men are more fact oriented and statistical. Men appreciate a colder more scientific approach, while women sensibilities tend to be more personal, human, and literary."

24.3.1 Background

A father brought his 15-year-old son to the emergency department because of a large bruise over the son's lower left ribs from being struck by a lacrosse ball during a high school game.

In addition to complaining of pain in the upper portion of his left side of the abdomen—the area of the spleen, the patient also has pain in his left shoulder also a sign of splenic injury, which appeared to hurt more when moved. He could walk and was in no acute distress. The triage nurse orders a chest x-ray, which was normal.

The patient was screened to be managed by the fast-track care section of the emergency department.

24.3.2 Physical Examination

On physical examination, the patient has a blood pressure of 125/78 mmHg, a heart rate of 106 beats per minute, and a respiratory rate of 12 breaths per minute. His temperature was normal. He had no trouble walking, but he seemed to have a lot of pain while positioning him on the bed. Findings from examining his heart and lungs were unremarkable. But he had diffuse abdominal tenderness that was most pronounced in the left upper quadrant—the upper quarter of the left side of the abdomen just where the spleen is located. No signs of intraabdominal infection were observed. The patient had no tenderness when putting pressure over the left shoulder or clavicle, and he had full range of motion of that shoulder, which indicated that there was really no shoulder injury and more likely than not, the "pain" he felt in his shoulder was just being felt there from a pain elsewhere a condition known as referred pain—probably from injured spleen.

24.3.3 Medical Course

When a needle was put in to his vein in the emergency department, the patient's blood pressure temporarily decreased to a systolic pressure of about 90 mm Hg. At the time, this change was thought to be due to a possible near faint (at the sight of blood) because his blood pressure soon returned to normal.

However, suspicion of injury to the spleen, which is found in the upper part of the abdomen on the left side, prompted bedside US (a sonogram of the abdomen similar to the pictures taken in a pregnant woman to see the baby). This showed fluid in the space all around the spleen and more fluid (probably blood) flowing around also to the kidney, which is near the spleen.

The patient was immediately transferred from the fast-track area to the trauma section of the emergency department, where a CT scan confirmed an injury to the spleen with a grade II–III rupture.

Blood was seen by the CT scan inside the abdominal cavity, with active bleeding seen coming from the spleen into the abdominal cavity.

Instead of abdominal surgery, the doctors chose to insert a very thin flexible plastic tube into a vein in which to control the bleeding. Through this tube, they placed chemically treated coils in the mid portion of the artery of the spleen to obstruct the flow of blood.

On repeat imaging of the blood vessels, the spleen artery, which was obstructed by the procedure to stop the bleeding, was now being replaced other nearby blood vessels so that the doctors did not have to worry that the spleen would not be nourished by a cessation of blood flow to it.

The patient's condition was stabilized without any blood transfusions. He did well afterward, went home, and is now playing baseball.

> Care more for the individual patient than for the special features of the disease . . . Put yourself in his place . . . The kindly word, the cheerful greeting, the sympathetic look—these the patient understands.
>
> —**William Osler**

24.3.4   Standard of Medical Care Discussion

24.3.4.1   Introduction

In blunt trauma, to the abdomen, the abdominal organ most commonly injured is the spleen—an organ in the left part of the upper abdomen next to the stomach.

These injuries occur with motor vehicle crashes, assault, sports injuries, and bicycle injuries. Even minor trauma can cause rupture of the spleen in patients with large spleens due to certain diseases, which occurred to the patient in the past like mononucleosis, malaria, and leukemia. The spleen has many blood vessels going to and from it, and is surrounded by blood vessels so the spleen can easily bleed a lot after. Patients with spleen injuries may develop only left upper quadrant pain or diffuse abdominal tenderness and nothing else to indicate a spleen injury.

The "pain" to the left shoulder that the patient complained about was not due to a direct shoulder injury but instead occurred by an irritation of the diaphragm from blood coming from the torn bleeding spleen. This symptom of pain in the shoulder, not from any problem within the shoulder, but instead, from irritation elsewhere has been named the "Kehr sign."

If we wait more than 48 h after trauma, we may see additional findings such as jaundice (yellow eyes and skin) or left pleural effusion (fluid within the left chest but still outside the lung), and severe hemorrhage may cause abdominal swelling and shock.

Traumatic spleen injuries are graded Roman numerals I–V according to how severe, as evaluated on CT scans:

I. A grade I injury is a subcapsular hematoma (blood clot still within the spleen near the surface of its covering) of less than 10% of the surface area or a laceration that is less than 1 cm (2.2 cm = 1 in.) deep.

II. If both of these findings are present, the injury is grade II. A grade II injury is also a subcapsular hematoma (blood clot) of 10–50% of the surface area, an intraparenchymal (a clot of blood deep inside the spleen in contrast to the former seen just below the surface of the spleen) of 5 cm diameter, or a laceration 1–3 cm deep.

III. If two grade II injuries are present, the severity is grade III. A grade III injury is also defined as a blood clot, not deep in the spleen but near the surface of the spleen of greater than 50% of the surface area, a parenchymal hematoma that is larger than 5 cm in diameter, or a laceration that is deeper than 3 cm or that involves the deep blood vessels within the spleen.

IV. A grade IV injury is a laceration to the very crux of the spleen that produces >25% loss of blood vessels due to the clot pressure on the vessels.

V. A grade V injury is a completely shattered spleen.

24.3.4.2 *Standard of Medical Care*

Details: Most patients with spleen injuries have stable vital signs but should always undergo an imaging study for accurately diagnosing and defining the injury.

1. Patients with low blood pressure, which even goes lower when sitting up and with signs of bleeding into the abdominal cavity, should receive fast I.V. rehydration and blood transfusions.
2. These patients should be sent directly to the operating room, a technique known as FAST.
3. Sonograms at the bedside are useful to follow the course of intraabdominal bleeding.
4. CT scan of the abdomen is the best way to make an accurate diagnosis.
5. For patients in stable condition, serial lab blood level determinations and serial bedside sonographic studies are performed as part of conservative nonsurgical management.
6. As part of stabilization after potential intraabdominal injuries, two I.V. lines should be placed in all patients.
7. And a patient's blood sample should be sent to the blood bank for typing and screening if the patient is stable.
8. Or for the preparation of 4–6 units of blood to be at the ready if the patient has any signs falling blood pressure and red blood count and blood levels.
9. Abdominal surgery needs to be done if the blood pressure falls, or if the patient requires massive transfusion (transfusion of packed red blood cells of >40 mL/kg in a child or of >2 units in an adult).
10. Overall, less than 10% of children with spleen injuries ultimately require surgery.
11. But even in the stable patient with normal blood pressure and pulse, the higher the grade of injury, the more likely the need for surgery.
12. Most grade IV or V injuries require surgical care, as do some low-grade injuries depending on a variety of circumstances, including other illnesses of the patient, or even lack of hospital resources, and capabilities to make an accurate diagnosis and to regularly assess the patient's status.
13. Acceptability of blood transfusions is also a factor because some religious patients (like Jehovah's Witnesses) refuse blood transfusions; thus, we may have to act earlier to avoid a time delay when more blood is lost that the patient may not allow to be replaced.
14. Nonsurgical observation is a safe practice that improves outcomes in for stable patients with blunt solid-organ injuries as opposed to sharp knife like injuries.
15. In addition, if we keep the spleen instead of removing it as one would have to do in surgery; it avoids the subsequent risk of infections with the resultant difficulty of the patient to combat germs.

16. Some grade III injuries and all grade IV or V injuries should be initially managed in an intensive care setting—with many nurses to check the patient all the time (ICU setting) because sudden deterioration is an ever-present possibility.

17. Most grade I or II injuries can be observed in a step-down unit or a regular surgical unit.

18. Spleen injuries in stable patients that used to be treated surgically are increasingly being managed nonoperatively in trauma centers with 24-h surgical capabilities.

19. Obstructing the bleeding vessel in the method used in this case may increase the likelihood for success, especially when a "vascular blush" (classic sign seen on x-ray which indicates active bleeding) is seen on CT scans, as this procedure may help to stop bleeding and avoid surgery.

20. Medical resources must always be available to take the patient to the operating room quickly if unexpected or sudden deterioration occurs in his medical condition.

References

1. Mintz D. What's in a word: the distancing function of language in medicine. Medicalese v. English. *J. Med. Humanit.* 1992 Winter; 13(4): 223–233.
2. e-Medicine, www.medicinal.com, last visited, 7/6/2006.
3. Lutz F. Words that Work—It's not what you say, it's what people hear. New York: Hyperion ISBN 1-4013-0259-9.

Lessons from My Expert Testimony Mistakes

25

25.1 Introduction

The medical expert witness plays an important role in medical malpractice and liability cases. The expert assesses medical information and interprets and explains medical uncertainty, medical research, and customary practice for a nonscientific jury. Recently, several of the medical specialist organizations have developed codes of conduct for their members.

These organizations have asserted the premise that giving expert testimony by a physician for either plaintiff or defendant is not only a required civic duty, but also part of the practice of medicine as well. Medical experts now have been given a clearer guideline, and should adhere to the ethical principles of the code of conduct developed by their professional organizations.

These codes of conduct should govern their activities in their case preparation, reports, letters, and, especially, testimony.

A compendium of most medical society's codes of conduct for their members is given in Section 25.2. To date, these programs have received judicial praise and have withstood court challenges. This, it is hoped, will be an important step toward improving the quality and fairness of expert witnesses.

25.2 Summary of Medical Expert Rules and Code of Ethical Conduct for the Physician Expert Witness

1. All expert witnesses and trial attorneys should obtain and study the recommended practices for professionals and scientists engaged as physicians for the review of other professional's work and practices, and providing testimony in public forums.
2. Physicians should always be truthful and conduct themselves in a professional manner.
3. Physicians should conduct a thorough, fair, and impartial review of the facts and the medical care provided.
4. Physicians should serve only when qualified and should provide evidence or testify only in matters in which they have clinical experience and knowledge.
5. Physicians should not be influenced by conflicts of interest, and should actively seek information about the issue at hand and limit reliance on other's assumptions.

6. Physicians should evaluate the medical care provided in light of the generally accepted practice standards that prevailed at the time of occurrence and should discuss the standard of care only with knowledge of the standard of care that applies.
7. Physicians should not condemn performance that falls within generally accepted standards, nor endorse or condone performance that falls below these standards.
8. Physicians should make a clear distinction between departure from accepted practice standards and an untoward outcome; and should make every effort to determine whether there is a causal relationship between the alleged substandard care and an untoward outcome.
9. Physicians should reject preprepared or other's research and insist upon personally conducting their own research from which they will render informed opinions.
10. Physicians, according to several medical professional organizations including the American College of Gastroenterology, should offer fact or expert opinions based on the U.S. Supreme Court guidelines of *Daubert v. Merrell Dow*, that is,
    a. Evidence will be based on scientific knowledge that has given rise to testable and tested hypotheses.
    b. Evidence has been subjected to peer review and publication.
    c. Evidence is generally accepted by the scientific community.
    d. The known or potential rates of error are made known to the court.
11. Physicians should eliminate sensational, exaggerated, or disparaging statements from their opinions and should address other physicians' opinions about the issues under consideration [respectfully].
12. Physicians should be compensated only for their time; and never accept compensation that is contingent upon their opinion(s) or the outcome of the litigation.
13. Physicians should supply information to the news media only when authorized to do so.
14. Physicians should acknowledge that their rendering of medicolegal testimony be considered the practice of medicine and subject to peer review (according to the American Medical Association [AMA H-265-993]).

Now, let us see how this applies in my trial testimony of one case where I was retained by the plaintiff's attorney. The case was about a woman who had not been hospitalized in a timely way after developing abdominal pain secondary to a duodenal perforation subsequent to an endoscopic sphincterotomy (endoscopic retrograde cholangiograph picture [ERCP]).

In fact, this postsphincterotomy perforation was seen on a KUB done immediately after the procedure for just that purpose, to rule out postsphincterotomy complications. These complications could easily have been spotted within minutes after the films were developed on the same morning prior to discharge. The endoscopist, several weeks later, testified that he could see the perforation on the KUB but did not bother to look at it after the procedure.

The ERCP and sphincterotomy, which took all of 8 min, was done for specious reasons and poor indications, and afterwards, the physician went on to perform another ERCP in another hospital.

The patient with the perforation causing abdominal pain subsequently traveled 100 miles to home. During this 100-mile auto trip she became septic from peritonitis and was admitted to a local hospital after the 3-day weekend that followed the ERCP.

Actually, there are literally dozens of such cases in the United States.

ERCP and sphincterotomy is a procedure being done by too many untrained (formally) physicians, and in many cases, the indications for this procedure are not adequate to the subjective symptoms and to the objective data. One of the foremost authorities in the field has researched the medical-legal aspects of this dangerous procedure.[1]

The study reports the analysis of a personal series of 59 cases in which ERCP malpractice was alleged.

Methods: Half of the cases involved pancreatitis; 16 suffered perforation after sphincterotomy (8 of which involved precutting), and 10 had severe biliary infection. There were 2 esophageal perforations. Fifteen of the patients died.

The most common allegation (54% of cases) was that the ERCP, or the therapeutic procedure, was not indicated. Most of these patients had pain only, usually after cholecystectomy. Negligent performance was alleged in 19 cases, with corroborating evidence in 8. Inadequate post-procedure care was alleged in 5 cases, including 3 with a delayed diagnosis of perforation.

Disputes about the extent of the education and consent process were common.

Results: The final outcome was available in 40 cases. Sixteen were withdrawn and 14 were settled. Of the 10 that came to trial, half were defense verdicts.

Conclusions: The lessons are clear. ERCP should be done for good indications, by trained endoscopists with standard techniques, with good documented patient-informed consent and communication before and after the procedure. Speculative ERCP, sphincterotomy, and precuts are high-risk for patients and for practitioners.

This is echoed by Testoni PA.[2]

The authors stated that post-ERCP pancreatitis can also be prevented by patient selection. Patient-related risk factors are now well known, so an increased risk of developing pancreatitis is predictable *a priori* in these subjects, independent of the type of endoscopic procedure performed. Furthermore, the risk of pancreatitis escalates when multiple risk factors occur in the same patient or some technique-related risk factor comes up during the procedure. In these patients, diagnostic ERCP should be avoided in routine practice and magnetic resonance cholangio-pancreatography should be used as the first diagnostic step. When either diagnostic or therapeutic ERCP is indicated, these high-risk patients should be informed about their own specific risk of postprocedure pancreatitis.

I had been retained by the plaintiff's attorney to review the case and give my expert opinion, which I stipulated in a signed agreement would be in accordance with the Summary of Medical Expert Rules and Code of Ethical Conduct for the Physician Expert Witness—and, in particular, points #1, 3, and 6:

1. All expert witnesses and trial attorneys should obtain and study the recommended practices for professionals and scientists engaged as physicians for the review of other professional's work and practices, and providing testimony in public forums.
3. Physicians should conduct a thorough, fair, and impartial review of the facts and the medical care provided.
6. Physicians should evaluate the medical care provided in light of the generally accepted practice standards that prevailed at the time of occurrence and should discuss the standard of care only with knowledge of the standard of care that applies—usually what a prudent physician of similar education, training, and expertise would do under similar circumstances.

After a thorough review of the medical records, my verbal, then written report included the following conclusions:

1. There was no valid indication for performing this ERCP and especially the sphincterotomy; that is, a prudent physician under a similar circumstance would not do this procedure.
2. There was no clinical or laboratory evidence to suggest that the patient had any common bile duct obstruction.
3. There was no evidence of sphincter of Oddi (SOD) dysfunction based on any objective studies.
4. Indeed, these very same symptoms were diagnosed almost 10 years previously as being secondary to nonalcoholic steatohepatitis, and therefore, a sphincterotomy should not have been performed on this diabetic female with severe hypertriglyceridemia, and nonalcoholic fatty liver disease; with probably (postcholecystectomy) hyperalgesia.
5. Thus, I stated my opinion based on a reasonable degree of medical probability that there was no proper indication for the sphincterotomy.

The sphincterotomy was the proximate cause of the duodenal perforation with all the resultant complications that ensued.

I also stated in my letter/report that in the event other information is brought to my attention, I reserve the right to supplement and modify my opinion, if necessary.

The standard of care for a physician who performs endoscopic procedures such as an ERCP/sphincterotomy is to provide the level of care that a reasonable and prudent physician would provide under the same or similar circumstances. That means that the medical/surgical indications for the procedure (ERCP/sphincterotomy) should be appropriate. And even if we assume that an objective study used by Dr. Salvador was positive along with any other justification to perform the sphincterotomy, he should have at least looked at the last film taken during his procedure—the KUB that was available to him prior to his exit from the scene. This would have immediately made the diagnosis of perforation and mitigated the subsequent severe peritonitis sustained by the patient over a 3-day period after traveling 100 miles to home, without the knowledge of the perforation that occurred during the procedure.

The standard of medical care for a gastroenterologist such as Dr. Salvador, who has claimed to have performed 10,000 ERCPs in his relatively short career and who stated publicly that he is a world-renowned gastroenterologist required him to ensure the prompt and thorough review of x-ray films taken in association with performing this surgical procedure. A prudent physician would not release a patient to travel 100 miles to home until after the final x-rays of the procedure were reviewed and shown to be without complications.

In accordance with the Summary of Medical Expert Rules and Code of Ethical Conduct for the Physician Expert Witness, point 2, physicians should always be truthful and conduct themselves in a professional manner. Dr. Salvador had testified that he could have indeed reviewed these x-rays and could have diagnosed the complicating perforation "in a split second" had he seen the films ordered in his name for the indication stated on the x-ray requisition, "right upper quadrant abdominal pain." However, he also testified that he did not review these films taken within minutes of the ERCP procedure he performed and which he easily could have looked at prior to his leaving the scene and prior to the patient's discharge.

Since the standard of medical care is for early diagnosis and treatment and to recognize, diagnose, and treat as early as possible any medical complications of any gastroenterology/medical/surgical procedures, before discharge of the patient, any physician on the staff of a hospital or ambulatory surgical center must do so personally, or at least delegate the task of reviewing the x-rays of the procedure in a timely manner.

Had Dr. Salvador done so, he would have seen on the x-rays the major complications, that is, obvious extravasation and perforation, suffered by Ms. Taft during the procedure and prior to discharge. He thus would have made a more timely diagnosis of a major complication, and thus instituted more timely treatment of the major complications experienced in this particular procedure by Ms. Taft rather than waiting until after the weekend for the diagnosis of the complication. Indeed, it was not until 3 days after discharge of the patient that these films were reviewed and the complications were discovered by the staff of Harris Hospital.

It is a known rule in medical care that the earlier a complication is treated, the better the outcome for the patient—and the converse is also true, that the later the patient is properly diagnosed and treated, the worse the outcome. Memorial Harris Hospital thus breached the standard of care by failing to

1. establish an organizational/feedback system that would assure compliance with its policies and procedures that it had or should have had in place to satisfy JCAHO requirements;
2. have a radiologist present during the procedure and failing to have the radiological films read/reviewed by a radiologist physician in a timelier manner;
3. have a radiologist in the room, while an endoscopic surgical procedure requiring fluoroscopy was being performed;
4. have a radiologist sign out the films prior to the patient's discharge;
5. ensure that the treating physician was aware of the complications. The x-ray report stated that these findings of perforation were discussed with Dr. Salvador, "who was aware of them at the time of the procedure." Dr. Salvador denies this. "Someone is not telling the truth," I concluded.

It was not until 3 days after discharge of the patient, Ms. Taft, that these films were reviewed and documented by dictation and transcription of the report.

The report documented the extravasation and perforation by a Harris Hospital radiologist, thus delaying the diagnosis of a major complication, and thus delaying the timely treatment of this complication. In conclusion, my opinion, based on a reasonable degree of medical probability, was that the failures and breaches of the standard of care as set forth earlier by both Dr. Salvador and the facility in which the procedure (ERCP) was performed—the Harris Hospital—were the proximate cause of her increased severity of complications. This medically unnecessary procedure and the increased delay in medical diagnosis and treatment of the procedure's complications, more likely than not, were proximate cause(s) of her multiple severe complications and prolonged hospitalization, including severe pain and discomfort, increased gastroparesis, and increased sepsis.

After a period of 2 years, I was called to give testimony—video deposition testimony. And I did so.

Let us review the goals of the retaining attorney for the plaintiff and the retaining attorney for the defendant to point out, in actual testimony, how to avoid the tricks and traps laid by both to ensnare you. Do not forget: deposition and trial testimony is not so much designed to find the truth as it is designed specifically for two adversarial opponents to make their case to a jury so that the jury will choose the side telling most of the truth.

So, what is the goal of the plaintiff's retaining attorney who has hired you to give testimony—here in the direct examination, that is, the interview of questions and answers that will establish his side of the story?

Let us examine my direct testimony—questions asked of me by the attorney who has hired me to give my opinion he already knows. This will be prior to the cross-examination to be given for the opposing side, that is, the retained attorney for the defendant.

25.2.1   *Taft v. Salvador* I

25.2.1.1   *My Testimony with Commentary*

In our next and more advanced text for advanced medical expert witness testimony including advanced strategies in responding to very aggressive cross-examination from hyper-combative opposing attorneys, we will cover the applications of questions and answers in more detail and from the point of view of more assertive defensive and offensive strategies in your medical expert testimony. But now for introductory purposes, we will explore how and why this case of *Taft v. Salvador* is important in forearming the physician and medical expert witness in the subject of direct and cross-examination testimony.

The direct testimony, which follows, is what I have named the "puff and stuff" questions. "Puff" to puff up for the jury the expert's importance, his impeccable credentials, his unbiased opinion, his vast store of knowledge and experience, his Oslerian expertise, his many awards as a scientist and statesman, and not least his world-shaking research and publications, for which he deserves to win the Nobel Prize. The "stuff" is what the attorney wants the jury to hear about his case—a consistent story line with simple questions and direct answers—so that even the most disinterested juror becomes alert to the wrongs done to his client. Note that it always occurs in two phases.

During the direct examination, you can expect that the opposing cross-examining attorney will aim to do just the opposite—what I have named "search and destroy."

First the "puff," then the "stuff" of the direct examination, then the "search and destroy" cross-examination.

25.2.1.2   *Direct Examination by Counsel for Plaintiff*

By Mr. Gordon:

First, the puff, which I asked to keep at a minimum.

Q: Would you please state your full name for the record?
A: Perry Hookman.

Q: Dr. Hookman, my name is John Gordon. As you know, I represent Mr. and Mrs. Taft and this lawsuit that has been brought against Dr. Salvador. I would like the jury to get to know you a little bit. I think they already know that we are up here in Rockville, Maryland to take your videotape deposition in this case. You are a medical doctor?
A: Yes, I am.

Q: Licensed to practice medicine in how many states?

A: I am licensed to practice medicine in Maryland, DC, Virginia, and Florida.

Q: And as I understand it, you see patients. You consult with medical doctors in the areas of your specialty that we will get into in a minute, and you teach.

A: Yes.

Q: Let us give the jury an idea of your educational background, at least after you got out of college. Take us through medical school and take us through your practice.

If the attorney does not ask, I do not review my awards, professional positions, or publications. I do not think it seemly to blow my own horn. If the jury wants details, they will find it in my cv, which is an exhibit.

A: Well, after four years of medical school, I did my training as an assistant resident in medicine at the Johns Hopkins Hospital in Baltimore, Maryland. Then I became a fellow, postgraduate fellow, in gastroenterology also at the Johns Hopkins Hospital in Baltimore. I am licensed in those states as you see. I do not practice anywhere else but Florida, but I keep my license in these states mostly for sentimental reasons. I had a practice in Maryland for about 30 years as a gastroenterologist, moved to Florida in 1997, and teach at the _____ Medical Center, which is a major affiliate of the University of _____ School of Medicine.

I am a diplomate of the American Board of Internal Medicine and the American Board of Gastroenterology. I am a Fellow of the American College of Gastroenterology. I am a Fellow of the American College of Physicians, the American College of Physician Executives, and the American Gastroenterological Association. My current position is that from 1997 to present I am on the teaching staff and gastroenterology outpatient clinic at the _____ Medical Center. And my previous practice was in Maryland, as I said, in a private practice of gastroenterology and internal medicine with offices in DC, Maryland, which I did until the mid-'90s, before I moved to Florida.

I have had several professional positions. I will not go into them unless you ask me.

Q: For instance, do you currently serve as an assistant professor at a medical school?

A: Yeah, well I was just promoted to Associate Professor of the University of _____ School of Medicine.

This was relatively mild and limited at my request. I've had attorneys ask about each award, why I won it, who gave it, etc., and list all of what they think are the most prestigious past positions; also, they want to show that a fellow in medicine and gastroenterology is an elected position with an appointment by his peers so as to puff up this friendly expert witness.

Now to the stuff.

In accordance with the Summary of Medical Expert Rules and Code of Ethical Conduct for the Physician Expert Witness

4. *Physicians should serve only when qualified and should provide evidence or testify only in matters in which they have clinical experience and knowledge.*

7. *Physicians should not condemn performance that falls within generally accepted standards, nor endorse or condone performance that falls below these standards.*

8. *Physicians should make a clear distinction between departure from accepted practice standards and an untoward outcome; and should make every effort to determine whether there is a causal relationship between the alleged substandard care and an untoward outcome.*

And, in addition

14. *Physicians should acknowledge that their rendering of medicolegal testimony be considered the practice of medicine and subject to peer review (according to the American Medical Association [AMA H-265-993]).*

Therefore, anything I say is a matter of public record and is subject to review of my peers as to the accuracy and the veracity of my medical opinions. As was said by another expert, I start with the attitude that this is to be one of the best clinical consultations I have ever done.

In the following testimony, notice how deliberate the questions are. Note also that each question divulges another part of the story that this plaintiff's advocate wants to present to the jury, starting with definitions and gradually proceeding through the case.

Q: You mentioned gastroenterology, and I think most folks have some idea of what that is. It is a recognized specialty of medicine. Is it not?

A: Yes.

Q: Would you tell us what the specialty of gastroenterology involves?

A: The specialty of gastroenterology involves the digestive tract and digestive tract diseases and the appendages that come from the digestive tract like the pancreas, the liver, etc.

Q: We're going to be talking today about a procedure called an ERCP?

A: Yes.

Q: What is an ERCP?

A: An ERCP is an endoscopic retrograde cholangiograph picture, which I can show you using Dr. Salvador's diagram, which is an excellent one. And this is the—

Mr. Gordon: We're putting up on the Elmo a diagram that we're going to mark as Exhibit 2 to your deposition.

(Deposition Exhibit No. 2 was marked for identification.)

The witness: Well, it says Exhibit 3 for Dr. Salvador's.
Mr. Gordon: That's right. But it's going to be Exhibit 2 for your deposition today.
The witness: All right.

Note that I attempt as much as possible to utilize any exhibit used by the defendant before I add my own. The jury has or will see it as part of the other side's case. I am also respectful to the physician defendant, perhaps overly so, because whenever possible I try to compliment him.

Mr. Gordon: It was previously marked as Exhibit 3 during Dr. Salvador's deposition.

By Mr. Gordon:

Q: You have been retained in this case, have you not, to evaluate what Dr. Salvador did with respect to Mrs. Taft.

A: Yes.

Q: Is this the very first time that you have done that?

A: The very first time I have done this for Dr. Salvador and your law firm?

Q: Is this the very first time that you have been called upon to evaluate whether a doctor acted within the standard of care or whether he breached the standard of care?

A: No, this is not the first time.

Q: Okay. Can you tell me approximately how many times you have been called upon to do that?

A: Well, I'm called upon to testify about two to three times a month. I don't accept all those cases to testify in. I do accept two to three testimonies a year and I presented, if you want, as another exhibit, my six-year history of testifying.

Q: All right. In this case you have been retained on behalf of Mrs. Taft, have you not?

A: Yes.

Q: She is what's called the plaintiff in this case.

A: Yes.

Q: Have you been retained in prior cases and have you given testimony in prior cases on behalf of defendants? That is, such as the defendant in this case.

A: Yes.

Q: Can you give me and then the jury some idea of what percentage of your time has been devoted to evaluating cases on behalf of the injured party as compared to evaluating the care of the defendant that has been sued in a case?

A: About half and half.

Q: All right. By the way how old a man are you?

A: Do I have to tell you?

Q: You do.

A: I feel like I'm 40, but I play golf like I'm 90. Now you can figure out what I am in between.

Q: How long have you been practicing medicine?

A: I practiced medicine for 30 years in Maryland and I've actually been in practice since 1965.

Q: So about 40 years.

A: About 40 years.

Q: All of it devoted to the specialty of gastroenterology?

A: And internal medicine.

Q: I think you also touched on, and I want to talk a little bit more about it right now, that you have just been elevated to being an Associate Professor?

A: Couple years ago, yeah.

Q: Who do you teach?

A: I teach postgraduate physicians, nurses, x-ray people, visiting medical students, etc.

Q: What do you teach them about?

A: I teach them about the standard of care when it comes to medical and gastrointestinal problems.

Q: Have you also been published in the area of gastroenterology?

A: Yes.

Q: Have you been published in what are called peer-review literature?

A: Yes.

Q: What is peer-review literature?

A: Peer-review literature are medical articles that have to pass a test before they get published in medical journals and that is a review by the peers, people of the same training to see if: (a) if it appears to be accurate, and (b) whether there's anything worthwhile that should be presented in the article.

(Deposition Exhibit No. 1 was marked for identification.)

By Mr. Gordon:

Q: I'm going to hand you what we've marked as Exhibit 1 to your deposition, which is the curriculum vitae of yourself. Is that curriculum vitae up to date and accurate, and does it contain in the last few pages of it a listing of the various articles that you were just referring to that's been published in peer-review literature?

A: Yes.

Q: All right. Let's turn our attention more specifically to Mrs. Taft's case. Have you been provided a number of materials with respect to this case?

A: I've been provided with thousands of pages which [are] about this case.

Q: Can you give the jury just a general description, summary if you will, of those thousands of pages?

A: Well, my summary of those pages and the medical records are that Mrs. Taft was wrongly selected to do a hazardous procedure, the ERCP. She should not have had it done and had problems since. I think the standard of care that we call it, what a prudent physician would do with similar training, under similar circumstances . . . of what we call a breach of the standard of care if he doesn't do it. And I think Dr. Salvador's has breached the standard of care in several instances.

Q: All right. We'll get into them in some detail in just a minute. But while we talk about that, you've used the term standard of care. What does that mean to you as a gastroenterologist?

A: Well, a standard of care is very simple. It's what a prudent physician would do with similar background and training and under similar circumstances. So, in this case, a certified gastroenterologist, a prudent physician would be a certified gastroenterologist who, when evaluating a patient such as Mrs. Taft, would or would not attempt this procedure. And I believe that a prudent physician would not [have done what was done here].

Q: Now, with respect to this case, what work have you done and what training do you have to determine what the standard of care would be for a physician like the defendant in this case? That is, what have you done with respect to this case to express the opinions that you're going to today with respect to the standard of care, the breach thereof by Dr. Salvador?

A: Well, first I reviewed my own education, training, experience, and expertise and I have—and I went through and looked up all the literature involved with this type of case to support my opinion on the standard of care.

In accordance with the Summary of Medical Expert Rules and Code of Ethical Conduct for the Physician Expert Witness:

10. *Physicians, according to several medical professional organizations including the American College of Gastroenterology, should offer fact or expert opinions based on the U.S. Supreme Court guidelines of Daubert v. Merrell Dow; that is,*
    a. *Evidence will be based on scientific knowledge that has given rise to testable and tested hypotheses.*
    b. *Evidence has been subjected to peer review and publication.*
    c. *Evidence is generally accepted by the scientific community.*
    d. *The known or potential rates of error are made known to the court.*

Many times the retaining attorney wants you testify on the cheap—without spending any billable hours pertaining to the review of medical literature supporting your opinion. Always point them to this passage if you have incorporated it into your agreement as I have. (See agreement.)

Q: Now, based on your training and experience, based on the review of the literature that you just described, based on the review of the documents in this case, which would include, would it not, for instance, the medical records of Harris Memorial in Houston where the ERCP was performed?

A: What's your question?

Q: Have you reviewed the Harris Hospital records?

A: Yes.

Q: Where he performed it?

A: Yes.

Q: Dr. Salvador has also given a deposition in this case. Have you reviewed that?

A: Yes.

Q: And you've reviewed the deposition of Mrs. Taft?

A: Yes.

Q: And her husband?

A: Yes.

Q: So, based on your training and experience, based on your review of the medical records in this case, based on your review of the depositions of the case, including the deposition of Dr. Salvador's, do you have an opinion as to whether Dr. Salvador fell below the standard of care with respect to his care and treatment of Mrs. Taft?

A: Yes.

Q: And what is that opinion?

A: My opinion is that he did, Dr. Salvador did breach the standard of care as it pertains to this patient and this problem.

Q: In what way or ways did Dr. Salvador breach the standard of care in his treatment of Mrs. Taft?

A: He breached the standard of care: (1) by inappropriately doing a risky procedure on a patient that did not need this risky [procedure] or at least was not documented to need this procedure. That (2) once he did this procedure and the patient developed the complication following this procedure, several hours after the procedure, he advised the patient rather than coming in to get an emergency x-ray to see if there was a perforation, he advised the patient to simply take narcotics which would cover up this pain. And basically I would say that is the crux of the problem here.

Q: All right. I believe you—

A: There's a third one, if I may.

Q: All right. What is the third one?

A: If I may. The third one is he really should have reviewed the KUB or x-ray that was taken as a matter of policy by the Harris Digestive Disease Center and would have seen right then and there that this patient had a perforation and that the patient should have gotten emergency treatment right then and there.

Q: Was that the KUB x-ray that was performed toward the end of Dr. Salvador's ERCP procedure there at Harris Hospital?

A: Yes, it was the KUB that was done at around 9:10 a.m., right before she went to the treatment, the treatment area post the ERCP, the recovery room.

Q: Now, what I'd like you to do is in the three areas that you have discussed where Dr. Salvador fell below the standard of care, let's talk about them now each in some detail. Okay. First, let's take them in the order in which you were describing them. I think you testified that he breached the standard of care in inappropriately performing this procedure on her. Is that correct?

A: That's correct.

Q: Please explain to the jury what you mean by that.

A: All right. I can explain to the jury what I mean by that. I'm simply showing a diagram of the standard of care. This is the standard of care as outlined in the peer-review literature.

In accordance with the Summary of Medical Expert Rules and Code of Ethical Conduct for the Physician Expert Witness:

10. *Physicians, according to several medical professional organizations including the American College of Gastroenterology, should offer fact or expert opinions based on the U.S. Supreme Court guidelines of Daubert v. Merrell Dow; that is:*
    a. *evidence will be based on scientific knowledge that has given rise to testable and tested hypotheses;*
    b. *evidence has been subjected to peer review and publication;*
    c. *evidence is generally accepted by the scientific community;*
    d. *The known or potential rates of error are made known to the court.*

Q: All right. Is this something you've prepared?

A: No. This is from the peer-review published literature.

The witness: Well, let me just show you. This is an algorithm which is the standard of care, written up—

Ms. Riley: And I apologize, Doctor, for the interruption. But since I'm not there with you, could I get an identifying source and date, please.

The witness: All right. The identifying source is *UpToDate* and it was in the latest *UpToDate*. But it's also supported by articles that I have here prior to 2006 which will confirm this.

In accordance with the Summary of Medical Expert Rules and Code of Ethical Conduct for the Physician Expert Witness:

6. *Physicians should evaluate the medical care provided in light of the generally accepted practice standards that prevailed at the time of occurrence and should discuss the standard of care only with knowledge of the standard of care that applies.*

Ms. Riley: Okay. I'm just trying, I'm sorry. I just need to make sure I know that this is the standard of care as you believe it exists in 2006?

The witness: Yes. In 2006—

Ms. Riley: Thank you.

The witness: —and 2005 and 2003, and 2002, and 2001, and in 1999.

Mr. Gordon: All right. Let me clarify for the record—

The witness: Yes.

Mr. Gordon: —just what we have here, particularly with counsel's comments also. We have put up on the view box so the jury can follow along with what you're saying an exhibit that we've marked as Exhibit 4 to your deposition.

By Mr. Gordon:

Q: Is that correct?

A: That's correct.

Q: And as I understand it, this is, I think you called it, an algorithm.

A: Algorithm.

Q: Algorithm of the standard of care that existed with respect to Dr. Salvador's ERCP procedure as of the date that he performed it?

A: That's correct.

Q: Okay. Now, by referring to Exhibit 4 when you need to, why don't you just take us down through it. And if we need to, hone in on it because I'm not sure the jury can actually see some of it.

A: All right. Let me zoom in on the top part. Okay. So that everybody can see it. Now, we're talking about sphincter of Oddi dysfunction (SOD) which Dr. Salvador did the sphincterotomy on, cut the sphincter. Okay. He cut the sphincter and I'm going to show you the sphincter after I show you this.

Q: What is biliary pain?

A: Biliary pain is the type of pain that this patient had, which typically is right upper quadrant pain radiating to the back. And this is the algorithm that one uses, which means the standard of care that one uses developed by the people that developed the sphincterotomy for this SOD or sphincter of Oddi dysfunction, the Milwaukee people with the Milwaukee criteria that I'm sure the jury will hear about and the Milwaukee people who have done the most work in this area. This is a diagram by Dr. Walter Hogan who is the father of sphincter-otomy for SOD in this country.

Q: Let me stop you there. Is the diagram that's marked as Exhibit 4 the type of diagram, the type of information that a gastroenterologist such as yourself would customarily rely upon on expressing opinions dealing with ERCP, the decisions that should be made with respect to ERCPs and the standard of care with respect to doing an ERCP in a patient such as Mrs. Taft?

A: Yes.

Q: Okay. Go ahead. Sorry.

A: So, we have a patient with biliary pain. The standard of care is to exclude certain processes. The standard of care is to exclude, let me see if I can widen it a little bit. The standard of care is to exclude irritable bowel syndrome, that's IBS, which affects about 30 percent of patient visits in gastroenterologists' office or functional dyspexia and I won't go into these right now. And if the diagnosis has to be proven, you've got to rule out sphincter of Oddi dysfunction, which I'm going to call SOD.

Now, you then have two pathways to go. One is when the gallbladder is intact. And in this case, the gallbladder was taken out when Dr. Salvador saw this patient. So when he saw this patient, this was a patient with biliary type pain, which is right upper quadrant pain related to what people could think is the biliary tract or gallbladder area or the bile duct area. And one has to, according to the standard of care, do the ultrasound, fat meal sonography, or qualitative hepato-biliary scintigraphy.

Q: Let me stop you just right there, just to be clear.

A: Right.

Q: When Dr. Salvador first saw Mrs. Taft, she had previously had her gallbladder removed by another physician at another time. Correct?

A: Correct.

Q: Okay. And that's why we're on this side of the page?

A: Correct.

Q: All right. Please continue.

A: Now, just making it short, if these tests, both of them together are positive and symptoms persist, then we have to go into SO manometry (SOM).

Q: What's that?

A: SO manometry is sphincter manometry, which determines whether you have sphincter of Oddi dysfunction due to muscle contractions. And I'll show you what those muscle contractions look like.

Q: Yeah.

A: If the sphincter of Oddi manometry is positive then you can go on and do what Dr. Salvador did, the endoscopic sphincterotomy. If the sphincter of Oddi manometry is negative, then you've got to cease according to this standard of care algorithm. You cannot do a sphincterotomy in a patient that does not have the positive pressure criteria for the sphincter. This is very important. Because it's been shown that the efficacy of this procedure in patients who do not have positive pressure is equal to a sham procedure. In other words there is no effect, or a placebo, that occurs and there is no better results without the SO manometry in people who are cut and have the sphincterotomy than people who have the positive SOM.

Now, let me explain to you what we're talking about.

Q: All right. What are you about to put up there?

A: I'm going to show you what the sphincter is, what's cut.

Q: All right. Before you do, let's mark what you're about to show as Exhibit 5 to your deposition.

(Deposition Exhibit No. 5 was marked for identification.)

By Mr. Gordon:

Q: Would you please identify what Exhibit 5 is?

A: The Exhibit 5 is the muscle anatomy around the sphincter of Oddi. This is the papilla. This is the nipple that I said I remember telling you protrudes into the duodenum where you have to put a tube or catheter in here and actually cut with a papillitone, you cut this area. This is the pancreatic duct. This is the bile duct and this is where the bile and pancreatic juices meet. And this is where they come out into the duodenum. And this is where the gastroenterologist puts a tube with a knife in her or actually a cutting instrument and he cuts this area so that this opens up and fails to contract like it did.

Now, the whole rationale for this, the whole reason for doing this is if you think you have positive manometry. In other words, if the manometry, if the pressure in this area, shows that you have spasm and increased pressure greater than 40 millimeters of mercury; less than 40 millimeters is negative, greater than 40 millimeters is positive. There are certain things we call tachydonia and other things that make sure that this is documented to the SOD.

Then and only then is it cut. But Dr. Salvador did not have the documentation to make this cut.

Q: All right. Let's stop right there, but let's keep the, no keep the diagram on the screen. I want to talk just a little bit with the jury looking at the diagram. I want to go back before the surgery started, actually started, and go over a little bit, two or three of the things that you've been talking about. Now, you were just talking about Dr. Salvador did not have the benefit of the manometry. That is the benefit of knowing what the pressure was. Is that correct?

A: That's correct.

Q: Now, what I want you to explain to the jury in a little more detail is that when a doctor such as Dr. Salvador and Mrs. Taft his patient are talking together about a patient's problems, first what was the patient's problem that Mrs. Taft expressed to Dr. Salvador or that he determined she had?

A: Well, I'm sure, as Dr. Salvador puts in his notes, that she complained of right upper quadrant pain. Her referring physician referred the patient for right upper quadrant pain with some increased liver function tests that were abnormal. Dr. Salvador, I'm sure, told the patient that in order to evaluate whether this sphincter should be cut to improve her symptoms, he told her that he must do sphincter manometry, a pressure study. And it's very simple. You just put a little catheter in there and check to see whether the pressure is up or not.

Q: I want to stop now. Was Mrs. Taft's complaints consistent with at least or was one of the possible reasons she was having those complaints something having to do with that sphincter and the muscles that control that sphincter?

A: Yes.

Q: Okay. Now, is there a way to determine if there's really anything wrong with that sphincter or the muscles controlling that sphincter without having to take a cutting tool and cut those muscles in what you've described as a sphincterotomy?

A: Yes.

Q: Is that the manometry?

A: Yes.

Q: Is the manometry a way in which a physician can, utilizing a tube or apparatus, determine whether there really is anything wrong with that sphincter or not?

A: Yes.

Q: Now, tell the jury how the manometry would be done first.

A: All right. The manometry is done with a little catheter, pressure catheter, a pass through the gastro scope which is already in the duodenum. And it's hooked up to a pressure transducer which simply tells you when you withdraw the catheter out, what the pressure is of this area. The catheter will go into here and then will come, as you draw it out, you will get a pressure study. And I will show you the pressure study.

Q: Why don't we do that then so the jury will understand how the doctor learns about the pressure during the course of what you've been describing as the manometry procedure.

A: All right. You get a pressure study that looks like this.

Q: All right.

Mr. Gordon: We're going to mark this as Exhibit 6.

(Deposition Exhibit No. 6 was marked for identification.)

By Mr. Gordon:

Q: What is Exhibit 6?

A: Exhibit 6 is sphincter of Oddi manometry. And the sphincter of Oddi pressure profile obtained by a catheter pull through from the common bowel duct into the duodenum. There are three recording tips, proximal to distal which encompasses only a 4 mm length. The basal sphincter of Oddi pressure superimposed on phasic waves are demonstrated in all the tests. So—

Q: First off, this is not on Mrs. Taft.

A: That was not done on Mrs. Taft.

Q: Right. Where did this come from, the exhibit?

A: This comes from Dr. Hogan's article on *UpToDate*.

Q: Okay. Now, and *UpToDate* is a publication?

A: Yes.

Q: To which gastroenterologists such as yourself refer?

A: Yes.

Q: Now, so do I understand that somewhere in the room when a physician is, if they're doing a manometry, there's going to be some type of a readout where when he's got the manometry tube positioned like you just showed us on the diagram, this will show up on some kind of a readout?

A: Yes.

Q: And then does this readout assist him in determining the pressure?

A: Yes.

Q: Can you sort of tell us what we're, some of us would look at this, it doesn't mean much. Can you sort of—

A: Okay.

Q: —give us your expertise as to what this would show with respect to pressure.

A: All right. This is the normal. Right here is what you normally see. Notice that as you pass through the sphincter you get these pressure waves which are normal. They're not over 40 millimeters of mercury. This is abnormal.

Q: And this you're referring to, we're marking as Exhibit 7 to your deposition.

A: Right.

(Deposition Exhibit No. 7 was marked for identification.)

The witness: Right. Now notice that you have here peaks which occur which are over the normal pressure that you want to see, the difference between the sphincter of Oddi and the duodenum. And notice that you have high pressures when you pass by. This is courtesy of Dr. Walters.

By Mr. Gordon:

Q: Would you back up. The jury's not seeing what you're doing. Okay. There you go.

A: This is what we're seeing. This is abnormal. These are called elevated sphincter of Oddi pressures and when you see that you know that that's the problem with the patient. And you know that that's the reason why you've got to cut the sphincter. If you don't see this—

Q: Hold on, hold on. Would you put Exhibit 6 back up there, the normal. Now, I take it you did a manometry first.

A: Correct.

Q: So that you determine the pressure.

A: Correct.

Q: If you get a normal pressure reading like we see here in Exhibit 6, do you need to thereafter do a sphincterotomy?

A: No.

Q: Why not?

A: Because it won't work.

Q: What do you mean it won't work?

A: A sphincterotomy done with the normal pressure doesn't work. The patients will continue to have their recurrent, their continued, right upper quadrant pain.

Q: Okay. Now, in this case, did Dr. Salvador ever do a manometry on Mrs. Taft?

A: No.

Q: He never did.

A: No.

Q: What did he do?

A: Actually he, I don't think I've seen anything that he did do other than tell the patient he was going to do a manometry to evaluate the sphincter. And then—

Q: Let me stop you there. You've seen evidence in the record that says that he told Mrs. Taft before this procedure began that he was going to do a manometry study?

A: Yes.

Q: But he did not?

A: No.

Q: Okay. Now what did he do?

A: Well, in eight minutes, he simply went in during this eight-minute period and cut the sphincter without doing any diagnostic work.

Q: Do you see any evidence in the medical record, any objective medical evidence in the medical record, that she needed a sphincterotomy? That is the cutting of these muscles to this sphincter of Oddi?

A: Nothing.

Q: Was it during this procedure where he had a cutting device in her to cut the muscles around the sphincter of Oddi that the perforation occurred in your opinion?

A: More likely than not, yes.

Q: Okay. Now, I think we started this discussion with me asking you to elaborate and discuss in some detail the first area where you expressed your opinion that he had fell, that Dr. Salvador had fell, below the standard of care. That is inappropriately doing the procedure. Do you recall that?

A: Yes.

25.2.2   *Taft v. Salvador* II

Q: Now, let me ask you another question a little bit further down the time line. If you assume with me that when Mrs. Taft called Dr. Salvador the same afternoon of February 21st and told him about her pain, when she talked with him on the telephone, and we assume at that point in time that Dr. Salvador had brought her back to the hospital, either read the KUB that was done at the end of his procedure or had another one done, would the standard of care be the same in the sense of bringing in the surgeon to do the type of procedure that you described earlier?

A: No, as soon as you make the diagnosis, the standard of care is to bring in a surgeon on the case. The standard of care is to do everything that Dr. Salvador testified to.

Rather that expound on my research of the standard of care, I repeat the standard of care testified to by the opposing attorney's client, Dr. Salvador, in his previous deposition so that there is no questions objected to by the opposing attorney.

Q: And if we assume that he had followed the standard of care at that time, such that the surgery would have been occurring again on the afternoon of February 21st or in

the early evening hours of February 21st, do you have an opinion based on reasonable medical probability as to whether that surgery done on February 21st would have had different conditions for which the surgeon would have been encountering as opposed to the conditions that existed in her body several days later when Dr. Tracy operated on her?

A: Yes.

Q: What is that opinion?

A: My opinion is the opinion supported by the peer-review literature—and you know, it's common sense. The earlier you do this, the earlier you counteract it, the better the results. I'll even go a little further. 20 to 40 percent of duodenal perforations may not even have to be treated with surgery if you do the right things very quickly, nasogastric intubation, antibiotics, all the things that will prevent fluid from coming out of this thing.

Note: See previous rulings on the Daubert documentation of "the earlier the better." When used by three physicians testifying in another malpractice case, this "common sense reasoning" was cast out by the judge because it was not documented in the medical literature.

It might seal by itself and there might not be any surgery. That's why you have to be following this thing very closely. The time you do surgery is when you realize that you've got a sepsis, when you've got an abscess that's forming outside of the GI tract. And when you want to, when you definitely have to clean out and sew up the perforation.

So I can tell you that in a minority of cases you don't need even surgery. So had this been discovered an hour or two after the procedure and had this been discovered before the patient went home and started drinking fluids and started pouring stuff out of the duodenum, the results would have been much, much better.

Q: Now, let me ask you in terms of reasonable medical probability, if the KUB x-ray had been read by Dr. Salvador at the end of his procedure or was read later on in the afternoon, or early evening after she called in, and if therefore the detection of the perforation had been discovered earlier on February 21st, do you believe that she would have needed to be hospitalized for 29 days as she was ultimately?

A: I believe—

Ms. Riley: Object to form.
The witness: My opinion—
Mr. Gordon: Let me clean that up.

By Mr. Gordon:

Q: Doctor, if you assume with me that Dr. Salvador discovered the perforation before Mrs. Taft was discharged from the facility or if you assume with me that Dr. Salvador discovered the perforation later on February 21st after Mrs. Taft talked with him on the phone and instituted the standard of care procedures that I believe both you and he have testified in the fact of that perforation, do you have an opinion based on reasonable medical probability as to whether Mrs. Taft would have needed the care and treatment she ultimately received at Jefferson Hospital and ultimately at St. Elizabeth's Hospital for, I think, it was roughly 29 days thereafter?

A: Yes.

Q: What is that opinion?

A: My opinion is she would have needed much less hospital days than she actually showed because "the earlier the better."

Q: Have you read the St. Elizabeth records on Mrs. Taft?

A: Yes.

Q: Have you read the surgical reports of Dr. Tracy, her treating surgeon, during that hospitalization?

A: Yes.

Q: Either by using the color, the diagram, or any other diagram you have here today or if you can do it verbally, can you tell us what Dr. Tracy was faced with in his first operative procedure? What Dr. Tracy did in the face of what he discovered in his first operative procedure?

A: Well, I'm not going to go through the entire surgical procedure except to say what Dr. Tracy had to do. Because the cut and the perforation was now sepsis. There was a lot of abscess and infection and swelling in this area. He had to have a diversion procedure, which is doing a gastrojejunostomy with getting the—I'm not going to go into all those details. But, he had to do extensive surgery in order to prevent more abscesses from forming.

Q: All right. Well, let me ask you some questions while we're still on the diagram. Would you point in the area where the perforation was again.

A: It—

Q: All right. I'm just going to be hypothetical. Why couldn't he just go in and close where the perforation was? What did he find?

A: Well, as Dr. Tracy himself says in his operative report, it was too close to this area. This is a dangerous area to be sewing around, especially when you're getting swelling and you have a few days worth of swelling and infection and friable tissue, you really can't go here and start doing a simple closure for fear of involving, making more complications occur in, this area. So he had to go and do what he did.

Q: Now, you mentioned something earlier, that had she developed sepsis by the time he operated on her?

A: Yes.

Q: What is sepsis?

A: Sepsis is generalized infection in the bloodstream and everywhere else.

Q: Did she have the same generalized, in your opinion, did she have the same generalized infection, i.e., this sepsis, on the morning of February 21st right after the procedure was finished or on the afternoon of February 21st when she called Dr. Salvador?

A: Not likely.

Q: Why is that?

A: Because she didn't have fever.

Q: Okay. She had fever by the time Dr. Salvador saw her?

A: Yes.

Q: Okay.

A: Well, Dr. Salvador didn't see her—

Q: I'm sorry.

A: —until, as a matter of fact, I'm not even sure Dr. Salvador saw her ever again.

Q: Yeah, I misspoke. I meant Dr. Tracy. Did she have fever by the time Dr. Tracy saw her?

A: Yes.

Q: Okay. Is fever an indication of infection going on?

A: Yes.

Q: Was she treated with antibiotics?

A: She was treated with, I have no problems with what she was treated with by Dr. Tracy or St. E's admission and discharge.

Q: Based on your training and experience, based on your review of the medical records in this case, based on your review of the depositions in this case, based on your review of the medical literature in this case that you have identified, do you have an opinion that the care and treatment that Mrs. Taft received at St. Elizabeth's Hospital after she was admitted, after the discovery of the perforation was care that was reasonable and necessary because of the perforation caused by Dr. Salvador and the complications that developed due to the delay in the discovery of that perforation?

A: Yes.

Q: What is that opinion?

A: My opinion is that there was, that the St. G's doctors and staff met the standard of care. And they treated her correctly.

Q: And was the standard of care that they provided and treated her correctly, was that care necessitated in reasonable medical probability because of the perforation caused by Dr. Salvador and the complications that developed as a result of that complication including the delay in that treatment at St. Elizabeth's?

A: Yes.

Q: Now, before I pass you to Ms. Riley, there were some other references. I'm not sure that we have specifically identified them on the record. I'd like to do so at this time. What other references do you have? Where, for instance, [is] the exact reference for the algorithm that you did and the Milwaukee studies that you were referring to?

A: Well, I think I listed it and it's under *UpToDate*. And if you want I can give you the serial number of the one I was looking at. But it's the 2006, latest *UpToDate*. They do their reviews, almost every doctor I think has access to *UpToDate* either on the Web or on a CD—

Q: All right. Possibly when we take a break we can identify it specifically.

A: All right.

Mr. Gordon: At this time I'll pass the witness.

25.2.2.1 *The Cross-Examination*

This is the part of the testimony I call "search and destroy," with the expert being the target of the opposing cross-examining attorney.

Litigation lawyers are taught that the cross-exam should consist of two parts:

1. *The constructive part, in which you attempt to get the opposing expert to agree with certain parts of your case, which she will string together in her summation to the jury.*

2. *The destructive phase, in which she will attempt to discredit you and your testimony—
what is called in the parlance "impeachment."*

*Impeachment is the process by which the cross-examiner establishes a biased or sinister rea-
son in the minds of the jurors for the expert's opinion. These sinister motives include bias and
prejudice against her client (the defendant, if the cross-examiner is the defendant's attorney,
or the plaintiff, if the cross-examiner is the plaintiff's attorney).*

*Some attorneys flit from one phase to the other. Some will stay with the constructive
phase as long as possible to gain every last cooperative concession before the destructive
phase alienates the physician, who should never take this personally. Remember, just like in
the godfather, "I'm killing you not for personal but for business reasons."*

What is the opposing attorney trying to do?

*Of course, she wants to build up her case to the jury; so that the jury will vote for her side
of the story. In addition, she is trying to piece together like pearls in a necklace her closing
arguments to the jury when you are not there. You must always be alert to the fact that she
will use salami tactics (i.e., take one small concession from you after another) to build a logical case for her summation to the jury—an ironclad case she hopes will completely demolish
any argument against her client, and more important, she must obtain quotations from the
opposing expert—you—to help her do this.*

> *The firmest line drawn on the smoothest paper is still jagged edges if seen through a microscope.
> This does not matter until important decisions are made on the supposition that there are no
> jagged edges.*
>
> **—Samuel Butler**

And Vauvenargues wrote in his 1746 Reflections and Maxims:

> *a striking expression with the aid of a small amount of truth, can surprise us into accepting a
> falsehood.*

*It is this small amount of truth that the opposing attorney wants to quote from you to use
in her summation to the jury to hide the jagged edges.*

*However, in answering questions honestly, you may have to make an occasional conces-
sion. If you make the concession graciously and move on, you will exude confidence, integrity, and flexibility. If, however, you stubbornly refuse to give an inch, you may come off as
rigid, prejudiced, and a partisan advocate instead of the neutral expert you should be.*

*So, try not to make the error of "failure to concede an obvious fact" out of misguided
loyalty to one side of the case. This makes it appear you are indeed biased and an advocate
for the client instead of an advocate for the truth. When the expert fights the concession
every inch of the way and concedes only when left no reasonable alternative explanation, the
opposing attorney will point to your pigheadedness and biased prejudice against her client.
So you are damned if you do and damned if you do not. There is a delicately balanced fine
line between the two, which you will see I tried to walk in this cross-exam.*

25.2.2.2 *Additional Rules for Physician Testimony
I Learned the Hard Way*

*Avoid absolute words such as "always" and "never." The opposing attorney will attempt
to damage your credibility by first getting you to make an absolute statement and then
making an effort to show the inevitable weakness of the absolute statement.*

Avoid using namby–pamby words like "I guess," "I believe," "it seems," "it's possible," and "I would say." The opposing attorney may be able to make a motion to have your entire testimony stricken because speculation is not allowed under the rules of evidence.

Avoid the words "possibility" and "possible." Testifying that something is merely "possible" is ineffective, because your opinion must be "based on a reasonable degree of medical probability." If your opinion is only a mere possibility, the judge will most likely not allow it to be presented to the jury as evidence and may exclude your opinion from being admitted into evidence at trial.

So what do I say when pinned to the mat after repetitive questioning like the drip drip drip of a leaky faucet? I usually say, "Counselor, anything is possible—even flying pigs" or I use the rule of the zebras (Chapter 26) that usually ends that line of questioning without making it appear that I am refusing to answer her question.

Of course, if you say "yes, it is possible," you can be sure she will use your quote in her summation to the jury and make it look like you—the opposing expert—agrees with her case.

There is also no place for you to "guess" in your expert testimony. Your "guesses" are not admissible in evidence. Guessing can only hurt your credibility. It should be avoided. If asked about a fact, situation, or occurrence that you do not remember, do not guess. The best answer is, "I do not remember" or "I don't recall." If you do not know, do not guess, simply say "I don't know." Do not say "I do not know, but. . . ." If you answer you do not know, then any other information you provide after the "but" is mere speculation, and you may be volunteering damaging information after the "but."

If you are thinking of using humor that occurs to you in the shower the night before you testify—stop!!! Do not even think about it! Usually after everyone laughs, including the jurors and judge, a pall will be cast by the opposing attorney who does not laugh at all. He does not even crack a smile. Instead, he waits, for what seems to be an interminable time, and then points to his crippled, injured client, or widow dressed in black, sitting forlornly at the front table and asks you "do you really think my client's problems are funny?"

"Are you making a joke at my client's expense?"

Everybody wipes the smile off their faces.

You are left sitting there alone stared at by all in another eternal period of silence before the questions start.

If you are determined to use humor (and sometimes it works to establish more rapport with the jury), you may use it under questioning by the attorney who retained you. You should be very gentle, self-effacing, and only make self-deprecatory comments, never humor directed against anyone else.

Follow along with the following testimony I made during the cross-examination to see how I sometimes fail to fulfill the above and make an ass of myself. This occurred at the beginning of the cross-examination—the search and destroy mission of the opposing attorney.

Ms. Riley: Thank you, Alan.

Q: Doctor, so you knew that today the testimony you would be giving today would be your trial testimony.

A: That's correct, as I understand it.

Q: I reviewed your curriculum vitae and I notice you do several things professionally.

Here comes the same question asked by every attorney in every testimony I have given—and you'd better be prepared to answer this too.

Q: About what percentage of your personal income is comprised by income derived from expert witness work?
A: Less than 10 percent of my net income comes from any legal, combination legal expert witness work.

Make sure you answer truthfully. If an automobile salesman can do it, the opposing attorney certainly can research your credit rating, and finances.

Also, you must be alert to the fact that law firms have great researchers and the law search engines can unearth every one of your cases, including previous deposition and trial testimony. (See Chapter 13) Also, the opposing medical experts have researched your writings and submitted proposed questions to ask you.

More than 20–30% of your income from testifying indicates that this is an important part of your income and you may be, heaven forbid, a professional witness—and thus raises the possibility that you may be selling your opinion instead of your time. This decreases your credibility with the jury.

I also have a policy of stating, at the appropriate time, that I do not accept more than one case to testify for any attorney, firm, or client. This is to ensure I am not beholden to any attorney to make him happy with my opinion(s) and thus to establish and maintain continuing and future "business." This also serves to show my independence and credibility to the jury.

In accordance with the Summary of Medical Expert Rules and Code of Ethical Conduct for the Physician Expert Witness:

   5. *Physicians should not be influenced by conflicts of interest, and should actively seek information about the issue at hand and limit reliance on other's assumptions.*
  11. *Physicians should be compensated only for their time; and never accept compensation that is contingent upon their opinion(s) or the outcome of the litigation.*

Always, the next question is another attempt at impeachment. And, in most cases, some junior law associate has done the research so that she thinks she knows the answer before she asks, which by the way is one of the rules of the cross-examiner—never ask a question you do not know the answer to. Also, keep the witness on a short leash; do not permit the physician witness to repeat anything he said during the direct exam; if the witness is able to explain again his opinion or the reasons for his opinions you are not in the control you should be.

Q: You do not advertise your medical services in any form, do you?—your work with patients, clinical work with patients?

Here, if I answer "yes" to the last part of the question, it will also apply to the first part of the question. She will then stop this line of questioning, happy with my quote, which she will weave into her closing summation to the jury without me there to contradict her story. If I answer "yes," she will immediately stop this line of questioning so that I will not have a chance to say I do not advertise on all the media, newspapers, radio, TV, movie screens, etc. This question also suggests that I am offering each of my medical patients my medicolegal services so they can sue their referring doctors. This makes me a professional expert witness in the eyes of the jury. So here is my answer to draw out exactly what she is asking me.

A: I don't know what you mean by advertise my medical work.

Q: I mean do you market your medical services? Do you maintain a, do you run ads in the newspaper? Do you in any way market your services directly to patients who might come to you for medical treatment?

Q: You personally, however, do market yourself on at least 12 Web sites who offer expert witness services. Do you not?

A: Correct.

See, she has done her research on me. She also brought in printouts of my listings in case I said I don't recall. But I knew the question was coming and did my own preparation to prove my listings are equally dispersed between plaintiff and defendant directories.

Q: Are there more than 12?

A: I think there are 12 approximately.

Q: All right. And those would—

A: Half would be for—

Q: I'm sorry?

A: May I continue?

Q: Of course.

A: Half would be for defense attorneys and the other half for plaintiff attorneys to retain me. So they know that I'm available—

Q: All right.

A: —for record review.

Q: And, Doctor, you've got ExpertPages.com. Is that a plaintiff or a defense site?

A: Well, I don't know. I'd have to look at the, let me see. I could tell you right now that the ones that I remember for the defense side is DRI, which is a Defense Research Institute, which is for the defense, and the American Health Lawyers Association, which also lists me as a medical expert.

Thank heaven I try to list myself with both defense and plaintiff directories. This usually stops this onslaught of questions directed to the advertising witness intent on getting business primarily from only one side.

A: There are some that are other defense. I'm not sure who. And then there are plaintiffs like plaintiff areas. Now, I really don't know. I'm not prepared to go through a background of everyone of these directories.

Q: All right. Your testimony is or was on direct a moment ago, however, that you believe that you were advertising on 50 plaintiff, 50 percent defense sites.

This is a misquote I did not catch at the time. It was 12 sites, not 50 sites for one side and 50 sites for the other. It was 50% (50–50) of 12 sites.

A: Yes, I'm listed on approximately half and half of sites that would be seen by both plaintiff and defense attorneys.

If you make a mistake, try to catch it right away and correct it.

This documents that my "advertising" is limited to directory listings—not to radio, TV, newspapers, and People magazine—and what's more important, half for the defendant and half for the plaintiff to show no bias to either one. So you see I still make stupid mistakes. She can now go to the jury on her summation and allege that I advertise on 100 sites instead of 12.

Now she's temporarily switching to the constructive "search" phase of the cross-exam.

Q: You said in your earlier testimony that ERCPs are not "done anymore for diagnostic reasons." In your opinion when did that cease to be the case?

A: That ceased to be the case shortly before the NIH consensus came out that "diagnostic ERCPs are no longer indicated for the majority of the procedures that they used to be indicated for."

Q: And when did that—go ahead.

A: The NIH consensus agreement and consensus statement came out in 2002, January 2002. And if you don't mind I can place this here. And notice what it says. It states that, patients with type I sphincter of Oddi dysfunction respond to endoscopic sphincterotomy. That's ES. Patients with type 2 SOD, which is what Dr. Salvador states this patient had, should not undergo diagnostic ERCP alone. What they're saying is that it should have sphincter of Oddi manometry.

If sphincter of Oddi manometry pressures are greater than 40 mmHg endoscopic sphincterotomy is beneficial in some patients.

Avoidance of unnecessary ERCP is the best way to reduce the number of complications. That's basically the NIH consensus statement in which all surgeons and gastroenterologists and ERCP people took as the consensus statement in January 2002.

By Ms. Riley:

Q: All right. So there are, . . . there are some conditions for which diagnostic ERCP is still recommended even after January 2002.

A: Those I listed are the only ones that are recommended.

Q: So the answer to my question is "yes."

A: Yes.

Q: And actually sphincterotomy manometry can be performed during an ERCP procedure. Can it not?

A: Yes.

She's gotten me to make a concession and agree that there are exceptions to my statement that no diagnostic ERCPs are indicated anymore. Now her goal is to get me to agree that diagnostic ERCP is sometimes allowed under the NIH guidelines to lessen the impact of "no diagnostic ERCP."—even though under very narrow conditions, conditions that she will leave out in her summary to the jury—and that the SOM manometry that needed to be done would first need an ERCP.

Q: In fact, Dr. Salvador's operative plan was to perform with an ERCP.

A: True?

Q: All right. So are you saying that Dr. Salvador would have had to do manometry, could have only done manometry with an ERCP?

Here, my mistake is allowing her to maintain that manometry needs the ERCP when actually it needs only a side-viewing gastroscope. The reason an ERCP instrument is used is that you do not have to use more than one instrument.

A: Yes.

Q: And you're telling the ladies and gentlemen of the jury that manometry you believe was what Dr. Salvador should have done in order to diagnose Ms. Taft's condition or evaluate her condition.

A: I'm telling the jury that that's the standard of care, not just what I believe.

Now this is a subtle but important point—the law in some states makes a clear differentiation between what the doctor personally believes and the standard of care. What you personally believe is not important and can be thrown out by the court, so you must clearly enunciate that your opinion is based on the standard of care and supported by the peer-reviewed literature, not just your personal viewpoints.

Q: All right. So the standard of care would require Dr. Salvador to perform an ERCP at least for the purpose of conducting the manometry study. Correct?

A: Correct.

Q: So Mrs. Taft was going to have an ERCP. If Dr. Salvador had followed the standard of care as you defined it, she would have had an ERCP. Correct?

A: Correct.

My mistake here is not correcting her on the ERCP issue, which she is moving to show that the patient must, at a minimum, be subject to complications because of the ERCP too. She is confusing the ERCP procedure with the side-viewing scope needed to perform the SOM.

Q: And even with a perfectly performed ERCP, there could still be a perforation. True?

A: True. Not a perforation, but complications. You don't usually get a perforation from an ERCP. You usually get pancreatitis but not a perforation.

She tried to show here that the post-sphincterotomy perforation would have occurred anyway because the ERCP was the vehicle to do the SOM.

Now, she switches to the post-ERCP debacle in which her client advised narcotics for the post-sphincterotomy abdominal complication rather than getting her into the hospital while she was still spending the night in a local motel at his previous instructions.

Q: All right. And you understand that Dr. Salvador has no recollection of any phone call with Mrs. Taft on the 21st. True?

A: True.

Q: And you understand that the medical records of his office and answering service do not reflect any phone call from Mrs. Taft on the 22nd. Correct?

A: No, I don't know that.

Q: Has anyone shown you any records of his answering service or office which would purport to contain a telephone call from Mrs. Taft on the 21st?

A: Yes.

Q: And what would that be?

A: That would be the phone records of the 21st from Mrs. Taft and from Dr. Salvador's office.

Q: All right. Which specific records are you referring to? Can you show them to us in your file.

Mr. Gordon: Mo, what I put up there was the subpoenaed telephone records of Verizon that I showed him before the deposition.

Ms. Riley: Those are Mrs. Taft's records?

Mr. Gordon: Yes.

Ms. Riley: All right. That's fine. Can we flip to where we've got some records.

This was a surprise pulled on her by the plaintiff's attorney who had gotten the phone records documenting the calls to the doctor from the patient within hours of the procedure. He had shared this with me in the 1 hour pre-testimony conference.

Mr. Gordon: The actual phone records themselves?

Ms. Riley: Yes. Whichever records purport to show a call on the 21st. Okay. Why don't we zoom in on that so the doctor can discuss it with me for a moment.

Mr. Gordon: There are several, but there's two that I've highlighted here that I showed him.

Ms. Riley: Okay. The two that you showed him—

By Ms. Riley:

Q: Doctor, the records that you have before you, when was the first time you saw these records?

A: This morning.

Q: You did not have them when you completed the report. Correct?

A: Correct.

Q: And were you shown any other records this morning related to phone calls made to or from Dr. Salvador?

A: No.

Q: These are the only rec—you said a moment ago I thought that you had also seen records from Dr. Salvador's answering service or office. Have you?

A: No. I haven't seen any records other than these.

And according to Mr. Gordon, they contain—and showed me records from her phone number going to Dr. Salvador's number and these calls were about two minutes and then there was one, a 10-minute conversation between she and Dr. Salvador.

Q: All right. And it appears to me that the highlighted entry is, I can't really see.

Ms. Riley: Alan, could you slide it to your left just a little bit so I can see the rest of the highlighted entry.

Mr. Gordon: Yes.

Ms. Riley: Okay. I see the highlighted entry says area code (_____)*—I think that's_____*—incoming, 10 minutes.

Mr. Gordon: That is correct, meaning it was a call coming to her.

Ms. Riley: Right. Coming to her but coming to her from the number _____*? Is that the one—

---

*Actual phone numbers are purposefully omitted.

Mr. Gordon: No, no. That thing is the called phone, the phone that is receiving it, i.e.,—

Ms. Riley: Okay.

Mr. Gordon: Let's put it this way. I don't want to interpret them but it is on the column that is called phone number.

Ms. Riley: That's what I was confused about. Thank you. All right. So that phone call shows the called phone number, Doctor, but it does not show the number from which the call is coming.

By Ms. Riley:

Q: Correct?

A: I'm not a phone call expert. I can only go by the bottom line and the report to me by Mr. Gordon that this is what it shows. Now, I'm not going to make this my opinion because I'm not an expert on phone calls. So I'll leave that to the physicians whoever they call on that.

Here, I wisely stay in my own sandbox. I do not attempt to offer an expert opinion in any other field.

By Ms. Riley:

Q: And all you needed to see was the radiology reports and the x-ray itself from Dr. Smith and Roberts. True?

A: All I needed to see was the time of the performance of the procedure, which was 9:10 a.m. of the 21st and the time of reading this procedure, which was three days later. So this has to be, in my opinion, based on a reasonable degree of medical probability a breach of the standard of care of those doctors who waited three days to read and report on a film like that.

Q: All right. That's a breach in the standard of care by Dr. Smith and Roberts, the radiologists.

A: Correct.

Some states have a "shared liability doctrine" and here she is attempting to show that her client may have only part of the responsibility—certainly not all the negligence.

Q: And you also say that, further on in the body of the opinion, you say that these failures, and you're including Dr. Salvador's failure which you discussed, but you're also saying Dr. Smith and Dr. _____'s failure to read the x-ray caused Mrs. Taft to be denied necessary medical attention and thus her proximate cause of her injury. True?

A: On a timely basis, yes.

Q: And you've agreed with Mr. Gordon in his direct examination that Dr. Salvador appropriately set out in his deposition what should have been done and what he would have done once made aware of a perforation. True?

A: True.

Frequently, attorneys attempt to confuse the expert by asking compound questions; that is, two or more questions combined. Sometimes the manner of wording is difficult to comprehend. When faced with such questions, the appropriate responses include: "You have asked me several questions. Can you simplify the question?" and "I don't understand the question. Could you please rephrase it?" Or you may choose as I did to break down the compound question into its components.

Here is one example of such a compound question.

Q: And the assumption I suppose would be from reading your report that had either of these doctors read the report timely the standard of care would have been for them to contact the physician, the attending physician, Dr. Salvador, and make him aware of the perforation. True?

A: That's a compound question. Would you let me break it down if I can.

The standard of care was breached, number 1. The standard of care was breached by the doctor, the radiology doctors who did not read this and report out this film on time and contact the doctor. Although the film does say, the report does say, that they did talk to Dr. Salvador and that he understood that the abnormality had taken place on the morning that they say this was done. However, Dr. Salvador has a written note in this report stating that it's not true.

So, I don't know who to believe here.

But, at any rate, that's one part of the breach of the standard of care.

The other part of the breach of the standard of care is the fact that Dr. Salvador himself, knowing that this was a routine film and may not be read from Friday to Monday, the breach of the standard of care was Dr. Salvador should have read the film to make the split-second diagnosis that he said he could have made that this was a perforation and treatment should have begun immediately on this patient.

Beware of open-ended questions: the opposing attorney may be trying to get you to volunteer information not called for by the question. If you do volunteer information, it may be used against you. You should, therefore, answer open-ended questions as concisely as possible, being careful not to provide information that was not asked.

She may also attempt to trap you by the use of expressions or opinions he did not use, or rewording one of his previous answers that he does not immediately recall, either during a deposition or even at the beginning of the cross-exam. If you do not call her on it ASAP, it looks like you agree with the attorney's characterization or mischaracterization. You are, in effect, letting the attorney put words in your mouth. Speak up right away when you feel the attorney is doing this, as I demonstrate here:

Q: Is it your testimony that the standard of care for a gastroenterologist performing an ERCP is that he request that a KUB be done stat and that he read it immediately after each and every ERCP?

A: That's not what I said and that's not what the standard of care is on a national basis.

What I did say was that if a KUB is done at the end of a surgical procedure like the ERCP with sphincterotomy, that the doctor responsible for the ERCP should be the one to make sure that that KUB, since it's available, that that KUB is reviewed by him prior to the patient's discharge. Now, not all hospitals—

Q: Go ahead.

A: I say not all hospitals have this policy. But this hospital did have this policy, which is a good policy.

Q: Did you review Dr. Salvador's deposition and do you recall the portions in which he testified that he did not believe the review of the KUB would have been available to him unless he ordered that test stat?

Mr. Gordon: Objection to form.

By Ms. Riley:

Q: You may answer.

25.2.3 *Taft v. Salvador* III

A: He, when the question was directed to him that he could have ordered, he could have seen the film before he left on a stat basis. There's nothing wrong with that statement. However, he could have ordered the film stat. He didn't order the film stat. But since he knew that the film would be taken anyway, because it was routine, and since it doesn't take more than minutes to develop the film, and since Dr. Salvador was there and he could have made the diagnosis on the basis of this film, for heaven's sake, why not? Why didn't he see the film to make sure that treatment couldn't have been started and on a timely basis.

The floundering bird ploy:

Do not help her when she is miscommunicating a technical question by either real or feigned ignorance. Let her make all the mistakes in the questions without you using chivalry to help her formulate the question. I mistakenly was too chivalrous in previous testimony. You are there to answer her specific questions, not to assist her in framing her questions correctly.

Q: All right. So the standard of care, first of all to be clear, does to require that the film be ordered stat. True?

A: As I say, the national standard of care does not require every hospital to order a stat film nor every doctor should order a stat film. Again, let me reiterate that when the film is taken, when it's a matter of hospital policy to check the patient prior to discharge to make sure no complications have occurred, then that's where there's a breach in the standard of care that the doctor does not take advantage of that policy.

She foolishly opened up for my explanation.

Ms. Riley: Objection. Nonresponsive to everything after the word film.

By Ms. Riley:

Q: Doctor, did Dr. Salvador take a film at the end of the procedure during the endoscope?
A: Yes.

What to do when you suddenly realize you have made a mistake?

During an intensely difficult deposition, you may misspeak or make a mistake or error. If you do make a mistake, you should correct the error on the record as soon as you recognize your error. "I want to correct a statement I made a few minutes ago." If you are challenged by the mistake before you have an opportunity to correct it, promptly admit your error. What you want to avoid after making a mistake is making the matter even worse by a cover-up of your mistake.

Remember the motto in my hometown of Washington, DC is that the subsequent cover-up is usually worse than the initial mistake, as can be attested to by numerous politicians.

Also, not admitting the mistake makes you look biased.

The witness: No, no, no, let me check this because I'm curious.

Ms. Riley: No, Doctor, I can finish my question. Your attorney said that I didn't read the entire portion so I'm going to continue.

Be careful not to let the cross-examiner associate you with the attorney who has retained you.

Here, she is trying to show that the plaintiff's attorney is also your attorney and thus you are biased to his side. Always correct this attempted impression.

The witness: Wait a minute, let me make a—please understand, Mr. Gordon is not my attorney. This is the first time I met him this morning. He is the—

Ms. Riley: I'm sorry, plaintiff's attorney.

The witness: Okay.

Ms. Riley: I know how this works, Doctor. I know he's not your attorney. I misspoke.

Here, the cross-examining attorney wants me to read from her client's testimony.

Ms. Riley: 110, line 5.

The witness: Okay. 110, line 5.

Ms. Riley: 110, line 5.

The witness: I don't understand what he means by this. I mean the film that he took prior to this last film of the ERCP is a spot film. They're all spot films. He doesn't take the entire film of the abdomen. So I don't know what he's talking about. The film, the reason why they do a KUB of the entire abdomen is because these are—that you can't tell from a spot film unless you're very lucky and you're in the place where there's air, you can't tell from a spot film. That is not accurate as far as the perforation. So, I mean I don't know what he's really talking about. He doesn't really expect that he's going to see the entire abdomen on a spot film that he takes from the ERCP. I mean I don't believe that.

By Ms. Riley:

Q: You choose to disbelieve Dr. Salvador's testimony on that point.

A: I would say that it's impossible to see the entire abdomen from the ERCP pictures that he takes from the ERCP. He is taking spot films and he's not taking an entire KUB. That's why you have to have a radiology technician take the KUB or Dr. Salvador can take the KUB. But he doesn't say it was a KUB.

Q: Do you still hold the opinion that you put in your report that was given to us and filed with the court that Dr. Smith and Roberts were negligent in their treatment of Mrs. Taft?

Mr. Gordon: Objection. Form.

The witness: I haven't changed my opinion since I last stated it to you.

Again, she's trying to get the responsibility for the negligence shifted to or at least shared by two other doctors.

By Ms. Riley:

Q: So you believe as you sit here today that if the plaintiffs are going to hold Dr. Salvador for his actions in this case you also believe that Dr. Smith and Roberts bear some responsibility.

A: Well, I'm not, I don't know who bears what. All I can tell you is that that film should have been read. Dr. Salvador is the captain of a ship here. He is the one that ordered the film. Or at least he is the one that knows the film is there. Doctor—the other two radiology doctors that follow routine, and they just read a film that's on a stack of x-rays and they read them in order. It's not a stat film, so they just read them in order. This is a Friday, right before the weekend. Dr. Salvador should have realized that this film may not have been read like it happened until the next Monday. And my point is it's inexplicable how and why Dr. Salvador himself did not look at the film. He could have and he could have made the diagnosis.

Again, I take advantage of an opening to give my opinion, which she attempts to strike with an objection.

Ms. Riley: Objection. Nonresponsive.

By Ms. Riley:

Q: Do Drs. Smith and Roberts bear responsibility, some responsibility for Mrs. Taft's damages?

Mr. Gordon: Objection to form.
The witness: I don't know how to answer that question. I really don't. I don't know.

If you are asked a question that you do not know the answer to, your answer should be, "I don't know." You should not hesitate or try to avoid saying, "I don't know." Reply, "I don't know," and then sit quietly and wait for the next question, or for the question to be rephrased, which gives you some time to think about your answer.

By Ms. Riley:

Q: Well, let's—
A: I don't know what you mean by bear responsibility. If you tell me what that means—

Q: Okay.
A: I don't understand.

Q: Let me try and rephrase the question.

With the "I don't know" response, she is forced to rephrase the question or move on.

A: Is there some Texas law that talks about—

Q: I'll tell you.
A: —or defines bearing responsibility?

She is very determined to get the responsibility shared between her client and others. She realizes it will be a long haul, so she now goes to my previously written report, which does indicate that the radiology department should have had some system in place, especially before the weekends, to see to it that the films were reviewed earlier.

Q: All right, Doctor, let's do it your way. Your report number 10, page 2. Let's look at that.
A: And we're talking about the November remember.

Mr. Gordon: March report.

The witness: The March report is 10. Okay.

Ms. Riley: Number 10, March report.

The witness: All right.

Mr. Gordon: Exhibit 10.

By Ms. Riley:

Q: You say that Drs. Smith and Roberts breached the standard of care. Do you not?

Here, in retrospect, I think I'm overdoing it. I'm not following my own advice above. I should give her the concession and get it over with instead of withdrawing one inch at a time and prolonging the inevitable. My opinion is that the hospital radiology department is partly responsible, but not as responsible or negligent as the endoscopist who failed to even glance at the post-ERCP KUB.

A: What paragraph are we talking about?

Q: Well, it would be the third full paragraph.

A: The third full paragraph says this abnormal finding was apparently missed or ignored by Dr. Salvador—

Q: I'm sorry. Go ahead there.

A: —and by, pardon?

Q: Go ahead. Go ahead.

A: How this abnormal finding was apparently missed or ignored by Dr. Salvador and by Drs. Smith and Roberts who reviewed the films, thus causing Mrs. Taft to be prematurely discharged.

Q: All right. You go on to say, and you break it down into three things: The failure to thoroughly review this x-ray. That's a failure of Dr. Smith and Roberts. True?

A: That's a failure of three doctors, Drs. Smith, Roberts, as I say in my note, and Dr. Salvador.

Q: All right. And the second is a failure to recognize the extravasation and perforation. You also attribute that to Dr. Smith, Roberts, and Salvador. True?

A: Yes.

Q: And the third criticism, the failure to notify the physician and act on the extravasation and perforation that's a failure only on behalf of Smith and Roberts. True?

A: That's a failure of the radiology department, yes.

Q: Because the physician who was supposed to be notified is Dr. Salvador. True?

A: True.

Q: Is there any evidence to suggest in his testimony or anywhere else that you see in this record that had Dr. Salvador been timely notified that he would have not known what appropriate steps to take to address the perforation.

A: According to Dr. Salvador's testimony, he says had he known about this perforation he would have taken immediate steps which were correct.

Having finally achieved this concession, which she will use in her jury summation, she now tries for yet another concession.

Q: You say in your report, let's look back again at page, Exhibit 10, page 1. You say that Mrs. Taft had been very well worked up for prior, well several times in the past, for the abdominal pain for which she complained. Correct?

A: Correct.

Q: And she actually was very well worked up January 14th, 1994 with another ERCP. Correct?

A: That's correct.

Q: Do you believe that that ERCP then was unnecessary like Dr. Salvador's was?

A: I believe that in 1994 had they had MRCP available that the ERCP would not have been done. The ERCP here was done as a diagnostic procedure, which in 1994 was not a breach of the standard of care.

Q: All right. So in 1994 it wouldn't have been a breach of the standard of care for the doctor to perform an ERCP. Do you think it was prudent for Dr. Salvador to rely on nine year studies of any kind for Mrs. Taft's diagnosis?

A: I don't think it would be prudent for Dr. Salvador to rely on any studies prior to the time he actually had to evaluate her.

Q: So, the fact that she was "a 30-year report very well worked up in 1994" should not have had any bearing on Dr. Salvador's conclusion. Should it?

A: Well, not if he had to evaluate her de novo.

Q: And you think he should have evaluated her de novo.

A: Absolutely.

Q: So, for the benefit of the ladies and gentlemen of the jury, since de novo is one of the few terms that doctors and lawyers both know, you think Dr. Salvador should have looked at her with fresh eyes, not relying on the very well workup or very good workup that you believe she had in January of 1994.

A: Well, he didn't have to ignore the workup of 1994. No doctor ignores a workup. You use that at least for a baseline. But, the patient does deserve to have evaluation. She's being sent to him for an evaluation by a gastroenterologist, by the way. So he ought to do an evaluation that is an evaluation, not just simply what he did.

Q: All right. Was it fair and was it appropriate for Dr. Salvador to rely on the diagnostic studies that had been undertaken by Dr. Wield?

A: Well, at least in part, yes. I say you can—if you let me finish. You can review other studies, but the reason she's being sent to me and I get referrals from other gastroenterologists is to find out if there is enough—pair of fresh eyes that can diagnose this problem, which essentially, and be able to come up with a treatment program for this problem. Now, in 1994 her diagnosis was fatty infiltration of the liver. And that was a good diagnosis. I mean she's diabetic.

She has, . . . am I okay to continue this or do you want to wait and ask me the question?

It is better to answer by being brief and succinct to open-ended questions. If she has follow-up questions, let her ask them. Don't do the job for her. Here, I violated this good rule. I should have waited to respond to her question. As you see, I actually helped her formulate these questions, but this fortunately did not detract from my opinion, which I continued to hold despite the destroy methods.

Q: Go right ahead. Go right ahead.

A: So in 1994 and earlier and during the '90s she was diagnosed as having had fatty infiltration of the liver, which is NAFLD. We call it, or NASH for short. NASH actually means steatohepatitis. She was a perfect candidate for this. She's diabetic. She's hypertriglyceridemic. She's got a lot of fat in her blood. Most patients have with this, with these abnormalities of liver chemistry and right upper quadrant pain and distress, have the correct diagnosis, most of them would be fatty infiltration of the liver. This was documented by imaging studies and Dr. Salvador should have taken a pair of fresh eyes and seen whether this diagnosis ought to have been documented with a liver biopsy by the way, or to go into something else. But, he did not.

Q: All right. Let's take those one at a time. Fatty infiltration of the liver or NASH result in an abnormal HIDA scan.

You should not permit yourself to be tricked, cajoled, or forced into speculating when answering questions under oath. There is nothing wrong with the response, "I'm sorry, but I'm not going to speculate on that." Always make her define the terms she is using in her question.

A: Wait a minute, let's not confuse things. Fatty *liver*, is this a question, does it result in an abnormal HIDA scan?

Q: Yes.

A: Oh.

Q: That's the question.

A: The question, does fatty liver result in an abnormal HIDA scan?—It can or it does not have to.

Q: Okay. So an abnormal HIDA scan could be the result of fat infiltration of the liver or could be one indicator of sphincter of Oddi dysfunction. True?

Again, she's trying to put words in my mouth, which I've got to call her on ASAP.

A: No. An abnormal HIDA, you have to define what you mean by an abnormal HIDA scan. If the dye is not picked up in the liver that could be an abnormal HIDA scan. If the dye is not picked up—and I'm calling it dye. It's actually radioactive, radioisotope.—If the dye is not seen in the gallbladder, that could be an abnormality. If the dye is not seen in the cystic duct, that could be an abnormality. If the dye has a very slow transit from the liver to the intestine, that's another abnormality. So you have to define what you mean by abnormal.

Q: You read Dr. Salvador's deposition. Correct?

A: Yes, I did.

Q: You understand that one of the findings which put him on the diagnostic path he undertook was a recent prior abnormal HIDA scan taken of Mrs. Taft. Did you review that scan?

The denouement of her client's premise that the HIDA scan showed SOD.

A: Yes, I did. I review the report.

Q: And did you believe that to be a normal report?

A: Well, for his purposes, yes. Let me show it to you. This is a HIDA scan that Dr. Salvador relied on. The date, notice the date is _____. This is about a year prior to the time he saw her. All right. Now, let's take a look at this HIDA scan and see it's abnormal for biliary activity, which it should be if what Dr. Salvador says is true. What this says is the exact opposite to what Dr. Salvador said [and used as an indication for sphincterotomy].

He said that it was positive and it showed that the dye did not get to the intestinal tract in time, which meant to him that there was a hold up at the sphincter of Oddi.

But look what this really says.

This [report] says there is prompt radionuclide activity in the liver [which means] and then extrahepatic biliary ducts and intestinal tract. So what this is saying is that Dr. Salvador is not correct. This is saying, if he relied on this report and I don't know whether he saw this report, he would have seen that the dye was found from the liver. It went from the liver to the intestinal tract promptly. The only abnormality here was a small contracted gallbladder with a low ejection fraction. That's why she had a [previous] gallbladder operation.

So, even on this score, Dr. Salvador was relying on wrong—at least interpreted this information incorrectly.

And now the helpless bird technique—stalling for time as she recovers from the denouement.

Q: And, Doctor, you'll have to forgive me because my picture is keeping me from reading the bottom of the report.

A: The bottom of the report says, let me read you the impressions. (1) Delayed radionuclide filling of the contracted gallbladder. So that's the abnormality, not the delay in the radionuclide filling of the intestine, which would be an SOD problem, a sphincter problem. (2) The ejection fraction is 33 percent. And that's considered less than optimal and (3) Cholecystitis is suspected, probably chronic.

Now, based on that she had her cholecystectomy, which was an acalculus cholecystitis since there weren't any gall stones there. But this report that Dr. Salvador says was abnormal from the point of view of his impression that the patient should have a sphincterotomy because of a positive HIDA study is absolutely wrong. And he should have gotten another one.

She avoids the client's denouement and changes the subject.

Q: All right. You know that Mrs. Taft had her gallbladder removed. Correct?
A: Correct.

Q: And this HIDA scan to which you've just referred us, I forget the date. I know it's 2001.
A: Yes.

Q: That HIDA scan was clearly taken before her gallbladder was removed. True?

Here, she wants only a one word answer "true" or "false." She does not want me to explain my opinion again, but I take this opening to do just that.
Remember the proverb that "small truths make up big lies."

A: True, all the more reason if I may explain that Dr. Salvador should have ordered another hepatic biliary scan. According to the standard of care diagram or algorithm that I showed you, let me have that please. The algorithm, I think it's marked, here we go. Here's the algorithm and it says you've got to do in a cholecystectomized patient what you've got to do when the gallbladder was absent as it was when Dr. Salvador saw Mrs. Taft was he had to do two things. He had to evaluate her with an ultrasound fatty meal or what we call a quantitative hepato-biliary scintigraphy, which is like the HIDA scan. If both are positive—because either one has a bad sensitivity and specificity. But together they're more accurate.—So if they're both positive, that's when you do the sphincter of Oddi manometry. So you've got to do three things before you cut that sphincter. You've got to have two positive tests join an ultrasound, fatty meal and quantitative hepato-biliary scintigraphy, which is like the HIDA scan I just showed you. And if those are positive, you still can't cut the sphincter until you check the SO manometry to see if the pressure is increased. Only then can you cut the sphincter. Until then you can't. It's just absolutely, totally against the standard of care.

She fumbles around hoping against hope that there is a more recent HIDA scan that will corroborate her client's story and protect her option if and when this is found—an unlikely possibility.

Q: You have not seen any other HIDA scan for Mrs. Taft other than the one that you just put up on the board?

A: Do you know how many times I, no I haven't. Do you have one?

Q: Sir, I'm not answering questions. I'm—

A: No, I'd like to see it. I've been calling, I wanted to give Dr. Salvador the benefit of the doubt. And so I've been calling Mr. Mallory, is that how you pronounce his name, Mallory? I've been calling his chief nurse. Her name is Walters. I've been calling her over and over again to find me, in the thousands of documents which I've been looking through, find me a recent HIDA scan or a HIDA scan that was done by, after she had her gallbladder out. And it's not in the records. I can't find it. The nurse can't find it. If you can find it I'd appreciate looking at it.

She tries to blame the plaintiff's attorney for purposefully withholding the more recent HIDA scan—vital information—from me.

Q: My question to you was you have not been provided by plaintiff's counsel thus far a HIDA scan that was taken in 2002 which Dr. Wells felt was abnormal and thus caused Dr. Wells to call Dr. Salvador for a consultation. You have not seen any such document?

A: The only document I've seen is the one I've shown you February 26, '01. But let me go one step further.

Q: All right.

I plunge the sword in deeper . . .
*   This is an unusual thing for a cross-examiner to permit: another explanation augmenting my opinion and also telling her the truth about a latter HIDA scan even if one is found.*

A: Let me go one step further. Even if another HIDA scan was done, which I haven't seen, and even if that HIDA scan was positive, that's only one third of the way.

If that HIDA scan, which we call hepatic scintigraphy, was positive, there's a very poor correlation between that alone and increased sphincter of Oddi manometry. You've got to do both, the ultrasound fatty meal, which Dr. Salvador doesn't even mention—I don't know if it was done—and the qualitative scintigraphy, and only then, if both are positive or even if either is positive, you got to go through the SO manometry. Okay. So he didn't do what had to be done. So even if it was, even if there was another one which I haven't seen, and even if it did show a decrease transit from the liver—excuse me, to the intestine—he still did not do the gold standard which is SO manometry. Because without it you cannot cut the sphincter.

So now she attempts to trap me with a trick question—equating the standard of care with the gold standard.

Some physicians may take the bait. After all, is not the best of all medical tests part of the standard of care? No. The standard of care is what a prudent physician would do in a similar situation. If a prudent physician decides that a test, even a gold standard (e.g., liver biopsy), does not have a good risk/benefit ratio then it is not the standard of care.

Here, I turn this question around to show that in some cases the gold standard is not the standard of care—if it is more dangerous for the patient than the benefit, that is, a risk/benefit judgment.

Q: Your earlier testimony that sphincter of Oddi manometry (SOM) is the gold standard.—Is the gold standard and the standard of care the same thing?

A: No. I'm testifying that the standard of care is what a prudent physician would do. And a prudent physician would not do something contrary to this algorithm that I put up on the screen written up by the very people who are the pioneers in this problem.

And that's Hogan and his group in Milwaukee. And as a matter of fact, they call—Dr. Salvador refers to the Milwaukee criteria, so he relies on this too.

Q: You will at least concede that if Dr. Salvador was relying on a recent HIDA scan that you would withdraw your criticism of him for failing to do that. True?

Now desperate, she clings to the hope that a new and recent HIDA scan will somehow appear in the records she apparently has not studied as I have—nor has she had a complete opinion from her own expert who must have missed this. She wants to vindicate her client by getting a quote from me to use in her jury summation that "if the HIDA scan is found, I will withdraw my criticism," so she attempts the "true," "false," "yes," or "no" responses.

If an attorney tries to get you into a one word answer that should not be answered in that fashion, you should not do so. As pointed out earlier, volunteering information is also a mistake. Generally, an expert should answer only the questions asked and not volunteer information. The volunteering of information will almost always result in new lines of cross-examination. It may also disclose unnecessary information, as I have done here.

A: That's not—that's exactly the opposite of what I just said.

If Dr. Salvador had done a recent HIDA scan, which I have not seen, and if that HIDA scan was positive, which I don't know, he still has to do—that indicates the procedure known as SO manometry, which he said he would do and which he did not do.

Q: All right. And perhaps my question was impossibly unclear. But what I asked you is if Dr. Salvador was relying on the results of a recent, and by recent I mean within four or five months, HIDA scan, you would at least, one would hope, withdraw your criticism of Dr. Salvador for failing to have a HIDA scan done.

A: Oh, for failing to have a HIDA scan done, absolutely. I would withdraw that criticism.

Here, she finally got what she wanted from me—an admission that I would withdraw that criticism, which she will read as my testimony in her summation to the jury—but only if an improbable HIDA scan shows up.

Here I should have added and "only if that HIDA scan shows SOD and then if the standard of care is followed by SOM."
So I continued:

The witness: The only thing left was whether, the only question left with the sphincter was whether there were pressure problems. And the only way to do that is to slip a small catheter in here like I told you before and take the pressure. That was not done. He says he looked at the sphincter, determined that there were no structural problems. There's nothing else and therefore he did the sphincterotomy not using the pressure studies that is indicated by the standard of care.

Now, he gave his reasons. I really can't figure out what he means by the fact that he would have hyperalgesia. He mentioned hyperalgesia. He mentioned all kinds of things. I don't know what he was talk—frankly, I don't know what he was talking about in his testimony. You can't rule out pressure problems unless you actually do the pressure studies. That's why the standard of care requires it. Look at all the muscle around here. Look at the muscle here and there. You've got to find out whether there are pressure reasons. And you've got to rely on two, three things, three tests. The first two are what we said before, was the time it takes to go through the sphincter with radioactive isotope, which is the scintigraphy or the fatty meal study. And if that's positive, that's when you go into sphincter of Oddi manometry. That, for some reason, I have no idea. It's inexplicable to me why that was not done.

Q: Are you finished, Doctor?
A: Yes.

Q: The third type of sphincter of Oddi function, which you have not mentioned, could also be caused in addition to structural abnormality and perhaps this is a subset of structural abnormality, the scar tissue around the sphincter could cause sphincter of Oddi dysfunction. True?
A: That's structural. That's part of the structural abnormalities.

Q: It's a subset of structural abnormalities. It's certainly feasible, is it not, that Mrs. Taft could have developed scar tissue between 1994 and 2003. Isn't it?
A: Not according to Dr. Salvador.

Q: Well, why?—because Dr. Salvador—he saw it on the ERCP?
A: No, he said he saw no structural problems. Let me see if I can find it for you.

Q: No, Doctor, I understand what he said. What I'm asking you to confirm for me is that he saw it while he was doing the ERCP procedure. True?
A: Again, let me point out in his deposition what he says and unless he has a later HIDA, he's talking about—

Mr. Gordon: What page?
The witness: Page 35. He says, page 35, line 6, when there was a delay in the emptying of that radionuclide from the bowel duct into the intestine that it suggests the possibility that the sphincter of Oddi is not working properly. Now, I just showed you that the HIDA scan

shows the opposite. That the HIDA scan shows that it was a normal transit time. So he's relying, if he doesn't have anything else, he's relying on the wrong impression for whatever reason. Let's take a look on page 33. He also mentions the possibility of fatty liver as the cause of this abnormality. I don't know why he didn't go on and do—

Ms. Riley: I'm not interested really, I apologize, but I want to go back to my original question.

By Ms. Riley:

Q: Which was what he visualized during the ERCP. And I think you'll find that on pages 53 and 54 of his deposition.

A: All right. All right. Let me just take a look.

Q: Specifically really lines 13 to 25, but also on page 54 there's some overlap.

A: Okay. Let's take a look at page 51. That summarizes it. Question: Line 14. And you saw no blockages in Mrs. Taft. Correct? 15, Answer, None. So if we're talking about structural problems he says no, there aren't any.

Q: Okay. I understand what he says. I'm asking you, let me ask you my original question. When he said did you see and he says he saw none, during what event, procedure or other activity did Dr. Salvador not see any blockages? That was the ERCP. Was it not?

A: I assume so. He doesn't say that but I assume it was the ERCP. I don't know what he's referring to here.

Q: Okay. So he couldn't have known without being inside her, the ERCP, whether or not around the sphincter of Oddi there were any structural abnormalities or scar tissue. Could he?

A: Yes, he could have. He could have looked at the 1994 ERCP report and told him this, and said the same thing.

Q: All right. So that would have required Dr. Salvador to rely on or to believe that there could have been no accumulated scar tissue or other structural abnormalities that developed in the last nine years. Is that the standard of care?

A: I don't know what you're talking about as far as standard of care goes. Dr. Salvador saw no—there were no blockages seen in 1994. There were no blockages seen in 2003. And in order to see blockages you don't have to do an ERCP. You do an MRCP. Which has no invasive risks. So if he wanted to see blockages that developed since 1994 or any structural abnormalities, he could have done an MRCP and that would have solved the problem.

Q: All right. So are you now adding a criticism of Dr. Salvador that you believe he should have done an MRCP instead of an ERCP?

A: No, I'm not. I'm simply saying, I'm answering your question as to how Dr. Salvador would know there were no structural abnormalities. And I'm saying to you Dr. Salvador would know by simply doing an MRCP x-ray. That would have told him there were no structural abnormalities. But [what] Dr. Salvador was interested in though, was doing the manometry through the ERCP. And that wasn't done. He just simply went ahead and cut the sphincter.

Q: But what you've told us is obviously there's no way to do a manometry without the ERCP. Correct?

A: Correct. That's the way you do it.

Q: So if he was already going to be inside doing the manometry that was his initial plan, if he was inside doing the manometry with the ERCP, then the best thing for him to do would be to visualize the sphincter at that time through the ERCP and not put the patient through an additional MRCP. Correct?

A: We're talking apples and oranges, counselor. Don't you understand what I'm saying? What I'm saying is a structural abnormality was not part of a differential diagnosis. A structural abnormality would have presented a different way and would have been worked up a different way. What Dr. Salvador was doing or at least planned to do was a pressure study through the ERCP. Now remember one thing. Don't confuse the complications of an ERCP involving the intubation of a pancreatic duct and the bile duct and everything else. An ERC—a manometry is done simply with a small catheter in this area. Okay. Let's not confuse the issue here. Manometry is simply doing a, putting a small tube in here. We're not, here we go. Manometry is simply putting a small tube in here to check the pressures. ERCP involves, an ERCP is actually a misnomer of this because an ERCP means doing dye studies of the common bowel duct, the pancreatic duct, the intrahepatic ducts, etc. Which he did. But the point is that manometry doesn't involve that. All it means is doing a pressure study.

25.2.4   *Taft v. Salvador* IV

Q: Doctor, do you have Dr. Salvador's report in front of you?

By Ms. Riley:

Q: Are those or any or all of those symptoms consistent with sphincter of Oddi dysfunction?

A: With that and others, and other syndromes.

Q: Okay. And can you understand why that constellation of symptoms would have Dr. Salvador include sphincter of Oddi dysfunction in his differential.

A: As one of three or four differentials. That's my point.

Q: All right. And well, forgive me, Doctor, but she had been extensively worked up in the recent past as well with EGD, colonoscopy, and Cat scan. Had she not?

A: She had been worked up in the past few years with EGD, colonoscopy, Cat scan, and HIDA scan. That's correct.

Q: Well, actually the EGD, colonoscopy, and Cat scan, you've also seen those from just a couple of months before the procedure. True?

A: True.

Q: And the negative findings on those diagnostic tests ruled out a number of the other disorders which could be included on a differential for the type of symptoms she was describing. Correct?

A: It could have ruled out, it did not rule out SOD which is sphincter of Oddi dysfunction or tube—

Q: Right.

A: —or tube post-cholecystectomy syndrome. There are many patients that have this and only one percent of them have SOD. 14 percent in the latest Israeli study, so only 14 percent of patients with these constellations of symptoms have SOD. Or you could have hyperalgesia, which Dr. Salvador referred to as one of the reasons paradoxically he did the cutting of the sphincter. Or it could be a number of other things. But I wouldn't go when you, you know, there's a saying in medicine that when you hear hoof beats outside your door in New York think of horses before you think of zebras. Now if you were in Nairobi and you hear hoof beats out there you think of zebras.

Now, what I'm saying to you, the most common things that were not ruled out by Dr. Salvador and he had a duty to the patient to see, do a de novo evaluation of this patient so that she would not fall under the risk of going with the rare entities or uncommon entities or the zebras.

Q: Let me ask you with respect to the symptoms that she had, can you tell the jury with reasonable medical probability what was causing Mrs. Taft's pain?

A: I just went through the differential diagnosis. I would have to have—

Q: Is there any way to help her? Is there any way to stop that pain?

A: The first thing is to make a diagnosis. And so far the diagnosis has not been made. If it is fatty liver, which accompanies diabetes and hypertriglyceridemia, then there are many different treatments that one could do. But you have to document the diagnosis.

Q: All right. So are you telling the ladies and gentlemen of the jury that all of the doctors who have seen Mrs. Taft since February of 2003 have failed to make the correct diagnosis, which you can now make for us based on having seen her records?

A: No. I'm saying, I'm telling the members of the jury that the doctors who are seeing her now are calling it fatty infiltration of the liver. As a matter of fact, the latest note calls for a liver biopsy to be done. And this is the notes from the doctors who are seeing her in 2004. If you take a look at the notes you'll see the ones I have indicated says that a Cat scan shows the impression is fatty infiltration of the liver with no other abnormalities. The—in addition to her other co-morbidities she has coronary artery disease and all that stuff. And she does have an increase in her liver function studies. ASD is a 119. Alkaline phosphatase is elevated and this was as late as December '04. There is a—I have a whole series of lab work here which shows what her—and her lab work is exactly the same as it was before she had the sphincterotomy. So it was of no use. And the doctor, the last doctor who saw her, talked about doing a liver biopsy. So if you're asking me what the medical probability is or what diagnosis she has, I think it's the horses. The diagnosis that occurs most with diabetic, diabetes mellitus, and high blood fats is fatty liver. And that can cause all the symptoms.

Q: Assuming that—

A: Pardon?

Q: Assuming that that diagnosis is made or confirmed by a liver biopsy, what treatment, and that was really only my question, what treatment can be undertaken to stop her pain?

A: Well, I'm glad you asked. Let me show you why I'm glad you asked.

Q: Well, let me just ask you, this ought to be a pretty simple "yes" or "no" question. Are there treatment modalities that can provide relief of pain to Mrs. Taft today?

Never speculate.

A: The short answer is "I don't know."

Q: Okay. So you, as the expert witness for the plaintiff who apparently provided a two part report or summary of your work with fatty liver disease and your study of the fatty liver disease in the short answer, can't say whether or not there is a particular treatment modality that would be helpful to Mrs. Taft.

A: I can tell you that the question you asked me, "Is there a treatment modality that will take away her pain?"—the answer is "I don't know." But if you ask me: "Is there a treatment modality that will decrease her risks of having cancer of the liver?" the answer is "yes."

Q: Okay. And with respect to the literature that's currently available, no one, in other words the negligence of Dr. Salvador did not cause Mrs. Taft to have fatty liver disease. True?

A: True.

Q: You think she had that well before as a consequence of her diabetes among other things?

A: True.

Q: And fatty liver disease, if I understand what you just told me correctly, fatty liver disease can lead to liver cancer.

A: Fatty liver disease can lead to cirrhosis, which can lead to liver cancer.

Q: All right. So in some ways fatty liver disease can be a progressive or part of a progressive journey to liver cancer if left untreated.

A: Correct.

Q: All right. In terms of dealing with the day to day pain and the issues with which Mrs. Taft currently concerns herself, just the pain, the constellation of symptoms before, there's no treatment you know of which would definitively address that.

I stay in my own sandbox

A: Well, I'm not a pain specialist, but there are people who deal with this. It's called hyperalgesia. Dr. Salvador mentions this as part of his differential diagnosis and one of the reasons paradoxically he did not do a manometry study. And I can't figure out what the link is. But at any rate—

Q: Do you know why—

A: Pardon?

Q: Go ahead.

Mr. Gordon: Finish your answer, please.

By Ms. Riley:

Q: Go ahead.

Mr. Gordon: You said "I don't know why."
The witness: I don't know why, what?

Mr. Gordon: I don't know. That's the way you finished your answer.

The witness: Okay.

Mr. Gordon: Before you got interrupted.

The witness: So there are pain specialists that can deal with this question. I'm not a pain specialist. I can't deal with this question, but I'm certain that once the diagnosis is made, once the diagnosis of fatty liver is documented and once the treatment program starts on fatty liver to prevent her from having liver cancer, which is a very strong possibility if left untreated, then someone else can be treating the pain, the chronic pain syndrome.

By Ms. Riley:

Q: Have you completed your answer?

A: Yes.

Q: Do you know why Mrs. Taft was taking Vicodin on a regular basis between 1999 and 2003?

A: She had arthritis and orthopaedic problems. And I think I saw the orthopaedic notes and she had a lot of orthopaedic problems which necessitated the use of pain pills.

Q: Is Vicodin a narcotic?

A: Yes.

Q: Is Vicodin addictive?

A: Yes.

Q: What sorts of effect, if any, what sort of effect I should say, if any, can narcotics have [on] the function of a sphincter of Oddi?

A: That's a very broad question. I can't answer that without going through the physiology here. It can and cannot cause contractions. It can and cannot, which is why I'm surprised that Dr. Salvador told her to take Vicodin after having the sphincterotomy. It can or cannot have a lot of other symptoms, constipation, ostipation. I mean there are a lot of things that go with Vicodin that I don't think is relevant right now. But if you want me to go through, if you want me to go through all the side effects of Vicodin, I can do that too.

Q: No. I don't think my question asked that. I think what I specifically asked you was can Vicodin have an effect on the function of the sphincter of Oddi, yes or no?

A: Yes.

Q: In Mrs. Taft's case, you believe that the only explanation for her pain in reasonable medical probability is fatty liver.

A: With a reasonable degree of medical probability, yes.

Q: Have you seen any records reflecting treatment undertaken by Mrs. Taft since December 2004?

A: No.

Q: Do you know whether or not she has had any procedures or studies as we sit here today June of 2006, any procedures or studies related to the ERCP and its aftermath?

A: I don't know how to answer that question. I've got everything up to 2004. I don't know about 2005—

Q: I'm sorry, between 2004 and 2006?

And as we sit here today, is it your testimony that had Mrs. Taft not undergone the ERCP, had a diagnosis of fatty liver been made in 2003 that she would still have the same pain today that she had prior to any biopsy done in 2003?

A: Can you break down—

Mr. Gordon: Objection to form.
The witness: Can you break down the question?

Always ask the attorney to rephrase a compound question.

Ms. Riley: Sure.
The witness: There's too many questions in there.
Ms. Riley: You're right. You're absolutely right. You don't need to explain. Just ask me to break it down.

By Ms. Riley:

Q: If she hadn't had the ERCP and they had just diagnosed her with the fatty liver as you contend should have been done, she'd still have pain today. Wouldn't she?

A: I don't know.

Q: Well, would the biopsy disclose the presence of fatty liver? Would that biopsy have somehow relieved the pain?

A: Of course not.

Q: Patients with fatty liver disease tend to have pain which is chronic and as you point out in your earlier testimony not something that's easily treatable. True?

A: What I said was there are pain specialists who will treat chronic pain, which she has. I'm not even sure this is fatty liver, the pain I mean. The pain could be due to hyperalgesia, which is a distinct syndrome referred to by Dr. Salvador. Now there are pain specialists that will treat hyperalgesia. Now whether the fatty liver is causing the pain or not I'm not sure. To a reasonable degree of medical probability, it probably is part of the constellation of symptoms referred to by Dr. Salvador, including abnormal liver chemistries. But the reason I'm calling it a fatty liver is because that's what the objective studies show. The Cat scan showed a fatty liver. And these constellation of symptoms can fit fatty liver as we described in our articles.

By Ms. Riley:

Q: Doctor, did you keep any handwritten notes or typewritten notes—
A: No.

Q: —of your thoughts—
A: Not that I recall.

Q: All right. And what other document, you've got the medical records. Other than the medical records, the deposition of Mrs. Taft, the deposition of Dr. Salvador, and the journal articles which you showed to opposing counsel, is there any other category that would describe the set of documents you reviewed?

A: You know, I've told you before, I have thousands of documents here. I can't go through, I mean we have a box here you're not seeing in a chair. They include everything I guess that's in this case, so—

Q: All right. Have you issued any bills to the plaintiff's lawyer?
A: Oh sure, are you kidding, after three years of work on this case?

Q: Do you have copies of those?
A: No, but I can tell you what the total is.

Q: That's fine. Tell me what the total is so far.
A: Total far excluding today is $_____.

Q: And then today was $600 per hour—
A: Is $_____.

Q: Three hours, $_____.
A: Well, it's an eight-hour day, if it goes a full eight hours it's $_____ minimum.

Q: Okay. So that will be roughly $_____ total you've been paid for your involvement in this case.
A: Correct. I've spent . . . about three hours a month for the past three years—

Q: Have you—
A: —106 hours, 110 hours on this case.

Q: Will you read this?
A: All right. So what you wrote was Dr. Carter will testify that the ERCP with sphincterotomy is the accepted treatment for biliary dyskinesia.

But that's not true. Only if SOD documented, the accepted treatment of biliary dyskinesia with sphincterotomy must be documented by manometric studies of the sphincter.

You also say that Dr. Carter disagrees with the plaintiff's expert, Dr. Hookman regarding his opinions in this matter and will testify as such. You say that Dr. Carter will also testify that the hospital course that Mrs. Taft undertook would likely have been the same had she been explored on the 21st versus the early morning of the 23rd.

I've already shown you evidence that this is wrong. In Dr. Carter'—

Q: Doctor, not to break your flow, but do you have his report?
A: Yes, I have his report. It says—

Mr. Gordon: Hold on.

In accordance with the Summary of Medical Expert Rules and Code of Ethical Conduct for the Physician Expert Witness:

10. *Physicians should eliminate sensational, exaggerated, or disparaging statements from their opinions and should address other physicians' opinions about the issues under consideration [respectfully].*

There is to be no disparagement of the expert's witness' opinion.
In accordance with this, I first wanted to show where the opposing expert agreed with me in his written report.

Q: Can you now continue your discussion of that as it relates to the procedure and the diagrams that you have shown here so that we can get your complete opinion and the reasons behind it.

A: Well, I think I've given you my reasons. There's no reason to do a cutting of the sphincter, which is dangerous basically. At least it has a risk. There's no reason to put a patient through a risky procedure without any rationale, without having—by breaching the standard of care he put the patient at increased risk.

Q: You've talked about increased risk earlier and I want to see if we're talking about the same thing. I thought I heard you tell the jury some time ago there were certain types of procedures that Dr. Salvador utilized on her. You've got a risk of pancreatitis.

A: Correct.

Q: And I think you also talked about the risk of perforation.

A: Right.

Q: And I think you also talked about the risk of bleeding.

A: Correct.

Q: Which of those risks exist with just a manometry?

A: Perforation doesn't usually exist with manometry. Bleeding does not usually exist with manometry.

Q: If you go one step further though and skip the manometry and not do it as Dr. Salvador skipped it and you go right to the ERCP—

A: Well, he did the ERCP.

Q: I'm sorry.

A: Right to the—

Q: Right to the sphincterotomy.

A: Yes.

Q: Do you increase those risks to a patient such as Mrs. Taft?

A: Yes.

Q: You obviously do, I take it from having no risk of perforation in the manometry to the risk of perforation with the sphincterotomy.

A: Yes.

Q: Is that correct?

A: Yes.

Q: What about the risk of bleeding? Is there an increased risk there?

A: There's an increase risk, of course, of bleeding with the sphincterotomy. You're cutting into tissue.

Q: Is there an increased risk in pancreatitis with a sphincterotomy as compared with just a manometry?

A: Yes.

Q: Okay. Have you now completed your discussion to the jury of the breach of the standard of care by Dr. Salvador as it relates to selecting the procedures that he did select and leaving out the manometry, which he did not do?

A: I think so.

Q: Let's move to your second criticism, which I think had something to do with—was it the delay in not doing a study, a KUB study.

A: The second criticism was not doing, not looking at the KUB, which is abdominal film done in certain hospitals as a matter of policy to make sure there's no perforation.

Q: All right. Let's talk about that if we can for just a minute. First, how long did Dr. Salvador's procedure on Mrs. Taft last on February 21st?

A: Eight minutes.

Q: Toward the end of that procedure was an x-ray performed called a KUB?

A: Yes, I think it was performed at 9:10.

Q: What is a KUB x-ray?

A: A KUB x-ray is a flat plate of the abdomen, usually it's flat and upright. And the reason it's done is to detect whether there is any air under the diaphragm. That tells you that there's a perforation.

Q: Is that the purpose of the KUB done at the end of the procedure and before the patient leaves the hospital?

A: I don't know what other purpose it would serve.

Q: Okay. Since perforations are a known complication of a sphinctectomy.

A: Sphincterotomy.

Q: Excuse me, sphincterotomy and what Dr. Salvador was doing that day, does it make sense that a KUB is done at the end of the procedure?

A: Certainly.

Q: Did Memorial Harris Hospital back on February 21st, 2003 have a policy whereby if a physician like Dr. Salvador was doing the procedure that he was that a KUB x-ray would be done at the end of the procedure whether Dr. Salvador wanted to do one or not.

A: Yes.

Q: And is that why one was done in this instance?

A: Yes.

Q: Dr. Salvador I take it did not order it.

A: Well, his name is on the order sheet, but he says in his testimony he did not order it.

Q: Right. In his testimony, does Dr. Salvador admit that he knew that the KUB x-ray was being done at the end of the procedure?

A: Yes.

Ms. Riley: Object to form.

By Mr. Gordon:

Q: What is your recollection as to whether Dr. Salvador was aware at the time that his procedure was going on and at the end of the procedure that a KUB x-ray was being done on Mrs. Taft?

A: He testified that he knew that it was there.

Q: All right. Did Dr. Salvador make any effort to your knowledge to determine what the x-ray showed before Mrs. Taft was discharged from the hospital?

A: No.

Q: Did Dr. Salvador indicate in his deposition whether he was trained and proficient in reading KUB x-rays to determine if they showed perforations or not?

A: Yes, as a matter of fact I remember seeing in his testimony that he recognized the perforation in a split second after looking at the KUB.

(Deposition Exhibit No. 8 was marked for identification.)

By Mr. Gordon:

Q: Now, I'm going to show you what's been marked as Exhibit 8, which is the KUB study, that is, the written interpretation of the KUB. Let me put that up on the Elmo at this time. Do you recognize this as the report that was ultimately done with respect to Mrs. Taft on that KUB x-ray that was performed on her and was available at the end of her procedure?

A: Yes.

Q: Let's go in and see what we see here. Follow along, if you will. If we assume that under the comment section it reads and I quote, "spot film and prone KUB are submitted. The ERCP was performed by Dr. Salvador, cholecystectomy—

A: Clips are seen.

Q: Let me get back her. Clips are seen. The common bowel duct demonstrates no evidence of filling defect. Contrast extravasation is seen at the most proximal portion of the common bowel duct, right sided retroperitoneal air, is identified on the prone KUB." Let me stop there. Were those findings confirmed, a perforation has occurred?

A: Yes.

Q: Now, in the records, there's the word iatrogenic before the word perforation. What does iatrogenic mean?

A: Iatrogenic means caused by the doctor.

Q: Okay. And in your opinion was the perforation that this KUB x-ray confirms, taken at the end of the procedure, confirm that the puncture was caused by Dr. Salvador?

A: Yes.

Q: Okay. Does the same x-ray report conclude these findings were discussed with Dr. Salvador on February 24th, who was aware of them at the time of the procedure—

A: Yes.

Q: Now, this report was not actually prepared until when?

A: This report was prepared and dated _____ as the final report, transcribed at 10:59. That's _____.

Q: All right. Let's see if we can set up our dates here for a minute. The procedure was performed in the morning of February ____?

A: Correct.

Q: The procedure was finished about, would you say, 9:08, 9:10 a.m.?

A: Correct.

Q: What day of the week was that?

A: Friday.

Q: Can you tell from Dr. Salvador's deposition, his sworn testimony, whether he ever made any attempt to see or read the KUB x-ray himself before he left the facility that day?

A: Yes.

Ms. Riley: Objection to form.

By Mr. Gordon:

Q: Did Dr. Salvador attempt to read the KUB x-ray before he left the facility that day?

A: No.

Q: To your knowledge, would the KUB x-ray be available for him to review before he left the facility that day?

A: Yes.

Q: Tell us about that.

Ms. Riley: Object to form.

The reason for the objection by the opposing attorney is most probably that this is a leading question, that is, a question with the answer suggested within the question, or a guess not involving speculation and an opinion based on a reasonable degree of medical probability or certainty. If the judge agrees, then the jury is told to disregard the question (and answer).

The witness: The KUB was done at 9:10. I don't know, even if you assume it takes an hour for the film to develop, usually you could do that in 10, 15 min. But assuming the longest time you could look at that before the patient left. The patient left or was discharged after 11.

Mr. Gordon: Let's talk about that just a little bit.

By Mr. Gordon:

Q: Are you familiar with the KUB type of x-rays that are discussed here?

A: Yes.

Q: In your experience and in your personal knowledge, if Dr. Salvador wished to view the KUB x-ray himself before he left the facility that day, approximately how long would it take for that development process to occur and express it in terms of a range if you see fit.

A: Well, I think it's highly—

Ms. Riley: Objection to form.

The reason for the objection by the opposing attorney is most probably that this is a leading question, as defined earlier.

The witness: I think it's highly likely that Dr. Salvador could have checked that KUB within a couple of hours and certainly before the 11:15 hour in the morning that the patient was discharged from the recovery room.

By Mr. Gordon:

Q: Do you believe that Dr. Salvador, as I think you testified, fell below the standard of care in failing to read that x-ray that day before Mrs. Taft was discharged from the hospital?
A: Yes.

Q: Explain that to the jury in a little bit more detail, please.
A: Well, if you're at a facility where the policy is to do a final x-ray to see if you have perforated and perforation is a complication which is discussed with the patient prior to the procedure, then if you have the opportunity to look at the film, you certainly should look at the film. As Dr. Salvador himself said, he made the diagnosis when he looked at the film days later in a split second. So had he done so at the time prior to the discharge of the patient, a lot of time could have been saved with this patient.

Q: Back on _____-st, 200_, was the standard of care for Dr. Salvador in a facility where the KUB x-ray was performed at the end of the procedure to read the x-ray before either the doctor left the facility or the patient was discharged?
A: Well, either Dr. Salvador or a radiologist should have read the film and give it the final check before the patient was discharged.

Q: Does a physician like Dr. Salvador have the ability to order, if he's not going to read it himself, that a radiologist read it stat?
A: Yes.

Q: And what does stat mean?
A: Stat means right away.

Q: Is it commonplace for physicians to order tests or certain radiological studies stat?
A: Certainly.

Q: If Dr. Salvador had ordered Mrs. Taft's KUB x-ray to be read stat, based on your training and experience and your experience in the various hospitals that you've worked in the states that you've talked to us about, in reasonable medical probability, would the x-ray have been read either by Dr. Salvador or a radiologist before Mrs. Taft was discharged from the facility?
A: Yes.

Q: Now, I want you to assume with me that Dr. Salvador testified that the reason he did not read the KUB x-ray was because he did not think he had perforated anything during his procedure. Is that a recognized excuse in not reading an available KUB x-ray that is taken and is available to the physician after the procedure?

A: No, and may I add—

Ms. Riley: Objection to form.

The reason for the objection by the opposing attorney is most probably that this is a leading question, as defined earlier.

The witness: May I add that that excuse is similar to the excuse that my daughter made to me once and I asked her why she wasn't wearing a seatbelt and she said I didn't think I was going to get into an accident.
Ms. Riley: Objection. Responsiveness.

Here, the objection by the opposing attorney is that the answer does not answer the specific question asked.

By Mr. Gordon:

Q: I believe you had a third area of criticism pertaining to Dr. Salvador and the breach of the standard of care. Is that correct?

A: Yes.

Q: And what was that area?

A: The third episode was when the patient called him, called his office, and called him several hours after the procedure and told him that she was in pain. And instead of getting the KUB or going back and reading the old KUB, preferably he should have gotten a new KUB at that time.
    He did not.
    He simply said take some narcotics that she had in her pocketbook at the time and for other problems. And he said just take those, which covered up the symptoms of pain.

Q: Why is that a breach of the standard of care?

A: Well, it's a breach of the standard of care because abdominal pain following a sphincterotomy procedure usually could be a complication and should be looked into earlier rather than later.

Q: If you assume with me that the medical records at Harris Hospital show that Mrs. Taft was discharged sometime maybe about 18 minutes after 11, 11:18 in the morning, approximately two hours or so after the procedure, generally speaking, what is your familiarity with what the condition of the patient should be with respect to pain or abdominal pain in order to be discharged?

A: A patient should be pain free, essentially pain free.

Q: If we assume that that was her condition and the nurses discharged her in that situation, did Dr. Salvador to your knowledge tell Mrs. Taft that if the pain increased any that she should call him?

A: Yes. He even told her to stay overnight [in the area so that he can check her out before she traveled 100 miles to her home].

Q: And if you assume with me that later that same day, that is the day of the procedure, after she had been discharged from the facility that afternoon she experienced increased pain and called Dr. Salvador, is that in your opinion what she was supposed to do?
A: Yes.

Q: And do you see evidence in the record that the telephone call was made by Mrs. Taft to Dr. Salvador? In other words did she testify to it?
A: It's in her testimony, yes.

Q: Okay. And what do you recall with respect to her testimony with respect to the conversation between she and Dr. Salvador?
A: I recall that Dr. Salvador told her to take Vicodin, which is a narcotic, for the pain.

Q: Now, if you assume with me that Dr. Salvador in the course of the telephone conversation with her asked her whether she had a pain medication, if you assume with me that she said "yes, you know, I can take some Vicodin," and if you assume with me that Dr. Salvador in that conversation said, "well go ahead and take the Vicodin," do you have an opinion whether that would be a breach of the standard of care given the complaints that Mrs. Taft had on the afternoon of February 21st?
A: Yes.

Ms. Riley: Object to form.

Again, the reason for the objection by the opposing attorney is most probably that this is a leading question, as defined earlier.

By Mr. Gordon:

Q: And what is that opinion?
A: That was a breach of the standard of care. What he should have done—

Q: All right. Let me just stop you. Why was it a breach of the standard of care?

Here he stops me before I continue because he wants no further objections from the opposing attorney. The physician expert witness is supposed to answer only the question asked and not to expand on it unless asked to by another question, otherwise the opposing attorney will raise an objection, which may bar my testimony on this subject.

A: Because the standard of care calls for an urgent x-ray to rule out complications after such a procedure in the complaint of pain.

Q: If a patient such as Mrs. Taft, having had a procedure performed between 9:00 o'clock and 9:10 roughly on the morning of _____, is thereafter discharged from the facility around 11:18 a.m. and experiences increased pain the very same afternoon, does the concept of a differential diagnosis come into play with respect to Dr. Salvador when that is brought to his attention?
A: Sure.

Q: What is a differential diagnosis?
A: Oh, a differential diagnosis in a patient like that who complains of pain is something that's related to the surgical procedure which was done or something that is not related to the surgical procedure that was done. Either way you've got to have a KUB.

Q: And if a patient is expressing to Dr. Salvador on the afternoon of February 21st that she is experiencing increased pain, is one of the possibilities that there is a perforation?

A: Oh, sure.

Q: Now, let's talk about that for a minute. When a perforation occurs, such as occurred with Mrs. Taft, what actually has happened? I don't know whether the use of these diagrams would again be of any assistance. But, I think I would like the jury to understand what physically is happening inside the patient's body because of the perforation.

A: Well, very simple, what's physically is happening, do you have that color photograph?

Q: I think you may have it here somewhere.

A: Yeah.

Q: If you want to put that back up. And you may have to adjust the—

A: What physically is happening is this. There is a perforation right here. And that's where she had it, right here [pointing to the diagram of the sphincter]. Right where he cut. And he himself talks about a fold here that you should not go further because that's where perforations occur. Apparently that's what happened with him. But what happens is you have a hole now in this intestine. And through this hole pours out fluid from the bile and the pancreas. Fluid pours out into your abdomen. In addition to that, you're getting a lot of bacteria that's pouring out and you are getting a lot of fluids that's pouring out. And the longer you wait, the more sepsis or the more infectious it becomes.

If you know that you have a perforation, the main thing to do is to put a nasogastric tube or a nasal-duodenal tube which will aspirate, suck up all the fluids that are coming here so that it doesn't go, it doesn't leave the intestine. That's one of the early things you've got to do. You've also got to put the patient on antibiotics because you know there's going to be an infection. So that's what's happening physically when you have a hole in your intestine.

Q: So, literally, do you have the contents, if you will, of our intestine being emptied into inside our body?

A: Exactly.

Q: In Mrs. Taft's situation, if we assume that Dr. Salvador read the KUB right after the procedure was over, maybe around the time that he was writing his report of what he did during his procedure, and as he testified, saw in a split second that there was a perforation evident on that x-ray, what would the standard of care have been at that time for him to follow with respect to dealing with the perforation that he caused?

A: Well, I agree with Dr. Salvador. He testified that the standard of care, he went through all the details of what he would do. Nasal gastric intubation, suction, antibiotics, etc., fluids, calling the surgeon to follow the patient with you so that you don't have a late cause with sequalae that makes it worse. The longer you wait in a case like this, the worse it becomes.

Q: If Dr. Salvador had followed the standard of care at that time and did the things that you talked about such as surgical procedure would what—probably occur on the 21st?

A: Yes.

Q: Is that correct? If he had followed the standard of care and the surgery had been performed on the 21st, do you believe that Mrs. Taft would have been in the condition she was ultimately determined to be in when she was ultimately evaluated and operated on by Dr. Tracy several days later?

A: Absolutely.

Ms. Riley: Object to form.

The reason for the objection by the opposing attorney is most probably that this is a leading question, as defined earlier.

The witness: She would have been better off.
Mr. Gordon: I'm sorry, did you object—
Ms. Riley: I did.
Mr. Gordon: Okay. Did you object to form?
Ms. Riley: I did.
Mr. Gordon: Can you elaborate on your objection?
Ms. Riley: Sure. It's patently speculative what would have happened. We don't know that. And the doctor cannot know that.
The witness: Well, I do know that. It's in the literature.
Mr. Gordon: All right. Let me rephrase the question.

Now he asks the question the correct way according to trial procedure rules.

By Mr. Gordon:

Q: If Dr. Salvador had read the KUB on the 21st, either at the end of his procedure around the time that he was writing his report or before Mrs. Taft was discharged from the facility, do you have an opinion based on reasonable medical probability as to whether what the surgeon would have faced that date in doing the repair would be the same as what Dr. Tracy faced several days later when he was doing the repair?
A: Well, I can best—

Q: First, do you have an opinion?
A: Yes, I do.

Q: What is your opinion?
A: My opinion reflects the peer-review literature with the one statement which says, which is backed up by papers which I'll give you. Early surgical consultation and careful observation is mandatory since the outcome may be poor in patients who do not receive prompt and appropriate treatment. And the references for that, I'll give them slowly.

Q: All right. Let me just do it in Q&A form. Are the references that you're going to be giving the references that you deem to be authoritative?
A: Yes.

Q: For that matter, the references that you have talked about today whether it was the people from Milwaukee that we'll get the specifics on or the algorithm that you did with respect to that, Doctor, are the authorities that you're referring to today and you have referred to today in your deposition all authorities that you would deem to be authoritative?
A: Yes.

Q: And are they authorities to which gastroenterologists such as yourself would customarily turn and rely upon with respect to not only the facts and circumstances of a case such as this—
A: Yes.

Q: —but in addition the opinions that you are expressing in a case such as this?

A: Yes.

Q: Now, what authorities are you referring to when you were answering my question about the difference between the surgery that if it had been done on the 21st as compared to what her condition would have been and was when Dr. Tracy operated on her several days later, which authorities are you referring to?

A: I'm referring to three peer-review articles which go into those details as to the benefits of early versus late surgery with perforations.

Q: Would you cite those, please.

A: I will cite one. I will cite all three. I specifically cited, the earliest ones were in the journal *Surgery* 1999, volume 126, page 658; also 1996 *The Annual Review, The College of Surgeons*, volume 78, page 206; and the *American Journal of Surgery*, 1993, volume 23, page 1018.

These articles I researched were not the same as those enclosed in the packet of medical records and other information I reviewed on this case. My research documents that early surgery is better than delayed surgery in perforation, but also documents the standard of care at the time of the perforation in accordance with the Summary of Medical Expert Rules and Code of Ethical Conduct for the Physician Expert Witness:

> 9. *Physicians should reject preprepared or other's research and insist upon personally conducting their own research from which they will render informed opinions.*
> 5. *Physicians should not be influenced by conflicts of interest, and should actively seek information about the issue at hand and limit reliance on other's assumptions.*
> 6. *Physicians should evaluate the medical care provided in light of the generally accepted practice standards that prevailed at the time of occurrence and should discuss the standard of care only with knowledge of the standard of care that applies.*

25.2.5 *Taft v. Salvador* V

Ms. Riley: All right. And you were going to show me how Dr. Carter actually agreed with you.

The witness: Dr. Carter [the plaintiff's expert] assumes that all the tests have been done accurately. And it's just not been done. Dr. Carter doesn't realize that the treatment rendered for biliary dyskinesia, the biliary sphincterotomy [did not have] the workup that he says was done. There was no documentation for the SOM pressure and he says that . . . and other than the disagreement that we have about earlier rather than better, the earlier there does not appear to be great disagreement because I would agree that if he had the documentation with SOM then it was okay to do [the sphincterotomy]. In his letter he says ERCP with sphincterotomy is the acceptable treatment for biliary dyskinesia. He didn't add, which has been documented by SOD, because I'm sure Dr. Carter knows the standard of care.

Here, I'm treating the opposing expert as gently as possible, trying to find a rational reason for his statements that the sphincterotomy was indicated despite the lack of evidence that the literature requires to document SOD prior to a sphincterotomy in certain classes of patients (Milwaukee class II and III patients). In fact, one cannot tell from Dr. Salvador's ERCP report exactly what was done.

And so, and he says the procedure was, there's no information that would suggest that in any way the procedure was not performed in a proper manner. I don't know about that because Dr. Salvador's note is pretty sketchy. He doesn't say whether, how he cut the sphincter. He doesn't say what he used to cut the sphincter. He doesn't say whether he did a precut sphincterotomy. I mean I don't know. I mean this is what he should have put in the report. And—

By Ms. Riley:

Q: Well, let's, I'm sorry. I can shorten this by asking you specific questions about Dr. Carter' report.

Mr. Gordon: Let's shorten it.

Now she will attempt to get me to disagree with her expert or co-opt every concession she can get from me about her expert's report for her pearl necklace, or perhaps a Mme. DeFarge knitted noose.

In this next exchange, she will attempt to get me to either agree with each sentence of her expert's report, or if not, for me to vouch that her expert is a good gastroenterologist, perhaps of a higher academic grade, a higher position, and with more experience.

Thus, his report, according to her thinking and summation to the jury, should take precedence over mine. Watch the interplay.

Q: No, that's not what I asked you, sir. What I asked you was do you agree that Dr. Carter is the best person to tell the jury what he thinks as opposed to you.
A: Oh, absolutely. Dr. Carter is his own man, I'm sure.

Again, with respect for her expert.

Q: All right. Let's look at page 2 of his report, from which you were just reading to me.
A: Uh-huh.

Q: You didn't read the—you read the first sentence. ERCP with sphincterotomy.—This is under number 1—is the accepted treatment for biliary dyskinesia. Do you agree or disagree with that statement?
A: Only if he added with documented by SOM.

Q: Okay. So you can disagree on that one.

No concession there.

Q: He goes on to say this diagnosis is supported by clinical history and laboratory studies. Do you agree or disagree with Dr. Carter on that point?
A: Agree.

Concession. Trying not to one up her expert. I have already testified that her expert is under the (mis)impression that the complete workup and evaluation of the patient was performed by Dr. Salvador, her client.

Q: Okay. Therefore it is my opinion that the procedure was performed for the proper indication. You obviously disagree with Dr. Carter on that point.
A: That's right because Dr. Carter apparently doesn't know that the HIDA scan was an old one pre-cholecystectomy and that there were no recent HIDA scans nor was there any SOM pressures performed so as to document the indication for the procedure.

Q: Right. And you're saying, you say that because Dr. Carter has the opinion that the procedure was performed for proper indications, Dr. Carter must not know about the HIDA scan and you just know that?

A: You know, you're putting words in my mouth and I don't know how to answer that.

I mean, if Dr. Carter didn't know about the HIDA scan, if Dr. Carter assumes that the HIDA scan was there and was done at post-cholecystectomy then Dr. Carter has an opinion of his own.

I'm trying hard to be as courteous as possible about her physician expert. At this point, however, I must point out the differences.

But if Dr. Carter agrees with the standard of care as outlined by Dr. Hogan and the Milwaukee group, it's hard to understand how we could disagree. It's not a personal disagreement here. I agree with the standard of care and I don't make any assumptions because when I look at the HIDA scan I saw that it was not what Dr. Salvador said it was.

No concession here.

Q: All right. Dr. Carter' report you just told me, it doesn't mention the HIDA scan one way or the other anywhere in it as part of the basis for his conclusions. Does it?

A: That's correct. That's the problem.

Point I made as a reason her expert holds the wrong opinion.

Q: What he says is my opinion that the procedure was performed for the proper indications and that the diagnosis is supported by clinical history and laboratory studies. Clinical history is not a HIDA scan. Is it, sir?

A: No. And that's against the standard of care. Because clinical history means that it could be one of four things. How do you choose the zebra out of all the horses?

Q: Okay. So now you're changing your position that you agree with Dr. Carter's statement that this diagnosis is supported by clinical history and laboratory studies?

A: I don't disagree because I said before this is one of the constellation. This is the one diagnosis that supports all these constellations. But there are three and four, and maybe five others which is mentioned here.

No concession here. Still being courteous and sensitive to her expert, I don't want to show the jury there is a "battle of the experts" which she so earnestly wants.

Q: Let's look at number 2. Perforation is a recognized complication of ERCP. You disagree with that statement?

A: No.

Q: Because I asked you about it before and you said it wasn't.

A: I'm not sure I said it wasn't. I said perforation is a complication of sphincterotomy. Of course perforation should not be a complication of ERCP unless you actually go through the wall. That would be extremely uncommon, much less common than perforations secondary to a sphincterotomy, but I guess it could happen.

The next sentence says the fact that this occurred is not in and of itself an indicator of negligence in performance of the procedure. Agree or disagree?

A: I disagree because, do you want to know why?

She took the bait and now is going to let me put in an explanation.

Q: Sure.

A: All right. I disagree because the procedure was not indicated. Had she not had the procedure she would not have had the complication.

Q: Okay. Well, let's take us out of the realm of that possibility and just say, let's assume that we're not talking about Dr. Salvador. We're talking about you performing an ERCP. Do you agree with Dr. Carter that if you have a perforation during an ERCP that that is not in and of itself an indicator of negligence in your performance of that procedure.

A: Regardless of my performance or anybody else's it's a recognized complication of the procedure.

Q: So you are telling the jury and confirming for the jury that the mere fact that a perforation occurred does not mean that Dr. Salvador was negligent.

A: Of course not. He was negligent not by anything he did during the exam.

This was an unnecessary concession of mine because I am trying hard to be considerate of her client in front of the jury. Perhaps this is too considerate, because she's going to read that concession of mine to the jury in her summation. I really do not know that Dr. Salvador was not negligent during the ERCP since his note was so sketchy. For instance, why did he fill up the pancreatic duct so many times? It certainly was not necessary and can lead to a whole lot of other complications.

So I now try to recoup any losses.

He was negligent for doing the exam in the first place. That's the problem here.

Q: Well, Doctor, I can promise you that I understand your opinion on that ad nauseam at this point. My question is you are not critical of Dr. Salvador's performance of the procedure. True?

A: I—

Q: The actual mechanical performance of the procedure.

A: I am not critical Dr. Salvador's actual performance of the procedure. Correct.

But she gets me again. Why? I don't know, maybe she's wearing me out and I'm tiring. This was an unnecessary concession on my part.

Q: And you can tell the jury that the mere fact that a perforation occurred during the procedure, that perforation is not the negligence of which you complain. True?

A: True, that is true.

Another concession, in which she will tell the jury my opinion that perforation does not mean negligence in such a way that it will sound like a simple accident in which the nonindication for the procedure in the first place will be forgotten.

A: So Dr. Carter agrees with me that there's no picture that Dr. Salvador could have taken that could have seen the perforation.

I should have mentioned here, which I did not, that it was the endoscopist's reason for leaving, that is, his ERCP spot films did not see the perforation, which is a highly unlikely event.

So, another concession.

Q: And do you agree where he says interpretation by a radiologist viewing the printed films after the procedure may be required for final diagnosis.

A: I agree that it could be a radiologist, as I said before, or Dr. Salvador, who said he could recognize it in a split second.

No concession.

Q: ERCP and sphincterotomy are routinely performed as an outpatient and hospitalization is not required. Is that a correct statement?

A: That's correct.

Q: Number 5, some time after the procedure when Mrs. Taft developed abdominal discomfort, she was appropriately offered emergency evaluation but elected to try pain medicine at home with the advice to contact Dr. Salvador if her pain worsened or did not resolve. Did I read that correctly?

She purposely left out the last sentence in the report, which makes it more agreeable to her side of the story.

A: Yes, but—

Q: Do you agree or disagree with that?

A: I disagree with the last sentence which you didn't read, which says this is appropriate advice. That's not appropriate advice.

Q: Sir, excuse me. I'm going to ask you if you agree with one statement and then I'll read you the other one as I had been doing for the last ten minutes.

A: Excuse me.

Mr. Gordon: Read it again, please.
The witness: I can't, go ahead, please.

By Ms. Riley:

Q: Do you agree with the first sentence of item 5?

I do not let her reinterpret the expert's report. No concession.

A: Do I agree with the paragraph which is the whole point that says here item 5 is sometime after the procedure when Mrs. Taft developed abdominal discomfort she was appropriately offered emergency evaluation, but elected to try pain medication at home with the advice to contact Dr. Salvador if her pain worsened or did not resolve. This is appropriate advice. And I'm saying that's not appropriate advice.

That's why she omitted the last sentence—if I agreed with the preceding sentence, she would have discontinued this line of questioning to keep another pearl.

Q: Okay. I know what your position is on the second sentence, sir. I'm asking you about the first sentence. Do you agree with Dr. Carter' rendition of the facts?

No speculation.

A: I don't know. I don't know whether she told Dr. Salvador that she did not want, and I don't know exactly what happened there. I did not go through that conversation as Dr. Salvador says he didn't remember.

Q: So you agree that she was appropriately offered emergency evaluation. Yes or no?

A "yes" or "no" answer is not appropriate here for me—only small truths for her to use with a striking statement to the jury to get them to believe her story.

A: I don't know. When somebody calls you with pain after a procedure, you don't give them a choice. You say head to the nearest emergency room for an x-ray. Come back. You're only 10 minutes away. You're staying over in Houston. You're 10 minutes from me, from the facility. Come back and get an x-ray. You don't give them a choice, take narcotics and see if it works or something else. That's not good advice.

Q: Now, Dr. Carter goes on to say that the patient was treated in the hospital and told the hospital force it was not unexpected given the type of procedure she underwent. This is the sentence I want to ask you about. He says, in my opinion, the procedure performed in the hospital course would likely have been the same had she been explored on the 21st versus the early morning of the 23rd.

A: I don't agree.

Q: Do you agree?

Can you believe she's hoping the hour is late and I will agree based on fatigue and the desire to get all this over with?

A: I don't agree.

Q: And what is your basis for disagreement?

A: The citations I cited earlier. The evidence shows in the peer-review literature that the earlier you tackle this problem the better.

From the peer-reviewed literature, see my prior testimony supporting my opinion and going against her expert's opinion. Now she'll have to find articles supporting an opposite position that earlier surgery is not better than late delayed surgery for intestinal perforation. Thus, no concession.

Now she wants a puff piece from me on her expert to quote from me to the jury.

Q: All right. And have you undertaken any independent review of Dr. Carter' credentials?
A: No.

Q: Do you know what Dr. Carter' academic position is?
A: Well, I've seen his cv.

Q: Does he hold an academic position or rank superior to the one which you hold?

She should not have asked a question to which she did not know my answer.

Again, the jury is watching me comment on an opposing expert. I'll try to be as respectful as I can.

A: Oh, let's see. He says he's Assistant Professor of Medicine, so that makes him junior to me, I guess. I don't think that's important.

Q: He's Chief of the Section of Intestinal Endoscopy at the Abbott Clinic in Abbott Memorial Hospital in Abbott, Texas.
A: Okay.

Q: Is he?

A: It says it, yes, he's Chief of the Section of the Endoscopy. Correct.

Q: Do you know how many endoscopic procedures Dr. Carter has performed?

A: I don't know. I may have missed it possibly, almost, I hope it's not 10,000.

Sarcastic comment that nobody else will understand, except maybe another gastroenterologist, because Dr. Salvador is a gastroenterologist in a very small farming community in the southwest, who appears to be performing up to 10 ERCPs daily including weekends.

And now I'm faced with critiquing another expert.

Q: You assume that as the Chief of a Division Endoscopy he's probably performed five or six times more than you have. Wouldn't you?

By this time I'm biting my tongue, but I will not let the jury see me criticize another doctor like she wants. So, my understated answer is:

A: As a Chief of a Division of Endoscopy like I was at a 600-bed hospital, you don't perform any. You teach it. So I don't know whether he's performing it or not. He could be teaching his postgraduate fellows how to do it like I did it when I was exactly in that position.

By Ms. Riley:

Q: But my question is only about your opinion. Do you have any reason to tell this jury, based on your review of Dr. Salvador's credentials, that he is not a well-qualified gastroenterologist?

A: I am certain, as I told you before, he's a well-qualified gastroenterologist.

She wanted this quote from me, but what else could I do?

"... he's a well-qualified gastroenterologist" is a concession.

Just because he made a mistake in this case doesn't detract from him. The error isn't a character error. It's a medical error. I must be certain not to disparage the other doctor.

Now, get this, she's really trying my patience. Should I express anger? An inexperienced physician might, but not me.

Q: Have you ever made a medical error in your 40, I guess, years of practice?

A: I've been in practice for 40 years. I'm sure I've made medical errors, but none that led to this kind of disaster that I remember.

Q: Can you give me an example of any medical error you've made in 40 years of practice?

A: There's no way I can tell you all—I'm sure I've made dozens of medical errors, but none that led to this kind of thing. I don't remember anything like this.

You see this is a "when was the last time you beat your wife?" question.

I think my retaining attorney is asleep because he's not objecting, but I turn her wrath away with gentle humor, which she can't trump without looking bad to the jury.

Q: Can you give me an example of one error you believe you've made that you would consider to be an error?

A: I can't recall and I'm not going to guess. My wife would probably tell you. Why don't we call my wife in, she'll go through all the errors I've ever made in the 40 years of our great marriage.

No concession here either.

Under stress, perhaps another physician might start to review most of his errors, even the last few fresh in his mind.

No one on the jury believes I can't remember any errors, but given the circumstances and with humor with which every member of the jury can identify, I turned off that line of questioning.

Further questions from her like that would have been interpreted by the jury as harassment and she was now afraid to continue on with this line of questioning for fear of jurors sympathizing with me.

In addition, an endless string of "I don't recalls" (or even one that may seem hard to believe) that you see above may tend to damage credibility. Had I not turned this off, she may then have attempted to refresh my memory, with what I don't know. This is permissible under the rules of evidence.

So, you must turn off that line of questioning with a shared experience that everyone on the jury would know (e.g., the loving but critical spouse who recalls all mistakes by the husband). That identification with every juror's experience is a bonding that the opposing attorney wants to avoid. She'll often stop that line of questioning immediately. As seen here, in this case, she was forced to drop this line of inquiry and move on.

Her next gambit in the search and destroy questioning was this:

Q: Have you ever been sued for medical malpractice?
A: Once in my 40 year career I have been sued, myself and several other doctors on a case of terminal and inflammatory bowel disease in which the patient developed every complication of inflammatory bowel disease and died. And the jury found in our favor. It was a defendant's verdict.

Q: I take it in that case you took the position that you had not committed negligence. Correct?
A: Correct.

Q: And the plaintiffs that hired physicians who said that you had. True?
A: True

Q. And it was an expert witness who took the patient, irrespective of his questionable credentials and the fact that he was being paid, took the position that you were negligent and you availed yourself of your right to defend yourself. Didn't you?
A: Exactly. That's the American way.

Q: And you don't contest Dr. Salvador's right to contest your findings in this case. Do you?
A: Absolutely not. I mean the jury is the judge of the facts in this case. The jury's going to have to figure out who to believe. Whether to believe this, my research and my review of the case, or any other expert that testifies. It's the right of the jury. That's what our system is like.

While making this statement, I looked squarely at the jury with an unmistakable belief in myself, and my opinions.

Now, an attempt to impeach by suggesting I'm a "professional" witness.

By Ms. Riley:

Q: How many depositions have you given this calendar year beginning in January of 2006?

A: Let me see, I have everything prepared here for you.

Q: I want to attach that list as Exhibit, where are we 18?

By Ms. Riley:

Q: How many did you do this year?

A: Two.

Q: Okay. So far?

A: That's correct.

Q: When is the last time you testified against another Florida physician?

A: Let's see here, November 15th of 2005.

Q: And what were the circumstances of that case?

A: I don't recall.

Q: You testified against the physician?

She would have loved it if I had said "yes." Instead, I said:

A: Well, I don't testify against a physician. I'm a retained expert by the either the defense or the plaintiff. And I don't advocate for either one. I advocate for my medical opinion. So my opinion was that that physician was outside the standard of care. I had another case where I defended—what you'll see here—a doctor in the Mayo Clinic, where I took the position that there was no deviation in the standard of care. So when you look through this thing you'll see that it has a fair representation of defendants and plaintiffs.

She did not like my equalizing my testimony in both defense's and plaintiff's cases.

Ms. Riley: Objection. Nonresponsive.

By Ms. Riley:

Q: My question about the November 15th, 2005 case you referenced, Doctor, was simply did you testify against the defendant and on behalf of the plaintiff?

A: I was retained by the plaintiff's attorney.

Q: You believe that what you're doing is a service because what you're doing is advocating for the truth.

A: That's correct.

Here comes the money part.

Q: It's just not free.

A: Of course not. My time is just as valuable as yours and the attorneys.

She helped my image, unknowingly I assume, with the next questions.

Q: Have you ever volunteered to give testimony without payment to a medical board about a particular situation—

A: Oh sure—

Q: —or your deposition?

A: Sure, I've been on the Medical Arbitration of the State of Maryland for several years and we've done medical legal consultations for free.

Q: And you've done that without compensation throughout?

A: Correct.

Q: And do you keep statistics of how many times you find that there has been malpractice and how many times there has not been malpractice in your tenure in that job?

A: I can't remember. There's just too many cases that came through our board. And besides I was just one of several specialists on that board.

Q: One of several gastroenterologists on that board?

A: Yes.

Q: How many cases a year did you see then?

A: Maybe two or three. We rotated.

Q: And during what years did you fulfill that function

A: 1987 to 1993.

Q: Approximately how many patients do you see a week?

A: Well, I see about a dozen in the GI clinic and maybe one or two of my own private patients.

Q: 12 to 13 patients a week—

A: Correct.

Q: —approximately?

A: Correct.

Q: And I note from your cv that you have a permanent residence which is in Boca Raton, Florida. Correct?

A: Ten months of the year. The academic year—

Q: And then you have a summer home?

A: Yes. The academic year, which goes from—goes for 10 months is every month in the year except for July and August. And I'm here a little earlier for my summer vacation to help my wife handle my two daughters, one pregnant with twins and the other with one baby. And they're due in a few weeks.

This is my shameless currying to the jury, but totally true.

Q: Congratulations.

A: Thank you.

Q: Doctor, have you authored any—I looked through your cv for your publications. Have you authored any specific articles related to diagnosis of sphincter of Oddi dysfunction?

A: Let's see here. Indirectly I've authored the article "Oxygen Desaturation during Ambulatory Endoscopy," number 27. I've authored checklist to justify endoscopy problems, number 33. I've authored number 38, which is called "Pancreatic Sphincter Hypertension Increases the Risk of Post ERCP Pancreatitis." I've authored number 42, the diagnosis of acute right lower quadrant pain, which encompasses the area we're talking about. I've authored—

Q: Did she have upper or lower quadrant?

A: Lower.

Q: Okay.

A: I've authored number 44, "Laparoscopic Cholecystectomy Should Be Routinely Performed with Intraoperative Cholangiogram."

I have authored number 49, "Current Chemical Studies of Non Alcoholic Fatty Liver Disease and Non Alcoholic Steatohepatitis Suggest a New Therapeutic Approach." And I showed you one of those articles.

I've authored 50, the "Up Date on Current Standards of Care and the Diagnosis Management of Fatty Liver Disease"; number 51, part 2 of the "Update on Current Standards of Care and the Diagnosis of Management of Fatty Liver Disease."

And that's about all of my 56 published medical articles I can find that directly or indirectly relate to the subject in this case.

Q: So your only meeting with anyone for this case has been with Mr. Gordon?

A: Just today.

Q: And then you had a number of telephone conversations with Ms. Walters?

A: Yes, mostly to get information that she sent me. And of course, most of the calls I made to Ms. Walters to find out where the HIDA scan was, the latest HIDA scan. And she went through the records. I went through the records. I thought it was missing from my thousands of records and I went, I asked her and she went through it over again and couldn't find it. Anything else other than what I had.

Q: Would your conversations or the time for your conversations with Ms. Walters be reflected in your bills?

A: No. I usually don't charge for administrative type calls.

Ms. Riley: Alan if we can agree that the doctor can attach a copy of his bills generated at the time he reviews the deposition, that would be great.
The witness: I don't know whether I have copies. You have my permission to get that from Mr. Gordon. I'm sure he has all the bills I've ever sent.
Mr. Gordon: I don't, but the law firm that's been on it since day one I'm sure does.
The witness: All right. Well whoever has it, you have my permission to get copies.
Mr. Gordon: Okay.

By Ms. Riley:

Q: Doctor, other than the $_____ which will be due and owing you from your time today, have you been paid in full for your time expended thus far in this case?

A: I've been paid in full even with the $_____.

I insist on being paid in full before I testify so that the question, if it's ever asked, "do they still owe you money?"—the answer is no.

Because not only do they not owe me money for this case, I can testify any way I want. But I will never be working for this firm again or for this attorney again.

As I told them, my policy is never to work for an attorney more than once.

Great! She finally gave me an opening to let that into my testimony for the jury to see that I am an independent expert that cannot be bought.

Q: All right. And have you undertaken any independent research of any kind in your review of this material? Have you, in other words, other than the literature which you provided Mr. Gordon during your direct, is there any other literature or internet searches or anything, literature searches that you've done that comprises your file?

A: I'm sure that most of the research I did is on the Web and reading in the library. But everything I have right now you've got.

Q: Okay. All right. Doctor, is there any infor—other than the HIDA scan which we've mentioned, is there any information, other information which you requested from plaintiff's firm which you have not been provided?

A: No.

Q: And do you feel that you have, that at the time you authored your reports, Exhibits 9 and 10 as you've told us, that the medical records you had were sufficient to allow you to form a report about Dr. Salvador, about the care and treatment of Dr. Salvador, Smith, and Roberts.

A: Everything I—all my reports are accurate up to the day of my reports and today, of course, if I get any other information like any medical records of this patient between 2004 and today I reserve the right to modify my testimony and also to talk about or discuss any of the auxiliary issues that come up with any new information.

Q: All right. And based on—do you have any understanding about why Memorial Harris Hospital or Drs. Roberts and Smith are not defendants in this case?

A: No. I understand they—

Ms. Riley: That's all I have.
The witness: —were dropped from the case but I don't know why.
Ms. Riley: All right. That's all I have for you, Doctor. Thank you.
The witness: Okay. It was nice meeting you.

Still courteous to the last drop. Happy that I satisfied all 13 of the medical expert rules and code of ethical conduct throughout this entire trial testimony while still being an advocate for my medical opinion, not an advocate for the attorney or his client.

Now comes the redirect. Anything that remains unclear in my retaining attorney's case must now be cleared up for the records.

One of my medical research citations bears the date of 2006. He wants to make sure the jury knows it also applied as the standard of care during the date of the alleged negligence.

Mr. Gordon: Doctor, I have one—
Ms. Riley: Thank you.
Mr. Gordon: I just have one follow-up question and then I believe we'll be through.

25.2.6 Further Examination by Counsel for Plaintiff

By Mr. Gordon:

Q: It has to do with Exhibit 4, which is this approach to suspected sphincter of Oddi dysfunction, Milwaukee Class 3 that you previously walked us through. This is the—what did you call it—the algorithm?

A: The algorithm.

Q: The algorithm. It has down at the bottom of it copyright 2006 *UptoDate*, which I think you told us is a publication.

A: Correct.

Q: My question to you is is this standard of care that you have testified to a number of times today, is this the standard of care that was in place at the time Dr. Salvador did his surgery or his procedure, his ERCP on Mrs. Taft back at that time even though it has a date of 2006 on this particular page?

A: Yes.

Q: That's all I've got.

Mr. Gordon: Thank you.
Ms. Riley: We'll reserve.

25.3 Critique of Hookman Testimony in Salvador Case by Tim Junkin, Esq. (Medical Malpractice Attorney)

25.3.1 Direct Examination

Dr. Hookman was asked about how many times Dr. Hookman had been called to testify as an expert. Dr. Hookman's answer was, "I am called upon to testify about two to three times a month. I don't accept all those cases to testify in. I do accept two to three testimonies a year." He could have given a more effective answer and in fact Dr. Hookman's actual answer was very vague.

"I'm called upon to testify about two to three times a month. I don't accept all those cases to testify in." What the heck does that mean? Dr. Hookman only accepts the ones where Dr. Hookman gets paid a lot of money? Dr. Hookman only accepts the ones where Dr. Hookman's brother-in-law is involved? Dr. Hookman did not explain better.

I think Dr. Hookman could have given a much better answer because Dr. Hookman already made clear that he believed that he had a professional responsibility to agree to review cases.

So, it would be a very easy opportunity at this point in time to say,

"Well, I believe as a number of medical schools have suggested, and as our state medical and professional organizations have suggested, a physician has a responsibility to participate in reviewing cases whether there is a potential for a mistake on either one side or the other."

Dr. Hookman also should have said, "I feel that as part of practicing medicine, I have that obligation. So I review cases for both sides. I only take and accept the cases and agree to be an expert in the cases that I think have merit for the person who has asked me to review them. So, yes, I have participated in many, many cases. I have only testified in maybe a small percentage of the ones I have participated in because I believe I have an ethical and professional obligation to do so."

So, Dr. Hookman could have done a better job there, by saying "the physician has an ethical obligation to review records to see if the standard of care was adhered to and the cases that I take are those only with merit."

As to the question "What work has Dr. Hookman done and what training did Dr. Hookman have to determine what the standard of care would be." First of all, it is a compound question. So, Dr. Hookman needed to take it to two parts, which he did not do.

The first part really has to do with what training Dr. Hookman had to determine what the standard of care would be. This would be an opportunity for the expert to explain that "not only was I trained as a doctor, an intern, and a resident in the specialty and then went on to become board certified in this specialty, but I also have practiced for 20 years. I have had thousands of similar cases. I have discussed those cases with other physicians both here and also nationally in national conferences. I have lectured on this issue and so I have, over this period of time for this experience, become intimately familiar and completely familiar with what is expected of a physician given these symptoms in these circumstances to meet the standard of care."

That would be the first part of the question. The second part of the question is, "What has Dr. Hookman done with respect to this case to express the opinions?"

I think, at this point, it is important for the expert to look at the jury and say, "Well, first of all I've carefully reviewed all the critical records in this case and I would list the ones—a particular importance would be the medical record of Dr. Salvador; the medical record from the hospital; the testimony of Dr. Salvador, which he gave under oath trying to explain what he did and why and what he didn't do and why; the testimony of the plaintiff's; the tests, which explained from their point of view what happened; the nurse's notes, the x-ray reports. I have reviewed everything that is important."

He should then have said, "After I reviewed those, I understood completely what happened in this case, but to further buttress my own opinions I went to the medical literature and read about similar cases, case studies, and things of this nature to just further support what I already knew was the obvious answer here."

Again Dr. Hookman did not do that.

In Dr. Hookman's opinion there was a breach of the standard of care. I think one of the problems that Dr. Hookman had and a lot of medical experts make is that they sometimes try to put too much into a case when one particular breach is so clear and the real reason for the harm, they try to bring in too many things.

For example, in this case, the question of whether the procedure was necessary to begin with is probably a harder question than the simple obvious fact that the defendant did not even read the x-ray to rule out a complication when he could easily have done so.

Now, why is a picture taken after the procedure? It is taken to make sure that there was not any unknown damage done to the patient. That is the whole reason the defendant had that x-ray done postoperatively? Well, if the defendant did not bother to read the x-ray, what is the point of even taking the x-ray?

It is clear, and obvious medical malpractice, that the defendant never even bothered to read the x-ray, which would have shown that the patient had been injured and needed to be immediately treated.

So, to get into a more difficult question such as well, "Was this procedure even appropriate to begin with?" is just to invite a lot of fighting on something that is nowhere near as clear and nowhere near as important.

Another thing is, in giving Dr. Hookman's answer as to why there was a breach in the standard of care in failing to review the x-ray, I would explain why just like I did previously—for a jury to understand, of course, the reason the defendant did an x-ray and why an x-ray is required. Obviously, if the defendant had created an injury, there could be bleeding or could even be infection that could be a catastrophic problem for the patient. So, a very simple procedure is to take a picture to make sure. The defendant did not do that. Obviously, it is clear that the person who ordered the picture must look at the picture. That is pretty obvious.

Also, another criticism I have of Dr. Hookman is his use of not very simple words, which I'm sure the jury would not understand. When Dr. Hookman came to using the word algorithm, Dr. Hookman should have explained what an algorithm was. Instead of using algorithm, perhaps the use of the words "a plan of action according to the standard of medical care" is more appropriate.

Before Dr. Hookman explained why he was using the algorithm or "plan of action," he should have explained in very succinct and simple terms what the symptoms were of the patient and why Dr. Hookman was using that algorithm, which matches the symptoms of the patient to show that the defendant did not follow the algorithm.

It is important that Dr. Hookman did use diagrams and in this case he used a diagram of the anatomy of the area that is involved. That was good so the jury could understand very completely what it is that Dr. Hookman was talking about and where in the area Dr. Hookman was talking about.

The lack of indications should also be part of Dr. Hookman's reasons why there were deviations in the standard of care. You can say that, but also saying "that was bad enough not doing a procedure, which was not indicated, but it is compounded by the fact that the doctor did not even bother to see the x-ray and pick up what could have amounted to a much earlier treatment of this patient."

In the question asked of Dr. Hookman as to whether, if the perforation had been discovered early on February 21st, Dr. Hookman believed that the plaintiff would have needed to be hospitalized for 29 days as she was ultimately, Dr. Hookman's answer was, "I believe so." That response is wrong.

The other attorney objected because that's the wrong terminology. Dr. Hookman then saved himself when he said, "My opinion." That is what Dr. Hookman should have started with in the beginning, saying "your opinion" and not starting with "I believe."

Dr. Hookman, however, did a nice job on the cross-examination—a nice job in responding to the questions about advertising and marketing to make sure the jury understood that Dr. Hookman did an equal amount of work for the defense and for the plaintiff and he did not let him be cut off.

The lawyer asked Dr. Hookman in telling the ladies and gentlemen of the jury about manometry, whether Dr. Hookman believed that was what Dr. Salvador should have done in order to diagnose the plaintiff's condition or evaluate her condition. Dr. Hookman's answer was, "I am telling the jury that is the standard of care and not just what I believe." That's good.

He also did a nice job in making sure that the jury knew that Mr. Gordon "was not my attorney. He was my retaining attorney."

Also, I like Dr. Hookman's use of the "captain of the ship." This is a good analogy.

Dr. Hookman did a very good job on cross-examination because he was constantly making his points despite the questions.

Dr. Hookman also did a very good job when Dr. Hookman said, "Let me go one step further." Dr. Hookman, in constantly hammering in his opinion, was excellent.

The use of the term gold standard is a very good term to use. Dr. Hookman also made the cross-examining attorney break down most [but not all] of the compound questions.

Do not forget that the negligence was not the perforation of the duodenum, but the negligence was the failure to detect it afterward. Puncture of the bowel is a known complication.

The seatbelt analogy used by Dr. Hookman is a not a great analogy because you can drive 60 years without an accident. When Dr. Hookman uses medical literature to support Dr. Hookman's opinion, I hope he makes sure he reads every single one of those articles, because the other side can find something in any of those articles to damage Dr. Hookman's opinion.

Dr. Hookman made an error when he answered the question asked him about the opposition's expert witness. The correct answer to the question as to whether Dr. Hookman agreed that the defendant's expert Dr. Carter was the best person to tell the jury what he thinks, as opposed to Dr. Hookman, Dr. Hookman answered wrongly, "Oh, absolutely. Dr. Carter is his own man, I'm sure." However, Dr. Hookman, this is not the right way to go.

Dr. Hookman should never defer to another expert. He should say "I've got over 35 years of experience as a doctor with reviewing cases exactly like this and treating cases like this. I wouldn't defer to another doctor's opinion. My opinion is correct. I don't care what the other doctor says. I respect the witness, but I can also tell the jury I know what I'm talking about."

The proper response to the question as to whether the perforation was caused by negligence would be, "It is impossible to tell from the sketchy operative report whether the perforation was caused because he performed the procedure in a negligent way or because he performed it technically correct, but it was simply a complication that sometimes does occur."

The problem is that because these complications do occur even without negligence, that is why it is so critically important to postoperatively, immediately, before the discharge of the patient, to take an x-ray to make sure there has not been an injury to the bowel. Because an injury to the bowel can be catastrophic to the patient—it allows material to leak out into the abdomen. This can cause severe catastrophic infection.

In a case like this, the defendant's lawyer and the defendant are in trouble because if it is a known complication and the consequences of a complication are as severe as they are in this case, then it just stands to reason that you must test if you can to make sure you are doing the right thing and do not have the complication. If you're going to test, you've got to look at the test.

Remember that lawyers can ask leading questions and all the leading questions she wants during a cross-examination, the retaining plaintiff attorney could not raise an objection. Leading questions are like: "Isn't it a fact, Dr. Hookman, when you have a radiologist perform a scan and review the scan that you routinely rely on that radiologist to interpret the scan and provide you information concerning the scan particularly if there is a problem?"

On the question: "Isn't it a fact, Dr. Hookman, that you charged over $15,000 for your opinion on this case?" That is a leading question. A question that suggests the answer is a leading question. As opposed to "Dr. Hookman, please tell me what your fee is," which is nonleading.

If you said to someone, "What color was the stop light when you first saw it?" That is a non-leading question. If you said, "The stop light was red when you first saw it, wasn't it, sir?" That is a leading question.

Dr. Hookman should have said, "I've been practicing medicine for over 35 years. I've handled thousands of patients with similar types of problems to the one involved in this case. I teach other doctors routinely how to handle these kinds of situations. I lecture nationally and locally. I don't know what kind of position this other doctor has, I don't know how he got that position, maybe he is older than I am, maybe he has got political connections, I don't know, but I know what I'm talking about."

However, I love Dr. Hookman's response, "you should call my wife. She'll give you all the mistakes I've made in the past 40 years," or Dr. Hookman could have said "everyone makes mistakes, but I have never made a mistake like this that endangers the life of a patient and where it is so easy to ensure that the patient is not at risk. This is laziness—to not have the time to take 10 seconds to review the x-ray."

Also, what I liked is that Dr. Hookman talked about all the medical malpractice work Dr. Hookman has done for free for the Maryland Arbitration Board, etc.

In summary, if I had to grade Dr. Hookman's testimony in this case I would break it up between the direct and the cross.

Direct examination grade: I think on the direct testimony, I would give Dr. Hookman a 6 out of 10. I think Dr. Hookman could have done a better job in emphasizing the time he had spent reviewing the critical materials, his experience he had as a practicing doctor, and also in explaining the pathology of the patient, why she came in, what should have been done, and being a little stronger on clarifying the obvious malpractice.

Cross examination grade: However, I think on the cross-examination, on a scale of 1–10, his testimony was more like a 9.

I think Dr. Hookman did an excellent job, and as often happens, Dr. Hookman's cross was much stronger than his direct and the foolish defense attorney allowed Dr. Hookman to really strengthen Dr. Hookman's opinions and explain them, which Dr. Hookman did an excellent job on cross notwithstanding the ineffectual questions.

I think though that by the time that Dr. Hookman had finished the direct, the jury would not have been as nearly as impressed with his testimony as it was by the time Dr. Hookman finished both the direct and the cross.

Critiqued by Tim Junkin, Esq. November 4, 2006.

References

1. Cotton PB., from Digestive Disease Center, Medical University of South Carolina, Charleston. Analysis of 59 ERCP lawsuits; mainly about indications. *Gastrointest. Endosc.* 2006; 63: 378–388; quiz 464.
2. Testoni, PA., Preventing post-ERCP pancreatitis: where are we? *JOP* 2003; 4: 22–32.

Critiques and Golden Nuggets for Physician Defendants and Medical Expert Witnesses

26

26.1 Introduction

It is difficult enough to beat down challenges to your medical opinion. We have seen how to prepare and win over these challenges in the last two chapters. Now as a testifying physician or medical expert witness, we have got to face a myriad of other challenges having nothing to do with our medical opinions; in fact having very little to do with medicine, surgery, or any of the subspecialties. What I am referring to are personal attacks on your personal character or *ad hominem* attacks. You also have to face a myriad of trick questions, questions designed to embarrass you and questions aimed at destroying your integrity. Like it or not that is what our adversarial litigation system is about. To paraphrase Winston Churchill—our litigation system is terrible—however, there is nothing better anywhere else in the world to protect the individual citizen from tyranny and false allegations. So where to look for methods that the medical expert can use that is fit for a physician yet at the same time helpful in countering the *ad hominem* attacks. Much of this also occurs in other "expert fields." However, what is appropriate for a lipreading or construction expert witness may not be for the physician who deals with life and death matters.

There are many generic books for expert witnesses, such as handwriting analysis, carpentry, engineering, publishing, accounting, animal husbandry, etc. When I was told that I had to testify at my own medical malpractice trial as a defendant, I looked through the library shelves and bookstores but could not find anything that was exclusively devoted to physician testimony. I thus read through several expert witness books more applicable to other trades than the profession of medicine, and did the best I could in extracting what I thought was appropriate information.

Now, after 35 years of experience in clinical medicine as well as in medical testimony and in reviewing medical records and risk management, I have used my experience as a colander by which to review, critique, and extract applicable information from most of the books out there. This is my book review of what is good and bad in those books. What is good, I think you should incorporate into your education as a medical expert witness. What I think is inappropriate or even dangerous for the testifying physician, I believe you should ignore and not bother to even try as a testifying medical expert. In summary, the appropriate material I have denoted as "nuggets" from the nonphysician generic expert books can be adapted for the testifying physician.

Not to be overly repetitive, I remind you that in reviewing these generic expert witness books I managed to sift out from the morass of information only what I believe will be useful to the testifying physician. My selections are entirely arbitrary but I trust my more than 30 years experience filter when sifting through these literally thousands of pages of information. I would like to have known all this prior to my first testimony experience, and I am sure you too will profit from my opinions on these texts. Of course no filtered information is complete. And along with all the other book reviews I have done for the reader, my advice to you is to go to the original and form your own conclusions. I encourage you to use your own developing experience filter when reading these books.

26.2   "Under Oath: Tips for Testifying" by William P. Isele[1]

I find that certain of the suggestions in this book will mislead the testifying physician. It is my opinion that some very wrong advice is given for the medical expert in this manual.

- *"It helps to be 'fashionably late,' for your deposition that is, waiting until everyone else is in the room before entering the deposition room."* The reason to come in late the authors state is "this allows the attorneys to discuss any procedural matters between themselves. It also does not hurt to enter standing when everyone else is sitting. If one of the attorneys is the type who uses intimidation as a tactic, at least you are not starting off in the subordinate position."

This recommendation is nonsense. In my experience, it is always better to get into the room first, find the chair that you are most comfortable, put away any file and organize any of your papers and materials and records, and usually have a conference with the retaining attorney for about 30 min prior to the deposition. Be available to hear all the dialogue that goes on between the attorneys. This business about not starting off in a subordinate position is ridiculous.

Other points with which I disagree—

Q: "Oh, come on now, you don't expect this court to believe that?"

A: The appropriate response as advised in this publication is to remind the attorney in a cool, calm voice of the oath you took, "Sir, when I took this seat I swore to tell the truth. What I expect isn't important. The court will decide what to believe. I can only tell you what I know to be true."

My strategic advice: Avoid the dramatic and defensive rhetoric. You are not making points with the jury with self-righteous answers. A better answer I think would be simply "Yes."

Q: "Doctor, are you being paid for your testimony here today?" The article correctly states that there is an implication in this question that somehow you have sold your *testimony* or are being paid for a particular opinion helpful to a particular party.

A: A good answer to this question advised by this publication is, "I am being compensated for my time and expertise *just as I suppose you are, counsel.*"

I do not agree with this answer. My strategic advice: Omit "just as I suppose you are, counsel." I think it is combative, aggressive, and somewhat too defensive.

Additional advice in this book is "Do not concede more than you have to." To which I must add that you should concede the obvious. Do not even give the perception that you are stubborn. The author's recommended answers may be interpreted by the jury as being a strong advocate for your side, rather than an objective medical expert willing to see both sides, and favoring your opinion only—not your client or attorney or case.

1. A good yes or no demand question can be answered, "I cannot truthfully (accurately, completely, etc.) answer the question with a yes or no. May I be allowed to explain?"

   Since, as an expert, you are sworn to tell the (whole) truth, no one can insist on something you have told them will not be truthful.

2. There are other attorneys who will try to run through your testimony recklessly, tossing answers aside and moving on to seemingly unconnected topics.

3. However, somewhere buried in this barrage is a question he really wants you to answer. He is attempting to catch you unawares hoping you will answer it in a way he can turn it to his advantage.

4. Often, these attorneys appear crumpled and disorganized, but he has really planned his questioning quite carefully and cleverly.

5. So, listen carefully to each question and think before you answer.

6. Answer only the question that is asked.

7. In this situation of "disorganized, seemingly inconsequential questions," answer yes or no.

8. Do not try to anticipate where these questions are taking you because they generally are not headed anywhere, at least most of them, because many of the questions are merely a smokescreen for the important one or two he is really interested in.

   I add to this advice: Just go with the flow. Do not get anxious thinking you are in the wrong case or in the wrong courtroom. You will not know which are the important questions anyway, until later, when his whole case/theme develops.

9. Also, you may be asked a question that seems harmless, but which later sets up some devastating point. Now he seems to be approaching the issues at hand in your opinions.

10. Again, listen carefully to each question and think about your answer before you respond, but this time try to anticipate what the ramifications your answer may have.

11. In a way, you have got to understand you are playing a chess game.

✓ Not only must you be alert to your opponent's plan of attack, but you must more importantly consider all the possible ramifications of each move you make.

12. Always ignore the bluff and bluster of the attorneys. Shakespeare said that, "All the world's a stage and all the men and women merely players." Lawyers usually adopt personae to achieve their purposes in litigation. There seems to be no good reason why the physician cannot adopt a suitable professional and "wise man" persona that your wife would not recognize, as long as she/he remembers that an oath has been taken to tell the truth, the whole truth and nothing but the truth.

13. Remember, the cross-examiner's job is to reduce your credibility and weaken your impact on the case.

A good lawyer is usually well prepared in trial, after the deposition, and he will certainly know the strengths and weaknesses of his case and your case. He will know which areas to pursue and which to leave alone. He will attempt to find your Achilles heel.

14. Do not fall into the trap of trying to answer compound questions.

   If the attorney interrupts you on any question, simply answer calmly, "Excuse me, but I would like the opportunity to finish my answer to the questions that you asked."

15. The first and foremost role of a physician in court is to conduct yourself as the professional that you are. If lawyers try to play intimidation games, do not sink to their level. You should appear relaxed, serious, and confident. Your purpose there is to assist the judge and jury in their search for truth.

Tell your story. Recognize that you are only one of several witnesses who will be called. Your testimony is contributory to an overall picture, probably not determinative of the entire case. Do not expect your expert testimony to make anyone close up their books and files and go home. Be direct, courteous and polite. That is your only role on the stage.

16. Do not lose your temper or get into fights with anybody.

17. Try to stay on point. If the attorney succeeds in getting you off your point, try to rephrase his questions. Rephrasing the question serves two purposes, it breaks his momentum, but it also causes him to stop and reformulate what he already asked. So, you also will have a chance to recollect your thoughts and the rephrasing might provide you with the keyword to use to get the questioning back on the track you want to take.

18. When talking to the jury, never talk down to them. Never use medicalese jargon. Always paint word pictures for the jury. Not only does it enhance your credibility, but it also helps keep them awake. An analogy to something with which the average person is familiar—the weather, cars, trucks, TV, Aesop's fables—can often explain the complex medical condition to which a jury may be baffled by the medical terminology.

19. If at all possible, answer in five words or less. With rare exceptions no sentence of yours should exceed 20 words.

20. You should try to use every chance you get on cross-examination to repeat and hammer home the one or two principal points you came to make on the direct examination.

26.3 "Succeeding as an Expert Witness: Increasing Your Impact and Income" by Harold A. Feder[2]

1. Feder succeeds in explaining to the expert witness a "Bill of Rights" in which he lists your rights as an expert witness. This is an excellent summary on page 243. A very good summary on how the expert witness can avoid abuse and a lot of good testimonial tips for both the experienced and novice expert witness is also provided (page 243–276).

2. Feder also summarizes ethical violations, which can be "avoided or used for attack as the case may be" on page 288. These include the following:
   • Outright false data
   • Purposely incomplete investigation of the medical records

- Altered data
- False testimony either from erroneously provided information or carelessly gathered information or intentionally ignoring data
- Recanting prior contrapositions from previous testimony or writings
- Assignments beyond competency
- Unauthorized attorney influence (premises in which the expert has relied in whole or in part on the attorney's statement, which is produced for examination)
- Reaching conclusions before complete review of the records and research, which is determined through cross-examination to uncover a fact that your expert opinion or conclusion was reached before all the records were reviewed or all the research was done
- Conflicts of interests
- Fraudulent credentials
- Contingency fee (page 290)

26.4 "The Trial Lawyers" by Emily Couric[3]

This book of interviews with 10 fabulously successful lawyers, including the late Arthur L. Liman and the late Edward Bennett Williams, provides an excellent look into the minds of the most prominent lawyers of twentieth century America (such as David M. Harney, an extremely successful medical malpractice lawyer). All of them agreed that courtroom battle (for justice) "is not an easy victory" . . . but is a fierce competition between lawyers, . . . one that demands the best minds, the most finely tuned skills, and the know-how that comes from the experience of many earlier battles.

One of these attorneys, the prominent medical malpractice attorney (second only to John Edwards in his awards) David M. Harney, did not surprise me when he stated that his strategy in at least one of his trials was to *help boost the jury award* by suing doctors for *punitive* as well as compensatory damages. Since medical malpractice insurance liability does not cover punitive damages, "this promotes early settlement," he says. Another of his strategic tactical decisions, and I am sure the tactical decisions of other malpractice attorneys also, is calling the defendant physicians themselves as adverse witnesses before any other plaintiff's witnesses can testify. Under the (California) law an attorney is able to question these physicians, "adverse witnesses" as if cross-examining them, which includes, therefore, asking leading questions, which cannot be done outside a cross-examination. As is understood, a leading question is one that suggests an answer in the wording of the question, such as "You went to the theater last night at eight?" Thus, he states, "The defendant physicians could not alter their testimony after hearing what their own medical expert said on the stand nor could the defense's experts try to explain the defendant's behavior in advance of the defendant's testifying."

So, after Harney had questioned the defendant doctors in this fashion, he called his own experts to offer their critical views on the doctor's care as the doctors, themselves, had described that care. Harney admits he changes personae in court—this time opting for an "attitude of outrage." Harney hoped that by choosing this particular persona and style, he would elicit in the jurors the same indignation and repulsion that he felt toward the doctors. And he did.

In one cross-examination, Harney was so merciless that in their appeal, the defendant physician's lawyers wrote, "Dr. M_____ was subjected to the most unwarranted cross-examination and personally attacked witness by trial of counsel. The viciousness of the attack cannot be overstated or overemphasized."

This (deliberate) courtroom verbal attack caused a very prominent cancer specialist to lose his composure on the stand and hence, "his respectability before the jury," said Haney.

Another Harney tactic is to build up speed while questioning an expert until the expert trips up under the grueling pressure and gives an answer Harney wants, "but that the expert had not planned to provide." Harney says he does that because "the cross-examination of the witness by an opposing party has been described as the greatest legal engine ever invented for the discovery of truth."

What I believe to be an extremely aggressive and perhaps unconscionable method of Harney and some other malpractice attorneys in states which place a legislative cap on medical malpractice awards is this: Caps apply only to noneconomic compensatory damages, not punitive damages. Harney believes there is a *built-in punitive amount for medical malpractices cases" because of the fiduciary obligation between the physician and the patient.*

Harney's witnesses will then testify (hopefully because they really believe it) that the defendant physician was "guilty of conscious disregard" of the plaintiff's safety. This is a prerequisite for awarding punitive damages in addition to compensatory damages. Harney as well as, I am sure, other medical malpractice lawyers *attempt to prove that punitive damages should be awarded by questions, which force the defendant physician to assume that each and every step of the patient's diagnosis and treatment are intentionally followed, which, when he puts it together in the summation, is the reasoning that "In order to do all of this deliberately and intentionally, therefore, had to be a conscious, awake disregard for the plaintiff's safety." All these to get punitive damages award from the jury because of California's (and other states) Supreme Court ruling upholding the constitutionality of the state's $250,000 cap on medical malpractice awards.* Since the cap applies only to awards to compensate for noneconomic losses such as pain, suffering, inconvenience, physical impairment, and disfigurement, the malpractice attorneys in those states purposely aim for loss of income or compensation or punitive damages. As of that 1998 interview with Haney, courts in Idaho, Illinois, Minnesota, Montana, New Hampshire, North Dakota, Ohio, Texas, and Virginia have found the caps unconstitutional. However, courts in California, Florida, Indiana, Nebraska, and Wisconsin have upheld the constitutionality of these award limitations.

In an interview this time with the experienced litigator James F. Neal, we learn from his long experience that, "Jurors will really understand only 50% of what they hear and remember 50% of what they understand. That gives you about 25% of everything that goes on. What you have got to do is to make sure that the jury understands—and remembers—the 25% that you want them to understand and remember."

Compare this with what Gilbert K. Chesterton said, "You take 12 people, lock them in a room and the Holy Ghost descends. They become something special. It is not 12 × 1 or 6 × 1, they become a unique organism. They are smarter than we are. They remember everything. They understand everything. They never make a mistake. They always come up with the right answer."

Neal, an aggressive cross-examiner, was also quoted as saying,

✓ *"Once a person makes a mistake (in cross-examination), never take your foot off his neck."*

It was the great Edward Bennett Williams's interview that I enjoyed most. What few people know, and perhaps the interviewer also did not know, was that in the last decades of his life Williams was battling with uncontrolled colon cancer. His trial schedules had to be interrupted several times by operations to remove metastatic lesions as they appeared in the liver and lungs. Despite the ravages of cancer, Williams worked till the last days and never let his defendant clients down.

In this interview, which had to occur within the last 2–3 years of his life, he stated that he believes that, "A trial lawyer stages a production that is designed to create an impression on the jury. The trial lawyer has no backdrop, no lighting, no effects to create illusions, there is only the bare stage." He was also quoted as saying, "For every hour an attorney is in court, as a rule of thumb, you need one hour of preparation during the trial. So, in other words, if you are in court seven hours a day, you need seven hours outside court to get ready for that day. There is no substitute for preparation. There should be no surprises. Nothing should ever happen in the courtroom that catches you unprepared or surprised. That is what you should strive for."

He also said, "Cross-examination is an art form where you *chip away and chip away and chip away at him until he is just a pile of little stones although he started out like the prudential rock. It is only on the Perry Mason shows where a witness collapses and confesses. However, the reality is, you chip and chip and chip and then collect all the pieces for your summation.*"

26.5 "The Expert Witness Marketing Book: How to Promote Your Forensic Practice in a Professional and Cost-Effective Manner" by Rosalie Hamilton[4]

I have copied from Ms. Hamilton, for my book, her excellent personal disclaimer to women, which also applies to me. She says on page v, *"For simplicity in this book, I have used "he," "him," and "his" throughout the book. Women readers, please overlook this usage. I look forward to a day when words will be coined in our society that apply to either gender."*

Unfortunately, this is the only passage I agree with in her book that applies to physicians. I cannot comment on whether all her marketing suggestions would be or not be effective for other experts who do not deal with life or death matters as do physicians. However, in knowing her great marketing experience, I would give her advice to nonphysician experts the benefit of the doubt. Experts in accounting, construction, business and financial, electronics, industrial, handwriting, lipreading, etc., may well benefit from her book.

It is my opinion, however, that little if anything in her book should be adopted by any testifying physician. Hers is the oft-touted marketing approach, which she defines as the process and technique of promoting, selling, and distributing a product or service. She believes that the expert witness should treat his activities as a business with a business plan and a marketing plan. She believes in creating a database of prospects, clients, and referral sources, and learn how to build on it.

When she recommends tailoring your curriculum vitae for the legal market, I do not think it is applicable to physicians. She also advises that, "You should master the art of networking: The developing of contacts or exchanging of information with others in an informal network." She instructs the reader on direct mailings and provides postal information as well as the different types of advertising and spending guidelines, which in my opinion may be beneficial to the handwriting expert but would be lethal to the budding medical expert.

I have seen her and heard her talks at various meetings. She is a charming, educated, and well trained in her marketing field and a very business savvy attractive woman. Her experience is that of the director of marketing for various legal publications with a background in advertising sales, in insurance advertising sales, and real estate. She is also an extremely honest person. I still have a returned invoice for her book with two dimes scotch taped to it because of an overpayment I did not even know I made. Her advice and recommendations may be excellent for a nonphysician and nonmedical experts. However, in my opinion as a physician, with 100% of my professional time concerned with the care of patients and the teaching of undergraduate and postgraduate medical students, the question I hate to hear in a cross-examination is,

✓ "Dr. Hookman, tell me all the things you have done to promote your expert witness business." And I would hate to ever admit to a letter writing marketing campaign to attorneys—one of whom may be cross-examining me.

Although Ms. Hamilton's recommended response to these questions is "what will impact the jury more is your evasion to the question rather than your direct answer," I still do not believe in direct mail campaigns to attorneys and the like, which is unsuitable, I believe, to physicians. Medical experts who deal with life and death situations almost on a daily basis must convince a jury of his impartiality and of being nonbiased and nonprejudiced.

For that reason, for maximum credibility a policy not to accept another case from the same attorney, law firm or client is important if that is what you also choose. And it is for that reason that your "marketing" activities is to list your name only in medical expert witness directories with equal access to both defendant and plaintiff attorneys.

26.6   "The Expert Witness Handbook: Tips and Techniques for the Litigation Consultant" by Dan Poynter[5]

This is an excellent book, especially for its glossary of terms in the appendix to explain to the novice what the legal terms and legal languages are all about. I, personally, am indebted to Dan Poynter's book, *The Expert Witness Handbook*, which is the first book I ever read (and one of the few) from cover to cover.

In his chapter on the trial, you cannot do any better than reading his suggested responses to these "trick questions" which attempt to "put words in your mouth." "Beware," Poynter says, "when the opposing attorney says, . . .

Q: "Is it fair to say?" for which you should answer, "It is better to say . . ."

Q: Now, you have stated?

A: No, that is not what I said. What I said was . . .

Q: If I can sum up your testimony?

A: Let me restate my position . . .

Q: Is it not true that . . .?

A: Not quite. What I said was . . . or that is almost correct or not exactly.

His section on hypothetical questions is excellent. His answer "that is a great hypothetical question, but it does not apply to these situations, so, "My hypothetical answer to your hypothetical question has to be . . ."

Also, his recommendations for yes or no answers with "I can't answer with a yes or no without leaving a false impression with the jury" or "Yes, but . . ." so that the jury knows there is more to the answer.

"Isn't it possible?" with his recommended response, "No, sir, it is not possible, not under the facts of this case, not from what I know" or his response to

Q: Is this book an authoritative source, a recognized source of professional knowledge?

A: If you mean by authoritative in this book with a lot of good information? Yes. But if you mean have I read the entire book recently and do I agree with everything in it? No.

Q: Are you not familiar with this article?

A: With over 600 journals and 30,000 articles each year, no one can read them all, but I will read it now and give you my opinion.

Q: Is Dr. Guru not the university-recognized authority on this subject?

A: I am familiar with Dr. Guru's writings, but not everyone agrees with every statement he has ever made.

His suggested answers to a passage being read out of one of your articles is to answer that "the article was published in 1978 and there have been a lot of changes since 1978." Articles and books can only reflect thought up to the day they are printed."

His answer to "Have you ever been wrong?" is "Of course, but not today."

His answer to "Wouldn't it be fair to say…" "What does fair mean?"

His answer to "Isn't it a fact that?" is "Under all circumstances?"

His answer to "Wouldn't you agree?" is "On a scale of 0–100?"

His response to "Do you really believe that position?" is "Yes, I', glad you asked me that question" and then go on to explain.

✓ His fundamental maxims for testifying in court are classic ones and as applicable to physicians as it is to parachutists:

Be a real expert, stick to what you know, tell the truth, never lie, listen to the whole question, answer the question exactly as phrased, you are being recorded, be respectful to everyone especially opposing counsel, do not argue or insult opposing counsel, let him or her beat up on you. Show the jury you know what you are talking about, help the jury to understand the complex nature of the case, explain buzz words and technical words that may not be common to them, be real, invite the jury to like you, be alive and enthusiastic, look the jury in the eye and speak forthrightly.

26.7 "Effective Medical Testifying: A Handbook for Physicians" by William T. Tsushima[6]

This is one of the very few good short manuals designed for physicians. The authors, one a psychologist and the other now a retired physician in Hawaii, explain the differences between scientific statistical significance of 95–99% probability versus reasonable medical probability, which is a less stringent and exacting standard. Their manual is very well referenced.

Their emphasis on not being an advocate saying, "I don't know" when you really do not know and turning a question around that, "If you're asking me—, then my answer is—," which is referenced to their source of SL Brodsky, "Testifying in Court: Guidelines and Maxims for the Expert Witness, Washington D.C., American Psychological Association, 1991."

✓ They also explain to the physician the legal definitions of causation, (which) precipitate, hastens, and aggravates. Their answer that, "Medicine is not nuclear physics, but medicine is based on scientific theory and research and the opinions I offered today are rooted in medical science" is a very good response to the attorney's question, "Doctor, isn't your profession simply an art and not a science?"

They also have good recommendations for dealing with difficult questions in cross-examinations to get you more time to think with recommended responses of the following questions:

- Can you repeat the question?
- I am sorry I do not understand the question.
- Could you please rephrase the question?
- The question is too general, can you be more specific?
- Can you define the word in your question of _____?
- I cannot answer that question without more information.

✓ Their point is to make sure the cross-examining attorney makes his question crystal clear to make sure you fully understand the question and its ramifications, and also to give you valuable time to contemplate your best answer. Their suggested answers to a question trying to elicit your bias is, "I don't know who favors my opinions. I know that I have based my conclusions on objective medical evidence and it is my duty to be an impartial medical expert who favors neither side of a case."

I am not sure, however, if I completely agree with their response to a question about an expert's fees being paid more per hour than the "judge" and certainly more per hour than any of the jury. Their suggested response is, "I have several reasons for charging my fees in court. Testifying in court is a much more demanding and rigorous process. The unpredictable scheduling of my appearance in court usually is also some lost time, thus, I feel compelled to charge more to come to court and to review records and talk with attorney's on the phone."

This response is weak-kneed. You should not have to go into all of those details, which the cross-examiner can use against you and dissect it out over numerous subsequent questions. I believe that all you really have to say is, "These are my fees for testifying per hour, based on my expertise, experience, training, and education and also, checked to be within the usual reasonable and customary fees of medical experts in my specialty as published in—."

I personally would have the statement in my signed agreement with the retaining attorney.

I like their recommended answer on the question to the medical expert about who is better qualified to render an opinion, the treating physician or the medical expert, "The treating doctor has more experience with the patient. Nevertheless, because of the vast research I've done on this case including the review of all the patient's past medical records, I am in the position to offer my expert opinion regarding the medical issues in this trial along with all the research, which supports my opinions from the peer-reviewed medical literature."

I also like their answers to the standard *ad hominem* attack on you being a "hired gun" by their suggestions of answers:

- "I do not advocate for patients in court.
- I am here to testify as to the standard of medical care in this case.
- I am not being paid for my testimony. I am being paid for my expertise based on the time I spend in court.
- I am not an advocate for anyone's side, as an attorney must be.
- If I am an advocate, I am an advocate for the truth as I know it."

I think their point is well taken that a medical expert, in offering opinions, should neither overstate the certainty of the conclusions reached nor understate the possibility of alternative viewpoints. The expert, the authors state, "should report the results of the available evidence as an educator, not as an advocate. On the other hand, the expert has no duty to provide educational services to the opposing attorney in a deposition, "a deposition is not grand rounds" because a deposition is entirely different than testifying in a courtroom. While at a trial, the physician in direct examination may assume the role of a teacher and be somewhat expansive in answering questions, at a deposition, which is a discovery procedure for the opposing counsel in search of how to discredit the expert's testimony, the medical expert is advised to be relatively brief and to the point and never volunteer unsolicited information."

Also, the medical expert is advised "to keep your guard up at all times." As to their recommendation "make them beat the answers out of you" suggestion, I cannot agree on the basis of my experience in testimony. Lastly, in answering the question that "In the past have you differed in your opinions with other doctors?"

Your suggested answer is "Doctors do not always agree in their diagnoses and opinions. I don't know about the other two doctors in this case, who are your medical experts, but I am certain that my diagnosis and evaluation is based on objective findings and a thorough evaluation of the medical records and research and peer-reviewed literature."

Their conclusion is "Your best insurance for a successful deposition is to be prepared to support your opinions with solid scientific evidence and cogent medical reasoning, not speculation or unsupported assumptions. You will help yourself most by providing a clear, succinct, accurate, and intelligible presentation of your findings and you may, in the process, also hope the attorneys on both sides reach a satisfactory out-of-court settlement of a legal dispute.

This appears to be in conflict with their previous opinions of let them pull it out of you, but otherwise, I believe this book is a very good start for the medical expert prior to his testimony. In fact I discussed the book with both William T. Tsushima, PhD, and Kenneth K. Nakano, MD, at their homes in Hawaii to ask for advice before putting my thought to paper through my book. Both were extremely gracious and the advice I received from them, which I have used in my book, was to have experienced attorneys review and contribute to the drafts.

26.8 "Malpractice: A Trial Lawyer's Advice for Physicians" by Walter G. Alton Jr.[7]

In this book, the author gives a thorough explanation of pretrial, trial, and posttrial activity, including settlements and appeals. Also, he instructs on how to be prepared and how to truthfully field questions posed in legal proceedings.

The book is somewhat dated being over 30 years old. It does not cover the most recent changes in expert witness's testimony necessitated by the most recent Supreme Court rulings as well as new legislation, including HIPAA. I discussed this point with Mr. Alton and offered him a chance to submit an updated chapter in this book. He said he would try. His busy schedule has, up to now, precluded it. Perhaps, we will have it by the next edition.

26.9 "Clinicians in Court: A Guide to Subpoenas, Depositions, Testifying, and Everything Else You Need to Know" by Allan E. Barsky and Jonathan W. Gould[8]

The heart of their advice is in their rules of testifying, which also applies to physicians, "regardless of who is asking the questions."

1. Tell the truth, the whole truth and nothing but the truth
2. Convey professionalism
3. Respect the formalities of the court
4. Speak slowly, loudly, and without hesitation
5. Provide clear and concise answers
6. Let the attorney lead (with his) questions
7. Just give the facts
8. Keep your composure
9. Maintain eye contact
10. Use notes to refresh your memory, and
11. Be prepared during the cross-examination for questions challenging your
    - Credibility
    - Establishing doubt
    - Trying to nudge you in a particular direction by "a logic funnel" in which you must answer yes to either an all or a never question and then you are led down the path so that you become inconsistent in this particular case. Also,
      - Prepare for leading questions
      - Guard against the power of suggestion
      - Coping with the feigned ignorance of the cross-examiner
      - Preparing for the cut-off in your testimony to stop you from providing further information that is detrimental to the attorney's case
      - The rapid fire tactics of the attorney, which is likely an attempt to get you to speak without having time to think about how to formulate your responses
      - The intentional ambiguity of some questions to confuse you if you did something that you did not intend to. The last two, which is implying impropriety with the intimation that you may have done something dishonest such as "Have you spoken to anyone about the answers you are giving today?" in the hopes that you may feel some guilt in breaking some code of confidentiality or rule of evidence, and last, the attempt to rattle you, which may include ridicule, insult, sarcasm, and intimidation, which though are questionable tactics and may backfire on the cross-examiner resulting in some sympathy for you. It may still be allowed in many courts.

The authors advise, of course, is to ignore

- intimidation,
- close physical proximity,
- piercing eye contact,
- loud voices, and
  - if your space is being violated, feel free to move back,
  - avoid threatening eye contact by casting your eyes toward somewhere else (but not down), and
  - maintain your composure and do not get thrown off your course.

The above suggestions are excellent, but I believe this book is particularly weak in suggesting responses for the medical expert in challenging qualifications, impartiality, factual bases, theoretical bases, reliability and validity.

It is strong in instructing the general physician in avoiding malpractice with their advice of

1. Ensure that you have proper education, experience and supervision for the type of clinical practice in which you are engaged.
2. Stay within your area of expertise.
3. Keep up to date with theory, research, and ethical standards in your field.
4. Maintain timely, accurate, and thorough records.
5. Have your patient sign a consent form that discloses the type of treatment with adequate informed consent.
6. Know when to call an attorney or your professional association or colleague for assistance with your ethical or legal issues.
7. Do not be embarrassed to ask for help.
8. If an allegation is true, consider admitting fault and offering the appropriate remedy depending on the severity of the issues *after, of course*, legal advice is sought, and lastly
9. Be particularly cautious with patients who have a proclivity for bringing legal actions (e.g., people with paranoia, personality disorders or a history of frequent litigation involved).

26.10 "Testifying in Court: Guidelines and Maxims for the Expert Witness" by Stanley L. Brodsky[9]

This book, as the two others by Stanley Brodsky—*Coping with Cross Examination and Other Pathways to Effective Testimony*, 2004, ISBN: 1-59147-094-3 plus the *Expert Witness: More Maxim and Guidelines for Testifying and Court*, 1999, ISBN: 1-55798-597-9—are the recommendations of a psychologist with some good advice but also some bad recommendations as far as I am concerned.

First, the good advice summarized.

✓ "Handle loaded and half-truth questions by first admitting the true part in a dependent clause and then, strongly denying the untrue part in an independent clause." On the reverse side, his suggestions of answers to antagonistic questions on his fees as he suggests, "Your question seemed to imply that my opinions in this matter are for sale for the price of my fee. It has been said that whose bread we eat, his song we sing. It is exactly for those reasons I bend over backwards to double and triple check my findings to ensure that there is no hint of bias interfering with my conclusions."

I believe this response is too defensive. It may insert into the juror's mind that the idea that maybe the bread you are eating really is being paid for *by* the song you are singing. This is what he calls an assertive presentation of the foundations of your objectivity (but, I do not believe this will go well in court or with the jury).

✓ It might be a good idea, however, to adhere to one of his maxims, that is, "prepare a list of professionally relevant and complete qualifying questions for the retaining attorney to use in his opening of your direct examination." Yet at the same time, another one of his maxims is to "Comfortably agree with accurate challenges to your credentials or for narrative explanations only when they are nondefensive and unforced."

This seems contradictory to his first recommendation.

I also do not agree with Brodsky that one should tell jokes in court, but his maxim that "If you are humorous at all on the witness stand, keep it gentle, good natured and *infrequent.*" I would modify infrequent to *rare.* His advice perhaps is more fitting for a psychologist as a response to a cross-examining attorney's poor attitude by actually stating to the attorney, "I notice you are raising your voice a lot now. Are you okay? You seem to be losing control."

I do not believe this is not an appropriate statement for an expert on the stand— especially from a physician. However, his psychologist background makes for good advice when he states, "Cross-examination probes for guilt and shame are effective only if you (the expert) respond with guilt and shame. Stay on task and be nondefensive."

✓ I also agree with his maxim that "an expert should recognize the voluminous nature of the content from which the final verdict will be drawn by the jury and if you sit through the entire trial including all the summations, then you *will truly understand that you are only a small cog in a multifaceted and complex process.*"

His maxim is that a witness's self-centeredness about the importance of his testimony can serve as blinders that interfere with clarity, self-assurance, and nondefensiveness, which I find to be true by experience.

I guess the only maxim I cannot remember from Brodsky's next book *More Maxims and Guidelines* is the word, which he says was devised by George Bernard Shaw and allegedly found in the Oxford English Dictionary, "floccinaucinihilipilification," which defines its meaning as the action of estimating "worthlessness." This word, he says, "is made by combining four separate word roots that captured the notion of judging things worthless—flocci, nauci, nihil, and pilfy."

Brodsky says this is the motive of the cross-examining attorney, i.e., to make your testimony or, at least parts of it, *worthless (and) to destroy the apparent worth of your testimony just given during direct examination.*

This cross-examining tactic takes the form of "comparing your opinion with the existence of contradictory opinions in the literature as well as diminishing your testimony through a sarcastic questioning manner and also take apart the words and metaphors that you may have used to attack you." Particularly, "this is done when the substance seems unassailable," says Brodsky.

Also, interesting is that Brodsky introduces the concept found in the 1981 publication of the *Bulletin of the American Academy of Psychiatry and the Law* by Edward Colbach. Colbach advocated measuring devices to check on an expert's integrity:

1. A contrary quotient, CQ
2. A validity quotient, VQ, of which the CQ is equal to the number of your opinions contrary to the preferences of the requesting attorney divided by the total amount of attorneys requesting you to review a case

Brodsky thinks the CQ should be used by the expert during challenges to one's integrity as a "hired gun." Brodsky suggests that to the usual opposing attorney's question "Doctor, how many times have you testified for the defense as in this case and how many times for the plaintiff in medical malpractice cases?" answer "I have calculated just how many times I have come up with an opinion that supports the case of the potential retaining attorney. I get calls about four to five times a month (or 50 times a year) by an attorney who wants me to testify. In the last 50 consecutive cases, over a 12-month period, I have found my opinion was in agreement with the potential retaining attorney 50% of the time and in disagreement 50% of the time." "Of course," Brodsky continues, "counsel, you must realize that I am called only to be a witness when my opinion fits with the case of the retaining attorney. For attorneys to call me, otherwise, when my opinions differ from their case, they would have to be desperate or incompetent. Most of my disagreements never make it to court and almost all my agreements make it to court. In all these instances, my case do not include the many cases in which attorneys have asked my opinion over the phone about whether they may have a case well before I even reviewed the records." Brodsky, however, issues his caveat that "on the CQ (the contrary quotient) that if the expert does choose to calculate his CQ, he would hope not to do it primarily to protect himself on the stand against adversarial questioning, but rather because it is a useful piece of information."

This kind of a response may be variable with each medical expert. But as far as this pertains to me I usually, do not even get to review the records if on the first 3 min of the conversation I tell the potential retaining attorney that I do not think he has a case.

Only when I suspect that the case may have merit do I then give the attorney permission to send me the records for a flat review fee of three billable hours. After the review I then give the potential retaining attorney my telephone judgment on whether or not the case is worth pursuing and not whether they want to engage me as a testifying expert.

When I offer a negative opinion, sometimes they settle and sometimes they keep looking for other experts. Whatever they do, I am not in a case at that point, often with the appreciation of those attorneys who say that they "saved a considerable time, travel, and expense."

Some good advice by Brodsky is on the response to "*ad hominem*" attacks on your integrity. His excellent advice is to "never attack back in kind and never exchange insults, . . . maintain (your) dignity and poise." Also, he advises that you may use negative assertions, i.e., begin your responses with statements like "No, quite to the contrary," or "That's not so at all. You have it completely wrong."

Lastly, great advice from a psychologist, "do not act battered because if you do the personal attacks have appeared to work (and) the expert will look diminished on the stand. Maintaining a solid presence means avoiding the defeated look, having your consistent voice quality and body language of a confident expert and not a battered witness."

Brodsky, a good psychologist, notes the traps of a cross-examiner's alleged "common sense" questions to what the cross-examiner hoped would be a helpful conclusion to his case and client. Brodsky's maxim is, "do not be immediately agreeable to affirmations of common sense until you think through the specific meanings of the questions for your conclusions and opinion" so as to neutralize *the cross-examiner's "common sense" questions*.

Q: Doctor, your opinion is only just that, an opinion, is it not?

A: No, it is my best professional judgment.

Q: Doctor is it not true that Dr. PMD had much more exposure to the patient that you had?

A: Yes.

Q: Is it not true that your knowledge was only based on the documentation and medical records?

A: Yes. Most certainly, because the patient is dead.

Q: Is the clinical interview and physical examination with its direct personal contact with the patient not the best source of knowledge about a patient?

A: No.

Q: What could you possibly know from documentation that would be good or better than a personally performed, clinical history and physical examination?

A: The patient's medical records contain the patient's history along with the results of laboratory tests and the results of x-rays administered by different individuals. The whole unfolding of this patient's disease as his pathology developed became visible and made its way into a pattern of abnormalities all documented in the medical records. It is at least as good and much better than a personal history and physical.

Brodsky's last book, *Coping with Cross Examination*, published in 2005, is about the psychology of cross-examination within the totality of "testifying in court." In this book, he states (testifying) about mastering the fear of being on the stand. Brodsky also recommends to the expert "to tell the story of what you have found and believed in a way that makes the technical material accessible and that enhances that jury's understanding of your opinion. Build a narrative bridge between your findings and the actual experience of the defendant or plaintiff, so that the testimony comes alive to *create a meaningful story.*"

In explaining *how to tell a story*, Brodsky reminds us of what he learned from a writer about the "*in medias res,*" which literally means in the middle of the thing. Brodsky suggests that "you start in the middle of the story," the lesson is so that you can get people caring about what happens right away and then, tell what you wish. He believes in telling in metaphors, which can clarify and simplify technical parts of the testimony . . ., and challenges to metaphors are best met by defining the limits of the metaphor and by placing it in an illustrative context.

✓ However, my colander just will not let this advice through. I cannot agree with this. May be it is a good idea for novels but not for telling a story to a jury, who can be easily confused with all the data that must also be remembered. And can anybody interpret for me the statement ". . . defining the limits of the metaphor and by placing it in an illustrative context?"

26.11 "Testifying in Court: The Advance Course" by Jack E. Horsley[10]

This book contains several nuggets in the suggested answers to "trick questions."

Q: Why is it doctor that physicians have so much difficulty in agreeing on points of medicine?

A: Probably for the same reason that the U.S. Supreme Court has so much difficulty in agreeing on points of law.

Q: Doctor, you are something of a professional witness, aren't you?

A: No, my profession is the practice of medicine. It just so happens I am frequently called to testify on medical matters for both defendants and plaintiffs.

A. First beware of the cross-examiner's demeanor.
   1. The bartender sort who is all smiles and friendliness. He may be trying to lull you into a false sense of security before zapping you with a devastating question.
   2. The lawyer who specializes in silent threats, who will approach you on the witness stand while grimly going through a pile of papers. Ignore the paper shuffling; he is only trying to make you think he has a pile of damaging information on you.
   3. The courtroom actor who simulates profound amazement, indignation, disbelief, and outrage while questioning you. Disregard his antics. They are principally designed to upset you. Do not change your demeanor or tone of voice when any of those personas take over.
B. Never attack the medical expert for the opposing side. Simply state the points on which you disagree. It will sound vindictive if you attack the expert. That is the job of the attorneys.
C. Be glad that the cross-examination is very prolonged and if the cross-examiner's questions seem tortuous and time-consuming. This usually means that the cross-examiner has not been able to weaken your testimony and he is getting desperate. Keep your head. Keep your cool, but do not leave the witness stand until you are dismissed because your retaining attorney may have some further questions.
D. Address the jury as you would your patients. Do not patronize them. Do not talk down to them, but do as you would with your own patients, trying to explain or get informed consent for a procedure.

26.12 "Effective Expert Testimony" by David M. Malone and Paul J. Zwier[11]

Q: You have no qualm with Dr. Peterson's qualifications to treat Crohn's disease, do you, Doctor?

A: No.

Q: And you agree with his diagnosis of Crohn's disease in this patient, don't you, Doctor?

A: Yes.

Q: And in fact you agree with his treatment of Crohn's disease for this patient, don't you?

A: Yes.

Q: And you certainly agree that Dr. Peterson, Professor of Medicine at the Harvard Medical School, has written extensively and is an authority on the subject of Crohn's disease, don't you, Doctor?

A: Yes.

Q: Well, Doctor, why don't you agree completely with my expert, Dr. Peterson in this entire case? Why do you stubbornly differ with him on these few aspects?

A: Sometimes doctors disagree on certain issues just like Supreme Court Justices will disagree on certain issues and in this situation and clinical condition I disagree with the distinguished Dr. Peterson.

26.13 "Legal Answer Book for Managed Care Aspen Health Law Center" by Patricia Younger[12] et al.

26.13.1 Adapted Cross-Examination Nuggets for Physicians

Be careful with these cross-examiner's techniques and demeaning questions:

1. Repeating the question twice or thrice after your answers to show the jury that you are not answering the question completely.
2. Are you saying Dr. Hookman that there are . . .
3. So, Dr. Hookman we can agree that . . .
4. Thank you, Dr. Hookman, you have answered my question.
5. Do you understand Dr. Hookman what I am asking you? I am asking you whether or not . . .
6. Do understand the difference between a question which asks X and not Y, Dr. Hookman?
7. Dr. Hookman, the question I asked you which you have not yet answered is did you perform a blood test? This can be answered yes or no, can't it?
8. Dr. Hookman, you have been so responsive to your retaining attorney, Mr. Jones. May I ask you to be as responsive to me as you have been to him?
9. Dr. Hookman, can't you reasonably concede that . . .

10. Dr Hookman, did you come in to this courtroom favoring one side or did you come in to answer whatever questions were asked by whatever lawyer asked them?

11. Dr. Hookman, the question I asked you was did you actually read the EKG, the answer to which is either yes I did or no I did not, why can't you cooperate?

26.14 "The Effective Deposition: Techniques and Strategies That Work" by David M. Malone and Peter T. Hoffman,[13] "Deposition Practice Handbook: How to Take and Defend Depositions" by LJ. Chris Martiniak,[14] "The Art of Cross Examination" by Francis L. Wellman[15]

26.14.1 Summary of Points That I Find Interesting in These Books

Cross Examination—the rarest, the most useful, and the most difficult to be acquired of all the accomplishments of the advocate . . . It has always been deemed the surest test of truth and a better security than the oath.

—Cox

Wellman related a cross-examination of a well-known, successful physician by a cross-examiner who was a good friend.

Q: Doctor, you say you are a practicing physician, have you ever practiced your profession in the city of Chicago for any length of time?
A: Yes, I have been in practice here in Chicago now for about 40 years.

Q: Well, doctor, during that time I presume you have had occasion to treat some of our most prominent citizens, have you not?
A: Yes, I think I have.

Q: By any chance, doctor, were you ever called as a family physician to prescribe to the elder Marshall Field?
A: Yes, I was his family physician for a number of years.

Q: By the way, I haven't heard of him lately. Where is he now?
A: He's dead.

Q: Oh, I'm sorry. Were you ever the family physician of the elder Mr. McCormick?
A: Yes, also for many years.

Q: Would you mind my asking where he is now?
A: He is dead.

Q: Oh, I'm sorry.

"After the cross-examiner proceeded in the same vein to make inquiries about 8–10 of the most leading Chicago citizens whom he knew this physician had attended, all of whom were dead and having exhausted the list, he sat down quietly amid the amused chuckles of the jurors with the comment, "I don't think it is necessary to ask you any more questions. Please step down.""

With friends like that—you do not need enemies.

Wellman also states that the "taming of a hostile witness, forcing him to tell the truth against his will is one of the triumphs of the cross-examiner's art. ... The cross-examiner will use rapid-fire questions that are negative to the memory, character, and disposition of the expert. Some of the witnesses under this style of examination lose their tempers completely and if the cross-examiner only keeps his own and puts his questions rapidly enough," Wellman states "he will be sure to lead the witness into such a web of contradictions as to entirely discredit him with any fair-minded jury. A witness in anger often forgets himself and speaks the truth; his passion benumbs his power to deceive. Still, another sort of witness displays his temper on such occasions by becoming sullen. He begins by giving evasive answers and ends by refusing to answer at all. He might as well go a little further and admit his perjury at once, so far as the effect on the jury is concerned."

"The cross-examiner will select the weakest points of your testimony and the attendant circumstances that you would least be prepared for. He will not ask the questions in logical order, but dodge him and pin down direct and precise answers on all the incidental, nonsignificant circumstances directly or indirectly associated with his medical opinion. The cross-examiner will ask questions very rapidly, asking many unimportant ones to one important one and all in the same voice in the hope that you will never be able to answer as quickly as he can frame your questions, and at the same time he hopes that you cannot correctly estimate the significance of your present answer on those answers that have preceded it. He is hoping to land you into a maze of self-contradictions from which you will never be able to extricate yourself."

The cross-examiner hopes to stop his questioning "with a victory." This is one of the maxims of cross-examination, "Stop with a victory," and if nothing more is accomplished by the cross-examiner, then in showing that you made a serious omission or a serious contradiction in your documented testimony, he believes he has gone a long way toward discrediting you with the jury. "If the jury distrusts you on one part, they are likely to disregard your testimony altogether, even though much of it has been true" says Wellman.

26.15   "Cross Examination: The Comprehensive Guide for Experts" by Steven Babitsky and James J. Mangraviti[16]

Good reading for anyone unfamiliar with the adversarial customs of cross-examination.

26.16   "How to Become a Dangerous Expert Witness: Advanced Techniques and Strategies" by Steven Babitsky and James J. Mangraviti Jr.[17]

Q: Doctor, are you using the same standards of scientific validity and certainty testifying here today as you use in your practice?

A: In my medical practice, I'm constantly dealing with the probable, not the certain. As you know, medicine is an art. Have you ever gone to a doctor who tells you I am sure you have such and such and will ask exactly three days and you will feel exactly this much pain?

It doesn't work like that. Some people have side effects to certain medications, others don't. Some people heal quicker than others. When you are pregnant, the doctor gives you the due date, but as we all know, babies come when they want to. As Benjamin Franklin frequently said, "The only things certain in life are death and taxes." Yes, in court I deal with the probable, just like I do when practicing medicine (Page 314).

Another good suggestion is the response to the question, "Doctor, what assumptions did you make in reviewing the records in this case?" And instead of saying "none," or "I assume that I was sent all the materials I requested," your suggested response should be, "I assume good faith as to the material and if you're asking did I just take these documents I received just at face value, my answer is no. What I did was I started with the documents I was sent. I then interviewed the retaining attorney to make sure that I received all of these documents. I reviewed all the records, I conducted a research into the evidence-based medicine standard of cares that I obtained, any additional documents and reports as they became available such as the depositions of Dr. ____ and nurse ____. I reviewed all of the additional documents for either corroboration or dis-corroboration of the original documents I reviewed."

✓ However, I have serious exceptions to the recommendations made by the authors of this book *who* in their preface define the dangerous expert witness as an expert witness *"who puts fear into opposing counsel."* "Dangerous experts," the authors state, *"understand how to defeat opposing counsel's tactics and are capable of turning the tables on the opposing attorney."*

My warning:

1. This may be good advice to the generic expert in business or political consulting. The jury expects to see the same fighting banter from their talking head shows on Sunday morning. However, this is entirely inappropriate for a physician.
2. Let us not lose sight of who the medical expert is and remind ourselves of the definition of a medical expert witness.
3. A medical expert witness is an individual who in his day-to-day practice may deal with life and death decisions. He must have special knowledge, skill, training, education, or experience that she/he can bring to bear to assist the attorney, judge, or jury in understanding the evidence or in determining a fact at issue.
4. While fact witnesses are generally limited to testifying regarding matters they have personally observed or about which they have personal knowledge, an expert witness may offer opinion testimony based on his reviews, study, observations, and analysis on virtually any source of what he believes to be relevant information. And this includes hearsay* in making and in arriving at his conclusions.
5. This is the primary distinction between an expert and a fact witness. Federal Rule of Evidence 702 defines expert testimony as, "Scientific, technical, or other specialized knowledge (that) *will assist the trier of fact to understand the evidence or to determine a fact in issue, a witness qualified as an expert by knowledge, skill, experience, training, or education, may testify thereto in the form of an opinion or otherwise*, if
   - The testimony is based upon sufficient facts or data.
   - The testimony is the product of reliable principles and methods.
   - The witness has applied the principles and methods reliably to the facts of the case."

I have always agreed that a good expert witness is

1. Able to communicate effectively with the judge and the jury orally and in writing clearly and concisely and in plain English that every juror could understand.
2. Exhibits confidence through his verbal and physical communication and presents an overall professional image.
3. Open to suggestion and willing to work collaboratively on developing a case with the attorney.
4. That the expert should not be a "yes man" and should be comfortable in challenging fixed ideas about the case.
5. A good expert will not hesitate to point out weaknesses in the case or even to let you know that the case may not succeed.
6. It is crucial to the physician defendant or medical expert witness that the expert is percieved as truly unbiased, an independent third party whose only true allegiance in the case is to his field and its principles.

However, I believe that the authors, though excellent teachers of the rudiments of "generic one size fits all" expert witnessing, have missed the point in the above definition of a good medical expert, and have also missed the boat in this book—at least for the physician testifier. Perhaps looking at the best-case scenario for their suggested techniques, it may very well fit in with other kinds of experts.

We are used to TV political pundits yelling at each other or playing one-upmanship. We have all watched the John McLauglin show where sometimes you cannot tell who is talking over the din. And perhaps a jury might enjoy seeing a battle of wits between experts of an assorted variety—e.g., politics, salesmen, business consultants, and maybe even the lipreading experts and hand writing analysts—and even learn something from that brouhaha.

However, it is simply nonprofessional for a physician to do this, especially when an injured plaintiff is sitting in the courtroom next to his distraught family. A physician must not under any circumstances get into verbal or other slugfest with the opposing attorney. Attempted a "bridge too far" by advising the use of what amounts to intimidation of the opposing attorney by the expert, in this case is a *role inappropriate to a medical expert*.

In my opinion based on over 30 years of medical expert testimony, it is very difficult to beat an attorney at his own game. And that is what the authors are suggesting that the medical expert do with the cross-examiner. There is no way a full time practicing physician or academician who does not spend most of his time in court, can pull off any of these tricks on an opposing attorney, or even attempt them without a strong counterattacks from the attorney detrimental to the physician.

What I am specifically referring to are the following suggestions made to potential medical expert witnesses, in this dangerous "witness" book. To wit

- "Push back on fee questions by pointing out the fees paid to opposing counsel and his experts. Justify your fees by challenging the cross-examining attorney about his fees.
- Point out the opposing counsel's attempts to mislead the jury; thus, causing opposing counsel to lose credibility.
- Lull the opposing counsel into a false sense of security prior to striking.

- Incite the opposing counsel to lose his cool by picking up on things that annoy him and push his buttons by repeating these.
- Point out the hypocrisy of the opposing counsel (to the jury).
- Try to "turn the tables on the cross-examiner" by implying attorneys "and not physicians are taught to manipulate people" and that it is the attorney and not the physician who is trained in the art of persuasion.
- Give a *sarcastic* answer to an "irrelevant" or "foolish" question asked by the cross-examiner to show "that the lawyer does not know what he is talking about."
- *Challenging the cross-examiner* about his advertising when answering question about yours.
- Baiting the cross-examiner into asking open-ended questions; and trying to bait the cross-examiner into asking too many questions; or wrong questions; or one question too many.
- Also baiting the cross-examiner with a handwritten note called "*baiting the interrogator*" into demanding the document that you are writing upon while you are being cross-examined, and then showing him some insulting remark you have written on the note he has asked for.
- Directing an *ad hominem* attack on the cross-examiner by telling him you have formed an (unfavorable) opinion about him in response to his question about whether you formed any additional opinions in the case.

I do not know who will have the last laugh in these situations. However, I can guess.

I believe from over 30 years of medical expert experience that this is far more dangerous to the medical expert than it will be to the opposing attorney. Remember the quotation in the Themes chapter "*I learned long ago never to wrestle with a pig, you get dirty and besides, the pig likes it.*" *(For those experts who choose to engage in a battle of wits with the cross-examiner.)*

I also remember the words of the late, great litigator Edward Bennet Williams who repeatedly warned his expert witnesses and also junior associates about not getting into a battle of wits with the attorney and certainly *not* using tricks. He said, "To have any chance at all of pulling a rabbit out of a hat in a trial, you have to come to court armed with fifty rabbits, fifty hats, and a lot of luck. If the luck is with you, you may get to use one rabbit and one hat."

Thus I believe the testifying physician should take much of the above advice with what Yogi Berra says is a "grin of salt." The author's have made other inappropriate suggestions in the book for the generic expert:

- *Keep watching for the opposing attorney's weak point before striking.*
- Use backhanded compliments to chip away at opposing counsel's credibility.
- Use a statement revealing damaging information about opposing counsel and as part of a response.

My advice about this to testifying physicians:

- *Do not do any of these!*
- *You are risking too much!*
- *Do not even think about these tricky moves even at home or in the shower!*
- *The moment the jury senses "a battle of wits or tricks" with the attorney, the medical expert witness and not the opposing attorney loses.*

26.17 "Anatomy of Cross Examination: A History and the Techniques of an Ancient Art" by Leonard E. Davies,[18] "Expert Rules: 100 and More Points You Need to Know about Expert Witnesses" by David M. Malone and Paul J. Zwier,[19] "Expert Witnesses" by Faust F. Rossi[20]

26.17.1 More Nuggets and Points of Interest from the above Generic Expert Books

26.17.1.1 What to Expect from Cross-Examination?

On a learned treatise, the opposing attorney will try to get at least one concession from you, either that it is generally reliable or that the author is qualified or that the author's institutional affiliation is respectable.

It does not matter to him whether or not you have read or heard of the contradictory material and taken it into account. If you have not read it, then he will intimate that you are guilty of not having considered all the relevant literature. If you have taken it into account, and even if you have good reasons for rejecting the contradictory material, the cross-examiner has injected the idea that there can be a fair debate among professionals about the matter at issue.

Having made the point that the issue(s) is subject to a "fair debate" he will then revert to questions stressing that the jury will ultimately decide this question.

✓ The ending of a cross-examination should always be a strong one, say these attorney's instruction manuals.

At the end of cross-examining, they advise the attorney that at the end of cross-examining an expert that the ending questions must focus on *bias, ineptitude, cupidity, greed, the conflict of expertise, the limitations of the particular expert's knowledge, the mutability of the expert's factual assumption, or all of these.* A variation of the ending cross-examination could be

Q: So, Dr. Hookman, if the jury finds the facts or what you assumed them to be, you think they should agree with you, right?
A: Yes.

Q: And if the jury finds the facts are different from what you assumed them to be, they will probably disagree with you, right?
A: Yes.

Q: *And either way it's their call, isn't it?*

26.17.1.2 Questions to a Teaching Medical Expert or University Medical Expert

Q: Dr. Hookman, in addition to your teaching responsibilities, could you tell us just generally since the time you have become a doctor approximately how many colonoscopies you have engaged in?

A: If you now teach others to do the procedure your response can be—In some fashion or another, either as being the one who did the procedure or who directed the procedure or who assisted someone else doing the procedure, an average of at least 20 a week for approximately 30 years.

26.17.1.3 *What to Expect about the Issue of Your Fees?*

Impeachment is usually used demonstrating some partiality on the witness, on your part. The cross-examiner will try to get you to admit that your hourly fee in court is substantially higher than what you charge for patient care and actually bears no relation to your normal professional fees. He will try to demonstrate any improper financial relationship or show an inordinate frequency of prior testimony *for the same attorney or issue. He will attempt also to show that the vast majority of annual income is derived from lawsuit participation.*

26.18 "How to Excel During Depositions: Techniques for Experts That Work" by Steven Babitsky and James J. Mangraviti Jr.;[21] "Art of Advocacy: Cross Exam of Non-Medical Expert" by Matthew Bender;[22] "ABA's Practice Checklist Manual on Taking Depositions" by Gregory P. Joseph;[23] "Defense Counsel Journal," Rex K. Linder[24]

26.18.1 Nuggets from These Generic Expert Books Adapted for Testifying Physicians

Q: Doctor, do you agree that this textbook edited by Dr. Nobel Prize is authoritative?

A: The answer to a question about a *learned treatise or authoritative writing* is, "as with most any published work, the authors or editors state things which many in the field agree and other things which many in the field disagree. Similarly, there may be things where in which I agree, and other things with which I may disagree. If you would like me to comment on a specific portion of the text, please ask me about that.

Impeachment by inconsistent prior sworn testimony:

- When you testify at a deposition or a trial to a fact or opinion that is inconsistent with your oral or sworn transcribed written statements or in a transcribed testimony either in this case or in a prior case, the cross-examiner will set the trap and spring it.
- Remember that all your prior deposition and trial testimony transcripts are readily available to attorneys.

Q: If you are questioned about even a small mistake in a wrong citation from an article, the answer should be

A: "I'm sorry if I made an error reporting this citation. I can try to get you an accurate citation if you'd like."

- A comprehensive list of all your writings is also available to attorneys through electronic search engines and the court's examiner will probably do a lot of homework by reviewing all your writings. What the attorney is trying to do is to seize on any small and seemingly inconsequential bit of inconsistency or contradiction in an attempt to undercut your credibility.
- *The cross-examiner is trying to show the jury that you could be wrong on one fact, thus you can then be wrong on others and therefore your entire opinion may be suspect.*

- Remember a simple, single discrepancy can damage your credibility, so get all your facts straight prior to any testimony you do.
- A cross-examiner will also try to interrupt your answer to his question. Remember that you are entitled to finish your answer to any question and you should never permit the cross-examiner to cut you off when you are about to deliver some unexpected or unwanted testimony. Your response should always be, "I have not finished my answer, counsel. As I was about to say, a full …"
- Remember your credibility is an important issue. It is all right and proper to ask the cross-examiner to rephrase his questions or to define any word that he is using in his question. However, the reply to a question by the cross-examiner, "Do you have any prior relationship with Mr. retaining attorney?" should not be "It depends on what your definition of *any* is" or "What your definition is of a retaining attorney?"

Examples of items and issues you think may appear very insignificant as far as you are concerned are just the items that will be pounced on by the opposing attorney. First thing is to check and recheck and check again any unnecessary mistakes on your CV, especially typographical errors. Example of questioning for typographical errors:

Q: Did you carefully check your CV for accuracy before you sent it to me?
A: Yes.

Q: Are you aware the court, the jury, and everyone depend upon accuracy of your CV?
A: Yes.

Q: Dr. Hookman, you state that your article on "Crohn's disease in Adolescents" appeared in the Journal of Gastrointestinal Endoscopy, do you not?
A: Yes.

Q: Is it not true, Dr. Hookman, that the journal was not the Journal of Gastrointestinal Endoscopy, but instead it was the Journal of Digestive Diseases?
A: Well, yes. That must be a typographical error.

Q: That article shows that your CV is not complete and accurate, does it, Dr. Hookman?
A: I'm sorry for the typographical error.

Q: Do you know if there's anything else you forgot to add or omit or change or modify on your CV?
A: I don't know.

Other questions on your CV along this vein for inconsistent statements or omissions could be:

Q: Dr. Hookman, are you a careful expert?
A: Yes.

Q: Were you careful when you drafted your CV?
A: Yes.

Q: I have one question on your CV, if you could help me.
A: Okay.

Q: On page one it says you received your MD degree in 19588?
A: I'm sorry, that's a typo.

Q: Are you saying, Dr. Hookman, that's a mistake?
A: Yes.

Q: Like everyone else, Dr. Hookman, you make mistakes?
A: Yes.

Q: But you do not know what year it is now?
A: Yes.

Q: And do you know the actual year you received your MD?
A: Yes.

Q: Do you know how many other mistakes you had made on your CV?
A: No, I hope there were none.

Q: Dr. Hookman, you have at the head of your CV the statement that this is your Curriculum Vitae?
A: Yes.

Q: Do you know what the term Curriculum Vitae means?
A: Well, you know, I'm not really sure. I'm not a Latin student.

Q: It means, "academic life." Did you know that?
A: No, I just learned that today.

Q: Dr. Hookman, do you ordinarily title papers with expressions you do not understand?
A: Well, this is an exception.

Q: Doctor, you're saying this is an exception? How do we know that?

Questions and your responses stating that the fees you charge for testifying is similar to the fees you charge in your office:

Q: Dr. Hookman, you say that the fees you charge the attorneys for testifying is similar to what you charge in your office?
A: Yes.

Q: What are you charging an hour for testimony here in this court?
A: $600 per hour.

Q: If we multiply $600 per hour with 2,000 hours, which is a usual 40 hour a week of 50 weeks a year, allowing you two weeks for vacation, does that mean Dr. Hookman, that just on your office visits you actually make $1,200,000 per year?
A: I guess not.

Q: So, you are making much more by testifying, Dr. Hookman, than you would be by practicing medicine, in your office aren't you?
A: Well, I guess if that's the way you put it, yes.

Q: So Dr. Hookman, in a way, you are overcharging us, aren't you?
A: Well, okay, if you put it that way, yes.

Q: You realize that people who overcharge the government can go to prison?

A: But, but, but . . . This is not a criminal act, these are my fees (visibly agitated).

Q: Do you demand a certified check or will you accept personal checks?

A: No, personal checks are okay. I don't demand any certified checks.

Q: Do you accept Master Card?

A: No.

Q: Visa?

A: No.

Q: American Express?

A: No.

Q: And that's an economic decision you've made not to accept credit cards because you do not want to spend any of the costs involved and you want to make even more money and the maximum profit from your legal activities?

A: I can't answer that question.

Q: Why not, Dr. Hookman? You seemed to be very verbal in all the other answers you have given.

Checkmate!

On the difference between your opinion and the opposing expert's opinion:

Q: Dr. Hookman, you disagree with my client's (the plaintiff's) medical expert, don't you?

A: Yes, I do.

Q: You don't disagree however, that he is a distinguished professor at Harvard University and a physician widely published in his field?

A: No, I have great respect for the doctor. However, I disagree with his opinion. I disagree with his opinion because . . . Now you should offer substantive and credible reasons as to why you disagree.

Questions on draft reports:

You should throw away your stamp called "draft" permanently. Never send a report marked "draft" to any retaining attorney.

Q: Your draft report is dated 01/01/05, correct?

A: Yes.

Q: You faxed it to your retaining attorney on that date?

A: Yes.

Q: It says "draft" on the top of the report?

A: Yes.

Q: Do you have any subsequent reports?

A: Yes.

Q: What date?

A: Well, I have another draft on 01/07/05 and a third draft on 02/01/05.

Q: Did your retaining attorney talk to you in the interim between these drafts?

A: Yes, but we did not discuss the substantive parts of the reports.

Q: Come now, Dr. Hookman, you're telling me that he never asked you to change or modify any parts of the report?

A: Yes, well there was one change, one small, insignificant modification that I changed having to do with the correct date of his last hospitalization.

Q: Come now, Dr. Hookman, that's not all the suggested changes and tell me why you made 15 different changes that appear on your final draft and did not appear on all your other three preliminary drafts?

Checkmate! There is intimation here to the jury that you have been influenced by your retaining attorney.

Direct testimony during the direct examination

You must ask your retaining attorney to deal with any potential problems you yourself recognize to be a potential problem, and other issues that the cross-examiner will attempt to intimate, e.g., being a hired gun, skeletons in the closet, etc. To take the sting out of the cross-examination, these issues should be dealt with by the "sympathetic" retaining attorney:

1. Questions of your fees
2. The time, records you spent on the case
3. How many times you have testified before in legal matters, whether they apply to cases like what is at issue?
4. And that you have been qualified as an expert in a court of law in your specialty of—a few dozen times.

This will take any surprise away from the cross-examiner's questions. It shows you are not defensive about the amount you charge or the number of times you have testified and that other courts and judges have found you to be qualified to testify in the dozen or so cases you already have testified in. It also limits where the cross-examiner can go with the "hired gun" theory of you.

26.19   "The Psychiatrist as Expert Witness" by Thomas G. Gutheil[25]

This author states the following:

- The most common error the beginning expert makes in testimony is the failure to concede an obvious and irrefutable point out of misguided loyalty to his or her side of the case.
- Also papering over the possible exceptions or equivocating in some way does not help your testimony.
- You should also never permit yourself to be tricked, cajoled or forced into speculating when answering questions under oath. There is nothing wrong with the response, "I'm sorry but I'm going to speculate on that."

- Remember that if you are making a video testimony, some unethical lawyers might attempt to gain some tactical advantages. These techniques at videotape testimony may include:
  1. One, pacing to force the expert's eyes to move back and forth which makes the expert look shifty.
  2. Pointing the camera up at the expert to make him look sinister.
  3. Lighting to wash out the witness or placing the expert in shadows.
  4. Using an extreme close-up to make the expert look harsh and to emphasize facial expressions and movements.
  5. Getting the expert angry or upset so the jury can see his "true nature."

Try to avoid these nonverbal behavior and body language no-no's: appearing impatient; clearing your throat excessively; drumming on the table; blinking your eyes frequently; fidgeting with pens, pencils, and any other items on the table—coffee cups, saucers, spoons, whatever; gritting your teeth; nodding your head too often; impatiently looking at your watch (remember the first President Bush on his TV debate); looks of disgust; playing with your hair, your fingers, or any other facial areas; rocking back and forth in your chair; shifting your eyes; slouching; smirking; wringing your hands; appearing evasive, suspicious, nervous and anxious; and being ill at ease.

26.20 "Cross Examination of Witnesses: The Litigator's Puzzle" by T. Aron[26]

26.20.1 Summary of the Only Points That I Agree with in This Book

Aron believes that the goals of cross-examination for the cross-examiner are at least to

1. create an impression for the jury that the cross-examination was successful.
2. establish the examiner's thesis on subjects not covered expressly by the direct examination.
3. induce the expert to modify conclusions expressed on direct examination.
4. discredit his conclusions expressed on direct examination.
5. discredit the expert personally:
   - The cross-examiner would love to get you agitated in an attempt to get you to lose your cool.
   - He would also love to make you get evasive or defensive.
   - He would like to trick you into making a mistake by cross-examining you from a document you have never seen before.
   - He would like to push you away from your true area of expertise and to push you to an extreme and illogical position.
   - He is hoping you have a lack of relevant experience to the issues at hand.
   - He will pounce on any mistakes in your reports.
   - He will get you nervous by interrupting you and not letting you finish your answer.
   - He will try to take your material out of context.

- He will take a quote or some prior testimony at a context to use it to attempt to trap you during the cross-examination. These out of context quotations can be from your own testimony or out of an authoritative text.

Anticipate these tactics and be prepared for it: *forewarned is forearmed.*

26.21 "The Deposition Handbook" by Dennis R. Suplee and Diana S. Donaldson[27]

26.21.1 Report Writing

- Write your report drafts as a single document on your word processor because there appears to be no rule obliging you, the expert, to create multiple electronic documents when drafting, editing, or revising a report.
- However, if you create multiple documents named with different folder titles, you will certainly be obliged to retain all of your files and they can be discovered.
- You must remember that if you have multiple copies of the same document or different drafts, the cross-examiner will have a field day in questioning you and will try to intimate that you made all the changes based not on your opinion but on what your retaining attorney told you to do with his "suggested changes, corrections, and modifications."
- This is especially significant if on the same dates that you wrote those modifications to the document, there are telephone calls to the attorney.
- Also understand that one way to discover the changes you make on a single word processing document is a forensic examination of your hard drive.

26.21.2 Deposition Transcripts Points

Make sure you put on the record the following after taking the oath:

1. You do not waive your right to review, correct, and certify the transcript.
2. And that you wish to review the transcript for correctness and to obtain a copy of the final certified transcript, including all attachments.
3. The answer to who will be paying for all this and when you will be receiving it.
4. At what time a testimony was previously scheduled to end and offer to make yourself available at a mutual, agreeable date and time for continuation if insufficient time has been allotted.
5. Do not accept any kind of communications from either your retaining attorney or the opposing attorney that the deposition will go on day after day until completed.
6. Insist that you only have a limited time.
7. Usually make it four hours and to start no later than four hours prior to an event that you must attend, whether it is related to a business, professional, or even a family matter.
8. However, if the opposing attorney insists that four hours is not enough, then ask it to be four hours per day and multiply by the number of days to calculate an advance fee to cover all those hours.

9. You would be surprised how quickly the opposing attorney, if he is paying for it, then changes his mind to say, "Well, four hours for one day is probably enough."

10. The reason to limit it to four hours per day is to avoid the "fourth-hour fatigue factor" in which your mind is now too tired to focus enough to answer the questions as confidently as you would during the first hour.

26.22 "Talk Is Cheap: Using the Pretrial Deposition to Advantage an Examining Expert's Trial" by R. Dietz[28]

26.22.1 Depositions Points

What is the purpose of a deposition?

1. To get the opposing expert's story out completely.
2. To get all the facts and have the medical experts cement themselves into a story to be dealt with later at trial.
3. The deposition is to develop areas to use during the cross-examination in the trial but not to rehearse the witness to respond better next time.
4. The chances for a witness being impeached on deposition are very low unless the deposition is going to be read into evidence.
5. The difference between a deposition is to find out all a witness knows before the cross-examination.
6. During trial the attorney will let the jury know only such portions of the expert's knowledge as will help or hurt the case.
7. The opposing attorney is seeking statements from you that can be used against you later.
8. The deposition is intended to exhaust the expert on all relevant points, to fix his testimony, and also to provide a basis for impeachment.
9. While deposition is encyclopedic, the cross-examination is specific, focused, and intended to make valuable points, *not* to acquire information.
10. During the deposition, all open-ended questions are asked.
11. However, at the cross-examination there is no question asked that the attorney does not know the answer to.
12. "The clincher" is never used in deposition. The kill is saved for the courtroom.
13. While in deposition, detailed answers are sought, many more questions are asked and ever would be at a trial.
14. At a deposition, the opposing attorney tries to discover all the information he can and to pin the expert down to one version of the facts.
15. A typical question would be "what are the biggest weaknesses in your opinion?" Answer, "There are no weaknesses in my opinion."
16. The opposing attorney will try as much as possible to elicit any response that is inconsistent with previous answer interrogatories or in the expert's report.
17. The opposing attorney will try as much as possible to get as many inconsistencies out as possible because inconsistencies will later damage your credibility as an expert in the trial.
18. You can expect your entire report to be covered and all the interrogatories put out by your retaining attorney to see if there are any inconsistencies.

19. A mistake is to answer yes to a question being read in a document by the opposing attorney when you really mean "yes, that is exactly what the article states" instead of "yes, I agree with what the articles states."

20. *The retention letter from the retaining attorney* will be looked at when the opposing attorney examines your file to see whether the letter from their attending attorney assess forth his theory of the case or does it limit your assignment in some way or does it ask you to assume a certain set of facts, some of which may be disputed.

21. He will check to see what materials were made available to you to review in forming your opinion and whether you will inquire as to whether there were other materials and whether you asked to see them, if not why not, if so what were you told.

22. He will want to know whether there were any drafts to the reports and what changes you made in your report before it was finalized; why were the changes made; and whether the retaining attorney suggested any of the changes, which ones? Did the lawyers suggest any change that you refused to make—either an affirmative or negative answer will be useful to him.

23. Even though the rules now state that the opposing attorney's expert can declare a treatise authoritative and as a reliable authority, cross-examination based upon an authoritative text, no matter how skillfully done, will not have the same impact if you have not conceded the authoritativeness of that text.

- Therefore, at deposition, the opposing attorney might seek concessions from you as to the authoritativeness of the treatise, article book, etc., before you are really on guard as to such questioning.
- The opposing attorney can conceal his objective by asking not only about the several texts he plans to use on cross-examination at the trial but about another dozen other texts he does not really care about, making him more likely to win at least some concessions that he wants because he thinks you "certainly can't declare nothing is authoritative."
- Since the attorney taking the deposition of the opponent's expert witness will concentrate only on securing information from the expert rather than telegraphing the expert, an attempt to discredit him and what the discrediting information will be,
  - You can expect the attorney during that part of the deposition to ask you whether you expect to testify at trial as to any facts or opinions besides those set forth in your report (or answers to interrogatories).
  - Or have you formed any opinions concerning this case other than those set forth in your report (or answers to interrogatories).

If you answer either question "yes," you can expect to be asked all the relevant information concerning the additional facts and opinions. *If you answer "I don't know, I will be getting more information and continuing to do research," then you maintain enough wiggle space.*

Here is how one judge instructs a jury at the end of the case—*Judge Allen Van Gestel, Massachusetts Superior Court, June 25, 2004*: "The Rules of Evidence provide that a witness qualified as an expert may testify and state his or her opinion concerning the subject matter of his or her expertise. You have heard testimony given by the expert witnesses in this case. The testimony of these experts may be helpful in determining issues beyond your everyday experience.

You should consider each expert opinion received in evidence in this case and give it such weight as you think it deserves. You may give weight to the expert's opinion only if you find that all the facts on which expert rely are true. The foundation of the expert's opinion—that is, the information relied upon by the expert—does not have to be admitted into evidence. As with all other witnesses, you will have to determine which experts to believe and how much weight to give to their testimony.

You may consider an expert's demeanor on the witness stand, his or her frankness or lack of frankness in testifying and whether his or her testimony is reasonable or unreasonable, probable or improbable. You may also consider an expert's motive in testifying and whether he or she has any interest in the outcome of the case or otherwise that might call his or her credibility into question. Just like all other witnesses, you may believe all that an expert says, some of what an expert says or none of what an experts says."[29]

26.23   Irving Younger's "The Art of Cross Examination"[30]

Most memorable line*

Is it not a fact doctor, that you commit sodomy every night with a parrot?

Now if you really want to get frightened, read Irving Younger's "The Art of Cross Examination." Younger states that impeachment by prior inconsistent statement is the most frequently used mode of impeachment and the simplest. Younger states he has great respect for the jury's intelligence. Therefore, he recommends that you should always respect the jury and especially their intelligence.

- *However, he then reveals one of his impeachment methods that take unfair advantage of the jury.*
- The crux of this well-renowned cross-examiner's teachings to his fellow attorneys are to *impeach the witness by asking a question which has nothing directly to do with the subject matter of the testimony given on direct examination.*
- A cross-examiner, he reiterates, will never want the witness to repeat on cross-examination what he said on direct.
- This principle to Younger "is elementary."

Younger will ask "Mr. Witness, is it not a fact that you commit sodomy every night with a parrot?"

- *Shock strikes in the courtroom!*

"The judge calls you into the sidebar conference and says, "What the hell are you doing?" "You simply say, "I'm testing credibility." The answer, he believes, really is irrelevant as long as *the jury heard the question.*

However, since the law requires that the cross-examiner must have a good faith basis for asking the question, Younger's advice is to *encompass either bias, prejudice, interest, or corruption into the question and impeachment process of the expert.* Bias, he defines as being in an irrational predisposition in favor, prejudice being an irrational predisposition against, interest is having a stake in the outcome, and corruption he defines as bribery.

He continues that a witness may also be impeached by questions relating to prior bad acts, which are defined as acts of immoral, criminal, or vicious nature. His questions:

Q: "Mr. Witness, did you beat your wife last night?" "Did you commit sodomy with a parrot?"

Although the question really stretches credibility, Younger maintains that, "to render the question permissible, the relationship is so slight that we will not listen to independent evidence to show that the denial was false." How do you as a medical expert defend against an attorney like that? I do not know.

✓ Younger's commandments of Cross-Examination as taught to his fellow attorneys are:

- Be brief.
- Use plain words.
- Use only leading questions (those questions which suggest the answer), may put words in the witness' mouth. Nothing could be worse than allowing the witness to repeat his story in his own words.
- Be prepared. Never ask a question to which you do not already know the answer.
- Listen to the answers.
- Do not quarrel.
- Avoid repetition. Never allow the witness to repeat on cross-examination what he said on direct examination.
- Never permit a witness to say something twice. The reason is simple. If the jurors hear something once, they may or may not believe it; if they hear it twice, they will probably believe it; if they hear it three times, they will certainly believe it.
- The key to effective impeachment lies in asking questions, which had nothing to do with the direct examinations, questions which do not allow the witness to repeat what he has said.
- Never give the witness an opportunity to repeat on cross what he said on direct.
- Ask instead
    - Have you been bribed to give your testimony?
    - Have you been convicted of a crime?
    - Did you beat your wife last night?
- Disallow witness explanation.
- Never allow the witness to explain anything on cross-examination.
- Limit questioning by avoiding asking one question too many.

Save the ultimate point for summation, he advises cross-examiners. "The temptation," Younger says, "is to have it explained on the cross-examination." How do you explain it? By asking the witness a question that permits the witness to explain, that will always be the one question too many, and the force of impeachment will disappear. *You must save it.*

It is at the summation that you would give the jury the entire story even though the entire story was not developed on your cross-examination of the witness and left key questions out just so that you would not let him explain.

This, my dear reader, is what we can be faced with. So I advise never be retained by an attorney who will be unable either with education, expertise, or experience to neutralize this type of lawyer—or bring your own attorney to court with you.

26.24 "Medical Malpractice Law" by Angela Roddey Holder,[31] "Medico-Legal Forms with Legal Analysis"[32] Published by the American Medical Association, "Malpractice Solutions, Coming to Doctors' Defense" by James Rosenblum,[33] "Expert Testimony: A Guide for Expert Witnesses and the Lawyers Who Examine Them" by Steven Lubet[34]

Steven Lubet, is Professor of Law at Northwestern University in Chicago, Illinois, and directs the school Program on Advocacy and Professionalism. In my opinion, this is the very best book for expert witnesses on the market. Lubet's views on depositions and cross-examination bears intensive study by the testifying physician. I would strongly advise you to get this book and read it at least twice.

26.24.1   Depositions

26.24.1.1   Theory Testing

26.24.1.1.1 Functions of depositions.   The deposition process by the opposing attorney is used to explore several alternative theories in the process of his preparing the case for trial. He wants to see how various theories will work with you. Therefore, he will pose a series of fairly intricate hypotheticals to determine which one seems the most promising for development at trial.

The questions will often start out at deposition with "Dr. Hookman, I would like you to make the following assumptions one, two, and three. Assuming assumptions number one, two, and three, how would your opinion in this case be affected?"

Some lawyers use depositions as settlement tools and as such, the deposing lawyer may be eager to test your nettle by engaging in what has become known as "phantom cross-examination." This is conducted in recognition of the fact that more than 90% of all cases are settled before (unintelligible) court. If your opinions can be undermined or impaired at deposition, your retaining attorney will have to be more forthcoming in the settlement negotiations.

Lubet offers five principles for coping at depositions:

1. Avoid universal commitments.
2. Do not argue with the counsel.
3. Resist free association.
4. Do not fill silences with words.
5. Do not hide mistakes or errors.

- The "universal commitment" is answering yes to always or never.
- Arguing with or attempting to convince and educate the opposing attorney is an impossible task because the opposing attorney will never be persuaded.
- It is not his job to be persuaded by you, but rather to locate the gaps and weaknesses in your opinions.
- As Lubet says, jousting with a proficient lawyer is a contest that the expert cannot win. The lawyer always gets to ask the final question. Even if the expert succeeds in concealing information or evading a question, the impression will be negative and therefore counterproductive.

- If you as an expert continue to challenge the lawyer's word choices or ask for too many definitions or try to find ambiguities, the lesson is not that you have outsmarted the attorney, but rather it is that you are slippery and therefore not to be trusted, says Lubet.
- "Free association" is simply the lawyer remaining silent while the expert is tempted to fill the silence by offering all kinds of unrequested testimony and volunteered information, which may be subject to misinterpretation or misconstruction.
- Everything done by the opposing attorney at deposition is done "for the record" since the very purpose of the deposition is to create an account that can be later used for preparation or at trial.
- If the deposing lawyer asks you a question which your retaining attorney thinks should not be answered because it is confidential, your retaining attorney will object by saying "this is not subjected to discovery, I'm going to instruct the witness not to answer." The deposing attorney will say, "The witness is not your client, you cannot instruct him. Dr. Hookman, unless you are personally represented by the plaintiff's lawyer, please answer my question that I just asked you." What should you do? Accepting the instruction may appear to compromise your independence, but answering the question might jeopardize perhaps undiscoverable information.
- So, you have got to know that Rule 26(c) of the Federal Rules of Civil Procedure states that a party may protect sensitive information from discovery by seeking "a protective order" from the appropriate court. Therefore, as a responsible expert who wants to best respect the rights of all concerned, you should decline to answer the question until every party has had an opportunity to bring the issue before the judge. Therefore, your answer will be

Q: Dr. Hookman, on what basis are you refusing to answer my question?

A: An objection has been raised to the discoverability of that information. If I answer now, I will preclude the retaining attorney from seeking the protective order, which would not be fair. So, I am temporarily declining to answer until all of the attorneys agree or until there has been a ruling by the judge.

- According to Lubet, the expert should always be sensitive to the need to shield privileged information.
- If there is an argument between the two opposing attorneys as to whether or not you can answer a question, once information has been revealed by you, it may lose its protective nature even if the opposing attorney was never entitled to it in the first place.
- This "cat out of the bag" rule requires extreme caution in responding to questions that have drawn objections and while it is true that the retaining attorney cannot instruct you to refrain from answering, that does not mean that you should not answer.
- The solution is, according to Lubet, that if you as the expert improperly declined to answer the information, it can always be provided later.
- Thus, there is relatively little harm in refusing to answer a particular question pending resolution by the lawyers or ruling by the court. However, information can never be retrieved once it has been disclosed and great damage can be done by ignoring an objection and proceeding to reply.
- *So the best approach for you is to decline to answer questions once your retaining attorney has objected on the basis of privilege or confidentiality.*

Q: Dr. Hookman, are you going to follow your lawyer's instructions and refuse to answer my question?

A: First of all, Mr. Smith is not my attorney and I am not following anyone's instructions, but I decline to answer that question. It is not my job to resolve this fuse between lawyers about privilege or discoverability.

✓ What I filtered out for the testifying physician from the above publications are these points:

- *The cross-examiner's attempts at your tight control.*
- *You have got to think at least three chess moves ahead.*

The cross-examiner's whole purpose is to tightly control the course of your testimony on cross-examination. So how are you as the medical expert able to defend the integrity of your opinion while the cross-examiner is making this well-planned campaign of maneuvers to confine and control every one of your answers?

- While you cannot wrest control of the cross-examination away from the attorney, you also want to protect your ability to function as something more than a yes person.
- It may be a good idea during cross-examination to start out at least with full sentences rather than just yes or no because should the cross-examination become more contentious later, once you have set the pattern of answering in full sentences rather than yes or no, the cross-examiner cannot simply abruptly attempt to change your pattern because it may reveal them as unfair.
- In other words, you want to ensure some measure of your ability to explain yourself and your opinion and to escape from being completely under the thumb of the cross-examiner.
- You, therefore, must always be alert for opportunities or "invitations" to explain your answers.
- This does not mean that you should attempt to disrupt the cross-examiner by interjecting explanations at every turn.
- Indeed, this will be counterproductive and will ultimately result in negative remarks by the judge (see chapter on my mistakes in testimony).
- Answer yes or no when such an answer is fair and complete.
- However, you may answer when you recognize the situation and an "invitation" from the cross-examiner who will occasionally, either by mistake or intentionally, solicit an explanation from you. Although it breaks all the "rules of cross-examination" some attorneys make the mistake of requesting explanations even when they start with tight leading questions.

26.24.2   Strategy

- *You must wait for that mistake as you would a mistake from your chess match opponent.*
- Wait till it happens.
- Plan to wait for a mistake, a misstep in the cross-examiner's tight control.

- Whenever and whatever that form of invitation during the course of the cross-examination, there is one appropriate response.
- When and if the question from the cross-examiner contains either the word "how" or one of the five "Ws"—who, what, when, where, or why—you have got the opening and invitation.
- Your answer is, "I'll be glad to explain."
- You then will have your answer ready for that question and explain again what you explained on direct testimony.
- You might even be lucky enough to ask permission which will be granted to you, certainly not by the cross-examiner but perhaps by the judge to step down from the witness chair, to go down to the exhibits, and to teach to the jury from those exhibits—like the teacher you are.

26.24.3 Incremental Questions

- The most frequent cross-examination techniques are performed with *incremental questions*.
- These are short, steady, "baby" step questions, with each area of questioning divided into even smaller components and finally into the smallest and simplest component parts.
- These sequential questions begin with the most undeniable aspects, that are well documented or make "common sense" to which it is impossible not to answer either yes or no without looking stubborn or even biased to one point of view (see "common sense" questions above).
- Once the cross-examining attorney has artfully laid the groundwork, he then proceeds to the difficult areas. In that fashion he hopes to get to the top step—the impeachment of your opinion or your character and preferably both.
- The cross-examiner will ask no *ultimate* questions because "it's best (most cross-examiners believe) to make the ultimate point only by implication" and in that manner denying the witness an opportunity to explain.
- Your goal as a testifying physician, therefore, is to explain and support your opinion, but not to defend it at all cost and certainly not to *defeat* the cross-examiner.
- Therefore, you should be prepared and willing to answer all questions whether reasonable or silly, legitimate or ill-founded.
- Your best answers will often refer back to your theory (and theme) explaining why you formed your opinion and why that opinion is reliable.

26.24.4 Concessions to "Common Sense" Questions

Do not fear making concessions. A competent cross-examiner may ask for any number of sound, reasonable concessions from you and those requests should never be fought simply for the sake of foiling the examination. He may actually be asking these questions, which are so obvious as to be answered yes or no for the benefit of the jury, to show them your stubbornness.

Some experts have a tendency to fight concessions apparently on the theory that it always hurts to give ground to the cross-examiner and in the heat of the battle does not want to yield one inch—even to questions whose answer yes or no may make a lot of common sense—at least to the jury.

Willingness to concede to the obvious is most often taken as a sign of true objectivity. The expert who resists at every turn only damages his own credibility. As a matter of fact, very skilled cross-examiners do not want to see the expert concede the obvious because they will try to ask for these concessions in a tone or voice calculated to seem patronizing or condescending just to get you riled. This strategy is intended to bait you into the (unintelligible) common sense conclusion. The cross-examiner wants you on a limb where you have to defend an irrational position.

26.24.5   Ambiguous Questions

You should never answer a question that has even the slightest bit of ambiguity in a sentence or in a word. Always have the attorney explain what he means in that question. That ambiguity can be used later against you, because the term usually means one thing to you and another to him. He will use his term in his summation to the jury—when you are not there to contradict him. Perhaps, you can also make use of the ambiguous question as an opportunity for a short explanation. When you ask the cross-examiner to explain what he means by the ambiguous term, you can then say, "May I explain then what I believe about this?"

The best response is to take the role of the teacher for the cross-examiner with a succinct explanation that is not contentious and truly answers the question by explaining your conclusions without answering yes or no.

26.24.6   Argumentative Questions

During the cross-examination, the cross-examiner will also ask questions that are somewhat argumentative. This may be done in an attempt to intimidate you and imply that you have made a mistake or even insinuate that the cross-examiner is about to smash you with some hidden fact or stunning revelation. The intimidating questions are usually asked for effect more than anything else.

These questions are frequently recognized by their typical makeup, i.e., "You *still believe* Dr. Hookman that . . . or *Yet still*, Dr. Hookman, *you really believe* . . ." He may ask this in a sarcastic way in the hopes that he might intimidate you about thinking that there was something wrong about your choice or opinion.

If you say yes, it might suggest your acceptance of the innuendo of your stubbornness. If you answer no, then you have made his point. If you become argumentative, he will again ask you the *yet still* question showing your stubbornness. Your best response to this is never a yes or no but "May I explain what I believe?"—and go on to make your points. If he does not give you permission to explain— you have turned the tables and now it is he that looks evasive.

26.24.7   Cross-Examination Challenges to Your Credentials

You the medical expert are a Nobel Prize winner in Medicine. You are board certified in internal medicine and three other subspecialties. You have written many books and hundreds of articles about a specific disease. However, if you have not treated more patients than the opposing medical expert or with an uncommon medication possibly used in this severe disease (e.g., with _____ in severe ulcerative colitis) your credentials can be challenged on those contrasting credentials. You can be challenged on the lack of specifically relevant expertise, your limited scope of expertise, your missing credentials, or the contrast in credentials between you and the opposing medical expert involved in the case.

The cross-examination on your credentials will usually begin *not* with the challenge to your credentials. It will start when the cross-examiner attempts to obtain favorable information from you about the opposing expert in a cordial nonconfrontational way, being "friendly first."

You will be asked whether you will acknowledge the reliability of the opposing expert, his credentials, his data, his assumptions, and perhaps even find out how much you agree with much of his opinion. He will attempt to get concessions from you on the merits of the case, trying to get you to agree with several of the major premises even though your ultimate conclusion is unfavorable to the cross-examiner's case.

Learned treatises are discussed in another section.

26.24.8   Impeachment from Prior Contrary Opinions

There are several possible sources of impeachment from your prior opinions—your own testimony or writings, either in your depositions, written report, testimony in prior cases, publications, or public statements (*see* chapter on Investigation of the Expert).

If you feel that the cross-examiner appears to have made headway on this subject do not argue. Do not antagonize by insisting you have to explain. Don't fret. You have got to depend on your retaining attorney to ask you the appropriate questions on re-direct to neutralize any impeachments made by the cross-examiner. He may be able to do this by a so-called *Rule of Completeness*. In most courts you may be allowed to add any of the part of the statement or document "which ought in fairness to be considered contemporaneously" with the impeachment (Rule 106, Federal Rules of Evidence—so-called "*Rule of Completeness*"). This means that once you have been impeached on cross-examination, do not fret—the expert's retaining attorney (the direct examiner) may request the immediate reading of additional explanatory portions of the same statement. Or if not, he will certainly ask a question which will allow you to give a full and complete explanation.

26.24.10   Impeachment from Biased, Nonapplicable, or Otherwise Wrong Published Clinical Guidelines

As the medical expert, do not fall into the trap of testifying on the basis of wrong guidelines or biased statistics or randomized control studies compiled from the literature without a careful analysis of potential bias and possible unreliability of the data and its testability. Remember the T in PEAT from Daubert (*see* chapters on Daubert and on biased guidelines and standard of care).

You can be questioned by a knowledgeable cross-examiner or one that has been well prepared by the opposing medical expert on the reliability of the data you are depending on to support your opinion.

26.24.11   Need I Say This? Do Not Trust the Cross-Examiner

Always distrust the cross-examiner. It is not rare for a cross-examiner to try to trick you by showing you a document that has been marked "Defendants' Exhibit 3" and asking whether you recognize it. It may be one you never reviewed, with a file front cover similar to the records you did review.

You should never just glance at the document, perhaps only at its first page or so, and then respond "yes, I recognize it." You should actually take the entire document in hand and read it through in its entirety—even if you need to request a full 30 min to do so. Or if permission is not granted you can simply respond with "this patient-record folder contains 162 pages. I've just skimmed through them and they seem to be in order, but I haven't had time to read everything."

26.24.12 Predicate or Partial Truth Questions

As an example the cross-examiner may ask you this question, which will include an implicit predicate. An answer to such a question can tend to be misleading since your answer may be understood as accepting the assumed fact.

Q: "Dr. Hookman, the fact that this patient had congestive heart failure, isn't it true that diuretics would have helped him?"

Since the question contains the implication that the patient had congestive failure, an answer "yes" suggests that you are accepting not only the diagnosis of congestive heart failure but also that diuretics can help in congestive heart failure, thus diuretics would have helped the patient. These are partial truth questions. They are questions in which the predicate of the question may be true but the conclusion false or vice versa. In either case, you probably will be tempted to give a "yes but" answer. However, this may be misleading and will be responsible for your later downfall.

You should attempt to uncouple the predicate question by simply answering only the part of the question that is true leaving out the part that is not true. Therefore, the best response to a partial truth question is simply to state the whole truth rather than agree with only half of it. You should clearly identify the nature of the assumption by simply answering "I cannot agree that the patient had congestive failure which I believe is an inaccurate impression, but if you want me to answer the question on diuretics in heart failure, I'll be glad to do so."

26.24.13 The Perfection Fallacy/the Ideal Test/the Gold Standard Question

There is a Latin maxim, Lubet reminds us, which warns that "best can become the enemy of good," meaning that inflexible insistence on perfection may prevent one from accepting perfectly decent alternatives. In cross-examination, this type of question seeks to exploit the expert's gold standard tests and treatments.

Q: Dr. Hookman, can we agree that it is best to measure blood alcohol levels within one hour after ingestion?

A: Yes, that is the goal.

Q: However, in this case, no blood was taken from the plaintiff until three hours after the accident, right?

A: I believe that is correct.

Q: Which would be at least four hours after any possible ingestion, correct?

A: Correct.

Q: So, it took four times as long as the ideal before any blood was taken from the plaintiff in this case?

Of course, what is ideal in a laboratory may be impossible in real life, but the "perfection fallacy" makes no such allowances. You should frame your answer within the context of the case. So, in answer to the "gold standard" question "can we agree that it is best to measure blood alcohol levels within one hour after ingestion," you should be thinking three chess moves ahead by answering that the blood alcohol can be reliably measured for at least six hours following ingestion and if the cross-examiner keeps pressing, "but isn't it best (the gold standard) to do it within one hour?"

Your answer should be *"what is best will always depend upon the medical circumstances involved,"* i.e., the fact that some test or procedure is named the "gold standard" does not mean that the "gold standard" can be used in every medical situation or circumstance—especially not when the risk/benefit ratio is against using the "gold standard" in the patient with co-morbidities which are contraindications to the gold standard procedure/test.

26.25   The Chess Match

- As in a chess match, you should see several moves ahead and recognize and deal with questions to set you up with an accurate but hedged response or by asking for clarification from the cross-examiner.
- The kinds of questions that you should hedge your answers to are asking you yes or no whether you are an (adjective) expert.
- Q: For example these adjectives:
  1. Are you a *careful* expert?
  2. Are you an *ethical* expert?
  3. Is your CV *accurate*?
  4. Is your CV *complete*?
  5. Do you conduct a *thorough* review of all the medical records in this case?
- You should not answer "yes" or "no" to either of these because then the cross-examiner will find exceptions to your yes or no reply and attempt to discredit you.
- Always answer these questions not by a yes or no, but by either saying, "I try" or "I tried" or "I hope so."
- Because the next cross-examiner's question to a yes will be to question some of the adjectives, e.g., "What do you mean by accurate? What do you mean by complete?"
- He will return the question by saying, "How do you define accurate, doctor? How do you define complete?"
- You can respond by simply saying, *"This is your question, counsel, and I'd like to know the definition of what the word in your question means to you so I can answer it as accurately as I can."*
- *Facing a more qualified opposing medical expert(s):*

Q: Dr. Hookman, can you explain why 20 distinguished faculty members of the Medical School of Harvard University have an opinion that is completely different than yours?

A: I don't think that any of the 20 faculty members that you speak of took the amount of time that I took in reviewing all the records and studying up on all the randomized control trials and standards of care plus evidence-based medicine articles which support my opinion which is based on my education, training, and expertise.

Q: Are you saying then, Dr. Hookman, that my opposing expert who holds the Nobel Prize in Medicine, has five medical degrees, has been given honorary degrees from 14 other universities around the world, and has published more than 1000 articles in the field on gastroenterology *is not* more qualified than you are, Dr. Hookman, in this case and shouldn't you defer to his extensive experience?

A: While your expert physician is a distinguished member of the Harvard faculty and certainly has an impressive resume, I have spent a lot of time studying the facts and all the records in this case and have polled an evidence-based medicine compendium of articles which support my opinion and, therefore, I believe I am more qualified in this case to offer an opinion.

✓ You have therefore turned the question from his Nobel prize winning qualifications to you, who has done more work in the case. Therefore, the one who has done more work in the case is more qualified to offer an opinion. You have not deferred to his expert with the very impressive resume.

Questions aimed to agitate you

It is not below the belt tactics for the cross-examiner to try to agitate you by distracting you or getting you to lose your temper, to goad you into fighting with him, to force you to take contrary but untenable positions just to show up the cross-examiner.

However, you should not lose your cool.

Q: Doctor, aren't you really a professional expert since you have testified 175 times in the past 4 years?

A: I have been found qualified by each of the courts where I have testified 175 times in the past four years. Correct.

Q: Doctor, are you acting as an advocate for your client?

A: I do not have a client if that term means someone for whom I advocate. If you call the retaining attorney a client or his client my client, that is not true since I do not advocate for him. I'm an independent expert and an advocate for the truth and opinions in this case, the truth and opinions supported by the peer-reviewed medical literature which I have expressed here today.

Q: Dr. Hookman, do you mean to tell me that you're holding yourself out as the authority above and beyond the 20 professors from Harvard University Medical School who hold opposing opinions?

- Your reply should encompass the response that should remind the jury that you are not holding yourself out as an authority, but since the judge has ruled that you could testify as an expert, you are so qualified to testify.
- You will remind the cross-examiner and the jury what your role is—that the lawyers ask the questions and as an expert you just answer the questions.
- An alternative to the question as to who is your client, you can say, "Technically, I was hired on behalf of the (plaintiff-defendant) by his legal representative, Mr. Smith. My

duty to the client, however, is not to advocate for him, but to provide my truthful expert opinions to help this jury decide the case. Further, I call cases as I see them. I have been retained by parties at different times to whom I had provided unfavorable opinions. I believe it is a great service to the attorneys because it has made those attorneys realize the problems with their cases and encourage settlement or the dropping of a claim which I believe they are only going to lose."

Q: Are you saying, Dr. Hookman, that the 20 Harvard University professors are wrong and that you are right and that all those experts departed from the standards of their profession?

A: This is a compound question with many questions in it, I'd like to answer these questions one at a time. Would you please ask me those many questions one at a time?

- When he starts asking them one at a time, the information you will impart is that you disagree with the Harvard faculty, but whether they all departed from the standards of medicine is not for you to say.
- You will not level any accusation against any of your colleagues.
- This is against the ethical standards of medical testimony proclaimed by most medical societies.
- However, in saying it is not for me to say, *you leave open the possibility to the jury that they may have indeed not looked at the case as intensively as you have and may have violated the standards of care.*

Q: Did you go over with your retaining attorney the questions he was going to ask you and the answers you were going to give?

A: As you know, sir, the retaining attorney has an ethical duty to prepare his expert witness before a testimony, so yes we obviously discussed his questions and my replies.

Q: Is there anything that you requested from your retaining attorney that you did not receive?

A: No, I followed my standard procedures and requested all the following records which you can read off again, present in this room, all were provided to me, including A, B, C, D . . .

Q: Is it possible you are just plain wrong?

A: I base my opinions on education, training, experience, reviewed documents, analysis, and research. I arrived at my opinion to a reasonable degree of medical probability and while it is possible that I am wrong, in my opinion I am not wrong.

Q: Don't you agree with me, Dr. Hookman, that the doctors that were involved in this patient's care are in a better position to give information with regard to her diagnosis and treatment than you basing all your opinions on the medical records?

A: The doctors did not have the opportunity to review all the medical records, the time to research and the benefit of hindsight as I did, plus I am in a better position than they are to offer my opinions on the patient's condition. This is the typical way a peer review medical evaluation takes place either at a morbidity and mortality conference in a hospital or in a peer review meeting outside the hospital.

✓ **Q: Dr. Hookman, did you not write a book on how to testify in medical malpractice cases?**

In this case, I will recognize that the cross-examiner wants to tie me to a book that teaches physicians on how to testify to get enough of an admission to have permission from the court to cross-examine me about every single thing in the book. And if he can portray me as more of a professional witness who studies the art of testimony rather than a practicing physician he will accomplish an important goal.

My answer will be, "Yes, I did write this book. You'll note that I emphasized in this book to "Always tell the truth while testifying," and as a matter of fact, counselor, I gave "Always tell the truth" as the 10 Commandments of medical testimony and I agree with that advice. Counselor, don't you?"

The book I wrote is a compendium of notes taken from many books on generic expert testimony, many books and articles written on generic expert testimony, which I translated for the testifying physician. Testimony, you know is now thought to be part of the practice of medicine, thus I believe that treating physicians should adequately be prepared not only to testify as defendant physicians, but also as medical expert witnesses.

Further Nuggets from Generic Expert Books Adapted for Testifying Physicians:

Q: Dr. Hookman, are you telling me these 20 Medical School Harvard professors, one of whom has won the Nobel Prize, are not more qualified to testify than you are?
A: That's not for me to say.

Q: You're telling me, Dr. Hookman, again, that you are more knowledgeable about the subject than the 20 Harvard professors?
A: Based on my education, experience, training, and the 64 hours of research, review, analysis, and evidence-based medicine articles I reviewed in this case, and that I have devoted to this case, I am confident that I am the most knowledgeable about these issues.

Q: So, Dr. Hookman, you consider yourself smarter than not only the Harvard professors but also most people, especially some people here on the jury.
A: I will leave up to the jury to determine how smart I am and how my education, training, experience, and testimony will assist them when they decide this case.

Q: How many drafts of preliminary reports did you do based on conversations with your retaining attorney before you finalized your final report in this case?
A: My practice is to wait until I have reviewed all the documents, completed my research and analysis, and formed my opinions before I write my report. For that reason, I do not write any draft or preliminary reports. I did, however, discuss this case with the counsel before I wrote my report.

References

1. Isele WP. *Under Oath: Tips for Testifying.* LRP Publications, 1995.
2. Feder HA. *Succeeding as an Expert Witness: Increasing Your Impact and Income.* Tageh Press, 2000 (first printing 1991, second printing 1993), ISBN: 0-9638385-3-9.
3. Couric E. *The Trial Lawyers.* New York: St. Martin's Press, 1988, ISBN: 0-312-051727.

4. Hamilton R. *The Expert Witness Marketing Book: How to Promote Your Forensic Practice in a Professional and Cost-Effective Manner.* Expert Communications, 2003, ISBN: 0-9723237-3-2.
5. Poynter D. *The Expert Witness Handbook: Tips and Techniques for the Litigation Consultant.* Para Publishing, 1st ed. 1987, 2nd ed. 1997, ISBN: 0-915516-45-4.
6. Tsushima WT, Nakano KK. *Effective Medical Testifying: A Handbook for Physicians.* Boston and Oxford: Butterworth-Heinemann, 1998, ISBN: 0-7506-9986-8.
7. Alton WG., Jr. *Malpractice: A Trial Lawyer's Advice for Physicians.* Boston, MA: Little Brown, 1977, ISBN: 0-316-03500-9.
8. Barsky AE, Gould JW. *Clinicians in Court: A Guide to Subpoenas, Depositions, Testifying, and Everything Else You Need to Know.* New York and London: Guilford Press, 2002, ISBN: 1-57230-788-9.
9. Brodsky SL. *Testifying in Court: Guidelines and Maxims for the Expert Witness.* Washington, DC: American Psychological Association, 1991, ISBN: 1-55798-128-0.
10. Horsley JE, et al. *Testifying in Court: The Advance Course.* Oradell, NJ: Medical Economics Company, 1972.
11. Malone DM, Zwier PJ. *Effective Expert Testimony.* The NITA Practical Guide Series. University of Tennessee College of Law, 2000, ISBN: 155681-564-6.
12. Younger P, Conner C, Cartwright KK, Kole SM. *Legal Answer Book for Managed Care Aspen Health Law Center.* 1995, ISBN: 0-8342-0700-1.
13. Malone DM, Hoffman PT. *The Effective Deposition: Techniques and Strategies That Work.* 2nd ed. Lincoln, NE: University of Nebraska, National Institute for Trial Advocacy, the NITA Educational Services Committee, 1995, ISBN: 1-55681-504-2.
14. Martiniak LJC. *Deposition Practice Handbook: How to Take and Defend Depositions.* 2nd ed. Aspen Law and Business Publishers, ISBN: 0-7355-0437-7.
15. Wellman FL. *The Art of Cross Examination.* 4th ed. The Macmillan Company, 1903, 1904, 1923, 1956.
16. Babitsky S, Esq., Mangraviti JJ, Esq. *Cross Examination: The Comprehensive Guide for Experts.* Falmouth, MA: Seak, Inc., Legal and Medical Information Systems, 2003, ISBN: 1-892904-23-3.
17. Babitsky S, Esq., Mangraviti JJ, Jr. *How to Become a Dangerous Expert Witness: Advanced Techniques and Strategies.* Seak Publishers, 2005, ISBN: 1-892904-27-6.
18. Davies LE. *Anatomy of Cross Examination: A History and the Techniques of an Ancient Art.* 2nd ed. Xlibris, 2003, ISBN: 1-4134-3199-2.
19. Malone DM, Zwier PJ. *Expert Rules: 100 and More Points You Need to Know about Expert Witnesses.* National Institute for Trial Advocacy, Notre Dame Law School, 1999, ISBN: 1-55681-649-9.
20. Rossi FF. *Expert Witnesses.* American Bar Association, 1991, ISBN: 0-89707-675-3.
21. Babitsky S, Esq., Mangraviti JJ, Jr. *How to Excel During Depositions: Techniques for Experts That Work.* Falmouth, MA: Seak, Inc., 1999, ISBN: 1-892904-00-4.
22. Bender M. *Art of Advocacy: Cross Exam of Non-Medical Expert.* New York, 1998.
23. Joseph GP. *ABA's Practice Checklist Manual on Taking Depositions.* Pennsylvania: American Law Institute, 1995.
24. Linder RK. *Def. Counsel J.* April 1991; 58(2).
25. Gutheil TG. *The Psychiatrist as Expert Witness.* Washington, DC: American Psychiatric Press, 1998.
26. Aron. *Cross Examination of Witnesses: The Litigator's Puzzle.* West Group, 1989.
27. Suplee DR, Donaldson DS. *The Deposition Handbook.* 3rd ed. Aspen Law and Business Press, 1999.
28. Dietz R. Talk is cheap: using the pretrial deposition to advantage an examining expert's trial. *Chronicle* 1992; 38: 71.
29. Wright M. A view from the bench. *13th Annual SEAK, National Expert Witness Conference,* Hyannis, MA, June 2004.

30. Younger I. The art of cross examination. *American Bar Association's Annual Meeting in Montreal*, Canada, August 12, 1975. Library of Congress Catalog Card No. 76-02426.
31. Holder AR. *Medical Malpractice Law*. Wiley, 1975, ISBN: 0-471-40615-5.
32. *Medico-Legal Forms with Legal Analysis*. American Medical Association, 1991, ISBN: 0-89970-402-6.
33. Rosenblum J. *Malpractice Solutions, Coming to Doctors' Defense*. Whittle Direct Books, 1993, ISBN: 1-879736-13-6.
34. Lubet S. *Expert Testimony: A Guide for Expert Witnesses and the Lawyers Who Examine Them*. NITA Press, National Institute for Trial Advocacy, 1998, ISBN: 1-55681-595-6.

For Further Reading

Alan ES. *The Expert Witness Guide for Scientists and Engineers*. Krieger Publishing Company.

Carol AJ. *Expert Witnesses*. Cary, NC: Oxford University Press.

Charles M. *Marketing Your Expert Witness Practice*. National Forensic Center.

Charlotte H. *Witness Guide to Testifying in Court*. Texas: Pale Horse Publishing.

Daniel B. *Law for the Expert Witness*. Lewis Publishers.

Douglas D, Larry V. *Expert Witness Checklist*. Rochester, New York: Thomson Professional Publishing and Bancroft-Whitney Company.

Expert Witness's Books: A Guide to Expert's Fees. Lawrenceville, NJ: National Forensic Center.

Expert: A Guide to Service as a Forensic Professional and Expert Witness. Silver Spring, MD: ASFE, 1995.

Frank JM, Charles C. *The Expert Witness Survival Manual*. Thomas Publisher.

Handling Expert Witnesses in California Courts. Berkeley, CA: California Continuing Education of the Bar.

Jack VM. *Effective Expert Witnessing: A Handbook for Technical Professionals*. Lewis Publishers, 1994.

Jeffrey LL. *The Consultant's Kit*. Cambridge, MA.

Katherine K. *How to Be a Credible Witness*. Joppa, MD.

Mark AD. *Expert Witnesses in Civil Trials: Effective Preparation and Presentation*. Thomson Legal Publishing and Lawyers Cooperative Publishing.

Michael ES, Esq. *An Overview of the Law: A Guide for Testifying and Consulting Experts*. Horsham, PA: LRP Publications.

Michael PR, Philip SK. *The Expert Witness and His Evidence*. Cambridge, MA: Blackwell Scientific Publications.

Richard A, Connor, Jr., Jeffrey PD. *Marketing Your Consulting and Professional Services*. 2nd ed. Wiley, 1990.

Robert CC. *Qualifying and Attacking Expert Witnesses*. James Publishing Company.

Sam B. *Forensic Engineering*. ISI Publications.

Sonya H. *What Makes Juries Listen*. 2nd ed. Little Falls, NJ: Glasser Legal Works.

Terry L. *Vocational Expert Primer*. Athens, Georgia: Blackwell, Elliott, and Fitzpatrick.

Thomas V. *The Consultant's Guide to Litigation Services: How to Be an Expert Witness*. Wiley.

William GM. *Expert Witnesses: Direct and Cross Examination*. Wiley.

Medical Expert Witness Rewards

27

27.1 Academic and Teaching Rewards of a Testifying Medical Expert Witness

> When you have made and recorded the unusual or original medical observation or when you have accomplished a piece of research in laboratory or ward, do not be satisfied with a verbal communication at a medical society. Publish It!
>
> **—Sir William Osler**

During the past few years of taking on medical expert reviews and testimony; and despite more than 30 years experience as a clinician and teacher, I have learned a lot of medicine from literature reviews to support my medical testimony and medical expert opinions. Each case prompts me to do the evidence based medicine (EBM) research to first formulate, then establish, and then support my opinions prior to writing any reports of giving my expert opinion and testimony.

And in doing so I find occasional gray areas in the medical literature dealing with the standard of care. It is tempting me to help clarify those gaps with the appropriate clinical research and reviews. Using the clinical data of the patients at my teaching hospital, I and several colleagues, students and house officers make a point of investigating the literature for the standard of care which would make the right fit for a generic patient with complex of symptoms similar to the legal case at hand.

The medicolegal cases I review prompts seminars on the issues that I encounter in these case reviews and testimony (without names of course). These medicolegal cases have proven to be a rich lode of medical teaching material. I also note that a pioneer in my field of gastroenterology has published on his endoscopic retrograde cholangiopancreatography (ERCP) legal experiences, which has also sharpened the field for his gastroenterologic colleagues when it comes to proper selection of cases for certain procedures—and perhaps also more important the appropriate selection of physicians and facilities doing this procedure. We will review Dr. Peter Cotton's important writings dealing with his own testimony experiences on ERCP in the chapter on "malpractice prevention" by gastroenterologists.

I too have been extremely rewarded in several ways using this method of study of cases in my medical-legal reviews of medical records.

27.2 Rewards of My Medicolegal Case Reviews

1. Using the material for clinical teaching seminars for undergraduate and post-graduate physicians as to the medical aspects of the diagnosis and treatment of the clinical problem.
2. Using the case as one in risk management for postgraduate physicians in their care of patients. Research documents state that successful problem solvers must possess comprehensive knowledge, but that the way they organize and understand their knowledge is even more critical. (Skilled and experienced physicians use) "schemes" for both learning and problem solving.

   A "scheme" in this context is a mental categorization of knowledge that includes a particular organized way of understanding and responding to a complex situation. "Schemes" provide the advantage of combining the creation of a knowledge structure and a search-and-retrieval strategy *into a single operation*. The implication for medical education is that the "hypothetico-deductive" strategy traditionally used may be replaced at times by "scheme-driven search strategies" so that students develop a more organized and logical approach to problem solving.[1]

Similarly, Schmidt et al.[2] states that contrary to some conventional views, research shows that (gaining medical diagnostic and treatment) expertise is not so much a matter of superior reasoning skills or in-depth knowledge of pathophysiological states as it is based on *cognitive structures that describe the features of prototypical or even actual patients.*

These cognitive structures, referred to as "illness scripts," contain relatively little knowledge about pathophysiological causes of symptoms and complaints but a wealth of clinically relevant information about disease, its consequences, and the context under which illness develops. By contrast, intermediate-level students without clinical experience (and who have lesser diagnostic skills) typically use pathophysiological, causal models of disease when solving problems. The more exposure/experience to clinical cases—i.e., examples of medical errors—the more the physician can take the fast track of "direct automatic retrieval of pattern recognition." The authors review evidence supporting this theory and discuss its implications.

Also documented is the fact that knowledge of a given category is structured in memory around key cases or clear examples, referred to as the prototypes, which capture the core meaning of the category. It is argued that the prototype view may help facilitate the understanding of the learning and problem-solving process in medicine.[3]

In the Introduction to this book I summarized the following points:

- More physicians should serve as expert witnesses.
- The irresponsible expert witness is the product of failure of our current biomedical graduate medical education.
- Review and scholarly study of medical negligence cases should be an essential part of medical school and residency programs.
- All physicians must learn the minimum core common denominators in decreasing litigation risks in all fields of medicine.

The critical element in teaching young physicians may be deliberate practice with multiple examples which, on one hand, facilitates the availability of concepts and conceptual knowledge (i.e., transfer) and, on the other hand, adds to a storehouse of already solved problems.[4]

Therefore, in my opinion there is no better way to teach medical students and post-graduate physicians in how to avoid medical errors but to instruct them in these (malpractice) case presentations so as to establish in their minds what it would take many years of experience—trial and error—to learn. Establishing these prototypes and illness scripts early in their careers is the "one stitch in time that can save nine."

The literature devoted to medical education agrees with me.

In these days of doctors, lawyers and lawsuits, chances of an American physician finishing his or her career without a malpractice claim are growing more remote. Every physician executive overseeing the activities of a group of peers knows this and should be prepared to assist (educate and pre-train) the physician who is sued.[5]

It would be a "valuable experience to similarly review medical malpractice cases and the associated testimony by medical experts." When available, the cases reviewed in residency programs would be those in which faculty members at the same institution had testified. The faculty member in such cases would be intimately familiar with the case and able to share the knowledge necessary to take part in the legal process. This case review process would expose residents to the legal realities of medical practice, provide a forum for peer review of legal testimony by experts, and show residents how to participate in the legal system should the need arise."[6]

The American Medical Association (AMA) has also advocated that medical expert physician testimony should be part of "the practice of medicine." The American College of Physicians in 1990, and the AMA in 1998, adopted a policy that medical expert witness testimony by physicians be considered "part of the practice of medicine subject to peer review."

It was thus also my stated opinion at the beginning of this book and now, that the principles of the medical expert witness must be taught in medical and graduate school during formal courses. The greater visibility of medical experts and their testimony ("light of day policies") should raise the quality of expert witness testimony and encourage the desired goal of more qualified physicians to participate as expert witnesses-thus meeting the objective of all major medical professional organizations.

In this malpractice climate, potentially every medical student, house officer, practicing clinician, and full-time as well as part-time academician will testify in court at least once; either as a defendant physician or as an expert. And every testifying physician is either a potential defendant physician, a potential medical expert, or any physician asked by the legal system to help sort out medical facts for an attorney or a jury.

And even if the above was not the case, Physicians have a responsibility to society, their peers, and patients to participate in malpractice litigation in a manner that ensures that medical malpractice cases are properly evaluated. But physicians are reluctant to involve themselves as expert witnesses in medical malpractice litigation because they simply are not educated or trained in "this practice of medicine."

Studdert has also written that:

Resident physicians, attending physicians, and graduate medical education (GME) institutions share a collective responsibility. The law does not offer concessions in quality of care to accommodate GME. Resident physicians are generally held to the same standard of care as attending physicians in their respective specialties. Attending physicians face malpractice exposure not only for the care they provide but also for the care they direct. In addition, they may be held vicariously liable for the negligence of resident physicians working with them, or directly liable for inadequate supervision. . . . GME institutions and programs bear legal responsibility for both the care they deliver and the negligence of their employees. . . .[7]

Thus these cases in which I have testified and also reviewed for alleged medical malpractice not only have been good teaching material to my medical student and post-graduate physician seminars, but have also been a rich source of publishable medical material as it pertains to clinical guideline "weaknesses" and the improvement of the standard of medical care.

It permits with help of my medical colleagues publishing aids to current clinical professional guidelines and helps with understanding more about the standard of medical care in several entities.

Example, of these publications based on my medicolegal activities and medical quality assurance studies are listed in "For Further Reading" section.

The latter two publications[8,9] have in the opinion of the many letters we have received contributed greatly for the earlier diagnosis and treatment of this deadly new mutation of *C. difficile*—an infectious agent that causes severe diarrhea and colitis—so severe that several patients needed a colectomy and colostomy for toxic megacolon.

I have also noted where the published standards of care in long term care facilities (LTCFs) surveillance and treatment of this deadly disease can be helped when reviewing the medical literature in this *C. difficile* case in which I testified.

With my medical colleague, we consolidated into two published articles the standard of care for prevention, detection, and earlier treatment of this deadly disease.

In addition to enabling an increased contribution to the peer-reviewed medical literature, I find that my teaching abilities have improved. I also have a richer experience and may I say some increased wisdom in my clinical management of patients.

So I encourage other teaching physicians (and who among us are not teaching physicians?) to enter this rich field of teaching cases to better educate yourself and your students. Remember "Praemonitus, praemunitus"—forewarned is forearmed.

References

1. Mandin H, et al. Helping students learn to think like experts when solving clinical problems. *Acad Med.* 1997 Mar; 72(3): 173–179.
2. Schmidt HG, et al. A cognitive perspective on medical expertise: theory and implication. *Acad Med.* 1990 Oct; 65(10): 611–621.
3. Bordage G, Zacks R. The structure of medical knowledge in the memories of medical students and general practitioners: categories and prototypes. *Med Educ.* 1984 Nov; 18(6): 406–416.
4. Norman G. Research in clinical reasoning: past history and current trends. *Med. Educ.* 2005 Apr; 39(4): 418–427.
5. Gorney M. Coping with bad news: the physician executive's role in a lawsuit. *Physician Exec.* 2002; 28: 26–29.

6. Fish R, et al. Review of medical negligence cases: an essential part of residency programs. *J Emerg Med.* 1992 Jul–Aug; 10(4): 501–504.

7. Kachalia and Studdert. Professional liability issues in graduate medical education. *JAMA* 2004; 292: 1051–1056.

8. Hookman P, Barkin J. Guidelines for prevention, surveillance, diagnosis, & treatment, and, in this new era of more virulent strains of antibiotic associated diarrhea (AAD), *C. difficile* associated diseases/diarrhea [CDAD] and *C. difficile colitis* [CDAC]. *Pract. Gastroenterol.* June 2006; 30(6): 65.

9. Hookman P, Barkin J. *C. difficile* associated disorders/diarrhea (CDAD) and *C. difficile colitis* (CDAC): The emergence of a more virulent era. *Digest. Dis. Sci.* March 2007; 52(4): 1071.

For Further Reading

Cabon V, Hookman P, Barkin J. Post-cholecystectomy recurrent acute pancreatitis secondary to sump syndrome. *Am. J. Gastroenterol.* September 2005; 100(8): Abst. S236.

Hookman P. Checklist used to justify endoscopy problems. Models for cost management and health care quality. In: *Innovations '92.* Pinellas Park, FL: Publication of the American College of Physician Executives, Promocom Printing, Inc., May 1992. ISBN: 0-924674-1.

Hookman P. Establishing a successful performance appraisal system for health services organization personnel. In: *Perspectives in Medical Management '92.* Published by the American College of Physician Executives, May 1992, pp. 43–144. ISBN: 0-924674-16-4.

Hookman P. Practice guidelines: The second generation of utilization review: How to make it work for the health service organization. In: *Perspectives in Medical Management '92.* Published by the American College of Physician Executives, May 1992, pp. 145–146. ISBN: 0-924674-16-4.

Hookman P. Pro-active feedback loops in the management of clerical and clinical personnel of a medical group practice. In: *Perspectives in Medical Management '92.* Published by the American College of Physician Executives, May 1992, pp. 19–22. ISBN: 0-924674-16-4.

Hookman P, Barkin J. Pancreatic sphincter hypertension increases the risk of post-ERCP pancreatitis. *Gastrointest. Endosc.* November 1998; 48(5): 546–547.

Hookman P, Barkin J. Surgical complications of fundoplication for gastro esophageal reflux disease. *Am. J. Gastroenterol.* November 2000; 95(11): 3305–3307.

Hookman P, Barkin J. Recommendations for greater accuracy in the standard of care for the detection of early barrett's esophageal cancer. *Am. J. Gastroenterol.* May 2002; 97(9): 1246–1249.

Hookman P, Barkin J. What should be the standard of care for the surveillance of cancer, the diagnosis of dysplasia, and the decision for colectomy in chronic inflammatory bowel disease. *Am. J. Gastroenterol.* May 2002; 97(9): 1249–1255.

Hookman P, Barkin J. Current biochemical studies of non-alcoholic fatty liver disease (NAFLD) and non-alcoholic steatohepatitis (NASH) suggests a new therapeutic approach. *Am. J. Gastroenterol.* February 2003; 98(2) 495–499. Published also in *Am. J. Gastroenterol.* September 2003; 98(9): 2093–2096.

Hookman P, Barkin J. Update on current standards of care in the diagnosis and management of non-alcoholic fatty liver disease (NAFLD) and non-alcoholic steatohepatitis (NASH). *Pract. Gastroenterol.* September 2004; 38(9): 70–88. Part I Diagnosis.

Hookman P, Barkin J. Update on current standards of care in the diagnosis and management of non-alcoholic fatty liver disease (NAFLD) and non-alcoholic steatohepatitis (NASH). *Pract. Gastroenterol.* October 2004; 38(10): 82–90. Part II Medical therapy.

Hookman P, Barkin JS. The role of vigorous detection of recurrence after curative resection of colorectal cancer. *Am. J. Gastroenterol.* December 1998; 93(12): 2624–2627.

Hookman P, Barkin JS. The diagnosis and management of unexplained chest pain—Is less more? *Am. J. Gastroenterol.* August 1999; 94(8): 2310–2313.

Hookman P, Barkin JS. Diagnosis of acute right lower quadrant pain and appendicitis by CT scan: Do we still need the clinician? *Am. J. Gastroenterol.* May 2000; 95(5): 1355–1357.

Hookman P, Unger S, Barkin J. Laparoscopic cholecystectomy should be routinely performed with intraoperative cholangiography. *Am. J. Gastroenterol.* November 2000; 95(11): 3299–3305.

Philips R, Hookman P, Barkin J. Early diagnosis and treatment of hepatitis C (HCV). *Am. J. Gastroenterol.* September 2000; 95(9): Abst. 2597.

Pyrsopoulos N, Hookman P, Barkin J. Update on the causes and standards of care for the diagnosis and treatment of hepatocellular carcinoma. *Pract. Gastroenterol.* April 2005, 29(4): 98–116.

Slate J, Hookman P, Barkin J. Systemic autoimmune disorders associated with celiac disease. *Digest. Dis. Sci.* September 2005; 50(9): 1705–1707.

Slate JA, Hookman P, Philips RS, Barkin J. Systemic autoimmune disorders associated with celiac disease (CD): A case report. *Am. J. Gastroenterol.* September 2002; 97(9 Suppl.): 136–137.

Appendix
CD Table of Contents

An update today is just a click away

Index

A

ABA's Practice Checklist Manual on Taking Depositions, 503–507
abuse of medical experts, guidelines for management, 337–343
academic medical experts
  information sources for, 502–503
  rewards for, 527–530
access to health care
  managed-care organizations liability and, 157
  tort litigation and, 17
accounts-receivable financing, asset protection and, 197
acute abdomen, delayed surgery and mortality rates from, 87–88
ad hominem attacks on expert witnesses, 479–480, 489–490, 493–494
admiralty jurisdiction, maritime medical malpractice and, 71–72
admissibility standards, federal and state rules on, 293–294
advance directives, guidelines for, 106–107
adverse drug events (ADEs)
  dosage and labeling errors, 128–129
  HIPPA disclosure provisions, 46–50
  in hospitalized patients, 125–126, 175–176
  in nursing homes, 125–126
  in office patients, 126–128
  in outpatients, 112–113
  patient nonadherence and compliance and, 113–116
  preventive and proactive strategies for, 119–120, 124–125
  in psychiatric malpractice, 144–145
advertising by medical experts
  resources for, 485–486
  warnings against, 233–235
advocacy, avoidance by medical experts of, 309
Aesop's fables, use in malpractice trials, 380–382
AGA Compliance Plan Template for GI Practices, 44
agency-by-estoppel claims, maritime medical malpractice and, 70
airway management errors, anesthesia morbidity and mortality, 88–89

allergic reactions, anesthesia morbidity and mortality, 88–89
alternative dispute resolution (ADR)
  attorney's role in, 208–209
  basic principles, 201–202
  decision criteria for, 207
  definitions, 205–206
  litigation *vs.*, 207–208
  managed-care malpractice and, 153
  medical experts' guidelines concerning, 226–227
  national practitioner databank, 210–212
  peer-reviewed literature sources on, 212–214
  pretrial screening panel, 211
  terminology, 204–205
  time and money savings with, 206–207
Alton, Walter G., 489–490
ambulatory surgical centers (ASCs), physician partnerships with, 36–37
analgesics medications, avoidance of medical errors with, 122–124
analogy
  attorneys' use of, 373–374
  examples of, 377
Anatomy of Cross Examination: A History and the Techniques of an Ancient, 502–503
anesthesia morbidity and mortality, medical errors and, 88–89
answer, legal definition of, 290
antibiotics, adverse events in pregnancy from, 85
anticoagulants, in office patients, adverse drug events from, 127–128
anti-kickback laws, joint physician/hospital ventures, 36–37
apology-and-offer programs, malpractice management and, 18, 181–182
"apparent or ostensible agency," vicarious liability and, 297
arbitration, alternative dispute resolution and, 204–205
arrogant experts, avoidance of, 308
Art of Advocacy: Cross Exam of Non-medical Expert, 503–507
Art of Cross Examination, The, 512–513
asset protection, malpractice litigation and, 196–198
assumption, legal definition of, 290

535